T5-BQA-359

A Garland Series

CLASSICS OF
ENGLISH LEGAL HISTORY
IN THE MODERN ERA

One Hundred and Forty-Two
Rare and Important Titles
Reproduced in Facsimile
in One Hundred and Eleven Volumes

Selected by

David S. Berkowitz
Samuel E. Thorne

T. E. Tomlins

LYTTLETON, HIS TREATISE OF TENURES

Garland Publishing, Inc.
New York & London • 1978

Bibliographical note:

This facsimile has been made
from a copy in the British Library
(1380.d.10)

*The volumes in this series are printed on
acid-free, 250-year-life paper.*

Library of Congress Cataloging in Publication Data

Littleton, Thomas, Sir, d. 1481.
Lyttleton, his treatise of tenures.

(Classics of English legal history in the modern era)
Text in English and French.
Reprint of the 1841 ed. published by S. Sweet, London.
Includes index.
1. Land tenure--Great Britain--Law.
2. Real property--Great Britain. I. Tomlins, Thomas Edlyne, 1804-1872. II. Title. III. Series.
KD833.L5713 1978 346'.42'0432 77-89237
ISBN 0-8240-3172-5

Printed in the United States of America

Lyttleton,

HIS

TREATISE OF TENURES.

Lyttleton,

HIS

TREATISE OF TENURES,

IN FRENCH AND ENGLISH.

A NEW EDITION,

PRINTED FROM THE MOST ANCIENT COPIES, AND COLLATED WITH THE VARIOUS READINGS OF THE CAMBRIDGE MSS.

TO WHICH ARE ADDED

The Ancient Treatise of The Olde Tenures,

AND

The Customs of Kent.

BY T. E. TOMLINS, ESQ.

"Est non magnus, verùm aureolus, et ad verbum ediscendus, libellus."—
Cic. Quæst. Acad.

LONDON:
S. SWEET, CHANCERY LANE, FLEET STREET.

1841.

LONDON:
W. M'DOWALL, PRINTER, PEMBERTON-ROW,
GOUGH-SQUARE.

TO

THE RIGHT HONORABLE

HENRY LORD LANGDALE,

BARON LANGDALE OF LANGDALE,

IN THE COUNTY OF WESTMORELAND,

THE

MASTER OF THE ROLLS,

THIS EDITION

OF

Lyttleton's Tenures,

IS,

WITH HIS LORDSHIP'S PERMISSION,

MOST RESPECTFULLY DEDICATED,

BY HIS OBLIGED AND HUMBLE SERVANT,

THE EDITOR.

ADVERTISEMENT.

THE Editor in presenting to the Public a new and correct Edition of Lyttleton's Tenures sincerely regrets, that some person, better qualified than himself, has not undertaken the task, which, at this day, considering the changes that have been wrought since Lyttleton wrote, and especially in the Law of Real Property, during the last eight years, seems to involve something more than a mere collation of texts.

Although the Editor did not undertake his self-imposed task without being fully sensible of his own disadvantages, he has not shrunk from performing, to the uttermost of his small ability, what he has deemed a responsible, and some may consider a presumptuous, effort—the addition of notes and introductory remarks to each Chapter, so that the General Reader and Student, (for whose use this Edition has been prepared), may be apprised of the extent of those alterations that have lately taken place, and are now prospectively coming into operation. The Editor has also carefully reduced the text into marginal notes.

With regard to the text of Lyttleton, which the Editor trusts is now rendered perfect, every possible attention and care has been expended; and no trouble has been spared by the Editor, in either gaining complete access to, or procuring, every copy of Lyttleton in print*.

The present Edition contains the text of the earliest Edition by *Lettou & Machlinia* minutely collated with the Edition by *Machlinia,* and with that known as the *Rohan* Edition. The orthography adopted has been that of the two latter; the spelling of these being more uniform and correct than that of the former.

It has not been thought necessary to encumber this Edition with one-tenth part of the various readings of Lyttleton; therefore, only those which appeared to the Editor material have been noticed; and in forming his judgment upon the materiality or importance of those variations, he has been guided chiefly by a desire to strengthen the authenticity of the acknowledged text, and to demonstrate its preciseness of expression, when placed in juxta-position with those parts which, from their inconsistence with previous text, or other causes, may be deemed questionable, if not absolutely spurious.

From an anxious desire that nothing should be noted but what is necessary or material, every sheet has been minutely revised, with the original and other Editions, twice, and sometimes thrice, (pursuant to the plan adopted in printing the authentic Statutes of the Realm),

---

* The three small Editions by Pynson (see p. xlvii), must be excepted; the absence of these, the reader will not have occasion to regret, as most of the corruptions of the text originated in these and the preceding Edition of 1516. The Editor has never given a reading from any Edition of Lyttleton, without having actually seen and collated the copy described or alluded to.

each revision retrenching or compressing the contents of the former copy, so that considerable portion of the labour actually expended does not appear before the public, whilst the expense of the publication has been necessarily increased.

The Translation has been taken from that used by Sir Edward Coke, varied occasionally with one of the ancient Translations, which also formed the foundation of his; and, indeed, as the public, by long and frequent use, has been so familiarized with that Translation, that it has obtained, in some degree, the credit of an original, the Editor has conformed to the deference paid to it, in following it, but he has not scrupled to deviate from it, when he found (as was not unfrequently the case) that text faulty, or, where more precise and critical modes of expression became necessary.

The Editor has not given the original text of *The Olde Tenures*, but a Translation by *William Rastell*, the text being very unsettled.

T. E. TOMLINS.

4, Halton Place,
Cross Street, Islington,
18*th October*, 1841.

PREFACE.

IT has been remarked, that neither *Lyttleton,* or his great Commentator, *Sir Edward Coke,* ever once mention or allude to the doctrines of feudal law, although the learned persons who have illustrated their works have been constantly under the necessity of referring to the doctrine of *fiefs.* The fact seems to have been, that *Lyttleton* presupposed, in some measure, a knowledge of this learning in his reader, and *Sir Edward Coke* as a Commentator confined himself to the text which treats more of the practical effect of the feudal system, as applied to the Laws of England, than of the doctrine itself; and as the feudal restraints, which operated chiefly as a bar to alienation, were vanishing even when *Lyttleton* wrote, there was little occasion to refer to doctrines which were then growing out of practical knowledge, and which did not seem, at first sight, to be closely connected with the Law of Real Property.

The consequence, however, has been, that *Lyttleton's* Treatise has been misunderstood and undervalued by Foreign Jurists, at the head of whom appears *Hottoman,* who, in his Treatise "*De Verbis Feudalibus,*" thus expresses himself:—"*Stephanus Pasquerius excellenti vir*

ingenio, et inter Parisienses causidicos dicendi facultate præstans, libellum mihi Anglicanum Littletonium dedit, quo Feudorum Anglicorum Jura exponuntur, ita inconditè, absurdè, et inconcinnè scriptum, ut facilè appareat, verissimum esse, quod Polydorus Vergilius, in Anglicâ Historiâ, de Jure Anglicano testatus est, stultitiam in eo libro, cum malitiâ (*a*), *et calumniandi studio, certare*." This passage from *Hottoman* is cited without any disapprobation in the 6th edition of "*Struves*' *Bibliotheca Juris Selecta;*" but in the 8th edition of that work (*Jenæ* 1756) it is qualified by the words "*Singularia sed* parum apta sunt, *quæ Franciscus Hottomanus profert, &c.*" (*b*). *Gatzert*, another Foreign Jurist (*c*), notices *Lyttleton* with somewhat more consideration; but has erred in supposing that the Book was published in French and Latin (*d*), and by a misprint has confounded the date of

---

(*a*) It is difficult to account for *Hottoman's* imputing "malitia" to *Lyttleton*, other than by supposing that the reason given for barring a right in some of the cases of *Lyttleton* is "folly" in the party. This reason *Hottoman* may have deemed capricious, and especially by him, as a professor of the Roman law, which is calculated to embrace a most comprehensive system of equity.

(*b*) When *Dr. Cowell*, in his *Law Dictionary*, cited the passage in question from *Hottoman*, it raised universal indignation, and he expunged it from the later editions of his book. It certainly was unjust to impute it as a crime to *Dr. Cowell*, that he inserted this citation in his work; but the manner in which it was received is a striking proof of the high estimation in which *Lyttleton's* Treatise was held.—*Butler's Pref. to* 13*th Edition Co. Lytt.*

(*c*) In his "*Commentatio Juris exotici Historico-Literaria de Jure communi Angliæ*."—*Gottingen*, 1765.

(*d*) The only mode of accounting for this mistake the Editor can suggest is, that *Gatzert* had been carelessly informed of the edition of the *Tenures*, in French and English, 1671, in double

Lyttleton's decease, and in other ways he shews that he had never attentively considered the Book of which he professes to give an account. The great repute which this Treatise of *Lyttleton* had obtained in England had reached *Gatzert*, for he concludes his derogatory notice of *Lyttleton* by adding, " *Cæterùm liber ob methodi brevitatem, argumentandi subtilitatem, atque dictorum ordinem, laudem omnino meretur; sed nec minus fatendum est, adeò sæpissime obscuritati bonum hominem studuisse, ut ænigmata legum maluisse, quàm præcepta, tradere videatur. Multa jam immutata esse, plura inveterata atque obsoleta, non urgeo. Interim communis ICtorum Anglorum hæc vox est perfectissimum et absolutissimum hoc opus esse ex omnibus quæ unquam in ullâ scientiâ humanâ scripta sint quæ unquam proferre potuerit hominis ingenium; non intelligere qui culpent. Ita parum abest, quin credant, falli eum fuisse nescium!*"

Any person who is acquainted with the feudal law prevailing on the Continent, and which till the year 1790 was in full vigour in France (*e*), will find on com-

---

columns; and it is possible that the Latin Translation of the first section of the *Tenures*, and an allusion to the first words of the chapter on fee-tail, also rendered into Latin by *Hottoman*, in his *De Verbis Feudalibus*, latterly printed as an Appendix to *Calvin's Lexicon Juridicum*, may have led to this error.—See *post*, p. 3, n.

(*e*) By a decree of the National Assembly, 4th August, 1790,

1. *Ils detruisent le regime feodal.*

2. *Ils abolissent la main-morte, la servitude et les droits qui les representent, ou qui y tient.*

3. *Ils declarent racheletter les autres droits et devoirs tant feodaux que casuels, meme les simples préstations et charges foncieres.*

4. *Enfin, Ils suppriment sans indemnité les Justices seigneurales.*

French feudality may yet be witnessed in Lower Canada; and

paring the same with our own system of jurisprudence, that jurisdiction of the lord (an inseparable incident to

---

as we derived the form of our tenures from Normandy, the *coutumier* whereof did not differ in essentials from the *coutumier* of Paris or other cities or districts in France, no apology need be made for offering to the reader what has been noticed on this subject.

When Lower Canada was first settled by the French, the feudal tenure was in full vigour on the continent of Europe, and naturally transplanted by the colonizers to the new world. The King of France, as feudal lord, granted to nobles and respectable families, or to officers of the army, large tracts of land termed "seignories," the proprietors of which were termed "seigniors," and held immediately from the king *en fief*, or *en roture* [corresponding to the knight's service and socage of *Lyttleton*], on condition of rendering fealty and homage on accession to seignorial property; and in the event of a transfer, by sale or gift, or otherwise (except in hereditary succession), the seignory was subject to the payment of a *quint*, or fifth part of the whole purchase-money; and which, if paid by the purchaser immediately, entitled him to the *rabat*, or a reduction of two-thirds of the *quint*. This custom still prevails, the King of Great Britain having succeeded to the claims of the King of France.

Quints is a fifth part of the purchase-money of an estate held *en fief*, which must be paid by the purchaser to the feudal lord, that is, to the king. If the feudal lord believes the *fief* to be sold under value, he can take the estate to himself, by paying the purchaser the price he gave for it, with all reasonable expenses. *Reliefe* is the rent or revenue of one year for mutation fine when an estate is inherited by collateral descent. *Lods et ventes* are fines of alienation of one-twelfth part of the purchase-money, paid to the seigneur by the purchaser on the transfer of property, in the same manner as *quints* are paid to the king on the mutation of *fief;* and are held *en roture*, which is an estate to which heirs succeed equally. *Franc aleu noble* is a *fief* or freehold estate held subject to no seignorial rights or duties, and acknowledging no lord but the king. The succession to *fiefs* is different from that of property held *en roture* or by *villainage*.

pure feudal tenure), and restraint of alienation by the the tenant, are the most prominent features, of which,

---

The eldest son by right takes the chateau, and the yard adjoining it; also an *arpent* of the garden joining the manor-house, and the mills, ovens, or presses, within the seigniory, belong to him, but the profit arising from these is to be divided among the other heirs. Females have no precedence of right; and where there are only daughters, the *fief* is equally divided among them. When there are only two sons, the elder takes two-thirds of the lands, besides the chateau, mill, &c., and the younger one-third. When there are several sons, the eldest claims half the lands, and the rest have the other half divided among them. *Censive* is an estate held in the feudal manner, subject to the seignorial fines or dues. All the Canadian *habitans*, small farmers, are *censitaires*. Property, according to the laws of Canada, is either *propre*, that is, held by descent; or *acquits*, which expresses being acquired by industry or other means [*scil.* purchase].

Dower in Canada is either customary or stipulated. The first consists of half the property which the husband was possessed of at the time of marriage, and half of all the property which he may inherit or acquire: of this the wife has the use for life, and the children may claim it at her death. If they be not of age, the wife's relations can take it out of the father's hands for them, and may compel him to sell his property to make a division. Stipulated dower is a portion which the husband gives instead of the customary dower.

Those farmers who hold land from the seigneur *en roture*, and who are termed *tenanciers* or *censitaires*, do so subject to certain conditions, *viz.* a small annual rent, and are also bound to grind their corn at the *moulin banal*, or the seigneur's mill, when one-fourteenth is taken for the lord's use as *mouture*, or payment for grinding. The *lods et ventes* [fines upon alienation] form another part of the seigneur's revenue: it consists of a right to one-twelfth part of the purchase-money of every estate within his seignory that changes its owner by sale; this twelfth to be paid by the purchaser, and is exclusive of the sum agreed on between the latter and the seller; and if promptly paid, a reduction of one-fourth is usually made (in the same manner as two-thirds of

in our remains of the feudal system, we retain but the bare reflection or image.

---

the *quint* due to the crown is made). On such an occasion a privilege remains with the seigneur, but seldom exercised, called the *droit de retrait* [*jus retractus*], which confers the right of preemption at the highest bidden price, within forty days after the sale has taken place.

All the fisheries within the seignories contribute also to the lord's income, as he receives of the fish caught, or an equivalent in money for the same. The seigneur is also privileged to fell timber, any where within his seignory, for the purpose of erecting mills, constructing new or repairing old roads, or for other works of public and general utility, and repairing churches, parsonage-houses, &c.

The duties of the seigneur to his tenants are also strictly defined. He is bound, in some instances, to open roads to the remote parts of his *fiefs*, and to provide mills for the grinding of the feudal tenants' corn. He cannot dispose by sale of forest lands, but is bound to concede them; and upon his refusal to do so, the applicant may obtain from the crown the concession he requires, under the usual seignorial stipulations, in which case the rents and dues appertain to the king.

The seigneurs were formerly entitled to hold courts in what was termed *haut-moyenne et basse-justice;* which took cognisance of all offences except murder and high treason.—*Martin's Hist. Brit. Colonies.* 8vo. Lond. 1834.

About thirty years after the British conquest of Lower Canada, in 1759, the common socage tenure was introduced, which is analogous to the *franc aleu roturier*, which, according to the *coutume* of Paris, is "terre sans justice ou seignieurie pour laquelle le detenteur ne doit cens, rentes, lods et ventes, ou autres redevances:" in fact, a fee-simple holden of the king in free and common socage, and being the same tenure by which land in England is ordinarily held, since the stat. 12 Car. 2, c. 24.

However, in Lower Canada, the land holden by seignorial grants preponderates in the proportion of 11 to 7, there being 11,000,000 acres seignorial, and 7,000,000 socage tenure.

The statute 6 Geo. 4, c. 59, was passed for the purpose of facilitating the gradual extinction of these feudal tenures, which are

Mr. Butler remarks, there is no doubt but our laws respecting landed property are susceptible of great illustration from a recurrence to the general history and principles of the feudal law. This is evident from the writings of *Lord Chief Baron Gilbert*, particularly his Treatise of Tenures, in which he has very successfully explained, by feudal principles, several of the leading points of the doctrines laid down in the works of *Lyttleton* and *Sir Edward Coke*, and shewn the real grounds of several of their distinctions, which otherwise appear to be merely arbitrary. By this he has reduced them

---

opposed to present habits and opinions; but the descendants of the original French grantees do not seem to avail themselves of the modes pointed out by the statute for converting the *seignorial fiefs* into the *franc aleu roturier*, or socage tenure.—*Id.*

It may be remarked that some remains of the *droit de retrait*, or *jus retractus*, a very copious subject in continental tenure, appear to have existed here. For example, the custom of Clivenor, p. 104, (*h*); and a custom that exists in some ancient demesne manors, of admitting a tenant to a new purchase without fine, p. 106, n., as at *Lambeth*.

To these observations may be added, as a well known fact, that in some parts of the United States of America the law of our lately abolished real actions, which were derived from the forms of feudal jurisprudence, and were a consequence of tenure, continues at the present day in full operation. *Mr. Hoffman*, in his *Course of Legal Study*, Baltimore, 1817, p. 184, states that, in the states of Massachusetts and New York, most of the real remedies have been preserved, with but little modification. The writs of right, dower, waste, assise, *formedon* in remainder, descender, and reverter; of entry in the *per*, *cui*, and *post*, &c., are, in Massachusetts particularly, in daily use, with all their concomitants of voucher and counterplea of voucher, imparlances, sole-tenure, non-tenure, disclaimer, aid, view, defaults, distress, summons, and severance, &c. &c. An American edition of *Booth on Real Actions* has been published, the Editor believes, by the same author.

to a degree of system, of which till then they did not appear susceptible. His treatise, therefore, cannot be too much recommended to every person who wishes to make himself a complete master of the extensive and various learning contained in the works of those writers. The same may be said of the writings of *Sir William Blackstone*, [*The Introduction to the Law of Tenures by Sir Martin Wright, and the Lectures on the Constitution and Laws of England, by Dr. Sullivan.*] Much useful information may be derived also from other writers on this subject.

But the reader, whose aim is to qualify himself for the practice of his profession, cannot be advised to extend his researches upon those subjects very far. The points of feudal learning, which serve to explain or illustrate the jurisprudence of England, are few in number, and may be found in the authors we have mentioned.—*Butler's Preface to* 13*th Edition of Co. Lytt.*

In 1766, *Mons. Houard*, an Avocat in the Parliament of Normandy, and Conseiller Echevin of the Town of Dieppe, published at Rouen, in two quarto volumes, the text of *Lyttleton*, with a French *Traduction* or paraphrase, notes, a glossary, and *Pièces justificatives ;* the object of this work is to shew the connexion that exists between our feudal law, and that comprised in the Norman *Coutumier*, in which he successfully demonstrates that the Tenures of *Lyttleton* are to be deduced from that source. This work, which is by no means scarce, may assist that student who is desirous of pursuing the subject of our Tenures to that fountain.

The reader need scarcely be reminded, that any system of jurisprudence derived from the maxims or doctrines of feudality, are utterly at variance with the

Roman law, whose rules of succession to real property, whilst they do not make any distinction between that and what we term personal property, are also in accordance with the most just and generally received notions of equity, so far as respects the division or inheritance of property (*f*).

With regard to property itself, the most simple mode of distinguishing or classifying it, is that which is derivable from its nature and incidents, either as moveable or immoveable; and every system of jurisprudence, whatever notion may prevail as to the inheritance and transmission of property, necessarily recognises these simple and marked distinctions. *Immoveable* property is land and hereditaments, *moveable*, goods and chattels (strictly so termed), and this classification is modified or subdivided according to the notions jurisprudents may entertain, or which from other causes may happen to prevail in every state as to these broad divisions or classes of property. In our law of property, which is derived from the principles of tenure, every thing that is or can be the subject of an express holding or tenure, whether land itself, or its honorary adjunct—a descendible title, is a " tenement," and, being heritable, is termed a hereditament; whereas moveable property, *viz.* goods and chattels, are not the subject of tenure or service,

---

(*f*) The *casus omissi* of the feudal law have, however, been supplied by the interpretation of the civil lawyers, and, consequently, gloss superincumbs gloss; and that fact doubtless has led some to suppose that there exists some close association between the feudal and Roman law: a notion that has been repudiated by the best authorities.

either actual or honorary. These two classes of property are in our law peculiarly distinguished; as, 1. Real; 2. Personal.

1. *Real property* comprises lands, tenements, and hereditaments. The term " tenements " comprehend all three, whilst the term " land " is only denominative of the soil, and " hereditament " means any thing inheritable.

2. *Personal property*, in addition to goods and chattels, extends to things which, though they may be collateral to, or connected with, land, yet could not be recovered *in specie*, *i. e.* the real thing itself could not be recovered in the same manner as land might have been, for which reason a peculiar form of action or process against the *land* was invented, termed a real action; whilst in respect of moveables and things not necessarily involving the actual right or title to the land, as leases or other inferior interests, the remedy to recover them lay in damages, *i. e.* the action was directed against the *person;* from hence has arisen the distinction between *real* and *personal* property, these terms "real" and " personal" having direct association with, and reference to, the means by which each kind of property was recoverable by law, *viz.* the form of action or process adopted by our ancient system of jurisprudence, so that those things which can be comprehended under the first division are known as *realty*, whilst that species of property which is comprehended under the second division are termed *personalty*, the first comprising land and interests in or profits out of land, as tithes, fisheries, rents, &c.; the latter containing property of a more transient and less durable nature, and in its turn modified and subdivided into

things that are said by our lawyers to " savour of the realty," *i. e.* interests which are carved out of land, such as leases and inferior interests termed chattels real, and into things purely personal, as cattle, furniture, plate, and whatever else is the object of manual occupation, sight, touch, and enjoyment, and being at the same time moveable, also termed chattels personal.

Property being thus classed under these easily recognised distinctions, the reader will perceive that the following Treatise of Tenures is solely concerning " tenements " *i. e.* lands holden, and hereditaments *i. e.* things inheritable, and inseparably or permanently annexed to land; for personal property, as well as those inferior estates called chattel (or rather prædial) interests in land, are only mentioned as of an inferior nature, and somewhat incidentally.

Lyttleton has commenced his Treatise by first discoursing on the estates which may be acquired in land, a subject so far as the qualities of such estates are concerned, resumed in the third book; the second book treats of the tenures and services upon which lands were formerly holden, with their incidents; and in the third, the operation of derivative or secondary conveyances, and the various means by which the course of descent may be interrupted or restored to the heir by act of the party, or by operation of law, are fully discussed in their order.

Even if the reader has not diligently addressed himself to the study of feudal law, he will not have much to regret, so far as concerns continental feudality; and with regard to the origin of English tenure, he will readily perceive that the English tenures were derived from a system already perfected at the time of its introduction here, and consequently well understood by the Norman Jurists, but which were not illustrated by reference to the *jus feodorum* of other nations, further than by the application of those rules or principles upon which all feuds were created, and which had reference to the general system: those rules had not long previously been reduced into the form of a *Coutumier*, and were introduced hither by our kings of the Norman race, as a model for tenures. The preservation of the estates and acquisitions of the Normans, which, in those ages, it was thought could only be supported by an institution strictly feudal, seems to have been the chief motive of introducing the Norman tenures here. However, those tenures having been transplanted from Normandy, where feudal polity had been much cultivated, they grew to their full vigour here, but were verging towards their declination when *Lyttleton* wrote, *temp.* Edw. IV. The reader will, therefore, have to consider the nature of an Anglo-Norman fief or feud, as distinguished from continental tenure generally, the latter being governed by certain undeviating principles, although diverging or declining into special customs or usages, to suit the genius of the nation or district adopting it.

The essential principles of feudal tenure were, that all land was holden of some superior lord, being the person first acquiring the land by succession or conquest, and who granted out portions to his followers upon condition to perform certain military services, retaining so much for his own tillage or *demesne* as was necessary for his own support; his followers and feudatories, the better to enable themselves to follow their lord in his wars according to the tenor of their service,

land granted in the same manner as their chief lord had done, upon render of similar services to themselves, and committed their *demesne lands* to their inferior tenants or *serfs,* who were bound to the land, and performed what were termed *base* and uncertain services, in contradistinction to *military* and *socage* services, which were certain and free. From these two kinds of tenure have arisen the two distinctions of free tenure and base tenure, from which a variety of more modern tenures sprang up, and form the subject of *Lyttleton's* treatise.

CONTENTS.

BOOK III.

ERRATA ET CORRIGENDA.

Page 9, *in n.*, *for* Catesby, J., *read* Catesby, (he was not created a judge till 22 E. 4).

38, *in n.*, *for* deforciat, *read* deforciant.

538, *in marg.*, *for* and of my right, *read* and release of my right.

636, *in n.*, *for* origninal, *read* original.

661, *in marg.*, *for* issue, *read* assets.

693, sixth line from the bottom, *for* serront, *read* ferront.

MEMOIRS

OF

LYTTLETON,

FROM

SIR EDWARD COKE'S PREFACE TO THE COMMENTARY.

The name and degree of our author.

OUR Author, a gentleman of an ancient and a fair descended family de Littleton, took his name of a town so called (*a*), as that famous chief justice, Sir John de Markham, and divers of our profession, and others, have done.

His arms.

Thomas de Littleton, Lord of Frankley [in Worcestershire], had issue Elizabeth, his only child, and did bear the arms of his ancestors, *viz.* argent a chevron between three escalop-shells sable (*b*).

Thomas Westcote.

With this Elizabeth married Thomas Westcote, Esquire, the king's servant in court, a gentleman anciently descended [from a family of that name in Devonshire], who bare argent, a bend between two cotisses sable, a bordure engrayled gules, bezanty.

(*a*) South Lyttleton, in Worcestershire; however, it appears that there were other families of note of that name in the counties of Dorset, Somerset, Bedford, and Bucks, as early as the reign of H. 3.

(*b*) A Thomas de Lyttleton, or L*u*ttleton (for so the family spelt their name before the reign of H. 6), about the 19 H. 3, married Emma, sole daughter and heir of Sir Simon de Frankley, knight.

But she being of a fair and of a noble spirit, and having large possessions and inheritance from her ancestors de Littleton, and from her mother the daughter and heir of Richard de Quatermains, and other her ancestors (ready means in time to work her own desire), resolved to continue the honour of her name (as did the daughter and heir of Charleton, with one of the sons of Knightley, and divers others), and therefore prudently, whilst it was in her own power, provided, by Westcote's assent before marriage, that her issue inheritable should be called by the name of de Littleton (*c*).

Our author bore his mother's surname.

Thomas the eldest [of that issue] was our author, who bare his father's Christian name Thomas, and his mother's surname de Littleton, and the arms de Littleton also; and so doth his posterity bear both name and arms to this day.

Camden.

Camden, in his Britannia, saith thus:—Thomas Littleton, *alias* Westcote, the famous lawyer, to whose Treatise of Tenures the students of the common law are no less beholden, than the civilians to Justinian's Institutes.

He was of the Inner Temple (*d*), and read learnedly upon the statute of W. 2, *De donis conditionalibus*, which we have. He was afterwards called *ad statum et gradum servientis ad legem*, and was steward of the court of Marshalsea of the king's household (*e*), and for his worthiness was made by

---

(*c*) On this marriage, Westcote settled at Frankley, and served the office of escheator there, the 29 H. 6, 1450; soon after which he died, leaving issue four sons and as many daughters: 1, Thomas, our author; 2, Edmund; 3, Guy; 4, Nicholas: which three last retained the name of Westcote, though often solicited by their mother to call themselves Luttleton. It is said, she once, expostulating with them, asked whether they thought better of themselves than their elder brother? They answered, "that he had a fair estate to alter his name; and if they might share with him, they would do the like."

(*d*) Sir Edward Coke states Lyttleton to have come from an university to the study of the common law.—*Co. Lytt.* 235. b.

(*e*) The name of Lyttleton does not appear in the *Year Books* before 28 H. 6, 145. However, in the *Paston Letters*, iii. 37,

King Henry the Seventh his serjeant, and rode justice of assise the Northern Circuit, which places he held under King Edward the Fourth, until he, in the sixth year of his reign, constituted him one of the judges of the Court of Common Pleas, [and granted him out of the customs of London, Bristol, and Hull, 110 marks yearly, *ultra consuetum feodum*,

King's serjeant, Rot. Pat. 33 H. 6, part 1, m. 16. Mich. 34 H. 8, fol. 3. a.
Judge of the Common Pleas, Rot. Pat. 6 E. 4, part 1, m. 15.

---

the following letter is given, which shews that he was then (*circa* 1445) fast rising in importance as an advocate, *viz.*:

"*To the Most Reverend Father in God, the Archbishop of Canterbury, Chancellor of England;*

"Beseecheth meekly your gracious Lordship, your own servant and orator, John Hauteyn, chaplain, that whereas he hath divers suits and actions in law, to be sued against Agnes, that was the wife of William Paston, of the manor of Oxnead, in the county of Norfolk; and forasmuch as your said beseecher can get no counsel of men of court to be with him in the said matters, because that the said W. Paston was one of the king's justices, and John Paston, son and heir to the said William Paston, is also a man of court, that it please your good Lordship to assign and most strictly to command John Heydon [recorder of Norwich], *Thomas Lyttylton*, and John Olston, to be of counsel with your said beseecher in the said matters, and other that he hath to do against the said Agnes and others, and your said beseecher shall content them well for their labour; and that this be done in the reverence of God, and by way of charity.

"John Hauteyn, Chaplain."

Lyttleton also appears to have been Recorder of Coventry *anno* 1450, when Hen. 6 paid that city a visit. The mode of the king's reception is entered in a *Leet Book* belonging to the corporation. The ceremonies used on that occasion are stated to have been adopted by *advice of counsel;* and by the manner in which "Thomas Lytelton, then Recordour, who seyde unto the Kynge such wordes as was to his thynking most plesaunt," is spoken of, it is not unlikely that he compiled the account of a ceremonial, of which, in all probability, the arrangement had devolved upon him.—See *Gent. Mag.*, Nov. 1792, lxii. part 2, p. 985, where the entry is given at full length.

ut statum suum decentius teneret, et expensas sustinere valeret, and moreover the sum of 106*s.* $10\frac{1}{2}$*d.* for a robe and furs, and 66*s.* 6*d.* for a summer robe called *linura*]; and he then rode Northamptonshire Circuit. The same king, in the 15th year of his reign, with the prince, and other nobles and gentlemen of ancient blood, honoured him with the knighthood of the Bath.

Knight of the Bath, 15 E. 4.

When he wrote this book. 14 E. 4, tit. Garranty 5.

He compiled this book when he was judge, after the fourteenth year of the reign of King Edward the Fourth (*f*),

---

(*f*) It is suggested that Sir Edward Coke had formed this opinion from the circumstance that many of Lyttleton's *cases* are vouched by the judgments decided by the *Year Books* from that time to the 18th Ed. 4. However, it is certain that the book, in a complete state, was published in MS. in Lyttleton's life-time; for there are now two MS. copies of Lyttleton's *Tenures* in the Public Library of the University of Cambridge, the distinguishing references whereof are *D d* 11. 60., and *M m* 52.; the first is written on vellum, and is imperfect at the beginning and in the Chapter of Warranty; and the second, which seems to be the most valuable, is written on paper, and has only one leaf torn, and its antiquity appears from the following note in the first page:

Iste liber emptus fuit in cæmeterio Sti. Pauli.
London, 27*th die Julii, anno regis E. 4ti.* 20*mo.* 10*s.* 6*d.*

This date shews that the manuscript is of Lyttleton's time, July 20, E. 4, being in 1480. In referring to the manuscripts, that in vellum is distinguished by Vell. MS., and that in paper, by Paper MS.; and both MSS. as *Camb. MSS.*

Sir William Jones noted the differences between these copies and the later printed copies; and the result is that these MS. copies confirm the general correctness of the three earliest printed copies, which, as well as some of later date, were printed from MSS. However, the Editor does not deem these MS. copies of greater authenticity than the three earliest printed copies, which were doubtless published with great care and circumspection, as the early printers were accustomed to bestow the most scrupulous revisal on their works.

but the certain time we cannot yet attain unto, but (as we conceive) it was not long before his death, because it wanted his last hand; "for that tenant by *elegit*, statute-merchant, and staple, were in the table of the first printed book, and yet he never wrote of them" (*g*). Litt. Sect. 692, 729, and 740.

Our author, in composing this work, had great furtherance in that he flourished in the time of many famous and expert sages of the law. Sir Richard Newton, Sir John Prisot, Sir Robert Danby, Sir Thomas Brian, Sir Pierce Ardern, Sir Richard Choke, Walter Moyle, William Paston, Robert Danvers, William Ascough, and other justices of the Court of Common Pleas: and of the King's Bench, Sir John June, Sir John Hody, Sir John Fortescue, Sir John Markham, Sir Thomas Billing, and other excellent men flourished in his time.

(*g*) That Lyttleton did intend to write of those tenancies, is plain from the 291st and 324th sections; but it may be justly questioned whether the fact alleged by my Lord Coke, to support his opinion, be true; because in the copy of the Rohan edition, now in Lincoln's-Inn Library, and in that at this time in the bookseller's custody, the table mentions nothing concerning these tenancies: nor does it seem probable that there ever was any other table, both the copies appearing, on the nicest examination, to be complete.—*Note to the* 11*th edition. See also page* 279 *of the present edition.*—The same remark equally applies to the copy in the Inner Temple Library, and to that copy *penes Ed.*

It may perhaps be assumed that Lyttleton abandoned his intention of treating upon the subject of Tenant by Elegit and Statute-Merchant; since the Old Tenures, which it was the object of his Treatise to illustrate, treats of these tenancies very copiously, considering the general meagreness of that tract. The book, either in MS. or in print, appears perfect. It may be collected from the Introductions to the 1st and 3rd books, and the concluding passage of the 3rd book, which supersedes the address to his son at the commencement of the 1st book, that the work was prepared in separate portions.

His marriage.

He married with Johan, [widow of Sir Philip Chetwynd of Ingestre, in the county of Stafford], one of the daughters and co-heirs of William Burley, of Broomscroft Castle, in the county of Salop, a gentleman of ancient descent, and bare the arms of his family, argent, a fess checkie or and azure, upon a lion rampant sable, armed gules; and by her had three sons, Sir William, Richard the lawyer, and Thomas.

His issue.

In his life-time, he, as a loving father and a wise man, provided matches for these three sons, in virtuous and ancient families.

His last will.

He made his last will and testament the 22nd day of August, in the 21st year of the reign of King Edward the Fourth, whereof he made his three sons, a parson, a vicar, and a servant of his, executors; and constituted supervisor thereof, his true and faithful friend, John Alcock, doctor of law, of the famous university of Cambridge, then bishop of Worcester; a man of singular piety, devotion, chastity, temperance, and holiness of life; who, amongst other of his pious and charitable works, founded Jesus College in Cambridge; a fit and fast friend to our honourable and virtuous judge.

His executors; his supervisor.

His age. His departure.

He left this life in his great and good age, on the 23rd day of the month of August, in the said 21st year of the reign of King Edward the Fourth (*h*): for it is observed

---

(*h*) Lyttleton's name appears in the *Year Book* of Michaelmas Term, 21 Edw. 4, as a Justice of C. P. (in the first *placito* of that term); so that it seems he was alive in October, 1481, for Michaelmas Term then began in that month. Sir John Catesby appears, by the *Chronica Juridicialia*, to have been made C. J. C. P. 20 Nov. 1482. The first Editor of Coke's *Reports* has, in the margin of the Preface to the 10th Report, referred to this *Life of Lyttleton*, by Sir Edward Coke; but he adds, "Note therein divers errors" The inscription on the tomb might easily lead to such a mistake, by the omission of a *minim* in engraving the date: assuming the inscription to have been truly copied.

for a special blessing of Almighty God, that few or none of that profession die *intestatus et improles*, without will, and without child; which last will was proved the 8th of November following, in the Prerogative Court of Canterbury, for that he had *bona notabilia* in divers diocesses. But yet our author liveth still *in ore omnium jurisprudentium* (*i*).

(*i*) Lyttleton's Will.

In the name of God, Amen. I, Thomas Lyttelton, knight, oon of king's justice of the Common Place, make my testament, and notifie my wille, in the manner and forme that followeth. First, I bequeth my soule to Almighty God, Fader, Sonne, and Hollye Ghost, three Persons and oon God, and our Lorde, Maker of heven and erth, and of all the worlde; and to our most blessed Lady and Virgin, Seynt Mary, moder of our Lord and Jesu Christ, the only-begotten Sonne of our said Lorde God the Fader of heven, and to Seint Christopher, the which our said Lord did truste to bere on his shoulders, and to all the saints of heven: and my bodie to be berried in the tombe I lete make for me on the south side of the body of the cathedrall-church of the monasterë of our said blessed Lady of Worcester, under an image of St. Christopher, in caas if I die in Worcestershire. Also, I wulle and specially desire that immediately after my decesse, my executors find three gode preests for to singe iij. trentals for my soule, so that everich preest by himself sing oon trental, and that everich such preest have right sufficiently for his labor; also that myn executors find another gode preest for to singe for my soule, five masses and rowe; the office of which begynneth, *Humiliavit semel ipsum Dominus Jesu Christus usque ad mortem.* Also I give one hundred shelings by yere to the priour and covent of the said monasterë, out of certain messuages and landes in the citë of Worcester, and to their successors, to sing at the altar hallowed for the worship of St. George and Saint Christopher, daily, at vii. in the morning, for the soules of my fader and moder, and for the soule of William Burley, my fader-in-lawe, and for the soule of Sr. Philip Chetwin, and for all soules that I am most specially bounden to praye, and specially for myn own soule after my decesse; and that everich such monk sing everich Friday, a mass of *requiem*, and ij*d.* for his troubel to be paid him by the handes of the sexton; and I wulle that whenever the co-

1 H. 7, fol. 27. 21 H. 7, fol. 32. Littleton is named in 1 H. 7, and 21 H. 7. Some do hold, that it is no error either in the reporter or printer;

---

vent singe the annual *placebo* and *dirige* and *requiem* for my soule, and that of my ancestors, that they have vis. viii*d*. for their disport and recreation. I wulle that the said covent have C.*lib*. for performyn this dyvin servyce.

Also I wulle, that the feoffees to myn use, of and in the halfyndele of the manor of Baxterley and Bentley, in Warwickshire, and in Moselĕ, in the lordship of Kingsnorton and in Stonebesyd-Keddermyster, in Worcestershire, make a sure estate unto Richard Lyttelton, my sonne, and to the heirs of his bodie, with all chartours, muniments and evidences concerning the same.

Also I wulle, that he have the reversion of the manor of Molstou-besyde-Clybery, in the county of Shrewsbury. Also I wulle, that my said sonne Richard have all my state, title and interest that I have in a messuage in the parish of St. Sepulchre's of London, on the north side of the said church, which I hold of the Abbot of Leicester for term of yeres. Also I wulle, that the feoffees to myn use of and in the manor of Spechley, in Worcestershire, make a sure estate to my sonne Thomas Lyttelton and the heirs of his body, with all chartours, &c., concerning the same, and all other lands, rents, reversions and services that I have in Spechley, Cuddelly, Bradicot and Whitelady Aston, with the lands and tenements in Weddesbury in com' Stafford.

I wulle, that my wyf have a bason, in the myddes whereof been myn arms, and an ewer of silver, two great salt-salers, and a kever weying 93 ounces and ½; a standing plaine gilt peece, with a plaine gilt kever weying 24 ounces and ½; six bolles of silver in the myddes of which been enamelled for her using six months of the yere, a standing peece with kever weying 19 ounces and ½, two peeces of silver covering another the which I occupie at London, a powder boxe of silver, a paxe borde, two cruetts and a sakering bell, all of silver. Also I wulle, that William Lyttelton my sonne and heire shall have a depe washing-bason of silver weying 41 ounces, and two salt-salers of silver, with a kever to oon of them weying 31 ounces and ½, with another peece all over gilt in the myddes of which be iij. eagles, a kover weying 33 ounces, also a lowe peece of silver with a kover embossed in the likeness of roses weying 29 ounces, also a standing gilt nutt and the best dosein of the second sort of my spones.

but that it was Richard the son of our author, who in those days professed the law, and had read upon the statute of

---

Also I wulle, that Thomas Lyttelton my sonne have two salt salers of silver weying 27 ounces, a standyng peece weying 21 ounces gilt and myn arms in the myddes of the same, also a boll of silver embossed with gold bosses outward weying 11 ounces and three quarters, also he shall have a dosein spones of the third sorte.

Also I bequeth my gode littel mass book and gode vestment with the apparel to an auter of the same sorte of vestments which were my moder's, and also a gilt chalës, I geve them to the blessed Trinitë, to the use and occupation of my chapel of Frankley in honour of our said most blessyd Trinitë ; inasmuch as the said chapel of the blessyd Trinitë and an aulter thereof is halowed in the worship of the said blessyd Trinitë, for to have masse songen there on Trinitë Sunday and other high festivals and other days to the pleasure and honour of our said most blessyd Trinitë. I wulle, that a bigger cofer and locke and key be provyded for the safe keping of these vestments and chalës, within the chapel of Frankley; and the Lord of Frankley for the time being have the keping of the said key by himself, or som true and faithful person, so that he se that the said masse book, vestments, chalës and apparyl be surely kept as he will answer to the blessed Trinitë. Also I wulle, that my great antiphoner be ever more had and surely kept in worship of God and St. Leonard to the use and occupation of and for the chapel church of St. Leonard of Frankley. Also I wulle, that all my utensils of myn houshold, except silver plate, as beds, matraces, blanquetts, brushes, tables, all pots and chaldrons, and all such things that longith to my kechyn, after the third part geven to my wyf, be equally devided between my three sonnes.

Whereas I have made certaigne feoffees of my manour of Tixhale, in Staffordshir, for terme of the lif of my wyf, the which manour she had a jointour for terme of her lif, with me, neverthelater my wille is, that my said wyf do not hereafter trouble, vexe, ne disturbe my wille and ordenance that I have and will mak of and in or for certaigne lands and tenements within the citë of Worcester ; now my will and ordenance is, that she shall have the saide manour of Tixhale, with the revenuz thereof, during her lif, or else that the profitts thereof shall be taken and

W. 2, cap. 11. W. 2, *quia multi per malitiam*, and unto whom his father dedicated his book: and this Richard died at Pilleton Hall

---

disposed in alms deeds for my soule by myn executour or by such other as I wulle thereto assigne during her lif.

I wull that my three sonnes and Sr. Xtopher Goldsmyth, parson of Bromsgrove, Sr. Robert Bank, parson of Enfield, and Robert Oxclyve, be myn executours; that the three first have xx. *lib.* in money apeece, toward their increce and profit, the latter v. marcs each of money, trusting in them that they wull do their diligent labor to se that my will be performed; the which as they know well the performyng thereof in godely hast and tym, that shall be to the hasty remedie of my soule, and the long tarying thereof is to the retardation of the meritts of my soule: wherefor I wull that everich of my said sonnes to whom my grete specyal trust is, as kind nature wull, for to performe and execute my will aforesaid.

I wulle that my wyf have my best plough, and all apparyl thereto, and ten of my best plough oxen, and my best waine; and that William Lyttelton have my second best waine, two ploughs and ten oxen. Also I wulle and specially desire all the money, debts, goods and catells that be myn at tym of my deth, over and above the cost and expensys of myn exequies and funeral, and over that that is bequethed by me in my lyf, be sould and disposed for my soule, in alms and charitable deeds, that may be most profitable and merit to my soule. Also I wulle that all my beests and quick cattel not afore bequethed, after myn exequies and funeral, be sold by myn executours, and to be disposed as they think most expedient for my soule.

I wulle and bequeth to the abbot and convent of Hales Oweyn, a boke of myn called *Catholicon*, to theyr oun use for ever; and another boke of myn, wherein is contaigned the *Constitutions Provincial*, and the *De gestis Romanorum*, and other treatis therein, which I wulle be laid and bounded with an yron chayn in some convenient part within the said church at my costs, so that all preests and others may se and rede it when it plesith them. Also I wulle and bequeth to Sr. Richard my preest xl. *s.* in money, and the same to my servant Hawkins. Also I bequeth to Dame Jane my wyf, xx. *lib.* in money in recompense of a silver bason, the which was somtyme her husband's Sir Philip Chetwin's; to the said Dame Jane my best habyt, that is to

in Staffordshire, in 9 H. 8. [The family became extinct, 1812].

The body of our author is honourably interred in the cathedral church of Worcester, under a fair tomb of marble, with his statue or portraiture upon it, together with his own match, and the matches of some of his ancestors, and with a memorial of his principal titles; and out of the mouth of his statue proceedeth this prayer, *Fili Dei miserere mei,* which he himself caused to be made and finished in his life-time, and remaineth to this day (*k*). His wife Johan, Lady Littleton, survived him, [dying in 1505], and left a great inheritance of her father, and Ellen her mother, His sepulchre.

---

saye, my goun, cloke and hode. Also to my daughter Elyn my second best habyt, in lyke forme. Also to Alice my second daughter my third best habyt, in lyke forme. Also I bequeth my gloset saulter to the priorie of Worcester. Also I bequeth a boke called *Fasciculus Morum* to the church at Enfield. Also I bequeth a boke called *Medulla Grammatica* to the church of Kingsnorton. Also I wulle that my grete English boke be sold by myn executors, and the money thereof to be disposed for my soule.

I bequeth to Thomas Lyttelton, my sonne, a little flatte peece of silver, with a kover, all over gilte. Also to Edward Lyttelton, my god-sonne, a little standing goblet of silver, with a kover to the same all over gilt. And I wulle and specyally desire my moost betrusted Lord, my Lord Bishop of Worcester, to be overseer of this my will, to be performed as my moost special trust is in his gode Lordship. In witness whereof to this my will I have sett my seale, these being witnesses, Sir Richard Howson, priest, Roger Hawkeyns, Thomas Parkess, and others. Written at Frankley, 22 August, the yere of our Lord Jesu Christ MCCCCLXXXI.

(*k*) These figures, with various shields in brass, containing the heraldic memorials of his family, were torn off in the civil war, and nothing left but the following inscription on brass, round the verge of the tomb:—*Hic jacet corpus Thome Littleton de Frankley, Militis de Balneo, & unus Justiciariorum de Communi Banco, qui obijt* 23 *Augusti, Anno. Dom. MCCCCLXXXI.* The tomb has been subsequently restored.

daughter and heir of John Grendon, Esquire, and other her ancestors, to Sir William Littleton her son.

When this work was published.

This work was not published in print, either by our author himself, or Richard his son, or any other, until after the deceases both of our author and of Richard his son. For I find it not cited in any book or report, before Sir Anthony Fitzherbert cited him in his *Natura Brevium*, who published that book of his *Natura Brevium* in 26 Hen. 8. [1534]. Which work of our author, in respect of the excellency thereof, by all probability should have been cited in the reports of the reigns of E. 5, R. 3, H. 7, or H. 8, or by St. Jermyn in his book of the Doctor and Student, which he published in the three and twentieth year of H. 8, if in those days our author's book had been printed (*l*). And yet you shall observe, that time doth ever give greater authority to works and writings that are of great and profound learning, than at the first they had. The first impression that I find (*m*) of our author's book was at Roan in France, by William de Tailier (for that it was written in French) *ad instantiam Richardi Pinson*, at the instance of Richard Pinson, the printer of King Henry the Eighth, before the said book of *Natura Brevium* was published; and therefore upon these and other things that we have seen, we are of opinion, that it

F.N.B. 212. C.

Note.

When this work was first imprinted.

(*l*) The poet Skelton, who died in 1529, notices Lyttleton's *Treatise* as a work well known in his time:

> After old segnyours
> And the learning of Littleton Tenours.
>
> *Boke of Colin Clout.*

(*m*) Sir Edward Coke appears to have had various opinions as to the time when Lyttleton's *Treatise* first appeared in print, see *post*, p. xlv. The Editor believes that what Sir Edward Coke terms the *Original* was a MS. copy; for it is certain that some of the readings he supplies from the *Original* (see pp. 329 (†), 210 (*), 255 (*), 588 (†), 591 (†)), are not given in the three earliest printed copies mentioned at §§ 35, 172, 221, 277, 283, 619, 621, 684, 702.

was first printed about the four and twentieth year of the reign of King Henry the Eighth, since which time he had been commonly cited, and (as he deserves) more and more highly esteemed (*n*).

Account of the editions of Littleton without the Commentary.

(*n*) This opinion of my Lord Coke's, concerning the time of the first impression of Lyttleton's *Tenures*, although it hath been followed by Sir William Dugdale, in his *Origines Juridiciales*, and by Bishop Nicholson, in his *Historical Library*, is certainly erroneous; for it appears, by two copies now in the bookseller's custody, that they were printed twice at London in the year 1528: once by Richard Pinson, and again by Robert Redmayne; and that was the nineteenth year of the reign of H. 8. To determine certainly when the Rohan edition was published is almost impossible; and before any conjectures can be offered on that subject, it will be necessary to consider how conclusive the arguments his Lordship draws from our author's not being cited as authority in the books he mentions may be: it either proves what his Lordship uses it for, or else that Lyttleton's authority was not then so well established as it is now (for which he gives us here a very good reason): and that this last is true, the aforesaid editions do sufficiently evince, for their titles and conclusions run thus: "Lyttleton's *Tenures*, newly and most truly corrected." And in the end, "Expliciunt Tenores Littletoni cum alterationibus eorundem et additionibus novis, necnon cum aliis non minus utilioribus:" nay, these very additions are incorporated into the book itself, nor are they distinguished by any mark from the original. The weakness of this argument will further appear, if it should be applied to the discovering the time my Lord Coke's *Commentary on Lyttleton* was first published; for this was not cited as authority for some time after its publication. The old editions above mentioned, Pynson's and Le Talleur's name, and the manner Lyttleton is printed in at Rohan, seem to be the only means of discovering what we seek. From those editions we may collect, not only that the Rohan impression is older than the year 1528, but also, by what occurs in the beginning and end of them, that there had been other impressions of our author. From Pynson's name at the end of the Rohan edition, it may be concluded that he would not have engaged his friend William Le Talleur to have printed Lyttleton

His picture.

He that is desirous to see his picture, may in the churches of Frankley and Hales-Owen see the grave and reverend

---

at Rohan, had he ever before printed any books in French; and that he printed an *Abridgment of the Statutes*, part of which is in French, in the year 1499, appears by one of those books now in the same person's custody. Statham's *Abridgment* has his name to it, but there is no date; yet it being printed with the same types, and in the same manner Lyttleton was at Rohan, and as it is a larger book, it is highly probable it was printed some time after the publication of Lyttleton's *Tenures;* and that Pynson's success in the lesser undertaking induced him to venture on the greater, which in those days was the work of two or three years. William Le Talleur printed a *Chronicle of the Duchy of Normandy*, as appears by his name and cypher at the end thereof, and the date in the beginning in the year 1487. The book itself is printed without any title-page, initial letter of the chapters, number of the leaves or year, and in a character much resembling writing, and with such abbreviations as are used in manuscripts: all which, it is well known to those who have seen many old books, are undoubted proofs of a book's being printed when that art was in its infancy. Upon the whole it may certainly be concluded that the book was printed some years before 1487; because the above-mentioned *Chronicle*, which hath not so much marks of antiquity, was printed in that year; and from what has been observed concerning the manner it is printed in, it will be thought by those who are versed in ancient books to have been published ten years before that time.—*Note to the* 11*th Edition.*

It has not yet been settled, and perhaps cannot now be settled with any degree of precision, when the first edition of Lyttleton's work was printed. Sir Edward Coke's mistakes respecting the Rohan edition are pointed out in the note taken from the 12th edition to that part of his Preface. Dr. Middleton, in his *Account of Printing in England*, conjectures the edition by J. Lettou and W. Machlinia to have been printed in 1481, and that it is the first edition. This makes the printing of the book to have been within six or seven years after Caxton's introduction of the art into England, and within twenty-four years after the first invention of it. Dr. Middleton's conjecture is supported by the concurrent circumstance of the time when those printers appear to

countenance of our author, the outward man. [A copy of this picture in line engraving, which represents *Lyttleton* in

---

have been in partnership; and no other edition bears evidence of a prior title to antiquity. Another edition, of nearly equal pretensions to precedence with the Lettou and Machlinia edition, has lately appeared from the library of the late William Bayntun, Esq. It has remained hitherto undescribed, and was probably unknown to all who have undertaken to notice the several editions of this work. At the end it is said to be printed by Machlinia alone, then living near Fleet-bridge; from which, and other circumstances, it is clearly distinguishable from the former edition. The letter used in printing it is less rude, and more like the modern English black letter than the letter used in the joint edition of Lettou and Machlinia, and the abbreviations are much less numerous. These circumstances afford some, though but a faint ground to suppose it posterior in date to the former.

At the end, both of the edition of Lyttleton by Lettou and Machlinia, and of that by Machlinia only, Lyttleton's work is called the "*Tenores Novelli,*" to distinguish it (it is presumed) from the Treatise of "*Olde Tenures.*"—*Butler's Preface to* 13*th Edition of Co. Lytt.*

Many editions of Lyttleton, in French and English only, have been published in small octavo, twelves, sixteens, and twenty-fours: they are all of them very inaccurate. Considering the universal estimation in which Lyttleton's work is held, and that it generally is the first work put into a student's hand, it is very singular that, since the editions by Lettou and Machlinia and the Rohan edition, no correct edition without the *Commentary* has yet been published.

The following is an account of the numerous editions of this work published since the introduction of printing, collected from Dr. Dibdin's edition of *Ames's Typographical Antiquities*, and from the Editor's inspection.

An Account of the Editions of "Lyttleton's Tenures."

Tenores Novelli, Empressi per nos Johez Lettou et Willz de Machlinia, ĩ c̃itate Londonia℞, juxta ecc̃az oĩm sc̃o℞: i.e. *The New Tenures, printed by us, John Lettou and William de Mechlin, in the city of London, near the church of All Hallows.*

This book is a thin small *folio*. It has no title, the above being a copy of the *colophon*, which commences, *Expliciunt*—&c. On

the act of prayer in his oratory, has been prefixed to every edition of *Sir Edward Coke's* Commentary, previous to the 13th, since which time this memorial has been discontinued.

---

the reverse of the first leaf is, *Incipit tabula huj' libri.* The table, or general index, gives the reference to each tenure according to the *signatures* a i. a ii. a iij. &c. On the *recto* of the second leaf commences "Tenant en fee-simple"—&c. This book has neither numerals or catchwords. The omission of the printed initial letters is supplied by the illuminator; the type is very barbarous, and made (as was the case long afterwards with the French printers) to resemble the set writing of MSS. This specimen of type, which appears to have been used by no other printer, although difficult to describe, may be deemed a coarse kind of *secretary-gothic.* The abbreviations are very numerous, and correspond to those used in MSS. No stops except the period or full stop, which, however, is used rarely.

The date of the publication of this edition is uncertain: it has been suggested by Dr. Conyers Middleton that it was printed about 1481; from the opinion of others who notice this edition, who attempt to fix a date by referring to contemporary publications by these printers, an earlier date may be assigned to this edition. The reader may perhaps form a better judgment than the Editor, as to the antiquity of this book, by consulting Dr. Conyers Middleton's *Dissertation on the Origin of Printing,* 1735; Ames's *Typographical Antiquities,* p. 76; and Dr. Dibdin's edition of the above, Lond. 1810—1816, ii. p. 6. Sir Thomas Tomlins, in his Introduction to the Account he prepared in print (not published) of the *Printed Collections of Statutes,* (for the use of the Record Commission, 1810,) gives it as his opinion that these printers published, in or before 1481, an *Abridgment of the Statutes* hereafter mentioned. Mr. Cay, in his Preface to the *Abridgment of the Statutes,* 1739, had expressed a similar opinion: and his data may perhaps lead to the conclusion that these printers published as early as 1471.

Tenores Novelli. Impressi per me Wilhelmũ de Machlinia in opulentissima civitate Londoniaꝝ, juxta pontem qui vulgariter dicitur Flete brigge: i.e. *The New Tenures, printed by me, William de Mechlin, in the most wealthy city of London, near the bridge which is commonly called Fleet-bridge.*

This book is of the size of the preceding, and commences in

In the copies of *Sir Humphry Davenport's* Abridgment of the Commentary, this print has also been given. The society of the Inner Temple, whereof *Lyttleton* was a member,

---

the same manner, having no title-page (the above being the *colophon*), and has, in like manner, the *Tabula*, referring each tenure to the leaves, according to their several signatures, a i. a ii., &c. The initial letters are either left in blank, or filled up by the illuminator, the illuminator being directed by a small letter placed at the corner of the blank space. The type resembles black letter, and is tall and full, but appears slightly ragged and unfinished, and of that description which is observable in early Mentz or Cologne printed books. Dr. Dibdin, whose labours prevented him from bestowing a minute collation on this book, states (*Bibl. Spenceriana*, iv. 385), that it is an exact reprint of the preceding; but this is not the fact: there is not only a difference in the spelling, which is much more uniform and less abbreviated, but these editions differ in §§ 10, 28, 35, 133, 168, 170, 172, 174, 177, 210, 225, 226, 231, 240, 260, 261, and subsequently; the paragraphs also are differently arranged at §§ 174, 202, 204, and in other instances. On the other hand, some errors by the preceding edition appear also in this, in §§ 107, 177, 222, 240, 246, 262, 415, and 694. It is agreed on all hands that this edition is of a later date than the preceding; but as to the exact period of publication, no precise information can be given. Conjecture has supplied the date of 1483, by a comparison with other publications from his press.

Tenores Novelli. Impressi per me Wilhelmū le Tailleur in opulentissima civitate Rothomagensi juxta prioratum Sancti Laudi ad instantiam Richardi Pynson: i. e. *The New Tenures, printed by me, William le Tailleur, in the most wealthy city of Rouen, near the priory of Saint Eloy, at the instance of Richard Pynson.*

This book is like the two preceding editions, in thin small folio, with a broad margin. There appears to have been some reprints or copies of this edition closely succeeding each other; for some copies are said to have a *Tabula*, as in the two preceding editions, and some have none; and the same with regard to the *colophon*. All the copies are said to have no title-page, whilst a copy, *penes Ed.* (which is without the *Tabula*), has what supplied the place of a

had his arms and quarterings painted in the windows of their dining-hall, which remained till the Civil War;

---

title-page*, *viz.* the device of Pynson, a small rude square wooden cut, not corresponding in appearance to any one of the *fac-similes* given by Dr. Dibdin. However, all agree that this edition (or editions) is printed with the same type as Statham's *Abridgment*, which was also printed at Rouen.—See Dibdin's *Ames*, ii. 461.

The Editor concludes, from the result of a minute collation, that this edition was compared with, if not reprinted from, the last preceding edition by Machlinia: the mode of spelling is not only more uniform than the two preceding, but there is a remarkable similarity in the spelling to the Machlinia edition, and, in some particular instances, peculiarities of spelling and errors have been copied (§ 308). The orthography is like that of the two previous editions, capricious and far from being entirely uniform; but there is a greater tendency to uniformity than in the Machlinia edition, and the blank, which is left in the commencement of the previous chapters, is, in the Chapter on Warranty, filled up by 𝔍 𝔏; which may perhaps shew an advancement in the art of printing; though it is to be remarked that the small letters inserted in *Machl.* at the corner of the blanks, to guide the illuminator, are not to be found in this edition. Common consent has placed this edition later in date than Machlinia, and various circumstances identify it closely with the two preceding copies; whilst some variations and omissions, such as are peculiar to MSS., seem to favour the idea that this book was also collated by the press with a MS. copy of Lyttleton.

This book is printed in a very small delicate type, resembling the writing used in MS., and is of that kind denominated *secretary-gothic*. The Editor considers that the date of this edition cannot be later than 1490, though this notion is at variance with the opinion of Dr. Myddleton and Dr. Dibdin, who both assign a somewhat later date. Dr. Dibdin is of opinion that the reasons assigned by the Editor of the 11th edition of *Co. Lytt.*, for the antiquity of this Rohan edition, namely, for its being printed in

* Title pages do not appear before 1488, or 1490; they first consisted of the printer's *device*; the next step was to place the title of the work on one, or perhaps two lines, over the device. Also see *Dibd. Bibl. Decameron*, ii. 297-8.

and they have at this time a fine picture of him at full length, painted by *Cornelius Jansen*, from the portrait (as it

1487, do not appear conclusive. This editor, Dr. Dibdin asserts, was ignorant of the history of printing at Rouen. All the present Editor ventures to remark is, that several Rouen-printed books, which he has seen of the date of 1500, display considerable perfection in the art of printing; whilst the appearance of the Rohan edition denotes its impression at a time when the art was far from perfect. Dr. Dibdin informs us that Pynson did not print *here* till 1493. Taking the sum of all the observations on this subject, it may not be unreasonable to assume that this edition was printed about 1490, although its comparison with the *Chronicle*, printed by Tailleur, is much in favour of its having been printed at an earlier date.

Sir Edward Coke, in attributing the date of 19 H. 8 to this book, which he deemed the earliest edition, was evidently guided by the only book of Pynson's printing he was acquainted with, having a date or some distinctive mark denoting the time of its impression; in *that* instance (for he was not always of the same opinion, as will presently be seen,) he was guided by an *Abridgment of the Statutes*, which included the statutes of 19 H. 8, printed by Pynson in 1528, as appears by the title-page of that book. This mode of computing the date of a book by such a reference or association appears very natural in that age, which, although so much nearer the invention of printing, was exceedingly deficient in typographic intelligence. In 1 *Rolle*, 317, (temp. Jac. 1,) *Davenport*, Serjt., says, "*Jeo aie un auntient Littleton, imprimee* 33 *H.* 6 [1455] per *Lettou*. *Coke*, C. J.:—"*Jeo aie le primer impression que fuit temps E.* 4." Davenport, in referring the publication of his antient copy to Lettou, in 33 H. 6, was guided by the fact of Lettou and Machlinia having printed an undated book, the *Vieux Abreggement des Statutes*, which concludes with the stat. 33 H. 6, c. 13 [1455], and which he might have concluded was printed soon afterwards. Another circumstance also may, in both instances, have more firmly induced the belief expressed, *viz.* that the earliest editions of *Lytt. Tenures* were seldom sold singly, but were bound with other books, chiefly the *Abridgments*, *Year Books*, *Olde Tenures*, or later statutes, instances of which are now observable*.

* *Worrall's Bibl. Legum*, p. 6. *Dibd. Bibl. Spencer*, iv. 284.

is conjectured) in the church windows of Frankley or Halesowen. Indeed, that learned society paid such respect to his

---

With regard to Serjt. Davenport's observation concerning his "auntient Littleton" (which it was utterly impossible could have been printed so early as 33 H. 6, as there is a case in that edition of Lyttleton, § 103, of 35 H. 6), it is to be noticed that an undated book by Lettou, *viz.* an edition of the *Vieux Abreggement des Statutes* and the *Tenures* is printed on similar paper, and paragraphed by the illuminator in precisely the same manner; and it is also known that the *Tenures* have been discovered bound up with it. Now, with respect to Coke's "*primer impression quc fuit temps H.* 4," his belief had relation to Statham's *Abridgment*, printed by William le Tailleur at Rouen, for Pynson, in the same type and also bound up with other early-printed books, as was the case with MSS., and most probably with the *Tenures*. Now *Statham's Abr.* contains all the cases of H. 6; consequently was printed since that time. Coke, in the Preface to his 10th Report, speaks of that book as having been first published in the reign of H. 6; but speaking more cautiously on this occasion, he ascribes the date of E. 4 to this edition of the *Tenures*, which was associated in his mind with the date of *Stath. Abr.* However, in the Preface to his *Commentary*, he acted upon what he thought a surer guide, by referring to the first dated book he had seen of Pynson's printing. Thus these discrepancies of Sir E. Coke may in some measure be accounted for.

Upon similar grounds, *viz.* the type, and the date of the latest case in *Stath. Abr.*, an anonymous commentator on Lyttleton, lately published, ascribes the publication of the *Tenures* to the period of H. 6, and refers to a similar statement made at the end of Ashe's *Table to the Reports**.

Leteltun Tenuris new correcte.

This is the title (printed on one line) of the next edition of Lyttleton, in *sm. folio*, and placed over the arms of France and England, supported by a dragon and greyhound, and surmounted with two angels, bearing an inscription encircling a rose. At the back of the title-page is a description of H. 7 and his court. At the end of the last page is a "Table," referring to the chapters,

---

* See Commentary on Lytt. edited by H. Cary, 8vo. 1829, p. 525.

memory, that, in 1639, Mr. Thomas Lyttelton, a collateral descendant of the judge, was admitted freely and without

---

as in the later and common editions; and at the conclusion, in addition to the barbarous verse which concludes the *Tenures*, is another still more rude, *viz.* Litilton Tenorum Lector jam cernitio finem. *Colophon:* Impressum per me Richardum Pynson, Anno Dni. MCCCCCXVI.

This book was printed at London, and not, as most of Pynson's legal publications were (*viz.* the *Year Books*, &c.), at Rouen. The text is most corrupt and vicious, and has, therefore, been seldom referred to in the present edition. A copy of this book, formerly belonging to the late Mr. Hargrave, is now in the British Museum, together with that learned gentleman's copies of the two first editions.

Pynson printed three other editions of Lyttleton, in a small form: the first two 16mo. and the last in 24mo. The title of the first of these latter copies is, Lytylton Tenures newly and moost truly correctyd and amendyd, placed over the king's arms crowned. *Colophon:* Londini in ædibus Richardi Pynsonis regij impressoris quarto idus Octobris MCCCCCXXV.—Dibd. *Ames*, ii. 460. On the last leaf is Pynson's invective against his brother printer and rival, Redman, in roman letter, thus:

"Richardus Pynsonus regius Impressor Lectori salutem.

"En tibi candide Lector jam castigatior (ni fallor) Littiltonus occurrit, Curavi ut e calcographia mea non solum emendatior verum etiam elegantioribus typis ornatior prodeat in lucem: quam elapsus est e manibus Rob. Redman, sed verius Rudeman, quia inter mille homines rudior*um*, haud facile invenies. Miror profecto, unde nunc tandem se fateatur typographum, nisi forte quum diabolus sutorem nauclerum, et illum calcographum fecit. Olim nebulo ille profitebatur se bibliopolam tam peritum quam unquam ab Utopia exiluit: Bene scit liber est qui præ se speciem libri fert, præterea fere nihil: tamen ausus est scurra polliceri, sua cura reverendas ac sanctas Leges Angliæ scitè verèque omnes imprimere. Utrum verba dare usus, an verax sit, tu Littiltono legendo. s. sua cura ac diligentia excuso, illico videas. Vale."—This abuse was repeated in an edition by Pynson of *Magna Charta*, 1527; but Redman appears to have taken this virulence in good part, returning no other answer, at least in print, than, *Si Deus vobiscum quis contra nos?* and, if we may believe the en-

fine to a chamber in that house, as a testimony of respect to his ancestor]; but he hath left this book, as a figure of that

The figure of his mind.

---

tertaining typographical gossip of Dr. Dibdin (who gives the cause of this quarrel), these printers were afterwards reconciled.

The next edition, being the fourth printed by Pynson and the third of his English-printed edition of Lyttleton, is in the same form as the last, with the following *colophon:* Explicitunt Tenores Littletoni cum alterationibus eorundem et additionibus nobis necnon cum aliis non minus utilioribus. Londini in ædibus Rich. Pynsonis, anno Dni. MCCCCCC xxviij, die vero xviij Junij, cum privilegio.

The last edition 24mo. is of the same date, concluding with *cum privilegio a rege indulto.*

These editions are very faulty, and some of the misreadings and interpolations date their origin from them; one especially at § 569, which had been noticed by the editor of the 11th edition of *Co. Lytt.* as an error manifestly corrupting the sense, and which has kept its place in H. Butterworth's faulty edition, which has been held out as printed from the Rohan edition. Pynson printed from about 1493 to about 1528.

The next printer who published the *Tenures* in French was Robert Redman, or Redmayne: he printed from 1522 to 1539, during which time he published two editions, one in sm. folio, and the other 12mo.: both without date. The title-page of both is, *Les Tenures de Lyttleton, novelment imprimes, et ovesque toute diligence revises, coriges, et amendes: et ensement ove plusours authoriteis annotes et marques en le marge de cest lyver ou mesmes les cases sount overtement debatus et purparles pluis a large,* placed over the king's arms crowned, and supported at the bottom by a dragon and a greyhound standing on the ground. On the back of this leaf, which is printed separate, is the Analysis of Estates, which has appeared in every subsequent edition of Lyttleton, (see p. lvi), intituled, *A Figure of the Division of Possessions.* This book is printed in a neat long primer roman, in double columns, has running titles, catchwords, and the leaves numbered: contains 52 leaves. The vergil (*vergule*) stop much used, and but few commas. *Colophon:* Emprinted at London by me Robert Redman. Cum gratia et privilegio regali.

This book, it has been conjectured, was printed about 1540 (which was the year of this printer's decease); but the

higher and nobler part, that is, of the excellent and rare endowments of his mind, especially in the profound knowledge

---

editor of the 11th edition of *Co. Lytt.* has ascribed to it the 19 H. 8, 1527-8. The invective of Pynson evidently alludes to a *Lyttleton* recently published, *viz.* the 12mo. ed.; and certainly the adoption of a roman type was more likely to prove attractive than the thick black letter of his rival. It seems certain, however, that the *sm. fo.* edition was printed after the 19 H. 8; for in the margin, and in the interpolated § 509, there is a case cited of that year.

The 12mo. edition of Redman's *Lyttleton* is in the style and type of the folio edition, without date, and, in other respects than the size, is much the same as the folio, which it seems to have preceded, *viz.* in 1525. The title is printed over a king's arms crowned.—See Dibd. *Ames*, iii. 236—239.

Lyttylto̅ Tenures newly imprinted. This is the title of a 24mo. edition of Lyttleton, published by Berthelet. *Colophon:* Londini in edibus Thome Bertheleti Reg. impressoris in Fletestrete prope aquagium sitis, sub signo Lucrecie Romane. Anno domini MD. xxx.

This book is printed with Venetian type, in a small round Gothic letter, and contains, almost in every respect, the same text with Redman. The vergil stop is much used, no commas. It contains, together with *Redm.*, a few cases which do not appear in other editions, except those that are reprints or copies of this edition. This text and that of *Redm.*, which it closely follows, is evidently taken from a MS. of the *Tenures*, later than that from which the earliest copies were printed, and which in the two first books varies in idiom and style from the four earliest printed copies, but not materially, or so as to affect the sense.

This edition was followed by impressions, in not dissimilar type, by *William Middleton*, 1545; *Henry Smyth*, 1545; *William Powel*, 1553; and *Richard Tottyl*, 1554. The title-page to these editions, which are mere reprints of *Berth.*, is, *Lytylton Tenures, newly revised and truly corrected, with a Table after the alphabete, to finde out briefely the cases desired in the same, thereto added, very necessary to the readers.* The latter edition, by *Tottyl*, is printed in the very same type as that of *Berth.*, and much worn, the other reprints are of the same type as that of *Middl.* These editions abound with corruptions, and are much interpolated.

of the fundamental laws of this realm. He that diligently reads this his excellent work, shall behold the child and

This state of the text of Lyttleton's *Tenures* appears to have induced Tottyl, the king's printer, to publish an expurgated edition; and accordingly we next find, in a small black letter character, *Lyttleton's Tenures*, conferred with divers true wrytten copies, and purged of sondry cases, having in some places more than then the autour wrote, and lesse in other some. *Apud Richardum Tottel. Cum privilegio* 1557. In this edition the place of the expunged interpolations is denoted by a small *asterisk*. The edition is neatly printed on a fine Dutch paper, and had been either preceded or succeeded in the same year by an edition of Lyttleton in every respect the same as the preceding, except the advertisement in the title-page denoting the purgation: indeed it would seem that the expunging of the "sondry cases" had been any thing than acceptable; for the next edition by Tottyl (17 May, 1567,) has for its title-page, LES TENURES de Monsieur Littleton, ovesque certein cases addes per autres de puisne temps, queux cases troverres signes ovesque cest signe [a *flower*] al commencement & al fine de chescun deux, au fine que ne poyes eux misprender pour lez cases de Monsieur Littleton: pur quel inconvenience, ils fuerent derniermemt tolles de cest livre et icy un foits pluis admotes al request des gentilhomes students en le ley dengleterre. (⁂). *Cum privilegio.* These editions, with some variations (for, on close collation, scarcely any two are exactly alike), were continued in 1569, 1572, 1577, and *1579, when, in 1581, West, the author of the *Symboleography*, furnished an index (a rude sort of table had been given in *Middl.*, *Sm.*, and *Powel*), and subdivided the text into *sections*, which, however injudiciously marked in this edition, have been ever since retained for the convenience of citation; at the end of this index, to which the editor adds, *Ingenij cibus studium, per W. West*, is his *Epilogus:*

"Lectori studioso VV. VVest, S.

"Animaduertas quæso (candide lector) me Littletonum (quo facilius quicquid in eo continetur invenias) in 749. partes dissecuisse, huncque in ipsum qualemcunque indicem ita congressisse,

* This edition is very neatly printed on very fine thin paper, and was, by Sir William Jones, deemed more correct than the other editions by *Tottyl.*

figure of his mind, which the more often he beholds in the visual line, and well observes him, the more shall he justly

vt singuli eius numeri, singulas libri sectiones designent. Errata autem (prudens lector) si qua forte, vel meâ, vel typographi incuria, pretermissâ sunt, amice corrige, ceterisque mecum, in tuum commodum fruere & vale. Ex interiori Templo, duodecimo calendas Iulij anno restitutæ salutis. 1581."

The restoration of the additions and notes, the adoption of the mode then in use of subdividing the text by sections, and the convenience of the index, seem to have driven away all competitors; and Tottel, or Tott*y*l (for he prints his name both ways), appears as the only publisher of *Lyttleton* in French, for he published these sectioned editions in 18mo. with some English copies† (of which more hereafter) till 1591; and then the publication was, on Tottyl's decease, taken up by *Charles Yetsweirt*, who published a 32mo. edition in 1591, and subsequently by the *Stationers*, who, in 1604, published an 18mo. edition, which has been rendered notorious by a misprint in § 712, more especially as Sir Edward Coke appears to have taken his text from this corrupted edition. See also p. 665. The title-page of these editions was the same as Tottyl's.

In or about 1594 (the edition is *sans* date), *Charles Yetsweirt* published another edition of *Lyttleton*, in 32mo., with the same title-page used by Tottyl, but with this addition, "*Revieu et corrige en divers lieux queux vous troveres signes ovesque ceux signes* * *." And he adopted a different mode of subdividing the text by numbered sections, the number commencing and concluding with each chapter. This mode of subdivision appears more judicious than that adopted by West, and certainly is more convenient as a mode of citation; but only one other edition appeared with this new and more rational mode of sectioning, published (*sans* date) by *Jane Yetsweirt* about 1597.

The *Stationers*, into whose hands the publication of the *Tenures* fell, naturally adopted the more saleable form; and they almost exclusively published the *Tenures* in French to 1627, and also in English till 1661, with the only exception of an edition in 32mo. 1621, and another *printed for the assigns of John More, Esquire*, 1639, to whose index the following address is prefixed: "*In tuam gratiam* (*candide Lector*) *Indicem* (*omnibus continuatis sectionibus*

†. Viz. in 1583, 1585, 1588.

admire the judgment of our author, and increase his own. This only is desired, that he had written of other parts

---

congruentem) nunquam antea impressum huic Littletono *apposui. Vtere, fruere: Errata amicè corrige et vale.* 1621."

The last edition of the *Tenures* in French was published in 1671, in tall 18mo., by an association of booksellers, who gave the text with the translation, in opposite columns, without the analysis or diagram usually prefixed to the tenures, and without subdividing the text by sections. The text of this edition differs from every other edition, and is evidently composed of the French of Redman's edition, and Sir Edward Coke's translation; but it has been carelessly put together, and the translation disagrees in many instances from the text. There is also prefixed a table or index of the principal matters: with all its faults, this edition is more creditable to the booksellers than those of late years, which are indeed beneath notice. One edition, which appears to have had the largest sale, printed by H. Butterworth, 1825, is extremely faulty, although it has found a place in Lowndes's *Bibliographer's Manual*, 1140, as being taken from the Rohan edition, and as bearing the name of the late Mr. Roscoe: qualifications to which its pretensions appear very slender.

Notice of the English editions, Littleton.

The *Tenures* appear to have been first translated by *John Rastell*, author, printer, and serjeant-at-law, who printed from about 1514 to 1533. There are two editions of this translation by him, one in *octavo*, the other in *sm. folio:* both *sans* date. Since that time, *William Rastell*, 1534 (two editions, 4to. and 12mo.); *Petyt*, who printed from 1536 to 1551; *Berthelet*, 1538; *Wyer*, 1542; *Middleton*, 1544; *Smyth*, 1545; *Powell*, 1548, 1551; and *Marshe*, 1556, have printed editions in 12mo., and these editions contain all that is in the earliest French editions; but in 1556 *Tottyl* published an 18mo. edition of this translation, which is very faithful and correct, and in almost every instance has anticipated Mr. Ritso's emendation of the text of what has been termed *Sir Edward Coke's Translation;* and in particular supplies a true reading where all the French copies seem to err (§ 432). Tottyl's edition, however, demands attention from the fact that §§ 459—461, 474, 521, 527, 552, 554—559, 568—570, 576, 577, 583, 584, 590, 591, 605, 609—612, 620—623, 625, 626, part

of law, and especially of the rules of good pleading, (the heartstring of the common law), wherein he excelled; for of him might the saying of our English poet be verified:

> Thereto he could indite and maken a thing; Chaucer.
> There was no wight could pinch at his writing:

so far from exception, as none could pinch at it. This skill

---

of 637, 638—642, 649, 650, all inclusive, part of 652, and the whole of 658, are not given, besides other small portions of text; and, as it seems, with good reason, as some of these sections are against law, and inconsistent with what Lyttleton had previously stated, or, at least, are repetitions of cases already put.

This translation was published by Tottyl, J. Yetsweirt, Wight, and other printers, to 1604; after whom the Stationers published this edition to 1661.

The translation commonly called *Sir Edward Coke's Translation*, is chiefly taken from some copy previous to Tottyl's first edition of 1556; but it often deviates from the text, and is in many instances very imperfect, loose and inaccurate: but as Sir Edward Coke always comments on the words from the French text, he evidently did not intend his translation, which was imperfectly collated, should supersede the text ofLyttleton.

The translation given in the English and French edition of 1671, set opposite to Redman's text, varies in many instances from the text, the French having several cases and passages not noticed in the translation, which is very plain to the most careless observer; and the translation, taken from some copy printed previous to Tottyl's edition, 1556, is altered by copying the defects of what has been termed *Coke's Translation* (§§ 352, 370); and a peculiar omission in that translation is also presented in this, see § 325.

None of the translations have ever been sectioned or subdivided for purposes of reference.

With respect to the editions of the Treatise called "The Olde Tenures," (which Sir Edward Coke, in the Preface to the Tenth Report, attributed the date of Hen. II., and in his Commentary, that of Edw. III., *post*, p. 92), the copies are scarce. The best account of them is in *Dibd. Ames*, and *Worrall's Bibl. Legum*. The present translation was made by William Rastell, who divided it

Good pleading.

of good pleading, he highly in this work commended to his son, and under his name to all other students sons of his law. He was learned also in that art, which is so necessary to a complete lawyer; I mean of logick, as you shall perceive by reading of these Institutes, wherein are observed his syllogisms, inductions, and other arguments; and his definitions, descriptions, divisions, etymologies, derivations, significations (*o*), and the like. Certain it is, that when a great learned man (who is long in making) dieth, much learning dieth with him.

Logick. [*Year-Book, Pasch.* 15 E. 4, *Forger de faux faits*]. Seneca.

The commendation of his work.

That which we have formerly written (*p*), that this book

---

into sections, and then appended it to the editions of his "Olde Termes de la Ley," 1571, 1576, 1579. *Serjeant Hawkins* also published this translation with *Coke's Tracts* in 1764. The editor has obtained an edition by Berthelet, 1531, which he considers more correct than the faulty editions by Pynson, or the still more faulty copy thereof prefixed to the Tenth and Eleventh Editions of Co. Lytt. With this assistance, the present translation of this ancient Tract has been given in the form it now appears.

(*o*) Sir William Jones remarks that although the great commentator on Lyttleton thought that excellent learning might be extracted from every "&c.," and that his "Notas" and "Items" had a peculiar force; yet, that in the *Camb.* MSS. many "&cas" are omitted and many added through the whole work, and very often *Item* is written for *Nota*, and vice versâ. This observation equally applies to the earliest printed copies of Rastell's Translation. In the three earliest French editions the "Item" preponderates. In *Pyns.*, 1516, *Item* most commonly occurs, as the commencement of every paragraph in the first two books, while *Nota* is almost always given in the third book. *Redm.*, *Berth.*, and the subsequent editions to Tottyl, 1554, inclusive, almost always adopt the "Nota," and in some instances place *Auxi* for the *Item*. Many of the "&cas." upon which Sir Edward Coke has commented do not appear in the three earliest copies; but these are retained in the present edition.

(*p*) Littleton's Tenures, a book of sound and exquisite learning, comprehending much of the marrow of the common law, written and published by Thomas Littleton, a grave and learned

is the ornament of the common law, and the most perfect and absolute work that ever was written in any human science; and that it is a work of as absolute perfection in its kind, and as free from error, as any book that I have known to be written of any human learning.

And albeit our author in his Three Books cites not many authorities, yet he holdeth no opinion in any of them, but is proved and approved by these two faithful witnesses in matter of law, authority and reason. Certain it is, when he raiseth any question, and sheweth the reason on both sides, the latter opinion is his own, and is consonant to law. We have known many of his cases drawn in question, but never could find any judgment given against any of them, which we cannot affirm of any other book or edition of our law. In **Note.** the reign of our late sovereign lord, King James, of famous and ever blessed memory, it came in question upon a demurrer in law, whether the release to one trespasser should be available or no to his companion? Sir Henry Hobart, that honourable judge and great sage of the law, and those reverend and learned judges, Warburton, Winch, and Nichols, his companions, gave judgment according to the opinion of our author, and openly said, that they owed so great reverence to Littleton, as they would not have his case disputed or questioned.

Mich. 3 Jac. in communi banc inter Cock et Ilnours.

---

judge of the Common Pleas, some time of the Inner Temple, wherein he had great furtherance by Sir John Prisot, Lord Chief Justice of the Court of Common Pleas, a famous and expert lawyer, and other the sages of the law who flourished in those days.—*Pref. to 10th Rep. page* 6.

A FIGURE

OF

THE DIVISION OF POSSESSIONS.

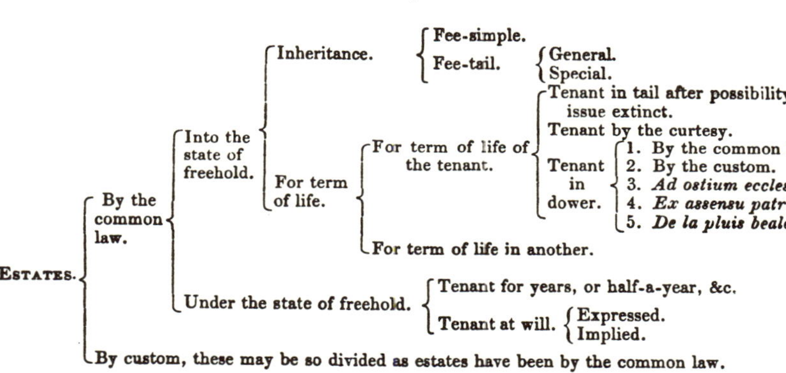

Ung brief Table, Exposicion et Division, par qui sont declares touts les Estates et Possessions des queux Lyttleton fait mencion en son Primer Lyver.—Redm., see p. xlviii.

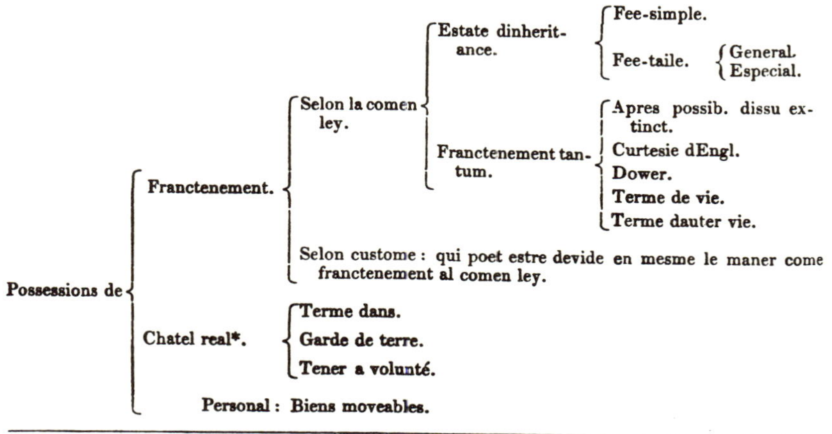

[* Potius predial ; car RES continet etiam res mobiles †.]

† MS. note by Sir Edward Coke, in a copy of *Lyttleton's Tenures*, 1572, formerly in his possession. This shews Sir E. Coke's great attention to accuracy in the definition of terms.

LYTTLETON'S TENURES (a).

BOOK I.

CHAPTER I.

FEE-SIMPLE.

LYTTLETON commences his Treatise by discoursing of fee-simple, (an estate of the highest degree in our law (§ 11)), which he informs us is a pure, rightful, and absolute estate descendible to a man's heirs, as a *fee* or fief (§ 1); he proceeds to shew what persons shall inherit (§ 2), distinguishing the course of descent from those who have taken by purchase or voluntary acquisition, and from those who themselves had succeeded by course of inheritance or descent) (§ 3—5). The peculiarities which till very recently subsisted in our law of descent: viz. the prohibition of lineal ascent, and the exclusion of the half-blood, are next noticed and illustrated by cases (§ 6—8). The distinction between those things which are said to *lie in livery,* and those which *lie in grant,* with an exposition of the term *purchase,* closes the chapter (§ 12).

(*a*) Tenure is in Latin *Tenor,* and is the same as *Tenor investituræ,* viz. the terms of a feudal donation or investiture, and is described by *Hotoman* (*de verb. feud. in verb. Tenor. Feud. Lib.* 2, *tit.* 2, § 2), as, *pactio contra communem feudi naturam ac rationem in contractu interposita. Craig,* (*de Jur. Feud.* 50), and *Zasius* (*in Usus Feud. p.* 123), also both interpret this word thus: *Tenor est qui dat legem feodo, et plerumque naturam feudi mutat.* English jurists use the word to signify the service reserved, or the express terms upon which any tenant holds his land, which in this country is either holden mediately or immediately of the king.

A BOOK of explanation of part of the Tenures, made for thee my son, for the better comprehending and understanding the Tenures*.

UN lyver de exposicion de parcell de les teneures fait a toy mon fitz, de plus melior apprendre et entendre les teneures *.

Tenancy in fee-simple defined.

1 Tenant in fee-simple (*b*) is he who hath lands or tenements to hold to him and to his heirs for ever. And it is called in Latin, *feodum simplex,* for *feodum* (*c*) is the same that

1 *Tenaunt en fee-simple est celuy qui ad terres ou tenementes a tener a luy et a ses heires a toutz jours. Et est appelle en Latin,* feodum simplex, quia feodum idem est

---

* Paper MS. See note at commencement of Book 3, § 241, where a similar introduction is given from the vellum MS.

(*b*) To hold in fee-simple, is to hold to any man or woman, to him and to his heirs and his assigns for ever. *Olde Tenures,* § 7. To hold in frank-fee is to hold in fee-simple, lands, pleadable at the common law. *Id.* § 15.

It seems, that the lands which were in the hands of Edward the Confessor, and as such mentioned in Domesday Book, are ancient demesne, and that all the rest of the realm is called *frank-fee. Brooke, Abr. tit. Demesne,* 32; *F. N. B.* 161; and the author of *Termes de la Ley* defines frank-fee to be a tenure in fee-simple of lands pleadable at the common law, (viz. not holden of any manor), and not in ancient demesne:—*feudum francum,* in the language of the foreign feudists, means, that fief for which no service is rendered; and in like manner, those lands which were held in frank-fee were exempted from all services, save homage.

(*c*) *Origo vocis est fe-od: id est, stipendii possessio. Grotius in flor. spars.* AD LIBRUM DE FEUDIS. See also B. C. ii. 45. n. (*f*),

inheritance is, and *simplex* is as much as to say, lawful or pure; and so *feodum simplex* signifies a lawful or pure inheritance.

Fee-simple, highest degree of estate.

quod hereditas, et simplex idem est quod legitimum vel purum, et sic feodum simplex idem est quod hereditas legitima, vel hereditas pura.

---

for the etymology of "*feodum.*" It has been already noticed in the Introduction, that the doctrines of feudal tenure here differed exceedingly from those maintained on the continent, so much so, that Lyttleton has not only been misunderstood, but contemptuously spoken of by *Polydore Vergil*, *Hotoman*, and *Gatzert*. The following is extracted from an Appendix (*De Verbis Feudalibus*) to *Calvin's Lexic. Jurid. Cologne, fol.* 1734:—" *Feodum pro feudum dixerunt multi, et in his Angli*: *Fortasse ab illa notatione Germanicæ vocis* FEUD, *de qua diximus* eodem Disput. cap. *Itaque vulgari lingua scribunt* FEE: *longissime tamen a Longobardici juris ratione et instituto, feoda namque generaliter appellant prædia omnia, quæ perpetuo jure tenentur, etiam Allodia, quæ a parentibus et majoribus hæreditate relicta sunt. Et aliquando feodum ipsis hæreditatem significat.* Hotomann. in Lexic. Feud. *Stephanus Pasquerius excellenti vir ingenio, et inter Parisienses causidicos dicendi facultate præstans, libellum mihi Anglicanum* Liteltonium *dedit, quo feudorum Anglicorum jura exponuntur: ita incondite, absurde, et inconcinne scriptum, ut facile appareat, verissimum esse, quod* Polydor. Vergilius *in Anglicana Historia de jure Anglicano testatus est, stultitiam in eo libro cum malitia et calumniandi studio certare. Sed operæ prætium, quas feudi species constituant, ipsorum verbis exponere. Feudum enim appellatur aliud simplex, aliud talicum.*" (Hotoman here transcribes the *first section of Lyttleton*, and adds his translation or paraphrase of it, which perhaps might have induced Gatzert hastily to believe there was a Latin edition of Lyttleton's Treatise). "*Id est: Feudatarius simplex is dicitur, qui prædia perpetuario jure possidet. Nam Latine feodum simplex vocatur, quia feodum idem est, quod hæreditas; et simplex, idem est, quod hæreditas legitima, vel hæreditas pura. Nam si quis prædia jure feodi simplicis adquirere velit, hac formula uti eum oportet: ut sibi suisque hæredibus habere et tenere licet. Hæc enim verba,* SUIS HÆREDIBUS, *faciunt rem hæreditariam, sive perpetuariam. At si utatur his verbis. ut tibi habere et tenere, perpetuo habere tenereque liceat: his duobus casibus ad vitæ tempus duntaxat acquiritur. Tum aliquanto post,* cap. 2. Fee-*taile: feudum taile*

In purchase-deed the word, "heirs" is indispensable, if an estate in fee simple is to be created.

For if a man would purchase lands or tenements (*d*) in fee-simple, it behoveth him to have these words in his purchase, "To have and to hold to him and to his heirs;" for these words "his heirs" make the estate of inheritance.

Qar si home voille purchaser terres ou tenementes en fee-simple, il covient avoir ceulx parolx en son purchace, A avoir et tener a luy et a ses heirez: Qar ceulx parolx, ses heires, *fount lestate denheritaunce.*

---

dicitur, cum prædia donata sunt alieno viro, et ipsius hæredibus ab ipso nascituris."

(*d*) Land (in a general signification) is any ground, soil, or earth whatsoever; whether arable, meadow, pasture, moor, marsh, ground covered with water, or producing wood, furze, heath, or other things, together with the water, (while it remains on the ground), and the wood, furze, heath, and other things growing thereon, or permanently affixed thereto; and the castles, houses, and other buildings, standing or being thereon; and as well all the ground, soil, earth, and other things, between the surface thereof and the centre of the earth, as the air and light, &c., above the surface thereof indefinitely. B. C. ii. 17, 18; Co. Lytt. 4. *a.*

Land (in a restrained sense) is arable land. Co. Lytt. 4. *a.* In deeds, the word *land* is used in the general signification before-mentioned; but in the parcels of a fine or recovery, this word was used in a restrained sense, and signified arable land.

Tenement is a large word to pass not only lands and other hereditaments and inheritances which are holden, but also offices, rents, commons, profits apprender out of lands, and the like, wherein a man may have a frank-tenement and whereof he can be said to be seised *ut de libero tenemento.* But hereditament is the largest word of all in that kind; for whatsoever may be inherited is an hereditament, be it corporeal or incorporeal, real, personal, or mixed. Co. Lytt. 6. *a.*

As to what are termed corporeal and incorporeal hereditaments, some mention is made in the concluding remarks to this chapter. Hereditaments are also generally classed as 1st, real, viz. lands and tenements; 2nd, personal, as an office or annuity; 3rd, a dignity, by name of a place.

The *feodum legitimum* or rightful or lawful fee of which Lyttleton speaks, is opposed and spoken in contradistinction to what are termed tortious or wrongful estates, which, though in cases before the operation of the stat. 3 & 4 *Gul.* 4, c. 27, § 39, they might pass a fee and in-

For if any man purchase lands by these words, "To have and to hold to him for ever;" or by these words, "To have and to hold to him and his assigns for ever:" in these two cases he hath no estate but for term of life, for that there lack these words "his heirs," which words only make an estate of inheritance in all feoffments and grants (*e*).

Collateral descent.

2 And if a man purchase land in fee-simple, and die without issue, he which is his next cousin collateral of the whole

Qar si ascun home purchace terres per ceulx parolx, A aver et tener a luy a toutes jours: ou per tielx parolx, A avoir et tenir a luy et a ses assignes a toutz jours: en ceux deux cases il ny ad estate forsque pur terme de vie, pur ceo quil faut ceulx parolx, ses heires, *queux parolx tantsoulement fount lestate denheritaunce en toutz feoffementes et grauntz.*

2 *Et si home purchace terres en fee-simple et devia sauns issue, chescun qui est son prochein cosin collaterall del entier sank,*

---

heritance, yet were deemed in law but oppressions and injuries. (See remarks of *Ed.* prefixed to chapter of Discontinuance, Book 3, § 592).

(*e*) The law has ordained certain ceremonies to be used in the change and transmutation of things from one to another, (and especially in the case of freeholds which are of greater price and estimation in our law than other things), in order to know the certain times when things pass; and, therefore, in every feoffment, the law has appointed that livery and seisin shall be had, and in every grant of reversion or rents, &c., that attornment shall be made, which are certain points containing the time when and to whom such estates do pass. *Plowd.* 25. Since the Statute of Uses, 27 *H.* 8, *c.* 10, by which estates of inheritance vest in possession without livery, the operation of that statute being to transmute all uses into possession, or, in other words, to vest the possession in the same person to whom the use is given, the ceremony of livery is not so frequent as formerly; neither since the statute 29 *Car.* 2, *c.* 3, can estates be created by livery and seisin only without writing. The ceremony of attornment is also taken away by stat. 4 *Anne*, *c.* 16: *Id. in nota.* See *post*, § 551. Also concluding remarks on this chapter.

—proximity of blood. blood, how far soever that he be from him in degree, may inherit and have the land as heir to him. *Exception in case of lineal descent.* [3] But if there be father and son, and the father hath a brother who is uncle to the son, and the son purchase land in fee-simple, and die without issue, living his father, the uncle shall have the land as heir to the son, and not the father, yet the father is nearer of blood (*unto the son*); because it is a maxim in law, that inheritance may descend, but not ascend * (*f*). *Yet by circuity* Yet if the

de quel pluis longe degree que il soit de luy, poet enheriter et avoir mesme la terre come heire a luy. [3] *Mes si soit pere et fitz, et le pere ad un frere qui est uncle a le fitz, et le fitz purchace terre en fee-simple, et mourust sauns issue vivaunt son pere, luncle avera la terre come heire al fitz et nemy le pere, unqore le pere est pluis proschein de sank; pur ceo que est un maxime en ley, que enheritaunce poet descendre, mes nemy ascendre *. Unqore si le fitz en tiel cas morust*

---

* *Pyns.* 1516, *Redm.*, *Berth.*, *Middl.*, *Powel.*, *Sm.*, and *Tottyl*, 1554, read this passage thus, *que enheritaunce puit* LINEALMENT *descendre, mes nemy* LINEALMENT *ascendre*, and the copies of the Translations by *Rastell*, render it accordingly. All the other copies omit the second *linealment*.

(*f*) This maxim of descent is contrary to the Salic law, by which the father or mother succeeded if the son died issueless. To the establishment of fiefs was owing this preference of ascendants to descendants. The course of descent and succession imposed on the chief lords, and the course of descent which attached on their sub-infeudations, seems to have been different; indeed, the land of the chief lords, as it in many respects was subject to no other service than that of homage, in fact a *francum feodum*, might have been deemed allodial, for the essence of feudality was military service. In this light Hotoman considers our fee-simple, (*see* n. (*c*), *p.* 3, *ante*); for, as it is discharged from service, and is by right hereditary, he terms it "*allodia.*" See *Houard*, i. 15. This portion of the first κανων of descent, though it prohibited the father or mother (*as such*) from inheriting immediately from the son, who died issueless, yet permitted either of them to succeed as cousin to the son; and Lyttleton himself tells us, that, by

son in such case die without issue, and his uncle enter into the land as heir to the son, as by the law he ought, and after the uncle dieth without issue, living the father, the father shall have the land as heir to the uncle, and not as heir to his son, for that he cometh to the land by collateral descent, and not by lineal ascension.

the lineal ancestor may inherit.

4 And in such case, where the son purchases land in fee-simple, and dies without issue, they of his blood on his father's side, shall inherit as heirs to him, before any of the blood on his mother's side. But if he hath no heir on his father's side, then the land shall descend to the heirs on his mother's side * (*g*).

Purchase. *The paternal line shall always be preferred to the maternal, and the heirs on the mother's side shall never succeed till those on the father's side are exhausted.*

sauns issue, et son uncle entra en la terre come heire a le fitz, sicome il devoit per la ley, et apres luncle devia sauns issue vivaunt le pere, donques le pere avera la terre come heire al uncle, et nemye come heire a son fitz, pur ceo que il veigne al terre per collaterall discent et nemy per lineall ascencion.

4 *Et en tiel cas lou le fitz purchace terre en fee-simple, et devie sauns issue, ceux de son sank de parte son pere, enheriterount come heires a luy, devaunt ascun de sank de parte sa mere: mes sil ny ad ascun heire de parte son pere, donques la terre descendera a les heires de part sa mere* *.

---

* In the editions by *Redm.*, *Berth.*, *Middl.*, *Powel*, *Sm.*, the English and French edition, 1671, and all the copies of *Rastell's* Transl. to 1656,

---

circuity, the father, on decease of his brother, the uncle of the deceased son, might have inherited. This part of the rule of descent is now altered, as will be seen in the editor's concluding remarks on this chapter.

(*g*) A purchaser of land died without issue, leaving no heir on the part of the father, and the heir on the part of the mother entered, and the lord entered claiming it by escheat, and the heir on the part of the mother brought an assise, and upon the general issue pleaded, all this matter was found by verdict; and it was then adjudged that the plaintiff should recover, because when the inheritance never came in descent, nor in the degrees, but the

But if a man take a wife inherited of land in fee-simple, who have issue a son, and die, and the son enter into the te-

Mes si home prent feme enherite en fee-simple, queux ount issue fitz, et devieront, et le fitz entra en les tenementes, come

---

there appears a particular reference to, as well as an abridgment of, the Year-book, *Mich.* 12 *E.* 4. In these editions also, as this portion of the text is burdened with an interpolation, in order to avoid a manifest redundancy, a part of the purer text, placed between brackets, (*see p.* 10), is thrown aside. The spurious text according to those copies reads as below*. In *Tottyl*, 1557 (both editions), the reference as well as the abridgment is omitted, and an *asterisk* is placed to denote the vacancy of the excluded interpolation; but the editions of *Tottyl* from 1567 to 1591 place the reference between two *flowers*, and in the editions by other printers from 1591 to 1639, a similar index is adopted. In *Redm.* where this false arrangement of the text first appears, the reference to the folio, 14, which is that of the earliest *printed* Year-book, is marginal; but the reference in the body of the text is to the term and year generally, which seems to indicate that *Redm.* edition was taken from a manuscript. In many of the copies of *Rastell's* Transl. the reference is to *fol.* 34 and *fol.* 35 of that Year-book, which evidently refers to a MS. Year-book; from all which it may be concluded, that this interpolation, spurious text, or misarrangement, is very ancient.

---

* " And this was the opinion of all the justices. M. 12 E. 4. But it was there held, if land descend to a man on the part of his father, who dies without issue, that his next heir on the part of his father shall inherit to him, that is, to wit, the next who is of the blood of the father on the grandfather's side: and for default of such heir, those who are of the blood of the father on the part of the mother of the father, viz. the grandmother, shall inherit. And if there is no such heir on the part of

---

purchaser was the first that had it, there, although this is a failure of one branch of heirs, viz. of those on the part of the father, it is reasonable that the heirs on the part of the mother should have it, rather than that it should escheat to the lord. 49 *E.* 3, *in assise.*

In descent to the next heirs on the mother's side, the heirs of the blood of the male line, from whom the mother is descended, ascending, are to be preferred before the blood of the female line, &c., ascending. Co. Lytt. 12. *b.*, in the case of *Fairfield* there put. *Plowd.* 445.

nements, as son and heir to his mother, and after dies without issue, the heirs on the mother's side ought to inherit, and never * the heirs on the father's side. And if he **Escheat.**

fitz et heire a sa mere, et puis devie sauns issue, les heires de parte sa mere doient enheriter les tenementes et jammes * *les heires de parte le pere. Et sil ny ad ascun heire de part la*

---

the father, then the lord shall have the land by escheat,—and so it is if a man take a wife inherited," &c. (*omitting that part of the text which is between the brackets, (see p.* 10), *and concluding with, et sic vide diversitatem, &c.*) The case referred to is thus :—viz. 'Note well, that it was holden by all the justices of the Common Bench, that, where a man purchases land and dies without issue, and without heir on the father's side, his next heir on the mother's side shall have the land, &c. And if a man purchase land and have issue and die, and the issue enter and die without issue, and without heir on his father's side on the part of his grandfather, *scil.* the father of his father, that, in this case, the heir on the side of his father's mother, *scil.* on the side of his grandmother, ought to inherit; for he who ought to inherit to the father, ought to inherit to the son, (*cesty qui doit enheriter al pere, doit enheriter al fitz*). *Catesby*, J., put the case, that when the issue was once inherited, this descent was in the blood of the father, through which recourse shall not be had to the blood of the mother of his father, &c., no more than where a man purchases land, &c., and dies without issue; here if the land descends to the heir on the father's side for the worthiness of blood, and he is seised, and afterwards dies without issue and without heir, yet the blood on the mother's side ought not to inherit, for that is a different blood. To which it was answered, that the cases are not alike, for where there is a descent to the collateral blood, recourse shall not be had to a different blood, &c. But it was holden that if a man (A.) purchase land and has issue (a son, B.), who has the land by descent, and afterwards the issue (B.) die issueless, and without heir on the father's side, that the heir on the side of the mother of the son (C.) ought not to inherit: for he (the heir on (C.) the mother's side) is not of the blood of him in whom the original possession commenced; *scil.* he is not of the blood of the father (A.), &c., but the heir of the son on the side of the grandmother (D.), *scil.* on the side of the mother of his father (A.), ought to inherit, &c. *Quod nota.*' *Year-Book, M.* 12 *E.* 4. *Year-Book, Mich.* 12 *E.* 4.

* *Jammes*, never, *Lettou & M.*; in *Machl., Roh., and Pyns.* 1516, *nemye*, not; which last is the translation given by *Rastell* as well as by *Sir Ed. Coke*, and is conformable to the ordinary copies.

hath no heir on the mother's side, then the lord, of whom the land is holden, shall have the land by escheat.

Descent.

[In the same manner it is, if tenements descend to the son on his father's side, and he entereth and afterwards dies without issue, this land shall descend to the heirs on the father's side, and not to the heirs on the mother's side. And if there be no heir on the father's side, then the lord, of whom the land is holden, shall have the land by escheat]. And *so ye may see the diversity*, where the son purchaseth lands or tenements in fee-simple, and where he cometh in to such lands or tenements by descent on his mother's side, or on his father's side.

Paternal line preferred.

Escheat.

Diversity.

Descent between brothers.

5 Also if there be three brethren, and the middle brother purchase lands in fee-simple, and die without issue, the elder brother shall have the land by descent, and not the younger.

And also if there be three brethren, and the younger purchase lands in fee-simple, and die without issue, the elder brother shall have the land by descent, and not the middle, for that the elder is more worthy of blood. 6 And it is to be

mere, donques le seignour, de qui la terre est tenus, avera les tenementes per eschete.

[*En mesme le maner est, si tenementes descendont a le fitz de parte son pere, et il entra et puis mourust sans issue, cel terre descendera a les heires de parte le pere, et nemy a les heires de parte la mere. Et sil ny ad ascun heire de part le pere, donques le seignour, de qui la terre est tenus, avera la terre per eschete*]. Et sic vide diversitatem, *lou le fitz purchace terres ou tenementes en fee-simple, et lou il vient einz a tielx terres ou tenementes per discent de part sa mere, ou de part son pere.*

5 Item, *si soient trois freres, et le mulnes frere purchace terres en fee-simple et devie sauns issue, leigne frere avera la terre per discent et nemy le puisne.*

Et auxi si soient trois freres et le puisne purchace terres en fee-simple et devie sans issue, leigne frère avera la terre per discent et nemy le mulnes, pur ceo que leigne est pluis digne

understood, that none shall have land of fee-simple by descent as heir unto any man, unless he be the heir of the whole blood. *Exclusion of the half-blood.*

For if a man hath issue two sons by divers venters, and the elder purchase lands in fee-simple, and die without issue, the younger brother shall not have the land, but the uncle of the elder brother, or some other his next cousin shall have it, because the younger brother is but of half blood to the elder brother (*h*).

7 And if a man hath issue a son and a daughter by one venter, and a son by another venter, and the son by the first venter purchase lands in fee, and die without issue, the sister

de sank. 6 *Et est assavoir que nul avera terre de fee-simple per discent come heire a ascun home, si non quil soit leire de lentier sank.*

Qar si home ad issue deux fitz per divers ventres, et leigne purchace terres en fee-simple quil mourust sauns issue, le puisne frere navera la terre, mes luncle leigne frere ou auter son proschein cosin ceo avera, pur ceo que le puisne frere est de demy sank al eigne frere.

7 *Et si home ad issue fitz et fille per un ventre, et fitz per autre ventre, et le fitz per le premier ventre purchace terres en fee, et morust sauns issue, la soer avera la terre per discent,*

(*h*) The common law required that a claimant by descent to the inheritance, should be of the whole blood to the last owner (§ 6), and in illustration of this rule, Lyttleton puts the case (§ 7); the term "whole blood" means, the blood of the father and mother of the person to whom he claims as heir, but this exclusion of the half-blood is now qualified by the stat. 3 & 4 *Gul.* 4, c. 106, *s.* 9, which allows the heirs of the half-blood to inherit, but postpones their succession till after the whole blood *in the same degree* is exhausted, "so that (in the words of the *stat.*) the brother of the half-blood on the part of the father shall inherit next after the sisters of the whole blood on the part of the father and their issue, and the brother of the half-blood on the part of the mother shall inherit next after the mother."

shall have the land by descent as heir (*to her brother*), and not the younger brother, for that the sister is of the whole blood to her elder brother.

8 And also where a man is seised of lands in fee-simple and hath issue a son and daughter by one venter, and a son by another venter, and die, and the elder son entreth, and die without issue, the daughter shall have the tenements, and not the younger son; and yet is the younger son heir to the father, but not to his brother: but if the elder son enter not into the land after the death of his father, but die before any entry made by him, then the younger brother may enter and shall have the land as heir to his father: but where the elder son in the case aforesaid entreth after the death of his father, and thereof hath possession, there the sister shall have the land (*i*). For the possession of the brother (*possessio fratris*) in fee-simple, maketh the sister to be heir.

Possessio fratris.

come heire, et nemye le puisne frere, pur ceo que la soer est de le entier sank a son eigne frere.

8 *Et auxi lou home est seisi de terres en fee-simple et ad issue fitz et fille per un ventre, et fitz per autre ventre, et morust et leigne fitz entra et morust sauns issue, la fille avera les tenementes, et nemy le puisne fitz, unquore le puisne fitz est heire a le pere, mes nemy a son frere: mes si leigne fitz nentra en la terre apres la mort son pere, mes morust devaunt ascun entre fait per luy, donques le puisne frere poet entrer, et aver la terre come heire a son pere. Mes lou leigne fitz en le cas avauntdit entra apres la mort son pere, et ad ent possession, donques la soer avera la terre.* Quia possessio fratris de feodo simplici facit sororem esse heredem.

(*i*) This doctrine, which is termed "*possessio fratris,*" has no place with regard to descents since 31st Dec. 1833; for, by *stat.* 3 & 4 *Gul.* 4, *c.* 106, *s.* 1, it is not necessary that the person last entitled should obtain the actual possession, *i. e.* be *seised* of the estate, and by s. 2 of the same statute, it is enacted, that, in every case, descent shall be

But if there be two brothers by divers venters, and the elder is seised of land in fee, and die without issue, [and his uncle enter as next heir to him, who also dies without issue *], now the younger brother may have the land as heir to the uncle, for that he is of the whole blood to him, albeit he be but of the half-blood to his elder brother.

9 And it is to be understood, that this word "inheritance" is not only intended where a man hath lands or tenements by descent of inheritance †; but also every fee-simple ‡, that

Mes si sont deux freres per divers ventres, et leigne est seisi de terre en fee, et morust sauns issue, [et son uncle entra come heire a luy, quel auxi morust sauns issue], ore le puisne frere poet aver la terre come heire al uncle, pur ceo quil est de lentier sank a luy, coment quil soit del demy sank a son eigne frere.*

9 *Et est assavoir, que cest parole* enheritaunce *nest pas tantsoulement entendus lou home ad terres ou tenementes per discent denheritaunce* †, *mes auxi chescun fee-simple* ‡ *que home*

* The words within brackets are omitted in *Machl.* and *Roh.*

† *Discent del heritage—Machl.*, *Roh.*, and *Pyns.* 1516.

‡ *Fee-simple ou taile—Redm.* and later copies.

traced from the first purchaser who shall be considered to have been the person last entitled, unless it be proved that he inherited the same; in which case, the person from whom he inherited the estate shall be considered to have been the purchaser, unless it be proved that he inherited the same, and so on *in infinitum*. The consequence of this rule is, that the brother of the half-blood, and not the sister of the whole blood, shall succeed to the inheritance which *descended* from their common father, the purchaser; for the brother of the half-blood is the heir to the father, from whom, according to the statute, the descent must be traced. The case in which the sister can now inherit, is where it cannot be proved that her brother took by descent; for if it can be proved that he so took, (*i. e.* was not a purchaser), her brother of the half-blood shall have the preference as heir to the common father. See *Watk. Desc. by J. Williams*, 50 [1].

a man hath by his purchase, may be styled inheritance, because his heirs may inherit him. For in a writ of right which a man bringeth of land that was of his own purchase, the writ shall say, *Quam clamat esse jus et hereditatem suam.* And so shall it be said in divers other writs which a man or woman bringeth of their own purchase, as appears by the Register (*k*).

Distinction of corporeal and incorporeal hereditaments.

10 And of such things as a man may have a manual occupation, possession, or receipt, as of lands, tenements, rents, and such like, there a man shall say in count countant, and in plea shall plead *, that such a one was seised in his demesne as of fee. But of such things that lie not in such manual occupation, &c., as of an advowson of a church;

ad per son purchace poet estre dit enheritaunce, pur ceo que ses heires luy purront enheriter. Qar en briefe de droit que home portera de terre que fuist de son purchace demesne, le briefe dirra, Quam clamat esse jus, et hereditatem suam. ***Et issint*** *sera dit en divers auters briefes, queux home ou feme portera de son purchace, demesne come il appiert per le registre.*

10 *Et de tielx choses que home poet aver un manuell occupacion, possession ou resceit, sicome des terres, tenementes, rentes, et* hujusmodi, *la home dirra en count countaunt, et en plee pledera * qun tiel fuist seisi en son demesne come de fee.* ***Mes*** *de tielx choses que ne gisount en tiel manuell occupacion, &c., sicome de advowson desglise,* et hujusmodi; *la il dirra que il*

---

* The reading as given in the text appears to be at variance with *Berth.*, *Powel*, *Sm.* and *Tottyl*, 1554, in which the reading is *en count countant, et per voye de barre ou auter enpleder*, which is rendered by *Rastell's* Trans. "shall say in his pleading and in way of bar." The common copies by *Tottyl*, and others of later date, give the reading, *en count countant et en plee pledant*, which the common translation follows.

(*k*) This ancient, and, as Coke terms it, excellent, book is mentioned at § 101, 234; in the latter section some account of this book will be given.

and such like, there he shall say, that he was seised as of fee, and not in his demesne as of fee. And in Latin it is in the one case, *Quod talis seisitus fuit, &c., in dominico suo ut de feodo, That such a one was seised in his demesne as of fee,* and in the other case, *Quod talis seisitus fuit, &c., ut de feodo, That such a one was seised, &c., as of fee.* 11 And note well, That a man cannot have a more large or greater estate or inheritance* than fee-simple (*l*).

Fee-simple, highest degree of estate.

12 Also purchase is called the possession of lands or tene-

Purchase defined.

fuist seisi come de fee, et nemy en son demesne come de fee, et en Latin il est en lun cas, quod talis seisitus fuit, &c. in dominico suo ut feodo, *et en lautre cas,* quod talis seisitus fuit, &c., ut de feodo. 11 *Et nota que home ne poet aver pluis ample ou pluis greindre estate ou enheritaunce**, *que fee-simple.*

12 Item, *purchace est appelle la possession de terres ou*

---

* Some copies since 1545 have corrupted *ou enheritaunce* into *en enheritaunce* and *denheritaunce*, and indeed the translation by Sir Ed. Coke renders it "of inheritance," although the editions of *Rastell's* translation give the true sense.

(*l*) Consequently it is permanent and endurable, though it may shift as to the person in whom it may vest, or it may be in abeyance, (§ 646, 647). Lyttleton has already informed the reader how it may be acquired, or rather of the two most ordinary modes of acquisition, viz. descent and purchase, and how it is descendible. The "fee-simple" is the term used to signify the absolute property of the land, and is opposed to base and determinable or qualified fees or estates of inheritance. The term "freehold," however confounded in common parlance with *fee-simple*, means an estate in possession, of land not inheritable; and in this sense Lyttleton uses the word frank-tenement, (§ 302), and the *Olde Tenures*, tit. *Frank-Tenure*, § 8, make the same distinction. The law renders the fee-simple subject to dower and curtesy, it is liable by statute to the owner's debts, and is forfeitable on an attainder for treason or murder.

ments that a man hath by his deed or agreement, unto which he cometh not by title of descent from any of his ancestors, of of his cousins, but [cometh in] by his own deed *.

tenementes que homme ad per son fait, ou per son agrement, a quel possession il ne avient per title de discent de nul de ses auncestres, ou de ses cosins, mes [vient eins] per son fait demesne *.

CONCLUDING REMARKS.

By the terms of feudal law, investiture or personal delivery of possession was always an indispensable requisite; indeed, the principles of feudal law strictly forbade the transfer of a feud, unless accompanied with the open and public delivery of the possession of the land upon the land itself. In ruder ages, the conveyance of land was perfected by this ceremony alone, which then and until the Statute of Frauds, (29 Car. 2, c. 3), was all that the law required; but the caution of later times superadded a charter or deed perpetuating the notoriety of the transfer, which was termed a "feoffment," which, although evidencing the terms of the conveyance, yet was not sufficient to pass the inheritance, unless accompanied by this delivery of possession, which is termed "livery of seisin."

This livery of seisin followed the principles on which feudal investiture had place; in former times it notified to the lord the person on whom he was to call for performance of the military services due in respect of his tenure or holding, and, in

---

* This passage in *Machl.* and *Roh.* is, *eins per son fait demesne, in by his own act;* not, *mes per son fait demesne*, the reading given by *Lettou & M.*, and followed by all the subsequent copies except the first-mentioned editions. It is most probable that this section originally concluded thus: *mes vient eins per son fait demesne, but* comes in *by his own act;* in accordance with the concluding passage of § 4.

the more modern "seisin," the person was designated against whom strangers or claimants were to bring their real actions for the recovery of the land. In either case, the *fief* or *fee* is said to be *full*, and in legal language, the tenant or holder is said to be *in* of the land holden, the *tenement* whereof such tenant is *seised*. As a feoffment can, according to these principles, only be made of corporeal hereditaments, or of those things of which the actual possession can be delivered to the feoffee, and which, according to the precise language of Lyttleton, are such things whereof a man may have a "manual occupation, possession, or receipt, as of lands, tenements, rents, and such like" (§ 10), these hereditaments are said to "lie in livery," in contradistinction to incorporeal hereditaments, which are said to "lie in grant," and which will be noticed presently.

The conveyance by feoffment, which was, from its necessary accompaniment (*m*), *livery*, notorious and open, appears not to have been suitable to the habits or inclinations of more modern times; and, in fact, the legal obstacles which for a long period presented themselves to private modes of conveyance, have been completely overcome through the medium of uses and trusts; and, consequently, the assurance of feoffment is in comparative disuse (*n*). The feoffment is one of that class of conveyances called Common Law Assurances, in opposition to those deeds which derive their effect from the Statute of Uses.

Incorporeal hereditaments consist of rights, or profits arising from or annexed to land, and principally may be said to consist of advowsons, tithes, commons, ways, offices, dignities, franchises, and rents, to which Sir William Blackstone

(*m*) A feoffment without livery passed nothing but an estate at will, § 283.

(*n*) This form of conveyance is mostly used for gifts, or in cases where no pecuniary consideration is given to the feoffor, or where the property of a corporation or charity is vested in a certain number of persons, of whom few survive; the survivors by this conveyance enfeoff some new trustees.

has added two others, corodies and annuities (*o*). These could only be conveyed by deed or grant, and their possession evidenced by such assurances, or what is in some cases deemed equipollent, prescription or long usage, which in themselves afford the reasonable presumption of a deed or grant (*p*). There are also other incorporeal hereditaments, viz. reversions and remainders, of which livery of seisin cannot always be had, and, consequently, are the subject-matter of a grant: to these grants, however, something equivalent to livery was required, viz. attornment by the tenant of the *particular* or previous estate, which, as it involved matter of notoriety, was considered tantamount to a feoffment with livery of seisin. In cases, however, where the *particular* estate and a remainder were created *by the same feoffment*, there, no grant or attornment was requisite, because the livery of seisin openly notified the terms of the conveyance; and the two estates, viz. the *particular* estate in possession and the future estate in remainder, are in contemplation of law but one subsisting estate of inheritance (§ 60 and 471). Incorporeal hereditaments are therefore said to "lie in grant," and the meaning of these words may be thus explained.

A grant, also, is the ordinary conveyance of moveable things or *personal* property, as goods, cattle, furniture, or the like; and the law requires, that the grant should be made upon or for valuable consideration, and that possession should accompany the things granted, in order to render it valid against creditors of the grantor, in respect of claims subsisting at the time of the grant.

When a tenant or owner of the fee-simple dies in possession actually *seised* of land, he is, as regards the person who claimed as his heir, to be deemed either a purchaser of the land descended, or as having himself succeeded by descent;

(*o*) B. C. ii. 20, 21.

(*p*) The distinction thus made between things corporeal and incorporeal, is a consequence of feudal doctrine. *Houard*, i. 29. See also § 10.

the maxim of law, *seisina facit stipitem,* equally applying to either origin or commencement of the last owner or tenant's possession; for, in the case of a purchase, the estate acquires a new inheritable quality, and is descendible to the owner's blood in general, consequently the inheritance must be traced from him. In the case of a descent it is descendible to the blood only of some particular ancestor, who was the original acquisitor or purchaser, who consequently is to be made the *terminus* or stock, from which the title by descent is to be traced by the claimant or heir.

If the person dying seised acquired the inheritance either as purchaser or as having taken by descent, the estate descends to the eldest or only son, or his descendants, if he should be dead leaving issue, and next to the second and other sons, according to priority of birth, and their descendants; in default of sons and their descendants it descends to daughters in equal shares, if more than one, and to the descendants of any deceased daughters, such descendants taking the share which would have gone to the parent if living.

When there is no lineal descendant, the estate goes to the eldest or only brother of the whole blood, that is, who was born of the same father and mother as the deceased proprietor, and to his descendants, if he should be dead leaving issue, and to the other brothers in succession and their descendants. If there be no brother or descendants of a brother, the sisters of the whole blood succeed in equal shares, and the descendants of deceased sisters, such descendants taking their parents' share as before.

Should there be a failure of brothers and sisters and their descendants, the estate then descends according to the rules laid down by Lyttleton in § 4, viz. if the last owner took by descent, the heir is to be sought for in the family from which the estate descended to the deceased proprietor; *i. e.* on the father's or mother's side, as it happened. If such last owner took by purchase, the preference is given to the relations on the paternal side; but if there be none such, then the inheritance descends to the relations on the maternal side, according to the following κανωνες or rules of descent, viz.—

1. Hereditaments shall lineally descend to the issue of such person *in infinitum;* but shall never lineally ~~descend.~~ ascend.

2. The male issue shall be admitted before the female.

3. Where there are two or more males in equal degree, the eldest only shall inherit, but the females altogether.

4. The lineal descendants, *in infinitum,* of any person deceased, shall represent their ancestor: that is, shall stand in the same place as the person himself would have done, had he been living.

5. On failure of lineal descendants, or issue of such person, the inheritance shall descend to his collateral relations, being of the blood of the first purchaser, subject to the three preceding rules.

6. The collateral heir of such person must be his next collateral kinsman of the whole blood.

7. In collateral inheritances, the male stock shall be preferred to the female; (*i. e.,* kindred derived from the blood of the male ancestors, however remote, shall be admitted before those from the blood of the female, however near); unless where the lands have, in fact, descended from a female.

If there be no lineal descending or immediate collateral heirs, the inheritance is to be traced to the 7th canon of descent, also subject to the 6th rule, which requires that collaterals be of the *whole blood* of the person from or through whom they claim. It is also requisite, that, before a person can be made the *stock* or *terminus* to whom the descent can be traced, he should be *actually* seised, *i. e.* not only have a right, but be actually in possession by himself or agents or lessees, before his *own* heirs can inherit; for if he die before some act of ownership, or actual seisin obtained, his brother of the half-blood succeeds to the inheritance, in exclusion of his sister of the whole blood; for, as before stated, the person claiming as heir must make himself heir to him who was last actually seised. This doctrine, which is termed *possessio fratris,* is illustrated at § 8.

And thus the law of descent as declared by Lyttleton still obtains; but so far only as regards descents of lands taking place on the death of any person dying before 1st Jan. 1834; for in respect of descents happening after 31st Dec. 1833, the stat 3 & 4 Gul. 4, c. 106, has framed new rules of descent, and has abolished the prohibition of lineal ascent, modified the doctrine whereby the half blood were excluded, and rendered the seisin of the person last entitled unnecessary; so that, although the distinction of descent and purchase (§ 4), so far as concerns the tracing of the inheritance, remains, the following may be now stated to be the leading rules which regulate title by descent at the present time, which only vary what Lyttleton has laid down in the three alterations last noticed, and by no means impair the consistency of the scheme of inheritance this chapter developes. These rules of inheritance substituted by statute for the old canons of descent, are in substance as follows:—

1. *That in every case descent shall be traced from the purchaser, and the person last entitled shall be considered to have been the purchaser, unless it be proved that he inherited the same; and in like manner, the last person from whom the land shall be proved to have been inherited, shall in every case be considered to have been the purchaser, unless it shall be proved that he inherited the same.*

2. Hereditaments shall lineally descend to the issue of the person last entitled, *whether he was in possession or not,* in infinitum; *and the ascending line shall come next after the lineal descending line.*

3. That the male issue shall be admitted before the female.

4. Where there are two or more males in equal degree, the eldest only shall inherit, but the females altogether.

5. The lineal descendants *in infinitum* of any person deceased shall represent their ancestor: that is, shall stand in

the same place as the person himself would have done, had he been living.

6. *The lineal descendants of a deceased ancestor, who would succeed to the inheritance through such ancestor, if the rule that inheritance shall not ascend were preserved, shall stand in the place of such ancestor in the order of inheritance.*

7. On failure of lineal descendants or issue of such person the inheritance shall descend to his collateral relations, *and as amongst kindred claiming through one and the same ancestor of the first purchaser, preference shall be given in inheritance to the whole blood of the first purchaser, subject to such preference, the whole and half blood shall stand upon equal footing as to inheritance;* also subject, however, to the *four* preceding rules.

8. In collateral inheritances, the male stock shall be preferred to the female; unless where the lands have in fact descended from a female.

N.B.—The Italic letter denotes the substituted, the Roman letter, the original rules of descent.

CHAPTER II.

FEE-TAIL.

LYTTLETON having discoursed of an absolute fee, now treats of a conditional fee at the Common Law, by the stat. *de donis* changed to a *fee-tail*, whereof the reader is informed there are several species, being either general (§ 14, 15), or special (§ 16, 26—29). These estates in general and special tail are also distinguished by the sexes of the issue in such entails, for they may either be *tail-male* or *tail-female*, according to the restriction imposed by the donor. An estate called *frank-marriage*, a peculiar species of *tail*, long in disuse, but (in essentials) capable of subsisting at the present day, is incidentally mentioned; and with various illustrations and examples of general and special tail, &c., this chapter concludes.

---

13 Tenant in fee-tail (*a*) is by force of the statute of *Westm.* 2, *cap.* 1; for, before the said statute, all inheritances were *Estates in tail.*

13 *Tenaunt in fee-taille est per force de lestatute de Westm. ii. Qar devant le dit estatute touts enheritaunces furent fee-*

(*a*) To hold in the taile is where a man holdeth certain lands or tenements, [and is enfeoffed upon condition*], to him and to his heires of his bodie begotten [&c.*]. And note wel, that if the land be given to a man and to his heires males and he hath issue male, he hath fee-simple; and that was adjudged in the parliament of our lord the king. But where lands or tenements be given to a man and to his heires males of his bodie begotten, [and he hath issue female*], then he

* The words within brackets do not appear in some editions.

Estates in tail. fee-simple; for all the gifts which be specified in that statute were fee-simple conditional at the common law, as appeareth by the rehearsal of the same statute (*b*). And now by this statute, tenant in tail is in two manners, that is to say, tenant in tail general, and tenant in tail special.

simple; qar touts les dones que sount specifies deins mesme lestatute furent fee-simple condicionell a le comen ley, sicome appiert per le rehersail de mesme lestatute. Et ore per cel estatute, tenaunt en le taille est en deux maners, cest assavoir, tenaunt en le taille generall, et tenaunt en le taille especiall.

---

hath fee-taile, and the issue female shal not be inherited as it appeareth the xiiij yeare of Ed. the iij. in assize.—*Olde Tenures*, § 18.

(*b*) The conclusion from § 13 and from Lyttleton's definition of a fee-simple is (§ 1, 731), that the only lawful or legitimate inheritance at common law, besides a fee-simple conditional, (an example of which occurs at § 350), was a fee-simple which was not conditional. A fee-simple conditional at common law resembles, in some respects, a fee-simple upon condition, that is to say, with a condition, that, on a given event, the grantor may defeat the fee-simple by his entry, and thereby be in of his former estate (§ 325). Yet a fee-simple upon condition differs in several respects from a fee-simple conditional; first, as to the course of descent, which in the case of a fee-simple upon condition is always to the heirs general, and in the case of a fee-simple conditional might be to a second son as heir male, and not to the daughter of the eldest son (deceased), though such daughter were heir general: secondly, as to the effect of the entry by the grantor in such cases; for, such entry for condition broken in the case of a fee-simple upon condition, determines the fee-simple till then subsisting in the grantee, and restores the grantor to his former estate; whereas entry in the case of a fee-simple conditional, merely restores the possession to the grantor, the fee-simple of the grantee being previously determined by failure of heirs inheritable. *The sections of Lytt. Tenures, subdivided, &c., by Canning, p. 9, in n.* The same maxims of descent apply to descents in tail as to inheritances in fee-simple, viz. that the male issue shall be admitted before the female; and where there are two or more males in equal degree, the eldest only shall inherit; but the females all together.—B. C. ii. 214.

14 Tenant in tail general is, where lands or tenements are given to a man, and to his heirs of his body begotten: In this case it is styled general tail, for that whatsoever woman such tenant taketh to wife, (if he hath many wives, and by each of them hath issue), yet each one of these issues by possibility may inherit the tenements by force of the gift; because that every such issue is of his body engendered. *Tail general.*

15 In the same manner it is where lands or tenements are given to a woman, and to the heirs of her body issuing, howbeit that she hath divers husbands; yet the issue that she may have by each husband may inherit as issue in tail by force of such gift (*c*), and therefore such gifts are called general tail.

16 Tenant in tail special is, where tenements are given to a man and to his wife, and to the heirs of their two bodies begotten; in this case none can inherit by force of the gift, *Tail special.*

14 *Tenaunt en le taille generall, est lou terres ou tenementes sont dones a un home et a sez heirez de son corps engendres: En ceo cas il est dit generall taille, pur ceo que quelconque feme que tiel tenant espousa, sil avoit plusours femes, et per chescun deux il ad issue, unquore chescun de les issues per possibilite poet enheriter les tenementes per force de le done, pur ceo que chescun tiel issue est de son corps engendre.*

15 *En mesme le maner est lou terres ou tenementes sont dones a un feme, et a les heirez de son corps issuants, coment que ele avoit divers barons, unquore lissue que ele poet aver per chescun baron, poet enheriter come issue en le taille per force de tiel done, et pur ceo tielx dones sont appellez generall taille.*

16 *Tenaunt en le taille especiall est lou tenementes sont dones a un home et a sa feme, et a les heires de lour deux corps engendres, en tiel cas null poet enheriter per force de le done,*

(*c*) The husband is entitled to his *curtesy*, and the wife to her dower, as either are tenants in tail. And tenant in tail is not liable to be called to account or *impeached* of *waste* in felling timber, pulling down houses, &c.

but those that be begotten between them two. And it is called especial tail, because, if the wife die, and he taketh another wife, and have issue, the issue of the second wife shall never be inheritable by force of such gift, nor also the issue of the second husband, if the first husband* die.

Frank marriage.

17 In the same manner it is, where tenements are given by one man to another, with a wife (*d*), which is the daughter or cousin (*e*) to the donor, in frank marriage, the which gift hath an inheritance by these words "frank marriage" annexed unto it, although it be not expressly said or rehearsed in the gift, that is to say, that the donees shall have the tenements to them and to their heirs between them two begotten. And this is called especial tail, because the issue of the second wife may not inherit, &c., *ut supra* (*f*).

This word passes estate in tail, though "heirs" not named.

forsque ceux qui sont engendres perentre eux deux. Et est appelle especiall taille, pur ceo que si la feme devie, et il prent autre feme, et ad issue, lissue del seconde feme ne serra jammes enheritable per force de tiel done, ne auxi lissue del second baron, si le premier baron devie.*

17 *En mesme le maner est lou tenementes sont dones per un home a un auter ove un feme, que est la fille ou la cosin al donour en frank mariage, le quel done ad un enheritaunce per ceulx parolx* frank marriage *a ceo annexe, coment que ne soit expressement dit ou reherce en le done, cestassavoir, que les donees averount les tenementes a eux et a lour heires perentre eux deux engendres: Et ceo est dit especiall taille, pur ceo que lissue del seconde feme ne poet enheriter, &c.,* ut supra.

---

* By a misprint in *Lettou & M.* the reading is *feme—wife.*

(*d*) And this may be as well after the marriage as before. *Kitchin, p.* 316, *ed.* 1675. And if a *divorce* be had, yet the wife, if daughter of the donor, shall hold the land, for she was the cause of the gift.—*Ibid.*

Frank marriage.

(*e*) Otherwise the estate is but for life.—*Olde Tenures*, § 20, *ad finem*.

(*f*) To holde in frank marriage is to hold in the second taile ly-

18 And note well, that this word, *Talliare* (*g*), is the same, as to set to some certainty, or else limit to some certain inherit-

Etymology of tail.

18 Et nota, quod verbum Talliare idem est quod ad quandam certitudinem ponere, vel ad quoddam certum here-

---

mitted in the Statute of Westminster ij. c. 1. And the feoffor* shal acquite the feoffee* of all maner of services, until the 4th degree be past, and the feoffor* shall performe all the services and suites during the said terme. And afterwards the heires of the feoffee* shal do them, for that the privitie of blood is past. And if he be distrained for services, he shall have a writ of mesne against him, supposinge that he held the lands of him, but he shal not have the forejudgment if it bee not in advantage of his issues. And note well, that after the fowerth degree be past, he shal be attendant of as much service to the donour as the donour is attendant to the lord paramount. And if he commit felony, for which he is attainted, the kinge shal have his landes for terme of his naturall lyfe. And after his death, his issue shal be inherited, as by force of the taile. And in this case, none shal have his land by way of eschete, no more than in any other taile, [*ut dicitur*†]. And in case the tenant die without heire of his bodie begotten, the land shal revert to the donor, as it should in the common tayle. And if a man let‡ hys land to another in franke marriage, yeldinge to him a certeine rent by yeare, he shal holde this land in the common tayle and not in franke marriage; for by the rent reserved, these words (*in liberum maritagium*) bee al utterly voyd, so that the tenure shal bee intended after the tenure in the common tayle. And note well, that the gift in franke-marriage hath a condicion annexed to it, notwithstanding that it be not

Frank marriage.

Reversion in the donor.

Gift in frank marriage, rendering rent, reservation void.

Estate tail by implication.

* Donor, donee, *ed.* 1579. ‡ Give, *Id.*

† The words within brackets do not appear in some editions.

(*g*) Or rather it might have the name of the French word, *tailler*, which is to cut wood, and because the estate is docked or cut off, (for before it was a fee-simple, and now the fee is cut off from it, and the estate thereby is docked, cut off, or made less), it may well be called an estate-*taille*, viz. an estate docked, cut off, or abridged, and immediately upon the making of the act, it had this name given it.—*Plowd.* 251.

ance. And for that it is limited and set in certain what issue shall inherit by force of such gifts, and how long the inheritance shall endure, it is called in Latin, *feodum talliatum, i. e. hæreditas in quandam certitudinem limitata.* For if tenant in general tail dieth without issue, the donor or his heirs shall enter * as in their reversion.

ditamentum limitare. *Et pur ceo que est limite et mys en certeyn quel issue serra enherite per force de tielx dones, et come longement lenheritaunce endurera, il est appelle en Latin,* feodum talliatum i. e. hereditas in quandam certitudinem limitata. *Qar si tenaunt in generall taille morust sauns issue, le donour ou ses heirez entreroun t* come en lour revercion.*

---

* *Enheriteroun t*, shall inherit, *Pyns.* 1516. *Redm. Berth. Middl. Powel, Sm. Tottyl,* 1554, *ed.* 1671, and *Rastell's Transl.*

---

openly declared in the deede of the gift, as it appeareth by the Statute of Westminst. ij. c. 1. *De donis condicionalibus.* And note well, that a man shall not give lands nor tenementes in franke marriage, but where the woman is privie of bloode to the donor, for else the man nor the woman shal have no other estate by the feoffement but for terme of lyfe.—*Olde Tenures*, § 20.

Gift made with a woman in frank marriage, not cousin to the donor, is but for life.

The form of a gift in frank marriage is thus: *Sciant, &c., me M. H. de W., dedisse et concessisse et presenti carta mea confirmasse J. A. filio meo et Margeriæ uxori ejus, filiæ veræ T. U., in liberum maritagium, unum messuagium, &c.*—*West Symbol.* part 1, lib. 2, § 303.

Maritagium is divided by *Glanvill* and *Bracton* into *liberum* and *servitio obligatum.* In *liberum maritagium* (frank marriage), after the fourth degree, the land was subject to all the former services; because it was supposed then to revert to the lord for want of heirs, so that it was exempted only to the fourth degree. Lands given in *maritagium servitio obligatum,* were, with a reservation of the services due to the lord, which the donee and his heirs were to perform for ever; but neither he nor the next two heirs were bound to do homage; that was to be done when it came to the fourth degree, and not before, and then both services and homage had to be performed.—*Cowell Int., edit.* 1727, *verbo Franke marriage.*

19 In the same wise it is of the tenant in especial* tail, &c., for in every gift in tail, without more saying, the reversion of the fee-simple is in the donor (*h*).

The tenure in tail is of the donor by the same services, but donees in frank marriage render no services till the fourth degree be past.

And the donees and their issues shall perform to the donor and to his heirs, the like services as the donor doth to his lord next paramount, except the donees in frank marriage, who shall hold quit of all manner of service, unless it be for fealty, until the fourth degree is past, and after that the fourth degree be past, the issue in the fifth degree, and so forth, the other issues after him shall hold of the donor, or of his heirs, as they hold over, as aforesaid (*i*).

19 *En mesme le maner est de le tenaunt en especiall* taille, &c.: Qar en chescun done en le taille, sauns pluis oustre dire, la revercion de fee-simple est en le donour.*

Et les doneez et lour issues ferrount al donour et a ses heirez, autielx services come le donour fait a son seignour proscheyn a luy paramont, forspris les doneez in frank mariage, les queux tiendront quitement de chescun manere de service, sinon que soit pur fealte, tanques le quart degree soit passe, et apres ceo que le quart degree soit passe, lissue en le quint degree, et issint oustre lautres dez issues apres luy, tiendront de le donour ou de ses heires come ils teignount oustre, come il est avaunt dit.

---

* *Despeciall*, of especial. *Roh.*

(*h*) A reversion is the undisposed of remnant of the original fee-simple of the grantor, remaining in him after the grant of any previous or *particular* estate in tail, life, or for years. *Vide post*, § 60, *in n.* where the subject of reversions is noticed.

(*i*) The reason assigned by *Fleta*, why the heirs do no service until the fourth descent, is: *Ne donatores vel eorum heredes, per homagii receptionem, a reversione repellantur:* and why, in the fourth descent and downward, they shall do no service to the donor: *Quia in quarto gradu vehementer presumitur, quod terra non est pro defectu heredum donatoriorum reversura.* Lib. 3, c. 11.

The intention of the parties to a gift in frank marriage with a

Computation of degrees by the canon law.

20 And the degrees in frankmarriage shall be accounted in such manner, *viz.* from the donor to the donees in frankmarriage the first degree, because the wife that is one of the donees ought to be daughter, sister, or other cousin to the donor. And from the donees unto their issue, shall be accounted the second degree, and from their issue unto their issue the third degree, and so forth, &c. And the cause is, that after every such gift, the issues of the donor, and the issues of the donees after the fourth degree past of both parties in such form to be accounted, may by the law of Holy Church intermarry (*k*). And that the donee in frankmar-

20 *Et lez degrees en frankmariage serount accomptz en tiell manere, cestassavoir, de le donour a les doneez en frank mariage, le premier degree, pur ceo que la feme que est une dez doneez covient estre fille, soer, ou autre cosin a le donour. Et de lez doneez tanques a lour issue, il serra accompte le seconde degree, et de lour issue tanques a son issue, le tierce degree, et issint oustre, &c. Et la cause est, pur ceo que apres chescun tiel done, les issuez queux veignont de le donour, et les issues queux veignont de les doneez apres le quart degree passe dambideux parties en tiel fourme destre accompte, poient, entre eux per la ley de Seynt Esglise entremarier. Et que le*

---

daughter of the donor, was understood to be, that the exemption from services should cease so soon as the lands should devolve from the donees to any of their descendants, who by possibility might intermarry with the issue of the donor by the canon law, though the event might be that no such intermarriage, could actually take place immediately (perhaps not at any time), if the four degrees were not then past on the part of the donor, &c.—*Canning's Sections of Lytt. p.* 15, *in n.*

(*k*) The computation of degrees Lyttleton alludes to, is that adopted by the *canon* law, which then had place; but the reader is referred to the statute 32 H. 8, c. 38, which, after being repealed, was revived by the stat. 1 Eliz. c. 1, § 11, 12. Assuming that an estate of frank marriage was created at this day, the issue of the donor and donees might legally intermarry after the

riage shall be said to be the first degree of the four degrees; a man may see in a plea upon a writ of right of ward, *P. anno* 31, *E.* 3 (*l*), where the plaintiff pleaded that his great-grandfather was seised of certain land, &c., and that same he held of another by knight-service, &c., who gave the land to one *Ralph Holland* with his sister in frankmarriage, &c. [21] And all these entails aforesaid be specified in the said statute of Westminster the second.

Estates tail by implication or by equity of the statute.

Also there be divers other estates in tail, howbeit that they be not by express words specified in the said statute, but they are taken by the equity of the said statute. As if lands be given to a man, and to his heirs males of his

donee en frankmariage serra le premier degree de les quatres degrees home poet veier en un plee sur un brief de droit de garde P. anno xxxj. E. iij.*lou le pleintif counta que son tresaiel fuist seisi de certeyn terre, &c., et ceo tenuyst dun autre per service de chivaler, &c., quel dona la terre a un* Rauf Holand *ovesque sa soer en frank mariage, &c.* [21] *Et touts ceux tailles avauntditz sont specifiez en le dit estatute de Westminster seconde.*

Auxi y sount dyvers autres estates en le taille, coment que ne sount especifiez per expresses parols en le dit estatute, mes ils sount prises per lequite de le dit estatute. Sicome terres

---

first degree (which corresponds with the *fourth* degree at common law), even if the donor and one of the donees were brother and sister; but *quoad* the tenure, the degrees might perhaps be said to subsist, for if there is a gift in frank marriage rendering rent, the reservation is void till the *fourth* degree (the *ninth* at common law) be past.—26 *Ass.* 66.

(*l*) The case cited by Lyttleton is fully stated in *Fitzherbert's Graund Abridgment*, tit. *Garde*, 116. Mr. Thos. Canning in his *Subdivision of the Sections of Lyttleton's Tenures. 8vo. Lond.* 1821, a work left unfinished at the decease of the learned author (to whom Mr. Butler acknowledges himself indebted for the Index prefixed to the last ed. of Co. Lytt. 1832), gives a translation of the case with a diagram of Pedigree and observations, to which the reader is referred, pp. liv. lx.

body begotten, in this case his issue male shall inherit, and the issue female shall never inherit, and yet in the other entails aforesaid it is otherwise.

Estate tail to heirs females, good.

22 In the same manner it is, if lands or tenements be given to a man, and to the heirs females of his body begotten: in this case his issue female shall inherit him by force and form of the gift, and not the issue male. For that in such cases of gifts in tail, as to who ought to inherit, and who not, the will of the donor shall be observed.

In descents of estates in tail-male or tail female, the special heir inheritable in exclusion of the general heir.

23 And in the case where lands or tenements be given to a man, and to the heirs male of his body issuing, and he hath issue two sons, and dieth, and the elder son enter as heir male, and hath issue a daughter and dieth; his brother shall have the land, and not the daughter, for that the brother is heir male. But otherwise it shall be in the other entails, which are specified in the said statute, [the daughter shall inherit before the brother *].

soient dones a un home et a les heires males de son corps engendres, en celle cas son issue male enheritera, et lissue female ne unques enheritera pas, unqore en les autres tailles avauntditz, autrement est.

22 *En mesme le manere est, si terres soient donez a un home et a les heires females de son corps engendres, en celle cas son issue female luy enheritera per force et fourme de le done, et nemye lissue male, pur ceo que en tielx cases de dones faits en le taille, les queux devoient enheriter, et queux nemye, la volunte le donour sera observe.*

23 *Et en le cas que terres ou tenementes sont donez a un home, et a les heires males de son corps issauntes, et il ad issue* ij. *fitz, et devie, et leigne fitz entra come heire male, et ad issue fille et devie, son frere avera la terre, et nemye la fille, pur ceo que le frere est heire male. Mes autrement serra en les autres tailles avauntditez queux sont specifiez en le dit estatute, [la fille enheritera devaunt le frere *].*

---

* The editions by *Pyns.* 1516. *Redm., Berth., Middl., Powel, Sm.*

24 Also if lands be given to a man and to the heirs males of his body begotten, and he hath issue a daughter, who hath issue a son, and dieth, and afterwards the donee die: in this case the son of the daughter shall not inherit by force of the tail, because whosoever shall inherit by force of a gift in tail made to the heirs males, it behoveth him to convey his descent wholly by the males. But in such case the donor shall enter, for that the donee is dead without issue male in the law, insomuch as the issue of the daughter cannot convey to himself the descent by heir male, &c†.

In tail-male, the heir must convey his descent wholly by males.

25 In the same manner it is, where lands are given to a man and his wife, and to the heirs males of their two bodies begotten, &c.

Tail-male special.

24 *Auxi si terres soient donez a un home, et a les heires males de son corps engendres, et il ad issue fille, le quel ad issue fitz, et devie, et puis apres le donee devie, en ceo cas le fitz de la fille ne enheritera pas per force de le taille, pur ceo que quiconque qui serra enherite per force dun done en le taille fait a les heires males, covient conveyer son discent tout per les males. Mes en cel cas le donour entrera, pur ceo que le donee est mort sauns issue male en la ley, entaunt que lissue de la fille ne puit conveyer a luy mesme le discent per heire male, &c †.*

25 *En mesme le manere est, lou tenementes sont donez a un*

Tottyl, 1554, and *ed.* 1671, omit the words, *auterment serra, it shall be otherwise*, and substitute the concluding words within brackets, which are not in *Lettou & M., Machl., Roh.* or the common editions. The Transl. by *Rastell* reads the passage thus—"*But it shall be otherwise in these other tailes aforesaid, which been especified in the said statute, the daughter shall inherit before the brother.*" In some of the first-mentioned editions, a reference is given to the year-book, *Trin.* 9 *H.* 6, *fol.* 24.

† PER *discent de heire male*—BY *descent of heir male: Redm., Berth., Middl., Powel, Sm. Tottyl*, 1554, and *ed.* 1671.

In what cases the husband takes an estate tail, and the wife for life only:

26 Also if tenements be given to a man and to his wife, and to the heirs of the body of the man begotten: in this case the husband hath an estate in the general tail, and the wife but estate for term of life.

27 Also if lands be given to the husband and to his wife, and to the heirs of the husband which he shall beget on the body of his wife: in this case the husband hath an estate in the special tail, and the wife but for term of life.

or è converso.

28 And if the gift be made to the husband and to his wife, and to the heirs of the wife of her body by the husband begotten, then the wife hath an estate in special tail, and the husband but for term of life.

In what cases both take an estate tail;

But if lands be given to the husband and the wife, and to the heirs which the husband shall beget on the body of the wife, in this case both of them have an estate-tail, because this word "heirs" is not limited to the one more than to the other. [And they have in this case such an estate as if

home, et a sa feme, et a les heires males de lour deux corps engendres, &c.

26 Item, *si tenementes soient donez a un home et a sa feme, et a les heires del corps del home engendres, en ceo cas le baron ad estate en le taille generall, et la feme forsque estate pur terme de vie.*

27 Item, *si terrez soient donez a le baron et a sa feme, et a les heires le baron, queux il engendra de corps la feme: en ceo cas le baron ad estate en le taile especiall, et la feme forsque pur terme de vie.*

28 *Et si le done soit fait a le baron et la feme, et a les heires la feme de son corps per le baron engendres, donques la feme ad estate en lespeciall taille, et le baron forsque pur terme de vie.*

Mes si terres sont dones a le baron et a sa feme, et a les heires que le baron engendra de corps la feme, en ceo cas ambideux ont estate en le taille, pur ceo que cest parole heires *nest limite a lun pluis que a lautre,* [*et ils ont en cell cas tiel*

lands had been given to them and to the heirs of their two bodies begotten *] (§ 352).

29 Also if land be given to a man and to his heirs which he shall beget on the body of his wife; in this case the husband hath an estate in special tail, and the wife hath nothing.

or the husband an estate tail and the wife nothing.

30 Also if a man hath issue a son and dieth, and land is given to the son, and to the heirs of the body of his father begotten, this is a good tail, and yet the father was dead at the time of the gift. And many other estates in the tail there be by the equity of the said statute, which be not here specified (*m*).

Gift to the heirs of the body of a man who is dead, a good estate tail.

31 But if a man give lands or tenements to another, to have and to hold to him and to his heirs males, or to his heirs

Words of procreation necessary, for heirs

estate sicome terres furent dones a ceux et a lez heires de lour deux corps engendres *].

29 Item, *si terre soit done a un home et a les heires quil engendra de corps sa feme, en ceo cas le baron ad estate en lespeciall taille, et la feme nad riens.*

30 Item, *si home ad issue fitz, et devie, et terre est done al fitz, et a les heires de corps son pere engendres, ceo est bone taille et unquore le pere fuist mort al temps de le done. Et moltz autres estates y sont en le taille per lequite de le dit estatute que icy ne sont specifiez.*

31 *Mes si home donna terres ou tenementes a un autre, a avoir et tenir a luy et a ses heires males, ou a ses heires*

---

* The words within brackets are in *Lettou & M.* only, and not in any other printed copy.

(*m*) The three estates limited in the preamble of the act, that is to say, especial tail, frank marriage, and general tail, are put there for examples, and not as containing all the entails intended in the statute, for the donor might make other entails by his limitation; for his will is a law as to the estates tail. *Plowd.* 251.

male *only, passes a fee-simple.*

females, he to whom such a gift is made hath fee-simple, because it is not limited by the gift, of what body the issue male or female shall be, and so it cannot in anywise be taken by the equity of the said statute, and therefore he hath a fee-simple, &c.

females, il a qui tiel done est fait, ad fee-simple, pur ceo que nest my lymyte per le done de quel corps lissue male ou lissue female issera, et issint il ne poet en ascun manere estre pris per lequite del dit estatute, et pur ceo il ad fee-simple, &c.

CONCLUDING REMARKS.

The inheritance arising from a grant or gift at common law to A. and the heirs of his body, or from such other like grant was called a fee-simple conditional, *i. e.* it was a fee-simple which, before issue had, could not be aliened; but the terms of the gift being interpreted as an implied condition, *scil.* that the donee had issue, upon issue had, the donee's estate, from a conditional estate, became an absolute fee-simple for the purpose of alienation, because the condition was deemed to have been performed.

To obviate the inconveniences arising from this construction, the stat. Westm. 2, 13 Ed. 1, (1285), c. 1, commonly termed the statute *de donis conditionalibus*, was passed, whereby it was ordained, "That the will of the donor according to the form in the deed of gift manifestly expressed, shall be from henceforth observed; so that they to whom the land was given under such condition, shall have no power to alien the land so given, but that it shall remain unto the issue of them to whom it was given after their death, or shall revert unto the donor or his heirs, if issue fail, so as there is no issue at all, or, if any issue be and fail by death, the heir of the body of such issue failing." 2. "Neither shall the second husband of any such woman from henceforth have anything in the land so given upon condition, after the death of his wife, by the law of England; nor the issue of the second husband and wife shall succeed in the inheritance; but immediately after the death of the husband and wife, (to whom the land was so given), it shall come to their issue, or return unto the giver or his heir, as before it is said."

By this statute a new sort of estate was cut out of (*taillé*) a fee-simple, upon the creation of which depended a right of reversion to the donor or his heirs, on failure of issue inheritable by force of the gift. On the creation of an estate tail, or indeed of any estate on which a reversion depends or is expectant, the *fee* is abstractedly divided into two essences; 1, the previous estate or immediate interest, viz. the fee-tail, which in reference to this doctrine is termed the *particular* estate, and in practice means a previous estate in possession; 2, the fee-simple in reversion, being the estate resting in the donor to take effect in future, and expectant or determinable on the destruction or determination of the *particular* estate, both interests forming in law one estate. So that the fee is divided into—1, the estate tail, viz. the *particular* estate passing to the donee; while 2, the reversion, viz. the undisposed remnant or residue, remains in the donor (§ 18), the donor having one inheritance, viz. a fee-simple; and the donee another inheritance of an inferior degree, viz. a fee-tail.

At the time this statute passed, the power of aliening land had become so absolute, that the lands of the nobles were continually diminishing; but the operation of this statute had a contrary effect, and rendered in time the nobility not only dangerously powerful, but abstracted land from the purposes of commerce; at last, however, the device of a common recovery (*n*) to bar an entail was supported by the decision of

---

(*n*) The form of a *recovery* is that of a collusive suit and judgment in a real action, and, therefore, under the very form of the

the Judges of the Court of Common Pleas in *Taltarum's case*, Mich. 12 Ed. 4; and the stat. 4 H. 7, c. 24, made a fine with proclamations conclusive against all persons, both "strangers" and "privies," excepting only such persons, not parties to the fine, as are women covert, persons under age, in prison, out of the realm, or not of sane mind; but saving the right of all persons which accrued after the engrossing of the fine, they pursuing their right within five years after it had accrued; the judges, by a decision upon a question which shortly afterwards occurred upon an ambiguity in the stat., decided that the issue were bound by the fine, which decision was confirmed by stat. 32 H. 8, c. 36, acting retrospectively. Estates tail in some instances could have been barred by release with warranty, and by the operation of discontinuance; but by stat. 3 & 4 Gul. 4, c. 74, s. 14, the doctrines of warranty and discontinuance do not apply to cases occurring after 31st. Dec. 1833.

The estates tail that have been created by the crown for public services, or on other considerations, are inalienable, as those estates are expressly exempted by the statutes of 32 Hen. 8, c. 26, and 34 & 35 Hen. 8, c. 20; which last statute enacted that no feigned recovery should operate against tenants in tail of the gifts of the crown, or where the reversion was in the crown; and by various later acts, a perpetual entail is still preserved in certain noble families, whose estates were originally granted by parliament in consideration of public services. With regard to estates tail in general, they are chargeable with debts due to the crown by record or specialty, 33 H. 8, c. 39, s. 75, and can be sold for

---

law itself, the law was eluded. See *Dalrymple's Essay on Feuds*, 135-6. A *fine* is an agreement of the parties on record, by which the lands are transferred from the *conusor*, the party aliening, to the *conusee*, the party purchasing or taking, with or without a render; it presupposes a suit in a real action, and a concord or agreement, by which the *deforciat* or defendant in this supposed suit acknowledges the right of the plaintiff.

debts contracted by a bankrupt or insolvent, by virtue of the Bankrupt and Insolvent Acts. The means of defeating an estate tail, and enabling the tenant in tail to alien and to bar the interest of his issue, as well as that of the reversioner, was effected by the methods before noticed, fine and common recovery; but these assurances which were extremely antiquated, very subtle, and depended upon principles nearly obsolete, have been substituted by more simple modes of assurance, provided by the stat 3 & 4 Gul. 4, c. 74; and the alienation other than by bankruptcy and insolvency of estates tail, is in fact regulated by that act, which amongst other essentials provides, ss. 40, 41, "That every such assurance (which is also to be under seal), shall be enrolled in the Court of Chancery within six calendar months after the execution thereof."

CHAPTER III.

TENANT IN TAIL AFTER POSSIBILITY OF ISSUE EXTINCT.

LYTTLETON having spoken of estates of inheritance (*a*), viz. fee-simple and fee-tail, now he treateth of tenants of free-hold *tantum* (*b*), that is, for term of life; and therein first

---

(*a*) The ordinary division of estates in fee is—1st. A fee-simple or absolute fee; 2nd. Limited fees, or such estates as are clogged and confined with conditions or qualifications of any sort, which are subdivided into conditional fees, at the common law afterwards turned to *fees-tail* by the statute *de donis* (already alluded to), and qualified fees, also termed base fees. Lyttleton does not notice a qualified fee which Blackstone describes as follows:—

"A BASE or qualified fee is such a one as has a qualification subjoined thereto, and which must be determined whenever the qualification annexed to it is at an end. As, in the case of a grant to A. and his heirs, *tenants of the manor of Dale*; in this instance, whenever the heirs of A. cease to be tenants of that manor, the grant is entirely defeated. So, when Henry VI. granted to John Talbot, lord of the manor of Kingston-Lisle in Berks, that he and his heirs, lords of the said manor, should be peers of the realm, by the title of barons of Lisle; here John Talbot had a base or qualified fee in that dignity, and the instant he or his heirs quitted the seigniory of this manor, the dignity was at an end. This estate is a fee, because by possibility it may endure for ever in a man and his heirs; yet as that duration depends upon the concurrence of collateral circumstances, which qualify and debase the purity of the donation, it is therefore a qualified or base fee." B. C. ii. 109. *Co. Lytt.* 27.

(*b*) To hold in freehold is to hold for terme of his owne lyfe, or for terme of another man's lyfe. And in this case the fee and the right remaineth in the person of him of whome he holdeth. And for that this tenaunt may not alien in fee nor for terme of lyfe. And if he do, it is well lawful to him in whom the fee and the right abideth to enter. *Olde Tenures*, § 8.

of tenant in tail after possibility of issue extinct (*c*); and he giveth unto him the first place, because this tenant hath eight qualities and privileges, which tenant in tail himself hath, and which lessee for life (§ 56) hath not: as first, he is dispunishable for waste (*d*); Co. Lytt. 27. b.—[*The remaining seven privileges are in respect of this tenant's appearance in a real action, and in respect of non-attornment, incidents obsolete and repealed.*] On the other hand, this tenant, as an ordinary tenant for life, forfeits his estate if he aliens in fee, (*Olde Tenures*, § 8, 19), and in some other respects he is treated as a mere tenant for life.—*Ibid.* Lyttleton informs us that this estate arises where one is (with or without his wife) tenant in special tail, (and no one else, § 34), and a person from whose body the issue was to spring, dies without issue; or, having left issue, that issue becomes extinct, in either case the survivor of such donees in special tail is tenant of this estate. The periphrasis in the description of this tenant is by Blackstone deemed absolutely necessary to give an adequate idea of this estate, viz. an estate tail in the survivor which cannot descend to any one; but Mr. Houard's appellation—"*Tenant in tail spe prolis extinctâ,*" seems sufficiently expressive.

(*c*) To hold in the taile after possibilitie of issue extinct, is where land is given to a man and to his wife and to the heires of their two bodies engendered, and one of them overlyveth the other without issue betwene them begotten, he shall holde the land for terme of hys owne life as tenant in taile after possibilitie of issue extinct. And notwithstanding that he do waste he shal never be impeached of that waste. And note that if he alien, he in the reversion shal not have a writ of entrie *in consimili casu*. But he may enter and his entre is lawfull. *Per Rob. Thorpe, Chief Justice.* 28 *E.* 3, 96, and 49 *E.* 3, 25. *Olde Tenures*, § 19.

(*d*) That is, he may cut timber, and is not accountable for it, but he is restrained from *malicious* waste, one species of which is the cutting of ornamental trees.

Tenancy in tail, apres, &c. defined.

32 TENANT in the tail after possibility of issue extinct is, where tenements are given to a man, and to his wife in especial tail, if one of them die without issue, he that surviveth is tenant in tail after possibility of issue extinct: and if they have issue, [and the one die, albeit that] during the life of the issue, he that surviveth shall not be said tenant in tail after possibility of issue extinct; yet if the issue die without issue, so as there be not any issue alive, which may inherit by force of the tail, then he that surviveth of the donees is tenant in the tail after possibility of issue extinct.

Gift to a man and his wife in special tail, viz. two donees.

Gift to man in special tail, viz. one donee.

33 Also if tenements be given to a man and to the heirs which he shall beget on the body of his wife; in this case the wife hath nothing in the tenements, and the husband is seised as donee in especial tail: And in this case, if the wife die without issue of her body begotten by her husband, then the husband is tenant in tail after possibility of issue extinct.

32 *Tenaunt en le taille apres possibilite dissue extient est, lou tenementes sont donez a un home et a sa feme en especiall taille, si lun deux devie sauns issue, celuy qui survesquist est tenaunt en le taille apres possibilite dissue extient. Et sils avoient issue, et lun devie, coment que durant la vie lissue, celuy qui survesquist ne sera dit tenaunt en le taille apres possibilite dissue extient; unquore si lissue devie sauns issue, issint que ne soit ascune issue en vie que poet enheriter per force de le taille, donques celuy qui survesquist de les donees est tenaunt en le taille, apres possibilite dissue extient.*

33 Item, *si tenementes sount donez a un home et a les heires quil engendra de corps sa feme, en ceo cas la feme nad riens en les tenementes, et le baron est seisi come donee en lespeciall taille: et en ceo cas, si la feme devie sauns issue de son corps engendre per son baron, donques le baron est tenaunt en le taille apres possibilite dissue extient.*

34 And note well, that none can be tenant in tail after possibility of issue extinct, but one of the donees, or the donee in an especial tail. For the donee in general tail cannot ever be said to be tenant in tail after possibility of issue extinct, for that always, during his life, he may by possibility have issue, which may inherit by force of the same tail. And so in the same manner the issue, which is heir to the donees in the special tail, cannot be tenant in tail after possibility of issue extinct, &c., for the reason abovesaid &c.*.

This tenancy occurs only in special tail, and is confined to the survivor of the donees or donee.

Therefore issue cannot be tenant in tail, apres, &c.

34 *Et nota que nul poet estre tenaunt en le taile apres possibilite dissue extient forsque un dez donees, ou le donee en un especiall taille. Qar le donee in generall taille ne poet estre unques dit tenaunt en le taille apres possibilite dissue extient, pur ceo que touts temps durant sa vie, il poet per possibilite aver issue que poet enheriter per force de mesme le taille. Et issint en mesme le manere lissue que est heire a les doneez en un especiall taille ne poet estre dit tenaunt en le taille apres possibilite dissue extient, &c.,* causa qua supra, *&c.**

---

* An addition to the text occurs here in the common copies, which, as it is according to law, is here given, viz.

"And note, that tenant in tail after possibility of issue extinct shall not be punished of waste, for the inheritance that once was in him. 10 *H.* 6, 1. But he in the reversion may enter if he alien in fee. 45 *E.* 3, 22." This and that which follows is not in the first edition (which I have). *Co. Lytt.* 28. b. Sir Ed. Coke evidently alludes to the copy of the Tenures printed at Rohan (*Rouen*), by *Pynson*, which he believed to have been the first edition, but the editions by *Lettou & M.*, *Machl.*, as well as this *Rohan* edition, do not give this addition. It was introduced by *Redm.* It also appears in all the copies of *Rastell's* Translation. The "&c.'s" in the concluding passage of this section are in *Lettou & M.* only.

CHAPTER IV.

TENANT BY THE CURTESY.

35 TENANT by the curtesy of England (*a*) is where a man taketh a wife seised in fee-simple, or in fee-tail general, or seised as heir in tail especial, and hath issue by the same wife, male or female [born alive], albeit the issue afterwards dieth or liveth, yet if the wife dies, the husband shall hold the land during his life by the law of England. And he is called tenant by the curtesy of England, because this is used in no other realm but in England only. And some have said, that

35 *Tenaunt per le curtosie Dengleterre est, lou home prent feme seisie en fee-simple, ou en fee taille generall, ou seisie come heire de le taille especiall, et ad issue per mesme la feme male ou female, [neez vife], soit lissue apres mort ou en vie, si la feme devie, le baron tiendra la terre duraunt sa vie per la ley Dengleterre. Et est appelle tenaunt per le curtosie Dengleterre, pur ceo que ceo nest ewe en nul auter roialme, forsque tantsolement en Engleterre. Et ascuns ount dit, que il ne*

(*a*) To hold by the curtesy of Englande is* there where a man taketh a wife inherited, and they have issue a son or daughter, and the wife dyeth, [by reason of this issue†], whether the issue be deade or alive, (*soit le issue mort ou en vie*), the husband shall holde this land for term of his life by the curtesy of England and by the law. And‡ in this case the fee and the right remaineth in the person of him of whom he holdeth; and, therefore, this tenant may not alyen in fee nor for terme of another's life, and if he do, it is lawful to him in the reversion to enter.—*Olde Tenures*, § 6.

* Is to hold where. *Berth.* 1531. † *Id.* ‡ For. *Id.*

he shall not be tenant by the curtesy, unless the child which he hath by his wife be heard to cry; for by the cry it is proved that the child was born alive, &c. (*b*). [*Quære, &c.**]

serra tenaunt per le curtosie, si non que lenfaunt quil ad per sa feme soit oye crye, car per le crier est le prove que lenfaunt fuist nee vife, &c. [*Quære, &c**.]

---

* The reading as given in the text, including the words placed within brackets, is according to *Lettou & M.;* but *Machl.*, *Roh.*, *Pyns.* 1516, *Redm.*, *Berth.*, *Middl.*, *Powel*, *Sm. Tottyl*, 1554, and *ed.* 1671, render the text without the words in the brackets, and so also do the copies of *Rastell's Transl.* Both the editions by *Tottyl*, 1557, give *oyes ou vis—heard or seen*, concluding, *nee vif, Ideo quære—born alive, therefore inquire. Tottyl*, 1567,—1577, has the same two readings, and also *oyes ou vife*, which in all subsequent editions to 1639, is by a misprint corrupted to *vife*. The copy of the Tenures in Co. Lytt. reads *oyes ou vife*, in the English rendered *born alive*, which shews that Sir Edward Coke did not minutely collate his Text, though he notices several false readings in the course of his comments.

(*b*) If it be borne alive it is sufficient though it be not heard cry, for peradventure it may be borne dumbe, and this is resolved clearly in *Paine's case*, [8 *Rep. fol.* 34]; for the pleading is, that during the marriage he had issue by his wife, and upon that point the trial is to be had, and upon the evidence it must be proved that the issue was born alive, for *mortuus exitus non est exitus*, so as the crying is but a proof that the chlld was born alive, and so is motion, stirring, and the like. And it is said by an ancient author, [*Mirrour*, *c.* 1, §. 3], that it was ordained in the reign of King Henry I., that all who survived their wives who had conceived by them, should hold the inheritances of their wives for life. *Co. Lytt.* 29. *b.*

If the issue be born living, notwithstanding that he die before he be heard cry, the husband shall be tenant by the curtesy; for the issue shall not be taken if the infant were heard cry after he was born, but if he were born alive or not.—*Kitchin*, 318, *ed.* 1675.

And it is to be understood, that if the issue which the husband has by his wife be born alive, notwithstanding that he die before that he be heard cry, and before that he be baptized, if neglect of baptism be not in the husband by wilfulness, the husband shall be tenant by curtesy; but if such neglect be by

CONCLUDING REMARKS.

With regard to this estate, Mr. Houard notices that the word *curtoisie* betrays its French origin. This right of the

---

wilfulness of the husband, some say that then the husband shall not be tenant by the curtesy. 13 *H.* 3. *Dower*, 188; *Perkins's Profitable Booke*, § 471. This ancient requisite of baptism may perhaps explain what Mr. *Hargrave* conceived an unaccountable peculiarity, viz. that the birth of a male was to be proved by men only, as it seemed to him on reference to a record from *Lord Hale's MSS.*, but *puer* means *issue* without reference to sex; and the naming the child by women was probably meant as a substitute for baptism by a man. The record as cited by Lord Hale is thus:—*Quia puer non fuit visus nec auditus clamare ab hominibus masculis, licet per feminas nominatus fuit Johannes.—Hill.* 5 *E.* 1, *rot.* 1, *Vigorn'.* Therefore husband not tenant by the curtesy.

But in this it is required that the child be vitall, that is to say, be born and brought forth into this world alive; and therefore the common saying is, and hath been, that unless the child be heard cry, the father shall not be tenant by the curtesy, for the only proof and argument of life in an infant born is the vagite [*vagitus*] and crying.—*Institutions of the Laws and Statutes of England*, (1541), *fol.* 7 *b*, *ed.* 1611.

Henrico adscribunt nonnulli legem, quam Curtoisé d'Angleterre, dicunt Icti. Hâc, vir susceptâ prole conjugis demortuæ herediis fruitur, in humanis scilicet dum egerit.—Selden, Janus Anglorum, § 38.

When a man shall take lands in marriage with a wife, if he have begotten of the same his wife, an heir, son, or daughter, which shall be heard to cry within the four walls, if the same husband overlive his wife, whether the heir live or not, the same land shall remain to the husband [for his life], and after the death of the husband, the lands shall return to the donor or to his heir; but if he have no heir by his wife, then after the death of the wife, it shall return to the donor or to his heir.—*Statutum de tenentibus per legem Angliæ—temp. incert.*

Cum consuetudo et lex Angliæ sit, quod si aliquis desponsaverit aliquam hæreditatem habentem, et ex eâ prolem habuerit, cujus clamor auditus fuerit infra quatuor parietes, et vir supervixerit uxorem, habebit totâ vitâ suâ custodiam hæreditatis uxoris, licet ea hæredem habuerit ex primo viro, qui plenæ ætatis est; præceptum est, quod eadem lex observetur in Hi-

husband to enjoy during his life the lands of his deceased wife, subsisted in France from the seventh century; and he traces the origin of this right to a moral recompense afforded the husband in respect of the dower to which the wife would have been entitled, had she survived her husband. The homage which the husband had to perform for his wife in her name was styled *courtesy,* as the homage which she had to render when unmarried was always distinguished by that name.

The Germans, according to Mr. Houard, acknowledged this right of the husband, before the seventh century.

Lyttleton, who never once throughout his Treatise alludes to the feudal law or its adoption here, imagined that this tenure was peculiar to England; and, in one sense, he is not to be accused of ignorance, for the *Curialitas Scotiæ,* the fragment styled the statute *de tenentibus per legem Angliæ,* and the precept or ordinance by Henry III., that this custom should have place in Ireland, are all secondary to and derived from the adoption of the feudal system, either introduced or perfected by William the Conqueror. Sir Martin

---

berniâ.—Rot. Claus. 11 *H.* 3, *membrana* 3, *cited also in Hale's Hist. C. L.* 180, *and in Wright's Tenures,* 192. [Cited in Hargr. n. and in B. C. ii. 116 (*g*), as *Rot. Patent.*]

Si habuit exitum qui auditus fuit clamare seu vocem edere infra quatuor parietes. Pasch. 9 *E.* 1, *rot.* 4. *Hale's MSS.* The husband of every female copyholder dying seised of any copyhold estate within this manor, by whom he hath had issue born alive, *and which has been heard to cry,* is entitled by the custom of this manor to hold his wife's copyhold estates for his life, in nature of tenant by the curtesy of England.—*Rot. Custumal. Maner. de Sedgley com' Staff.*

That is to say, that if, when she is delivered of child, the infant be heard to cry, and that the hue and cry be raised and the country be assembled and have the view of the child so born and of the mother.—*Custum. de Gavelk.* § 21. *Et puer ille visus fuit, aut cognitus, vel vagiens sive clamans audiatur.—Trin.* 17 *E.* 3, *coram Rege, Rot.* 32 *Kanc'.* cited by *Mr. Robinson* in his *Customs of Gavelkind,* 162—164.

Wright says—" Tenancies by the curtesy or *per legem terræ*, though so called as if they were peculiar to England, were known not only in Scotland but in Ireland, and in Normandy also," (he here refers to the *Ancien Coutumier*, c. 119, cited also by Mr. Houard, i. 51); " and the like law or custom is to be found amongst the ancient *Almain* laws (*c*); and yet it doth not seem to have been feudal, nor doth its original anywhere satisfactorily appear; some writers ascribe it to Henry 1, but Nathaniel Bacon calls it a law of *counter-tenure* to that of dower; "—which last opinion is justified by Mr. Houard, who speaks fully upon the origin of this tenure or right.

The circumstances necessary to create this estate are stated by Sir Edward Coke to be marriage, seisin of the wife, (and this seisin must be an actual seisin or a *seisin in fact*), issue, and death of the wife. But it is not necessary that these should concur altogether at one time. Lyttleton in the ensuing chapter on Dower, an analogous estate, tells us, " that in every case where a man taketh a wife seised of such an estate of tenements, &c., so as the issue which he hath by his wife can by possibility inherit the same tenements of such an estate as the wife hath, as heir to the wife (*d*); in

---

(*c*) *Si qua mulier qua hæreditatem paternam habet post nuptum pregnans peperit* puèrum, (by *puer*, a child of either sex is meant), *et in ipsâ horâ mortua fuerit, et infans vivus remanserit aliquanto spatio vel unius horæ, ut possit aperire oculos et videre culmen domus, et quatuor parietes, et postea defunctus fuerit, hæreditas materna ad patrem ejus pertineat; et tamen si testes habet pater ejus, quod vidissent illum infantem oculos aperire et potuisset culmen domus videre et quatuor parietes, tunc pater ejus habeat licentiam cum lege ipsas res defendere.—LL. Alemannorum, tit.* 92.

(*d*) *As heir to the wife.* This doth imply a secret of law, for except the wife be actually seised, the heir shall not make himself heir to the wife; and this is the reason that a man shall not be tenant by the curtesy of a seisin in law.—*Co. Lytt.* 40. *a.* [See 8 *Rep.* 36 *a.* where 11 *H.* 4, 11, and 40 *E.* 3, 9, are cited to prove this doctrine. *Hargr. n.* 40 *a.*]

such case, after the decease of the wife, he shall have the same tenements by the curtesy of England, otherwise not. § 52.

By the custom of Gavelkind, a man may be tenant by the curtesy without the having of any issue, but the custom restricts the curtesy to half of the wife's land, which is forfeited on the widower's marrying again.—*Customs of Gavelkind*, § 22.

The issue must be born alive (*e*); and a rule of evidence appears to have been established by our ancestors in determining this fact, which Lyttleton notices. It would seem that the ancient and prevailing rule of law was, that unless the child was heard to cry, the husband was not entitled as tenant by curtesy; and certainly almost the only evidence that could have been adduced in favor of the birth of a child which did not long survive, would have been the *vagitus* or cry; perhaps it was to this case the rule strictly applied, for, if the child survived any length of time, other evidence could have been adduced of a nature quite as conclusive. The Germans, by their law of curtesy, established a rule of evidence which steers clear of the arbitrary precision of that required by our old law; for if the infant was alive for any time, so that it could open its eyes and see the roof of the house and the four walls, and the father produced witnesses to that fact, he enjoyed the mother's estate.

But reason demanded that other evidence of the birth of the child than the cry should be receivable; and so it was adjudged at a very early period in the opposite instance of attainting a tenant in dower of gavelkind land of childbirth during her widowhood: for in the customs of gavelkind the cry of the child is mentioned as conclusive evidence, and by

(*e*) This is clear from the words of Lyttleton himself, independently of the words within brackets, for the word *apres*, *afterwards*, implies that the issue should be born alive.

Every word of Lyttleton is material.—*Co. Lytt.* 161. *a.*

that rule, it was contended to be the only evidence admissible of the birth; but then it was adjudged, as now it would be, that other evidence is receivable.—*Robinson Gavelk.* 167.

In either case, as the act of delivery is transient and frequently momentary, and in many instances not susceptible of proof by witnesses, therefore circumstantial evidence of a direct nature was sought for in this rule of proof; which, when coupled with the *quatuor parietes,* the four walls or house, as the place from whence the cry was to proceed, or in which the cry was to be heard, strongly points to the identity of the mother and child, and in all probability, with regard to tenancy by curtesy, was intended to prevent a *suppositio partûs,* a crime by no means uncommon in rude ages, the simplicity of which is not unfrequently tainted with gross frauds and outrageous impostures.

Sir Edward Coke (1 *Inst.* 8. *b.*), alludes to a prevention of a *suppositio partûs* by the widow, by exercise of the writ *de ventre inspiciendo;* and a recent instance occurred of this writ being obtained on behalf of some collateral heirs, who feared a supposititious offspring.

Magnas lites intulit olim
Falsum mendaci ventre puerperum.—*Catullus.*

CHAPTER V.

DOWER(*a*).

In this chapter Lyttleton divideth dower into five parts, viz.—dower by the common law (§ 37); secondly, dower by the custom (§ 38); thirdly, dower *ad ostium ecclesiæ* (§ 39); fourthly, dower *ex assensu patris* (§ 40); and fifthly, dower *de la pluis beale* (§ 48). And all these dowers were instituted for a competent livelihood for the wife during her life.—*Co. Lytt.* 33. *b.*

The reason why the law gave the wife a dower will appear, if we consider how the law stood anciently; for, by the old law, if this provision had not been made, and the party at the marriage had made no assignment of dower, the wife would have been without any provision, for the personal estates even of the richest were then very inconsiderable; and before trusts were invented, which is but lately, the husband could give his wife nothing during his own life, nor could he provide for her by will, because lands could not be devised, unless it was in some particular places by the custom, till the statute of 32 *H.* 8, *c.* 1.—*Note by Editor of* 11*th Edition of Co. Lytt.*

(*a*) To hold in dower, is where a man inherited taketh a wife and dieth, the heire shall enter and endow the wife of the third part of all that that was to her husband in his life in fee-simple or fee-taile, and shee shall holde these landes for terme of her lyfe as her freeholde.—*Olde Tenures*, § 9.

Tenancy in dower defined.

36 TENANT in dower is where a man is seised of certain lands or tenements in fee-simple or in tail general, or as heir in special tail, and taketh a wife, and dieth, the wife after the decease of her husband shall be endowed of the third part of such lands or tenements that were her husband's at any time during the coverture, to have and to hold to the same wife in severalty, by metes and bounds (*b*), for term of her life, whether

36 *Tenaunt en dower est lou home est seisi de certeyn terres ou tenementes en fee-simple ou en fee-taille generall, ou come heire de le taille especiall, et prent feme, et devie, la feme apres le decesse son baron, serra endowe de la tierce partie de tielx terres ou tenementes que furent a son baron en ascun temps duraunt la coverture, a aver et tener a mesme la feme en severalte, per metez et boundes, pur terme de sa vie, le quel*

(*b*) ***In severalty, by metes and bounds.***—The person whose duty it is to set out or assign the dowress her dower, is the heir, and if he does not do this, or he and the dowress cannot agree, she can sue out her writ of *dower unde nihil habet* against the heir, and recover her dower either in the County Court, or if the writ be removed, in the Court of Common Pleas. If the inheritance of which she is to be endowed be divisible, her dower is to be set out or assigned by *metes and bounds;* and this division, if made by the sheriff after judgment upon her writ of dower, must be strictly by metes and bounds, *i. e.* he is compellable to assign a third of such a meadow, a third of the arable land, a third part of the pasture, a third part of such a marsh, &c., so that a visible and known separation takes place, and this is called an endowment according to the common right. If the sheriff act maliciously or corruptly, the Court will award an attachment against him. Where dower is assigned by the heir, he may, by consent of the dowress, assign one part in lieu of another; and this, when accepted by the dowress, is termed an assignment against common right. Of inheritances that are entire, *scil.* not divisible in their nature, she must be endowed in a certain and special manner; (for she cannot be endowed of the thing itself), as of the third part of the profits of an office, the third presentation of an

she hath issue by her husband or no, and of what age soever the wife be, so as she be past the age of nine years at the time of the death of her husband; or else she shall not be endowed.

Dower at common law.

37 And note well, that, by the common law, the wife shall have for her dower but the third part of the tenements which were her husband's during the espousals; but by custom of some country she shall have the half, and by custom in some town or borough she shall have the whole. And in all these cases she shall be called tenant in dower.

Dower by custom or free-bench, see § 166.

38 Also there be two other kinds of dowers, *scil.* dower

ele avoit issue per son baron ou nemy, et de quele age que la feme soit, issint quele passe lage de ix. *ans al temps de le moriaunt son baron, ou autrement ele ne serra mye endowe.*

37 *Et nota, que per la comen ley la feme navera pur sa dower forsque la tierce partie des tenementes que furent a son baron duraunt lespousels, mes per custume dascun pays elle avera la moite, et per custume en asçun ville et borough ele avera lentierte. Et en toutes tielx cases, elle sera dit tenaunt en dower.*

38 *Auxi y sont deux autres maners de dowers,* scil., *dower*

---

advowson, the third part of tithes of corn, to be set out by the third sheaf, and so of other tithes, the third part of the profits of a court-leet or court-baron, the third part of a free fishery, by the third of the draught or the third cast of the net, &c.

The dowress being entitled to the one third part of the land, is to have her dower assigned according to the improved value. The dower, in some instances, may be assigned by a tenant seised of the freehold of the land chargeable with dower, or by the guardian of the heir; and in the latter case, if the heir was within age at the time of the assignment, and even if he assigned the dower himself, while under age, the dowress, if endowed of a greater part than she was justly entitled to, can be compelled to restore the surplusage, upon the heir's suing out his writ *of admeasurement of dower.*

which is called "dowment at the church-door," and dower called "dowment by the father's assent (*c*)."

Dower at the church door.

39 Dowment at the church-door, is where a man of full age seised in fee-simple, who shall be wedded unto a wife, and when he cometh to the door of the [monastery or*] church to be married, and there, after troth plighted be-

appelle dowment ad ostium ecclesiæ, *et dower appelle dowment* ex assensu patris (*c*).

39 *Dowment* ad ostium ecclesiæ, *est lou home de pleyn age seisi en fee-simple qui sera espouse a un feme, et quant il vient al huys* [*de monasterie ou**] *del esglise destre espouse, et la apres affiaunce entre eux fait, il endowa sa feme de sa entiere terre,*

* This passage reads in *Lettou & M.*, *Machl.*, and *Roh.*, as *al huys de monstr' del esglise;* while *Redm.* leaves out the words within brackets. In the next section (40), these words occur again, when *Lettou & M.* reads *al huys de monstr' de parcel;* and *Machl. al huys de monstr' del esglise. Pyns.* 1516, in this section reads *al huys del monastr' del esglise;* and so read *Middl.*, *Redm.*, and *Berth.*, in this section *al huys de monastr' de parcel.* The later and common editions read the words within brackets. In § 47, these words also occur, and a confused reading is given in all the early editions.

(*c*) These dowers at the church-door were of Norman origin, and, according to Glanvill, were in his time, the reign of Henry II., the most usual species of dower; and then the wife could not be endowed of more than a third part: but this rule was relaxed, for Lyttleton informs us in this section, that the wife may be endowed of the whole or any part of the husband's land. Marriages were before the Reformation solemnized at the church-door. *Chaucer* describes the *Wife of Bath* as having had five husbands at the church-door: "Housbondes at the churche-dore had she five."—*v.* 464.

These two dowers appear not to have been conclusive upon the wife, at least in Lyttleton's time, and were long obsolete, and were at last abolished by *stat.* 3 & 4 *Will.* 4, *c.* 105, *s.* 13.

The dower *de pluis beale*, mentioned at § 48, expired with the abolition of military tenures, by *stat.* 12 *Car.* 2, *c.* 24.

tween them, he endoweth his wife of his whole land, or of the half or other less parcel, and there openly doth declare the quantity and the certainty of his land that she shall have for her dower: In this case, the wife, after the death of the husband, shall enter into the said quantity of land of which her husband endowed her, without other assignment of any.

Dower ex assensu patris, *at the church-door.*

[40] Dowment by the father's assent is, where the father is seised of tenements in fee, and his son and heir apparent, when he is married, endoweth his wife at the door of the [monastery or*] church, of parcel of his father's lands or tenements, with the assent of his father, and assigns the quantity and parcels: In this case, after the death of the son, the wife shall enter into the same parcel without the assignment of any. But it hath been said in this case, that it behoveth the wife to have a deed of the father to prove his assent and consent of this endowment. [41] And if after the death of her husband she enter and agree to any such dower of the

Widow may elect after death of her

ou de le moyte, ou del autre meindre parcell, et la overtment declara le quantite et la certeynte de sa terre quele avera pur sa dower: En ceo cas la feme, apres le mort le baron, entrera en le dit quantite de terre dount le baron luy endowa sauns autre assignement de nulluy.

[40] *Dowment* ex assensu patris *est, lou le pere est seisi de tenementes en fee, et son fitz et heire apparaunt, quant il est espouse, endowa sa feme al huys [de monasterie ou*] del esglise, de parcel dez terrez ou tenementes son pere, del assent son pere, et assigna le quantite et les parcels: en ceo cas apres la mort le fitz, la feme entrera en mesme le parcell sauns autre assignement de nulluy. Mes il ad este dit en ceo cas, quil covient a la feme daver un fait de le pere provant son assent et consent de cel endowment.* [41] *Et si apres la mort le baron ele entra et agrea a ascun tiel dower de les dits* ij. *dowers* ad

---

* See *ante*, p. 54, *n.*

husband to abide by such dower or claim at common law.

said two dowers at the church-door, she is excluded from claiming any other dower, by the common law, of any the lands or tenements which were her husband's. But if she will, she may refuse such dower at the church-door, &c., and then she may be endowed according to the course of the common law.

Heir must be heir-apparent.

42 And note well, that no wife shall be endowed *ex assensu patris,* in form aforesaid, but where her husband is son and heir apparent to his father. Inquire of these two cases of dowment *ad ostium ecclesiæ, &c.,* if the wife at the time of the death of her husband be not past the age of nine years, whether she shall have such dower, or no.

In these dowers the wife might enter without assignment; but, in dower at common

43 And note well, that in all cases, where the certainty appeareth what lands or tenements the wife shall have for her dower, *there* the wife may enter after the death of her husband without assignment of any other (*d*). But where the

ostium ecclesiæ, *ele est exclude de claymer ascun autre dower per le comen ley, dascuns terres ou tenementes queux furent de son dit baron. Mes si ele voit, ele poet refuser tiel dower* ad ostium ecclesiæ, &c., *et donques ele poet estre endowe solonques le cours de le comen ley.*

42 *Et nota, que nul feme sera endoiwe* ex assensu patris, *en la fourme avauntdit, mes lou son baron est fitz et heire apparaunt a son pere.* Quære *de ceux* ij. *cases de dowment* ad ostium ecclesiæ, &c., *si la feme al temps de la mort son baron, ne passa lage de* ix. *ans, si ele avera tiel dower ou non.*

43 *Et nota que en toutz cases lou le certeinte appiert queux terres ou tenementes feme avera pur sa dower, la feme poet entrer apres la mort son baron, sauns assignement de nulluy. Mes lou le certeynte ne appiert, sicome destre*

(*d*) That is, she was not obliged to put her right in suit, but might enter without any formal process, as a jointress may now do, by the same reason.

certainty doth not appear, as to be endowed of the third part to have in severalty, or to be endowed of the half according to the custom to hold in severalty; in such cases it behoveth that her dower be assigned unto her, [because it doth not appear*] before the assignment what part of the lands or tenements she shall have for her dower.

law, assignment must first be made.

44 But if there be two jointenants of certain land in fee, and the one alieneth that which to him belongeth to another in fee, who taketh a wife, and after dieth, in this case the wife for her dower shall have the third part of the moiety which her husband purchased, to hold in common and occupy in common, as her part amounteth, with the heir of her husband, and with the other jointenant, who did not alien: for that in such case her dower cannot† be assigned by metes and bounds.

Dower may be had of an estate in common.

endowe de la tierce partie daver en severalte, ou destre endowe del moite solonques le custume de tener en severalte; en tielx cases il covient que sa dower soit a luy assigne, [pur ceo quod non constat*] *devaunt lassignement quel partie de les terres ou tenementes elle avera pur sa dower.*

44 *Mes si soient deux jointenaunts de certeyne terre en fee, et lun aliena ceo que a luy affiert, a un autre en fee, qui prent feme et puis devia; en ceo cas la feme pur sa dower avera le tierce partie de la moite que son baron purchasa, a tener en comen et occupier en comen, come sa partie amounta, ovesque leire son baron, et ovesque lautre jointenaunt qui ne aliena pas: pur ceo que en tiel cas sa dower ne† poet estre assigne per metez et boundez.*

---

* Instead of the words within brackets, *Pyns.* 1516, *Redm.*, *Berth.*, *Middl.*, *Powel*, *Sm.*, *Tottyl* 1554, read *apres la mort son baron, pur ceo que nest lymitte;* and with these agrees *Rastell's Transl.*, which renders these words, *after the death of her husband, because it is not limited.*

† Some copies of *Rastell's Transl.* after 1551 and before 1627, omit

but not of a joint estate.

45 And it is to be understood that the wife shall not be endowed of lands or tenements that her husband holdeth jointly with another at the time of his death: but where he holdeth in common, otherwise it is, as in the case next abovesaid.

Tenant in tail could not endow at the church-door, consequently cannot now make a jointure.

46 And it is to be understood, that if tenant in tail endoweth his wife at the church-door, as is aforesaid, this shall serve for little or nought to the wife, for this, that, after the decease of her husband, the issue in tail may enter upon the possession of the wife, and so may he in the reversion, if there be no issue in tail then alive*.

Infant would not give dower ad ostium, *but he might* ex assensu patris.

47 Also if a man, seised in fee-simple and being within age, endoweth his wife at the door of the [monastery or†] church, and dieth, and the wife enter: In this case the heir of the hus-

45 *Et est assavoir que la feme ne sera mye endowe de terres ou tenementes que son baron tient joint ovesque un autre al temps de son moriant: mes lou il tient en comen autrement est, come en le cas proscheyn avauntdit.*

46 *Et est assavoir que si tenaunt en le taille endowa sa feme* ad ostium ecclesiæ, *come est avauntdit, ceo servera pur petit ou pur nient a la feme, pur ceo que apres la mort son baron, lissue en le taille poet entrer sur le possession la feme; et issint poet celuy en le revercion si ne soit issue en le taille en vie*.*

47 *Auxi si home seisi en fee-simple et esteant deins age endowa sa feme al huys [del monasterie ou†] del esglise, et devia, et la feme entra, en ceo cas leire le baron luy poet ouster.*

---

this word *not*, but erroneously. *Tottyl* 1581, *J. Yetswiert* 1597, *Stationers'* ("perused and amended"), 1608.

* The concluding words *en vie, alive,* do not appear in *Machl.* or *Roh.*, but are supplied by an *&c.* Some later editions give these words and *&c.* also.

† See *ante*, p. 54, *n.*

band may oust her. But otherwise it is, as it seemeth, where the father is seised in fee, and the son within age endoweth his wife of his father's assent, the father being then of full age.

48 Also there is another dower which is called dowment *de la pluis beale.* And this is in such case where a man is seised of forty acres of land, and he holdeth twenty acres of the said forty acres of one by knight's service, and the other twenty acres of another in socage, and taketh a wife, and hath issue a son, and dieth, his son being within the age of fourteen years; and the lord of whom the land is holden by knight's service entereth into the twenty acres of land holden of him, and holdeth them as guardian in chivalry, during the nonage of the infant, and the mother of the infant entereth into the residue, and occupieth that as guardian in socage: if in such case the wife bringeth a writ of dower against the guardian in chivalry to be endowed of the tenements holden by knight's service, in the king's court or in any other court, the guardian in

Dower de la pluis beale.

Mes tout autrement il est come il semble, lou le pere est seisi en fee, et le fitz deins age endowa sa feme ex assensu patris, *le pere adonques esteant de pleyn age.*

48 *Auxi il y ad une autre dower, que est appelle Dowement de la pluis beale. Et ceo est come en tiell cas, que home seisi de quaraunt acres de terre, et il tient vint acres de les dits quaraunt acres de terre dun home per service de chivaler, et les autres vint acres de terre dun autre en socage, et prent feme, et ont issue fitz, et morust, son fitz esteant deins lage de* xiiij. *ans; et le seignour de qui la terre est tenus en chivalerie, entra en les* xx. *acres de terre tenus de luy, et les ad come gardeyn en chivalerie duraunt le nonnage lenfaunt, et la mere de lenfaunt entra en le remenaunt, et ceo occupia come gardeyn en socage: si en tiel cas la feme porta brief de dower envers le gardeyn en chivalerie, destre endowe de les tenementes tenus per service de chivalerie en le court le roy, ou en autre court, le gardeyn en chivalerie poet pleder en tiel cas tout cest matere, et monstrer coment la feme est gardeyn en socage,*

chivalry may plead in such case all the matter, and shew how the wife is guardian in socage, as aforesaid, and pray that it may be adjudged by the court, that the wife may endow herself *de le pluis beale*, i. e. of the fairest *part* of the tenements that she hath as guardian in socage, respect being had to the value of the third part that she claimeth to have of the tenements holden in knight's service by her writ of dower. And if the wife cannot gainsay this, then the judgment shall be, that the guardian in chivalry shall hold the lands holden of him during the nonage of the infant, quit from the woman, &c. [and that the wife may endow herself of the fairest part of the lands, that she hath as guardian in socage to the value, &c. *i. e. to the value of the third part that the guardian in knight's service has**].

49 And after such judgment given, the wife may take her neighbours, and in their presence endow herself, by metes

coment devant est dit, et prier quelle sera ajugge per la court que la feme luy mesme endowera de la pluis beale de les tenementes quele ad come gardeyn en socage solonques le value de la tierce partie quele claime daver de les tenementes tenus en chivalerie per son brief de dower. Et si la feme ceo ne poet dedire, donques le juggement sera fait, que le gardeyn en chivalerie tiendra la terre tenus de luy duraunt le nonage lenfaunt, quite de la feme, &c., [et que la feme poet endower luy mesme de le pluis beale partie de les terres quele ad come gardeyn en socage a le value, &c.]*

49 *Et apres tiel juggement done, la feme poet prendre ses vyceyns, et en lour presence endower luy mesme per metez et*

* The text is somewhat confused in the editions subsequent to the edition by *Machlinia;* in fact, the words within brackets are only the consequence implied by the *&c.* that precedes them. The words within brackets are the concluding words of the formula of judgment; but the *Rohan* edition and some later copies have interpolated at the commencement a *nota*, and so made this conclusion a separate sentence, thus: *And* note *that the wife, &c.*

and bounds, of the fairest part of the tenements that she hath as guardian in socage, to the value of the third part of the lands that the guardian in chivalry has, &c., and that, to have and to hold to her for term of her life; and such dower is called dower of the fairest *part**. [50] And note well, that such dowment cannot be but where the judgment is given in the king's court, or in some other court, that the wife can do this; and this is for the preservation of the estate of the guardian in chivalry, during the nonage of the infant. [51] And so ye may see five kinds of dower, *scil.* dower by the common law, dower by custom, dower at the church-door, dower by the father's assent, and dower of the fairest *part.*

[52] And be it remembered, that in every case where a man *To entitle a*

*boundez de la pluis beale partie de les tenementes quele ad come gardeyn en socage, a le value del tierce partie des tenementes que le gardeyn en chivalerie ad &c., et ceo aver et tener a luy pur terme de sa vie; et tiel dower est appelle dower de la pluis beale**. [50] *Et nota, que tiel dowment, ne poet estre, mes lou le juggement est fait en le court le roy ou en autre court, que la feme ceo poet faire; et ceo est pur salvacion del estate del gardeyn in chivalerie duraunt le nonnage lenfaunt.* [51] *Et issint poiez veier cinques maneres de dower,* scil., *dower par la comen ley, dower per le custome, dower* ad ostium ecclesiæ, *dower* ex assensu patris, *et dower* de la pluis beale.

[52] *Et* memorandum, *que en chescun cas lou home prent*

---

* In *Redm.*, *Berth.*, *Middl.*, *Sm.*, *Powel*, and *Tottyl* 1554, the following reference to the Year-book is placed between the 49th and 50th sections; in these French copies it appears as a concluding paragraph; though in *Rastell's Transl.* it is placed as the commencement of a new sentence: *Cum hoc concordat P.* xlv. *Ed.* 3, *fol.* 4. *But there it was said, that, after the time that the heir come to his full age, the wife shall have a new action of dower against the heir, to be endowed of the third part of all that the man died seised.*

husband as tenant by curtesy, the issue had must be such as can inherit the wife's estate.

So to entitle a woman to dower, her issue, if any, must be such as could inherit the husband's estate.

taketh a wife seised of such an estate of tenements, &c., so that the issue that he hath by the wife can by possibility inherit the same tenements of such estate that the wife hath, as heir to the wife: in such case, after the decease of the wife, he shall have the same tenements by the curtesy of England, and otherwise not. 53 And also in every case where a woman taketh a husband seised of such an estate of tenements, &c., so that by possibility it may happen that if the wife have any issue by her husband, and that the same issue may by possibility inherit the same tenements of such estate as the husband hath, as heir to her husband; of such tenements she shall have her dower, and otherwise not: for if tenements be given to a man, and to the heirs which he shall beget of the body of his wife; in this case the wife hath nothing in the tenements, and the husband hath an estate but as donee in special tail; yet if the husband die without issue, the same wife shall be endowed of the same tenements; because the issue that she by possibility might have had,

feme seisie de tiel estate dez tenementes, &c., issint que lissue que il y ad per la feme poet per possibilite enheriter mesmes les tenementes de tiel estate que la feme ad, come heire al feme: en tiel cas apres la mort la feme, il avera mesmes les tenementes per le curtosie Dengleterre, et autrement nemy. 53 *Et auxi en chescun cas lou la feme prent baron seisi de tiel estate dez tenementes, &c., issint que si per possibilite il puissoit happer que si la feme avoit ascun issue per son baron, que mesme lissue puissoit per possibilite enheriter mesmes les tenementes de tiel estate que le baron ad, come heire a son baron, de tielx tenementes elle avera sa dower et autrement nemy: qar si tenementes sont donez a un home, et a les heires quil engendra de corps sa feme, en tiel cas la feme nad riens en les tenementes, et le baron ad estate forsque come donee en lespeciall taille; unquore si le baron devie sauns issue, mesme la feme sera endowe de mesmes les tenementes, pur ceo que lissue quele per possibilite puissoit aver per mesme le baron puissoit enheriter mesmes les tenementes. Mes si la feme*

by the same husband, might inherit the same tenements. But if the wife die, living her husband, and after the husband takes another wife, and dies, this second wife shall not be endowed in this case, for the reason aforesaid (*e*).

devyast, vivaunt son baron, et puis le baron prent autre feme et mourust, cest seconde feme ne sera mye endowe en ceo cas, causa qua supra (*e*).

CONCLUDING REMARKS.

DOWER is a freehold tenancy arising by act of law, and gives the widow of a deceased proprietor of land an estate for life in one third, (but by special or particular custom she may have more, § 37), of all the lands and tenements whereof her husband was *solely* (not jointly, § 45), at any time during the marriage seised in fee, or in tail in possession, and whereto the issue of such widow by her husband may by possibility inherit, § 53.

These requisites have, of late years, been in *most* instances evaded or defeated by various artificial modes of conveyance; and some conventional modes of barring this interest of the widow have been used from a very early period,—for the dowers *ex assensu patris* and *ad ostium ecclesiæ*, were only antiquated modes of barring it. The stat. 27 H. 8, c. 10, also provides, that a jointure made in accordance with the terms of that act shall be a bar to dower. But, after all, dower could not be evaded in *every* instance; and in those

---

(*e*) Here follow two sentences, which in the common editions form the two concluding sections of this chapter, according to the subdivision of Lyttleton by *West*, 1581, and consist of two additions of spurious text. To the first addition Sir Ed. Coke remarks, "*That this shaft came never out of Lyttleton's quiver of choice arrowes;*" and with regard to the second addition, the concluding section, he states, "*Explosa est hæc opinio.*" These additions first appeared in *Pyns*. 1516.

cases, in later times, where dower did attach *invito marito*, it most frequently proved a very inadequate provision for the widow, while in some measure it restrained the alienation of the land so long as it was clogged with this incumbrance: as a provision for widows generally, since the increase of personal property, it was notoriously inappropriate; as that species of property chiefly consists of money and moveables, and much immoveable property consists of what are termed chattel interests, viz. leases, &c., which rank as mere personalty.

The most common methods of barring or defeating the wife's claim to dower were these: by obtaining the concurrence of the wife to a fine or to a recovery, which operated by estoppel, being a matter of record; by the creation of a trust or intervention of a trust or *equitable* estate, or a long term of years assigned to a trustee; for no dower could be had of an equitable estate by creating a joint-tenancy so as to prevent a *sole* seisin by the husband; or by putting the fee in *remainder*, so that the husband should not take an estate in possession.

The law of dower, so far as regards women married after the 31st December, 1833, is materially altered by the stat. 3 & 4 Will. 4, c. 105, ss. 4, 6, 7, 9; for by that act it is declared, that the husband may by deed or will deprive his wife of her dower, or may impose by his will any restrictions or directions he may please on the title of his widow.

Also, under the stat. 3 & 4 Will. 4, c. 74, s. 77, for the abolition of fines and recoveries, a married woman may, with her husband's concurrence, bar her right to dower in the same manner as the law allowed her to bar her dower by means of a fine or recovery.

The most usual mode of barring dower is by jointure under the provisions of the stat. 27 Hen. 8, c. 10, before alluded to. A widow is also barred of her dower by elopement, divorce, her being an alien, and by the treason of her husband; also, if she detains the title-deeds of the land or aliens in fee, her estate is forfeited; in the latter case the heir may enter upon the alienee.

CHAPTER VI.

TENANT FOR LIFE.

THE three last preceding chapters have described freeholds *tantum, scil.* estates for life arising by act of law. In the present chapter, Lyttleton treats of a similar interest (*a*), created by act of the parties, he divides tenant for life into two branches, viz. into tenant for term of his own life, and into tenant for term of another man's life; to this may be added a third, viz. into an estate both for term of his own life and for term of another man's life (§ 381).—*Co. Lytt.* 41. *b.*

---

56 TENANT for term of life is where a man letteth lands or tenements to another for term of the life of the lessee, or for term of the life of another man. In such case the lessee is tenant for term of life. *Definition of estate for life.*

But by common language, he that holdeth for term of his own life is called tenant for term of life, and he which *Different kinds of tenant for life.*

56 *Tenaunt pur terme de vie est* (*a*), *lou home lessa terrez ou tenementes a un autre pur terme de vie le lessé, ou pur terme de vie dun autre home, en tiel cas le lessé est tenaunt a terme de vie.*

Mes per comen perlaunce celuy qui tient pur terme de sa vie demesne est appelle tenaunt pur terme de vie, et cestuy

---

(*a*) The author of the *Olde Tenures*, § 8, distinctly classes this estate as a freehold, by the *name* of *Frank Tenure*. See *ante*, p. 40, n.; and *post*, § 57, *ad finem*.

holdeth for term of another's life is called tenant for term of another man's life.

-or and -ee have active and passive signification.

57 And it is to be understood, that there is feoffor and feoffee, donor and donee, lessor and lessee. Feoffor is properly where a man enfeoffs another in any lands or tenements in fee-simple: he who maketh the feoffment is called feoffor, and he to whom the feoffment is made is called feoffee. And the donor is properly where a man giveth certain lands or tenements to another in tail: he who maketh the gift is called donor, and he to whom the gift is made is called donee (*b*). And the lessor is properly where a man letteth to another lands or tenements for term of life or for term of years, or to hold at will: he who maketh the lease is called lessor, and he to whom the lease is made is called lessee. And every one, that hath estate in any lands or tenements for term of his own life or for term of another

Tenant for life has a freehold interest.

qui tient pur terme dautre vie, est appelle tenaunt pur terme dautre vie.

57 *Et est assavoir que il y ad feoffour et le feoffé, et le donour et le doné, et le lessour et le lessé. Le feoffour est proprement lou un home enfeoffa un autre en ascuns terres ou tenementes en fee-simple, celuy qui fist le feoffement est appelle feoffour, et celuy a qui le feoffement est fait, est appelle le feoffé. Et le donour est proprement lou un home done certeyn terres ou tenementes a un autre en le taille, celuy qui fist le done est appelle donour, et cestuy a qui le done est fait est appelle doné* (*b*). *Et le lessour est proprement lou un home lessa a un autre certeyns terres ou tenementes pur terme de vie, ou pur terme dez ans, ou a tener a volunte: celuy qui fist le lees est appelle lessour, et celuy a qui le lees est fait, est appelle le lessé. Et chescun qui ad estate en ascun terres ou tenementes pur terme de sa vie ou pur terme dautre vie, est ap-*

(*b*) Serjt. *Hawkins*, in his *Abr. Co. Lytt.*, styles a female donee a *doness*.

man's life, is called tenant of freehold, and none other of a less estate can have a freehold, but they of a greater estate have a freehold: for tenant in fee-simple hath freehold, and he in fee-tail hath freehold, &c.

pelle tenaunt de franktenement, et nul autre de meindre estate poet aver franktenement, mes ceux de greindre estate ont franktenement; qar tenaunt en fee-simple ad franktenement, et celuy en fee-taille ad franktenement, &c.

CONCLUDING REMARKS.

THIS estate at common law should be created by livery; and the term 'let' or 'lease' implies this accompanying solemnity or its equivalents, or some conveyance carrying the freehold. The incidents to this *conventional* estate for life are the same as those belonging to *legal* estates for life; viz. that this tenant is entitled to *estovers* and his executors to *emblements* (*c*); he is, as in the cases of dower and curtesy, punishable for waste, and his *tortious* alienation is a forfeiture.

(*c*) Estovers (from *estoffer*, to furnish) is a liberty of taking necessary wood, for the use or furniture of a house or farm, from off another's estate. The Saxon word, *bote*, is of the same signification with the French *estovers;* and therefore *house-bote* is a sufficient allowance of wood, to repair, or to burn in, the house; which latter is sometimes called *fire-bote; plough-bote* and *cart-bote* are wood to be employed in making and repairing all instruments of husbandry; and *hay-bote* or *hedge-bote* is wood for repairing of hays, hedges, or fences. These *botes* or *estovers* must be reasonable ones; and such any tenant or lessee may take off the land let or demised to him, without waiting for any leave, assignment, or appointment of the lessor, unless he be restrained by special covenant to the contrary.—*B. C.* ii. 35.

Emblements signify properly the profits of lands sown; but the word is sometimes used more largely for any products that arise naturally from the ground—as grass, fruit, &c.—*Vide post*, § 68, and in note.

At common law, a tenancy for life could not be created to take effect *in futuro*, because this estate is a *franktenement* (§ 57), *i. e.* a freehold in possession, though, by the operation of the Statute of Uses, an estate for life may now be limited to commence *in futuro.*

An estate for life may be conditional or determinable in the same manner as a fee-simple.

CHAPTER VII.

TENANT FOR TERM OF YEARS.

THIS chapter treats of estate for years, an interest which confers a title to the possession of the land, independent of the seisin or freehold (*a*). Lyttleton's definition embraces the ordinary application of this estate to a lease for years, with a reservation of rent, without noticing the creation of terms of years for any other purpose, for they were not known or used in his time. As this estate is but a chattel interest, and was deemed of little importance when Lyttleton wrote, he does little else than inform his reader, that, to a term of years, which might be created either by deed or without deed (*b*), livery of seisin was not requisite (§ 59);

(*a*) Nor indeed does the bare lease vest any estate in the lessee; but only gives him a right of entry on the tenement, which right is called his *interest in the term*, or *interesse termini:* but when he has actually so entered, and thereby accepted the grant, the estate is then, and not before, vested in him, and he is *possessed*, not properly of the land, but of the term of years; the possession or seisin of the *land* remaining still in him who hath the freehold. Thus the word *term* does not merely signify the time specified in the lease, but the estate also and interest that passes by that lease; and, therefore, the *term* may expire during the continuance of the *time*, as by surrender, forfeiture, and the like. —*B. C.* ii. 144.

(*b*) By the Statute of Frauds, (29 *Car.* 2, *c.* 3), no such term (except it does not exceed three years from the making of it, and whereon the rent reserved shall amount to two-thirds at least of the full improved [annual] value of the thing demised,) shall be created, assigned, granted, or surrendered, unless by deed or note in writing, signed by the party, or his agent authorized by writing, or by act or operation of law.

and digresses to state, that, though, as a rule of law, livery of seisin is necessary to pass an estate of freehold; yet that some freehold estates may pass without livery, as in exchange (§ 62—65, and see § 349). The interest which a lessee has before entry is noticed at § 59, 66; and with an allusion to the description of this estate in pleading, the chapter is concluded.

Estate for term of years defined.

If lessor reserve rent, he may either distrain or bring action of debt; but lessor in such case should have the seisin, else lessee may plead nil habuit in tenementis; *unless*

58 TENANT for term of years is (*c*), where a man letteth lands or tenements to another for term of certain years, according to the number of years that is accorded between the lessor and the lessee. And when the lessee entereth by force of the lease, then is he tenant for term of years; and if the lessor in such case reserve to him a yearly rent upon such lease, he may chuse to distrain for the rent in the tenements letten, or else he may have an action of debt for the arrearages against the lessee; but in such case it behoveth that the lessor be seised of the tenements at the time of his lease, for it is

58 *Tenaunt pur terme dez ans, est lou home lessa terres ou tenementes a un autre pur terme de certeins ans solonques le nombre dez ans que est accorde perentre le lessour et le lessé: et quant le lessé entra per force de le lees, donques il est tenaunt pur terme dez ans. Et si le lessor en tiel cas reserva a luy un annuell rente sur tiel lees, il poet eslier a distreigner pur le rente en les tenementes lessez, ou il poet aver une accion de dette pur les arrerages envers le lessee; mes en tiel cas il covient que le lessour soit seisi des tenementes al temps*

(*c*) To hold for terme of years is not but chattel in effect, for no action is maintainable against the termour for the recovering of the freehold, for no freehold is in him. A lease for terme of years is chattel real, and the other chattel [personal, all*] goods which are moveable [are chattels personal*].—*Olde Tenures*, § 10.

* The words within brackets do not appear in some copies.

a good plea for the lessee to say, that the lessor had nothing in the tenements at the time of the lease, except the lease be made by deed indented, in which case such plea lieth not in the mouth of the lessee to plead (*d*).

the lease was by deed indented, when lessee would be estopped from pleading thus.

59 And it is to be understood, that, in lease for term of years by deed or without deed, there needs no livery of seisin to be made to the lessee, but he may enter whensoever he will by force of the same lease. But of feoffments made in the

Livery of seisin not requisite to pass estate for years:

although abso-

de le lees, qar il est bon plee pur le lessee a dire, que le lessour naveroit rienz en les tenementes al temps de le lees, sinon que le lees soit per fait endente, en quel cas tiel plee donques ne gist en le bouche le lessé a pleder.

59 *Et est assavoir que en lees pur terme dezans per fait ou sauns fait, il ne besoigne ascun liverë de seisin destre fait a le lessé, mes il poet entrer quanques il voet per force de mesme le lees. Mes de feoffementes faitz en pays, ou dones en le*

Estoppel.

(*d*) Whenever a person has stated a fact by writing under his seal, or on record, he is *estopped* at law from denying the truth of his assertion, on account of the solemnity with which it was made; but according to Lyttleton in this section, and at § 693, this estoppel or closing the mouth of the party can only be where there is a deed *indented:* but this doctrine, which excludes a deed-*poll*, is now questionable, indeed it has lately been denied. The reason Sir Edward Coke gives for the superior efficacy of a deed indented; or, in his own expressive language—"wherefore a deed indented shall conclude the taker more than the deed-poll, is, for that the deed-poll is only the deed of the feoffor, donor, and lessor; but the deed indented is the deed of both parties, and therefore as well the taker as the giver is concluded."—*Co. Lytt.* 363. *b.* Perhaps the doctrine of *Acceptance* may be said to operate in the case of a deed-poll, and thus bind the *taker* by way of estoppel. There certainly seems no reason why the maker of a deed-poll should not be *estopped;* and upon that principle it was lately most distinctly held, that the obligor of a *bond* was estopped from denying the truth of a statement contained in the condition of such bond.—3 *Nev. & M.* 603.

lutely necessary to pass a freehold, but *see* § 349.

country (*e*), or gifts in the tail, or leases for term of life, [and*] in such cases where a freehold shall pass, if it be by deed or without deed, it behoveth to have livery of seisin, &c. (*f*).

taille, ou leses pur terme de vie, [et] en tielx cases ou franktenement passera, si ceo soit per fait ou sauns fait, il covient daver un liverë de seisin &c.*

* *Machl.* and *Roh.* omit this *et.*

(*e*) Assurances by matter *in pais* are transacted between two or more private persons *in pais, in the country*, that is, (according to the old common law), upon the very spot to be transferred; it is a term used to distinguish ordinary conveyances from matters of record, such as fine or recovery, statute, recognisance, &c.

(*f*) But since the introduction of uses and trusts, and the statute of 27 *H.* 8, c. 10, for transferring the possession to the use, the necessity of livery of seisin for passing a freehold in corporeal hereditaments has been almost wholly superseded, and in consequence of it the conveyance by feoffment is now very little in use. Before the Statute of Uses, *equitable* estates of freehold might be created through the *medium* of trusts, without livery, and, by the operation of the statute, *legal* estates of freehold may now be created in the same way. Those who framed the Statute of Uses evidently foresaw, that it would render livery unnecessary to the passing of a freehold, and that a freehold of such things as do not lye in grant, would become transferable by *parol* only, without any solemnity whatever. To prevent the inconveniences which might arise from a mode of conveyance so uncertain in the proof, and so liable to misconstruction and abuse, it was enacted in the same session of parliament, that an estate of freehold should not pass by bargain and sale only, unless it was by indenture inrolled. *See* 27 *Hen.* 8, *c.* 16. The objects of this provision evidently were, first, to force the contracting parties to ascertain the terms of the conveyance by reducing it into writing; secondly, to make the proof of it easy, by requiring their seals to it, and consequently the presence of a witness; and lastly, to prevent the frauds of secret conveyances by substituting the more effectual notoriety of inrolment for the more ancient one of livery. But the latter part of

60 But if a man let lands or tenements by deed, or without deed to one for term of years, the remainder over to another for life, or in the tail, or in fee; then in such case it behoveth, that the lessor make livery of seisin to the lessee for term of years, or else there shall nothing pass to them in the remainder, though the lessee enter into the tenements. And if the [termor*] in such case enter before any livery of seisin made to him, then is the freehold and also the reversion in the lessor (*g*): but if livery of seisin be made to the lessee, then is the

Livery may be made to termor when a remainder is created of the freehold, for a particular estate and the remainders over are but one estate in law, consequently require but one livery.

60 *Mes si home lessa terrez ou tenementes per fait, ou sauns fait, a un pur terme dez ans, le remaindre oustre a un autre pur terme de vie, ou en le taille, ou en fee, donques en tiel cas il covient que le lessour fait un liverë de seisin a le lessé pur terme dez ans, ou autrement riens passera a ceux en le remaindre, coment que le lessee entra en les tenementes. Et si le [termor*] en tiel cas entra devant ascun tiel liverë de seisin fait a luy, donques est le franktenement et auxi la revercion en le lessour: Mes si soit fait liverë de seisin a le lessee, donques est le franktene-*

---

* *Machl.* and *Roh.* read *tenant.*

---

this provision, which if it had not been evaded, [*See B. C.* ii. 338-9], would have introduced almost an universal register of conveyances of the freehold in the case of corporeal hereditaments, was soon defeated by the invention of the conveyance by lease and release, which sprung from the omission to extend the statute to bargains and sales for terms of years; and the other parts of the statute were necessarily ineffectual in our courts of equity, because these were still left at liberty to compel the execution of trusts of the freehold though created without deed or writing. The inconveniences from this insufficiency of the statute of inrolments are now in some measure prevented by the 29 *Car.* 2, *c.* 3, which provides against conveying any lands or hereditaments for more than three years, or declaring trusts of them, otherwise than by writing.—[*Hargr. in n. Co. Lytt.* 48. *a.*]

(*g*) A *reversion* is the residue of an estate left in the grantor, to commence in possession after the determination of some *particular* estate granted out by him. [Be-

Definition of a reversion.

See the consequences of this doctrine § 153, 470, 471, 557, 590.

freehold, [*i. e.* the estate in possession] together with the fee to them in the remainder, according to the form of the grant

ment ove le fee a ceux en le remaindre, solonques la fourme del graunt et la volunte de le lessour. 61 *Et si ascun home*

---

fore the statute *de donis conditionalibus*, no reversion remained in the grantor or donor after he had created a conditional fee; because the grantee of such an estate was considered as having the absolute property of it, and the grantor had only a possibility of reverter. But as soon as the statute was made, the judges determined, that an estate given to a man and the heirs of his body was only a particular estate; and, therefore, there remained an estate in reversion in the donor.—*Thomas's Syst. Arrangement of* 1*st Inst.* ii. 140, *in n.*] Sir Edward Coke (*Co. Lytt.* 22), describes a reversion to be the returning of land to the grantor or his heirs after the grant is over. As, if there be a gift in tail, the reversion of the fee is, without any special reservation, vested in the donor by act of law: and so also the reversion, after an estate for life, years, or at will, continues in the lessor. For the fee-simple of all lands must abide somewhere; and if he, who was before possessed of the whole, carves out of it any smaller estate, and grants it away, whatever is not so granted remains in him. A reversion is never therefore created by deed or writing, but arises from construction of law; a remainder can never be limited, unless by either deed or devise.

Incidents to reversion are fealty and rent.

The doctrine of reversions is plainly derived from the feodal constitution. For, when a feud was granted to a man for life, or to him and his issue male, rendering either rent or other services, then, on his death, or the failure of issue male, the feud was determined and resulted back to the lord or proprietor to be again disposed of at his pleasure. And hence the usual *incidents* to reversions are said to be *fealty* and *rent.* When no rent is reserved on the particular estate, fealty however results of course, as an incident quite inseparable, and may be demanded as a badge of tenure, or acknowledgment of superiority; being frequently the only evidence that the lands are holden at all. Where rent is reserved, it is also incident, though not inseparably so, to the reversion. The rent may be granted away, reserving the reversion; and the reversion may be granted away, reserving the rent, by *special* words: but by a *general* grant of the reversion, the rent will pass with it, as incident thereunto; though by the grant of the rent generally, the reversion will not pass. The in-

and the will of the lessor *(h)*. 61 And if any one will make a feoffment by deed or without deed, of lands or tenements

voille faire feoffement per fait ou sauns fait, de terrez ou tenementes quil ad en plusours villes en un countee, le liverë

---

cident passes by the grant of the principal, but not *e converso:* for the maxim of law is, "*accessorium non ducit, sed sequitur, suum principale.*"

These *incidental* rights of the reversioner, and the respective modes of descent, in which remainders very frequently differ from reversions, have occasioned the law to be careful in distinguishing the one from the other, however inaccurately the parties themselves may describe them. For if one, seised of a paternal estate in fee, makes a lease for life, with remainder to himself and his heirs, this is properly a mere reversion, to which rent and fealty shall be incident; and which shall only descend to the heirs of his father's blood, and not to his heirs general, as a remainder limited to him by a third person would have done: for it is the old estate, which was originally in him, and never yet was out of him. And so likewise, if a man grants a lease for life to A., reserving rent, with reversion to B. and his heirs, B. hath a remainder descendible to his heirs general, and not a reversion to which the rent is incident; but the grantor shall be entitled to the rent, during the continuance of A.'s estate.

By these incidents the law distinguishes remainders from reversions.

[Reversions are vested interests; for a person entitled to an estate in reversion has an immediate fixed right of future enjoyment, which may be aliened and charged much in the same manner as an estate in possession; and, when expectant on an estate tail, is liable to the judgments of all those who were at any time entitled to it, whenever such reversion comes into possession, for these are securities attaching on all the estates of the debtor; and is also liable to the leases made by those who at any time were entitled to it, and to the covenants in such leases whenever it comes into possession.]

In order to assist such persons as have any estate in remainder, reversion, or expectancy, after the death of others, against fraudulent

---

(*h*) The meaning of the text is, that the freehold and fee *both* pass only in those cases where the remainder over is in fee-tail, or in fee-simple, and not in the cases where the remainder is for life only.

Livery of part for all, good; unless lands lie in several counties.

which he hath in many towns in one shire, the livery of seisin made in one parcel of the tenements in one town, [in the name of all]*, is sufficient for all other the lands or tene-

de seisin fait en un parcell de les tenementes en un ville [en le nome de toutz] suffist pur toutz lez autres terres et tene-*

---

* The words within brackets are not in *Lettou & M.*, *Machl.*, or *Roh.*; but they appear in *Redm.*, and in every edition since, as well French as English.

---

concealments of their deaths, it is enacted by the statute 6 *Ann. c.* 18, that all persons on whose lives any lands or tenements are holden, shall (upon application to the Court of Chancery and order made thereupon) once in every year, if required, be produced to the court, or its commissioners; or, upon neglect or refusal, they shall be taken to be actually dead, and the person entitled to such expectant estate may enter upon and hold the lands and tenements till the party shall appear to be living. [And in other respects the law is as careful of the rights of the reversioner, as of those of the tenant in possession; and will, therefore, allow an action to be brought by the reversioner, as well as by the tenant in possession, for an injury done to the inheritance.—4 *Burr.* 2141. Equity will also interfere, by granting an injunction to prevent waste or irremediable injury, on behalf of a reversioner.]

Merger of estates.

Before we conclude the doctrine of reversions, it may be proper to observe, that whenever a greater estate and a less coincide and meet in one and the same person, without any intermediate estate, the less is immediately annihilated; or, in the law phrase, is said to be *merged*, that is, sunk or drowned, in the greater. Thus, if there be tenant for years, and the reversion in fee-simple descends to or is purchased by him, the term of years is merged in the inheritance, and shall never exist any more. But they must come to one and the same person in one and the same right; else, if the freehold be in his own right, and he has a term in right of another (*en auter droit*) there is no merger. Therefore, if tenant for years dies, and makes him who hath the reversion in fee his executor, whereby the term of years vests also in him, the term shall not merge; for he hath the fee in his own right, and the term of years in the right of the testator, and subject to his debts and legacies. So also, if he who hath the reversion in fee marries the tenant for years, there is no merger; for he hath the inheritance in his

ments comprehended within the same feoffment, in all other towns within the same shire; but if a man maketh a deed of feoffment of lands or tenements in divers shires, there it behoveth to have a livery of seisin in every shire. 62 And in some cases a man shall have by the grant of another a fee-simple, fee-tail, or freehold, without livery of seisin. As if there be two men, and each of them is seised of one quantity

Some estates of freehold may pass without livery as in exchange.

mentes comprehendus deins mesme le feoffement en toutz les autres villes deins mesme le countee. Mes si home fist un fait de feoffement de terres ou tenementes en divers countees, la il covient daver en chescun countee un liverë de seisin. 62 *Et en ascun cas home avera per le graunt dun autre, fee-simple, fee-taille, ou franktenement sauns liverë de seisin; sicome deux homes y sont, et chescun deux est seisi dun quantite de terre*

---

own right, the lease in the right of his wife. An estate-tail is an exception to this rule; for a man may have in his own right both an estate tail and a reversion in fee; and the estate tail, though a less estate, shall not merge in the fee. For estates tail are protected and preserved from merger by the operation and construction, though not by the express words, of the statute *de donis;* which operation and construction have probably arisen upon this consideration; that, in the common cases of *merger* of estates for life or years by uniting with the inheritance, the particular tenant hath the sole interest in them, and hath full power at any time to defeat, destroy, or surrender them to him that hath the reversion; therefore, when such an estate unites with the reversion in fee, the law considers it in the light of a virtual surrender of the inferior estate. But, in an estate-tail, the case is otherwise: the tenant for a long time had no power at all over it, so as to bar or destroy it; and now can only do it by certain special modes, by [the modes of assurance prescribed by the stat. 3 & 4 *Gul.* 4, *c.* 74, as substitutes for] a fine, a recovery, and the like: it would therefore have been strangely improvident, to have permitted the tenant in tail, by purchasing the reversion in fee, to merge his particular estate, and defeat the inheritance of his issue; and hence it has become a maxim, that a tenancy in tail, which cannot be surrendered, cannot also be merged in the fee.—B. C. ii. 175—178.

All particular estates merge in the reversion, whenever the same person becomes entitled to both; except an estate tail.

For some notice of *remainders,* see *post,* § 216, *in n.*

of land in one county, and the one granteth his land to the other in exchange for the land which the other hath, and in like manner the other granteth his land to the first grantor in exchange for the land which the first grantor hath. In this case each may enter into the land of the other, so [taken*] in exchange without any livery of seisin (*i*), and such exchange, made by words, of tenements within the same shire without any writing is good enough. 63 And if the lands or tenements be in divers counties, *scil.* that which the one hath is in one county, and that which the other hath is in another county, there it behoveth to have a deed indented made between them of such exchange of such lands, &c. (*k*).

Entry must be had on both sides.

If objects of exchange lie in different counties a deed is requisite.

deins un countee, et lun graunta sa terre a lautre en eschaunge pur la terre que lautre ad, et en mesme le manere, lautre graunta sa terre a le premier grantour en eschaunge pur la terre que le premier grantour ad; en ceo cas chescun poet entrer en lautre terre issint [prise] en eschaunge sauns ascun livere de seisin, et tiel eschaunge fait per paroll de tenementes deins mesme le countee sauns ascun escripture est assetez bon.* 63 *Et si les terres ou tenementes, soient en divers countees,* scil. *si ceo que lun ad, est en un countee, et ceo que lautre ad est en autre countee, la il covient de aver un fait endente destre fait entre eux de tiel eschaunge de tielx terres, &c.*

---

* *Mys, put*—*Machl.* and *Roh.* and all the copies by *Tottyl.* But *Redm.*, *Berth.*, *Sm.*, *Powel*, all the copies of *Rastell's Translation* to 1656, and the *edition* 1671, give the reading as above, which is conformable to the edition by *Lettou & M.*

(*i*) Exchange is a livery in law. *Per Moyle, J., Trin.* 9 *E.* 4.

(*k*) An *exchange* is a mutual grant of equal interests, the one in consideration of the other. The estates exchanged must be equal in quantity (§ 64, 65); not of *value*, for that is immaterial, but of *interest*; as fee-simple for fee-simple, a lease for twenty years for a lease for twenty years, and the like. And the exchange may be of things that lie either in grant or in livery. But no livery of seisin, even in ex-

64 And note, that in exchange it behoveth that the estates, which both parties have in the lands so exchanged, be equal; for if the one willeth to grant that the other shall have his land in fee-tail, for the land which he should have of the grant of the other in fee-simple, though that the other agree to this, yet this exchange is void, because the estates be not equal.

Interests must be equal in quantity;

65 In the same manner it is, where it is granted and agreed between them, that the one shall have in the one land fee-tail, and the other shall have in the other land but for term of life; or if the one shall have in the one land fee-tail general, and the other in the other land fee-tail especial, &c. So, once

i. e. fee-simple for fee-simple.

64 *Et nota que en eschaunge il covient que les estatez, que ambideux de les parties averount en les terres issint eschaungez, soient owelx; qar si lun voloit graunter que lautre averoit sa terre en le taille, pur le terre quil averoit de graunt de lautre en fee-simple, coment que lautre soit agree a celle, cest eschaunge est voide, pur ceo que les estatez ne sont mye owelx.*

65 *En mesme le manere est, lou il est graunté et agree entre eux, que lun avera en lun terre fee-taille, et lautre avera en lautre terre forsque pur terme de vie; ou si lun avera en lun terre fee-taille generall, et lautre en lautre terre fee-taille especiall, &c. Issint* [*toutdytz**] *il covient que en eschaunge*

* *Machl.*, *Roh.* and some copies read *toutdys;* all the copies by *Tottyl*, and the ordinary copies, read *toutz foitz*, which means the same thing.

changes of freehold, is necessary to perfect the conveyance: for each party stands in the place of the other and occupies his right, and each of them hath already had corporeal possession of his own land. But entry must be made on both sides; for, if either party die before entry, the exchange is void, for want of sufficient notoriety. If, after an exchange of lands or other hereditaments, either party be evicted of those which were taken by him in exchange, through defect of the other's title, he shall return back to the possession of his own, by virtue of the implied warranty contained in all exchanges.—*See B. C.* ii. 323.

for all, it behoveth that in exchange the estates of both parties be equal, *scil.*, if the one hath a fee-simple in the one land, that the other shall have like estate in the other land; and if the one hath fee-tail in the one land, the other ought to have the like estate in the other land. And so of other estates.

The relative value of the lands not material.

But it is nothing to charge of the equal [*i. e. the relative*] value of the lands, for although that the land of the one be of a far greater value than the land of the other, this is nothing to the purpose, so that the estates made by the exchange, be equal. And so in exchange there be two grants, for each party shall grant his land to the other in exchange, &c., and in each of their grants mention shall be made of the exchange.

Exchange is vocabulum artis, *consequently cannot be supplied by any other mode of expression.*

Interesse termini, *see also* § 459.

66 Also, if a man letteth land to another for term of years, albeit the lessor dieth before the lessee enter into the tenements, yet he may enter into the same tenements after the death of the lessor, because the lessee by force of the lease hath right forthwith to have the tenements according to the

les estatez dambideux parties soient egalx, scil., *si lun ad fee-simple en lun terre, que lautre avera tiel estate en lautre terre; et si lun ad fee-taille en lun terre, il covient que lautre, avera semblable estate en lautre terre,* et sic de aliis statibus.

Mes nest mye riens a charger del owell value des terres, qar coment que la terre lun vault mult pluis que la terre de lautre, ceo nest riens a purpose: issint que les estatez per leschaunge faits, soient owelx. Et issint en eschaunge ils y sont deux grauntes, qar chescun partie grauntera sa terre a lautre en eschaunge, &c., et en cheseun de lour grantez mencion sera fait de leschaunge.

66 *Item, si home lessa terre a un autre pur terme dez ans, coment que le lessour morust devant que le lessé entra en les tenementes, unquore il poet entrer en mesmes les tenementes apres la mort le lessour, pur ceo que le lessé per force de le lees ad droit maintenant daver les tenementes solonques la*

form of the lease. But if a man maketh a deed of feoffment to another, and a letter of attorney to one to deliver to him seisin by force of the same deed, yet if livery of seisin be not made in the life of him who made the deed, it availeth not, for that the other hath not any right to have the tenements according to the [purport*] of the said deed before the livery of seisin. And if no livery of seisin be made, then after the decease of him who made the deed, the right of those tenements is forthwith in his heir, or in some other.

Livery must be made in lifetime of feoffor, whether in person or by attorney.

67 Also, if tenements be let to a man for term of a half year, or for a quarter of a year, &c. In this case if the lessee commit waste, the lessor shall have a writ of waste against him, and the writ shall say: *Qui tenet ad terminum annorum:* but he shall have a special declaration upon the truth of this matter, and the count shall not abate the writ, because he cannot have any other writ upon the matter, &c.

Every tenancy of a definite duration is a term, and of the nature of a term of years, though for a less period than a year.

Writ may be general, and count special. S. C. § 381.

fourme de le lees. Mes si home fist fait de feoffement a un autre, et un lettre dattourney a un home a delyverer a luy seisin per force de mesme le fait, unquore si la liverë de seisin ne soit fait en la vie celuy qui faisoit le fait, ceo ne vault rienz, pur ceo que lautre nad pas ascun droit daver les tenementes solonques le [purport] du fait, devaunt le liverë de seisin. Et si nul liverë soit fait, donques apres la mort celuy qui fist le fait, le droit de tielx tenementes est maintenaunt en son heire, ou en ascun autre.*

67 *Item si tenementes soient lessez a un home pur terme de demye an, ou per le quart de un an, &c. En tiel cas, si le lessé fist wast, le lessour avera envers luy brief de wast, et le brief dirra:* Qui tenet ad terminum annorum: *Mes il avera un special declaracion sur le verité de son matere, et le count ne abatera le brief, pur ceo que il ne poet aver nul autre brief sur le matere, &c.*

---

* *Machl.* and *Roh.* read this word *purpos—purpose.*

CONCLUDING REMARKS.

ESTATES that are less than freehold are generally classed as—1, Estates for years; 2, Estates at will; 3, Estates by sufferance.

An estate for years is denominated by the law a term (*terminus*), because its duration is bounded or confined. Lyttleton's definition of this estate is the case of a contract to let lands, &c., to another for a term of a certain number of years agreed upon between the lessor and lessee, and therefore every contract which is intended to operate as a lease for years, ought to have certainty in three limitations or essentials, *viz.* in the commencement of the term, in the continuance of it, and in the end of it; for these three things are in effect, as Plowden reports, but one matter, shewing the certainty of the time for which the lessee shall have the land (*l*). So that this estate differs from an estate for life, fee-simple, or fee-tail; for either of those estates is dependent upon an *uncertain* event, that is, upon the death of the individual, or extinction or failure of heirs, either special or general; whereas every estate for years or lease must have a certain beginning and certain end. "But *id certum est, quod certum reddi potest:* therefore, if a man make a lease to another, for so many years as J. S. shall name, it is a good lease for years; for though it is at present uncertain, yet when J. S. hath named the years, it is then reduced to a certainty. If no day of commencement is named in the creation of this estate, it begins from the making or delivery of the lease. A lease for so many years as J. S. shall live, is void from the beginning; for it is neither certain, nor can ever be reduced to a certainty, during the continuance of the

(*l*) So that all these ought to be known at the commencement of the lease; and words in a lease which do not make this appear, are but babble, as *Brown* said.—*Plowd.* 272.

lease. And the same doctrine holds, if a parson make a lease of his glebe for so many years as he shall continue parson of Dale; for this is still more uncertain. But a lease for twenty or more years, if J. S. shall so long live, or if he shall so long continue parson, is good; for there is a certain period fixed, beyond which it cannot last; though it may determine sooner, on the death of J. S. or his ceasing to be parson there."—B. C. ii. 143.

But although it be essential to the very existence of this estate that there be a time absolutely prefixed, *beyond which it cannot continue,* yet it may be made subject to a condition [depending on the dropping of any life or lives, or on any other contingent event], for its determination before the period prefixed: as for ninety-nine years if A. B. live so long. Here if A. B. die before the ninety-nine years expire, the term shall cease; but though A. B. should survive the ninety-nine years, the lease, on the expiration of the ninety-nine years, would be absolutely at an end.—(*Watk. Conv.* 32).

An estate for years is assignable, unless there be an express condition or provision in the lease to restrict the power of alienation which the law gives; and such assignment may be made even before the lessee enter, as an *interesse termini* may be granted over. Or if a lease be made to two, one may release to the other before entry.

And as a lessee may grant over his *whole term,* so he may make an under-lease of *a part* of his interest. As if he have a term of ten years he may underlet for five; and the distinction between an assignment and an under-lease is where the lessee parts with his *whole* interest, and where *not.* In the latter case it is an *under-lease,* in the former an assignment.—*Id.* 35.

The origin of leases appears to have been the letting to farm or husbandry at a rack-rent by the proprietors of land; and as no livery of seisin was requisite to pass an estate for years, nothing but the mere term passed to the lessee, the *seisin* or *fee* continuing in the owner of the inheritance, the termor's interest vested in his executors; for a term of years, although it be for a 1000 years, is but a chattel; and, consequently, is deemed personal estate. "Hence it follows, that a lease for years may be made to commence *in futuro,* though a lease for life cannot. As, if I grant lands to Titius to hold from Michaelmas next for twenty years, this is good; but to hold from Michaelmas next for the term of his natural life, is void. For no estate of freehold can commence *in futuro;* because, it cannot be created at common law without livery of seisin, or corporal possession of the land: and corporal possession cannot be given of an estate now, which is not to commence now, but hereafter."—B. C. ii. 143.

Long terms of years, for reasons noticed by Sir William Blackstone (ii. 142), were not in use when Lyttleton wrote; but, since the reign of Henry VIII., they have been much used, on account of their convenience for family settlements, mortgages, and other purposes, continuing subject to the same rules of succession, and with the same inferiority to freeholds as when they were little better than tenancies at the will of the landlord.

At Common Law "tenant in fee simple might let leases of any dùration, for he hath the whole interest; but tenant in tail, or tenant for life, could make no leases which should bind the issue in tail or reversioner; nor could a husband, seised *jùre uxoris,* make a firm or valid lease for any longer term than the joint lives of himself and his wife, for then his interest expired. Yet some tenants for life, where the fee simple was in abeyance, might (with the concurrence of such as have the guardianship of the fee) make leases of equal duration with those granted by tenants in fee simple: such as parsons and vicars with consent of the patron and ordinary. So also bishops, and deans, and such other sole ecclesiastical corporations as are seised of the fee simple of lands in their corporate right, might, with the concurrence and confirmation of such persons as the law requires, have made leases for years, or for life, estates in tail or in fee, without any limitation or control. And corporations aggregate might have made what estates they pleased, without the confirmation of any other person whatsoever. Whereas now, by several statutes, this power, where it was unreasonable, and might be made an ill use of, is restrained; and, where in the other cases the restraint by the common law seemed too hard, it is in some measure removed. The former statutes are called the *restraining*, the latter the *enabling* statute (*m*)."—B. C. ii. 319.

(*m*) By the *enabling* statute, tenant in tail: husband and wife seised jointly of an estate of inheritance or in right of the wife; any person seised in the right of his church, except parsons or vicars; may by lease for 21 years, or three lives, bind the issue in tail, (but not the reversioners or remainder-men), the heirs or successors respectively; but certain requisites must be observed in the making of such lease.—32 *Hen.* 8, *c.* 28.

By the *restraining* or *disabling* statutes, all conveyances whatsoever made by ecclesiastical corporations, are made void, except leases for three lives, or 21 years *from* the time of the making, whereon the old yearly rent or more is reserved, subject to the requisites contained in the 32 Hen. 8, c. 28, except in two cases. 1 Eliz. c. 19; 13 Eliz. c. 10; also by statutes 14 Eliz. cc. 11 and 14; 18 Eliz. c. 11; and 43 Eliz. c. 29. The restrictions created by the 1 Eliz. c. 19, upon bishops, were extended to certain other inferior corporations, both *sole* and *aggregate*.—"From laying all which together, we may collect, that all colleges, cathedrals, and other ecclesiastical or eleemosynary corporations, and all parsons and vicars, are restrained from making any leases of their lands, unless under the following regulations:—1. They must not exceed 21 years, or three lives, from the making; 2. The accustomed rent, or more, must be yearly reserved thereon; 3. Houses in corporations or market towns may be let for forty years, provided they be not the mansion-houses of the lessors, nor have above ten acres of ground belonging to them; and provided the lessee be bound to keep them in repair: and they may also be aliened in fee simple for lands of equal value in recompense; 4. Where there is an old lease in being, no concurrent lease shall be made, unless where the old one will expire within three years; 5. No lease (by the equity of the statute) shall be made without impeachment of waste; 6. All bonds and covenants tending to frustrate the provisions of the statutes of 13 & 18 Eliz. shall be void."—B. C. ii. 321.

Concerning these restrictive statutes there are two observations to be made. First, that they do not, by any construction, enable any persons to make such leases as they

The lessee when not restrained by covenants, or an exception out of the lease, to the contrary, which is now usually the case, is entitled to *estovers;* and where the term is limited to determine on the happening of a collateral event, the lessee or his personal representatives are, when it so determines, entitled to *emblements* (§ 68). With respect to *waste* and *forfeiture,* the same doctrine generally applies to an estate for years as to tenant for life.

---

were by common law disabled to make. Therefore a parson, or vicar, though he is restrained from making longer leases than for 21 years or three lives, even *with* the consent of patron and ordinary, yet is not enabled to make any lease at all, so as to bind his successor, *without* obtaining such consent. Secondly, that though leases contrary to these acts are declared void, yet they are good against the *lessor* during his life, if he be a sole corporation; and are also good against an aggregate corporation so long as the head of it lives, who is presumed to be the most concerned in interest. For the act was intended for the benefit of the successor only; and no man shall make an advantage of his own wrong.—*Ibid.*

In addition to these statutes, (which were meant for the benefit of the successor), all leases by colleges and collegiate churches are void, unless one third of the old rent be reserved in corn, at the rate of a quarter of wheat for every 6*s.* 8*d.*, and a quarter of malt for every 5*s.* of the old rent.—18 *Eliz. c.* 6.

The leases of beneficed clergymen are further restrained in case of their non-residence, by stats. 13 Eliz. c. 20; 14 Eliz. c. 11; 18 Eliz. c. 11; and 43 Eliz. c. 9

CHAPTER VIII.

OF TENANT AT WILL.

This Chapter treats of tenancy at will, to which subject the doctrine of *emblements* is peculiarly incident, as the title to emblements accrues upon the determination of a tenure by death or other uncertain event; and, indeed, the instance cited by Lyttleton, which is that of an estate at will (§ 68), mainly turns upon the point of uncertainty of time in its determination. Any entry by the leave or will of the lessor creates this estate (§ 70). In respect of the uncertainty of his estate, this tenant is exempted from liability to repair; but for voluntary waste he is liable to an action, upon the same principle, as Lyttleton informs us (§ 71), that a bailee of goods is liable for misfeazance. In conclusion, Lyttleton observes, that the lessor may recover a rent reserved upon this tenancy, either by distress or action of debt (§ 72).

---

68 Tenant at will is, where lands or tenements are let by one man to another, to have and to hold to him at the will of the lessor, by force of which lease the lessee is thereof possessed: in this case the lessee is called tenant at will, because he hath no certain sure estate; for the lessor may put him

Tenancy at will defined.

68 *Tenaunt a volunte est ou terres ou tenementes sont lesses per un home a un autre, a aver et tener a luy a la volunte le lessour, per force de quel lees le lessé est en possessione: en tiel cas le lessé est appelle tenaunt a volunte, pur ceo que il nad ascun certeyn sure estate, qar le lessour luy poet oustre a*

Tenant at will entitled to emblements;

out at what time it pleaseth him: yet if the lessee soweth the land, and the lessor, after the sowing, and before that the corn be ripe, put him out, yet the lessee shall have the corn, and shall have free entry, egress, and regress to cut and carry away the corn, because he wist not at what time his lessor would enter upon him.

but not tenant for years.

Otherwise it is if tenant for years, [who knoweth*] the end of his term, doth sow the land, and the term is ended before that the corn be ripe; in this case the lessor, or he in the reversion, shall have the corn, because the termor knew well the certainty of his term and when his term should be ended (*a*).

quel temps quil luy plerroit: unquore si le lessé embleia la terre, et le lessour apres lembleier, et devaunt que les blees sont matures luy ousta, unquore le lessé avera les blees, et avera frank entre, egresse, et regresse a scier et de carier les blees, pur ceo que il ne savoit a quel temps son lessour voilloit entrer sur luy.

Autrement est si tenaunt pur terme dez ans [qui conust] le fyn de son terme embleia la terre, et le terme est finye devaunt que les blees sont matures; en ceo cas le lessour, ou celuy en la revercion avera les blees, pur ceo que le termour bien conust le certeynte de son terme et quant son terme serroit fynye.*

---

* *Lettou & M.*, *Machl.*, and *Roh.*, read *apres—after*, which, in a copy of the *Rohan* edition *penes Ed.*, is by a contemporary hand altered to *devant—before*; *Rastell's* translation renders this passage, '*before* the end of his term,' which it is apprehended is the true reading. *Pyns.* 1516, reads *conust le fin de son terme, et si emblea—knoweth the end of his term*, and if *he sow*: but *Redm.*, and all the subsequent copies, give the reading as in the text.

Emblements.

(*a*) Emblements (*emblemata*). Such vegetable produce and *chattels* as are not the spontaneous growth of the earth, but produced

69 Also if a house be let to a man to hold at will, by force whereof the lessee entereth into the house, into which house he brings his household stuff, and afterwards the lessor puts him out, yet he shall have free entry, egress, and regress into the

Tenant at will and executors have a reasonable time allowed for removal of their goods.

69 *Item si un mese soit lesse a un home a tener a volunte, per force de quel le lessé entra en le mese, deinz quel mese il porta ses utensiles de meason, et puis le lessour luy ousta, unquore il avera frank entre, egresse, et regresse en mesme le*

---

annually from the labour and industry of man, which, in the case Lyttleton mentions, belong to the tenant at will, and which he may, after his term, gather and carry away. Upon the same principle, the representatives of every tenant for life shall have the *emblements* to compensate for the tillage which produced them. As the object of this privilege is to prevent those whose estates are uncertain being prejudiced by their sudden determination; and because such determination is purely contingent, any determination of a tenancy or tenure by the tenant's *own act*, deprives him of the emblements. The doctrine of emblements is not extended further than corn sown, roots planted, or other *annual artificial* profit; for fruit trees, grass (not annual or artificial, as saintfoin, &c.), and the like, which are *permanent* and *natural*, will pass to the lessor or executor as the case may be; but to this an exception is made with regard to trees, shrubs, and other produce planted by gardeners and nueserymen in their grounds *for sale;* for these, upon principles in favour of commerce, are removable by the tenant or his executors.

The persons whose executors are entitled to emblements are tenants in fee, fee tail, for life, for years, for years *si tamdiu vixerint*, by curtesy, as jointresses; and Lyttleton's case, by parity of reason, includes executor of tenant at will.

In two instances emblements are given by statute: for by statute of Merton, 20 Hen. 3, c. 2, the representative of a dowress shall have emblements of the land assigned her for dower at her death, (indeed it has been said that other tenants are entitled to emblements by the equity of this statute, 37 Hen. 6), and by statute 28 Hen. 8, c. 11, the executors of an incumbent are entitled to the emblements of his glebe lands manured and sown by him with any corn or grain.

Under a devise of farming stock in general terms, the standing crops go to the executor.—6 *East*, 604, n.

If land sown by the husband is assigned by his heir to the wife for her dower, she shall have the crop.—2 *Inst*. 81.

said house, by reasonable time to take away his goods and utensils. As if a man seised of a mese in fee-simple, fee-tail, or for life, hath certain goods within the said house, and makes his executors, and dieth; whosoever after his decease hath the house, his executors shall have free entry, egress, and regress, to carry out of the house the goods of their testator by reasonable time.

A feoffment without livery passes only an estate at will.

70 Also if a man should make a deed of feoffment to another of certain land, and delivereth to him the deed, but not livery of seisin; in this case he to whom the deed is made, may enter into the land, and hold and occupy it at the will of him which made the deed, because it is proved by the words of the deed that it is his will that the other should have the land; but he who made the deed may put him out when it pleaseth him.

Tenant at will not bound to repair, yet

71 Also if a house be leased to hold at will, the lessee is not* bound to sustain or repair the house, as tenant for term of

mese per resonable temps, de carier ses biens et utensiles. Sicome que home seisi dun mese en fee-simple, fee-taille, ou pur terme de vie, le quel ad certeyns biens deins mesme le mese, et fait ses executours, et devie, quiconques apres sa mort ad le mese, unquore les executours averount frank entre, egresse, et regresse de carier hors de le mese les biens lour testator per resonable temps.

70 *Item si un home fesoit un fait de feoffement a un autre de certeyne terre, et delyvera a luy le fait, mes nemy liverë de seisin; en ceo cas, celuy a qui le fait est fait, poet entrer en la terre, et tener et occupier a la volunte cestuy qui fist le fait, pur ceo que il est prove per les paroles del fait, quil est sa volunte que lautre avera la terre, mes celuy qui fist le fait luy poet oustre quant il luy plaist.*

71 *Item si un mese soit lesse a tener a volunte, le lessé nest* pas tenus a susteiner ou repaireller les measons, sicome tenaunt*

---

* *Roh.* reads this passage thus—*a volunte le lesse* il *nest.*

years is holden to do: but if tenant at will commit voluntary waste, as in pulling down of houses, or in felling of trees, it is said that the lessor shall have thereof against him action of trespass. As if I deliver to one my sheep to [dung*] his land, or my oxen to ear his land, and he slayeth my beasts, I may well have an action of trespass against him, notwithstanding the delivery† (*bailment*) (*b*).

liable for voluntary waste, upon the same principle that a bailee is liable for misfeazance.

a terme dez ans est tenus: mes si le lessé a volunte fist voluntarie wast, sicome en abatement dez measons, ou en couper des arbres, il est dit que le lessour avera de ceo envers luy accion de trespas. Sicome jeo bayle a un home mes berbitez a [composter] sa terre, ou mes boefs a arrer sa terre, et il occist mes avers, jeo puis bien aver un accion de trespas envers luy nient contristeant le baillement*†.

---

* *A composter*. *Sir E. Coke's* Translation renders this word *to tathe*, *i. e.* to feed, fold, and manure; *Rastell's* Transl. *to dung or marle*.

† This word in *Lettou & M.*, *Machl.*, and *Roh.*, is given as *baille*, which may be a misprint. The word *bailment* is by no means a modern word, and is evidently *vocabulum artis*, for it occurs in the Old N. B., which was written *temp*. Hen. 6. In the editions of Lyttleton, *baylement* first occurs in *Redm.*, and is retained in all the subsequent editions. The text in *Pyns*. 1516, reads, *aient et conusaunt le baille*, which is absolute nonsense.

(*b*) A *bailment* is a delivery of goods to another person for a particular use; as in this case of Lyttleton, to a carrier to convey to London, to an innkeeper to secure in his inn, or the like. Here there is no absolute property in either the bailor or the bailee, the person delivering or him to whom it is delivered: for the bailor hath only the right, and not the immediate possession; the bailee hath the possession, and only a temporary right. But it is a qualified property in them both; and each of them is entitled to an action, in case the goods be damaged or taken away: the bailee on account of his immediate possession; the bailor, because the possession of the bailee is, mediately, his possession also.—B. C. ii. 396.

The word *bayle* has been translated by Lord Coke, *lend*; but *Rastell*, who is much more correct in his translation than *Sir E.*

Lessor at will may either distrain or sue in debt for his rent reserved.

72 Also, if the lessor upon a lease at will reserve to him a yearly rent, he may distrain for the rent arrear, or thereof have an action of debt at his election.

72 *Item, si le lessour sur tiel lees a volunte reserve a lvy un annuell rente, il poet distreigner pur le rente arere, ou aver de ceo un accion de dette a son eleccion.*

CONCLUDING REMARKS.

THE second species of estate less than freehold is a tenancy at will, which is so termed because it is a mere general letting; and, therefore, its duration is undefined and indeterminate; in fact, it has duration only but at the will or pleasure of either party. A tenant at will is not a *termor* in any sense of the word, for a term, it has been shewn, is dependent on a definite event. This estate is created and must commence by reciprocal and mutual agreement, and may determine at the will of either party, even when it is expressed to be at the will of one party only: but the law is careful that no sudden determination of the will by one party shall tend to the manifest and unforeseen prejudice of the other: hence the reason of allowing this tenant his *emblements*, the permission to carry

---

Coke, renders this word, *deliver*, which does not confine the case to a gratuitous permission to use a chattel; but goes further, and seems to shew that a bailee is answerable for misfeazance, whether there was any consideration for the bailment or not. The doctrine of bailments has been treated of by the late Sir William Jones, and another treatise on the same subject has appeared under the title of *Commentaries on the Law of Bailments, with Illustrations from the Civil and the Foreign Law, by J. Story, LL.D., Dane Professor of Law in Harvard University.*

away which, in all cases where allowable, turns upon the point of uncertainty in the determination or dissolution of the estate or tenancy; for the words of Lyttleton with respect to this tenant are, "he wist not at what time his lessor would enter upon him," consequently, could make no provision against such event; otherwise it is (and by parity of reason), where the determination of the estate arises from the act of the tenant, or he commits a forfeiture; for, in these cases, the landlord is entitled to the crops sown. This doctrine of emblements is also extended to all cases of determination of tenure by the decease of the tenant; for his executors are entitled to emblements as already noticed. This estate is very often confounded with the tenancy *from year to year, so long as both parties shall agree;* but this tenancy is a *term* which necessarily has a definite duration, and which requires a six months' notice to quit, expiring at that period of the year when the tenancy commenced. The Courts favour the construction of any holding for an indefinite period, being a tenancy from year to year, where there is an agreement to pay rent by the tenant, or a receipt of rent by the landlord under circumstances which may fairly induce that presumption, such as the lessor accepting yearly rent, or any rent measured by an aliquot part of a year.

There is a still lower estate than a mere tenancy at will, *viz.* an estate by sufferance, which is the third and last division of estates less than freehold. This tenancy can only arise where one comes into the possession of land, &c., by lawful title; but retains or holds over the occupation without any title at all. As if a man takes a lease for any period, and after the expiration of the term continues to hold the premises without any fresh lease or license from the owner; or if such owner let the premises at will and dies, the estate at will is thereby determined, and, if the tenant continue possession, he is deemed tenant at sufferance, and the owner or landlord may oust him, *i. e.* enter on the land; and, if the tenant at sufferance refuse to quit, recover the possession by action of ejectment; and by stat. 4 Geo. 2, c. 28, any person holding over after the determination of his term, after demand made and notice in writing given to him by the proprietor, is liable to pay double rent, which is recoverable in an action of debt; and with regard to tenants having power to determine their own tenancy giving notice to quit (by *parol* or otherwise) and not quitting at the time mentioned in their notice, they also are, by 11 Geo. 2, c. 19, liable to pay double rent, recoverable by distress or action. The operation of these statutes has almost put an end to the practice of tenancy by sufferance, unless by the tacit consent of the owner of the premises.

A person who enters on premises and takes possession without any license or authority is termed a "disseisor"—which is an estate wholly by wrong; for tenant at sufferance is where one enters by right or lawfullly, and holds over by wrong; but the estate of the disseisors is wrongful, or, as the law styles it, *tortious* from the beginning.

CHAPTER IX.

TENANT BY COPY.

LYTTLETON in the two following chapters treats of copyhold tenure, which is either free or base: with regard to *tenants by copy* and *tenants by the verge,* he does not appear to make much distinction, save that he expressly styles the latter base tenure (§ 81). In the chapter of *tenants by the verge,* Lyttleton is more explicit in the distinction between a mere tenancy at will and a customary holding (§ 82); and from both chapters the reader will collect that custom is the life of copyhold tenure, although the customs of each manor vary; for some tenants hold free copyhold inheritable, some base copyhold by payment of a fine, and some hold for lives only (§ 73); in which last case there is by custom a right of a perpetual renewal or payment of a fine *certain;* for tenants of copyhold land held at fine *uncertain,* stand in the same situation as other lessees for lives, whose leases are renewable or not at the pleasure of the lessor or landlord.

---

73 TENANT by copy of court roll is, as if a man be seised of a manor, within which manor there is a custom and hath been use, time out of mind of man, that certain tenants *Tenancy by copy defined.*

73 *Tenaunt per copye de court rolle est, sicome un home est seisi dun manor, deins quel manor il y ad un custome et ad este use, de temps dount memorie dez homes ne court, que*

within the same manor have used to have lands and tenements to hold to them and their heirs in fee-simple, or fee-tail, or for term of life, &c., at the will of the lord (*a*), according to the custom of the same manor. 74 And such a tenant may not alien the land by deed; for then the lord may enter as into a thing forfeit to him, but if he will alien his land to another, it behoveth him according to the custom to surrender the tenements at some court (*b*), &c., into the hand of the lord, to the use of him that shall have the estate, in such form or such effect.

Alienation of tenant by copy creates a forfeiture, for he must surrender into the lord's hands according to the custom, at some court.

certeyn tenauntes deins mesme le manor, ont use daver terres et tenementes, a tener a eux et a lour heires en fee-simple, ou en fee-taille, ou a terme de vie, &c., a volunte le seignour, solonques le custome de mesme le manor. 74 Et tiel tenaunt ne poet aliener la terre per fait, qar donques le seignour poet entrer come en chose forfaite a luy, mes sil voet aliener sa terre a un autre, il covient solonques ascun custome de surrendre les tenementes en ascun court, &c., en la mayn le seignour, al use celuy qui avera lestate, en tiel fourme, ou a tiel effecte.

(*a*) These words *at the will of the lord*, are material to express copyhold; for if these words be omitted in pleading, it shall be intended that the estate is a customary freehold.—*Hughes' case, Cro. Car.* 229; *Hal. MSS.* [*Hargr. in n. Co. Lytt.*]

The copyhold court being either court baron or customary court.

(*b*) And it is to be understood that this court is of two natures: The first is by the common law, and is called a court baron, as some have said, for that it is the freeholder's or freeman's court (for *barons* in one sense signify freemen); and of that court the freeholders being suitors (*i. e. those tenants who are bound by custom to pay suit or attendance at the lord's court*) are the judges, and this may be kept from three weeks to three weeks. The second is a customary court, and that concerns [mere] copyholders, and therein the lord or his steward is the judge. Now, as there can be no court baron without freeholders, so there cannot be this kind of customary court without copyholders or customary holders. And as there may be a court baron of freeholders only without copyholders, and then is the steward the register; so there may be a customary court of copy-

"To this court cometh A. of B., and surrendered in the "same court one mease &c., into the hands of the lord, to "the use of C. of D. and his heirs, or the heirs of his body "issuing, or for term of his life &c. And thereupon cometh "the aforesaid C. of D., and took of the lord in the same "court the foresaid mease &c. To have and to hold to him "and to his heirs, or to him and to his heirs of his body issuing, or to him for term of life, at the will of the lord, according to the custom of the manor, doing and yielding "therefore the rents, services and customs thereof before due "and of right accustomed &c., and giveth the lord for a "fine &c., and did unto the lord his fealty" &c. (*c*).

Form of surrender.

"*Ad hanc curiam venit A. de B. et sursum reddidit in "eâdem curiâ, unum mesuagium, &c., in manus domini, ad "usum C. de D. et heredum suorum, vel heredum de corpore "suo exeuntium, vel pro termino vitæ suæ, &c. Et super hoc "venit prædictus C. de D. et cepit de domino in eâdem curiâ, "mesuagium prædictum, &c. Habendum et tenendum sibi et "heredibus suis, vel sibi et heredibus de corpore suo exeuntibus, vel sibi ad terminum vitæ, &c., ad voluntatem domini, "secundum consuetudinem manerii, faciendo et reddendo inde "redditus, servitia, et consuetudines inde prius debita et de "jure consueta, &c. Et dat domino de fine, &c. Et fecit "domino fidelitatem,*" &c.

---

holders only without [a court baron for the] freeholders, and then is the lord or his steward the judge. And when the court baron is of this double nature, the court roll contains as well matters appertaining to the customary court as to the court baron. And forasmuch as the title or estate of the copyholder is entered into the roll whereof the steward delivers him a copy, therefore he is called a copyholder.—*Co. Lytt.* 58. a. b.

(*c*) It is now usual to enter a respite of fealty, but the rolls of many manors show entries of fealty since the stat. 12 Car. 2, c. 24, for military services were only abolished by that statute; and copyholds were expressly excepted. The *Editor* has seen this entry of fealty as late as 1754.—*Rot. Maner' de Send & Ripley, Com' Surr'.*

Reason why such tenants styled tenants by copy.

Tenants are to be impleaded for their lands in the lord's court.

75 And such tenants are called tenants by copy of court roll, because they have none other evidence concerning their tenements, but only the copies of the court rolls. 76 And such tenants shall neither implead nor be impleaded for their tenements by the king's writ: but if they will implead others for their tenements, they shall have a plaint entered in the lord's court in this form, or to such effect: "A. of B. complains against C. of D. of a plea of land, *viz.* of one messuage, forty acres of land, four acres of meadow, &c., with the appurtenances, and makes protestation to follow this plaint in the nature of the king's writ of assize of Mortdancestor at the common law, or of an assize of novel disseisin, or formedon in the descender at the common law (*d*), or in the nature of any other writ, &c.; pledges to prosecute F.

75 *Et tielx tenaunts sont appelles tenauntes per copye de court rolle, pur ceo que ils nount autre evidence concernant lour tenementes, forsque les copies des rolles del court.* 76 *Et tielx tenaunts ne emplederount, ne serront empledez de lour tenementes per brief le roy: mes sils voillent empleder autres pur lour tenementes, ils averont un pleint fait en le court le seignour en tiel fourme, ou a tiel effecte: "A. de B. queritur versus C. de D. de placito terræ, videlicet, de uno mesuagio, quadraginta acris terræ, quatuor acris prati &c., cum pertinenciis, et facit protestationem sequi querelam istam in natura brevis domini regis assisæ mortis antecessoris ad communem legem, vel brevis domini regis assisæ novæ disseisinæ ad communem legem, aut in natura brevis de forma donationis in descendere ad communem legem, ou en nature dascun autre brief &c. Plegii de prosequendo F. et G."* 77 *Et*

(*d*) By stat. 3 & 4 Gul. 4, c. 27, s. 36, these forms of real actions are abolished, writ of right of dower, and writ of dower *unde nihil habet*, and writ of *quare impedit* being the only writs retained. The process of *ejectione firmæ* or *ejectment* being that by which all titles to lands are now triable.

These tenants have an inheritance by the custom, though at law they are tenants at will of the lord.

Tenant's remedies against lord.

" and G." 77 And although that some such tenants have inheritance according to the custom of the manor, yet they have not estate but at the will of the lord according to the course of the common law. For it is said, that if the lord do oust them, they have no other remedy but to sue to their lords by petition (*e*); for if they should have any [other*] remedy, they should not be said to be tenants at will of the lord according to the custom of the manor. But the lord will not break the custom, which is reasonable in such cases (*f*).

coment que ascuns tielx tenaunts ount enheritaunce solonques le custome de manor, unquore ils nount estate forsque a volunte le seignour solonques le cours del comen ley. Qar, il est dit, si le seignour eux ousta, ils nount autre remedie forsque de suer a lour seignour per peticion, qar sils averont [*autre**] *remedye, ils ne serrount dits tenaunts a volunte le seignour solonques le custome del manor, mes le seignour ne voet enfreindre le custome que est resonable en tielx cases.*

---

* This word does not appear in *Machl.* or *Roh.*

(*e*) That is, by *bill* or *complaint*, a proceeding not according to the course of common law, but equity, which adopts this formulary. It has long been settled that equity will interfere to prevent the lord doing any act to prejudice his tenant; indeed, any unreasonable or vexatious conduct on the part of the lord, will render him amenable to the courts of law and equity; for any disputes between lord and tenant must necessarily be referred to those courts for their decision, the lord not being permitted to act as judge in his own cause, though he may act as a chancellor in deciding controversies arising upon title of copyhold land within his manor, especially upon matters of conscience and trust. *See Co. Copyh.* § 44.

(*f*) At this place occurs an addition, which first appeared in *Redm.;* for *Lettou & M.*, *Machl.*, and *Roh.*, have it not—*viz.* " But *Brian*, chief justice, said, that his opinion hath always been and ever shall be, that if such tenant by custom paying his services be ejected by the lord, he shall have an action of trespass against him. *Hil.* 21 *E.* 4. And so was the opinion of *Danby*, chief justice, in 7 *E.* 4, for he saith that tenant by the custom is as well inherited to have his land according to the custom, as he who hath a freehold at common law." This addition is not noticed as such by *Sir Edward Coke*, who cites 42 *E.* 3, 25, and *Britton*, 165, in confirmation of these opinions. The cases alluded to in this addition, are reported in the *Year-Book* as follows:

Year-Book, Mich. 7 *E.* 4. And it was moved in this matter [as an incidental point in the case, which was trespass for seizing a heriot], if the lord enter and oust his tenant at will according to the custom of the manor, hath he any remedy against the lord? *Danby*, J.—It seemeth that he hath, for if the lord oust him he doeth him a wrong; for he is as well inherited to have this land to him and to his heirs according to the custom of the manor, as any man is of lands at the common law, and *moreover* he pays fine when he enters. *Lyttleton*, J.—I once saw a subpœna brought by such a tenant against his lord, and it was holden by all the justices that he should recover nothing by it; for it was holden, that the entry of the lord upon him was lawful, insomuch as he is tenant at will, &c. And, Sir, neither writ of false judgment or writ of right shall he have, for no freehold [*frank-tenement* taken for the tenure] is in him, but the freehold is in the lord. *Danby*, J.—The judgment on the subpœna bears out what I say, he was to have recovery of the freehold [frank-tenement taken for the possession or *interest* in the land], for he could have no other writ for recovering of the freehold, &c.; but he shall have good writ of trespass against the lord, and he cannot justify his entry, &c. And, Sir, if the king enter in my land, I shall have no other remedy but my petition, &c.; but the king is bound of right to restore me; so in like manner is the lord bound to restore his tenant at will, according to the custom, &c. *Catesby* and *Pygot*.—In your case, if the king enter in my land, still the freehold is in me and not in the king; for he cannot have it but by matter of record, &c. *Danby*, J.—So I conceive, but put the case that he takes the profits, what remedy, &c.? *Catesby*.—None, &c. *Year-Book*, *Mich.* 7, *E.* 4; from which case *Kitchin* concludes, that the tenant shall have a subpœna. *p.* 159, *ed.* 1675.

Year-Book, Hil. 21 *E.* 4. Trespass for house and close broken.—The defendant says that the place where, &c., is two houses and a certain acre of land, and that the said land was customary land; and the two houses and land were let to the defendant for term of life, by force of which he was seised, &c., as of freehold according to the custom of the same manor, and gives colour to the plaintiff, &c. *Brigges*.—It is inconsistent with his estate to say that he is tenant by copy of court roll, and to say that he is seised of freehold. *Brian*, J.—He has said by force of the custom, and that is good enough, *quod cur' concessit*. *Brigges*.—If the lord will put him out he has no remedy, for he proves that he is but tenant at will. *Brian*, J.—That never was my opinion, nor do I believe ever will be; for then all the copyhold in England should be defeated; by which I mean it to be understood, that whilst the tenant performs his customs and services, if the lord put him out, he shall have action of trespass against him; [and by the conclusion of this report, it appears to have been settled that the lord could only justify expelling the copyholder who did not perform his services].—*Year-Book. Hil.* 21 *E.* 4, *secundum longum reportum.*

CHAPTER X.

TENANT BY THE VERGE*.

Tenancy by the rod defined.

Reason of this appellation.

78 ALSO there are other tenants who are called tenants by the verge (*g*) [and such tenants] are in [the like†] nature as tenants by copy of court-roll. But the reason why they be

78 [*Auxi* y sont autres tenauntes que sont appelles*] *Tenauntes per le verge,* [*et tielx tenauntes*] *sont en* [*autiel*†] *nature come tenauntes per le copy de court rolle. Mes la cause pur quel ils*

---

* In *Lettou & M.*, this chapter appears as a continuation of the paragraph, and not as the commencement of a new subject. In *Machl.* and in *Roh.*, the words *tenauntes, &c.*, are printed in capitals, but they do not form the commencement of a new chapter. In *Pyns.* 1516, these words are not printed in capitals, but only appear as the beginning of a new paragraph. In all subsequent editions, *tenants per le verge* form a separate chapter. The words within the two first brackets occur only in *Lettou & M.*

† This word *autiel* is, in *Pyns.* 1516, corrupted into *autre—other*, the very reverse of the sense.

(*g*) This tenant *by the verge* is a mere copyholder, and taketh his name of the verge.—*Co. Lytt.* 61, *a.* And this term which is now at this day called copy tenants or copyholders, or tenants by copy, is but a new-found term, for of ancient times they were called tenants in villenage, or of base tenure; and that appeareth by the ancient tenures, that those who hold by the rod, or in base tenure, or by copy of court roll, were then called and named tenants that held in the villenage: for tenants by copy of court roll are not specified nor named by such name; but yet at that time there were such tenants, but then they were called tenants in villenage or of base tenure.—*F. N. B. p.* 25, *C.*

called tenants by the verge is, for that when they will surrender their tenements into the hands of their lord to the use of another, they shall have a little [yard or] rod, by the custom and use in their hands, which they shall deliver to the steward, or to the bailiff, according to the custom of the manor, and he who shall have the land, shall take the same land in court, and his taking shall be entered upon the roll; and the steward, or bailiff, according to the custom, shall deliver to him that taketh the land the same rod, or another rod in the name of seisin; and for this cause they are called tenants by the verge, but they have no other evidence but copy of the court-roll. 79 And also in divers lordships and manors there is this custom, *viz.* if such a tenant that holdeth by custom will alien his lands or tenements, he may surrender his tenements to the bailiff, or to the reeve, or to two good men of the same lordship, to the use of him who shall have the land, to have in fee-simple, fee-tail, or for term of life, &c., and they shall present all this at the

Custom to surrender out of court, which surrender is to be presented at the next court.

sont appelles tenauntes per la verge, est pur ceo que quant ils voillent surrendre lour tenementes en la mayn lour seignour al use dun autre, ils averont un petit verge, per le custome et le use, en lour mayn, la quele ils bailleront a seneschall, ou al baillif solonques le custome et use del manor, et celuy qui avera la terre, prendra mesme la terre en le court, et son pris serra entre en le rolle, et le seneschall, ou le bailley, solonques le custome delyvera a celuy que prent la terre, mesme la verge, ou une autre verge en noun de seisin, et pur celle cause ils sount appelles tenauntes per la verge, mes ils nount autre evidence, sinon copye de court rolle. 79 *Et auxi en divers seignouries et manors, il y ad tiel custome, si tiel tenaunt qui tient per le custome voilloit aliener ses tenementes, il poet surrendre ses tenementes a le bailley, ou a le reve, ou a deux prudes homes del seignourie, al use cestuy qui avera la terre, de aver en fee-simple, fee-taille, ou pur terme de vie, &c. Et tout ceo ils presenteront al proscheyn court, et donques celuy*

next court, and then he, who shall have the land by copy of court roll, shall have the same according to the intent of the surrender. 80 And so it is to be understood, that in divers lordships, and in divers manors, there be many various customs in such cases; as to take tenements, and as to plead, and as to other things and customs to be done; and whatsoever is not against reason may well be admitted and allowed (*h*). 81 [And*] these tenants that hold according to the custom

Different customs exist in manors.

Tenants by

qui avera la terre per copye de court rolle, avera mesme la terre solonques lentent de surrendre. 80 *Et issint est assavoir, que en divers seignouries, et divers manors, y sont mults plusours divers customes en tielx cases; quant a prendre tenementes, et quant a pleder, et quant as autres choses et customes a faire; et tout ceo que nest pas enconter reason, poet bien estre admitte et allowe.* 81 [*Et**] *tielx tenauntes qui*

---

* This word *Et* is *en* in *Lettou & M.*, and is not the commencement of a new sentence as it is in all the subsequent editions, but the continuation of the preceding, viz. *admitte et allowe* en *tielx*, &c.

(*h*) The following are some of the particular customs which prevail in various manors as well of free as of base tenure, and are noted by *Kitchin*, 202, *ed.* 1675, as those he had "*seen allowed between copyholders within manors where he had been at courts:*" and with respect to the allowance of any custom, there ought to be precedents in the court rolls, or good proof of that to be shewn to the court accordingly, otherwise it is not to be allowed for a custom. —*Id.* 205.

With regard to customs of prescription between lord and tenant, and tenants and tenants, *Kitchin* has also collected several, respecting which no more need be said here, than his remark, that the prescription be—1, reasonable; 2, according to common right or law; 3, that it be upon good consideration.—*Ibid.*

Borough English.—See *Heir.*

Clivenor.—The copyholder, before he can enforce his lord to admit any one to his copyhold, is to make a proffer to his next of blood or clivenor, or to the next of his neighbours next adjoining to the land from the east of the sun, (*ab oriente solis*), who, on giving as much as the party to whom the surrender was made, shall have it. *See Coke's Copyholder*, § 33.

of a lordship or manor, albeit they have an estate of inheritance according to the custom of the lordship or manor, yet *custom have estate of inheritance by*

teignount solonques le custome dun seignourie, ou solonques le custome dun manor, coment quils ount estate denheritaunce

---

Curtesy and Dower.—That the wife shall have no dower, nor the husband be tenant by the curtesy.

Dower.—That the wife shall have the third part of the rent, and not any land for her dower, as at *Bush.*

That the woman being espoused a virgin, shall have all the copyhold whereof the husband *died* seised for her freebench; but the husband may alien all or part without the wife, and then she cannot claim dower.

That if a man marry a maid, and die seised of copyhold, his wife shall have all the land during her life for her dower; but if he marry a widow, and die seised, she shall have no dower.

Fine.—That a copyholder pay but one penny for a fine, though there be but a hundred acres or more; and in some manors, 6*s.* 8*d.* for every dwelling-house; and also for every acre, 6*s.* 8*d.*; and for every cottage, 6*s.* 8*d.*; and also 6*s.* 8*d.* for every hampsel, *i. e.* an ancient house or cottage decayed, 6*s.* 8*d.*; and in every manor the fine is uncertain; [but yet the lord then shall not take more for his fine than hath heretofore been taken for a fine; and if he do otherwise, the remedy for the copyholder is in the chancery against his lord.]

Gavelkind.—See *Heir.*

Heir.—That the youngest son or daughter of the first wife, being married a virgin, ought to inherit.

That the youngest son shall inherit as in *Borough English;* and if he have no son, his younger brother, as at *Edmonton.*

That all the sons and all the brothers shall inherit together as in Gavelkind, as at *Islington* (the Prebend Manor).

That if the tenant dies seised of five acres or less, then the youngest son ought to inherit; but if above, then all the sons, as in gavelkind, ought to inherit.

Heriot.—That where the copyholder is inheritable, the heir shall choose the best beast, and the bailiff of the lord shall seize two of the next best beasts; and for a cottage, two shillings in silver for heriot shall be paid, but no beast.

Custom of some manors is to pay 6*s.* 8*d.* for a heriot and no beast.

Inheritance, mode of.—See *Heir.*

Tenure of, where the surrender is of copyhold made *to him and his,* that is an estate of inheritance in fee by the custom, though it be not to him and his heirs; and in some manors it is *to him and his in villenage,* and it is a good estate of inheritance by the custom.

custom, but no freehold at law.

Distinction be-

because they have no freehold by the course of the common law, they are called tenants by base tenure (*i*). 82 And there

solonques le custome de seignourie ou de manor, unquore pur ceo quils nount ascun franktenement per le cours del comen ley, ils sont appelles tenaunts per base tenure. 82 *Et divers di-*

Jointenancy.—See *Lease.*

Lease.—That copyholder may let his copyhold by indenture for three years, without license of the lord, and in some for nine years, and in some manors for more; and in some manors from three years to three years for the term of 21 years, and it is no forfeiture.

If a man let to three for life, to have successively; yet this is a joint estate, and "successively," is void: but by custom of copyhold *successivé* holds place, and one shall have it after the other.—30 *Hen.* 8, *tit. Leases*, 54.

Parcenry by Custom.—See *Heir.*

Purchase.—That if one were no copyholder of the manor before, and purchase lands, at first the fine is arbitrable, and granted at the will of the lord; but neither he nor his afterwards shall pay a fine, but he shall be admitted free, without paying fine for all the lands which he afterwards purchase within the manor.

Relief.—That the copyholder shall pay for a relief upon a descent but half that which is due by common law; as if he held by sixpence, he shall pay but threepence for relief; but yet he ought to pay that relief by the custom: also if he came in by purchase, he ought to pay in the like manner half his rent as aforesaid: that is to say, 3*d.* where his rent was 6*d.*

Custom of some manors is to pay but one penny for relief, neither more nor less, though his rent be 10*s.*

Surrender.—That surrender may be made into the hands of the bailiff, in the presence of two tenants witnessing it; and in some manors, to the use of him to whom, &c. And in some manors, in the hands of one tenant, to the use of him who should have it. That surrender may be made into the hands of a tenant, in the presence of other persons, to the uses, &c., and is good.

Ward.—That if any copyholder die, that the custody shall be committed by the lord to the next of blood to whom the land cannot de-

---

(*i*) To hold in fee base, is to hold at the will of the lord.—*Olde Tenures*, § 16.

are divers diversities between tenant at will, which is in by lease of his lessor by the course of the common law, and tenant according to the custom of the manor in form aforesaid. For tenant at will, according to the custom, may have an estate of inheritance, as is aforesaid, at the will of the lord, according to the custom and usage of the manor. But if a man hath lands or tenements which be not within such a manor or lordship where such custom hath been used in form aforesaid, and will let such lands or tenements to another, to have and to hold to him and to his heirs, at the will of the lessor, these words "to the heirs of the lessee" are void. For in this case if the lessee dieth, and his heir

tween tenant by will and tenant by custom;

"heirs" rejected as to the former.

Lord cannot

versitees y sont perenter tenaunt a volunte, qui est eins per lees son lessour per le cours del comen ley, et tenaunt solonques le custome del manor en la fourme avauntdit. Qar tenaunt a volunte solonques le custome poet aver estate denheritaunce, come est avauntdit, al volunte le seignour solonques le custome et usage del manor. Mes si home ad terres ou tenementes, queux ne sount deins tiel manor ou seignourie, ou tiel custome ad este use en la fourme avauntdit, et voille lesser tielx terres ou tenementes a un autre, a aver et tener a luy et a sez heires a le volunte le lessour, ceux parolx, a lez heirez de le lessé, sont voidez. Qar en ceo cas si le lessé devie et son heire entra, le lessour avera bon accion

---

scend; and in some manors, the bailiff of the lord shall have the custody, and render the heir an account at 14 years of the profits; and by the custom of some manors, at 14 years, the heir may appoint a guardian to himself.

Waste.—That copyholder may cut his trees and wood and sell it at his pleasure; and also suffer the houses to decay; and yet it is not forfeiture as it is at *Islington*.

[Where this custom is not allowed, it is usual to present, 'That timber is at the will of the lord [*quod maremium est ad voluntatem domini*']. But tenant by copy is entitled to reasonable *estovers*. See *ante*, p. 67, *in n*.

Work.—To have certain days for labour in harvest, for a day or two days, and in some manors the copyholder shall pay fourpence in lieu of the labour.

have action of trespass against heir of copyholder for entering.

enter, the lessor shall have a good action of trespass against him, but not so against the heir of tenant by the custom, &c., [in any case*], for that the custom of the manor in some case may aid him to bar his lord in action of trespass, &c.

Custom as to repairs.

83 Also the one tenant, by custom in some places, ought to repair and uphold his houses, and the other tenant at will ought not.

As to performance of fealty.

84 Also the one tenant by the custom shall do fealty, and the other not, and many other diversities there be between them, &c. (*k*).

de trespas enverz luy, mes nemy issint envers leire del tenaunt per le custome, &c. [en ascun cas], pur ceo que le custome de le manor en ascun cas luy poet aider de barrer son seignour en accion de trespas, &c.*

83 *Item lun tenaunt per le custume en ascuns lieux doit reparelle r et susteiner sez measons, et lautre tenaunt a volunte nemye.*

84 *Item lun tenaunt per le custume ferra fealté, et lautre nemye. Et plusours autres diversitees y sont perenter eux, &c.*

---

* These words appear in *Lettou & M.*, and *Machl.*, and *Roh.*, but they confuse the text; and the translation of them by Sir Edward Coke as above, is evidently incongruous with the subsequent rendering of these words in the same paragraph. They do not appear in *Pyns.* 1516, *Redm.*, *Berth.*, *Middl.*, *Powel*, *Sm.*, *Tottyl* 1554, the French edit. of 1671, or in any of the copies of *Rastell's* Transl. to 1656; but they appear in all the editions of *Tottyl* from 1567 to 1591, and in other copies to 1639. Sir Edward Coke has adopted them in his Translation, which also forms the Translation in *ed.* 1671. In a copy of the *Rohan* edition, *penes Ed.*, these words are struck out by a contemporary hand, and certainly the sense requires it.

(*k*) Suit service is to come to the court from iij. weekes to iij. weekes by the whole yeare, and for that a man shall be distrayned and not amerced.

Suit real is to come to the court of leete, and that is not but ij. times in the yeare, and for that a man shall be amerced and not distrayned.—*Olde Tenures*, § 27.

CONCLUDING REMARKS.

As the law, more particularly at the time Lyttleton wrote, regarded copyholders as tenants at will, the freehold of their tenements not being in them, but in the lord (*l*), this tenure by copy has been treated of in the order it now appears, viz. next after tenant at will; though, for many purposes, its consideration may be referred to the second book, which treats of services strictly so called, their origin and incidents.

Copyholders are either those who are said to hold their land *according to the custom of the manor* (*m*), or are those who hold or are tenants *at the will of the lord according to the custom of the manor.* This tenure had its origin in the tenure of villenage, and the subjects of this tenure are those

---

(*l*) These kinds of copyholders have the frank-tenure in them, and it is not in their lords, as in case of copyholds in base tenure.—*Co. Copyhold.* § 32.

(*m*) Sir Edward Coke styles this interest copyhold of frank-tenure or freehold; and observes, that they are most usual in ancient demesne; though sometimes out of ancient demesne we meet with the like sort of copyholds; as in Northamptonshire there are tenants which hold by copy of court roll, and have no other evidence, and yet hold not at the will of the lord: a fact *Kitchin* also mentions, alluding to this Northamptonshire tenure 'out of ancient demesne,' (*p.* 162, *ed.* 1675), the existence of which can only be accounted for by those manors having been once in the hands of the crown: he also informs us in another place, that "in surrenders of land in ancient demesne of frank tenure it is not used to say, to hold at the will of the lord, in these copies, but to hold *according to the custom of the manor*, by the services therefore due, and it is not said there *at the will of the lord.*" *West* makes also the same distinction; for after defining a copyholder much in the language of Lyttleton, he tells us—"In some manors the tenants have the lands granted unto them and their heirs in fee, fee-tail, or for life or years, *according to the custom of the manor*, and not *at the will of the lord according to the custom*, in which case the rolls and copies ought to be made accordingly."—*Symbol.* § 603—5.

lands which formed the *demesne* of any honor or manor, for all other lands were holden by free tenure, *scil.* by military and socage services, the *demesnes,* as will be presently shewn, being held by base tenure or bond services.

Manors and tenures in the nature of copyholds or villenage, appear to have existed before the Conquest in essentials; but it seems to have been from the Normans that we had pure copyhold, or rather the form of manors as they have existed in this country, and as a consequence of the introduction of their feudal law by William I., the word *manor,* which occurs so frequently in Domesday Book, the word *ham* in the Saxon language, as well as the Norman word *manoir,* all three signifying a chief residence, (words not known to other nations where the feudal law had place), seems to shew this plainly enough.

The origin of manors appears to be this:—When the king granted a tract of land to any great person to hold as a feudal tenure, by homage or service, as the case might be, the grantee or feudatory granted part by subinfeudation to others, to hold of him by military service, as knight-service, or by rustic services, as socage, which last was not servile but privileged, because it consisted in *certain, i. e.* fixed and specific, services, since converted to a pecuniary render: the remnant the lord reserved to himself as his demesne, *i. e. his own,* and on this stood the *manor* or lord's house or court, where he resided and exercised those acts of jurisdiction which were inseparable from feudal dominion; and this word gave the title of manor to the whole. In the Saxon times, a separate jurisdiction was exercised in privileged manors or socs (*sokes*), which took their name from the word *soc,* a privilege or immunity, rather than from the word *soc,* a plough; though as plough or rural service of a fixed nature was the rent or render, legal etymologists might without any apparent inconsistency, derive the word *socagium* (socage) therefrom, though, according to both derivations, the meaning of the word *socagium* is the same, viz. a tenure not military, of a free and privileged nature, because certain in its services.

To return, however, to the subject of manors. This demesne or reserved portion set apart for the lord's maintenance, and which consequently was entirely and remained absolutely to his own use and purpose, was tilled by the villans, who were either *nativi, i. e.* bondmen by blood in respect of their persons, and who literally occupied their land at the will of the lord, and served him as slaves, possessing nothing, nor having the power to possess anything of their own; or *villans by tenure, i. e.* free persons of low degree, who took upon themselves to hold land upon performing servile offices with the *nativi* or bondmen, as a price for their occupation of some portion of the lord's demesne, and from which they could not be removed,—indulgence, custom, and long usage operating to secure them (as it did afterwards the bondmen or pure villans who encroached on the situation of those next above them), an inheritable interest in their tenements: from the latter proceed the freeholders or free tenants of a manor; from the former the customary tenants, who are still said to hold at the will of the lord according to the custom, &c., much in the same way as is mentioned hereafter concerning the tenants of ancient demesne.

It seems agreed by almost all writers, (though many different opinions prevail as to the fact of manors subsisting before the Conquest), that in the time of the Saxons, and especially a short time before the Conquest, a similar mode prevailed of allotting those portions of a lord's dominion or lordship which are called the demesnes or were reserved for home culture (*n*); though it may be doubted whether there

---

(*n*) Copyhold lands were before the Conquest, and it was called folk-land in the time of the Saxons, and the charter-lands are called book-land.—*Kitchin*, 177, *ed.* 1675. This is enlarged upon by *Sir Edward Coke*, in his *Complete Copyholder*, § 3—8, who there says, that book-land (*so called because it passed by book or writing*), differed nothing from freehold of this day; and that folk-lands, which passed by word of mouth, differed nothing from copyholds at this day; but he subsequently confesses, in discussing this subject, that he

was any such absolute and hereditary bondage and slavery as was introduced by the Normans under the style of *villenage*, (at least to the extent and universality of this tenure, which they created), for *villanus* (*o*), in strict feudal language, does not bear the same interpretation as the Norman word *villein;* the villans noticed in Domesday (*p*) rather signifying *coloni* (*tillers of ground*), and mere rustic drudges annexed to the soil or *adscriptitii glebæ*, it is true, but yet privileged, as enjoying certainty of tenure by a specific and fixed render of services; but after the Conquest, villenage bore a different sort of aspect, and in fact extended itself throughout the whole kingdom, for many freemen were forced to surrender and take back their own lands to hold by villein tenure; and others were reduced to a state of absolute bondage and hereditary servitude; and became, like cattle, the property of those who owned the lordship or manor, and could be sold by him to any other person, the only tie they had on their lords being that of sustenance, or rather a bare permission to dwell on the lord's demesnes as tenants at will, which was the state of many, even at the time Lyttleton

---

is "rashly running into an inextricable labyrinth;" and, indeed, what book-land and folk-land was, has been since made a matter of controversy with antiquarians.

(*o*) *Villani, inquit* Budæus, *dicuntur, quod villæ* (*unde villici dicti*) *ascripti, et colonariæ conditioni addicti, aut ipsi sunt, aut eorum majores fuerint quarum rerum vestigia non obscura multis in locis extant: quod tamen nomen loquentium inscitia in contumeliam jam vertit. Villanum enim, et vilem, vernacula simplicitas confundit.—Calvin. Lexic. Jurid. fol. Cologne*, 1734.

(*p*) In Domesday Book there are a great many descriptions of inferior tenants, some *villani*, some *servi*, *bordarii*, *cotarii*, *&c.*, in fact the Saxons seem to have infinitely subdivided the tenures, and consequently the conditions of men. Some *bondmen* there certainly were in the time of the Saxons, but to what extent it is difficult to ascertain, and the introduction of Saxon bondage has been ascribed to the Danes. The Normans appeared to have made villenage more extended and universal, and inferior estates and persons seem to have been arbitrarily reduced to this base and slavish tenure.

wrote, though they were then gradually disappearing. Something should be said about that tenure which is termed ancient demesne.

When William I. made grants of fiefs, or rather granted lands to hold *quasi-fiefs*, he reserved, or at least made no alteration in the tenure of those lands which had personally belonged to king Edward the Confessor, and which were thus peculiarly attached to the crown as *demesne* (*q*). These lands and manors are now called *ancient demesne*, to distinguish them from the demesne lands of the lords to whom grants had been made, or who had, from fear or other influence, been forced to accept their lands as a new grant, upon the condition of their bringing them in under the terms of the feudal law as used by the Normans. But boroughs which belonged to the king, and lands in the county of Kent which preserved its Saxon customs, were not granted as fiefs, or at least, if so granted, were granted subject to their ancient customs. These lands were termed *ancient socage*, to distinguish them from *modern socage;* (indeed it has been a question whether all land was not, before the Conquest, socage tenure, *i. e.* not subject to the *jus feudale*)*;* hence the customs still subsisting of Gavelkind, and Borough-English, and other customs evidently of Saxon origin in some manors.

Tenants in ancient demesne, viz. those who held of the king lands in villenage (*r*), were, from the circumstance of

---

(*q*) All the lands and manors which were in William the Conqueror's hands, and in Domesday-Book stated to have been in the seisin or possession of King Edward the Confessor, are ancient demesne and no other; for the lands stated in that book to be in other men's hands, under such titles as "Land of the Bishop," &c. are not ancient demesne. Those lands only are ancient demesne which are stated as *terra regis*.

(*r*) The tenants in ancient demesne found provision for the king, and the tenants by burgage tenure found cloth and other merchandize for him; and these provisions being valued at a certain rate, were afterwards in some returned into rents, and in some received in specie.—*Gilbert's Hist. Exch.* 42.

their holding *quasi in capite,* more favoured than other tenants of a like nature; indeed, the privileged sort were called socmen (*sokmanni* (*s*)), and, as their name imports, were freemen, though holding land by base tenure; in fact, they were a lower degree of socage tenants, and distinguished as *villan-socmen,* while the other villeins in ancient demesne held in pure villenage, and their successors, in old books are sometimes styled *tenants by the verge in ancient demesne:* but these pure villeins attempted to encroach upon the estate of those next above them, and sought to be recognised as *villan-socmen,* and in some instances to obtain their freedom altogether; to prevent which, the stat. 1 Ric. 2, c. 6, was enacted; the tenor of which Lyttleton notices at § 193.

These *villan-socmen,* or,—as they have been termed, socage tenants in base tenure—are peculiar to ancient demesne, and are now mostly, if not entirely, to be met with in manors of ancient demesne, or in manors originally derived from the crown. In such manors also the customs of Gavelkind or Borough-English not unfrequently hold place. The freeholders or *barons* (*t*) of such manors generally held by payment of a

---

(*s*) Note, that a socman is properly one who is a freeman, and holdeth of the king, or of the lord of ancient demesne, lands or tenements in villenage; and he is privileged in this manner, that no one ought to oust him from his lands or tenements, so long as he can do the services which appertain to those lands and tenements. And no one can increase his services, or make him perform more services than he ought to do. And no socman can implead another socman of lands or tenements within ancient demesne by any other writ than this writ of *right close.—Old N. B. tit. Brief de recto clauso.* See also *Olde Tenures, tit. Villenage, post,* § 172.

(*t*) Baron (*Baro-nis*), has many significations: in the Salic law (titul. 34), the word is taken for a male. So, in the laws of the Lombards (lib. 1, titul. 9). The word *homo* in the barbarous language of the middle ages, signified a vassal; and in this sense *baro* is also taken in the laws of the Lombards (lib. 1, titul. 14); subsequently those who were vassals of the king were termed *barones,* especially by the Scotch and the Germans: hence the tract allotted

small sum for relief, and a small quit-rent in the name of a *heriot;* and those who are the customary tenants or copyholders of such manors, hold *at the will of the lord* by payment of a *heriot,* which of itself shews their antiquity, for heriots are of Saxon, though by some supposed to be of Danish origin (*u*).

Modern demesne, as distinguished from *ancient demesne,* was the land which the lord retained for culture, and his own subsistence as already noticed, and was tilled by his bondmen or villeins, the predecessors of the ordinary and mere customary copyholders—tenants by the rod, who hold by payment of fines and services, and, generally speaking, by no means on such favourable terms as the tenants of manors in ancient demesne.

With regard to the customary tenant or mere copyholder, he is the successor of the pure villein; who, after the example of the socman, has been enfranchised and obtained an inheritance by custom; and the court which the lords of such manors still hold, and the holding of which are essential to the existence of such manors, is styled the *customary* court, to distinguish it from the court *baron,* which has relation to the free tenants of the manor; viz. the barons or freeholders who are inrolled, and who hold as their brethren the customary holders do, by copy of court roll. In the courts of ancient demesne manors, the free tenants or suitors are the judges (*x*); but if

---

to a feudatory was termed a barony, which is in many intents but another name for manor. *Baron and feme* in our law signifies husband and wife; but this phrase is getting into disuse.

(*u*) Sir William Blackstone, ii. 97, 422-3, advocates this opinion; but the Saxon word *herĕgeate,* which was a sum payable to the king on the death of a great person; and, subsequently, of inferior landholders, is mentioned in the rules of St. Benedict made in the time of King Edgar, and is there mentioned as a customary payment made on the decease of a great landholder. *Selden. Vita Eadmeri,* (*Spicilegium*), 153.

(*x*) That every freeholder holds his freehold land by certain yearly rent, fealty, and suit of court twice in the year, viz. at the two great courts; yet upon summons they

all the tenants are customary holders, *i. e.* hold *at the will of the lord,* termed tenants by the rod in ancient demesne, the steward is judge, for, as *Kitchin* observes, (p. 83, ed. 1675), these have but a base estate. In the common court baron and customary court, the steward is judge.

---

ought to appear upon trials between party and party.

That there are two sorts of copyhold lands and tenements in the manor of Sedgley: one sort held freely by copy of court roll, and is called free copyhold land; and the other is called base or customary copyhold land, and held by copy of court roll. The *free* copyhold lands and tenements are held by certain yearly rent, fealty, and suit of court twice in the year, viz. at the two great courts: and for every messuage, place, or tenement, the best beast of the tenant dying seised in fee, is due to the lord for a heriot. The *base* or *customary* copyhold lands and tenements are held by certain yearly rents, fealty, and for each messuage, place, or tenement, suit of court every three weeks' court, certain liens and oats yearly, and the best living beast; if none, the best household goods of the tenant dying seised of such messuage, &c., for an heriot, at every decease.

That there is only one year's chief rent due to the lord upon the admittance of every copyholder after the decease of his predecessor, as a *relief* for the *free* copyholder, and as a *fine* for the base or customary holder, and no other service except fealty, suit of court, and heriot.—*Rot. Custumal. Maner' de Sedgely, Com' Staff.*

EXPLICIT* LIBER PRIMUS.

INCIPIT LIBER SECUNDUS.

---

* The word *explicit*, generally used at the end of MSS. and early printed books, is a contraction of *explicitus*. The ancient books were nothing but rolls of parchment, (hence the Latin word, *volumen*, and our *volume*), which were unfolded by the reader in his progress through them. When they were quite *unfolded*, they were of course *finished;* and the word *explicitus*, which properly conveys the former sense, was afterwards used in the latter, when the books assumed a different form, to signify that they were *finished* or *ended*.

BOOK II.

CHAPTER I.

HOMAGE.

HOMAGE was rather a service incident to tenure, than a tenure of itself. Lyttleton opens his Second Book, which treats entirely of tenures and services, by stating the mode of performing this service, which was deemed the most honourable, although the most humble service, a tenant could render to his lord, and proceeds to shew how the formulary and mode of taking of homage was adapted to the cases of religious or professed persons (§ 86), women sole (§ 87), tenants holding of other lords (89), and married women (§ 90). It was a maxim or fixed rule, that this service (which was rendered but *once* by the tenant to the lord), could not be performed by or rendered to any other than a person having an estate of inheritance (§ 90); which, in all probability, is one of the reasons why Lyttleton commences with this service; and as this service was deemed the most honourable, and performed by those having the highest estate in the land, the priority in arrangement is fully justified.

This service was discharged by the stat. 12 Car. 2, c. 24, which abolished knight's-service and military tenures and their incidents, thereby reducing all tenures to *free* and *common socage*, i. e. *free*, as discharged from all service, and *common*, as not holden *in capite*, or of the crown, (one of the intents of that statute being to abolish the oppressive incidents of tenancies *in capite*), and as the statute only excepted frankalmoigne and copyhold, all other land is now holden by such free and common socage.

The mode of performing homage;

—by a freeholder.

85 HOMAGE is the most honourable service, and most humble service of reverence that a franktenant may do to his lord: for when the tenant shall make homage to his lord, he shall be [ungirt*], and his head uncovered, and his lord shall sit, and the tenant shall kneel before him on both his knees, and hold his hands [stretched forth†] joined together between (*a*) the hands of his lord, and shall say thus: I be-

85 *Homage est le pluis honourable service, et pluis humble service de reverence, que franktenaunt poet faire a son seignour. Qar quant le tenaunt ferra homage a son seignour, il serra [disceynt*], et son test discovert, et son seignour seera, et le tenaunt genulera devaunt luy sur ambideux genuez, et tiendra ses mainz [estendus†] joyntez ensemble entre les mayns le seignour, et issint dirra: Jeo deveigne vostre home*

* In *Rastell's* Transl. this word is rendered *he shall discend;* in *Sir E. Coke's* Transl. *he shall be ungirt*, i. e. not *gladio cinctus*. The three earliest editions have misprinted *disteynt* for *disceynt*, and *distent* appears in *Berth.*, *Powel*, *Sm.*, and *Tottyl* 1554. *Redm.* reads *discynct*, *ungirt*, which has been followed in all editions from 1557.

† This word appears in *Lettou & M.*, but not in *Machl.* or *Roh.*, or *Rastell's* Translation: almost all other copies retain it, reading the passage, *extendes* et *joynts*.

(*a*) This particular in the ceremony of taking the oath of homage is purely French. The *stationarii* or booksellers of Paris are stated to have been bound by oath "*entre les mains du Recteur de l'Université*," to publish a list of books as priced by the University. — *Mélanges d'Histoire et de Littérature*, ii. 187.

come your man from this day forward [for life, for member, and for earthly honour*], and unto you shall be true and faithful, and bear to you faith for the tenements that I claim to hold of you, saving the faith that I owe unto our sovereign lord the king: and then the lord so sitting, shall kiss him.

86 But if an abbot or a prior, or other man of religion, shall do homage to his lord, he shall not say: I become your man, &c., for that he hath professed himself to be only the man of God; but he shall say thus: I do homage unto you, and to you I shall be true and faithful, and faith to you bear for the tenements which I hold of you, saving the faith which I do owe unto our lord the king. *—by a religious.*

87 Also if a woman [sole†] shall do homage to her lord, she *—by a woman.*

de ceo jour en avaunt, [de vie, et de membre, et de terrene honor] et a vous seray foial et loial, et foy vous porteray des tenementes que jeo claime tener de vous, salve la foy que jeo doy a nostre seignour le roy: et donques le seignour issint seyant, luy basera.*

86 *Mes si un abbe, ou un prior, ou autre home de religion ferra homage a son seignour, il ne dirra: Jeo deveigne vostre home, &c., pur ceo que il y ad luy professe pur estre tant-solement le home de Dieu; Mes il dirra issint: Jeo vous face homage et a vous serray foial et loial, et foy a vous porteray des tenementes que jeo teigne de vous, salve la foy que jeo doy a nostre seignour le roy.*

87 Item, *si feme [sole†] ferra homage a son seignour, ele ne*

---

* These words do not appear in *Lettou & M.*, but *Machl.* and subsequent editions read them. These words form part of the oath of homage in the ancient tract or statute, (as it is generally termed), *Modus faciendi homagium et fidelitatem*, which has had the date of 17 *E.* 2, ascribed to it.—*Statutes of the Realm, fol.* 1810, *vol.* 1, *p.* 227, (*edited by Sir Thos. E. Tomlins*).

† This word appears in *Lettou & M.*, but not in *Machl.* or *Roh.*; almost all subsequent copies retain it.

shall not say, I become your woman, for it is not convenient (*b*) that a woman should say that she will become woman to any man but to her husband when she is married; but she shall say: I do to you homage, and to you shall be faithful and true, and faith to you shall bear for the tenements I hold of you, saving the faith I owe to our sovereign lord the king.

Homage performed by husband and wife.

88 *Also a man may see a note in M. 15, E. 3, where a man and his wife did homage and fealty in the Common Pleas,

dirra, Jeo deveigne vostre feme, pur ceo que nest convenient que feme dirra quele deviendra feme a ascun home forsque a son baron quant ele est espouse: Mes ele dirra, jeo face a vous homagè, et a vous serray foial et loial, et foy a vous porteray des tenementes que jeo teigne de vous, salve la foy que jeo doy a nostre seignour le roy.

88 *Item, *home poet veier en un note Anno* 15, *E.* 3, *lou un home et sa feme firent homage et fealté en le comen*

* In *Machl.*, *Roh.*, *Pyns.* 1516, *Redm.*, *Berth.*, *Powel*, *Sm.*, *Tottyl* 1554, and in *Rastell's* Transl., this section or portion of the text is transposed to the chapter of Fealty, as the commencement of, or as immediately preceding, § 94.

(*b*) Where the law is known and clear, though it be unequitable and inconvenient, the judges must determine as the law is, without regarding the unequitableness or inconveniency. Those defects, if they happen in the law, can only be remedied by parliament; therefore, we find many statutes repealed and laws abrogated by parliament, as inconvenient, which, before such repeal or abrogation, were in the courts of law to be strictly observed.

But where the law is doubtful, and not clear, the judges ought to interpret the law to be as is most consonant to equity and least inconvenient.

And for this reason, Lyttleton, in many of his cases, resolves the law not to be that way which is inconvenient, which Sir Ed. Coke, in his comment upon him, often observes, and cites the places.—*Vaugh.* 37.

The reasons *ab inconvenienti*, noted by Lyttleton, are to be found in § 138, 139, 231, 269, 440, 478, 665, 722, and 730. Sir Ed. Coke cites also the Year-Books, 21 H. 7, 13; 16 H. 7, 9; and also F.N.B. 230, D.

which is written in this form:—Note, that Johan Leuknor and Elizabeth his wife did homage to W. Thorpe in this manner: the one and the other held their hands jointly between the hands of W. Thorpe, and the husband said in this form: We do to you homage, and faith to you shall bear for the tenements which we hold of A. your conusor, who hath granted to you our services in B. and C. and other towns, &c., against all persons, saving the faith which we owe to our lord the king, and to his heirs, and to our other lords, and both the one and the other kissed him. And afterwards, they did fealty, and both of them held their hands upon the book, and the husband said the words, and both kissed the book.

89 Note well, if a man hath several tenancies, which he holdeth of several lords; that is to say, every tenancy by homage, then when he doeth homage to one of his lords, he shall say in the end of his homage done, saving the faith which I owe to our lord the king, and to my other lords.

—by tenant holding of several lords.

90 And note well, that none shall do homage but such as

None but those

bank, quel est escript en tiel fourme:—Nota, que Johan Leukenor et Elizabeth sa feme, firent homage a W. Thorpe en cest manere: lun et lautre tiendront jointement lour mayns entre les mayns W. Thorpe, et le baron dit en cest fourem: Nous vous fesons homage, et foy a vous porterons, pur les terres que nous teignons de A. vostre conusour, qui vous ad graunt nostre services en B. et C. et autres villes, &c., encountre toutz gentz, Salve la foy que nous devoiemus a nostre seignour le roy, et a ses heires, et a nostres autres seignours: et lun et lautre luy baiserount. Et puis, ils firent fealté, et lun et lautre tiendront lour mayns sur un lyver, et le baron dit les paroles, et ambideux baiserount le lyver.

89 *Nota, si un home ad several tenauncies queux il tient de severalx seignours;* scil., *chescun tenauncie per homage, donques quant il fait homage a un des seignours, il dirra en le fyn de son homage affaite, salve la foy que jeo doy a nostre seignour le roy, et mes autres seignours.*

90 *Et nota, que nul ferra homage mes tiel qui ad estate en*

who have an estate in fee or fee-tail shall either perform or receive homage.

Illustration of this maxim.

have an estate in fee-simple, or fee-tail in his own right, or in the right of another. For it is a maxim in law, that he that hath an estate but for term of life shall neither do homage nor take homage. For if a woman hath lands or tenements in fee-simple, or in fee-tail, which she holdeth of her lord by homage and taketh husband, and they have issue, then the husband in the life of the wife shall do homage, because he hath title to have the tenements by the curtesy of England if he surviveth his wife, and also he holdeth in right of his wife. [But before issue had between them, the homage shall be made in both their names*]. But if the wife dies before homage done by the husband in the life of the wife, and her husband holdeth himself in as tenant by the curtesy, he shall not do homage to his lord, because he then hath estate but for term of life.

More shall be said of homage in the tenure of homage auncestrel.

fee-simple, ou en fee-taille, en son droit demesne, ou en droit dun autre. Qar il est un maxime en ley quil qui ad estate forsque pur terme de vie, ne ferra homage, ne prendra homage. Qar si feme ad terres ou tenementes en fee-simple ou en fee-taille, queux ele tient de son seignour per homage, et prent baron, et ount issue, donques le baron en la vie la feme ferra homage, pur ceo quil ad title daver les tenementes per le curtosie Dengleterre sil survesquist sa feme, et auxi il tient en droit sa feme. [Mes devaunt issue ewe entre eux, le homage serra fait en lour ambideux nosmes.] Mes si la feme devie devaunt homage fait per le baron en la vie la feme, et son baron soy tient eins come tenaunt per le curtosie, il ne ferra homage a son seignour, pur ceo quil ad adonques estate forsque pur terme de vie.*

Plus serra dit de homage en le tenure per homage auncestrell.

---

* The words within brackets appear in *Redm.*, *Berth.*, *Middl.*, *Powel*, *Sm.*, *Tottyl* 1554, and *ed.* 1671, and in all the copies of *Rastell's* Transl.

CHAPTER II.

FEALTY.

91 FEALTY is the same that *fidelitas* is in Latin. And when a freeholder doeth fealty to his lord, he shall hold his right hand upon a book, and shall say thus: Hear you this my lord, that I shall be faithful and true unto you, and faith to you shall bear for the lands which I claim to hold of you, and that I shall lawfully do to you the customs and services which I ought to do at the terms assigned; so help me God and his saints: and he shall kiss the book. But he shall not kneel when he maketh his fealty, nor shall make such humble reverence as is aforesaid in homage. 92 And there is great diversity between the doing of fealty, and of homage, for homage cannot be done to any but to the lord himself: but the steward of the lord's courts, or bailiff, may take fealty for the lord.

The mode of doing fealty.

Diversities between homage and fealty.

91 *Fealté* idem est quod fidelitas *en Latin. Et quant franktenaunt ferra fealté a son seignour, il tiendra sa mayn dextre sur un lyver, et dirra issint: Ceo oyets vous mon seignour, que jeo a vous serray foial et loial, et foy a vous porteray des tenementes que jeo clayme a tener de vous et que loialment vous ferray les customez et services queux faire vous doy a termez assignez, sicome moy aide Dieu et ses seintz; et basera le lyver: Mes il ne genulera quant il fait fealté, ne ferra tiel humyle reverence, come avaunt est dit en homage.* 82 *Et graunde diversite y ad perenter feasaunt de fealté et de homage, qar homage ne poet estre fait forsque al seignour mesme: Mes seneschal dez courts de seignour ou bailly, poient prendre fealté pur le seignour.*

93 Also tenant for term of life shall do fealty, and yet he shall not do homage. And divers other diversities there be between homage and fealty.

94 [Also a man may see in 15 E. 3, how a man and his wife did homage and fealty in the Common Pleas, which is written before in the tenure of homage*.]

More shall be said of fealty in the tenure in socage, and in frankalmoigne, and in the tenure by homage auncestrel.

93 Item, *tenaunt a terme de vie ferra fealté, et unquore il ne ferra homage. Et divers autres diversitees y sont perenter homage et fealté.*

94 [Item, *home poet veier* 15 *E.* 3, *lou un home et sa feme firent homage et fealté en le comen bank, quel est escript devaunt en tenure de homage**.]

Pluis serra dit de fealté en le tenure en socage, et en le tenure en frankalmoigne, et en le tenure per homage auncestrell, &c.

CONCLUDING REMARKS.

It being a principle, that there must be a tenure of all lands in the hands of subjects, *scil.* that all the land in the kingdom is holden of some superior lord, the extinction of any service, or even its abolition, cannot extinguish tenure, but that fealty must remain for necessity of tenure. So that the abolition of military tenures, and tenures *in capite* by the stat. 12 Car. 2, c. 24, does not affect this service. Fealty is a service which was and still is strictly due from all tenants, save tenants in frankalmoign and tenants at will; and as Lyttleton in more than one place informs us, is incident to

---

* The words within brackets are an addition, and inserted while the book was in MS. by a later hand, in reference to the caption of homage, at § 88.

all services, consequently an inseparable incident of tenure (§ 99, 131, 135, 227).

Fealty, although incident to homage, was not always performed with it, and with respect to those tenants who were not freeholders, must necessarily have been performed apart from it, as none but tenants of the fee could perform homage (§ 90).

This service is due upon every change of the lord, and this with other differences forms one of the main distinctions between homage and fealty.

In other countries, where the feudal law prevailed, homage and fealty were blended; but in this country they have always been separated and kept distinct, homage and fealty being due from the freeholder, (*i. e.* the owner of a fee-simple or fee-tail) while fealty only was due from the inferior tenant. The fealty of copyholders is usually respited (*a*), and this ceremony as to other tenants has been long in disuse.

(*a*) See *ante*, p. 97, *n.* (*c*).

CHAPTER III.

ESCUAGE (*a*).

ESCUAGE was rather a service incident to or as a commutation of a tenure, rather than a tenure of itself; it varied also in its appellation and substance: for if it was uncertain, it was knight's-service; if certain, it became divested of its military attributes, and became socage (§ 98, 120). Tenure by escuage, indeed, appears to have been of a very amphibious nature, and if the expression may be allowed, was a military socage, which, on the subdivision of a knight's fee (§ 98), necessarily degenerated into an inferior tenure. *Scutum,* from which word Lyttleton in one sense derives the etymology of this tenure, was a term also used to signify money, and is the same as the French word *écu,* which is either denominative of a piece of money called a crown-piece, and in vernacular French means money, and also a shield. Lyttleton and his commentator prefer the latter derivation; but, like the etymology of socage (§ 119), the word escuage admits of both interpretations.

(*a*) To hold by escuage is to hold by knight's-service, and thereto belongeth ward, marriage, and reliefe. And marke well, that a man cannot holde by escuage unless that he holde by homage, for that escuage of common ryght draweth to it homage, as it was adjudged *anno* xxi. *Edvardi tertii.* And note well, that escuage is a certaine summe of money, and it ought to be levyed by the lord of his tenant after the quantitie of his tenure, according as escuage runneth by all Englande. And it is ordeined by all the counsell of Englande, how much every tenaunt shal give to his lord, and that is properlye for to mantayne the warres betwene Englande and them of Scotlande or of Wales, and not betwene other landes; because those forsayd lands should be of ryght belonginge to the realme of Englande.—*Olde Tenures,* § 4.

Etymology and description of escuage and tenure by escuage, a tenure by knight's-service.

Some tenants hold by the whole or the half of a knight's fee, and they ought to attend on a voyage royal forty days or less, as the tenure is.

95 ESCUAGE is called in Latin *scutagium;* that is, service of the shield; and that tenant which holdeth his land by escuage, holdeth by knight's service. And also it is commonly said, that some hold by the service of one knight's fee, and some by the half of a knight's fee, &c. And it is said, that when the king makes a voyage royal into Scotland to subdue the Scots (*b*), then he who holdeth by the service of one knight's fee ought to be with the king forty days, well and conveniently arrayed for the war; and he which holdeth his land by the moiety of a knight's fee, ought to be with the king twenty days; and he which holdeth his land by the fourth part of a knight's fee, ought to be with the king ten

95 *Escuage est appelle en Latine* scutagium, *i. e.* servitium scuti. *Et tiel tenaunt qui tient sa terre per escuage, tient per service de chivaler. Et auxi il est commenement dit, que ascun tient per un fee de service de chivaler, et ascun per le moyte dun fee de service de chivaler, &c. Et il est dit, que quant le roy face voyage royal en Escoce pur subduer les Scottes, donques il qui tient per un fee de service de chivaler, covient estre ove le roy per* xl. *jours, bien et convenablement arraye pur le guerre. Et celuy qui tient sa terre per le moyté dun fee per service de chivaler, covient estre ovesque le roy per* xx. *jours. Et il qui tient sa terre per le quart part dun fee per service de chivaler,*

(*b*) The *Olde Tenures* are very explicit as to the origin of this service; and Plowden reports, that it was invented on every occasion of the king making a 'voyage royal' against the Welsh, as it was when he made a 'voyage royal' against the Scots; for being within the sea, they were accounted as rebels.—*Plowd.* 126, 129. It seems to have been considered, that Scotland is only put for an example; for that if the tenure be in Wales, Ireland, Gascony, Poictou, &c., it is all one.—*Wright's Tenures*, 124. The meaning of the word *voyage* seems to have been a military expedition; and as taken in that sense, this word occurs in *Judith*, c. 2, v. 19.

days, and so he that hath more, more, and he that hath less, less. 96 But it appeareth by the pleas and arguments made in a good plea upon writ of detinue of a writing obligatory, brought by one Henry Gray, Trin. 7 E. 3, that it is not needful for him who holdeth by escuage to go himself, if he will find another able person for him conveniently arrayed for the war to go with the king. And this seemeth to be good reason. For it may be that he who holdeth by such services is languishing, so as he can neither go nor ride. And also an abbot, or other man of religion, or a feme sole, who hold by such services, ought not in such case to go in proper person. And Sir William Herle, then chief justice of the Common Pleas, said in this plea, that escuage shall not be granted but where the king goes himself in his proper person (*c*).

Service by a sufficient deputy adjudged sufficient.

Dictum *of Sir W. Herle, (see note,* infra).

covient estre ovesque le roy per x. *jours, et issint qui plus, plus, et qui minus, minus.* 96 *Mes il appiert per les pleez et argumentz faitz en un bon plee sur brief de detenue de un escript obligatorie, port per un Henry Gray, Anno* vii. *E.* iii., *quil ne besoigne a celuy qui tient per escuage de aler luy mesme, sil voilloit trover un autre person pur luy convenablement arraye pur le guerre de aler ovesque le roy. Et ceo semble estre bon reason: qar puist estre que celuy qui tient per tielx services est languissaunt, issint quil ne puist aler ne chivaucher. Et auxi un abbe, ou autre home de religion, ou feme soule que tient per tielx services, ne doit en tiel cas aler en propre persone. Et Sir William Herle, adonques chief justice de le comen bank disoit en tiel plee, que escuage ne serra graunte, mes lou le roy alast luy mesme en son propre persone.*

(*c*) Mr. Madox observes, that Sir William Herle's position, that escuage should not be granted but where the king goes to the war in person, is fallacious.—*Mad. Baron. Angl.* 226.

And so it abode in judgment in the same plea, whether the forty days should be accounted from the first day of the muster of the king's host made by the commons (*d*), and by the commandment of the king, or else from the day that the king first entereth into Scotland. *Therefore inquire of this.*

Computation of time as to tenants' attendance.

97 And after such voyage royal into Scotland it is commonly said, that, by authority of parliament, the escuage shall be assessed and put in certain, *viz.* a certain sum of money, [how much*] every one which holdeth by a whole

Escuage for non attendance to be assessed by parliament, [no assessment ever made since 8 R. 2.]

Et fuist demurre en juggement en mesme le plee, si les xl. *jours serront accomptez de le jour de le muster de host le roy, fait per les comens* (*d*), *et per commaundement le roy, ou de le jour que le roy primes entra en Escoce.* Ideo quære de hoc.

97 *Et apres tiel voyage royal en Escoce, il est comenement dit, que per auctorité de parlĕment, lescuage serra assesse et mys en certeyn,* scil. *certeyne somme dargent,* [*quant**] *chescun*

---

* *Roh.* reads this word *qar*—*for.*

(*d*) This word, which in every printed copy reads *commons*, is a corruption (by means of a well-known abbreviation) from *commissioners;* which is very evident by Sir Edward Coke's comment on the word *muster* in this same paragraph, viz.

"I find this word in the statute of 18 Hen. 8, c. 19, and the ancient military order is worthy of observation; for before and long after that statute, when the king was to be served with soldiers for his war, a knight or esquire of the country, that had revenues, farmers, and tenants, would covenant with the king by indenture enrolled in the Exchequer, to serve the king for such a term with so many men (especially named in a list) in his war, &c. An excellent institution that they should serve under him whom they knew and honoured, and with whom they must live at their return: these men being mustered before the king's *commissioners*, and receiving any part of their wages, and their names so recorded, if they after departed from their captain within the term, contrary to the form of that statute, it was felony. But now that statute is of no force, because that ancient and excellent form of military course is altogether antiquated; but later statutes have provided for that mischief."—*Co. Lytt.* 71. *a.*

Tenure by escuage to pay certain proportions or aliquot parts of sum so to be assessed, on account of the uncertainty, is deemed knight's service, secus, of escuage certain, see § 120.

knight's fee, who was neither by himself nor by any other with the king, shall pay to his lord of whom he holds his land by escuage. As put the case that it was ordained by authority of parliament, that every one which holdeth by a whole knight's fee, who was not with the king, shall pay to his lord xl*s*., then he who holdeth by the half of a knight's fee shall pay to his lord but xx*s*., and he who holdeth by the fourth part of a knight's fee shall pay but x*s*.; and so who more, more; and who less, less. 98 And some hold by the custom, that if escuage run by authority of parliament to any sum of money, they shall pay but the moiety of that sum, and some but the fourth part of that sum. But because the escuage that they should pay is uncertain, for that it is not certain how the parliament will assess the escuage, they hold by knight's service. But otherwise it is of escuage certain, of which shall be spoken in the tenure of socage. 99 And if one speak generally of escuage, it shall be intended by common speech of escuage

qui tient per entier fee de service de chivaler quil ne fuist per luy mesme ne per un autre pur luy ovesque le roy, paiera a son seignour de qui il tient sa terre per escuage. Sicome mettomus, quil fuist ordeigne per auctorité de parlëment, que chescun qui tient per entier fee per service de chivaler, qui ne fuist ovesque le roy, paiera a son seignour xl*s*., *donques celuy qui tient per le moite dun fee per service de chivaler ne paiera a son seignour forsque* xx*s*. *et celuy qui tient per la quart partie de fee per service de chivaler ne paiera forsque* x*s*., *et sic qui plus, plus, et qui minus, minus.* 98 *Et ascuns tenauntes teignount que si lescuage courge per auctorité de parlëment a ascun somme de moneye, quils ne paieront forsque la moite de ceo, et ascuns teignount quils ne paieront forsque la quart partie de ceo. Mes pur ceo que lescuage quils paieront est noncerteyne pur ceo quil est noncerteyne coment le parlëment voet assesser lescuage, ils teignount per service de chivaler. Mes autrement est de lescuage certeyne, de que serra parle en le tenure per socage.* 99 *Et si home parle generalment descuage, il serra entendus per la comen parlaunce descuage en*

uncertain, which is knight's service: And such escuage draweth to it homage, and homage draweth to it fealty; for fealty is incident to every manner of service, unless it be to the tenure in frankalmoigne, as shall be said afterward in the tenure of frankalmoigne. And so he who holdeth by escuage holds by homage, fealty, and escuage. 100 And it is to be understood, that, when escuage is so assessed by authority of parliament, every lord of whom the land is holden by escuage, shall have the escuage so assessed by parliament, because it is intended by the law, that, at the beginning, such tenements were given by the lords to the tenants to hold by such services, to defend their lords as well as the king, and to put in quiet their lords and the king from the Scots aforesaid. 101 And because such tenements came first from the lords, it is reason that they should have the escuage of their tenants. And the lords in such case may distrain for the escuage so assessed, or they [in some cases*] may have the

Incidents of escuage, see § 131, 135.

Fealty incident to every service but frankalmoigne, (§ 135, 138).

The lords entitled to have the escuage, when so assessed, of their tenants;

—and to distrain for the same or levy

noncerteyne, que est service de chivaler, et tiel escuage treit a luy homage, et homage treit a luy fealté; qar fealte est incident a chescun maner de service, forspris le tenure en frankalmoigne, come serra dit en apres en le tenure de frankalmoigne. Et issint il qui tient per escuage, tient per homage, fealté et escuage. 100 *Et est assavoir, que quant escuage est tielment assesse per auctorité de parlëment chescun seignour de qui la terre est tenus per escuage, avera lescuage issint assesse per parlëment, pur ceo que il est entendus per la ley, que a commencement, tielx tenementes furent donez per lez seignours a lez tenaunts de tener per tielx services a defendre lour seignours, auxi come le roy, et metter en quiete lour seignours et le roy, de les Scottes avauntdits;* 101 *Et pur ceo que tielx tenementes deviendront primez dez seignours, il est reason quils averont lescuage de lour tenauntes. Et lez seignours en tiel cas purront distreigner pur lescuage issint assesse, ou ils [en ascuns cases*] purront aver brief le roy, directz as viscontz*

---

* The words between brackets are an interpolation; they only appear in the later editions, and are not in *Rastell's* Transl.

by writ directed to the sheriff.

Of tenants in capite, *the king alone has the escuage.*

If tenant be unduly assessed where he had been with the king, it is to be tried by certificate of the constable of the host.

king's writs directed to the sheriffs of the same counties, &c., to levy such escuage for them, as it appeareth by the Register. But of such tenants as hold of the king by escuage, which were not with the king in Scotland, the king himself shall have the escuage.

102 Item, in such case aforesaid, where the king maketh a voyage royal into Scotland, and the escuage is assessed by parliament, if the lord distrain his tenant that holdeth of him by service of a whole knight's fee for the escuage so assessed &c., and the tenant pleadeth, and will aver that he was with the king in Scotland &c., by forty days, and the lord will aver the contrary, it is said, that it shall be tried by the certificate (*e*) of the constable of the king's host in writ-

de mesme lez countees, &c., de lever tiel escuage pur eux, sicome appiert per le registre. Mes de tielx tenauntes queux teignount de roy per escuage, queux ne fueront ovesque le roy en Escoce, le roy mesme avera lescuage.

102 Item, *en tiel cas avauntdit, lou le roy face un voyage royall en Escoce, et lescuage est assesse per parlement, si le seignour distreigne son tenaunt qui tient de luy per service dentier fee de chivaler pur lescuage issint assesse, &c., et le tenaunt pleda, et voet averrer que il fuit ovesque le roy in Escoce, &c., per* xl. *jours, et le seignour voet averrer le contrarie, il est dit, que ceo serra trie per le certificacion de con-*

(*e*) Baron Gilbert in his *Historical View of the Court of Exchequer*, notices, that "these certificates were generally before the division of the courts; and, therefore, when Lyttleton says that the certificate was sent to the justices, it seems to be a mistake in the printer; and that the certificate was sent to the *justiciar* and barons, under the seal of the marshal of the king's host; and so a *distringas* went out of the *Exchequer*, from the *justiciar* and barons, to distrain all the defaulters; and if any body was distrained where he had served, he might appear at the return of the *distringas*, and plead that he was *in servitio regis*, and [this] was to be tried by such indented certificate, remaining before the *justiciar* and barons, and nothing else. *Mad.* 468."

ing under his seal, [which shall be sent to the justices*], &c.

stable de le host le roy en escript southe son seale [que serra mys a les justices], &c.*

CONCLUDING REMARKS.

ESCUAGE was a service, but not personal, it consisting in the payment of a pecuniary aid or contribution in lieu of personal service, the better to enable the lord to bear the expense of his attendance upon the king, when he should have occasion to correct the Scotch or Welsh, or even foreign provinces of which he was lord, who were not so much deemed enemies as rebels. In this sense, it corresponds to the Norman *aide de l'ost*, mentioned in the *Custumier*, which some tenants who held *fiefs de Hautbert* were bound to perform; and this sum was not to be levied *devant que le prince leur ait ottroie le quantite de l'aide du fief*, which is the same as the assessment Lyttleton alludes to. In his time, however, it seems to have been considered a sort of mulct or penalty for defect of service on these occasions, which had, from lapse of time, settled into or become a mere matter of composition and agreement between the lord and his tenants, which last had to raise among themselves what the lord was assessed to pay. So

---

* In *Lettou & M.*, this concluding passage reads thus—*que ceo serra trie per le certificacion de constable de le host le roy en escript' south son seale, &c.* In *Machl.*, the "*&c.*" after *seale* is supplied by the words, *que serra mys a les justices.* In *Roh.*, *que ceo serra trie per le certificacion del mareschall hostell le roy en escript southe son seale que serra mys a lez justic';* and with this last reading agrees *Redm.*, *Berth.*, *ed.* 1671, and some other copies. The word *hostel* for *host*, may be deemed a corruption. The common copies, and *Sir Edward Coke's* Transl. read *marshal* for *constable;* while *Rastell's* Transl. gives *constable. Hostel, household,* does not occur in the common copies.

that, instead of paying an uncertain sum according to the parliamentary allowance or grant of escuage, which was escuage uncertain, the sum was ascertained and fixed; and because it discharged the tenants from all military service, such tenants are regarded as tenants in socage, and not deemed tenants by knight's service (§ 98, 120).

There seems some doubt whether tenant by escuage held by knight's service, in the strict sense of the word, although Lyttleton says in § 95, "*et tiel tenaunt qui tient sa terre per escuage tient per service de chivaler,*" or whether escuage was to be deemed, by reason of the occasion of its payment, a military tenure. Sir Martin Wright observes, that the ancient law writers have not so clearly distinguished them as might be wished; and he refers to a similar description of grand serjeanty, by Lyttleton (§ 158), where serjeanty, which is not a personal service, yet was deemed military by reason of the nature of the render.

The word *scutagium* is not known to foreign feudists, although the system of commuting military service for money was well known, and frequently alluded to in their books. Madox (Hist. Excheq. 432, *in margine*), notes that the word was used apart from tenure, to signify any payment assessed upon knights' fees, whether such payment was for the king's army or not; and that circumstance may perhaps account for knight's service being defined as a tenure by homage, fealty, and escuage (§ 103).

Escuage was expressly abolished by stat. 12 Car. 2, c. 24.

CHAPTER IV.

KNIGHT'S SERVICE (*a*).

In the present chapter, Lyttleton introduces his reader to the military tenure termed knight's service, or the tenure of a knight's fee, to which he names three leading incidents—wardship, marriage, and relief, matters formerly of great profit to lords. The discourse on these three subjects, which were the soul of this oppressive tenure, occupies the whole of this chapter, with the exception of *Castle-guard* (§ 111), about which some difference of opinion seems always to have prevailed.

(*a*) To holde by knightes service is to holde by homage, fealty, and escuage; and it draweth to it warde, marriage, and reliefe; and knowe thou, that knightes service is service of landes or tenementes, to beare armes in warre in the defence of the realme; and it oweth warde and marriage by reason that none is able nor of power, nor may have knowledge to beare armes before that he be of the age of twenty-one yeres. And forsomuch that the lord shall not leese that that of right he ought to have, and that the power of the realme nothing be made weake, the law willeth, because of his tender age, that the lord him shal have in his warde, till the full age of him, that is to say, twenty-one yeres.—*Olde Tenures*, § 1.

In *Rastell's* Transl., this chapter is intituled Homage, Fealty, and Escuage, from the six first words of the chapter.

Wardship in chivalry and age of marriage.

Heir male.

103 TENURE by homage, fealty, and escuage, is to hold by knight's service, and it draweth to it ward, marriage, and relief (*b*). For when such tenant dieth, his heir male being

103 *Tenure per homage, fealté, et escuage, est tener per service de chivaler, et treit a luy garde, mariage, et reliefe. Qar quant tiel tenaunt morust, son heire male esteaunt deins*

(*b*) Though guardianship in *chivalry* is now taken away by act of parliament, it may be useful to recollect some *general* things concerning it; and for the ease of the student in that respect, the following particulars, selected principally from the chapter of knight's service, are brought into one point of view:—Guardianship in chivalry could only be where the estate vested in the infant by *descent.*—All *males* under twenty-one at the ancestor's death were liable to it; but not *females*, unless they were then under fourteen.—It extended, not only to the *person* of the infant, but also to all such of the infant's *lands* or *tenements* as were within the guardian's seigniory; and if the king was guardian in respect of a tenure *in capite*, then to the *whole* of the infant's estate, of whomsoever holden, whatever the tenure, and whether lying in tenure or not.—If the infant heir held lands by knight's-service of several lords, each lord had the wardship of the land within his seigniory; and as to the body, the wardship of it belonged to that lord, of whom the tenure was most ancient, he being styled the lord by *priority*, and the others lords by *posteriority* (§ 103). But this must be understood with an exception of the king; for if any of the land of the infant were holden of the king by knight's service *in capite*, he was entitled to the wardship both of the infant's body and all his lands held of the crown *in capite*, or of others by knight's service.—It continued over males till *twenty-one*, over females till *sixteen* or *marriage.*—When it determined, if the tenure was of a *subject*, the heir might enter on the lord *immediately;* but if the king had the wardship, then the heir was not entitled to take possession of the land without suing to the crown for livery, which was a process both nice and expensive. It had a preference with respect to the custody of the infant's body over every other species of wardship, except only that of the *father*, where the infant was his *heir apparent;* even the *mother* being excluded (§ 114).—It entitled the lord to make a sale of the marriage of the infant, subject only to

within the age of twenty-one years, the lord shall have the land holden of him until the age of the heir of twenty-

lage de xxi. *ans, le seignour avera la terre tenus de luy tanques al age del heire de* xxi. *ans, lequel est appelle plein*

---

the restriction of not *disparaging;* and if the infant refused the marriage tendered by the lord, or married *after* such a tender and against the lord's consent; in the former case, the infant was liable to the payment of a sum equal to the value of the marriage, that is, to the profit which the lord might have made by the sale of it, [or in the words of Blackstone, so much as a jury would assess, or any one would *bonâ fide* give to the guardian for such an alliance]; in the latter case, the heir *female* paid the same sum as for a refusal, but the heir *male* was charged the *double* value, which was called a forfeiture of marriage (§ 110).—The guardian in chivalry was not accountable for the profits made of the infant's land during the wardship, but received them for his own private emolument, subject only to the *bare* maintenance of the infant. At least it doth not appear in any work we have seen, what means were provided for enforcing the guardian out of the profits of the estate in wardship, to support and educate the infant in a style and manner suitable to his rank and fortune.—Lastly, guardianship in chivalry, being deemed more an *interest* for the *profit* of the *guardian* than a *trust* for the *benefit* of the *ward*, was saleable and transferable, like the ordinary subjects of property, to the best bidder, and if not disposed of, was transmissible to the lord's personal representatives (§ 116). Thus the custody of the infant's person, as well as the care of his estate, might be devolved upon the most perfect *stranger* to the infant, one prompted by every pecuniary motive to abuse the delicate and important trust of education, without any ties of blood or regard to counteract the temptations of interest, or any sufficient authority to restrain him from yielding to their influence.—*Hargr. in n. Co. Lytt.* 74. *b.*

John Rastell, the printer and lawyer, in his *Olde Termes de la Ley*, written *temp.* Hen. 8, under the title *Gardeine*, after noticing the distinction between guardian in right and guardian in deed (see *post*, § 116), says—" And this gardein in deed may grant the heir to another also, but that other is not properly called gardein in deed, for that is the grantee of the gardein in right only; and here you may see, (brother Nicholas), what misery followeth the tenure by knight's service, if the tenant dyeth, leaving his heir within age, how the

one years, the which is called full age, because such heir by intendment of the law is not able to do such knight's service before his age of twenty-one years.

Marriage. Heir male.

And also if such heir be not married at the time of the death of his ancestor, then the lord shall have the wardship and marriage of him.

age, pur ceo que tiel heire per entendement del ley nest pas able de faire tiel service de chivaler, devaunt lage de xxi. *ans.*

Et auxi si tiel heire ne soit marie al temps de mort de tiel auncestre, donques le seignour avera la gurde et le mariage de luy.

---

poor child may be tossed and tumbled, chopped and changed, bought and sold like a jade in Smithfield; and what is more, married to whom it pleaseth his gardein, whereof ensue many evils.—*Fol.* 98, *ed.* 1579.

Although the evils of wardship were great, yet they were tolerated on account of its being evaded by sundry devices; and the Stat. of Wills, 32 Hen. 8, c. 1, gave the power of devising so as to deprive the lord of the wardship, so far as regarded two-thirds of the land devised; in which contracted state (as Mr. Hargrave notices), this odious species of guardianship was suffered to languish till abolished by the stat. 12 Car. 2, c. 24.

32 Hen. 8, c. 1, amended by 34 H. 8, c. 5.

If the heir on the death of his ancestor was of full age, he was stripped of the first emoluments arising from his inheritance, by way of *relief* and *primer seisin;* and, if under age, of the whole of his estate during infancy. And then, as Sir Thomas Smith very feelingly complains, "when he came to his own, after he was out of *wardship*, his woods decayed, houses fallen down, stock wasted and gone, lands let forth and ploughed to be barren," to make amends, he was yet to pay half a year's profits as a fine for suing out his *livery;* and also the price or value of his *marriage*, if he refused such wife as his lord and guardian had bartered for, and imposed upon him; or twice that value, if he married another woman. Add to this, the untimely and expensive honour of *knighthood*, to make his poverty more completely splendid. And when by these deductions his fortune was so shattered and ruined, that perhaps he was obliged to sell his patrimony, he had not even that poor privilege allowed him, without paying an exorbitant fine for a *licence* of *alienation*.—B. C. ii. 76.

But if such tenant dieth, his heir female being of the age of fourteen years or more, then the lord shall not have the wardship of the land, nor of the body, because that a woman of such age may have a husband able to do knight's service; but if such heir female be within the age of fourteen years, unmarried at the time of the death of her ancestor, then the lord shall have the wardship of the land holden of him until the age of such heir female of sixteen years. For it is given by the statute of Westm. 1, [c. 22], that by two years next ensuing the said fourteen years, the lord may tender a convenable marriage without disparagement to such heir female. And if the lord within the said two years do not tender such marriage, &c., then she at the end of the said two years may enter, and put out her lord. But if such heir female be married within the age of fourteen years in the life of her ancestor, and her ancestor dieth, she being within the age of fourteen years, the lord shall have only the wardship of the land until the end of the fourteen years of age of such heir female, and then her hus-

Heir female.

Two years after fourteen given by Westm. 1, c. 22, for tender of marriage.

If married before fourteen, wardship only extends to land till that age.

Mez si tiel tenaunt devie, son heire female esteaunt dage de xiiij. *ans, ou de pluis, donques le seignour navera my la garde de terre ne de corps, pur ceo que feme de tiel age poet aver baron able de faire le service de chivaler. Mes si tiel heire female soit deins lage de* xiiij. *ans, nient marie al temps de la mort son auncestre, donques le seignour avera la garde de la terre, tenus de luy, tanques al age de tiel heire female de* xvi. *ans, pur ceo quil est done per lestatute de Westminstre premier* [cap. 22], *que per* ii. *ans proschein ensuantz les dits* xiiij. *ans, le seignour poet tendre convenable mariage sauns desparagement a tiel heire female. Et si le seignour deins les dits* ii. *ans ne luy tendra tiel mariage, &c., donques ele a la fyn des dits* ii. *ans, poet entrer et ouster son seignour. Mes si tiel heire female soit marie deins lage de* xiiij. *ans en la vie son auncestre, et son auncestre devie, ele esteaunt deins lage de* xiiij. *ans, le seignour avera forsque la garde de la terre, jusques al fyn de* xiiij. *ans dage de tiel heire female, et donques son baron et luy poient entrer en la terre et ouster*

band and she may enter into the land, and oust the lord: for this is out of the case of the said statute, inasmuch as the lord cannot tender marriage to her which is married, &c. For before the said statute of Westm. 1, such issue female, who was within the age of fourteen years at the time of the death of her ancestor, and after she had accomplished the age of fourteen years, without any tender of marriage by the lord unto her, such heir female might then enter into the land, and oust the lord, as appeareth by the rehearsal and words of the said statute; so as the said statute was made (as it seemeth) in such case altogether for the advantage of lords. But yet this is always intended by the words of the same statute, that the lord shall have the two years after the fourteen years, as is aforesaid, [but only where such heir female is within the age of fourteen years, and unmarried at the time of the death of her ancestor*].

Tenure by

[Also, if a man holds a manor of another by knight's ser-

le seignour: qar ceo est hors de cas de le dit estatute, entaunt que le seignour ne poet tendre mariage a luy qui est marie, &c. Qar devaunt le dit estatute Westminstre premier, tiel issue female que fuist deins age de xiiij. *ans, al temps de mort son auncestre, et puis quele avoit accomplis lage de* xiiij. *ans, sauns ascun tendre de mariage per le seignour a luy, tiel heire female adonques puissoit entrer en le terre, et ouster le seignour, sicome appiert per le rehersail et parolx de le dit estatute; issint que le dit estatute de Westminstre premier fuist fait en tiel cas, tout pur lavantage de seignours, come il semble. Mes unquore ceo toutfoitz est entendue per les parolx de mesme lestatute que le seignour avera les deux ans apres les* xiiij. *ans, come est avauntdit, [mes lou tiel heire female soit deins lage de* xiiij. *ans, nient marie a temps de mort son auncestre*].*

[Item, *si un home tient un manor de un autre per service de*

---

* The words within brackets are not in *Rastell's* Transl. *Roh.* makes these words a separate sentence; they are surplusage, and consequently may be deemed apocryphal.

vice, and he holds another manor of another man by the same service, but holds one manor by priority, &c., and the other manor by posteriority, and has issue a daughter, and dies, and the manors descend to the daughter then being within the age of fourteen years, and the lord of whom one of the manors is held by priority seizes the wardship of the body of the heir and of the manor held of him, and the other lord seizes the wardship of the other manor held of him; in this case, when the daughter comes to the age of fourteen years, she shall enter on the manor held by posteriority although she be then unmarried.

priority and posteriority. (*See* **ante, p. 136** *in n.*)

For the words of the same stat. of Westm. 1, are in the form which followeth:—

And of heirs female after they have accomplished the age of fourteen years, and the lord (to whom the marriage belongeth) will not marry them, but from coveitise of the land will keep them unmarried: it is provided, that the lord shall not have nor keep, by reason of the marriage, the lands of such heirs female more than two years after the term of the

chivaler, et il tient autre manor de un autre home per un tiel service, mes il tient lun manor per priorite, &c., et lauter manor per posteriorite, et ad issue file, et devie, et les manors descendont al file adonques esteant deins lage de xiiij. *auns, et le seignour de qui un des manors est tenus per priorite, seisit la garde del corps del heire et de le manor tenus de luy, et lautre seignour seisit la garde del autre manor tenus de luy, en cest cas, quaunt la file vient al age de* xiiij. *ans, ele entrera en le manor tenus per posteriorite coment que ele soit adonques desmarie. Qar les parolx de mesme lestatute de Westm. primer sount en tiel fourme que ensuyst:—*

Les heires femels puisque eles avyrount complies age de xiiij. *ans, et le seignour a qui le mariage appent celes ne voudra marier, mes per coveitise de la terre celes voudra tener dismariez: Purview est que le seignour ne puis aver ne tener per encheson de le mariage les terres de celes heires femels outre deux ans apres le terme des avauntdits* xiiij. *ans, &c.,*

said fourteen years &c.; by which words it may be proved, that, after the age of fourteen years no one shall have the lands in such case &c., except him to whom the marriage belongs &c.; and because such marriage does not belong to him of whom the land is held by posteriority &c., such heir female, when she comes to the age of fourteen years, may well enter on such land which is thus held by posteriority, &c.*]

Age of marriage at common law, see § 259.

Age of discretion.

Guardian in chivalry to have marriage of his ward but once.

104 Note well, that full age of male and female, according to common speech, is said the age of twenty-one years. And the age of discretion is called the age of fourteen years. For at this age, the infant which is married within such age to a woman may agree or disagree to the marriage. 105 And if the guardian in chivalry doth once marry the ward within the age of fourteen years, and if afterward at his age of fourteen years he disagree to the marriage, it is said by some, that the infant is not holden by the law to be again married by his guardian, for that the guardian had once the marriage of him, and

per queux parolx il poet estre prove que apres les xiiij. *ans nul doit aver les terres en tiel cas, &c., forsque celuy a qui le mariage appent, &c., et pur ceo que tiel mariage nappent a celuy de qui la terre est tenus per posteriorite, &c., tiel heire femel quant ele vient al age de* xiiij. *ans poet bien entrer en tiel terre que issint est tenus per posteriorite &c.**]

104 *Nota, que pleyn age de male et female, solonques le comen parlaunce, est dit lage de* xiiij. *ans. Et lage de discrecion est dit lage de* xiiij. *ans, qar a tiel age lenfaunt qui est mari deins tiel age a un feme, poet agreer a le mariage, ou disagreer.* 105 *Et si le gardeyn en chivalerie maria un foitz le gard deins lage de* xiiij. *ans, et puis sil al age de* xiiij. *ans disagrea a le mariage, il est dit per ascuns, que lenfaunt nest pas tenus per la ley destre autrefoitz marie per son gardeyn, pur ceo que le gardeyn avoit un foitz le mariage de*

---

* The portion of the text within brackets is taken from the Year-Book, 35 Hen. 6, (52) (first printed by *Machlinia*), and occurs only in *Lettou & M.*, and the Paper MS.

therefore he was out of his ward as concerning the ward of his body. And when he had once the marriage of him, and he was once out of his wardship, he shall no more have the marriage of him. [Inquire of this*.] 106 In the same manner it is, if the guardian marry him, and the wife die, the infant being within the age of fourteen years, or twenty-one years. 107 And that such infant may disagree to such marriage [when he comes to the age of†] fourteen years, it is proved by the words of the statute of Merton, [c. 6], which saith thus:—"Concerning lords who shall have married those whom "they have in ward, to villeins, or others, as to burgesses, "whereby they be disparaged, if such heir shall be within "fourteen years, and of such age that he was not able to "consent to such marriage, then if his cousins complain, "let that lord lose that wardship until the lawful age of the "heir; and let all advantage that thereof was perceived be

If guardian disparage his ward by an improper marriage he is to lose the wardship.

luy, et pur ceo il fuist hors de sa garde, quant al garde de son corps. Et quant il avoit un foitz le mariage de luy et un foitz fuist hors de sa garde, il navera pluis avaunt le mariage de luy. [Quære de hoc*.] *En mesme le manere est, si le gardeyn luy maria, et la feme devie esteaunt lenfaunt deins lage de* xiiij. *ans, ou* xxi. *ans.* 107*Et que tiel enfaunt poet disagreer a tiel mariage,* [*quant il vient al age de*†] xiiij. *ans, il est prove per les parolx del estatute de Merton,* [*cap.* 6], *que issint dit:—"De dominis qui maritaverint illos quos habent in custodia, villanis, "vel aliis, sicut burgensibus ubi disparagentur, si talis hæres "fuerit infra* xiiij. *annos, et talis ætatis quod matrimonio "consentire non poterit, tunc si parentes illi conquerantur, "dominus ille amittat custodiam illam usque ad legitimam "ætatem hæredis; et omne commodum quod inde perceptum*

---

* This *quære* occurs only in *Lettou & M.* By this it appears that *Lettou & M.* has two *quæres*, at least, not found in *Machl.* or *Roh.*, for the *quære* at § 35, is in *Lettou & M.* only.

† The words within brackets are supplied by the word *deins—within*, in *Lettou & M.*

" applied for the benefit of him who is within age, according " to the disposal and providing of his cousins for the shame " put upon him. But if he was of fourteen years and above, " so that he was able to consent, and shall have consented " to such marriage, no penalty shall ensue." And so it is proved by the same statute, that there is no disparagement, but where he which is in ward is married within the age of fourteen years.

Comment upon the words of the Statute of Merton.

108 Also it hath been a question, how these words shall be understood. (*Si parentes* (c) *conquerantur*). ‖ And it seemeth to some, that, [considering*] the statute of *Magna Charta,* which willeth, *Quod hæredes maritentur absque disparagatione, &c.,* upon which, this statute of Merton upon this point is founded as it seemeth, and insomuch that it was never seen [or heard†], that any action was brought upon the sta-

" *fuerit convertatur in commodum ipsius qui infra ætatem est,* " *secundum dispositionem et provisionem parentum propter de-* " *decus ei impositum. Si autem fuerit* xiiij. *annorum et ul-* " *tra, quod consentire poterit, et tali maritagio consenserit,* " *nulla sequatur pœna. Et issint il est prove per mesme le-statute, que nul desparagement est, mes lou cestuy qui est en garde est mari deins lage de* xiiij. *ans.*

108 Item, *il soleit estre question, coment ceux parolx serroient entendus,* Si parentes conquerantur, &c. ‖ *Et il semble a ascuns que* [*consideraunt**] *lestatute de Magna Charta que voet,* Quod hæredes maritentur absque disparagatione, &c., *sur quel cel estatute de Merton sur cel point est fondus come il semble, et entaunt quil ne fuist unques viewe* [*ne oye*†] *que*

---

* *Redm.* reads *considerount—consider.*

† These words within brackets do not occur in *Rastell's* Transl.

(c) The word *parentes* signifies kindred or relations in general, according to the signification of the French word *parent;* and in this sense is the same word used in the Laws of Hen. I. c. 75.

tute of Merton for such disparaging against the guardian, &c. And if any action might have been taken upon such matter, it shall be intended [by common presumption before this time, at some time to be put in ure || that these words shall be understood] in such manner that these words should be understood thus, *Si parentes conquerantur, id est, si parentes inter eos lamententur,* which is as much as to say, if the cousins of such infant have cause to make lamentation or complaint among themselves, for the shame done to their cousin so disparaged, which is in a manner a shame to them all, then may the next cousin to whom inheritance cannot descend, enter and oust the guardian in chivalry. And if he will not, another cousin of the infant's may do this, and take the issues and profits to the use of the infant, and thereof to render an

ascun accion fuist porte sur cel estatute de Merton peur le disparagyng envers le gardeyn &c. Et si ascun accion puissoit estre pris sur tiel matere il serroit entendu [per comen presumpcion devaunt ceux heures a ascun foitz estre mise en ewre || que ceux parolx serront entendus] en tiel manere, Si parentes conquerantur, *i. e.* si parentes inter eos lamententur, *ou est a taunt adire, que si les cosyns de tiel enfaunt ount cause de faire lamentacion et compleynt entre eux pur le honte fait a lour cosyn issint disparage, quel est en manere un honte a eux, donques poet le proscheyn cosyn a qui leritage ne poet unques descendre, entrer et oustre le gardeyn en chivalerie. Et sil ne voille, un autre cosyn del enfaunt poet ceo faire, et les issues et profites prendre al use denfaunt, et de ceo rendre*

* The words and passage between the *parallels* occur in *Lettou & M.*, *Machl.*, *Roh.*, *Redm.*, *Berth.*, and in all the copies of *Rastell's* Transl. Yet in the two editions by *Tottyl* 1557, which first notice amendments of the text, by placing an *asterisk* in lieu of the expunged portion, this part of the text is excluded; and in all the subsequent editions of *Tottyl*, it is placed between two *flowers;* and is also noticed as an addition in all editions from *Tottyl* 1591 to 1639. The whole section is very questionable, for in every instance where the text is doubtful, the copies vary. The words within brackets, at the second *parallel*, appear only in *Lettou & M.*

account to the infant when he comes to his full age: or otherwise the infant within age may enter himself and oust the guardian &c. *Sed quære de hoc.*

Divers kinds of disparagements.

109 Also there be many other divers disparagements, which are not specified in the same statute. As if the heir that is in ward be married to one who hath but one foot, or but one hand, or who is deformed, decrepit, or having an horrible disease, or else great and continual infirmity. And, if he be an heir male, married to a woman past the age of child-bearing. And many other causes of disparagement there be: and inquire concerning them, for it is a good matter to learn. 110 And of heirs male which be within the age of twenty-one years after the decease of their ancestor not married, in such case the lord shall have the marriage of such heir, and have time and space to tender to him suitable marriage without disparaging within the said time of twenty-one years.

If heir refuse tender of marriage by the lord, the lord entitled to the single value of such marriage;

And it is to be understood, that the heir in such case may chuse whether he will be married or no; but if the lord, who is called guardian in chivalry, tender to such heir suitable

accompte al enfaunt, quant il vient a son pleyn age: ou autrement lenfaunt deins lage poet entrer luy mesme, et ouster le gardeyn, &c. Sed quære de hoc.

109 Item, *multes autres diverses disparagementz y sont, que ne sont especifiez en mesme lestatute. Come si leire qui est en garde est mary a un qui ad forsque un pee, ou forsque un mayn, ou qui est disfourme, decrepute, ou eiaunt horrible disease, ou graunde continuell infirmytë. Et, si leire male soit mary a feme que est passe lage denfauntere. Et multes autres cases de dysperagement y sont,* et quære de eis, *qar il est bon matere dapprendre.* 110 *Et dez heires males qui sont deins lage de* xxi. *ans aprez la mort lour auncestre nient mariez, en tiel cas le seignour avera le mariage de tiel heire, et avera temps et space de tendre a luy convenable mariage sauns disperagyng deins mesme le temps de* xxi. *ans.*

Et est assavoir, que leire en tiel cas poet eslier sil voet estre mari ou non; mes si le seignour qui est appelle gardeyn en chivalerie a tiel heire tendra convenable mariage deins lage de

marriage within the age of twenty-one years without disparaging, and the heir refuse, and doth not marry himself within the said age, then the guardian shall have the value of the marriage of such heir; but if such heir marrieth himself within the age of twenty-one years against the will of the guardian in chivalry, then the guardian shall have the double value of the marriage by force of the statute of Merton aforesaid, as in the same statute is more fully comprised.

but if heir within twenty-one marries against the lord's consent, then he forfeits the double value of the marriage.

Castle guard.

111 Also divers tenants hold of their lords by knight's service, and yet they hold not by escuage, neither shall they pay escuage. As they that hold of their lords by castle-guard (*d*); that is to say, to guard a tower of the castle of their lord, or a door, or some other place of the castle* upon reasonable

xxi. *ans sauns disperagyng, et leire ceo refusa, et ne soy mari deins le dit age donques le gardeyn avera le value de le mariage de tiel heire, mes si tiel heire luy maria deins lage de* xxi. *ans encounter la volunte le gardeyn en chivalerie, donques le gardeyn avera le double value de le mariage, et ceo est per force de lestatute de Merton avauntdit, come en mesme lestatute est compris pluis a pleyn.*

111 Item, *divers tenauntes teignount de lour seignours per service de chivaler, et unquore ils ne teignount per escuage, ne paieront escuage, come ceulx qui teignount de lour seignours per castell-garde,* scil. *a garder un toure de le chastell lour seignour, ou un huis ou un autre lieu de le chastell* per reason-*

* *Rastell's* Translation renders this passage; *to keep a tower of a castle, or a gayle, or some other place by reasonable warning.*

(*d*) To hold of the king by castle-guard, is knight's-service *in capite;* but to hold by certain rent for castle-guard, is but socage; but by F. N. B. 256 A, a tenure of the king, as of an ancient honor, by certain rent for the keeping of Dover Castle, is taken to be knight's-service *in capite;* but this seems no law.—*Ley's Wards and Liveries, pp.* 4, 5, *ed.* 1642.

warning, when their lord heareth that enemies will come or are come into England. And in many other cases a man may hold by knight's service, and yet he holdeth not by escuage, [nor shall pay escuage*], as shall be said in the tenure by grand serjeanty.

But in all cases where a man holds by knight's service, this service draweth to the lord, ward and marriage. 112 And if a tenant, who holdeth of his lord by the service of a whole knight's fee, dieth, his heir then being of full age, *i. e.* of twenty-one years, then the lord shall have 100*s.* for a relief, and of the heir of him which holds by the moiety of a knight's fee 50*s.*, and of him which holds by the fourth part of a knight's fee 25*s.*, and so he who holds more, more, and who less, less.

What relief payable by the heir of full age for one knight's fee.

113 Also a man may hold his land of his lord by the service of two knight's fees, and then the heir, being at full age at the time of the death of his ancestor, shall pay to his lord ten pounds for relief &c.

Relief for two knight's fees.

able garnissement, quant lour seignour oye que enemyes voillent vener, ou sont venus en Engleterre. Et en plusours autres cases home poet tener per service de chivaler, et unquore il ne tient per escuage [ne payera escuage], sicome sera dit en le tenure per graund serjantie.*

Mez en toutz cases lou home tient per service de chivaler, tiel service treit al seignour garde et mariage. 112 *Et si un tenaunt qui tient de son seignour per le service de entier fee de chivaler mourust, son heire donques esteant de pleyn age,* scil. *de* xxi. *ans, donques le seignour avera* c*s. pur relief, et del heire celuy qui tient per le moyte de fee de chivaler* l*s. et de celuy qui tient per le quart partie de fee de chivaler* xxv*s. et sic qui plus, plus, et qui minus, minus.*

113 Item, *home poet tener un mesme terre de son seignour per le service de deux fees de chivaler, et donques leire esteant de pleyn age al temps de mort son auncestre paiera a son seignour* x*l. pur relief &c.*

---

* The words within brackets are not in *Roh.*

Lord may have the wardship of the land; but not of the body of the heir vitâ patris.

114 Also if grandfather, mother*, and son, and the mother dieth, living the father of the son, and afterwards the grandfather, who holds his land by knight's service, dieth seised, and the land descend to the son of the mother as heir to the grandfather, who is within age: In this case, the lord shall have the wardship of the land, but not the wardship of the body of the heir, because none shall be in ward of his body to any lord, living his father, for that the father during his life shall have the marriage of his heir apparent, and not the lord. Otherwise it is where the father dieth, living the mother, where the land holden in chivalry descends to the son on the father's side &c. (*e*).

Secus, *with regard to the mother, for she is excluded from the marriage of the heir.*

Guardian in and right guardian in deed.

116 *Item,* there is guardian in right in chivalry, and guardian in deed in chivalry. Guardian in right in chivalry is,

114 Item, *si soit aiel, mere*, et fitz, et la mere morust vivaunt le pere le fitz, et puis laiel qui tient sa terre per service de chivaler moumst seisi, et la terre discendist al fitz la mere, come heire al aiel qui est deins lage : en ceo cas le seignour avera la garde de la terre, mes nemye la garde de le corps del heire, pur ceo que nul sera en garde de son corps a ascun seignour, vyvaunt son pere, pur ceo que le pere duraunt sa vie avera le mariage de son heire apparaunt, et nemye le seignour. Autrement est lou le pere est mort vivaunt la mere, lou terre tenus en chivalerie discendist al fitz de parte son pere &c.*

116 Item, *il y ad gardeyn en droit en chivalerie, et gardeyn en fait en chivalerie. Gardeyn en droit en chivalerie est,*

---

* All the editions from 1572 to 1639, read this passage, *Item, si soit aiel,* pere, *et fitz*—which is not only erroneous, but against the authority of every edition before that time, as well as *Rastell's* Transl. This corruption has kept its ground since, for it is in the ed. 1671, and in the copies of Coke's Transl. in Co. Lytt.

(*e*) An addition occurs here in the ordinary copies, which it seems of no use longer to preserve; it formed § 115, according to *West's* subdivision 1581.

where the lord by reason of his seigniory is seised of the wardship of the lands, and of the heir, *ut supra.* Guardian in deed in chivalry is, where in such case the lord after his seisin grants by deed, or without deed, the wardship of the land or of the heir, or of both, to another, by force of which grant the grantee is in possession; then is the grantee called guardian *in fait*, or guardian in deed &c.

lou le seignour per cause de sa seignourie, est seisi de garde del terre et del heire, ut supra. *Gardeyn en fait en chivalerie est, lou en tiel cas le seignour apres son seisin graunta per fait ou sauns fait la garde del terre ou del heire ou dambideux a un autre. Per force de quele graunte le graunté est en possession, donques est le graunté appel gardeyn en fait &c.*

CONCLUDING REMARKS.

THE first, most universal, and esteemed the most honorable species of tenure was that by knight's-service, called in Latin *servitium militare,* and in law-French *chivalry* or *service de chivaler,* answering to the *fief d'haubert* of the Normans (*f*), which name is expressly given it by the Mirrour:

(*f*) *Hauberticum feudum Gallica lingua vulgo dicitur pro Loricatum,* i. e. *datum vasallo ea conditione, ut ad edictum loricatus, sive cataphractus præsto sit. Nam ut Lorica Latinis proprie et minus usitate est tegmen de loro factum, quo majores in bellis utebantur, quemadmodum* Servius *scribit* 12 Æneid. *frequentissime autem pro ærea armatura integra usurpatur: sic apud Gallos* Haubert *proprie loricam anulis contextam significat, quam vulgus* Cotte de Maille *appellat, unde vetus proverbium Gallicum* De maille à maille on fait le haubergion. *Post vero integra equitis armatura eo nomine appellata est: videturque Normannicum verbum fuisse, cum in ea Galliæ parte frequentius illud verbum usurpetur: unde* Fiefs de Haubert *Feuda loricæ.*—Appendix (*de verbis feudalibus*) to *Calvins's Lexic. Jurid. fol.* 1734.

[the ancient Treatise, *Modus faciendi Homagium, &c.*, and the Customs of Kent, § 23]. This differed in very few points, as we shall presently see, from a pure and proper feud, being entirely military, and the genuine effect of the feodal establishment in England. To make a tenure by knight-service, a determinate quantity of land was necessary, which was called a knight's fee, *feodum militare;* the value of which, not only in the reign of Edward II. but also of Henry II., and therefore probably at its original in the reign of the Conqueror, was stated at 20*l. per annum;* and a certain number of these knight's fees were requisite to make up a barony. And he who held this proportion of land (or a whole fee) by knight-service, was bound to attend his lord to the wars for forty days in every year, if called upon; which attendance was his *reditus* or return, his rent or service, for the land he claimed to hold. If he held only half a knight's fee, he was only bound to attend twenty days, and so in proportion. And there is reason to apprehend, that this service was the whole that our ancestors meant to subject themselves to; the other fruits and consequences of this tenure being fraudulently superinduced, [by the subtlety and finesse of the Norman jurists], as the regular (though unforeseen) appendages of the feodal system.—B. C. ii. 62.

This tenure drew to it seven incidents; viz. aids, relief, primer seisin, wardship, marriage, fines for alienation, and escheat; all which, save wardship and marriage, appear to be necessary adjuncts and burdens to a tenure of this description: but wardship and marriage were by no means necessary incidents of a feudal tenure, but were merely a Norman custom affecting female wards; which, by mere encroachment, were made to extend to male wards, and, to make the imposition more grievous, were enforced long after the occasions which had formed the pretence for their introduction had ceased.

A distinction was also created very early between tenures of the king or *in capite*, and tenures of a common person; and although Mr. Madox observes, that the word tenant *in capite*, imports no more than *immediate* tenant, and that it may be predicated of tenant by knight-service and tenant in socage, and of a subject's tenant as well as of the king's; yet the ancient books and reports refer so frequently to this practical and then important distinction, that it may be necessary to note very precisely the difference between tenures *in capite* and tenures of inferior lords or persons; and first, the reader must be apprized that the ordinary division of tenures, so far as concerned their profits and fruits, was into knight-service and socage.

Knight-service was either *in capite* of the king, or in common knight-service:—*in capite* was of two kinds: one more special, viz. a grand serjeanty, the other, the general service. Knight-service was either of the king, as of some honor, castle, or manor, or was holden of common persons. So socage was either *in capite*, or common socage; *in capite* more special, as petty serjeanty, or else the general service. The common socage was either of the king, as of some honor, castle, or manor, which are species of *ancient demesne* and *burgage* of the king, or socage of a common person.

As to tenures *in capite*:—Tenure *in capite* by knight-service was, *properly*, where lands were holden of the person of the king and of his crown, as of a seignory itself in gross and chief above all other seignories; improperly, of him as of some ancient honor annexed to the crown.

And this description is understood as well of knight-service as of socage *in capite*.

To knight-service *in capite*, were incident not only ward, marriage, primer seisin, relief, livery, and license to alien, but the prerogative or priority of the wardships, and seisins of all other lands holden of inferior lords, whereof the tenant died seised; the king paying the rents to the *mesne* lords, by his officers appointed for that purpose.

Common knight-service of the king was where land was holden of the king as of some honor, castle, or manor, *per servitium militare*, expressly or impliedly upon the words of the grant. This tenure gave the king ward, marriage, relief, livery, but no primer seisin, nor license to alien: nor had the king thereby any prerogative to have other lands holden by the king's tenant of common persons in wardship.

Knight-service holden of a common person had incident to it, ward, marriage, and relief.

Socage *in capite* was the same as knight-service *in capite;* but the service that this tenure was known by, was, where the tenant held by certain or fixed services, not by knight-service; for all manner of services, to hold by fealty only, or by homage and fealty, or by homage, fealty and rent; fealty, whether expressed or not, being always applied as incident to every kind of service. More special socage *in capite* was petty serjeanty.

To socage *in capite* were incident relief, primer seisin, livery, and license to alien.

Common *socage* of the king, was, where land was holden of the king as of some honor, castle, or manor, by the services last mentioned; and this tenure yielded a relief but no wardship to the king, marriage, primer seisin, &c.

Socage of a common person, commonly known as *common socage,* is the tenure described by Lyttleton in the next Chapter, of which tenure all lands in England now are, in consequence of the abolition of military and other tenures *in capite.* To this tenure was incident a *relief,* the ward or guardianship of the heir being given to the next of kin, to whom the inheritance could not descend (§ 123), for the use of the infant, and this is the guardianship now subsisting, which, before the abolition of the ancient tenures, is in the books termed guardianship in socage (*g*), and upon which the present law in relation to *guardian and ward* is founded.

(*g*) Guardianship in socage is the guardianship by *nature* also alluded to in the books, which guardianship is confined by the common law to the heir apparent alone, and continues till he attain his age of twenty-one, and is not therefore to be confounded with guardianship by *nurture,* which is of all the children equally, and ceases at fourteen, in the case both of males and females.

So far as regarded the tenures *in capite,* the profits arising therefrom were carefully levied by the Crown, through its officers, termed *escheators,* one of whom, assisted by a subordinate officer, termed a *feodary,* or by commissioners appointed for this purpose, summoned a jury of twelve at least, whose inquisition was usually termed an "office," but more technically an *inquisitio post mortem;* and as these fruits of tenure formed no inconsiderable portion of the revenue, and also tended to enlarge the influence of the Crown, great oppressions and exactions were the consequence; indeed, it was by colour of inquisitions of this nature, that Henry VII. amassed so much wealth. However, in the reign of his successor, the court of wards and liveries was created (32 Hen. 8, c. 46), for the purpose of taking cognizance of all matters of this description, (previously, all matters of wardship had been decided in the superior courts), which was dissolved in the reign of Charles I. Finally by the statute 12 Car. 2, c. 24, it was enacted, "that the *court of wards and liveries,* and all *wardships, liveries, primer seisins,* and *ousterlemains,* values and forfeitures of *marriages,* by reason of any tenure of the king or others, be totally taken away. And that all fines for *alienations,* tenures by *homage, knight-service,* and *escuage,* and also *aids* for marrying the daughter or knighting the son, and all tenures of the king *in capite,* be likewise taken away. And that all sorts of tenures held of the king or others be turned into free and common socage; save only tenures in frankalmoign, copyholds, and the honorary services of grand serjeanty." The Commentaries of *Sir William Blackstone* (ii. 62, 77), give a very full account of this military tenure, with its burthensome and oppressive appendages, whereto the reader is referred for more conclusive information.

CHAPTER V.

SOCAGE (*a*).

LYTTLETON defines socage to be a certain or fixed service, to be rendered for performance of all services; so that such services do not constitute knight-service (§ 117), and he informs his reader immediately afterwards, that every tenure, which is not tenure by knight-service, is socage tenure (§ 118). The etymology and origin of the tenure is next explained; and its criterion, which is certainty of service or render, demonstrated (§ 119—122). The wardship of the infant heir, *i. e.* the right to the custody of such infant (§ 123—125), the payment of relief (§ 126—129), and the reason of fealty only being performed as a service, though of itself unproductive to the lord, concludes the Chapter.

(*a*) To hold in socage, is to hold of any lord, lands or tenementes yelding to him a certeine rent by the yeare for al maner of services. And note well, to holde by socage is not to holde by knight's-service, nor thereto belongeth warde, marriage, nor relyefe; but they shall double once their rent after the death of their auncestors, according to that that they be wont to pay to their lord*; and they shall not be over measure greved as it appeareth in the treatise of wardes and reliefes. And note well, that socage may be said in iij. maners: that is to say, socage in free tenure, socage in auncient tenure, and socage in base tenure. Socage in free tenure is to hold freely by certeine rent for all maner of services, as is before said, and of that the next kyns bodie (*le prochein amy*) shall have the warde, to whom the heritage cannot descend, till the age of xiiij. yeares; that it is to say, if the heritage come by the part of the father, they of the part of the mother shall have the ward; and contrary wise. And note wel, that if the gardein in socage do make waste, he shall not be impeached of

† *The which is in nature of a relief*, occurs in some copies.

Socage, a tenure by fixed and certain service.

117 TENURE in socage is, where the tenant holdeth of his lord his tenement by certain service for all manner of services, so that the service be not knight's service: as where a man holdeth his land of his lord by fealty and certain rent,

117 *Tenure en socage est, lou le tenaunt tient de son seignour son tenement per certeyn service pur toutz maners de services, issint que les services ne sount pas services de chivaler: Sicome lou un home tient sa terre de son seignour per fealté et*

---

waste; but he shal yelde accompte to the heire when he shall come to his full age of xxi. yeares. And see the statute of Marlbridge, *ca.* 17, for this matter*. Socage in ancient tenure is that where the people in ancient demesne helde, which use no other writ to have than the writ of right close, whych shall be determined according to the custom of the manor, and the *monstraverunt*, [for to discharge them where their lord distrayneth them for to do other service that they ought not to do, and this writ of *monstraverunt* ought to be brought agaynst the lord]; and those tenants hold at by one certain service, and these be free tenants of ancient demense†. Socage in base tenure is where a man holdeth in ancient demesne, that may not have the *monstraverunt*, and for that it is called base tenure.—*Olde Tenures*, § 13.

To hold in fee ferme, is to hold in fee-simple, yielding to the lord the value, or at least the fourth part, by the yeare, and he ought to do no other things but as it is conteined in the feffement, and he that holdeth in fee ferme ought to do feeltie and not reliefe‡.—*Olde Tenures*, § 14.

* Some copies add, *Quære, if he shall have action of account within the age of twenty-one years.* The words between brackets, also, are transposed to *socage in base tenure*, and are inserted after the third *monstraverunt*.

† Some copies read this sentence thus:—*Socage in ancient tenure is to hold in ancient demesne, where no writ runneth, but only the little writ of right close, which is called secundum consuetudinem manerii.* After the words within brackets, in some copies transposed to the second division of the section, such copies read as a conclusion to the sentence, *and these tenants hold not by any certain services, and for this they are not free tenants (frank tenauntz.)*

‡ Some copies add the following reference—*Come l'oppynyon Anno* 45 *E.* 3.

for all manner of services; or else where a man holdeth his land by homage and fealty for all manner of services; for homage by itself maketh not knight's service.

[118] Also a man may hold of his lord by fealty only, and such tenure is tenure in socage; for every tenure which is not tenure in chivalry is a tenure in socage. [119] And it is said that the reason why such tenure is called, and hath the name of tenure in socage, is this:—because *Socagium idem est quod servitium socæ, et hæc soca, socæ, idem est quod caruca, &c., i. e.* a soke or a plough*. And in ancient time, before the limitation of time of memory, great part of the tenants, that held of their lords by socage, ought to come with their ploughs, every of the said tenants for certain days in the year, to eare and sow the demesnes of the lord; and for that such works were done for the livelihood and sustenance of their lords, they were quit against their lords of all manner

Every tenure not in chivalry is socage, *see* § 119.
Etymology of socage.

See post, *as to limitation,* § 170.

per certeyn rent pur toutz maners de services, ou lou home qui tient per homage et fealté pur toutz maners de services; qar homage per soy ne fait pas service de chivaler.

[118] Item, *home poet tenir de son seignour per fealté tantum, et tiel tenure est tenure en socage. Qar chescun tenure que nest pas tenure in chivalerie, est tenure en socage;* [119] *et il est dit que la cause pur que tiel tenure est dit et ad le nome de tenure en socage, est ceo:* Quia hoc socagium idem est quod servitium socæ, et hæc soca, socæ, idem est quod caruca, scil. *un soke ou un charewe. Et en auncien temps devant le limitacion de temps de memorie graunde partie de lez tenauntz qui tiendrount de lour seignours per socage, devoient vener ovesque lour sokes, chescun de lez ditz tenauntz per certeyn jours per an pur arrer et semer les demeynes le seignour; et pur ceo que tielx overages furent faits pur le vivere et sustenaunce de lour seignours, ils furent quitez envers lour seignours, de toutz autrez maners de services, &c. Et pur ceo*

---

* *Rastell's* Translation renders these words—*one sok or one ploughland.*

of services &c. And, because that such services were done with their ploughs, this tenure was called tenure in socage. And afterwards these services were changed into money by the consent of the tenants, and by the desire of the lords, *viz.* into an annual rent &c. But yet the name of socage remaineth, and in divers places the tenants yet do such services with their ploughs to their lords; so that all manner of tenures which are not tenures by knight's service, are called tenures in socage.

Socage and escuage distinguished, see § 98.

120 Also if a man hold of his lord by escuage certain, *i. e.* in such form that when escuage runneth and is assessed by parliament to a greater or lesser sum, that the tenant shall pay to his lord but half a mark for escuage, and no more nor less, to how great a sum or to how little a sum the escuage runneth and is assessed &c. [in this case because the sum that he shall pay for escuage is in certainty before that any escuage be assessed*], such tenure is tenure in socage, and not

que tielx services furent faits ovesque lour sokez, tiel tenure fuist appelle tenure en socage. Et puis apres tielx servicez furent chaunges en denyers, per consent dez tenauntez et per le desire des seignours, scil. *en un annuall rente, &c. Mes unqore le nome de tenure en socage demoert, et en divers lyeux tenauntez unqore font tielx services ovesque lour sokez a lour seignours; issint que toutz maners de tenures que ne sont pas tenurez per service de chivalerie, sont appelles les tenures en socage.*

120 Item, *si home tient de son seignour per escuage certeyn,* scil. *en tiel fourme quant lescuage courge, et est assesse per parlëment a greindre somme ou a meindre somme, que le tenaunt paiera a son seignour, forsque demy marc pur escuage, et nient pluis et nient meins, a quel graunde somme, ou a quel petite somme que lescuage courge, et est assesse, &c. [en ceo cas pur ceo que la somme quil paiera pur lescuage est en certeyn devaunt que ascun escuage est assesse*], tiel tenure est*

---

* The words within brackets are not in *Lettou & M.;* but they appear in all subsequent editions.

knight's service. But where the sum which the tenant shall pay for escuage is uncertain, *i. e.* where it may be that the sum that the tenant shall pay for escuage may be at one time more, and at another time less, according as it is assessed, &c., such tenure is tenure by knight's service.

121 Also if a man holdeth his land to pay certain rent to his lord for castle-guard, such tenure is tenure in socage; but where the tenant ought by himself or by another to perform castle-guard, such tenure is tenure by knight's service.

Rent certain even for performance of a military service is socage for the certainty.

122 Also in all cases where the tenant holdeth of his lord to pay unto him any certain rent, this rent is called rent-service.

So all rent service is socage.

123 Also in such tenures in socage, if the tenant have issue and die, his issue being within the age of fourteen years, then the next friend of the heir to whom the inheritance cannot descend shall have the wardship of the land and of the heir, unto the age of the heir of fourteen years, and such guardian is called guardian in socage. For if land descend to the heir

Guardian in socage;—who shall have wardship and at what age.

tenure en socage, et nemy service de chivalerie. Mes lou le somme que le tenaunt paiera pur lescuage est non certeyn, scil. *lou il poet estre que la somme que le tenaunt paiera pur lescuage poet estre a une foitz le greindre et a autre foitz le meindre, solonques ceo que soit assesse, &c., donques tiel tenure est tenure per service de chivaler.*

121 Item, *si home tient sa terre pur paier certeyn rent a son seignour pur castell garde, tiel tenure est tenure en socage: mes lou le tenaunt mesme doit per luy, ou per un autre faire castell-garde, tiel tenure est tenure per service de chivaler.*

122 Item, *en toutes cases lou le tenaunt tient de son seignour a paier a luy ascun certeyn rent, cel rent est appelle rent-service.*

123 Item, *en tielx tenures en socage si le tenaunt ad issue et devie, son issue esteant deins lage de* xiiij. *ans, donques le proscheyn amy del heire a qui leritage ne poet descendre avera la garde de la terre et del heire jusques al age del heire de* xiiij. *ans, et tiel gardeyn est appelle gardeyn en socage.*

by the father's side, then the mother, or some other nigh cousin on the mother's side, shall have the wardship. And if land descend to the heir by the mother's side, then the father or next friend on the father's side shall have the wardship of such lands or tenements.

Guardian in socage accountable.

And when the heir cometh to the age of fourteen years compleat, he may enter and oust the guardian in socage, and occupy the land himself if he will. And such guardian in socage shall not take any issues or profits of such lands or tenements to his own use; but only to the use and profit of the heir; and thereof he shall render account to the heir when it pleaseth the heir, after that the heir hath accomplished the age of fourteen years. But such guardian on his account shall have allowance of all his reasonable costs and expences in all [things*], &c. And if such guardian marry the heir within the age of fourteen years, he shall account to the heir or his executors of the value of the marriage, although that he took

Allowance to socage guardian.

Qar si terre descendist al heire de part le pere, donques la mere, ou autre proscheyn cosin de parte la mere avera la garde. Et si terre descendist al heire de parte sa mere, donques le pere ou le proscheyn amy de parte le pere avera la garde de tielx terres ou tenementes. Et quant leire vient al age de xiiij. *ans complete il poet entrer et oustre le gardeyn en socage, et occupier la terre luy mesme sil voet. Et tiel gardeyn en socage ne prendra ascuns issues ou profitz de tielx terres ou tenementes a son use demesne, mes tantsoulement al use et profit del heire, et de ceo il rendra accompt al heire quant pleast al heire apres ceo que leire a complis lage de* xiiij. *ans. Mes tiel gardeyn sur son accompt avera allowaunce de touts ses resonable costez et expenses en toutz [choses*], &c. Et si tiel gardeyn maria leire deins le age de* xiiij. *ans, il accomptera al heire ou a ses executours de value del mariage,*

---

* *Cases, Roh. Rastell's* Translation renders this passage—*shall have allowance*——of *all things. Redm., Berth., Middl., Powel, Sm.*, and *Tottyl* 1554, read *en toutes cases, come de manger, boyer, et autres necessar' &c.* in all cases, as of eating, drinking, and other necessaries.

nothing for the value of the marriage; for that it shall be accounted his own folly, that he would marry him without taking the value of the marriage, unless that he marry him to such a marriage, that is worth in value as much as the marriage of the heir.

Folly of guardian.

124 Also, if any other man who is not the next friend, occupieth the lands or tenements of the heir as guardian in socage, he shall be compelled to yield an account to the heir as well as if he had been next friend, &c.; for it is no plea for him in the writ of account to say that he is not the next friend, &c.; but he shall answer whether he occupieth the lands or tenements as guardian in socage, or not. [But *quære*, if after the heir hath accomplished the age of fourteen years, and the guardian in socage continually occupieth the land until the heir comes to full age, *scil.* of twenty-one years, whether the heir at his full age shall have an action of account against the guardian from the time that he occupied after the said fourteen years, as guardian in socage, or against him as against his bailiff* ?]

So if a stranger occupy as guardian in socage, he must account to heir.

coment il ne prist riens pur le value del mariage, pur ceo que il serra rette sa folye demesne, quil luy voilloit marier sauns prendre le value del mariage, sinon que il luy maria a tiel mariage, que taunt vault come le mariage del heire &c.

124 Item, *si ascun autre home qui nest pas proscheyn amye, &c., occupia les terres ou tenementes del heire come gardeyn en socage, il sera compelle de rendre accompte al heire, auxibien sicome il fusoit proscheyn amye, &c. Qar il nest pas plee pur lui en briefe daccompte a dire, que il nest proscheyn amye, &c.; mes il respondra le quele il occupiast les terres ou tenementes come gardeyn en socage ou nemye.* [Sed quære, *si apres ceo que leire ad complis lage de* xiiij. *ans, et le gardeyn en socage continuelment occupiast la terre tanques leire vient a pleyn age,* scil. xiiij. *ans, si leire a son pleyn age avera accion daccompte envers le gardeyn del temps quil occupia apres les dits* xiiij. *ans, come envers le gardeyn en socage, ou envers luy come envers son bailly**.]

---

* *Sir Edward Coke* observes, on this *quære*, '*That it came not out of*

Wardship in chivalry and wardship in socage distinguished in reference to the interest of the guardian.

125 Also, if guardian in chivalry make his executors, and die, the heir being within age &c., the executors shall have the wardship during the nonage. But if the guardian in socage make his executors, and die, the heir being within the age of fourteen years, his executors shall not have the wardship, but another next friend, to whom the inheritance cannot descend, shall have the wardship &c. And the reason of this diversity is, because the guardian in chivalry hath the wardship to his own use, and the guardian in socage hath not the wardship to his own use, but to the use of the heir. And in such case, where the guardian in socage dieth before any account made by him to the heir, of this the heir is without remedy, for that no writ of account lieth against the executors, but for the king only. [But see 4 Ann. c. 16.]

At common law no action of account lay against executors.

Socage-relief is a year's rent on tenant's death;

126 Also the lord of whom the land is holden in socage, after the decease of his tenant, shall have relief in such

125 Item, *si gardeyn en chivalerie face ses executours et devie, leire esteant deins lage, &c., les executours averont la garde durant le nonage. Mes si gardeyn en socage face ses executours, et devie, leire esteant deins lage de* xiiij. *ans, ses executours naveront mye la garde, mes un autre proscheyn amye, a qui leritage ne poet mye descendre, avera la garde, &c. Et la cause de diversite est, pur ceo que gardeyn en chivalerie ad la garde a son propre use, et le gardeyn en socage nad la garde a son use, mes al use del heire. Et en tiel cas lou le gardeyn en socage devie devaunt ascun accompt fait per luy, leire est de ceo sauns remedie, pur ceo que nul briefe daccompt ne gist envers les executours si non pur le roy tantsoulement.*

126 Item, *le seignour de qui la terre est tenus en socage apres la mort son tenaunt, avera relief en tiel fourme, cestas-*

Lyttleton's quiver; for it is evident, that, after the age of fourteen years he shall be charged as bailiff at any time when the heir will, either before his age of twenty-one years or after;' notwithstanding this observation, the *quære* is in *Lettou & M., Machl., Roh., Pyns.* 1516, both the MSS., and in *Rastell's* Transl.

form: if the tenant holdeth by fealty, and certain rent to pay yearly &c., if the terms of payment be to pay at two terms of the year, or at four terms in the year, the lord shall have of the heir his tenant, as much as the rent amounts unto, which he payeth yearly: as if the tenant holds of his lord by fealty, and ten shillings rent, payable at certain times of the year, then the heir shall pay to the lord ten shillings for relief, over and beyond the ten shillings which he shall pay for the rent. 127 And in such case, after the death of the tenant, such relief is due to the lord presently, of what age soever the heir be*, because such lord cannot have the wardship of the body, nor of the land of the heir. And the lord in such case ought not to abide (*i. e.* wait for) the payment of his relief, according to the terms and days of payment of the rent, but he ought to have his relief immediately; and therefore he may forthwith distrain after the death of his tenant for the

which is due immediately,

and recoverable by distress.

savoir: si le tenaunt tient per fealté, et certeyn rent, a paier annuelment, &c., si les termez de paiement sont a paier per deux termes del an, ou per quatours termes del an, le seignour avera del heire son tenaunt tant come le rent amonta que il paia per an: sicome si le tenaunt tient de son seignour per fealté, et xs. *de rent, paiable a certeyns termes del an, donques leire paiera al seignour* xs. *pur relief, decoste oustre les* xs. *que il paiera pur le rent.* 127 *Et en tiel cas, apres la mort le tenaunt, tiel relief est due al seignour meyntenaunt, de quele age que leire soit**, pur ceo que tiel seignour ne poet aver la garde de corps ne de terre leire. Et le seignour en tiel cas ne doit attendre de le paiement de son relief, solonques les termez et jours de paiement de le rente, mes il doit aver son relief meyntenaunt, et pur ceo il poet incontinent*

* In *Pyns.* 1516, is an interpolation at this place, of the words *issint que il passa lage de* xiiij. *ans, so that he pass the age of fourteen years,* which is adopted by *Redm.*, *Berth.*, and indeed by almost every edition in French, since. *Sir Edward Coke* remarks (91 b), "that these words so added are against law, and no part of Lyttleton's work." They do not occur in *Rastell's* Translation.

So where a rose, a pound of pepper, a capon, &c., are reserved for rent, tenant must render double the first year;

relief. 128 In the same manner it is, where the tenant holdeth of his lord by fealty, and a pound of cummin by the year or by a pound of pepper, and the tenant dieth, the lord shall have for his relief a pound of cummin or a pound of pepper, besides the rent of cummin or pepper. In the same manner it is where the tenant holdeth to pay yearly a certain number of capons or hens, or a pair of gloves, or certain bushels of corn, and such like. (§ 222, 539). 129 But in some case the lord ought to abide to distrain for his relief until a certain time. As if the tenant holds of his lord by a rose, or by a bushel of roses to pay at the feast of St. John the Baptist, if such tenant dieth in winter, then the lord cannot distrain for his relief until the time that roses by the course of the year may have their growth &c., and so of the like &c.

but lord in some cases should stay for a season.

Escheats would be lost, but that fealty preserves the remembrance of

130 Also, if any peradventure will ask, why a man may not hold of his lord by fealty only for all manner of services, insomuch as when the tenant shall do his fealty, he shall swear to

distreigner apres la mort son tenaunt pur le relief. 128 *En mesme le manere est lou le tenaunt tient de son seignour per fealté, et per un lib. de cimine per an ou per un lib. de peper, et le tenaunt morust, le seignour avera pur son relief un lib. de cimine, ou un lib. de peper, oustre le rente de cimine ou de peper. En mesme le manere est lou tenaunt tient a paier per an certeyn nombre de chapons, ou de gelynes, ou un paire de gantes, ou certeyn busselx de frument,* et hujusmodi. 129 *Mes en ascun cas le seignour doit demurrer a distreigner pur son relief jusques a certeyn temps. Sicome si le tenaunt tient de son seignour per un rose, ou per un bussell de rosez, a paier al feste de nativite de Seynt Johan Baptist, si tiel tenaunt devye en yver, donques le seignour ne poet distreigner pur son relief tanques al temps que les roses per le cours del an poient aver lour crescer, &c.*, et sic de similibus, &c.

130 Item, *si ascun peraventure voille demaunder pur que home ne poet tener de son seignour per fealté tantsoulement pur toutz manerz des servicez, entaunt que quant le tenaunt ferra fealté il jurera a son seignour que il ferra a son seignour toutz les ser-*

his lord that he will do to his lord all manner of services due, and when he hath done fealty in such case no other service is due? To this it may be said, that where a tenant holds his land of his lord, it behoveth that he ought to do some service to his lord: for if neither the tenant or his heirs ought to do any manner of service to his lord or his heirs, then by long continuance of time it would grow out of memory of whom the land were holden, of the lord, or of his heirs or not; and then will men more often and more readily say, that the land is not holden of the lord, nor of his heirs, than otherwise: and hereupon the lord shall lose his escheat of the land, or perchance some other forfeiture or profit which he might have of the land. So it is reason that the lord and his heirs have some service done unto them, to prove and testify that the land is holden of them. 131 And for this that fealty is incident to all manner of tenures but to the tenure in frankalmoign, as shall be said in the tenure of frankalmoign, and because the lord will not at the beginning of the tenure

and evidences tenure.

Fealty an inseparable incident of tenure, § 99, 138, 227.

vices dues, &c., et quant il ad fait fealté en tiel cas nul auter service est due. A ceo il poet estre dit, que lou un tenaunt tient sa terre de son seignour, il covient que il doit faire a son seignour ascun service: qar si le tenaunt ne ses heires devoient faire nul manere de service al seignour ne a ses heires, donques per long temps continue il serroit hors de memorie et de remembraunce, de qui la terre fuist tenus, de le seignour, ou de ses heirez, ou nemye; et donques pluis tost et pluis redement voillont homes dire que la terre nest pas tenus del seignour ou de ses heires, que autrement: Et sur ceo le seignour perdera son eschete de la terre, ou per cas autre forfaiture ou profit quil poet aver de la terre. Issint il est reason que le seignour et ses heires ont ascun service fait a eux, pur prover et testifier, que la terre est tenus de eux. 131 *Et pur ceo que fealté est incident a toutz maners dez tenures forspris le tenure in frankalmoigne, sicome serra dit en le tenure de frankalmoigne, et pur ceo que le seignour ne voet a commencement del*

have any other service but fealty; it is reason that a man may hold of his lord by fealty only, and when he hath done his fealty, he hath done all his services*.

Tenants for life and years do fealty, but not tenants at will except according to the custom, &c. scil. copyholders.

132 Also, if a man letteth to another lands or tenements for term of life, without naming any thing to be reserved to the lessor, yet he shall do fealty to the lessor, because he holdeth of him. Also if a lease be made to a man for term of years, it is said that the lessee shall do fealty to the lessor, because he holdeth of him. And this is well proved by the words of the writ of waste, when the lessor hath cause to bring a writ of waste against him; which writ shall say, that the lessee holds his tenements of the lessor for term of years. So the writ proves a tenure between them &c. But he which is tenant at will according to the course of the common law shall not do fealty, because he hath not any sure estate (§ 84): but

tenure aver ascun autre service forspris fealté, il est reason que home poet tener de son seignour, per fealté tantum, et quant il ad fait son fealté, il ad fait touts sez services.*

132 Item, *si un home lesse a un autre pur terme de vie certeyns terres ou tenementes sans parlaunce de ascun rien rendre a le lessour, unqore il ferra fealté a le lessour, pur ceo que il tient de luy. Auxi si un lees soit fait a un home pur terme dez anz, il est dit que le lessé ferra fealté a le lessour, pur ceo que il tient de luy. Et ceo est prove bien per les parolx de brief de waste quant le lessour ad cause de porter brief de waste envers luy; le quel dirra, que le lessé tient les tenementes de le lessour pur terme dez ans. Issint le brief prova un tenure entre eux, &c. Mes celuy qui est tenaunt a volunté solonques le cours de comen ley ne ferra fealté, pur ceo que il nad nul certeyn sure estate. Mes autrement est de*

---

* *Rastell's* Transl. renders this passage thus:—*So it is reason that the lord and his heirs have some service done unto him for a proof and a witness that the land is holden* [§ 131] *in frankalmoign, as shall be said in frankalmoign, and because*—(concluding as above).

otherwise it is of tenant at will according to the custom of the manor; for that he is bound to do fealty to his lord for two causes: the one is by reason of the custom, and the other is, for that he taketh his estate in such form to do fealty &c.

tenaunt a volunté solonques le custome dun manor, pur ceo quil est oblige pur faire fealté a son seignour pur deux causez; lun est pur cause del custome, et lautre est pur ceo que il prist son estate en tiel fourme pur faire fealté, &c.

CONCLUDING REMARKS.

THE reader will have perceived on the perusal of this Chapter, that the distinguishing marks of this species of tenure are the having its services or renders specifically ascertained; consequently, under the denomination of *socage*, all free tenures of land by certain and invariable services or rents are included, and, in particular, *petit serjeanty*, *burgage*, and *gavelkind*, all hereafter mentioned.

As the tenure by knight's service has been abolished, it follows that all land which is not of base tenure or holden in frankalmoign is socage, and it is by this tenure that the greatest part of real property in England is held. This tenure is generally distinguished by the term *free and common socage*, an expression before alluded to: in fact it closely approaches the *allodium* of the foreign feudists, as being discharged of all services, save that of fealty, which must remain as an incident inseparably connected with tenure, (frankalmoign only excepted (§ 131)). The only incident that perfectly retains the impress of feudality, is that of *escheat* for default of heirs in cases of intestacy.

The great advantages of this tenure, which was a free tenure, although not military, consisted in the heir's not being burdened with the lord's right of wardship, as in knight's service, which was allowed upon the assumption, that the lord was most concerned in the heir's maintenance and education, in order to qualify him for the military services he was thereafter bound to render; but this principle did not apply to socage tenures, and therefore the guardian in socage is considered as a mere trustee for his ward, and accountable to the heir. As the heir may at fourteen nominate his guardian, an appointment not always exercised with judgment, the stat. 12 Car. 2, c. 24, after taking away wardship in chivalry or knight's service, enables the father by deed or will, attested by two witnesses, to appoint guardians to his children after his decease, until the infant attain twenty-one.

The doctrine of reliefs is still applicable, for the statute of 12 Car. 2, c. 24, reserves and excepts the reliefs incident to socage tenures; and, therefore, whenever lands in fee-simple are holden by a rent, relief is still due upon the death of the tenant.

The crown cannot, in future, create any other tenure than socage.—12 Car. 2, c. 24.

CHAPTER VI.

FRANKALMOIGN.

Frankalmoign is the tenure by which land is almost in every case held by the Church; and from the circumstance of no service (not even fealty) being reserved (§ 135), and from its being exempted from distress (§ 136), appears totally unconnected with feudal principles; however, neither this chapter nor the next are to be passed over hastily, as they develop many material features of tenure.

This tenure by frankalmoign could not be created by a subject after the statute of Westm. 3, *Quia emptores*, 18 E. 1; and, indeed, according to Lyttleton's expression, was created "in old time," *i. e.* before the statute of Magna Charta, which by chap. 36, prohibited gifts in mortmain, as well as the statute *De Religiosis*, 7 E. 1, to the same effect.

Although it has become impossible, since the Reformation, that the "orisons, prayers, masses, and other divine services" should be performed, yet the tenure still subsists; for, as Sir Edward Coke observes, "if the tenant saith the prayers now authorized, it sufficeth;" and the tenure is reduced to a certainty by the Book of Common Prayer. Lyttleton, however, makes a distinction between *tenure by Divine service* and *tenure in frankalmoign;* for the former was strictly a tenure, though, like the latter, it could not have been granted after the statute *Quia emptores*, which prohibited subinfeudatory grants. The distinction between frankmarriage and frankalmoign, both of them cases of free and voluntary gift, is noticed as to the incidents of fealty; and it is shewn, that, when the land given in frankalmoign, passed by alienation into secular hands, the universal incident of tenure, fealty, revived

(§ 138, 139). The mention of the doctrine of acquittal, which is parallel to that of warranty noticed in the next Chapter (§ 149), closes the account handed down to us of this tenure, which is expressly saved by the stat. 12 Car. 2, c. 24.

Definition of frankalmoign.

133 Tenure in frankalmoign (*a*) is, where an abbot or prior, or another man of religion, or of holy church, holdeth of his lord in frankalmoign, that is to say in Latin, *in liberam eleemosynam*, that is, in free alms. And such tenure began first in old time, in such form: when a man in old time was seised of certain lands or tenements in his demesne as of fee, and of the same land infeoffed an abbot and his convent, or a prior and his convent, to have and to hold to them and their successors in pure and perpetual alms, or in frankalmoign, or by such words, To hold of the grantor or of the lessor and his heirs in

Origin of this tenure.

A fee-simple passes without the word "successors," although the

133 *Tenure en frank almoigne est, lou un abbe ou priour, ou autre home de religion, ou de seynt esglise, tient de son seignour en frank almoigne, que est a dirè en Latin,* in liberam eleemosynam. *Et tiel tenure commenca a adeprimes en auncien temps en tiel fourme: quant un home en auncien temps fuist seisie de certeyns terres ou tenementes en son demesne come de fee, et de mesmes les terres ou tenementes enfeoffa un abbe et son covent, ou un priour et son covent, a aver et tener a eux et lour successours a toutz jours en pure et perpetuel almoigne,*

(*a*) To holde in frankalmoigne is to holde landes or tenementes for to serve God and holy church, to endow without doing any other manner of service.

And note well, that, in this case the donor is mesne, and ought to acquit him freely against the chiefe lorde, and also they that holde in frankalmoigne shall do no fealtie, but they that holde in frank marriage shall do fealtie.—*Olde Tenures.* § 21.

free alms: in such case the tenements shall be holden in frankalmoign (*b*).

corporation be sole, by the word "free alms."

134 In the same manner it is, where lands or tenements have been granted in ancient time to a dean and chapter, or to their successors, or to a parson of a church and his successors, or to any other man of holy church and to his successors, in frankalmoign, if he had capacity to take such grants or feoffments, &c. (*c*). 135 And they that hold in frankalmoign, are bound of right before God, to make orisons, prayers, masses, and other divine services for the souls of their grantors or feoffors, and for the souls of their heirs which are dead, and for the prosperity and good life, and good health of their heirs that

What persons may take in frankalmoign.

Services due by frankalmoign, see § 540.

ou en frank almoigne, ou per tielx parolx, A tener de le grantour ou de le feoffour et de ses heires en frank almoigne, en tielx cases les tenementes serront tenus en frank almoigne.

134 *En mesme le manere est, lou terres ou tenementes furent grauntes en auncien temps a un dean et le chapitre, et a lour successours, ou a un parson dun esglise, et a sez successours, ou a ascun autre home de seynt esglise, et a sez successours en frank almoigne, sil avoit capacité de prendre tielx graunts ou feoffementez, &c.* 135 *Et tielx qui teignount en frank almoigne sount obliges de droit devaunt Dieu, de faire orisons, praiers, messes, et autres divine services pur les almes de lour grantours ou feoffours, et pur les almes de lour heires queux sont mortes, et pur le prosperite et bon vie et bon salue de lour heires qui*

(*b*) Since Lyttleton wrote, all abbeys, priories, monasteries, and other religious houses of monks, canons, friars, and nuns, &c., have been dissolved, and their possessions given to the crown.—*Co. Lytt.* 94. *a.*

(*c*) *If he had capacity to take.*] For ecclesiastical persons have not capacity to take in succession, unless they be bodies politic; as bishops, archdeacons, deans, parsons, vicars, &c., or lawfully incorporate by the king's letters patent, or prescription; as deans and chapters, colleges, &c. But a college of religious persons, chantry priests, and such like, who are not lawfully incorporated, but only consist in vulgar reputation, have no capacity to take in succession. Therefore Lyttleton added materially (*if he had capacity to take*).—*Co. Lytt.* 95. *a.*

What ecclesiastical bodies have capacity to take.

are alive. And therefore they shall not at any time do fealty, because that this divine service is better for them before God, than any doing of fealty, and also because that these words, "frankalmoign," exclude the lord to have any earthly or temporal service, but to have only divine and spiritual service to be done for him, &c. 136 And if those that hold their tenements in frankalmoign will not, or fail to do such divine service, as it is called, the lord may not distrain them for this nonfeasance, &c. because it is not put in certainty what services they ought to do. But the lord may complain of this to their ordinary [or visitor*], praying him that he will lay some punishment and correction for this (*d*), and also provide that such negligence

No distress for non performance of the orisons, &c., because such services are uncertain.

But complaint (i. e. by course of law), lies to the visitor or ordinary.

sont en vie. Et pur ceo ils ne ferrount a nul temps ascun fealté, pur ceo que tiel divine service est melliour pur eux devaunt Dieu que ascun feasauns de fealté, et auxi pur ceo que ceux parolx, "frank almoigne" excludent le seignour daver ascune terrene ou temporell service, mes daver tantsoulement divine et spirituell service destre fait pur luy, &c. 136 *Et si tielx qui teignount lour tenementes en frank almoigne ne voillont ou faillont de faire tiel divine service come est dit, le seignour ne poet eux distreigner pur cel non-feasauns, &c., pur ceo que il nest mys en certeyn que les services ils doient faire: Mes le seignour de ceo poet compleigner a lour ordinarie [ou visitour*], luy priant quil voilloit metter punissement et correccion de ceo, et auxi de provider, que tiel negligence ne soit pluis avant fait,*

---

* The words *ou visitour, or visitor*, which occur twice in this section, are not in *Roh.*, although in *Lettou & M.*, and *Machl.*

(*d*) The meaning of this expression is, that, either the bishop or any person having in the language of the canonists ordinary (*i. e.* superior) jurisdiction, or, if the tenure were of royal foundation, that the chancellor may adjudicate upon the complaint. If a special visitor is appointed upon the foundation, complaint must be made to that visitor; but the ordinary and the chancellor are, *ex officio*, the visitors of pious or charitable foundations.

be no more done, &c. And the ordinary [or visitor] of right ought to do this, &c. 137 But if an abbot or prior holds of his lord by a certain divine service, in certain to be done, as to sing a masse every Friday in the week for the souls, *ut supra*, or every year at such a day to sing a *Placebo et Dirige, &c.*, or to find a chaplain to sing mass, &c., or to distribute in alms to an hundred poor men an hundred pence at such a day: in this case, if such divine service be not done, the lord may distrain, &c., because the divine service is in certain by their tenure what the abbot or prior ought to do. And in this case the lord shall have fealty, &c., as it seemeth. And such tenure shall not be said to be tenure in frankalmoign, but is called tenure by divine service. For in tenure in frankalmoign no mention is made of any manner of service: for none can hold in frankalmoign, if there be expressed any manner of certain service that he ought to do, &c.

Tenure in frankalmoign distinguished from divine service, which is certain, and for non performance of which lord can distrain, and to which fealty is incident.

138 Also, if it be asked whether tenant in frankmarriage shall do fealty to the donor or his heirs before the fourth

The cases of frankmarriage (§ 19)

&c. Et lordinarie [ou visitour] de droit ceo doit faire, &c. 137 *Mes si un abbe ou priour tient de son seignour per certeyn divine service en certeyn destre fait, sicome a chanter un messe chescun venderdy en le semaigne pur les almez,* ut supra, *ou chescun an a tiel jour a chanter* Placebo et Dirige, &c., *ou de trover un chapeleyn de chanter messe, &c., ou de distribuer a* C. *povers homes* C. *deniers a tiel jour: en tiel cas, si tiel divine service ne soit fait, le seignour poet distreigner, &c., pur ceo que tiel divine service est en certeyn per lour tenure, quel labbe ou le priour devoit faire. Et en tiel cas le seignour avera fealté, &c, come il semble. Et tiel tenure nest pas dit tenure en frank almoigne, mes est dit tenure per divine service. Qar en tenure en frank almoigne nul mencion est fait dascun maner de service: qar nul poet tener en frank almoigne, si soit expresse ascun manere de certeyn service que il doit faire, &c.*

138 Item, *si soit demande si tenaunt en frankmarriage ferra fealté a le donour ou a ses heires devant le quart degree passe,*

and frankalmoign in respect of fealty distinguished.

degree be past, &c., it seemeth that he shall; for he is not like as to this purpose, for tenant in frankalmoign, by reason of his tenure, shall do divine service for his lord, as is said before; and this he is charged to do by the law of holy church: and therefore he is excused and discharged of fealty: but tenant in frankmarriage shall not do by his tenure such service; and if he doeth not fealty to his lord, he shall not do any manner of service to his lord, neither spiritual nor temporal; which would be inconvenient, and against reason, that a man shall be tenant of an estate of inheritance to another, and yet the lord shall have no manner of service of him, as it seemeth: and so it seemeth he shall do fealty to his lord before the fourth degree be past, &c. And when he hath done fealty, he hath done all his services, &c. [139] And if an abbot holdeth of his lord in frankalmoign, and the abbot and convent under their common seal alien the same tenements to a secular man in fee-simple; in this case the secular man shall do fealty to

Fealty incident to every tenure.

But on alienation to a secular man fealty revives, for service is inseparably incident to tenure, and

&c., il semble que cy; qar il nest pas semblable quant a cel entent a tenaunt en frank almoigne, pur ceo que tenaunt en frank almoigne ferra, per cause de son tenure, divine service pur son seignour, come avant est dit, et de ceo il est charge a faire per la ley de seynt esglise; et pur ceo il est excuse et discharge de fealté: mes tenaunt en frankmarriage ne ferra per son tenure tiel service; et sil ne ferra a son seignour fealté, donques il ne ferra a son seignour ascun manere de service, ne spirituell ne temporell, le quel serroit enconvenient et encontre reason, que home serra tenaunt destate denheritaunce a un autre, et unqore le seignour navera nul manere de service de luy, come il semble: et issint il semble que il ferra fealté a son seignour devant le quart degree passe, &c. Et quant il ad fait fealté, il ad fait toutes sez services, &c. [139] *Et si un abbe tient de son seignour en frank almoigne, et labbe et le covent south lour comen seale alienount mesmes les tenementes a un seculer home en fee-simple; en ceo cas le seculer home ferra fealté a le seignour, pur ceo que il ne poet tener de son seignour*

the lord, because he cannot hold of his lord in frankalmoign. For if the lord should not have fealty of him, he should have no manner of service, which should be inconvenient where he is lord, and the tenement is holden of him.

where no service is specified fealty is due as incident to every tenure save the present.

140 Also, if a man grant at this day to an abbot or to a prior, &c., lands or tenements in frankalmoign, this word "frankalmoign" is void; for it is ordained by the statute, which is called *Quia emptores terrarum*, which statute was made *anno* 18 *E.* 1, that none may alien or grant lands or tenements in fee-simple to hold of himself. So that if a man seised of certain tenements, which he holdeth of his lord by knight's service, and at this day he, &c., granteth by licence, (*to alien in mortmain*) the same tenements, to an abbot, &c., in frankalmoign, the abbot shall hold immediately the tenements by knight's service of the same lord of whom his grantor held, and shall not hold of his grantor in frankalmoign, by reason of the same statute. So that none can hold in frankalmoign, unless it be by title of prescription, or by force of a grant made to any of his prede-

Frankalmoign cannot be created at this day, per Lytt. P. 12 E. 4, *by reason of the stat. Westm.* 3, *called* Quia emptores, *see* post, § 216.

So that frankalmoign must have subsisted all that time, or by prescrip-

en frank almoigne. Qar si le seignour ne doit aver de luy fealté, donques il avera nul manere de service, quel serroit enconvenient lou il est seignour, et le tenement est tenus de luy.

140 Item, *si home graunta a cel jour a un abbe ou a un priour &c., terres ou tenementes en frank almoigne, ceux parolx, "frank almoigne," sont voides, pur ceo que il est ordeigne per lestatute, que est appelle,* Quia emptores terrarum, *quel estatute fuist fait* anno xviij. Regis, E. primi, *que nul poet aliener ou graunter terres ou tenementes en fee-simple, de tener de luy mesme: issint si home seisi de certeyn tenementes queux il tient de son seignour per service de chivaler, et a cel jour il graunta per licence, mesmes les tenementes a un abbe, &c., en frank almoigne, labbe tiendra immediatly mesmes les tenementes per service de chivaler del seignour son grantour, et ne tiendra mye de son grantour en frank almoigne, per cause de mesme lestatute. Issint que nul poet tener en frank almoigne, si non que soit per title de prescripcion, ou per force dun graunt fait*

tion which presupposes such a grant. cessors before the same statute was made, in frankalmoign: but the king may give lands or tenements in fee-simple to hold in frankalmoign, or by other services, for he is out of the case of that statute.

Tenure in frankalmoign is of the grantor. 141 And note well, that none can hold lands or tenements in frankalmoign, but of the grantor, or of his heirs, [and this for the privity of the gift*]. And therefore it is said, that if there be lord, mesne, and tenant, and the tenant is an abbot, which holdeth of his mesne in frankalmoign, if the mesne die without heir, then the mesnalty shall come by escheat to the said lord paramount, and the abbot shall then hold immediately of him by fealty only, and shall do to him fealty, because he cannot hold of him in frankalmoign, &c.

In consideration of orisons, &c. (as in § 135). 142 And note well, that where such man of religion holds his tenements of his lord in frankalmoign, his lord is bound by

a ascun de sez predecessours, devant mesme lestatute fait, en frank almoigne: mes le roy poet doner terres ou tenementes en fee-simple, a tener en frank almoigne, ou per autres services, qar il est hors de cas del estatute.

141 *Et nota, que nul poet tener terres ou tenementes en frank almoigne forspris del grauntor, ou de sez heires [et ceo pur le privete del done*]. Et pur ceo il est dit, que si soit seignour mesne et tenaunt, et le tenaunt est un abbe qui tient de son mesne en frank almoigne, si le mesne devye sauns heire, donques le mesnalte deviendra per eschete al dit seignour paramont, et labbe adonques tient de luy immediatly per fealté tantum, et ferra a luy fealté pur ceo que il ne poet tener de luy en frank almoigne, &c.*

142 *Et nota, que lou tiel home de religion tient ses tenementes de son seignour en frank almoigne, son seignour est tenus per*

---

* ***Et ceo pur le privite del done—and this for the privity of the gift.*** These words first appear in *Redm.*, and are given in *Berth.*, *Middl.*, *Sm.*, *Powel*, and *Tottyl* 1554, and all the copies of *Rastell's* Transl. to 1656.

the law to acquit him of every manner of service, which any lord paramount will have or demand of him for the same tenements. And if he doth not acquit him, but suffereth him to be distrained &c., he shall have against his lord a writ of mesne, and shall recover against him his damages and the costs of his suit &c.

135), the grantor or lord is bound to pay to the chief lord, all rents and services issuing out of the land. And if the lord do not acquit the tenant, a writ of mesne is the remedy.

la ley de luy acquieter de chescun manere de service que ascun seignour paramount de luy doet aver ou demander de mesmes les tenementes: et sil ne luy acquita pas, mes suffra luy destre distreigne, &c., donques il avera envers son seignour un brief de mesne, et recovera envers luy ses damages et les costes de son suite, &c.

CHAPTER VII.

HOMAGE AUNCESTREL.

THE tenure by homage auncestrel appears to have been the homage chiefly alluded to in our earlier writers. The author of *The Olde Tenures* notices no other. Its chief peculiarity was the privity of blood, or rather succession time out of mind on the part of the tenant, and the privity of blood on the part of the lord. On alienation of the lord or tenant, whereby these connections or privities became dissolved, this tenure became simple homage. The doctrine of *voucher* is alluded to, and the reader is thus introduced to one of the consequences of real actions, viz. "recompense in value."

The statute of 12 Car. 2, c. 24, expressly abolished "all tenure by homage," thereby including the tenure by homage auncestrel, which doubtless had then long since expired, for *Sir E. Coke* doubted whether there was any relic of it even in his time.

This tenure described to exist in the

143 TENANT by homage auncestrel (*a*) is, where a tenant holdeth his land of his lord by homage, and the same tenant

143 *Tenure per homage auncestrel est, lou un tenaunt tient sa terre de son seignour per homage, et mesme le tenaunt et*

(*a*) To holde by homage auncestrel is, where I or my auncestors have holden of you and your auncestors from time out of mind, whereof no minde runneth, by homage, fealty, and certayne rent. And it is not to holde by knighte's-service, and there belongeth not warde,

and his ancestors whose heir he is, have holden the same land of the same lord and of his ancestors, whose heir the lord is, time whereof memory runneth not, by homage, and have done to them homage. And this is called homage auncestrel by reason of the continuance, which hath been by title of prescription in the tenancy in the blood of the tenant, and also in the seigniory in the blood of the lord. And such service of homage auncestrel draweth to it warranty, that is to say, if the lord which is living hath received the homage of such tenant, he ought to warrant his tenant when he is impleaded of the land holden of him by homage auncestrel. 144 And also such service by homage auncestrel draweth to it acquittal, *viz.* that the lord ought to acquit the tenant against all other

case where lord and tenant have both immemorially held by descent.

Warranty of lord incident to this tenure.

As also acquittal, (see § 142).

ses auncestres que heire il est, ont tenus mesme la terre del dit seignour et de ses auncestres que heire le seignour est, de temps dont memorie ne court, per homage, et ont fait a eux homage. Et ceo est appelle homage auncestrel, per la cause de le continuance que ad este per title de prescripcion en le tenauncie, en le sank le tenaunt, et auxi en le seignourie en le sank le seignour. Et tiel service de homage auncestrel treit a luy garrauntie, cestassavoir, si le seignour qui est en vie, ad receyve le homage de tiel tenaunt, il doit garraunter son tenaunt quant il est emplede de la terre tenus de luy per homage auncestrel. 144 *Et auxi tiel service per homage auncestrel treit a luy acquitance,* scil. *que le seignour doit acquiter le tenaunt enverz toutz autres seignours paramount, de chescun manere de ser-*

---

mariage, nor reliefe. And note well, that homage may be said to be in ij. maners: that is to say, homage auncestrel, and homage *de fait*. Homage auncestrel is where you or your auncestors have holden of me and mine auncestors during the time of man's remembrance, by homage, fealty, and rent. Homage *de fait* is where I enfeoffe yourselfe to hold of me by homage and rent; and insomuch that this homage beginneth by my deede, it is called homage *de fait*. And note well that homage auncestrell draweth to it voucher, that is to say, warranty of auncestors, but not homage *de fait*.—*Olde Tenures*, § 5.

If tenant be impleaded by a præcipe and vouch the lord, who comes in and asks why he is vouched, i. e. *called to warranty, and the tenant shews the tenure beyond memory, then if the lord has not received homage of tenant, he (the lord) may disclaim the seignory, and so deprive the tenant of his recovery over in value;*

But if the lord has received homage of tenant or tenant's ancestors, he is bound to warranty, and if tenant loses his land, he shall recover against the vouchee (i. e. the lord who is vouched), the value of the land, (i. e. so much land as the tenant has lost).

lords paramount, of every manner of service. 145 And it is said, that if such tenant be impleaded by a *præcipe quod reddat, &c.*, and he vouch to warranty his lord, who cometh in by process, and demands of the tenant what he hath to bind him to warranty, and he sheweth how he and his ancestors, whose heir he is, have holden the land of the vouchee and of his ancestors, whose heir he is, by *homage*, from time whereof memory runneth not; and if the lord who is vouched hath not received homage of the tenant, nor of any of his ancestors, the lord (if he will) may disclaim in the seignory, and so oust the tenant of his warranty. But if the lord who is vouched hath received homage of the tenant, or of any of his ancestors, then he cannot disclaim, but he is bound by the law to warrant the tenant: and then if the tenant loseth his land in default of the vouchee, he shall recover in value against the vouchee of the lands and tenements that the vouchee had at the time of the voucher, or any time after (*b*).

vice. 145 *Et il est dit, que si tiel tenaunt soit emplede per un* Precipe quod reddat, &c., *et il vouche a garrauntie son seignour, qui vient einz per proces, et demaunda del tenaunt quil ad de luy liere a la garrauntie, et il monstra coment il et sez auncestres, quil heire il est, ount tenus la terre del vouché et et de ses auncestrez quil heire il est, per homage, de temps dont memorie ne court; et si le seignour qui est vouche ne resceivast pas homage de le tenaunt, ne dascun de ses auncestres, le seignour (sil voet) poet disclaimer en le seignourie, et issint ouster le tenaunt de sa garrauntie. Mes si le seignour qui est vouche ad resceu homage de le tenaunt, ou de ascun de ses auncestres, adonques il ne poet disclaimer, mes il est oblige per la ley de garraunter le tenaunt: et donques si le tenaunt perde sa terre en defaute del vouché, il recovera en value envers le vouché dez terrez et tenementez que le vouché avoit al temps de le voucher, ou unques puis.*

(*b*) This doctrine of *voucher* or vouching to warranty will be better explained by recurring to the principles upon which feigned reco-

146 And it is to be understood, that in every case where the lord may disclaim in his seignory by the law, and of this he

On disclaimer the lord loses his seigniory as against the tenant;

146 *Et est assavoir, que en chescun cas ou le seignour poet disclaimer en son seignourie per la ley, et de ceo voet dis-*

The doctrine of voucher exemplified by the form of a common recovery.

veries lately had place. A *recovery* was, in fact, an action at law, and carried through every regular stage of proceeding as a real action; its efficacy in barring estates-tail, for which purpose it was chiefly used, turned upon the supposed "recompense in value," for the law contemplated the possibility of the vouchee making that recompense. The doctrine of voucher had its origin in that warranty and indemnity which a lord was bound to his tenant against claims of other persons or superior lords, and which are adverted to in this and the last chapter. It only remains to observe, that real actions (as has been already noticed), are, with two exceptions only, abolished, and that the mode of conveyance by fines and feigned recoveries are substituted by other forms of assurance (see *ante*, p. 39).

The following is *Sir William Blackstone's* narration of the suit in which the recoveror recovered against the tenant the land in question, who recovered over against the party whom he *vouched* or called to warranty, recompense (*i. e.* other land) in value—

" Let us, in the first place, suppose David Edwards to be tenant of the freehold, and desirous to suffer a common recovery, in order to bar all entails, remainders, and reversions, and to convey the same in fee-simple to Francis Golding. To effect this Golding is to bring an action against him for the lands; and he accordingly sues out a writ, called a *præcipe quod reddat*, because those were its initial or most operative words, when the law proceedings were in Latin. In this writ the demandant Golding alleges, that the defendant Edwards (here called the tenant) has no legal title to the land; but that he came into possession of it after one Hugh Hunt had turned the demandant out of it. The subsequent proceedings are made up into a record or recovery roll, in which the writ and complaint of the demandant are first recited: whereupon the tenant appears, and calls upon one Jacob Morland, who is supposed, at the original purchase, to have warranted the title to the tenant; and thereupon he prays, that the said Jacob Morland may be called in to defend the title which he so warranted. This is called the *voucher*, *vocatio*, or calling of Jacob Morland to warranty; and Morland is called the *vouchee*. Upon this, Jacob Morland, the vouchee, appears, is impleaded,

and then the tenant holds of lord next paramount.

will disclaim in a court of record, his seignory is extinct, and the tenant shall hold of the lord next paramount to the lord

claimer, son seignourie est extient, et le tenaunt tiendra del seignour procheine paramont le seignour, qui issint disclaime.

---

and defends the title. Whereupon Golding, the demandant, desires leave of the court to *imparl*, or confer with the vouchee in private; which is (as usual) allowed him. And soon afterwards the demandant Golding returns to court, but Morland the vouchee disappears, or makes default. Whereupon judgment is given for the demandant, Golding, now called the recoveror, to recover the lands in question against the tenant Edwards, who is now the recoveree; and Edwards has judgment to recover of Jacob Morland lands of equal value, in recompense for the lands so warranted by him, and now lost by his default; which is agreeable to the doctrine of warranty mentioned in the preceding chapter. This is called the recompense, or *recovery in value*. But Jacob Morland having no lands of his own, being usually the cryer of the court (who, from being frequently thus vouched, is called the *common vouchee*), it is plain that Edwards has only a nominal recompense for the lands so recovered against him by Golding; which lands are now absolutely vested in the said recoveror by judgment of law, and seisin thereof is delivered by the sheriff of the county. So that this collusive recovery operates merely in the nature of a conveyance in fee-simple, from Edwards the tenant in tail to Golding the purchaser. The recovery, here described, is with a *single* voucher only; but sometimes it is with *double*, *treble*, or farther voucher, as the exigency of the case may require. And indeed it is now usual always to have a recovery with double voucher at the least: by first conveying an estate of freehold to any indifferent person against whom the *præcipe* is brought; and then he vouches the tenant in tail, who vouches over the common vouchee. For, if a recovery be had immediately against tenant in tail, it bars only such estate in the premises of which he is then actually seised; whereas, if the recovery be had against another person, and the tenant in tail be vouched, it bars every latent right and interest which he may have in the lands recovered. If Edwards therefore be tenant of the freehold in possession, and John Barker be tenant in tail in remainder, here Edwards doth first vouch Barker, and then Barker vouches Jacob Morland the common vouchee; who is always the last person vouched, and always makes default: where-

which so disclaimeth. But if an abbot or prior be vouched by force of homage auncestrel, &c., albeit that he never took homage, &c., yet he cannot disclaim in this case, nor in any other case, a thing in fee which hath been vested in their house.

Lord cannot disclaim if abbot or prior hold of him.

P. 10 E. 4.

147 Also, if a man which holds his land by homage auncestrel alien to another in fee, the alienee shall do homage to his lord, but he holdeth not of his lord by homage auncestrel; because the tenancy was not continued in the blood of the ancestors of the alienee; neither shall the alienee ever have warranty of the land of his lord, because the continuance of the tenancy in the tenant, and in his blood by the alienation, is discontinued. And so see, that if the tenant that holdeth his land of his lord by homage auncestrel alien in fee, though he take an estate again of the alienee in fee, yet he holdeth the land by homage, but not by homage auncestrel.

Land holden by homage auncestrel, how affected by alienation, as to warranty, the privity of tenure being destroyed; scil. the alienee shall neither have warranty or acquittal against the lord, because he can vouch his feoffor, but tenant by homage auncestrel can vouch none but his lord; also see § 149.

Mes si un abbe ou prior soit vouche per force de homage auncestrel, &c., coment que il ne unques prist homage, &c., unqore il ne poet disclaimer en tielx cas, ne en nul autre cas, chose de fee que ad este vestue en lour meason.

147 Item, *si home que tient sa terre per homage auncestrel aliena sa terre a un autre en fee, laliené ferra homage a son seignour, mes il ne tient de son seignour per homage auncestrel, pur ceo que le tenauncie ne fuist continue en le sank de les auncestres laliené; ne laliené navera jamez la garrauntie de sa terre de son seignour, pur ceo que le continuance del tenauncie en le tenaunt et en son sank per lalienacion est discontinue.* Et sic vide, *que si tenaunt qui tient sa terre per homage auncestrel de son seignour, aliena en fee, coment que il reprist estate del aliené arrerement en fee, il tient la terre per homage, mes nemy per homage auncestrel.*

---

by the demandant Golding recovers the land against the tenant Edwards, and Edwards recovers a recompense of equal value against Barker the first vouchee; who recovers the like against Morland the common vouchee, against whom such ideal recovery in value is always ultimately awarded."—B. C. ii. 358-9.

Homage, once performed, excuses the tenant during his life.

[But see § 145, where although the tenant has performed homage to the father, yet the son can disclaim in the seignory, and so oust the tenant of his warranty and acquittal, because he had never received homage of the tenant].

148 Also it is said, that, if a man holds his land of his lord by homage and fealty, and he hath done homage and fealty to his lord, and the lord hath issue a son and dies, and the seignory descendeth to the son; in this case the tenant who did homage to the father shall not do homage to the son, because that, when a tenant hath once done homage to his lord, he is excused for term of his life to do homage to any other heir of the lord; but yet he shall do fealty to the son and heir of the lord, although he did fealty to his father.

Fealty due from tenant upon every grant; for fealty is due upon every attornment.

But where manor is recovered, the tenant shall do homage to the

149 Also, if the lord, after the homage done unto him by the tenant, grant the service of his tenant by deed to another in fee, and the tenant atturneth, &c., the tenant shall not be compelled to do homage; but he shall do fealty, although he did fealty before to the grantor. For fealty is incident to every attornment of the tenant when the seignory is granted, &c. But if any man be seised of a manor, and another holds of him the land as of the manor aforesaid by homage, which tenant hath done homage to his lord who is seised of the manor,

148 Item, *il est dit, que si home tient sa terre de son seignour per homage et fealté, et il ad fait homage et fealté a son seignour, et le seignour ad issue fitz, et devie, et le seignourie descendist a le fitz; en ceo cas le tenaunt qui fist homage al pere, ne ferra homage al fitz, pur ceo que quant un tenaunt ad fait un foitz homage a son seignour, il est excuse pur terme de sa vie de faire homage a ascun autre heire del seignour; mes unqore il ferra fealté al fitz et heire le seignour, coment que il fist fealté a son pere.*

149 Item, *si le seignour, apres le homage a luy fait per son tenaunt, graunt le service de son tenaunt per fait a un autre en fee, et le tenaunt attourna, &c., donques le tenaunt ne serra mye compelle de faire homage, mes il ferra fealté, coment quil fist fealté devant a le grauntor. Qar fealté est incident a chescun attournement del tenaunt, quant le seignourie est graunte, &c. Mes si ascun home soit seisi dun manor, et un autre home tient de luy sa terre come de le manor avauntdit per homage, le quele ad fait homage a son sei-*

if afterwards a stranger bringeth a *præcipe quod reddat* against the lord of the manor and recovereth the manor against him, and sues execution, &c.: in this case the tenant shall again do homage to him that recovered the manor, although he had done homage before; because the estate of him that received the homage [before], is defeated by the recovery; and it shall not lie in the mouth of the tenant to falsify or defeat the recovery which was against his lord. And so see a diversity in this case, where a man cometh to his seignory by recovery, and where he cometh by descent or grant to the seignory.

recoveror, for recovery supposes elder title, and this recovery binds the tenant; for it is a general rule that no one can falsify a recovery who cannot have the land recovered.

Diversity between acquisition by recovery and by grant.

150 Also, if a tenant who ought by his tenure to do his lord homage, cometh to his lord and saith unto him, Sir, I ought to do homage unto you for the tenements which I hold of you, and I am here ready to do homage to you for the same tenements, and therefore I pray you that you would now receive the same from me; 151 and if the lord shall then refuse to receive it, then after such refusal the lord cannot distrain the tenant for the homage, before that the lord require

After tender of homage,

lord cannot distrain.

gnour qui est seisi del manor, si apres un estraunge port un Precipe quod reddat *envers le seignour del manor et recovera le manor envers luy, et suist execucion, &c., en ceo cas le tenaunt ferra autrefoitz homage a celuy qui recovera le manor, coment que il fist homage devaunt, pur ceo que lestate celuy que resceut le homage, est defete per le recoverer; et il ne girra en la bouche le tenaunt a fauxer ou defeter le recoverer que fuist envers son seignour.* Et sic vide diversitatem *en ceo cas lou home vient a son seignourie per recoverer, et lou il vient per discent ou per graunt al seignourie.*

150 Item, *si un tenaunt qui doit per son tenure faire a son seignour homage vient a son seignour, et dit a luy, Sir, jeo doy a vous faire homage pur les tenementes que jeo teigne de vous, et jeo sue icy prist a vous faire homage pur mesmes les tenementes, pur que jeo vous prie que ore ceo voillez resceyver de moy;* 151 *et si le seignour adonques refusa de ceo resceyver, donques apres tiel refusell le seignour ne poet distreigner le*

the tenant to do homage unto him, and the tenant refuse to do it.

Homage auncestrel may belong as well to a tenure by escuage or knight's service, as to a tenure in socage, or to a tenure in nature of socage.

152 Also a man may hold his land by homage auncestrel and by escuage, or by other knight's service, as well as he may hold his land by homage auncestrel in socage, &c.

tenaunt pur le homage, devant que ceo le seignour requiroit le tenaunt de faire a luy homage, et le tenaunt a ceo faire refusa.

152 Item, *home poet tenir sa terre per homage auncestrel et per escuage, ou per autre service de chivaler, auxibien sicome il poet tenir sa terre per homage auncestrel en socage, &c.*

CHAPTER VIII.

GRAND SERJEANTY.

153 TENURE by grand serjeanty (*a*) is, where a man holds his lands or tenements of our lord the king by such services as he ought to do in his proper person to the king; as to carry the banner of the king, or his lance, or to lead his army, or to be his marshal, or to carry his sword before him at his coronation, or to be his sewer at his coronation, or his carver, or his butler, or to be one of his chamberlains of the receipt of his exchequer, or to do other like services, &c. And the cause why this service is called grand serjeanty is,

Definition of grand serjeanty.

153 *Tenure per graund serjeantie est, lou un home tient sez terrez ou tenementez de nostre seignour le roy per tielx services quil doit en son propre person faire al roy; come de porter le banere nostre seignour le roy, ou sa lance, ou de amesner son hoste, ou destre son mareschall, ou de porter son espee devavnt luy a son coronement, ou destre son sewer a son coronement, ou son carver, ou son butler, ou destre un de ses chamberleyns de le resceit de son eschequer, ou de faire autres tielx services, &c. Et la cause que tiel service est appelle graund*

(*a*) To hold by graund serjeanty is as if a man hold certein lands or tenementes of the king to go with him in his host, or to beare his banner with him in his warres, or to leade his host, [or to find a man at arms, or a horse or a hauberk, *i. e.* a coat of mail or brigandine], or such like, and thereto belongeth warde, marriage, and reliefe, as it appeareth in the treatise of wards and reliefes.—*Olde Tenures*, § 2.

for that it is a greater and more worthy service than the service in the tenure of escuage. For he that holdeth by escuage is not limited by his tenure to do any more especial service than any other that holdeth by escuage ought to do: but he that holdeth by grand serjeanty ought to do some special service to the king, which he that holds by escuage ought not to do.

What relief payable by heir.

154 Also, if a tenant which holds by escuage dieth, his heir being of full age, if he holdeth by one knight's fee, the heir shall pay but a c*s.* for relief, as is ordained by the statute of Magna Charta, c. 2. But if he, that holdeth of the king by grand serjeanty, dieth, his heir being of full age, the heir shall pay to the king for relief one year's value of the lands or tenements which he holdeth of the king by grand serjeanty, over and beside all charges and reprises. And it is to be understood, that *serjeantia* in Latin is the same *quod servitium,* and so *magna serjeantia* is the same *quod magnum servitium.*

Serjeanty same as service.

Difference between escuage

155 Also, they which hold by escuage ought to do their ser-

serjeantie est, pur ceo que il est pluis grand et pluis digne service que est le service en le tenure per escuage. Qar celuy qui tient per escuage nest pas limite per sa tenure de faire ascun pluis especiall service que ascun autre qui tient per escuage doit faire. Mes celuy qui tient per graund serjeantie doit faire un especiall service a roy, quil tient per escuage ne doit faire.

154 Item, *si tenaunt que tient per escuage morust, son heire esteant de pleyn age, sil tenoit per un fee de chivaler, leire ne paiera forsque* C*s. pur relief, come est ordeigne per lestatute Magna Charta,* [*cap.* 2]. *Mes si cesty qui tient de roy per graund serjeantie morust, son heire esteant de pleyn age leire paiera a roy pur relief, le value de les terrez ou tenementez per an, ouster lez charges et reprisez, queux il tient de roy per graund serjeantie. Et est assavoir, que* serjeantia *en Latin* idem est quod servitium; et sic magna serjeantia idem est quod magnum servitium.

155 Item, *ceux qui teignount per escuage doient faire lour*

vice out of the realm; but they which hold by grand serjeanty (for the most part) ought to do their service within the realm. *and knight's service.*

156 Also, it is said, that, in the marches of Scotland some hold of the king by cornage, that is to say, to wind a horn, to warn the men of the country when they hear that the Scots or other enemies are come, or will enter into England, &c. which service is grand serjeanty. But if any tenant hold of any other lord than of the king by such service of cornage, this is not grand serjeanty; but it is knight's service, and it draweth to it ward and marriage: for none can hold by grand serjeanty but of the king only. **Cornage.**

157 Also, it may be seen in *anno* 11 *H.* 4, that *Cockayne*, then chief baron of the Exchequer, came into the common place, and brought with him the copy of a record in these words:— "Talis tenet tantam terram de domino rege per serjeantiam, "ad inveniendum unum hominem ad guerram ubicunque [fu- "erit] infra quatuor maria," &c. And he demanded if this

servicez hors de roialme, mes ceux qui teignount per graunde serjeantie, pur le greindre partie, doient fair lour services deins le roialme.

156 Item, *il est dit, que en le marchez de Scotland ascuns teignount de roy per cornage,* scil. *per ventiler un corne, pur garner homes de pays, &c., quant ils oient que le Scottes ou autres enemyes veignont ou voillent entrer en Engleterre, &c., quel service est graunde serjeantie. Mes si ascun tenaunt tient dascun autre seignour que de roy per tiel service de cornage, ceo nest pas graunde serjeantie, mes est service de chivaler, et treit a luy garde et mariage: qar nul poet tener per graunde serjeantie si non de roy tantsoulement.*

157 Item, *home poet veier* anno xi. H. iiij. *que* Cockayne *adonques chief baron deschequer, vient en le comen bank, portant ovesques luy la copie dun recorde* in hæc verba:— "*Talis tenet tantam terram de domino rege per serjeantiam,* "*ad inveniendum unum hominem ad guerram ubicunque infra* "*quatuor maria,*" *&c. Et il demaunda sil fuist graunde*

were grand serjeanty or petit serjeanty. And *Hank.* (*b*) then said that it was grand serjeanty, because he had a service to do by the body of a man; and if he could not find a man to do the service for him, he himself must do it. *Quod alii justiciarii concesserunt.* Then, saith *Cockayne,* ought the tenant in this case to pay relief to the value of the land by the year? *Ad quod non fuit responsum.* [For they did not need to give him any answer to that point, because, if it was grand serjeanty, he might know by the usage in the Exchequer what sum he should pay; for from thence came the knowledge of the law in this point to the judges of the other courts, and, therefore, their silence to that question was more proper than an answer, and by their silence they attributed the knowledge of it to the Exchequer.—*Plowd.* 321.]

The usage of any one court in matters of which it has cognizance, ought to be affirmed for law in all courts.—Plowd. 321.

Tenure by grand serjeanty is a tenure by knight's service.

Escuage not incident, unless tenure is by escuage.

158 And note, that all who hold of the king by grand serjeanty hold of the king by knight's service, and the king for this shall have ward, marriage, and relief; but he shall not have of them escuage, unless they hold of him by escuage.

serjeantie ou petit serjeantie. Et Hank. *adonques disoit, que il fuist graunde serjeantie, pur ceo quil ad service a faire per corps dun home, et sil ne purroit trover nul home a faire le service pur luy, il mesme duyst le faire.* Quod alii justiciarii concesserunt. Cockayne. *Donques duist le tenaunt en ceo cas paier relief al value del terre per an?* Ad quod non fuit responsum.

158 *Et nota, que toutz que teignount de roy per graunde serjeantie teignount de roy per service de chivaler, et le roy pur ceo avera garde, mariage, et relief; mez le roy navera de eux escuage, sils ne teignount de luy per escuage.*

(*b*) This ridiculous abbreviation, which many may have taken for a true name, represents *William Hankford,* king's serjeant 1391, and a justice of *C. P.* 1398. Sir *William Dugdale* notices these abbreviations, which are to be found in the year-books and he gives many specimens of them, viz. *Mut.* for *Mutford, Shard.* for *Shardelow; Scorb.* for *Scorburghe,* &c.—*Dugd. Origin. Juridic. Preface, fol.* 1.

CHAPTER IX.

PETTY SERJEANTY.

159 TENURE by petit serjeanty (*a*) is, where a man holds his lands of our lord the king, to yield to him yearly a bow, or a sword, or a dagger, or a knife, or a lance, or a pair of gloves of mail, or a pair of gilt spurs, or an arrow, or divers arrows, or to yield such other small things belonging to war. 160 And such service is but socage in effect, because that such tenant by his tenure ought not to go, nor do anything in his proper person touching the war; but to render and pay yearly certain things to the king, as a man ought to pay a rent. 161 And note well, that a man can-

Petty serjeanty defined.

This is a socage tenure in effect.

This tenure can only be of the king.

159 *Tenure per petit serjeantie est, lou home tient sa terre de nostre seignour le roy, de rendre au roy annuelment un arke, ou un espee, ou un dagger, ou un cotel, ou un launce, ou un paire de gauntz de ferre, ou un paire desporrez dorés, ou un sete, ou divers setez, ou de rendre autres tielx petitz choses touchantz la guerre.* 160 *Et tiel service nest forsque socage en effecte, pur ceo que tiel tenaunt per son tenure ne doit aler ne faire ascun chose en son propre person touchaunt la guerre, mes de rendre et paier annuelment certeyns choses a roy, sicome home doit paier un rent.* 161 *Et nota, que home ne poet*

(*a*) To holde by petit serjeantie is, as if a man holde of the kinge landes or tenementes yelding to him a knife, a buckler, an arrowe, a bowe without stringe, or other like service at the will of the first feoffour, [as it appears in Magna Charta, cap. xxvi.*], and there belongeth not warde, maryage, nor relief. And marke well, that a man may not holde by graund or petit serjeantie, but of the king.—*Olde Tenures*, § 3.

* Some copies omit the words within brackets.

not hold by grand serjeanty, nor by petit serjeanty, but of the king, &c.

tener per graunde serjeantie, ne per petit serjeantie, sinon de roy, &c.

CONCLUDING REMARKS.

GRAND serjeanty was deemed knight's service *in capite*, and petty serjeanty, socage *in capite;* consequently the ruinous incidents of ward, marriage, primer seisin, livery and license to alien, with what was termed the king's prerogative to wardships and primer seisins of all other lands holden of subjects in knight's service, attached upon the tenure of grand serjeanty; but the tenant in petty serjeanty being a socage tenant, was chargeable with a relief only. The statute 12 Car. 2, c. 24, which abolished tenures in *capite*, relieved grand serjeanty of its burden, and in all other respects both these tenures remain the same as before the statute. The renders in petty serjeanty appear not unfrequently to have been services of convenience to the king in his progresses or journies (*b*).

(*b*) Penkelly Com' Cornub'.

Johannes de Treveilly tenet in Penkelly in com. Cornub' dimidiam acram terræ Cornubiensem, per serjantiam recipiendi unam capam de grisauco ad pontem de Panleton, cum rex fuerit in veniendo versus Cornubiam et intrando, de domino de Cabilia, qui eam in adventu domini regis ibidem deferre debet, et eam tradere eidem Johanni; qui quidem Johannes capam illam ferre debet cum domino rege per totam Cornubiam.

John de Treveilly holds in Penkelly, in the county of Cornwall, half a Cornish acre of land, by the serjeanty of receiving a grey riding-hood at Panleton Bridge, when the king should be coming towards Cornwall and entering, of the lord of Cabilia, who on the coming of the king ought to carry it thither, and deliver it to the said John; which said John ought to carry that hood with our lord the king throughout all Cornwall.

CHAPTER X.

TENURE IN BURGAGE.

BURGAGE is the tenure by which lands and tenements within boroughs and towns are holden of the king or of a subject. The form of this tenure is evidently Norman, though the course of customary descent is English; the render being certain, constituted this tenure a tenure in soccage (§ 162). The circumstance of Borough-English (*a*) being of English origin and before the Conquest, does not detract from its feudality, *burgage* signifying burgh-service, or that service upon which tenements in a borough are holden. The word "borough" is a Saxon word, pronounced *borhoe*, whilst the word burgh or *bourg* is French; whence it may be concluded, that the Normans engrafted their *tenure per burgage* upon those towns which were deemed capable of receiving, or reckoned of sufficient importance to be subjected to the terms of feudal tenure: in some towns or boroughs,

---

(*a*) The name [Borough-English] itself guides us to judge of the antiquity, and teaches us that this custom had its rise among the Anglo-Saxons; indeed, it is probable that it was not known by this title, until the Normans, who were strangers to any such kind of descent in their own country, on their settlement in this kingdom gave it the name of the *Custom of the Saxon Towns*, to distinguish it from their own law; and this may be collected from 1 E. 3, 12, where it is said, that in *Nottingham* there are two tenures, *Burgh Engloyes* and *Burgh Frauncoyes*, the usages of which tenures are such, that all the tenements whereof the ancestor dies seised in *Burgh Engloyes*, ought to descend to the youngest son; and all the tenements in *Burgh Frauncoyes* to the eldest son, as at common law.—*Appendix to Robinson on Gavelkind; Of the Custom of Borough-English.*

the ancient English course of descent was preserved; in others, the course of descent followed the Norman *custumier*. Those boroughs which were not subject to the imposition of a new custom, were in all probability the most insignificant, the tenants being little else than mean artificers; whilst in larger towns, the tenements were more valuable, consequently, the tenants more profitable to their lords. This tenure was never a military one, as the tenants, even of the better sort, were persons engaged in commerce and trade,—pursuits which were deemed ignoble by our ancestors in those warlike or rather barbarous times. The incorporation of boroughs or the creation of cities relieved the tenants and inhabitants from many burdens, imposed by the king or the lord to whom he had granted them, and as commerce gained ground, many boroughs obtained charters of incorporation; but this part of the subject properly belongs to the political history of boroughs, to which the reader is necessarily referred. The immunities of boroughs were in most instances obtained piecemeal and for money paid to their lords: for example, first the lord of the borough remitted a toll, then granted a market, then reduced the fines payable on alienation and decease; lastly, by payment of a fine, a charter of royal incorporation was by the interest of the lord obtained from the king as superior lord, who also had some share in the price paid for this last act of enfranchisement.

Burgage tenure appears to be noticed in the books as a species of ancient demesne, so far as concerns the tenure of those towns which were holden of King Edward at the time of the Conquest, or were *quasi* ancient demesne, as being granted by King William, which may account for the expression which occurs more than once in the year-books, *arguendo,* that London was ancient demesne of the king; a proposition that never was sanctioned, but rather repudiated. The tenements of a borough or a city, when freed from the burdens of tenure imposed by a lord, were then holden of the mayor, or those in whom the government as well as the property of the borough or city was vested.

Lyttleton's remarks on this tenure tend to explain what burgage tenure is, (for it is capable of subsisting, and does in many places subsist to the present day (§ 162)), and give the definition of a borough (§ 165). He next treats of the customs of such boroughs, especially as to testamentary alienation, (since extended by statute to all kind of real as well as personal property) (§ 168), and concludes with a dissertation upon custom, prescription, and the limitation of real actions; a subject resumed in the following chapter (§ 183), so far as concerns the mode of prescribing.

---

162 TENURE in burgage (*a*) is where there is an ancient borough, whereof the king is lord, and they that have tenements within the borough hold of the king their tenements, so that every tenant for his tenement ought to pay to the king a certain rent by year, &c. And such tenure is but tenure in socage. 163 In the same manner it is, where another lord spiritual or temporal is lord of such a borough, and the tenants of the tenements in such boroughs hold of their lord, to pay, each of them, an annual rent. 164 And it

Tenants in burgage hold by certain service of the king, which is socage.

And also may hold of a subject.

Why this te-

162 *Tenure en burgage est, lou un auncien boroghe est, de que le roy est seignour, et ceux que ont tenementes deins le boroghe teignount del roy lour tenementes, que chescun tenaunt pur son tenement doit paier a roy un certeyn rent per an &c. Et tiel tenure nest forsque tenure en socage.* 163 *En mesme le manere est, lou un autre seignour espirituell ou temporell est seignour de tiel boroghe, et les tenauntes dez tenementes en tielx boroghes teignount de lour seignour, a paier, chescun*

(*a*) To holde in burgage, is to holde as if the burgeis holde of the kinge, or of another lord, landes or tenements yelding to him a certeine rent by the yeare; or els there where another man then burgeis holdeth of any lord landes or tenements in burgage yelding to him a certeine rent by yeare.—*Olde Tenures*, § 12.

nure called burgage-tenure.

is called tenure in burgage, for that the tenements within the borough be holden of the lord of the borough by certain rent, [&c.*] (*b*).

And it is to wit, that the ancient towns called boroughs be the most ancient towns that be within England; for those towns that now be cities or counties, in old time were boroughs, and called boroughs; for of such old towns called boroughs come the burgesses of parliament to the parliament, when the king hath summoned his parliament.

Such boroughs have certain customs peculiar to themselves as that the youngest son shall inherit, which is Borough-English.

165 Also for the greater part such boroughs have divers customs and usages, which other towns have not, for some boroughs have such a custom, that, if a man have issue many sons and dieth, the youngest son shall inherit all the tenements which were his father's within the same borough,

deux un annuell rent. 164 *Et est appelle tenure en burgage, pur ceo que lez tenementes deins le boroghe sount tenuz del seignour du boroghe per certeyn rent,* [*&c.**].

Et est assavoir que les aunciens villes appellez boroghes sont les pluis aunciens villes que sont deins Engleterre; qar ceux villes que ore sont citees ou countees, en auncien temps furent boroghes, et appellez boroghes, qar de tielx aunciens villes appellez boroghes, veignount les burgeyses de parlëment, al parlëment quant le roy ad sommone son parlëment.

165 Item, *pur le greindre partie tielx boroghes ount divers customes et usagez que nount pas autres villes, qar ascuns boroghes ont tiel custome, que si home ad issue plusours fitz, et morust, le puisne fitz enheritera toutz les tenementes que furent a son pere deins mesme le boroghe, come heire a son*

---

* **This *&c.* first appears in *Roh.***

(*b*) By [&c.] here, is implied fealty or other service, as to repair the house of the lord, &c.—*Co. Lytt.* 109, *a*.

as heir unto his father, by force of the custom: and such custom is that *which is* called Borough-English (*c*).

166 Also, in some boroughs, by the custom, the wife shall have for her dower all the tenements which were her husband's. **Freebench.**

167 Also, in some boroughs, by the custom, a man may devise by his testament, his lands and tenements, which he hath in fee-simple within the same borough at the time of his death; and by force of such devise he to whom such devise is made, after the death of the devisor, may enter into the tenements so to him devised, to have and to hold to him according to the form and effect of the devise, without any livery of seisin to be made to him, [&c.*]

Custom to devise burgage tenements.

Livery superseded by this mode of alienation.

168 Also, though a man cannot grant or give his tenements to his wife, during the coverture, because his wife and he are but as one person in law, yet by such custom he can devise

So a man may devise to his wife because such devise takes effect after death.

pere, per force del custome. Et tiel custome est que appelle Boroghe-English.

166 Item, *en ascuns boroghes per le custome, feme avera pur sa dower toutes les tenementes que furent a son baron.*

167 Item, *en ascuns boroghes per le custome home poet deviser per son testament, sez terres et tenementes quil ad en fee-simple deins mesme le boroghe al temps de son moriant; et per force de tiel devise, celuy a qui tiel devise est fait, apres la mort le devisour, poet entrer en les tenementes issint a luy devises, a aver et tener a luy solonques la fourme et effect del devise, sauns ascun livëre de seisin destre fait a luy,* [*&c.**].

168 Item, *coment que home ne poet graunter ne doner sez tenementez a sa feme duraunt le coverture, pur ceo que sa feme et luy ne sount forsque un persone en ley, unqore per tiel cus-*

---

* This *&c.* first appears in *Machl.*

(*c*) The reason assigned by Lyttleton as the cause and original of this custom is given at § 211, and seems to be the most probable as well as the most reasonable.

by his testament his tenements to his wife, to have and to hold to her in fee-simple, or in fee-tail, or for term of life, or for term of years; for that such devise taketh no effect but after the death of the devisor. [For all devises do not take effect but after the death of the devisor*.] And if a man at divers times makes divers testaments and divers devises, &c., yet the last devise and will made by him shall stand (*d*).

Of several wills the last only is valid.

tome il poet deviser per son testament ses tenementes a sa feme, a aver et tener a luy en fee-simple, ou en fee-taille, ou pur terme de vie, ou pur terme des ans; pur ceo que tiel devise ne prent effect forsque apres la mort le devisour; [qar toutes devises ne prenount effecte forsque apres la mort le devisour]. Et si home fait a divers temps divers testamentez et divers devises, &c., unqore le darreyn devise et volunte fait per luy, estoiera.*

---

* The words within brackets appear in *Lettou & M.*, but are not in *Machl.* or *Roh.*

(*d*) This testamentary power is now extended to every description of real property. The progress of testamentary alienation has been very slow, though it commenced with statute of Ed. 1, called "*Quia emptores.*" The steps by which the genius of commerce has overcome the spirit of feudality are comprehensively detailed by the learned Mr. *Hargrave* in his note to *Co. Lytt.* 111. *a.*, and to which the studious reader is referred. Devises of land are now entirely regulated by the Statute of Wills, 1 Vict. c. 26.

The power of devising land, which was in use among our Anglo-Saxon and Danish ancestors, was incompatible with the feudal principles introduced by the Norman jurists. Mr. *Ritso* remarks—"The construction of testamentary alienation, for example, was originally adopted upon a purely commercial principle, and in relaxation of the rigour of the feudal system, which had a direct tendency to take lands out of commerce, and to render them inalienable. But here, again, the operation of a feudal principle interferes and requires a seisin in the devisor, analogous to that of the feoffor or grantor in the case of alienation by deed; so that, by the law of England, a will or devise of

169 Also, by such custom a man can devise by his testament, that his executors may alien and sell the tenements that he hath in fee-simple for a certain sum of money, to distribute for his soul. In this case, though that the devisor die seised of the tenements, and the tenements descend unto his heir, yet the executors after the death of the testator may sell the tenements so devised, and put out the heir, and thereof make a feoffment, alienation, and estate, by deed or without deed, to them to whom the sale is made. And so may ye here see a case where a man may make a lawful estate, and yet he hath nought in the tenements at the time of the estate made. And the cause is, for that the custom and

Devise to executors for sale.

169 Item, *per tiel custome home poet deviser per son testament, que ses executours poient aliener et vender les tenementes quil ad en fee-simple pur certeyne somme dargent, a distribuer pur son alme. En cest cas, coment que le devisour devyast seisi de les tenementes, et les tenementes descendount a son heire, unqore les executours apres la mort lour testatour poient vender les tenementez issint devises, et ouster leire, et ent faire feoffement, alienacion et estate, per fait ou sauns fait, a eux a qui le vende est fait. Et issint poies veier icy un cas lou home poet faire loial estate, et unqore il navoit riens en lez tenementes a temps de lestate fait. Et le cause est, pur ceo que la custome et usage ad este tiel, &c.* "*Quia*

---

lands does not operate by way of appointment of an heir generally, as in the Roman law, but by way of legal conveyance of the lands themselves; and, consequently cannot operate on any freehold lands, which, at the time of making the will of the party, had not this species of seisin."—*Introduction to the Science of the Law.* Lond. 8vo. 1815, p. 21.

By statute 1 Vict. c. 26, s. 24, which takes effect with regard to all wills and devises executed since 31st Dec. 1837, "Every will shall be construed, with reference to the real estate and personal estate comprised therein, to speak and take effect as if it had been executed immediately before the death of the testator, unless a contrary intention shall appear by the will."

usage has been such, &c. "For a custom used upon a certain reasonable cause barreth the common law."

No custom good without prescription.

170 And note well, that no custom is allowable, but only such custom as hath been [used*] by title of prescription, that is to say, from time whereof *the* memory *of man* runneth not *to the contrary*. But divers opinions have been concerning time of memory, &c., and of title of prescription, which is all one in the law. For some have said, that time of memory should be said from time of limitation in a writ of right, that is to say, from the time of King Richard the First after the Conquest, as is given by the statute of Westminster the first, for that a writ of right is the most high writ in its nature that may be; and in such a writ a man may recover his right of the possession of his ancestor of the most ancient time that any man may by any writ by the law, &c. And insomuch that it is given by the said statute, that in a writ of right none shall be heard to demand of the seisin of his ancestors

Time of memory and prescription all one.

Time of limitation for recovery in a real action, which by stat. of Westm. 1, is the time of Ric. 1.

"*consuetudo ex certa causa rationabili usitata privat communem legem.*"

170 *Et nota, que nul custome est allowable, mesque tiel custome que ad este [use*] per title de prescripcion,* scil. *de temps dont memorie ne court. Mes divers opinions ount este de temps de memorie, &c., et de title de prescripcion, que est tout un en ley. Qar ascuns ount dit, que temps de memorie serra dit de temps de limitacion en brief de droit,* scil. *de temps le roy Ric. le premier puis le Conquest, come est done per lestatute de Westminster premier, pur ceo que le brief de droit est le pluis haut brief en sa nature que poet estre; et en tiel brief home poet recoverer son droit de la possession son auncestre de pluis auncien temps que home purroit per ascun brief per la ley, &c. Et entaunt quil est done per le dit estatute, que en brief de droit nul soit oye a demaunder de le sei-*

---

* *Ewe*—had, *Lettou & M.*; *use*—used, *Machl.* and *Roh.*

of longer time than of the time of King Richard aforesaid; therefore this is proved, that continuance of possession, or other customs and usages [used*] since the same time, is the title of prescription, &c., and this is certain. And others have said, that well and truth it is, that seisin and continuance ever since the said limitation, &c., is a title of prescription, as is aforesaid, and by the cause aforesaid. But they have said that there is also another title of prescription, that was at the common law before any statute of limitation of writs, &c., and that it was where a custom or usage, or other thing hath been used for time whereof mind of man runneth not to the contrary. And they have said, that this is proved by the pleading: *for* where a man will plead a title of prescription of custom, &c., he shall say that such custom hath been used *from time whereof the memory of men runneth not to the contrary*, and that is as much as to say, when such a matter is pleaded that no man then alive hath heard any proof of the

Title by prescription at common law not confined or limited (when Lyttleton wrote), by any statute.

sin sez auncestres de pluis long temps que de temps le roy Ric. avauntdit; issint ceo est prove que continuaunce de possession, ou autres customez et usages [uses] puis le dit temps, est title de prescripcion, &c.,* et hoc certum est: *Et autres ount dit, que bien et verite est, que seisin et continuaunce puis le dit limitacion, &c., est un title de prescripcion, come est avauntdit, et pur cause avauntdit. Mes ils ount dit que il y ad auxi un autre title de prescripcion, que fuist a la comen ley devaunt ascun estatute de limitacion de briefes, &c., et ceo fuist lou un custome ou usage, ou autre chose, ad este use de temps dount memorie des homes ne court a le contrarie. Et ils ount dit, que ceo est prove per le pleder: lou home voet pleder un title de prescripcion de custome, &c., il dirra que tiel custome ad este use* de tempore cujus contrarii memoria hominum non existit, *et ceo est a taunt a dire, quant tiel matere est plede que nul home adonques en vie ne ad oye ascun*

---

* *Ewes*—had, *Lettou & M.; uses*—used, *Machl.* and *Roh.*

contrary, nor hath no knowledge to the contrary. And inasmuch that such title of prescription was at the common law, and not put out by a statute, *ergo*, it abideth as it was at the common law; and the rather, insomuch that the said limitation of a writ of right (*e*) &c., is of so long time passed [&c.*] *Ideo quære de hoc.* And many other customs and usages have such ancient boroughs.

prove a le contrarie, ne avoit ascun connusauns a le contrarie. Et entaunt que tiel title de prescripcion fuist a la comen ley, et nient ouste per ascun estatut, ergo, *il demourt come il fuist a la comen ley; et le pluis tost, entaunt que la dit limitacion de briefe de droit, &c., est de cy long temps passe,* [*&c.**]. Ideo quære de hoc. *Et plusours autres customes et usages ount tielx aunciens boroghes.*

* This *&c.* is in *Lettou & M.*, but not in *Machl.* or *Roh.*

(*e*) At the time Lyttleton wrote, there was no limitation of the time within which a real action for the recovery of a corporeal hereditament could be brought upon the seisin of an ancestor, except the reign of Richard the First (1189); and the same rule applied to the possession of incorporeal hereditaments; so that long enjoyment did not always secure a possessor of land, against adverse claims of a very ancient date. With regard to the correction of this evil, the stat. 32 Hen. 8, c. 2, s. 2, confined the writ of right, (which was termed a droitural action, viz. an action to try the mere right), on the seisin of an ancestor, to sixty years; by s. 3, a possessory action, viz. an action to recover the possession on the seisin of an ancestor, was confined to fifty years; and by s. 4, no real action, droitural or possessory, could be maintained by any person on his own seisin after a lapse of thirty years. Writs of *formedon* in reverter or remainder were required to be sued within fifty years; and by s. 6, no avowry or cognizance could be made for any suit or service after fifty years from the seisin of an ancestor or any other person.

By 21 Jac. 1, c. 16, s. 1, the period for all writs of formedon was limited to twenty years, and it enacted generally, that no person should make entry into any lands but within twenty years next after his right of entry had accrued, but by s. 2, persons under disability, viz. infancy, coverture, being abroad,

171 Also, every borough is a town, but not *e converso*. More shall be said of custom in the tenure of villenage.

A borough is a town, but not e converso.

171 Item, *chescun boroghe est un ville, mes nemy* e converso. *Pluis serra dit de customez en le tenure en Villenage.*

---

lunacy, and imprisonment, might make their entry within ten years after the cause of disability removed.

By 4 Hen. 7, c. 24, a fine levied with proclamations barred all present rights of entry after five years from the last proclamation, but a saving was made in favour of persons under disability and of rights to accrue, for these persons had five years after the disability removed and the accruer of the right. In actions of dower, escheat, and waste, and some other actions which did not arise upon the seisin of an ancestor, there was no period of limitation fixed.

With regard to advowsons, there was no limit to the time within which a writ of right of advowson could be brought. Tithes also were not affected by the statutes of limitation as is hereafter noticed.

With regard to rents, there was no other limitation than fifty years, according to the 32 Hen. 8.

This statute created no limitation to the rights of the Church, and a prescriptive right to incorporeal hereditaments could be established by proof of enjoyment of them for such a period, as would justify a jury, under the direction of a judge, to infer that the enjoyment had continued ever since the commencement of the reign of Richard the First.

By 53 Geo. 3, c. 127, s. 5, suits for the recovery of *the value* of tithes were confined or limited to six years; but in claims made by the church for tithes against a *modus decimandi* or ancient composition set up by the parishioners, the parishioners had to prove the existence of such *modus* at the time of Richard the First, or to prove such facts as led to that inference or presumption.

It being impossible in most cases to prove an enjoyment of incorporeal hereditaments, commencing from or in existence at that period, proof of enjoyment so far back as living witnesses could speak, raised a presumption of an enjoyment from the remote era of Richard the First; and this is the meaning of Lyttleton when he makes mention of " time whereof the memory of man runneth not to the contrary," and of the concluding passage of this section. This is known as the doctrine of presumption; for by evidence of the testimony of living witnesses or any other evidence of an ancient nature, an inference or presumption was raised that the subject of prescription had existed ever since the reign of Richard the First.

This time of legal memory as well as the *limitation*, or time within which actions for the recovery of corporeal or incorporeal hereditaments are to be brought, is now abolished, and other periods substituted; for by the stat. 3 & 4 Gul. 4, c. 27, s. 2, one period of limitation is established for all lands and rents; for after 31st Dec. 1838, no person shall make an entry or distress, or bring an action to recover any land or rent, but within twenty years next after the time at which the right to make such entry or distress, or to bring such action, shall have first accrued to some person through whom he claims; or if such right shall not have accrued to any person through whom he claims, then within twenty years next after the time at which the right to make such entry or distress, or to bring such action, shall have first accrued, (as is mentioned in the act), to the person making or bringing the same.

And with regard to *advowsons*, for the recovery of which no limitation existed, (the stat. 1 Mar. s. 2, c. 5, expressly declaring that the 32 Hen. 8, did not extend to them, so that the purchaser of an advowson was constantly liable to be evicted by very ancient titles), this statute further provides, that no advowson can be recovered by any person after three incumbencies, all of the incumbents having obtained possession thereof adversely to the right of presentation or gift of such person, or some person through whom he claims, and such additional time as will make up sixty years of adverse possession, or, as the extreme period, one hundred years adverse possession. s. 30-3.

With regard to *prescription*, by the act 2 & 3 Gul. 4, c. 71, a period of limitation for bringing actions and suits for the establishment of "incorporeal rights" (the usual subjects of prescriptive title), in which are not included rents or tithes, has been settled:—

1. By making the enjoyment of any right of common, or other profit or benefit from or upon land, (except tithes and rent), without interruption for thirty years, *primâ facie* evidence of a right, liable to be rebutted by proof, that during that time the owner of the land was under disability; and by making such enjoyment for sixty years *conclusive* evidence of a right, unless it appear to have been with some consent in writing.

2. By making the enjoyment of any way, or other easement or watercourse, or the use of water without interruption for twenty years, *primâ facie* evidence of a right, liable to be rebutted by proof that the owner of the land was under disability; and by making such enjoyment for forty years *conclusive* evidence of the right, unless it appear to have been with some consent in writing.

3. By making the enjoyment of lights for twenty years *conclusive* evidence of a right, unless it appear to have been had by some consent or agreement in writing.

With respect to prescription and claims for a *modus decimandi*, or exemption from tithes by composition, real or otherwise, by stat. 2 & 3 Gul. 4, c. 100, (amended by 4 & 5 Gul. 4, c. 83), s. 1, such prescription and claim shall be sustained upon evidence shewing, in case of a *modus*, the payment or render of such *modus*, and in cases of claim to discharge, shewing the enjoyment of the land without payment or render of tithes, money, or other matter in lieu thereof, for full thirty years next before the time of such demand, unless payment shall be shewn to have been made at some time prior to such thirty years, or that it was made by some consent or agreement expressly made for that purpose by deed or writing; and if such proof in support of the claim shall be extended to sixty years, the claim shall be indefeasible unless it shall be proved that such payment or render of *modus* was made or enjoyment of the exemption had, by some consent or agreement for that purpose by deed or writing.

CHAPTER XI.

VILLENAGE.

The tenure of villenage appears to have been introduced at or very shortly after the Conquest; and that, not so much as a consequence of the introduction of feudal tenure, but rather as a new kind of servile fief. Indeed, Sir Martin Wright, who is followed by Sir William Blackstone, considers this tenure as one of a mixed nature engrafted upon a Saxon bondage, and superseding it.

The estates holden by this, or rather by some analogous tenure, are stated by Sir Edward Coke and Sir William Blackstone to have been *folk-land* (see *ante*, p. 111, in n.); but what *folk-land* was, has since been made a matter of much disquisition and argument, and the subject is much obscured by those doubts which attach upon investigations which have no contemporary light afforded to clear them up; so that, after all, the reader must be contented with the account the author of *The Olde Tenures* and Lyttleton furnish on this matter; premising that the word *villein* is Norman, and that the word *villan* denotes a description of person constantly occurring in Domesday Book, and in the books of foreign feudists, (see *ante*, p. 112, in n.): so that, allowing a state of bondage to have existed among the Saxons or Danes, the Normans applied their notions of a feud so far as the same could be deemed applicable, to villenage, or the interest a villan could be said to possess; and in fact created a mongrel tenure, which, because it was a tenure, became ultimately a means of enfranchisement, and the foundation and origin of that estate known as a base fee or customary copyhold.

However, taking the account of villenage as we have it from *The Olde Tenures* and from Lyttleton, we find that it is treated of in both as a tenure, and as a state of bondage and absolute slavery; and there is nothing mentioned in Lyttleton to demonstrate that a base fee or copyhold at the will of the lord had its origin from villenage, although the author of *The Olde Tenures* makes a distinction between tenants in villenage and tenants by base tenure, *scil.* tenants by copy at the will of the lord, for there it is expressly stated that the former must do all the services their lord commands them, but that in regard to the latter it is otherwise.—pp. 106 *in n.*, and 208 *in n.*

Villeins, as Lyttleton divides his subject, were either *regardant*, *i. e.* annexed to the manor, or else they were *in gross* or at large, *i. e.* annexed to the person of the lord and transferable from one person to another, and could be restrained of their natural liberty, and also were claimed and recovered by action, like beasts or other chattels. In either case the villein could acquire no property whatever, but for the benefit of his lord or master; for if he acquired any property the lord might appropriate it, unless in the meantime a *bonâ fide* alienation had taken place before the lord's claim.

By the doctrine of *natural accession*, the children of villeins were bondmen or slaves, whence the appellation of *nativus* for a villein and *nativa* for a niefe: on the intermarriage of a freeman and a niefe, the issue followed the condition of the father; contrariwise of a free woman with a villein.

Lyttleton in this Chapter (§ 183, 209—212), resumes the subject of prescription from § 170; he also incidentally treats of pleas in disability to the person of the plaintiff (§ 196—202).

Villenage had long been extinct, when the statute 12 Car. 2, c. 24, was made; for even at the time of the Reformation there were but few villeins in the kingdom, and those were villeins regardant; indeed, Sir Thomas Smith, in his "Commonwealth," B. 3, c. 10, informs us, that the only villeins he ever knew of, (he wrote in the time of Edward the Sixth), were regardant, and were such as had belonged to bishops or ecclesiastical corporations in the time of popery.

Tenure in villenage is where tenure is servile.

172 TENURE in villenage (*a*) is most properly when a villein holdeth of his lord, to whom he is a villein, certain lands

172 *Tenure en villenage est plus proprement, quant un villeyn tient de son seignour a qui il est villeyn, certeynes terrez,*

(*a*) To hold in pure villenage is to do all that the lord will him command.

The definition of villenage is villein of bloud and of tenure. And it is he of whom the lord taketh redemption (*i. e. a fine*) to marrie his daughter, and to make him free, and it is he whom the lord may put out of his landes or tenementes at his will and also of all his goods and cattel. And note well that a sokeman is no pure villein; nor a villein oweth not warde, marriage, nor reliefe, nor to do any other services real. And note well, that tenure in villenage shall make no freeman villein, if it be not continued sith time out of mind, nor villein land shall make no freeman villein, nor free land shall make no villein free, except that the tenant have continued free sith the time of no minde; but a villein shall make free land villein by seisin or claim of the lord. And note well, that if a villein purchase certeine land and take a wife and alien, and dyeth before the claime or seisin of the lord, that the wyfe shall be endowed. And note well, that in case that the lord bring a *præcipe quod reddat* against the alienee, who voucheth to warranty the issue of the villein who is villein to the lord, he shall have the voucher, [and by protestation the lord may except (*saver*), that notwithstanding that he plead with his villein, yet his villein shall not be enfranchised*]. And note well, that a bastard shall never be judged villein but by acknowledgment in court of record. [*Quia est nullius filius*†]. And note well that if debt be due by a lorde to a freeman, and he maketh two men his executors, the which be villeins to the said lord, and dyeth, the villeins shall have an action of debt against their lord, notwithstandinge that he plead with them. And if he make protestation they shall not be therefore enfranchised, becanse they are to recover the debt aforesaid to the use of another person, that is to say, to the use of their testator and not to their own use. And if the tenant in dower have a villeine who

* Another reading of this passage is thus—*And by protestation can save* (saver) *the villenage, notwithstanding that he does not plead villenage. And for this his villein shall not be enfranchised.*

† Some copies do not retain these words.

or tenements, according to the custom of the manor or otherwise, at the will of his lord, and to do to his lord villein-service;

ou tenementes solonques le custome de manor, ou autrement a la volunte son seignour, et de faire a son seignour villeyn ser-

---

purchaseth certeine land in fee, and after the tenant in dower entreth, [she shall have the land to her and to her heires for evermore, and the same law is of tenant for terme of yeares of a villein*.] And note well that a lord may rob his villein, beat and chastise him at his will, save only that he may not maime him, for then he shall have appeale of maime against him. And note well, that a villeine may have three actions against his lord, that is to say, appeale of the death of his ancestor, appeale of rape done to his wife, and appeale of maime.· And note well, if two parceners bringe a writ of niefe, *(noiefe, noifte,)* and one of them be nonsuit, the nonsuit of her shall be judged the nonsuit of them both, so that, if that nonsuit be after appearance, they shall be put out from that action for ever, for the law is such in favour of liberty. And note well, if two have a villeine in common, and one of them make to him a manumission, he shall not be made free against both. And note well, that in a writ *de nativo habendo*, it behoveth that the lord shew how he cometh privye of the blood of the villeine of whom he is lord, &c. And if he nor none of his ancestours were not seised of none of his blood, he shall not gain by his action, if the villeine have not acknowledged himself in court of recorde to be his villein. And note well, that, in a writ of *niefe* may not be put more niefes than two, and this was first brought in for the hatred of bondage. But in a writ *de libertate probandâ* may be put as many niefes as

* In place of the words within brackets, some copies read as follows, viz.—*and alieneth in fee, he in the reversion can lawfully enter. And if he be estopped of his entry, he shall have a writ of entry* in casu proviso, ut dicitur.;

And note well, that if a man grant to another a manor (manoir) *to which many villeins are regardant, for term of twenty years by especialty, and one of the villeins purchase certain lands in fee-simple, the termor shall not have greater estate in the land purchased than that which he has in the manor which to him was first granted, [but otherwise it is, where land is aliened in mortmain, and the termor of the seignory enter, there he shall retain the land for ever].* (These last words within brackets do not appear in *Berth.* 1531, which, in other respects, adopts this substitution for the above-mentioned text within brackets).

as to bear and carry the dung of his lord out of the scite of his lord's manor, unto the land of his lord lying fallow, and to spread the dung of the lord lying upon the land, and such like*. And some [freemen †] hold their tenements according

vice; come de porter et de carier le fime le seignour hors del cyte de manor son seignour, jesques a la terre son seignour gisaunt warrette, et de spreder le fime le seignour gisaunt sur la terre, et hujusmodi*. *Et ascuns [frankes homes] teignount*

* The text, which is in conformity to the three most ancient printed copies by *Lettou & M.*, *Machl.*, and *Roh.*, differs from the text given by the common copies, as well as by the editions of *Redm.* and *Berth.*, (viz.)—*hors del cite* (subsequently corrupted to *city*), *ou del manor son seignour, jesques a la terre son seignour, en gisaunt ceo sur la terre, et hujusmodi;* which Sir Edward Coke thus translates, at least it appears in that translation given with his Commentary upon Lyttleton :—*As to carry and recarry the dung of his lord out of the city, or out of his lord's manor unto the land of his lord, and to spread the same upon the land, and such like.* Sir Edward Coke certainly observes that in the "original," the words are "*hors del scite del manor*" but goes no further, and does not mention the words "*gisaunt warrette*," which appear in the *Rohan* edition, which he had seen, and of which he takes such notice in the preface to his Commentary; so that it does not seem likely, that, in mentioning "the original" he alluded to the *Rohan* edition, although he might at one time have deemed it to be the *editio princeps;* for he gives readings from this "original," which are not to be found in *Roh.* or in the two earlier printed copies. (Co. Lytt. § 221, 241, 277, 283, (where he alludes to "a mistake in the imprinting"), and 621). Sir Edward Coke also, at various periods of the compilation of his Commen-

† For *freemen*, *Rastell's* Translation reads *tenants.*

the plaintife will. And note well, that if a villeine of a lord be in auncient demesne of the king or other town privileged within a yeare and a day, the lord may seize him, and if he dwells in the same towne or other place franchised by a yere and a daye, without seisin of the lord, he hath no power to seize him after, if he go not in estrey out of the aforesaid franchise.—*Olde Tenures*, § 17.

to the custom of certain manors by such services; and their tenure is called tenure in villenage, and yet they are not villeins. For no land holden in villenage, or villein land, nor any custom arising out of the land, shall ever make a freeman villein; but a villein may make free land to be villein land to his lord. As where a villein purchaseth land in fee-simple or in fee-tail, the lord of the villein may enter into the land, and oust the villein and his heirs for ever: and afterwards the lord (if he will) can let the same land to the villein, to hold in villenage, &c.*

Villenage follows the person (§ 187).

174 [But if any freeman will take any lands or tenements

Freeman not

*lour tenementes solonques le custome de certeyns manors per tielx services; et lour tenure est appelle tenure en villenage, et unqore ils ne sont pas villeyns. Qar nul terre tenus en villenage, ou villeyn terre, ne ascun custome surdaunt de la terre, ne unques ferra frank home villeyn; mes un villeyn poet faire frank terre destre villeyn terre a son seignour. Sicome lou un villeyn purchase terre en fee-simple ou en fee-taille le seignour du villeyn poet entrer en la terre, et ouster le villeyn et sez heirez a toutz jours; et puis le seignour, sil voilleit, poet lesser mesme la terre a le villeyn, a tener en villenage, &c.**

174 [*Mez si ascun frank home voille prendre ascuns terrez*

---

tary, seems to have had various impressions as to the antiquity of the early printed copies, which are undated; indeed, with respect to other ancient books of the law, his bibliography is not to be depended upon, for his account of such ancient books in the preface to the 10th Rep. is not in accordance with his commentary on § 749, so far as regards the authorship of the "Olde Tenures." To return to the text: the translation by *Rastell* renders this passage thus :—*As to beare, bring, and carry out the dung and filth of the lord, unto the land of the lord, there to lay it, cast it, and spread it abroad upon the land, and to do such other manner of service.*

* At this place, in the common copies, occurs an interpolation, which Sir Edward Coke notices is an addition to Lyttleton, with a reference to stat. 19 Hen. 7, c. 15.

made villein by payment of a fine for marriage.

to hold of his lord by such villein service, *scil.* to pay a fine to him [for his marriage, or] for the marriage of his sons or daughters, then he shall pay such fine for the marriage: yet notwithstanding that it be the folly of such freeman to take in such form lands or tenements to hold of the lord by such bondage, yet this maketh not the freeman villein*.]

Title to a villein is either by prescription or by confession.

After confession of villenage the post nati *bond.*

175 Also every villein is either a villein by title or prescription, to wit, that he and his ancestors have been villeins time out of mind of man; or he is villein by his own confession in a court of record; 176 but if a freeman hath divers issues, and afterwards he confesseth himself to be villein to another in a court of record, yet those issues, which he hath be-

ou tenementez a tener de son seignour per tiel villeyn service, scil. *a paier un fyne a luy [pur son mariage ou] per le mariage de sez fitz ou filles, donques il paiera tiel fyne pur le mariage: et nient obstaunt quil est la folye de tiel frank home de prendre en tiel fourme terrez ou tenementez, a tener de le seignour per tiel bondage, unqore ceo ne fait le frank home villeyn**].

175 Item, *chescun villeyn ou il est villeyn per title de prescripcion, cestassavoir, que il et ses auncestres ount estre villeyns de temps dount memorie ne court; ou il est villeyn per son confession demesne en court de record,* 176 *mes si frank home ad divers issues, et puis confesse destre villeyn a un autre en court de recorde, unqore lez issues que il avoet devaunt*

* Although this section appears in the earliest printed copies, yet it may be deemed spurious. *Tottyl* 1557 (both editions), excludes it, and places an asterisk to denote the place of the interpolation, and all the subsequent editions by *Tottyl* place this section between two *flowers.* All the other editions to 1639 adopt a similar mark of addition. In the *Paper* MS. and in the edition by *Lettou & M.*, this section is the concluding portion of the chapter, whilst in *Machl. & Roh.* it is placed as in the text. In the Vell. MS. it appears at both places. The words in the second line of the text included within brackets appear only in *Roh.* and *Rastell's* Translation; *Rastell's* Translation also reads—*marriage, &c. for that it is the folly.*—This case is vouched by the Year-Book, 41 E. 3, 9. See also § 209.

fore the confession, &c., are free; but the issues which he shall have after the confession, shall be villeins, &c.

177 Also if a villein purchase land, and he alien the land to another before that the lord enter, then the lord cannot enter, for it shall be adjudged his folly, that he did not enter when the land was in the hands of the villein. And so it is of goods: if the villein buy goods, and sell or give them to another before the lord seizeth them, then the lord cannot seize them: but if the lord before any such sale or gift cometh into the house of the villein where such goods be, and there openly amongst the neighbours claim them to be his own, and seizes part of the goods in the name of seisin of all the goods, &c., this is a good seizure in law, and the occupation that the villein, after such claim, hath in the goods, shall be taken in law in the right of the lord. 178 But if the king hath a villein who purchases land, and aliens it before the king enter, yet the king may enter, into whose hands soever the land shall come. Or if the villein buyeth goods and sell them before that the king seizeth them, yet the king may

Villein cannot retain property, for lord may seize it before alienation; for lord's title accrues on claim or entry.

See § 61, 417

Secus *with regard to villein of the king, for* nullum tempus occurrit regi.

la confession, &c. sont frankes ; mes lez issues quil avera apres la confession &c., serront villeyns.

177 Item, *si le villeyn purchasa terre, et il aliene la terre a un autre devaunt que le seignour entra, donques le seignour ne poet entrer, qar il serra ajugge sa folye quil nentra pas quant la terre fuist en le mayn le villeyn. Et issint est dez biens : si le villeyn achata biens, et lez venda ou dona a un autre devaunt que le seignour seisist les biens, donques le seignour ne poet eux seiser : Mes si le seignour devaunt ascun tiel vende ou done vient dedeins la meason du villeyn lou tielx biens sont, et la ouvertement entre les vyceyns, eux clayma estre les soens, et seisist parcell des bienz en noun de seisin de toutz lez biens, &c., ceo est dit bon seisier en ley, et le occupacion que le villeyn apres tiel clayme, ad en lez biens, serra pris en ley en le droit le seignour.* 178 *Mes si le roy ad un villeyn quel purchasa terre, et aliena devaunt que le roy entra, unqore le roy poet entrer, a que mayns que la terre aviendra. Ou si le villeyn achata biens, et eux vendast devaunt que le roy seisist*

seize the goods, in whose hands soever they be. Because *nullum tempus occurrit regi* (*b*).

Villein purchaser of a reversion.

179 Also, if a man let certain land to another for term of life, saving to himself the reversion, and thereupon a villein purchase of the lessor the reversion: in this case it seemeth that the lord of the villein can forthwith come to the land, and claim the reversion as lord of the said villein, and by this claim the reversion is forthwith in him. For in any other form he cannot come to the reversion; for he cannot enter upon the tenant for life. And if he ought to abide (*i. e.* stay) until after the death of the tenant for life, then perchance he should come too late. For peradventure the villein may will to grant or alien the reversion to another in the life of the tenant for life, &c. 180 In the same manner it is, where a villein purchases an advowson of a church full of an incumbent, the lord of the villein may come to the said church,

Lord must claim, before his title can accrue.

The like where villein is purchaser of an advowson.

lez biens, unqore le roy poet seisier lez biens en que mayns que lez biens sount. Quia nullum tempus occurrit regi.

179 Item, *si home lessa certeyne terre a un autre pur terme de vie, savaunt la revercion a luy, et issint un villeyn purchace de le lessor la revercion : en ceo cas il semble que le seignour del villeyn poet mayntenaunt vener a la terre, et claymer la revercion, come seignour le dit villeyn, et per celle clayme la revercion est mayntenaunt en luy. Qar en autre fourme il ne poet vener a la revercion, qar il ne poet entrer sur le tenaunt a terme de vie. Et sil doit demurrer tanques apres la mort le tenaunt a terme de vie, donques per cas il viendra trope tarde. Qar paraventure le villeyn voille graunter ou aliener la revercion a un autre en la vie le tenaunt a terme de vie, &c.* 180 *En mesme le manere est, lou un villeyn purchace un avowson dun esglise pleyn dun encombent, que le seignour de villeyn poet vener al dit esglise, et claymer le dit avowson, et*

(*b*) The chief statute which limits the king's title is the 9 Geo. 3, c. 16, by which the rights of the crown are barred by an adverse enjoyment for sixty years.

and claim the said advowson, and by this claim the advowson is in him. For if he ought to abide (*i. e.* stay) till after the death of the incumbent, and then present his clerk to the said church, then in the meantime the villein might alien the advowson, and so oust the lord of his presentment.

And how such claim is to be made.

181 Also there is a villein *regardant* and a villein *in gross.* A villein regardant is, as if a man be seised of a manor to which a villein is regardant, and he who is seised of the said manor, or they whose estate he hath in the same manor, have been seised of the said villein and of his ancestors as villeins regardant to the same manor, time out of memory of man.

Villeins are either regardant or in gross.

Examples.

And villein in gross is, where a man is seised of a manor whereunto a villein is regardant, and granteth the same villein by his deed to another, then he is a villein in gross, and not regardant.

182 Also if a man and his ancestors, whose heir he is, have been seised of a villein and of his ancestors, as villeins of

per celle clayme lavowson est en luy. Qar sil doit entendre tanques apres la mort lencombent, et adonques a presenter son clerke a le dit esglise, donques en le mesme temps le villeyn poet aliener le avowson, et issint ouster le seignour de son presentement.

181 Item, *il y ad villeyn regardaunt, et villeyn en gros. Villeyn regardaunt est, sicome home est seisi dun manor a que un villeyn est regardaunt, et celuy qui est seisi del dit manor, ou ceux que estate ad en mesme le manor, ount este seisis de le dit villeyn et de sez auncestres come villeyns regardaunts a mesme le manor, de temps dount memorie ne court.*

Et villeyn en gros est, lou un home est seisi dun manor a que un villeyn est regardaunt, et il graunta mesme le villeyn per son fait a un autre, donques il est villeyn en gros, et nemye regardaunt.

182 Item, *si un home et ses auncestres que heire il est, ount este seisis dun villeyn et de sez auncestres come villeyns en*

time whereof memory runneth not, such are villeins in gross.

Prescription in a que estate applies to those things only which will not pass at common law without deed.

183 And here note well, that of such things which cannot be granted or aliened without deed or fine, a man who will have such things by prescription cannot otherwise prescribe but in him and in his ancestors, whose heir he is; and not by these words, In him and those whose estate (*c*) he hath; (see § 170 as to pleading a prescription by custom (*d*)); for that

gros, de temps dount memorie ne court ; tielx sount villeyns en gros.

183 Et hic nota, *que de tielx choses que ne poient estre grauntez ne alienez sauns fait ou fyne, home qui voilleit aver tielx choses per prescripcion ne poet autrement prescriber forsque en luy et en sez auncestres que heire il est, et nemy per ceux parolx; En luy et en ceux que estate il ad ; pur ceo que il*

(*c*) *Whose estate* (que estate), *&c.*—*Quorum statum*, as much as to say, whose estate he has. Here *Lyttleton* declares an excellent rule, that a man cannot prescribe for any thing by a *que estate*, which lies in grant, and which connot pass without deed or fine; but in him and his ancestors he may, because he comes in by descent without any conveyance. Neither can a man plead a *que estate* in himself of any thing that cannot pass without deed; but in another he may, as in bar of an avowry, the plaintiff may plead a *que estate* in the seignory in the avowant. But Lyttleton's words are to be observed, (*a man who will have such things by prescription*). Therefore, when a thing that lies in grant is but a conveyance to the thing claimed by prescription, there a *que estate* may be alleged of a thing that lies in grant; as a man may prescribe, that he and his ancestors and all those whose estate he has in an hundred have, time out of mind, &c. had a leet, &c. this is good, &c.

(*d*) The distinction between custom and prescription is this: that custom is properly a *local* usage, and not annexed to any *person*; such as a custom in the manor of Dale, that lands shall descend to the youngest son: prescription is merely a *personal* usage; as, that Sempronius, and his ancestors, or those whose estate he hath, have used time out of mind to have such an advantage or privilege. As for example: if there be a usage in the parish of Dale, that all the inhabit-

he cannot have their estate without deed or other writing, the which it behoveth to be shewed to the court (*e*), if he will have

Prescription how pleaded; In the person

ne poet aver lour estate sauns fait ou autre escripture, le quele covient destre monstre a le court, sil voille aver ascun avaunt-

---

ants of that parish may dance on a certain close, at all times, for their recreation; this is strictly a custom, for it is applied to the *place* in general, and not to any particular *persons:* but if the tenant, who is seised of the manor of Dale in fee, alleges that he and his ancestors, or all those whose estate he hath in the said manor, have used time out of mind to have common of pasture in such a close, this is properly called a prescription; for this is a usage annexed to the *person* of the owner of this estate. All prescription must be either in a man and his ancestors, or in a man and those whose estate he hath: which last is called prescribing in a *que estate.* And formerly a man might, by the common law, have prescribed for a right which had been enjoyed by his ancestors or predecessors at any distance of time, though his or their enjoyment of it had been suspended for an indefinite series of years. But by the Statute of Limitations, 32 Hen. 8, c. 2, it is enacted, that no person shall make any prescription by the seisin or possession of his ancestor or predecessor, unless such seisin or possession hath been within threescore years next before such prescription made. [And by stat. 2 & 3 Gul. 4, c. 71, prescription is limited to shorter periods, see *ante*, p. 202, in n.]

I. Nothing but incorporeal hereditaments can be claimed by prescription: as a right of way, a common, &c.; but that no prescription can give a title to lands, and other corporeal substances, of which more certain evidence may be had. But, as to a right of way, a common, or the like, a man may be allowed to prescribe; for of these there is no corporeal seisin, the enjoyment will be frequently by intervals, and therefore the right to enjoy them can depend on nothing else but immemorial usage.

II. A prescription must always be laid in him that is tenant of the fee. A tenant for life, for years, at will, or a copyholder, cannot prescribe, by reason of the imbecility of their

---

(*e*) *The which it behoveth to be shewn to the court.*]—The reason why every deed that is pleaded ought to be shewn to the court is, because every deed must prove itself to have sufficient words in law, whereof the court only can judge: and also to be proved by others, as by witnesses or other proofs, if the deed be denied, which is matter of fact [to be tried by the jury].—*Co. Lytt.* 121. *b.*

Profert *required of all deeds pleaded.*

applies to any thing that lies in grant.

any advantage of it. And because the grant and alienation of a villein [in gross*] lieth not without deed or other

age de ceo. Et pur ceo que le graunt et alienacion dun villeyn [en gros] ne gist sauns fait ou autre scripture, home*

---

* The words within brackets are not in *Roh.*, *Redm.*, *Berth.*, *Middl.*, *Sm.*, *Powel*, *or Tottyl* 1554.

---

estates. For, as prescription is usage beyond time of memory, it is absurd that they should pretend to prescribe, whose estates commenced within the remembrance of man. And therefore the copyholder must prescribe under cover of his lord's estate, and the tenant for life under cover of the tenant in fee-simple.

III. A prescription cannot be for a thing which cannot be raised by grant. For the law allows prescription only in supply of the loss of a grant, and therefore every prescription presupposes a grant to have existed. Thus a lord of a manor cannot prescribe to raise a tax or toll upon strangers; for, as such claim could never have been good by any grant, it shall not be good by prescription.

IV. A fourth rule is, that what is to arise by matter of record cannot be prescribed for, but must be claimed by grant, entered on record; such as, for instance, the royal franchises of deodands, felons' goods, and the like. These, not being forfeited till the matter on which they arise is found by the inquisition of a jury, and so made a matter of record, the forfeiture itself cannot be claimed by any inferior title. But the franchises of treasure-trove, waifs, estrays, and the like, may be claimed by prescription; for they arise from private contingencies, and not from any matter of record.

V. Among things incorporeal, which may be claimed by prescription, a distinction must be made with regard to the manner of prescribing; that is, whether a man shall prescribe in a *que estate*, or in himself and his ancestors. For, if a man prescribes in a *que estate*, (that is, in himself and those whose estate he holds) nothing is claimable by this prescription, but such things as are incident, appendant, or appurtenant to lands; for it would be absurd to claim anything as the consequence or appendix of an estate, with which the thing claimed has no connexion: but, if he prescribes in himself and his ancestors, he may prescribe for anything whatsoever that lies in grant; not only things that are appurtenant, but also such as may be in gross (§ 183). Therefore a man may prescribe, that he, and those whose estate he hath in the manor of Dale, have used to hold the advowson of Dale as *ap-*

writing, a man cannot prescribe in a villein in gross without shewing forth a writing, but in himself who claimeth the villein, and in his ancestors whose heir he is. But of such things which are regardant or appendant to a manor, or to other lands and tenements, a man may prescribe, that he and they whose estate he hath, who were seised of the manor, or of such lands or tenements, &c., have been seised of such things, as regardant or appendant to the manor, or to such lands and tenements, &c., from time whereof memory runneth not. And the reason is, for that such manor or lands and

In the que estate is confined to things lying in grant and which cannot pass without deed as appendant or appurtenant to manors, land, &c.

ne poet prescriber en un villeyn en gros sauns monstraunce descripture, si non en soy qui clayma le villeyn, et en sez ancestres que heire il est. Mes de tielx choses que sont regardaunts ou appendantes a un manor, ou as autres terres et tenementes, home poet prescriber, que il et ceux que estate il ad, queux furent seisis de le manor ou de tielx terres ou tenementes, &c., ount este seisis de tielx choses, come regardaunts ou appendantes a le manor, ou a tielx terres et tenementes de temps dount memorie ne court. Et la cause est, pur ceo que

---

pendant to that manor: but if the advowson be a distinct inheritance, and not appendant, then he can only prescribe in his ancestors. So also a man may prescribe in a *que estate* for a common *appurtenant* to a manor; but, if he would prescribe for a common *in gross*, he must prescribe in himself and his ancestors.

VI. Estates gained by prescription are not, of course, descendible to the heirs general, like other purchased estates, but are an exception to the rule. For, properly speaking, the prescription is rather to be considered as an evidence of a former acquisition, than as an acquisition *de novo:* and therefore, if a man prescribes for a right of way in himself and his ancestors, it will descend only to the blood of that line of ancestors in whom he so prescribes; the prescription in this case being indeed a species of descent. But, if he prescribes for it in a *que estate*, it will follow the nature of that estate in which the prescription is laid, and be inheritable in the same manner, whether that were acquired by descent or purchase; for every accessary followeth the nature of its principal.—B. C. ii. 263-6.

Distinction between re-regardant and appendant.

tenements may pass by alienation without deed, &c. 184 And is to be understood, that nothing is named regardant to a manor, &c., but a villein: but certain other things, as advowsons and common of pasture, &c., are named appendants (*f*) to the manor, or to the lands and tenements, &c.

A man may be a villein by confession in court of record.

185 Also if a man will acknowledge himself in court of record to be a villein, who was not a villein before, such a one is a villein in gross.

tiel manor ou terres et tenementes poient passer pur alienacion sauns fait, &c. 184 *Et est assavoir que nul chose est nosme regardaunt a un manor, &c., forsque villeyn: mes certeyns autres choses, come avowsons et comen de pasture, &c., sont nosmez appendantes al manor, ou al terrez et tenementez, &c.*

185 Item, *si home voille en courte de recorde soy conustre destre villeyn, qui ne fuist villeyn adevaunt, tiel est villeyn en gros.*

Appendant and appurtenant distinguished and exemplified.

(*f*) *Appendants.*] — Appendant is any inheritance belonging to another that is superior or more worthy. Appendants are always by prescription; but appurtenants may be created in some cases at this day. As if a man at this day grant to a man and his heirs, common in such a moor for his beasts levant or couchant upon his manor; or if he grant to another common of estovers or turbary in fee-simple to be burnt or spent within his manor; by these grants these commons are *appurtenant* to the manor, and shall pass by the grant thereof. If A. be seised of a manor, whereunto the franchise of waifs, estrays, and such like are appendant, and the king purchases the manor with the appurtenances, now are the royal franchises reunited to the crown and not appendant to the manor. But if he grant the manor *in as large and ample a manner as A. had &c.*, it is said, that the franchises shall be appendant (or rather appurtenant) to the manor.— *Co. Lytt.* 121. *b.*, [for the words " in as ample a manner as A. had " &c., confer no new grant, and seem to avoid doing so, for a new grant would destroy the title by prescription, for writing determines prescription. — *Bro. Abr. tit. Prescripcion, pl.* 102].

For the learning of *appendants* and *appurtenants* the reader is referred to Co. Lytt. 121. *b.* 122. *a.*

186 Also a man that is villein is called a villein or nief, and a woman that is villein, is called a niefe: as a man who is outlawed is called outlawed, and a woman who is outlawed is called a waive.

Male villein. styled villein or nief (nativus); *female villein, niefe* (nativa).

187 Also if a villein taketh a free-woman to wife, the issue shall be villeins. But if a niefe taketh a freeman to her husband, their issue shall be free (*g*).

Issue of a villein by a free-woman is villein; secus e converso.

186 Item, *home qui est villeyn est appelle villeyn ou nief, et feme que est villeyne est appelle neife: sicome home qui est utlage est dit utlage, et feme que est utlage est dit wayve.*

187 Item, *si un villeyn prent frank feme a feme, lissue entre eux serra villeyne. Mes si une neife prent frank home a baron, lour issue serra franke.*

(*g*) In all the copies of Lyttleton since *Redm.* except *Tottyl* 1557, both editions, there occurs the following addition to this section: *Et cest contrarie a la ley civile, qar la est dit, partus sequitur ventrem*— *And this is contrary to the civil law, for there it is said, the issue followeth the womb.* But this rule only applied to the bondwomen of the Romans termed *vernæ*, and never was intended to be understood of any other. *Heineccius* in his *Elementa Juris Naturæ et Gentium, lib.* 1, § cclii. and in *lib.* 2, § lxxxi. explains by the doctrine of natural accession as well as by the principles upon which hereditary bondage was established, in what cases this rule operated; on referring to which, the reader will be satisfied that those born of parents joined in any recognised wedlock did not fall under this rule, whatever the *status* of the parents might be, and, consequently, that no one could be *dominus ventris* where *jura connubii* intervened.

The ascribing this maxim, which only had a partial application, to the civil law, as a general rule, is older than Lyttleton; who however possessed too much learning and sound knowledge to cite *Fortescue*, who in his *De Laudibus Legum Angliæ, cap.* 42, 43, assumes as a general proposition, that "the civil laws decree, that the issue ever followeth the womb," and represents his royal pupil as approving this rule, in terms not very favorable to the civil law. Justinian, *lib.* 1, *tit.* iv. *De ingenuis*, certainly states it as a rule, that the issue by a bondfather born of a freewoman was born free; and that where the father was uncertain, or the issue not born in wedlock, the issue followed the condition of the mother, because the issue could not be said

A bastard not villein unless by confession.

188 Also no bastard can be villein, unless he will acknowledge himself to be villein in court of record, for he is in law *quasi nullius filius*, because he cannot inherit to any.

A villein may sue any other person than his lord; yet

189 Also every villein is able and free to sue all manner of actions against every person, except against his lord, to whom

188 Item, *nul bastard poet estre villeyn, si non quil voille soy conustre estre villeyn en court de recorde, car il est en ley* quasi nullius filius, *pur ceo que il ne poet enheriter a nulluy.*

189 Item, *chescun villeyn est able et frank de suer toutz maners accions envers chescun persone, forspris envers son sei-*

---

to have a father (contrary to the principle stated at § 88); and in reference to this text of Justinian, *Redm.*, *Berth.*, *Middl.*, *Sm.*, *Powel*, (English 1551, as well as French edition), and *Tottyl* 1554, in the margin of the interpolated text, refer to this title, and cite the words, *sufficit autem liberam fuisse matrem;* the ancient writers on English law, who frequently animadvert on the civil law as being less equitable or just than the common law, are in this point set right by *Selden*, who in citing *Ulpian* in *π. tit. De Statu Hominum, l.* 24; and *tit. De his qui in potestate sunt*, repeats, that where *jura connubii* did not intervene, the issue followed the condition of the mother, for no marriage strictly could take place between bond persons (see in *π.*, *tit. De legatis* 3, *l.* 41, *Uxorem, sect.* 2, *Codicillis*, and *tit. De Incest. Nuptiis, l.* 3, *cum ancillis*, and *Heineccius, Elem. Juris.*, (*ut supra*), 2, § lxxxi); but where *jura connubii* did intervene, the children always followed the condition of the father.

Sir Edward Coke, although he states this interpolation to be an addition to Lyttleton, does not justify the civil law against this hacknied aspersion; but he merely says, "that, by the civil law, *partus sequitur ventrem*, as well where a freeman takes a bondwoman to wife, as where a bondman takes a freewoman to wife. In the first case, the issue is by the civil law bond, and in the other free. Both which cases are contrary to the law of England;" which, though strictly true, yet leaves the rule open to misinterpretation.

The editions by *Tottyl*, from 1561 to 1591, place this interpolation between two *flowers;* and in all the other editions to 1639, this passage is placed between two *asterisks* or signs. This passage also occurs in all the copies of *Rastell's* Translation.

he is villein. And yet certain actions he may have against his lord*. For he may have against his lord an action of appeal for the death of his father, or other his ancestor whose heir he is. 190 Also a niefe that is ravished by her lord, may have an appeal of rape against him (*h*). 191 Also, if a villein be made executor to another, and the lord of the villein was indebted to the testator in a certain sum of money which is not paid, in this case the villein as executor of the testator shall have an action of debt against his lord, because he shall not recover the debt to his own proper use, but to the use of the testator.

against his lord he might have had an appeal.

And the same of a niefe.

Villein executor may sue his lord by reason of his executorship.

gnour a qui il est villeyn. Et unqore certeyns accions il poet aver envers son seignour. Qar il poet aver envers son seignour un accion dappelle de mort son pere, ou dautre de son auncestre, qui heire il est.* 190*Auxi un niefe que est ravy per son seignour poet aver un appelle de Rape envers luy.* 191 *Auxi si un villeyn soit fait executour a un autre, et le seignour le villeyn fuist endette a le testatour en un certeyn somme dargent lequel nest mye paie, en ceo cas le villeyn come executour de le testatour avera accion de dette envers son seignour, pur ceo quil ne recovera le dette a son use demesne, mez al use de le testatour.*

---

* The text is given according to *Roh.*, for *Lettou & M.*, and *Machl.*, read this passage according to the ordinary copies, viz.—*Et unqore en certeyns choses, il poet aver accion envers son seignour; and yet in certain things he may have action against his lord. Rastell's* Transl. reads—*and yet in certain things he may have against his lord an action of appeal for the death of his father.* But *Redm.*, *Berth.*, *Middl.*, *Sm.*, *Powel*, and *Tottyl* 1554, read as in the text, which the editor conceives is the true sense.

(*h*) Appeals of rape, robbery, and murder, have been abolished. As to the nature and effect of the process of these appeals, which, though of a criminal nature, yet were at the suit of the subject. See B. C. iv. 310.

And the lord cannot seize testator's goods in villein's hands, for executors represent the person of villein testator, § 337.
But lord must plead protestando *with his villein.*

192 Also the lord may not take out of the possession of such villein, who is executor, the goods of the deceased; and if he do, the villein as executor shall have an action for the same goods so taken, against his lord, and shall recover damages to the use of the testator. But in all such cases it behoveth that the lord, who is defendant in such actions, make protestation that the plaintiff is his villein, or else the villein shall be enfranchised, although the matter be found for the lord, and against the villein, as it is said.

Trial of villenage in action where villein sues his lord, to be had in the county where action laid, not where the manor lies, to prevent consequence of which, stat. 9 Ric. 2, was passed.

193 Also, if a villein sue an action of trespass, or another action against his lord in one county, and the lord saith that he shall not be answered, because he is his villein regardant to his manor in another county, &c., and the plaintiff saith that he is free and of a free estate, and no villein; this shall be tried in the county where the plaintiff hath conceived his action, and not in the county where the manor is: and this is in favour of liberty. And for this cause a statute was made anno 9 R. 2, c. 2, the tenor whereof followeth in this form:

192 Item, *le seignour ne poet prendre hors del possession de tiel villeyn qui est executour lez biens le mort; et sil face, le villeyn come executour avera accion de trespas de mesmez lez biens issint prisez envers son seignour, et recovera damages al use de testatour. Mez en toutz tielx cases il convient que le seignour, qui est defendant en tielx accions, face protestacion que le pleintif est son villeyn, ou autrement le villeyn serra enfraunchise, coment que le matere soit trove pur le seignour, encountre le villeyn, come est dit.*

193 Item, *si un villeyn suist un accion de trespas, ou un autre accion envers son seignour en un countee, et le seignour dit que il ne serra respondu, pur ceo que il est son villeyn regardaunt a son manor en autre countee, &c., et le pleintif dit quil est frank, et de frank estate, et nemy villeyn; ceo serra trie en le countee lou le pleintif avoit conceyve son accion, et nemy en le countee lou le manor est; et ceo est* in favorem libertatis. *Et pur ceo cause un estatut fuist fait* anno ix. Regis Ricardii ii. *le tenor de quel ensuyst en tiel fourme:*

Also, for that where many villeins and niefs, as well of great lords, as of other folks, as well spiritual as temporal, flee and go into cities, towns, and places franchised, as into the city of London and other like places, and feign divers suits against their lords, [because they would make themselves free by the answer of their lords*]: it is accorded and assented, that the lords nor none other shall be fore-barred of their villeins, by reason of their answer in the law. By force of which statute if any villein will sue any manner of action to his own use in any county where he is powerful to try, &c. against his lord, the lord may choose whether he will plead that the plaintiff is his villein, or make protestation that he is his villein, and plead his other matter in bar. And if they be at issue, and the issue be found for the lord, then the villein is a villein as he was before, by force of the same statute. But if the issue be found for the villein, then

By this stat. 9 Ric. 2. lords were not forbarred of their villeins, but lord must plead villenage of the plaintiff, with a protestando to prevent enfranchisement of villein pleading the other matter in bar.

Item, *pur la ou plusours villeyns et neifes, sibien des graundes seignours, come des autres gentes, sibien espirituelx come temporelx, senfuent deins citees, villes, et lieux enfraunchises, come en la citee de Londres, et autres semblables, et feignount divers suits denvers lour seignours, [a cause de eux faire franks per le respons de lour seignours*:] Accorde est et assentus, que les seignours ne autres ne soyent forbarres de lour villeynes per cause de lour respons en la ley. Per force de quel estatut, si ascun villeyn voilleit suer ascun maner de accion a son use demesne en ascun countee, lou il est fort a trier, &c., envers son seignour, le seignour poet eslier de pleder que le pleintif est son villeyn, ou de faire protestacion que il est son villeyn, et de pleder autre matere en barre. Et sils sont a issue, et lissue soit trove pur le seignour, donques le villeyn est villeyn come il fuist adevaunt, per force de mesme lestatut. Mes si lissue soit trove pur le*

---

* The words within brackets are not in *Machl.* or *Roh.*

the villein is free; because that the lord took not at the beginning for his plea, that the villein was his villein, but took it by protestation, &c. (*i*).

villeyn, donques est le villeyn frank, pur ceo que le seignour ne prist a commencement pur son plee, que le villeyn fuist son villeyn; mes ceo prist per protestacion, &c.

(*i*) Now this section is to be thus explained:—while tenure in villenage subsisted it was not unusual for villeins to set up feigned actions against their lords, for the purpose of obtaining their enfranchisement; for, since the lord was not liable to be sued by his villein in a civil action, the very circumstance of his pleading thereto, was, by implication, an admission that the plaintiff was not his villein. At the same time it was a general rule of law, (for the law always favours liberty), that the plaintiff might bring his action in any other county he pleased, instead of confining himself to that in which the manor lay, to which he was regardant as a villein. But this rule gave rise to a manifest inconvenience; for if the villein brought his action in some distant county, where the enfranchisement of villeins was particularly favored, and consequently where he had the advantage of, and was strong in trial against his lord, then, if the lord took issue upon the question of villenage, it would be decided against him; and if, on the other hand, he pleaded to the special matter upon which the feigned action was brought, he necessarily admitted the enfranchisement of his villein by implication; so that, in either case, he lost his property in the villein. "For this cause," says Lyttleton, "it was enacted by the stat. 2 Ric. 2, that no advantage should be had of these feigned actions; but that the vassalage of the plaintiff should be still saved to the defendant, upon his protesting, by force of the above statute, 'that the plaintiff is his villein,' and then 'pleading the special matter in bar.'" The reader will observe that the words mistaken in the original are, "where he" the villein, "is powerful or strong in trial against his lord;" *où il est fort à trier envers son seignour.* It is almost needless to remark, that this section explains the doctrine of pleading with a "protestando," and which Lord Coke, therefore, accurately defines to be the *exclusion* of a conclusion.—*Ritso's Introducduction*, p. 107. A similar expression occurs in the *Year-Book*, 21 *E.* 4, 119, viz. *est fort que le tenaunt* (copyholder) *prescribera vers le seignour.*

194 Also the lord may not maim his villein. For if he maim his villein, he shall of that be indicted at the king's suit; and if he be of that attainted, he shall for that make grievous fine and ransom to the king. But it seemeth that the villein shall not have by the law any appeal of maihem against his lord; for in appeal of maihem a man shall not recover but his damages. And if the villein in that case recover damages against his lord, and hath thereof execution, the lord may take that which the villein hath in execution, from the villein, and so the recovery *is* void, &c.

The lord may not maim his villein.

Yet the villein cannot have his appeal, for by that process damages are recovered.

195 Also, if a villein be demandant in an action real, or plaintiff in an action personal, against his lord, if the lord will plead in disability of his person, he may not make full defence (*k*), but he shall defend but the wrong and the force, and demand the judgment if (*i. e.* whether) he shall be an-

To a villein plaintiff, his villenage may be pleaded in disability of the person.

194 Item, *le seignour ne poet maheymer son villeyn. Qar sil maheyma son villeyn, il serra de ceo endite a le suyte le roy; et sil soit de ceo atteynt, il ferra pur ceo grevous fyn et raunson al roy. Mes il semble que le villeyn navera pas per la ley un appelle de maheyme envers son seignour. Qar en appelle de mayheme home recovera forsque damages. Et si le villeyn en ceo cas recoverast damages envers son seignour, et ent avoit execucion, le seignour poet prendre ceo que le villeyn avoit en execucion de le villeyn, et issint le recoverer voide, &c.*

195 Item, *si un villeyn soit demandant en accion real, ou pleintif en accion personel, envers son seignour, si le seignour voille pleder en disabilite de son person, il ne poet faire pleyn defence, mes il defendera forsque tort et force, et demandera juggement sil serra respondu, &c.,* [*et monstrera son matere*

(*k*) The words *defence* and *defend* in our law pleadings do not mean a *justification*, but a *denial*.

wered, [and shew his matter forthwith how he is villein, and demand judgment if he shall be answered*].

Six disabilities of the person which may be pleaded to actions.

196 Also, there be six manner of men against whom if they sue judgment may be demanded, if they shall be answered, &c.

The first, villenage.

One is, where a villein sueth an action against his lord, as in the case aforesaid.

The second, outlawry.

197 The second is, where a man is outlawed upon an action of debt or trespass, or upon any other action or indictment; the tenant or the defendant may shew all the matter of record and the outlawry, and demand judgment if he shall be answered; because he is out of the law to sue an action during the time that he is outlawed.

The third, alien nee.

198 The third is, where an alien who is born out of the allegiance of our sovereign lord the king; if such alien will sue an action real or personal, the tenant or defendant may say,

meyntenant coment il est son villeyn, et demandera juggement sil serra respondu].

196 Item, vi. *maners de homes y sont contre queux sils suont accions &c. juggement poet estre demaunde sils serront responduz, &c.*

Un est, lou villeyn suist accion envers son seignour, come en le cas avauntdit.

197 *Le seconde est, lou home est utlage sur accion de dette ou trespas, ou sur autre accion ou enditement le tenaunt ou defendant poet monstrer tout le matere de recorde, et lutlagarie, et demaunder juggment sil serra respondu, pur ceo que il est hors de la ley de suer ascun accion duraunt le temps que il estoit utlage.*

198 *Le tierce est, lou un alien qui est nee hors de la liegeaunce nostre seignour le roy; si tiel alien voille suer un accion reall ou personell, le tenaunt ou defendant poet dire, quil fuist nee*

---

* The words within brackets are not in *Roh.*

that he was born in such a country which is out of the king's allegiance, and demand judgment if he shall be answered.

199 The fourth is, where a man who, by judgment given against him upon a writ of *premunire facias &c.*, is out of the king's protection; if he sue any action, and the tenant or defendant will shew all the record against him, he may ask judgment if he shall be answered; for the law and the king's writs be the things by which a man is protected and holpen, and so, during the time that a man in such case is out of the king's protection, he is out of help and protection by the king's law, or by the king's writ.

The fourth, premunire.

200 The fifth is, where a man is entered and professed in religion; if such a one sue an action, the tenant or defendant may shew that such a one is entered into religion in such a place, into the order of Saint Bennet, and is there a monk professed; or into the order of *friars-minors* or *preachers*, and is there a friar professed; and so of other orders of religion, &c., and demand judgment if he shall be answered. And the

The fifth, profession.

en tiel paiis que est hors de la liegeaunce le roy, et demaunder juggement sil serra respondu.

199 *Le quart est, lou un home qui per juggement done envers luy sur un brief de* premunire facias, *&c. est hors de proteccion le roy, sil suast ascun accion, et le tenaunt ou defendaunt monstrerast tout le recorde envers luy, il poet demaunder juggement sil serra respondu; qar la ley le roy et les briefs le roy sount les choses per queux home est protecte et eide, et issint durant le temps que home en tiel cas est hors de la proteccion le roy, il est hors destre eide ou protection per la ley le roy, ou per brief le roy.*

200 *Le quinte est lou un home qui est entre et professe en religion; si tiel suist un accion, le tenaunt ou le defendaunt poet monstrer que tiel est entre en religion en tiel lieu, en lordre de Seynt* Benet, *et la est moigne professe, ou en lordre des freres prechours, ou menours, et la est frere professe, et issint dez autres ordres de religion, &c. et demaunder juggement sil serra respondu. Et la cause est, pur ceo que quant home entra en*

cause is this, that, when a man entereth into religion and is professed, he is dead in law, and his son or next cousin incontinent shall inherit him, as well as though he were dead in deed. And when he entereth into religion he may make his testament and his executors &c., the which executors may have an action of debt due to him before his entry into religion, or any other action that executors may have, as if he were dead indeed. And if that he make no executors when he entereth into religion, then the ordinary may commit the administration of his goods to other, as if he were dead in deed.

The sixth, excommunication.

201 The sixth is, where a man is excommunicated* by the law of Holy Church, and he sueth an action real or personal, the tenant or defendant may plead that he that sueth is excommunicated: and of this it behoveth him to shew the bishop's letters under his seal, witnessing the excommunication, and ask judgment if he shall be answered, &c. But in

religion, et est professe, il est mort en ley, &c. et son fitz ou autre cosin meyntenaunt luy enheritera, auxibien sicome il fuist mort en fait. Et quant il entra en religion il poet faire son testament et sez executours, &c., les queux executours averont un accion de dette due a luy, devaunt lentre en religion, ou autre accion que executours poient aver, sicome il fuist mort en fait. Et sil ne fait ascuns executours quant il entra en religion, donques lordinarie poet committer ladministracion de sez biens as autres, sicome il fuist mort en fait.

201 *Et le sisme est lou home est excommenge* per la ley de seynt esglise, et il suist un accion reall ou personell, le tenaunt ou defendaunt poet pleder que celuy qui suist est excommenge: et de ceo covient monstrer lettres de levesque south son seale, tesmoignant lescommengement, et demaunder juggement sil serra respondu, &c. Mes en ceo cas, si le demaundant ou pleintif*

---

* *Rastell* translates this word *excommenge—accursed,* and *excommengement—accursing.*

this case, if the demandant or plaintiff cannot deny it, the writ shall not abate; but the judgment shall be, that the tenant or defendant shall go quit without day; for this, that when the demandant or plaintiff hath purchased his letters of absolution, and these are shewed to the court, he may have a resummons or re-attachment upon his original, after the nature of his writ. But in the other five cases the writ shall abate, &c., if the matter shewed cannot be gainsaid, &c.

Profession or entering into religion is a civil death, see also § 410.

Remedies of the lord if villein professed, or niefe married to a freeman.

202 Also, if a villein be made a secular [chaplain*], yet his lord may seize him as his villein, and seize his goods, &c. But it seemeth that if the villein enter into religion, and is professed &c., that the lord may not take nor seize him, because he is dead in law, no more than if a freeman take a niefe to his wife; the lord cannot take nor seize the wife of the husband, but his remedy is to have an action against the husband, for that he took his niefe to wife without his license and will. And so may the lord have an action against the

ceo ne poet dedire, le brief nabatera mye, mes le juggement serra, que le tenaunt ou defendaunt alera quite sauns jour, pur ceo que quant le demandaunt ou pleintif purchace ses lettres de absolucion, et ceux sont monstres a le court, il poet aver un resommons ou reattachment sur son originall, solonques la nature de son brief. Mes en les autres cinq casez le brief abatera, &c, si la matere monstre ne poet estre dedite, &c.

202 Item, *si un villeyn est fait un* [*chappeleyn**] *seculer, uuqore son seignour poet luy seisier come son villeyn, et seisier sez biens. Mes il semble que si le villeyn entre en religion, et est professe, &c., que le seignour ne poet luy prendre ne seisier, pur ceo que il est mort en ley; nient pluis que si un frank home prent un neif a sa feme, le seignour ne poet prendre ne seisier la feme de le baron, mez son remedie est daver un accion envers le baron, pur ceo que il prist sa neif a feme sauns son licence et volunte. Et issint poet le seignour*

---

* *Rastell's* Translation renders this word *priest.*

sovereign of the house that taketh and admitteth his villein to be professed in the same house without license and leave of the lord &c., and he shall recover his damages to the value of the villein. For he that is professed a monk shall be a monk, and as a monk to be taken for term of his natural life, unless he be deraigned by the law of Holy Church. And he is bound by his religion to keep his cloister, &c. And if the lord could take him out of his house, then he should not live as a dead person, nor according to his religion, which should be inconvenient &c. (*l*) 203 For if there be a guardian in chivalry of body, and of the land of an infant within age, if the infant when he comes to the age of fourteen years entereth into religion, and is professed, the guardian hath no other remedy, as to the wardship of the

Another case of civil death and its consequences.

aver accion envers le souveraigne del meason qui prist et admittast son villeyn destre professe en mesme le meason sauns le licence et la volunte le seignour, &c., et recovera sez damages a la valewe de le villeyn. Qar celuy qui est professe moigne, &c., serra un moigne, et come un moigne estre pris pur terme de sa vie naturell, sinon quil soit desreigne per la ley de seynt esglise. Et il est tenus per sa religion de garder son cloyster, &c. Et si le seignour luy puissoit prendre hors de sa meason, donques il ne viveroit come mort persone, ne solonques sa religion, le quel serroit inconvenient, &c. 203 *Qar si soit gardeyn en chivalerie de corps et de terre dun enfaunt deins age, si lenfaunt quant il vient al age de* xiiij. *ans entra en religion, et est professe, le gardeyn nad autre remedie quant a le garde le corps forsque brief de ravissement de*

(*l*) Lyttleton extends the liability of the sovereign (*i. e.* an abbot or prior), beyond the case stated in the text, for in 18 E. 4, he says, "And if my villein enter into religion, or if a man grant to me an annuity, and enter into religion, I shall have my action against the sovereign, for this, that it shall be judged (*serra rette*) his folly to receive those who are so indebted into his house," &c.—*Year-Book, Mich.* 18 *E.* 4.

body, but a writ of *ravishment of ward* against the sovereign of the house. And if any, being of full age, who is cousin and heir of the infant, entereth into the land, the guardian hath no remedy as to the wardship of the land, because the entry of the heir of the infant is lawful in such case.

204 Also in many divers cases the lord may make manumission and enfranchisement to his villein.

Manumission and enfranchisement of villein;

Manumission is properly, when the lord makes a deed to his villein to enfranchise him by this word, "*manumittere,*" which is the same as to put him out of the hands and power of another. And for that by such deed the villein is put out of the hand and the power of his lord, it is called manumission. [And so every manner of enfranchisement made to a villein may be said to be a manumission*] 205 Also if the lord make to his villein an obligation for a certain sum of money, or grant to him by his deed an annuity, or let to him

—by deed.

What acts of the lord operated as an enfranchisement.

garde envers le souveraigne del meason. Et si ascun esteant de pleyn age, qui est cosyn et heire del enfaunt, entra en le terre, le gardeyn nad ascun remedie quant al garde de la terre, pur ceo que lentre del heire lenfaunt est congeable en tiel cas.

204 Item, *en moultes dyvers cases le seignour poet faire manumission et enfraunchisement a son villeyn.*

Manumission est proprement quant le seignour fait son fait a son villeyn de luy enfraunchiser per hoc verbum "manumittere," quod idem est quod extra manum vel extra potestatem alterius ponere. *Et pur ceo que per tiel fait le villeyn est mis hors de sa mayn et de la poiar son seignour, il est appelle manumission. [Et issint chescun maner denfraunchisement fait a un villeyn poet estre dit manumission*].* 205 *Auxi si le seignour fait a son villeyn un obligacion de certeyn somme dargent, ou graunta a luy per son fait un annuite, ou*

* The words within brackets are not in the Paper MS.

Bond, obligation, annuity, or lease.

Feoffment.

by his deed, lands or tenements for term of years, the villein is enfranchised. 206 Also if the lord maketh a feoffment to his villein of any lands or tenements by deed, or without deed, in fee-simple, fee-tail, or for term of life [or years*], and delivereth to him seisin, that is an enfranchisement.

A letting at will no enfranchisement.

207 But if the lord maketh to him a lease of land or tenements to hold at will of the lord, by deed or without deed, this is no enfranchisement, for that he hath no manner of certainty or surety of his estate, but the lord may oust him when he will.

Suit by lord against villein in a real or personal action a manumission.

208 Also, if the lord sueth against his villein a *Præcipe quod reddat*, if he recover or be nonsuit after appearance, this is a manumission, for that he might lawfully have entered into the land without suit. In the same manner it is if he sue against his villein an action of debt or account, or of covenant, or of trespass, or of such like; that is an enfran-

lessa a luy per son fait terrez ou tenementez pur terme dez ans, le villeyn est enfraunchise. 206 *Auxi si le seignour fait un feoffement a son villeyn dascun terres ou tenementes per fait, ou sauns fait, en fee-simple, fee-taille, ou pur terme de vie [ou ans*], et a luy livera seisin, ceo est un enfraunchisement.* 207 *Mes si le seignour fait a luy un lees dez terres ou tenementes, a tener a volunte le seignour, per fait ou sauns fait, ceo nest ascun enfraunchisement, pur ceo que il nad ascun manere certeynte ne seurte de son estate, mes le seignour luy poet ouster quant il voilleit.* 208 *Auxi si le seignour suist envers son villeyn un* Præcipe quod reddat, *sil recover ou soit nounsue apres apparaunce, ceo est un manumission, pur ceo quil puissoit loyalment entrer en la terre sauns tiel suite. En mesme le manere est, sil suist envers son villeyn un accion de dette ou daccompt, ou de covenaunt, ou de trespas, ou hu-*

---

* The words *ou ans, or years,* are not in *Lettou & M., Machl.,* or *Roh.,* they first occur in *Redm.,* and appear in every subsequent edition.

chisement: for that he might imprison the villein and take his goods without such suit.

But if the lord sue his villein by appeal of felony, this shall not enfranchise the villein, albeit that the matter of appeal be found against the lord, for that the lord could not have the villein to be hanged without such suit. But if the villein were not indicted of the same felony before the appeal sued against him, and afterward is acquitted of this felony, so as he recover damages against his lord for the false appeal, &c., then the villein is enfranchised, because of the judgment of damages to be given unto him against his lord. And many other cases and matters there be by which a villein may be enfranchised against his lord, &c.*

Appeal of felony an exception, for villein could not be hanged without this process.

Yet if villein recover damages for the false appeal, it is otherwise.

209 Also, if the lord of a manor will prescribe, that there hath been accustomed within his manor time out of mind, that every tenant within the same manor, who marrieth his daugh-

An instance of a void prescription as being against reason.

jusmodi, ceo est un enfraunchisement, pur ceo que il puissoit emprisoner le villeyn, et prendre sez biens sauns tiel suite.

*Mes si le seignour suist son villeyn per appelle de felonye, ceo ne enfraunchisera pas le villeyn, coment que le matere de lappelle soit trove encounter le seignour, pur ceo que le seignour ne puissoit aver le villeyn destre pendu sauns tiel suite. Mes si le villeyn ne fuist endite de mesme le felonye devaunt lappelle suy envers luy, et puis est acquite de cest felonye issint que il recovera damagez envers son seignour pur le faux appelle, &c., donques le villeyn est enfraunchise per cause de le juggement de damagez pur luy donez envers son seignour. Et plusours autres cases et materes y sount per queux un villeyn poet estre enfraunchise envers son seignour, &c.**

209 Item, *si le seignour dun manor voille prescriber, que il y ad este accustume deins son manor de temps dount memorie ne court, que chescun tenaunt deins mesme le manor, qui maria*

---

* A spurious, *sed de illis quære* occurs here in *Redm.* and in all the subsequent copies, English as well as French. The *&c.* that precedes it is not in *Machl.* or *Roh.*

Marchet. ter to any man without license of the lord of the manor, shall make fine, at the will of the lord, [and have made fine*] to the lord of the manor for the time being, this prescription is void; for none ought to make such fine but only villeins. For every freeman may freely marry his daughter to whom it pleaseth him and his daughter. And because this prescription is against reason, such prescription is void. 210 But in the shire of Kent (*m*), concerning tenements holden in gavelkind, there, where by the custom and use of time whereof memory runneth not, the children male ought equally to in-

Gavelkind allowable because reasonable.

Post, § 265.

sa file a ascun home sauns licence de le seignour del manor, ferra fyne a le volunte le seignour [et ont fait fyne] al seignour del manor pur le temps esteant, cest prescripcion est voide; qar nul doit faire tielx fynes forsque tantsoulement villeyns. Qar chescun frank home poet franchement marier sa file a qui que pleast a luy et sa file. Et pur ceo que cest prescripcion est enconter reason, tiel prescripcion est voide.* 210 *Mes en le countee de Kent, de tenementes tenus en gavelkynde, la lou per la custome et use de temps dount memorie ne court, les fitz males doient owelment enheriter, ceo*

---

* The words within brackets do not appear in *Roh.* The preceding words, *a le volunte le seignour—at the will of the lord*, are in neither *Machl.* nor *Roh.*

(*m*) For that in no county of England, lands at this day be of the nature of gavelkind of common right, saving in Kent only. But yet in divers parts of England, within divers manors and seignories, the like custom is in force.—*Co. Lytt.* 140. *a.*

And in Kent, in gavelkind, "The father to the bough, the son to the plough;" there, all heirs male shall divide their inheritance, and likewise women; but women shall not make partition with men. And a woman after the death of her husband shall be endowed of the moiety; and if she commit fornication in her widowhood, or take an husband after, she shall lose her dower.—*Stat. Prerogativa Regis*, 17 *E*, 2. *Statutes of the Realm*, i. 226, *edited by Sir Thos. E. Tomlins.*

herit, this custom is allowable, because it standeth with some reason; because every son is as great a gentleman as the eldest son, and [by reason of this] to greater honour and valour will increase; and [if he had nothing] by his ancestor &c. peradventure he would not increase so much, &c.*

211 Also, where by the custom called Borough-English (*n*) *And so is Borough-English*

*custome est allowable, pur ceo que il estoit ovesque ascun reason : pur ceo que chescun fitz est auxi graund gentilhome come leigne fitz, et [ceo per cause] a pluis graunde honour et valour cressera, et [sil navoit] rien per son auncestre, &c., paraventure il ne puissoit tielment cresser, &c.**

211 Item, *lou per custome appel Borough-English, en as-*

---

* The text of *Lyttleton* is confused at this place. The reading above given is conformable to *Machl.* and *Roh.*, both which editions accord closely with each other. *Lettou & M.* reads *et per case; Machl.* and *Roh. et ceo per cause; Lettou & M.* again reads *et sil avoet; Machl.* and *Roh. et sil navoit; Rastell's* Translation is as follows:—*and because of that, more great honour and valour shall grow, than if he had nothing by his ancestors, where peradventnre he might not so grow, &c. Redm.*, and after him, *Berth.*, *Middl.*, *Sm.*, *Powel*, and *Tottyl* 1554, read *et per reason de cel, pluis graund honour et valour cressera a tiel enfaunt, que cresseroit, sil navoit rien per son auncestre, &c., ou* (lou) *paraventure il ne puissoit tielment cresser, &c. And by reason of this, greater honour and wealth* (valeur) *shall increase to such child, than would* [otherwise] *increase, if he had nothing from his ancestor, &c., where peradventure he could not thus increase, &c. Pyns.* 1516 reads, *et ceo est plus grand honor et valour et pluis honor cressera sil navoit rien per son auncestre ou peraventure* —— (as in the other editions. The Translation adopted by *Sir Edward Coke* is thus—*And perchance will grow to greater honor and valour, if he hath anything by his ancestors, or otherwise peradventure he would not increase so much, &c.*

(*n*) Of this custom Lyttleton has spoken before in the Chapter of Burgage. And in our books there is a special kind of Borough-English; as it shall descend to the younger son, if he be not of the

a good custom, and reason why. § 165, 735.

in some borough the youngest son shall inherit all the tenements &c. This custom also stands with some certain reason, because that the younger son, (if he lack father and mother), because of his younger age, may least of all his brethren help himself &c. 212 But if a man will prescribe, that if any cattle were upon the demesnes of his manor, there doing damage, that the lord of the manor for the time being hath used to distrain them, and the distress to keep till fine were made to him for the damage at his will, this prescription is void; because it is against reason, that, if wrong be done any

Unreasonable prescription void.

Example.

§ 265.

cun boroughe le fitz puisne enheritera toutz les tenementes, &c., cest custome estoit ovesque ascun certeyn reason, pur ceo que le fitz puisne, sil faute pere et mere, per cause de son juvente, poet le pluis meyns de toutz sez frerez luy mesme ëider, &c. 212 Mes si home voille prescriber, que si ascun avers furent sur les demeynez de son manor, la damage fesantz que le seignour del manor pur le temps esteaunt ad use eux destreigner, et le distresse reteigner tanques fyne fuist fait a luy pur le damage a sa volunte, cest prescripcion est voide, pur ceo quil est enconter reason, que si tort soit

---

Borough-English sometimes extends to daughters.

half-blood; and if he be, then to the eldest son. Within the manor of B. [Bray, 2 Watk. c. 410], in the county of Berks, there is such a custom, that if a man have divers daughters, and no son, and dies, the eldest daughter only shall inherit, and if he have no daughters, but sisters, the eldest sister by the custom shall inherit, and sometimes the youngest. And divers other customs there be in like cases. And herewith agreeth *Britton*, who saith, "*De terres des ancients demeynes soit use solonques le auncient usage del lieu; dount en ascun lieu le tient lieu per usage, que le heritage soit departable entre touts les enfaunts, freres et sores, et en ascun lieu que le eigne avera tout, et en ascun lieu que le puisne frere avera tout.*" *Concerning lands in ancient demesne let the custom be according to the ancient usage of the place; whereof in some places the usage holds that the heritage be departable between all the children, brothers and sisters, and in another place that the elder shall have all, and in some place, that the younger brother shall have all.—Co. Lytt.* 133. *a.*

Customs respecting inheritances in ancient demesne, gavelkind, and Borough-English.

man, that he thereof should be his own judge: for by such means, if he had damages but to the value of an halfpenny, he might assess and have therefore an hundred pounds, which should be against all reason. And so such prescription, or any other prescription used, if it be against reason, this ought not, nor will be allowed before judges (*o*): *Quia malus usus abolendus est**.

Malus usus abolendus.

fait a un home, que il de ceo serroit son juge demesne : Qar per tiel voie, sil avoit damages forsque a la valewe dun mail, il puissoit assesser et aver pur ceo, C. *lib. que serroit encounter tout reason. Et issint tiel prescripcion, ou ascun autre prescripcion use, si ceo soit encounter tout reason ceo ne doit ne voet estre allowe devaunt jugges :* Quia malus usus abolendus est.

---

* In *Lettou & M.* here follows that portion of the text which forms § 174, *ante*, p. 211.

(*o*) This expression of Lyttleton *devaunt jugges*, (*before judges*), is explained by a reference to the Year-Book, *Mich.* 1 *E.* 4, *pl.* 13, which is abbreviated in *Fitz. Abr. tit. Custome*, viz. That customs of cities or boroughs not affecting land or uses of land, *scil.* customs of inferior jurisdictions take their effect and are allowed before the judges of the courts within such jurisdictions, because they only are the judges of such customs and of the reasonableness thereof, and none other. So a feme covert, sole merchant by the custom of London, can maintain her action only there, and nowhere else, for such custom is not pleadable elsewhere, and, consequently customs arising within the limits of inferior jurisdictions are not pleadable in the courts above. In this particular instance in the text, Lyttleton informs his reader, that the custom he mentions as an example, is unreasonable, and not to be allowed before judges; that is, not before any judges whatever.

CONCLUDING REMARKS.

THE account that Lyttleton has given us of the slavish tenure of villenage, and the bondage to which the pure villein and villein in gross were subjected, although quite sufficient for the purposes of describing the tenure, and also of specifying the mode of acquiring the property of such a slave, yet leaves many particulars of this *status* of slavery unnoticed; a circumstance the reader can have no occasion to regret, as Bracton in his Fifth Book has been exceedingly copious in his description of the condition of the *servus* or bondman, whom he particularly distinguishes from the villein by tenure, who again is distinguished from the villein-socman and the villeins in ancient demesne, which last-named persons Bracton states were not *servi*, though holding by villein services. Glanvil has noticed villenage, but Bracton treats more amply of the subject, and his account of this *status* may be deemed a full description of it. In respect of the pure villeins, this authority states that these *servi* did not escape from their condition by going off the land of their lord, if they continued in the habit of returning; and sometimes they used to be permitted to absent themselves for a length of time from the lord's lands, and employ themselves in trade, upon paying to the lord a fine called *chevagium*, or chiefage, as an acknowledgment of their subjection and villenage. But if they left the lord's land without returning regularly, or ceased to pay their *chevagium*, they were then considered as fugitives; and when they were once become fugitive, they were to be pursued and demanded by the lord, both within liberties and without, for which purpose the aid of the king's officer might be had; and after such claim had been made, the *servus*, though he was not taken till after a year had elapsed might be detained; but if no such claim had been made, then, at the end of a year, the *servus* would be privileged, and considered as free. So strictly was claim required to be made, that if the lord, after the lapse of three or four days only, without making any claim, had taken him anywhere *extra villenagium*, *i. e.* without the bounds of the lord's manor, he would have been liable to an action for the imprisonment (*p*).

The Year-Books are full of cases relating to villenage, especially upon the facts which manumitted the pure villein; for in addition to the causes of manumission already noticed, such villein would become *ipso facto* free, if he had remained a year and a day in any privileged or corporate town or city, and had been received into their *gylda* or fraternity as a citizen of that town (*ante*, § 194); and the curious reader will observe a conflict of cases relative to the enfranchisement of a niefe married to a freeman or to her lord, and as to the operation of a villein's marriage with his *lady*;—questions now as useless to consider as it was then brutal and absurd to have raised them (*q*).

In ancient court-rolls villeins are distinguished as *villani capitis*, or villeins by blood, from the villeins *ratione tenuræ;* and indeed it is chiefly from the inspection of these evidences that the practical operation of villenage can be fully demonstrated (*r*).

(*p*) Reeve's Hist. i. 99, 268; B.C. ii. 93.

(*q*) Hargr. n. in Co. Lytt. 123. *a.*

(*r*) John Syrede of Croydon, husbandman, espoused Agnes, daughter of William Toller, one of the lord's villeins in gross, without license, he came and paid 6*s*. 8*d*.—3 Hen. 6, (1425).

Alice, daughter of Richard Colgrymme (or Grim the Collier, a nickname for a charcoal-burner), one of the lord's villeins in gross, remains at Chalvedon (Chaldon) with Richard Alleyn without *chivage* and without license.—Ordered to be seized.

Thomas Bassett comes and gives to the lord for the *chivage* of William Colgrymme the lord's villein for license to stay with him till Michaelmas next, 8*d.*

At the same court niefes (bondwomen) ordered to be seized.—9 Hen. 6, (1431). *Rot. Maner' de Coulsdon Com' Surr'.*

It was presented that John Prymme, who held of the lord one tenement and half a virgate of villein land (*de terrâ nativâ*) to him and his heirs, had removed out of the seignory (lordship or manor) and refused to hold the land, whereupon there happened to the lord for a heriot, one heifer, which remains in the hands of the lord.—*Id.* 19 Ric. 2, (1396).

CHAPTER XII.

RENTS.

Lyttleton, in this concluding Chapter of his Book of Services, treats of the substitution of service; viz. a pecuniary render as a commutation of service or fruits of tenure, termed rent-service. As a substitution must follow the nature of its original, it is an inevitable consequence, that rent must be issuing out of land; that it be recoverable by the same means as other fruits of tenure, *scil.* by distress; that fealty should be inseparably annexed to it; and, finally, that as a service it should be incident to, and run or descend with, the reversion.

Rent-charge, which is evidently a conventional assimilation of tenure, though, strictly speaking, no tenure of itself, (for it does not follow the reversion), is, where land is charged with an annual payment by deed with a clause of distress; for no power of distress is incident thereto at law.

A rent-seck must also be issuing out of land, in accordance with those principles upon which rents were created, and is in theory the same as rent-charge, but practically it differs from it in this, that a rent can only be termed "seck" when the remedy for its recovery is not commensurate with the amount, or the means of enforcing payment are gone or waived (§ 218); and a rent-service may be *quasi* rent-seck when there is no reversion in the person entitled to the rent, or where privity of tenure has ceased to exist (§ 225).

213 THREE manner of rents (*a*) there be; that is to say, rent-service, rent-charge, and rent-seck. Rent-service is, where

Rents described.

213 *Trois maners de rentz y sount, cestassavoir, rent-service, rent-charge, et rent-sekke. Rent-service est, lou le tenaunt*

(*a*) There be three maners of rentes: that is to saye, rent-service, rent-charge, and rent-secke.

Rent-service is, where a man holdeth of another by fealtie and for to do suit to his court, and yeldinge to him a certaine rent by the year for all maner of services.

And note well, that, if the lorde bee seised of the service and rent before saide, and they be behinde, and hee distraine, and the tenant rescue the distresse, hee may have assize or writte of rescous. But it is more necessarye for him to have assize than writte of rescous, inasmuch that, by assize he shall recover his rent and his damages: but by writte of rescous [he shall not recover but the reprises (*i. e.* the rent) and the damages*].

And note well, that, if the lorde be not seised of the rent and service, and they be behinde, and he distreine for them, and the tenant take againe the distresse, he cannot have assize, but writte of rescous, [for a man shall not have assize without seisin and possession in deed†], and it behoveth not the lord to shew his right.

And note well, that if the lorde distraine his tenant in socage for knight's-service [which is not denyed him‡], and avowe for the same service in court of recorde, he shall be charged by the same service, by Finch. (*Finchden*, Ch. J. *C. P.*) termino Hillarii, anno xlvj. [E. 3.]

And note well, that if the lord can not finde a distresse by two yeres, he shall have against the tenaunt, writte of *cessavit per biennium*, as it appeareth by the statute of West. ii. ca. xxj. And if the tenant die in the meantime and his issue enter, the lord shall have against the issue writt of *entre sur cessavit*; or if the tenant alien, the

* He shall not recover the arrearages, but damages for the rescue.—*Pyns.* The text as above is conformable to *Berth.* 1531.

† The words within brackets are only in *Pyns.*

‡ The text is the Translation of *Rastell*, which seems at variance with the French copy he gives; for that copy, literally translated, reads *which he supposes to be holden of him;* which accords with *Berth.* 1531, and with a slight variation, is according to *Pyns.*

the tenant holdeth his land of his lord by fealty and certain rent, or by homage, fealty, and certain rent, or by other ser-

tient sa terre de son seignour per fealté, et per certeyn rent, ou per homage, fealté et certeyn rent, ou per autres services,

---

lord shall have against the alienee the aforesaid writ. But if the lord have issue and die, and the tenant be in arrerages of the said rent and service, in the time of the lord father of the issue, [and not in the time of the issue*] he cannot distraine for the arrerages in the time of his father, nor shall he have any other recovery against the tenant [or his son†] or any other; for this, that such advantage is given by the law to the tenant. And note well, that rent-service is that to whiche belongeth fealtie, but to rent-charge or annual rent-seck there belongeth not fealtie, for it belongeth to rent-service of common right.—*Olde Tenures*, § 24.

Rent-charge is, where a man graunteth certeine rent issuing out of his landes or tenementes to another in fee-simple, or in fee-taille or for terme of lyfe by deed, upon condition that, at whatever time the rent be behind, it shall be well lawful for the grantee his heires or assignes to distrayne in the same landes or tenements. And note well, that, if the rent be behind, it is well lawfull to the grantee at his election to have writte of annuitie, or else he may distrayne, and if the distresse be rescued from him, and he was never seised before, he hath no recovery but by writt of rescous, for the distresse first taken giveth not to him seisin only, unless he happ (*i. e.* obtain) the rent before: for if he were seized of that rent before by receipt [*par happe*], and afterwards the rent be behind and he distraine, and rescous be to him made, he shall have assize or writte of rescous.

And note well, that in every assize of rent-charge and of annuell rent, and in writte of annuitie, it behoveth him that bringeth the writte to shewe forth an especialte: or els he shall not maintayne assize, but in *Mortdauncestre* or *Formedon en le discender*, and other writts in the whiche title is given or comprised, brought of rent-charge or annuell rente, it needeth not to shewe especialtye ‡.

And note well, that if a man graunt rent-charge to another, and

* The words within brackets not in *Berth.* 1531.

† The words within brackets not in *Rastell's* Copy.

‡ *And the same reason is in this case, as in rent-charge, tamen quere; vide de hoc*, 2 *H.* 6, 4; 4 *H.* 7; *and* 12 *H.* 1. This addition,

vices and certain rent: and if rent-service at any day that it ought to be paid, be behind, the lord may distrain for that of

et certeyn rent: et si rent-service soit a ascun jour, que doit estre paie, aderere, le seignour poet distreigner pur ceo de

---

the grantee purchase the halfe of the lande whereof the rent is issuing, all the rent is extinct; and if the grantee release to the grantour parcell of the rent, yet all the rent is not extinct. But in rent-service the law is otherwise; for notwithstanding that the lord shall have purchased the halfe of the land, whereof the rent is issuing, yet the rent is not extinct but for the moiety, [and also if the lord release even to the moiety of the rent, the rent-service is not extinct but for the moiety*], and the reason of the diversitie is, that rent-service may be severed as to one portion, but not rent-charge. And note well, that if rent-charge be granted to two jointly, and the one release, yet the other shall have the moiety of the rent. And also if one purchase the halfe of the lande whereof the rent is issuing, [he†] shall have the moiety of the rent from his companion. And if the disseisor charge the land to a stranger, and the disseisee bring assize and recover, the charge is defeated: but if he that hath right, charge the land, and a stranger feign a false action against him [who hath not right‡] and recover by default, the charge abydeth. And note well, that in case purpartie be made betwene two parceners, and more land be allotted to one than to the other, and she that hath more of the land chargeth her land to the other, and she happeth the rent, she shal maintain assize without especialtie. And if the grantee have [the rent‡] in fee-simple or in fee-taile, and hath issue and dyeth; if the issue bring *formedon* or assize of *mortdauncestre*, he shall never be charged to shew especialtie; [but if no purparty be made between them, then he is as in the case aforesaid. In the same manner if purparty be, and one give her land to the other, reserving to her a certain rent, or grant out of the same land an annuity to another of x*s*. of rent, never shall he who demands the

for such it seems to be, occurs in *Berth.* 1531; but that copy does not give the *Vide de hoc* with the references to the Year-Books, and these are to be found only in *Pyns.*

* The words within brackets are not in *Rastell's* Copy, but in *Pyns.* and *Berth.*

† *Rastell* reads *the other.*

‡ The words within these two brackets not in *Rastell's* Copy.

Rent service may issue out of estates tail, for life or years; and may be reserved without deed; for it is a rule

common right. [214] And if a man now will give lands or tenements to another in the tail, yielding to him certain rent,

comen droit. [214] Et si ore home voilleit doner terres ou tenementes a un autre en le taille, rendaunt a luy certeyn rent,

---

rent be compelled [*charged, Berth.*] to shew forth a deed, no more than of rent-charge as is aforesaid. And note well, that, in the aforesaid case where rent-charge is granted to two, he who has not released or purchased, can distrain for the rent upon the grantor, or his heir, or upon the land which is in the hand of his companion*, &c.]—*Olde Tenures*, § 25.

Rent-secke is, where a man holdeth of me by homage, fealtie, and other services; yelding to me a certeine rent by the yeare, and I graunt this rent to another, reserving to myself the services. [Or otherwise in this case, if a man be seised of certain lands which he holds of another lord paramount, and aliens the same lands or tenements to a stranger to hold of the chief lord, by the services due, reserving to him a certain rent by the year†]. And note well, that, in rent-secke if a man be seised of the rent, and the rent be behind, he cannot distreine, but he shall have assise of novel disseisine.

And note well, that, if rent-secke be granted to a man and to his heires, and the rent be behind, and the [grantour‡] dye, the heire cannot distreine, or recover the arrerages of the tyme of his father: as is aforesaide of rent-service.

And in the same manner it is in speaking of rent-charge or annuall rente. But in all these rentes beforesaide, the heire may have for the arrerages in his own tyme, such advauntage as his father had in his life. [*Vide statutum*, 32 *H.* 8, § 37]. And note well, that, in rent-secke, if a man be not seised of the rent and it be behind, he is without recovery, for that it was his own folly at the beginninge when the rent was granted to him or reserved, that he toke not seisin of the rent, as a penny or twopence.

And note well, that a man cannot have a *cessavit per biennium* or another writte of *entre sur cessavit*, for any rent-secke in arrear for two yeares, but solely for rent-service as it appeareth in the statute W. 2, c. xxj.

And note well, that, in rent-secke

* The words within brackets not in *Rastell's* Copy.

† The words within brackets are not in *Rastell's* Copy, but occur in *Pyns.* and *Berth.*

‡ *Home*, man, *Pyns.* and *Berth.*

§ This reference is given in *Rastell's* Copy.

he of common right can distrain for the rent in arrear, although such gift was made without deed, because that such

in law that a rent service may be reserved without deed.—Co. Lytt. 124. b.

il de comen droit poet distreigner pur le rent aderere, coment que tiel done fuist fait sauns fait, pur ceo que tiel rent est

---

it behoveth him that sueth for the rent-secke for to shewe a deed to the tenant, or else the tenant shall not be charged with the rent: except where the rent-secke was rent-service before, as in this case, *viz.* lord, mesne, and tenaunt are, and each of them holdeth of the other by homage and fealty, and [the tenant of the mesne*] x *s.* of rent; the lord paramount purchaseth the landes or tenements of the tenant, *in this case*, all the seignory [of the mesne*], but the rent is extinct. And for this reason this rent is become rent-secke and the rent-service changed, for he cannot distrain for this rent; for in this case, hee that demandeth the rent shall never be charged (chace, *driven, Pyns.*) to shew a deed, neither in case of *mortdauncestre*, *aiel*, or *besaiel*, there needeth not to shewe a specialtye, for that these writtes of possession do comprehend a title within themselves; that is to say, that the auncestour was seised of the same rent, and continued his possession, by reason of which seisin the law supposeth that it is also averrable by the country; yet learn (*tamen quœre*), for some suppose that it behoveth of necessitie to shew forth a deede, because rent-secke is a thing against common right, as well as rent-charge: but in assize of novel disseisin, and in writte of *entre sur disseisin* brought of rent-secke, it behoveth of necessitie (*il covient de fyne force*) to shewe forth a deed, because rent-secke is a thing against common right, except in the case beforesaide, where it was rent-service before. And assize of *novel disseisin* and a writte of *entre sur disseisin* do not contain within them a title, but *rather* suppose a disseisin done to the plaintiff. And by entendement of law, the disseisin giveth no cause of averment against common right, but of necessitie it behoveth to shewe forth a deede (*especialtye*).

[And note well, that rent-secke can in no wise be reserved to any one in tail; because no reservation can be against the tail, but would be adjudged no gift in law, for then it would ensue that men should owe rent to themselves, the which gift would be impossible in law, &c.†]—*Olde Tenures*, § 26.

* The words within these two brackets do not occur in *Pyns.* and *Berth.*

† This last paragraph is given in *Pyns.* and *Berth.* and is not in *Rastell's* Copy.

rent is rent-service. [In the same manner it is, if lease be made to a man for life or for term of years, rendering certain rent, &c.*]

In a grant of rent-service, the grantor must retain the reversion for reversion fait tenure, § 132, 225,

215 But in such case, where a man upon such a gift or lease will reserve to him a rent-service, it behoveth that the *ultimate* reversion of the lands or tenements be in the donor or lessor. For if a man will make a feoffment in fee, or will give lands in tail, the remainder over in fee-simple (*b*), without

rent-service. [En mesme le maner est, si lees soit fait a un home pur terme de vie, ou pur terme dans, rendant certeyn rent, &c.]*

215 *Mes en tiel cas lou home sur tiel done ou lees voille reserver a luy un rent-service, il covient que la revercion de lez terrez ou tenementes soit en le donour ou lessor. Qar si home voille faire feoffment en fee, ou voille doner terres en le taille, le remeyndre oustre en fee-simple, sauns fait, reservaunt a*

---

* The words within brackets do not appear in *Rastell's* Translation, although they appear in all the French copies; but they vary in the earlier copies—a certain indication of their questionable origin.

(*b*) An estate in remainder may be defined to be an estate limited to take effect and be enjoyed after another estate is determined. As if a man seised in fee-simple granteth lands to A. for twenty years, and, after the determination of the said term, then to B. and his heirs for ever: here A. is tenant for years, remainder to B. in fee. In the first place an estate for years is created or carved out of the fee, and given to A.; and the residue or remainder of it is given to B.: but both these interests are in fact only one estate; the present term of years and the remainder afterwards, when added together, being equal only to one estate in fee. They are indeed different *parts*, but they constitute only one *whole*: they are carved out of one and the same inheritance: they are both created, and may both subsist together; the one in possession, the other in expectancy.—B.C. ii. 164.

So much is premised for the purpose of drawing the reader's attention to the rules of law necessary to be observed in the creation of remainders, and which can be but very cursorily noticed in a work of

deed, reserving to him a certain rent, this reservation is void, for that no reversion is in the donor, and such tenant holds

else the reservation is void.

luy certeyn rent, tiel reservacion est voide, pur ceo que nul revercion est en le donour, et tiel tenaunt tient sa terre immedi-

---

this description: [remarking, that remainders of any kind in lands might at common law, as it stood before the Statute of Frauds, 29 Car. 2, c. 3, have been created without deed; but they could not after their creation be so conveyed from hand to hand. For if there were a demise for life or years, or a gift in tail with remainder over in fee, and livery of seisin were made accordingly, then says Lyttleton (§ 60, 215), is the freehold together with the fee to them in the remainder, according to the form of the grant. The immediate freehold indeed in these instances passes to the first taker, except in the case of the lessee for years. Likewise at this day, (now that a written deed is necessary), livery of seisin may be made to a lessee for years, in order to effectuate a freehold remainder over, that it may immediately vest, and may not be liable to an objection which would render it void, as to conveyances at common law; namely, that of being a freehold to commence *in futuro.—Flintoff's Introd. to Conveyancing*, 257.]

I. The first rule is, that there must be some *particular* estate precedent to the estate in remainder, [which precedent estate must be formed at the same time with the remainder, (as appears in the cases Lyttleton gives), and must be valid in its creation; for it is regularly true (to use Sir Ed. Coke's words), that, when the *particular* estate is defeated, the remainder shall be thereby also defeated]; as an estate for years to A., remainder to B. for life; or, an estate for life to A., remainder to B. in tail. This precedent estate is called the *particular* estate, as being only a small part, or *particula*, of the inheritance; the residue or remainder of which is granted over to another. The necessity of creating this preceding particular estate, in order to make a good remainder, arises from this plain reason,—that *remainder* is a relative expression, and implies that some part of the thing is previously disposed of: for, where the whole is conveyed at once, there cannot possibly exist a remainder; but the interest granted, whatever it be, will be an estate in possession.

An estate [therefore] created to commence at a distant period of time, without any intervening estate, is therefore properly no remainder; it is the whole of the gift, and not a residuary part.

There must be a particular estate before a remainder.

II. A second rule to be observed is this,—that the remainder must

The remainder must pass at the time of the

his land immediately of the lord of whom his donor held, &c. [216] And this is by force of the statute of [Westm. 3,

ate de le seignour de qui son donour tenoit, &c. [216] *Et ceo est per force de lestatute de* Quia emptores terrarum: *qar de-*

Otherwise it creation of the particular estate.

commence or pass out of the grantor at the time of the creation of the particular estate (§ 673). As, where there is an estate to A. for life, with remainder to B. in fee: here B.'s remainder in fee passes from the grantor at the same time that seisin is delivered to A. of his life-estate in possession. And it is this which induces the necessity at common law of livery of seisin being made on the *particular* estate, whenever a *freehold* remainder is created. For, if it be limited even on an estate for years, it is necessary that the lessee for years should have livery of seisin, in order to convey the freehold from and out of the grantor; otherwise the remainder is void (§ 60). Not that the livery is necessary to strengthen the estate for years; but, as livery of the land is requisite to convey the freehold, and yet cannot be given to him in remainder without infringing the possession of the lessee for years, therefore the law allows such livery, made to the tenant of the particular estate, to relate and enure to him in remainder as both are but one estate in law.

And must vest in the grantee during the continuance of the particular estate or* eo instanti, *that it determines.

III. A third rule respecting remainders is this; that the remainder must vest in the grantee during the continuance of the particular estate, or *eo instanti* that it determines. As, if A. be tenant for life, remainder to B. in tail; here B.'s remainder is vested in him, at the creation of the particular estate to A. for life: or, if A. and B. be tenants for their joint lives, remainder to the survivor in fee: here, though during their joint lives the remainder is vested in neither; yet on the death of either of them, the remainder vests instantly in the survivor: wherefore both these are good remainders. But, if an estate be limited to A. for life, remainder to the eldest son of B. in tail, and A. dies before B. hath any son, here the remainder will be void; for it did not vest in any one during the continuance, nor at the determination, of the particular estate: and, even supposing that B. should afterwards have a son, he shall not take by this remainder; for, as it did not vest at or before the end of the particular estate, it never can vest at all, but is gone for ever. And this depends upon the principle before laid down—that the precedent particular estate, and the remainder, are one estate in law; they must therefore subsist and be *in esse* at one and the same instant of time, either during the continuance of the first estate or at

cap. 1], *Quia emptores terrarum:* for before the said statute, if one made a feoffment in fee-simple by deed or without

was at common law before the stat. Quia emptores, *see* § 140.

vaunt le dit estatute, si home fesoit un feoffement en fee-simple per fait ou sauns fait, rendaunt a luy et a ses heires

---

the very instant when that determines, so that no other estate can possibly come between them. For there can be no intervening estate between the particular estate, and the remainder supported thereby: the thing supported must fall to the ground, if once its support be severed from it.

It is upon these rules, but principally the last, that the doctrine of *contingent* remainders depends. For remainders are either *vested* or *contingent*. *Vested* remainders (or remainders *executed*, whereby a present interest passes to the party, though to be enjoyed *in futuro*) are where the estate is invariably fixed, to remain to a determinate person, after the particular estate is spent. As if A. be tenant for twenty years, remainder to B. in fee; here B.'s is a vested remainder, which nothing can defeat or set aside.

Contingent or *executory* remainders (whereby no present interest passes) are where the estate in remainder is limited to take effect, either to a dubious and uncertain *person*, or upon a dubious and uncertain *event:* so that the particular estate may chance to be determined, and the remainder never take effect.—B.C. ii. 165, 169.

And these remainders may be *defeated* by destroying or determining the particular estate upon which they depend, before the contingency happens whereby they become vested; an occurrence which is obviated by the practice of appointing trustees to preserve the contingent remainders. Remainders also may in some measure be created not in accordance with the principles laid down by law with regard to these estates; though, in strictness they are not to be called remainders, being termed *executory devises, i. e.* devises hereafter to be executed.

Vested remainders.

The subtleties and refinements (as Sir William Blackstone expresses himself) into which the doctrine of remainders, as to their creation, limitation, and determination or destruction has been spun out and subdivided, and which have rendered the legal learning on this subject extremely abstruse, can be no more than barely alluded to in this place; but the Student is referred to Mr. *Fearne's Essay on Contingent Remainders and Executory Devises*, and those books which treat of the law concerning real property, and particularly those forming an introduction to the modern system of conveyancing.

Contingent remainders.

deed, yielding to him and to his heirs certain rent, this was rent-service, and for this he might distrain of common right. And if he made no reservation of any rent nor of any service, yet the feoffee held of the feoffor by the same service as the feoffor held over his lord next paramount. 217 But if a man by deed indented at this day make such a gift in the tail, the remainder over in fee, or a lease for life, the remainder over in fee, or a feoffment in fee, and by the same indenture reserveth to him and to his heirs a certain rent, and that if the rent be behind, that it shall be lawful for him and his heirs to distrain &c., such a rent is rent-charge; because such lands or tenements are charged with such distress by force of the writing only, and not of common right. And if such a man upon a deed indented, reserve to him and to his heirs certain rent, without any such clause put in the deed, that he may distrain &c.; then such rent is rent-seck; for that he cannot levy [or distrain] to have the rent, if it be denied, by the same distress. And if he were never in this case seised of the rent,

Rent-charge *is where there is a clause of distress and land to be charged with distress.*

Rent-seck *is where it is issuing out of land and no clause of distress, and as these two last are sums in gross and not annexed to the reversion, distress is not at common law incident to these charges.*

certeyn rent, ceo fuist rent-service, et pur ceo il puissoit distreigner de comen droit. Et sil fist nul reservacion dascun rent ne dascun service, unqore le feoffé tenuist del feoffour per autiel service que le feoffour tenoit oustre de son seignour procheyn paramount. 217 *Mes si home per fait endente a cel jour fait tiel done en le taille, le remeyndre oustre en fee, ou lees a terme de vie, le remeyndre oustre en fee, ou un feoffement en fee, et per mesme lendenture il reserva a luy et a sez heirez un certeyn rent, et que si le rent soit aderere, que bien lirroit a luy et a ses heires a distreigner, &c., tiel rent est rent-charge, pur ceo que tielx terres ou tenementes sount charges de tiel distresse per force de lescripture tantsolement, et nemye de comen droit. Et si tiel home sur fait endente reserva a luy et a ses heires certeyn rent, sans ascun tiel clause mys en le fait, quil poet distreigner, &c.; donques tiel rent est rent-sekke, pur ceo que il ne poet lever daver le rent, si ceo soit denye, per mesme le distresse : et sil ne fuist unques*

he is without remedy, as shall be said hereafter* (§ 341). 218 Also if a man seised of certain land grant by a deed-poll, or by indenture, a yearly rent to be issuing out of the same land to another in fee, or in fee-tail, or for term of life &c., with clause of distress &c., then that is rent-charge: and if the grant be without clause of distress, then it is rent-seck. And note, that rent-seck *idem est quod redditus siccus;* for that no distress is incident to it.

See § 235 and as to what is a sufficient seisin of rent.

Grant of rent with power of distress is a rent-charge;—without such clause it is a rent-seck.

219 Also, if a man grant by his deed a rent-charge to another, and the rent is behind, the grantee can choose whether he will sue a writ of annuity for this against the grantor, or distrain for the rent behind, and the distress to retain until

So, if one grant a rent-charge to another, the grantee may either avow or have a writ of annuity, and whichever of these he will use is maintainable, and yet at the beginning it was uncertain; but notwithstanding the uncertainty the grant is good;

*en ceo cas seisi de le rent, il est sauns remedie, come serra dit apres**. 218 *Auxi si home seisi de certeyn terre graunta per un fait polle, ou per endenture, un annuell rent issaunt hors de mesme la terre a un autre en fee, ou en fee-taille, ou pur terme de vie, &c., ovesque clause de distresse, &c., donques ceo est rent-charge. Et si soit graunte sauns clause de distresse, donques il est rente-sekke.* Et nota, *que rente-sekke* idem est quod redditus siccus, *pur ceo que nul distresse est incident a ceo.*

219 Item, *si home graunta per son fait un rent-charge a un autre, et le rente est aderere, le grauntė poet eslier sil voet suer un briefe dannuite de ceo envers le grauntour, ou distreigner pur le rent aderere, et le distresse retener tanques il soit de ceo*

---

* In *Redm.* this section concludes thus: *pur ceo que il ne poet avener a le rent, si ceo soit denie, per mesne* (meane) *de distr'. Et sil ne fuit unques en cest cas seisi de le rent il est sans remedye, come serra dit apres* [*in cel chapiter ad tale signum* (;)]*:* which reading is, with the exception of the words within brackets, literally followed by *Berth.*, *Middl.*, *Sm.*, *Powel*, and *Tottyl* 1554, and all subsequent editions give a similar reading, which is followed in *Sir E. Coke's* Translation; viz. 'for that he cannot *come* to have the rent, if it be denied, by way of distress.' The text as above given from the three earliest printed copies, is also in conformity with *Rastell's* Translation.

but grantee cannot have a writ of annuity and distrain also, for

he be thereof paid; but he cannot do or have both together, &c. For if he recovers by a writ of annuity, then the land is discharged of the distress, &c. And if he doth not sue a writ of annuity, but distrains for the arrearages, and the tenant sueth replevin, &c., and then the grantee avow the taking of the distress in the land, &c., in court of record, then is the land charged, and the person of the grantor discharged of the action of annuity.

Avowry on distress charges the land, and discharges the person.

Proviso restraining the grantee from bringing writ of annuity which fixes the person, is good.

220 Also, if a man will that another should have a rent-charge issuing out of his land, but he will not that his person be charged in any manner by writ of annuity, then he may have such a clause in the end of his deed (*c*): " Provided " always, that this present writing, nor anything therein spe- " cified, shall in any way extend to charge any person by writ

paie; mes il ne poet faire ne aver ambideux ensemble, &c. Qar sil recovera per brief dannuite, donques la terre est discharge de le distresse, &c. Et sil ne suist brief dannuite, mes distreigna pur les arrerages, et le tenaunt suist replegiare, &c., et le graunté avowa le prise de le distresse en la terre, &c., en court de record, donques est la terre charge, et le person del grauntour discharge daccion dannuite.

220 Item, *si un home voille que un autre averoit un rent-charge issaunt hors de sa terre, mes il ne voille que son persone soit charge en ascun maner per brief dannuite, donques il poet aver tiel clause en le fyn de son fait. " Proviso semper, quod presens scriptum, nec aliquid in eo specificatum, " non aliqualiter se extendat ad onerandum personam meam,*

How the word proviso operates.

(*c*) And here it is to be observed, that this word (proviso) has divers operations. Sometimes it works a qualification or limitation, and so it is taken here, and often in our books; sometimes a condition; and sometimes a covenant: whereof you shall read more hereafter, § 320.—*Co. Lytt.* 146. *b.* In this case the words *proviso semper* do not make a condition, but declare an agreement between the parties annexed to the thing granted. —*Dyer*, 5 *Eliz.* 222.

" or action of annuity, but only to charge the lands and tene- " ments with the yearly rent aforesaid," &c. Then the land is charged, and the person of the grantor discharged.

221 Also, if one make such a deed in this manner, That if A. of B.* be not yearly paid at the feast of Christmas for term of his life twenty shillings of lawful money, that then it shall be lawful for the said A. of B. to distrain for this in the

Power of distress may be reserved on the grant of a sum in gross, i. e. *not annexed to the reversion*,

" per breve, vel accionem de annuitate, sed tantummodo ad " onerandum terras, et tenementa prædicta de annuali red- " ditu prædicto," &c. Donques la terre est charge, et le person del grantour discharge.

221 Item, *si home fait tiel fait en tiel manere, que si A. de B.* ne soit annuelment paie a la feste de Nowel pur terme de sa vie* XX*s. de loiale moneye que adonques bien lirroit a mesme celuy A. de B. a distreigner pur ceo en le manor de*

---

* *Sir Edward Coke* remarks on this passage, which is in conformity to *Lettou & M.*, *Machl.*, *Roh.*, and *Rastell's* Translation, " Here want words to precede these, viz.—*Que il grant al A. de B. &c., que si A. de B. &c.*, as it appeareth in the original; and so it appeareth in the close of this section, viz. *mes granta tantsolement que il poet distreigner* —And without such a grant the clause should be imperfect." The Editor is inclined to think that *Sir Edward Coke*, when he alludes to the " original," speaks of some MS. copy; as the readings he gives from such " original" are doubtless the true readings (*Co. Lytt.* § 35, 172, 241, and 702); but they are not all, as in the present instance, to be found in *Lettou & M.*, *Machl.*, or *Roh.* (*Co. Lytt.* § 221, 241, (the second corrected reading), 277, 283, and 621). The Editor is strengthened in this opinion by expressions of *Sir Edward Coke* in his Commentary upon § 172, 241, and 283, where, in alluding to this " original" he suggests a false printing, and " a mistake in the imprinting:" *Sir E. Coke* has been supposed to have considered that the *Rohan* edition was the original, *i. e.* the first edition, from the words in his preface, viz.— " The first impression that I find of our author's book ——;" but this expression is by no means inconsistent with his correction of the text by a MS. copy.—See *ante*, p. 210.

which is a good rent-charge:

but person of grantor discharged.

manor of F. &c., this is a good rent-charge, because the manor is charged with the rent by way of distress, &c.; and yet the person of him who makes such deed, is discharged in this case of an action of annuity, because he doth not grant by his deed any annuity to the said A. of B.; but granteth only that he may distrain for such annuity, &c.

Extinguishment of rent-charge by purchase of part of the land, because it cannot be apportioned.

Contra *of rent service which is apportionable on purchase.*

222 Also, if a man have a rent-charge to him and to his heirs issuing out of certain land, if he purchase any parcel of the land to him and to his heirs, all the rent-charge is extinct and annulled*, because the rent-charge cannot in such manner be apportioned. But if a man that hath rent-service purchase parcel of the land whereout the rent is issuing, this shall not extinguish all, but for the parcel. For rent-service in such case may be apportioned according to the value of

F. &c., ceo est bon rent-charge, pur ceo que le manor est charge de le rent per voye de distresse, &c., et unqore le persone de celuy que fait tiel fait, est discharge en ceo cas daccion dannuite, pur ceo que il ne graunta per son fait ascun annuite a le dit A. de B.; mes graunta tantsolement, quil poet distreigner pur tiel annuite, &c.

222 Item, *si home ad un rent-charge a luy et a sez heires issaunt hors de certeyn terre, sil purchace ascun parcell de la terre a luy et a sez heires, tout le rent-charge est extient et anniente*, pur ceo que rent-charge ne poet per tiel manere estre apporcione. Mes si home qui ad rent-service purchace parcell de la terre dont le rent est issaunt, ceo nextiendra tout, mes pur le parcell. Qar rent-service en tiel cas poet estre apporcione solonques le valewe de la terre. Mes si*

---

* This word which in *Lettou & M.* is printed *anyenty*, and in *Machl.* and *Roh. anniente, annulled*, has been strangely corrupted in *lannuite auxi, the annuity also*. This corruption first appeared in *Pyns.* 1516, and has kept its place ever since. The text also is in conformity with *Rastell's* Translation. *Sir Edward Coke* in his Translation adopts the corrupted reading.

the land. But if a tenant hold his land of his lord by the service to render to his lord yearly at such a feast a horse, a red (or sorrell) hawk*, or a clove, and such like, if in such case the lord purchase parcel of the land, such service is gone, because such service cannot be severed or apportioned. 223 But if a man hold his land of another by homage, fealty, and escuage, and by certain rent, if the lord

But in this last case entire things cannot be apportioned.

Apportionment by act of the party,* scil. *if the lord

un tenaunt tient sa terre de son seignour per le service de rendre a son seignour annuelment a tiel feste un chival, ou un esperver sore, ou un clou de gylofre, et hujusmodi, si en tiel cas le seignour purchasa parcell de la terre, tiel service est ale, pur ceo que tiel service ne poet estre severe ne apporcione.* 223 *Mes si home tient sa terre dun autre per homage, fealté, et escuage, et*

---

* These words are confusedly printed in the three earliest editions, *Lettou & M.* reading *esper sore*, and *Machl.* and *Roh. esperner sore*, the *n* being formed by inverting the *u*, which had the power of a *v*. This may have given rise to the corruption in the subsequent editions of *esperon dor*, *a gilt or golden spur*, which in *Sir Edward Coke's* Transl. is rendered *a golden spear*. The words in the text evidently allude to a kind of hawk greatly in esteem at the time Lyttleton wrote, and in the Treatise on Falconry by *Markham*, *Turberville*, and *Latham*, named "*The Blood-red Rook from Turkey*." *Sir Edward Coke's* Translation reads the words *clove de gylofrer*, *a clove gilliflower*, which, it is conceived, is not the correct rendering of these words, which correspond to the modern French words *clou de girofle*, *a clove*, *i. e.* the spice known by that name; and this interpretation of the word renders the context here conformable to § 128, where a rent of spice is alluded to, which kind of rent although "exotica, the growth of outlandish countries," might be, as *Sir Edward Coke* there informs us, reserved, indeed there is in the Register, (Ed. 1531, fo. 2, part 1), the form of a writ of right:—" Of the rent of one pound of ginger, one pound of setwall, one pound of cinnamon, one pound of cloves [*clavorum gariophili*], one pound of mace and nutmegs, one pound of pepper, one pound of saffron, and one pound of cummin [*cimini*], one rose, one pair of gilt spurs, and of the third part of one garden," &c. The words of *Rastell's* Translation are *an horse, an hawke, or such thing semblable.*

purchase *part of the land, the rent is apportionable; but the homage and fealty abide entire.*

purchase parcel of the land, &c., in that case the rent shall be apportioned, as is aforesaid; but yet in this case the homage and fealty abide entire to the lord: for the lord shall have the homage and fealty of his tenant for the rest of the lands and tenements holden of him, as he had before, &c., because that such services are not annual services, and cannot be apportioned; but the escuage may, and shall be, apportioned according to the quantity and rate of the land, &c.

Apportionment by act of law, scil. *if part* descend *to owner of rent-charge, it may be apportioned as a rent-service is.*

Reason.

224 Also, if a man hath a rent-charge, and his father purchase parcel of the tenements charged in fee, and dieth, and this parcel descends to his son who hath the rent-charge, now this rent-charge shall be apportioned according to the value of the land, as is aforesaid, of rent-service; because such portion of the land, purchased by the father, cometh not to the son by his own act; but by descent, and by course of law.

Rent-seck. *Rent-service changed to rent-seck by the lord's grant*

225 Also, if there be lord and tenant, and the tenant holds of his lord by fealty and certain rent, and the lord grant the rent by his deed to another, &c., reserving to himself the

per certeyn rent, si le seignour purchasa parcell de la terre, &c., en ceo cas le rent serra apporcione, come est avauntdit; mez unqore en ceo cas le homage et fealté demurrount entier a le seignour: Qar le seignour avera le homage et fealté de son tenaunt pur le remenaunt de lez terres et tenementes tenus de luy, come il avoit adevaunt, &c., pur ceo que tielx services ne sount pas annuelx services, et ne poient estre apporciones; mez lescuage poet, et serra apporcione solonques lafferaunte, et rate de la terre, &c.

224 Item, *si home ad un rent-charge, et son pere purchace parcell de les tenementes charges en fee, et morust, et cell parcell descendist a son fitz, qui ad le rent-charge, ore cell rent-charge serra apporcione solonques le valewe de la terre come est avauntdit, de rent-service, pur ceo que tiel porcion de la terre purchace per le pere, ne vient al fitz per son fait demesne, mez per discent et per cours de ley.*

225 Item, *si soit seignour et tenaunt, et le tenaunt tient de son seignour per fealté et certeyn rent, et le seignour graunta le rent per son fait a un autre, &c., reservaunt a luy le fealté,*

fealty, and the tenant attorns to the grantee of the rent, now such rent is rent-seck to the grantee; because the tenements are not holden of the grantee* of the rent, but are holden of the lord who reserved to himself the fealty†. 226 In the same manner it is, where a man holds his land by homage, fealty, and certain rent, if the lord grant the rent, saving to him the homage, such rent after such grant is rent-seck. But there, where lands are holden by homage, fealty, and certain rent, if the lord will grant by his deed the homage of his tenant to another, saving to him the remnant of the services, and the tenant attorn to him according to the form of the grant; in this case the tenant shall hold his land of the grantee, and the lord who granted the homage shall have the rent but as rent-seck, and shall never distrain for the rent; because [that fealty cannot be severed from homage,

of the rent, reserving the fealty.

Or of the fealty, reserving the rent.

et le tenaunt attourna a le graunté de le rent, ore tiel rent est rent-sekke a le graunté, pur ceo que lez tenementes ne sont tenus del graunté de le rent, mes sont tenus del seignour qui reserva a luy le fealté†. 226 En mesme le manere est lou home tient sa terre per homage, fealté, et certeyn rent, si le seignour graunta le rent, savaunt a luy le homage, tiel rent apres tiel graunte est rent-sekke. Mes la lou terres sount tenus per homage, fealté, et certeyn rent, si le seignour voet graunter per son fait le homage de son tenaunt a un autre, savaunt a luy le remenaunt de les servicez, et le tenaunt attourna a luy solonques le fourme del graunt, en ceo cas le tenaunt tiendra sa terre del graunté, et le seignour qui grauntast le homage navera forsque le rent come rent-sekke, et ne unques distreignera per le rent; pur ceo [que fealté ne poet estre se-*

* The abbreviated word *graunt'* has in the edition 1585-8, been corrupted to *grauntor*, and *Sir Edward Coke's* Copy and Translation have adopted this corruption. All other copies that give the word unabbreviated, read *grauntee*, as the sense requires.

† In *Rastell's* Translation this passage is rendered, *but are holden of the lord that resceyveth to him fealty.*

and because*] homage, nor fealty, nor escuage, cannot be said seck, for no such service can be said to be seck. For he that hath, or ought to have homage, fealty, or escuage of his tenant†, may, by common right, distrain for it, if it be behind, &c. For homage, fealty, and escuage, are services by which lands or tenements are holden, &c., and are such *services* as in no manner can be taken but as services, &c. 227 But otherwise it is of rent that was once rent-service; because, when it is severed by the grant of the lord from the other services, it cannot be said to be rent-service, for that it hath not to
§ 99, 135. it fealty, which is incident to every manner of rent-service, and therefore it is called rent-seck, [if the lord cannot grant such a rent with a distress, as it is said‡].

*vere de homage et pur ceo**] *que homage, ne fealté, ne escuage, ne poet estre dit sekke, qar celuy qui ad ou doit aver homage, ou fealté, ou escuage, de son tenaunt*†, *poet per le comen droit distreigner pur ceo si soit aderere, &c. Qar homage, fealté et escuage, sount services per queux terres ou tenementes sont tenus, &c., et sont tielx que en nul manere poient estre prisez forsque come services, &c.* 227 *Mes autrement est de rent que fuist un foitz rent-service, pur ceo que quant il est severe per le graunte le seignour, de lez autres services, il ne poet estre dit rent-service, pur ceo que il ne ad a ceo fealté, que est incident a chescun maner de rent-service, et pur ceo est dit rent-sekke,* [*si le seignour ne poet granter tiel rent ove distresse, come est dit*‡].

---

* The words within brackets are in *Lettou & M.*, but do not occur in *Machl.* or *Roh.* In a French copy of Lyttleton, 1591, *penes editorem*, these words are supplied by a contemporary hand.

† In *Machl.* and the common copies, *terre, land,* is substituted for *tenant*, which, in *Lettou & M.*, *Roh.*, *Redm.*, and *Berth.*, is the reading given, and is the true sense.

‡ These words are not in *Lettou & M.*, *Machl.*, or *Roh.*, they first appear in *Redm.*—They do not occur in *Rastell's* Transl. In *Sir E. Coke's* Copy and Transl. this passage commences as a new sentence, *And the lord —— &c.*

228 Also, if a man let to another land for term of life, reserving to him certain rent, if he grant the rent to another by his deed, saving to him the reversion of the land so letten, &c., such rent is but rent-seck; because the grantee hath nothing in the reversion of the land, &c.; but if he grant the reversion of the land to another for term of life, and the tenant attorn, &c. (*d*), then hath the grantee the rent as rent-service, for that he hath the reversion for term of life; 229 and so it is to be intended, that if a man give lands or tenements in the tail, yielding to him and to his heirs a certain rent, or letteth land for term of life, rendering a certain rent, if he grant the reversion to another, &c., and the tenant attorn, all the rent and service pass by the expression of 'grant of the reversion,' because that all the rent and service in such case are incidents to the reversion, and pass by the grant of the reversion, &c. But albeit that he

Or by the lessor's grant of his rent, reserving rent; rent being incident to the reversion; [for nothing but the reversion gives the power of distress, 2 E. 4, 11].

Secus, *as to a grant of the reversion;—*

for services and rent run with the reversion, according to the rule at § 225, reversion fait tenure, 132, 314, 347, 572, 590.

The same distinction between granting the reversion and granting the rent is taken, post, § 572.

228 Item, *si home lesse terre ou tenementes a un home pur terme de vie, reservaunt a luy certeyn rent, sil graunt le rent a un autre per son fait, savaunt a luy la revercion de la terre issint lesse, &c., tiel rent nest forsque rent-sekke, pur ceo que le graunté ad riens en la revercion del terre, &c. Mes sil graunta reverciou del terre a un autre pur terme de vie, et le tenaunt attourna, &c., donques ad le graunté le rent come rent-service, pur ceo que il ad le revercion per terme de vie;* 229 *et issint est a entendre que si home dona terrez ou tenementes en le taile, rendant a luy et a sez heires certeyn rent, ou lessa terre pur terme de vie, rendant certeyn rent, sil graunta la revercion a un autre, &c., et le tenaunt attourna, tout le rent et le service passe per le parole del graunt del revercion, pur ceo que tout le rent et service en tiel cas sont incidentz a la revercion, et passont per le graunt de la revercion, &c. Mes*

(*d*) By the statutes of 4 & 5 Anne, c. 16, and 11 Geo. 2, c. 19, the efficacy of an attornment has been almost taken away.—See *post*, "Attornment," § 551.

granteth the rent to another, the reversion doth not pass by such grant, &c. (*e*).

Service of mesne tenant extinguished by lord paramount purchasing the tenancy, the seignory being thus extinct; for same person cannot be both lord and tenant.

231 Also, if there be lord, mesne, and tenant, and the tenant holdeth of the mesne by the service of five shillings, and the mesne holdeth over by the service of twelve pence; if the lord paramount purchase the tenancy in fee, then the service of the mesnalty is extinct; because, that, when the lord paramount hath the tenancy, he holdeth of his lord next paramount to him; and if he ought to hold this of him that was mesne, then he should hold one selfsame tenancy immediately of divers [lords by divers†] services, which should be inconve-

*coment que il graunta le rent a un autre, la revercion ne passa mye per tiel graunt, &c.**

231 Item, *si soit seignour, mesne, et tenaunt, et le tenaunt tient del mesne per les servicez de* vs. *et le mesne tient oustre per le service de* xii*d. si le seignour paramont purchasa la tenauncie en fee, donques le service de le mesnalte est extient, pur ceo que quant le seignour paramont ad le tenauncie, il tient del seignour proscheine paramont luy; et sil doit tener ceo de celuy qui fuist mesne, donques il tiendroit un mesme tenauncie immediatly de divers [seignours per divers†] services,*

---

* In *Redm.* and all subsequent editions of Lyttleton is inserted an addition, forming the 230th section of the text, as divided by *West* 1581. It merely contained a reference to *Pasch.* 21 *E.* 4, which in editions of 1621 and 1639, stands 12 *E.* 4, together with a cross reference to 26 *Ass.* which *Brooke, tit.* "*Grants,*" *pl.* 73, says is contrary to Lyttleton. *Sir Edward Coke* also states that the judgment in 26 *Ass.* was reversed.

† The above text is according to the common copies, but neither

---

(*e*) This needs no explanation; but is evident by that which formerly hath been said, saving by this (&c.), in the end is implied the old rule, that the incident shall pass by the grant of the principal, but not the principal by the grant of the incident, *accessorium non ducit, sed sequitur suum principale.—Co. Lytt.* 152. *a.*

nient, and the law will sooner suffer a mischief than an inconvenience; and for this *reason* the seigniory of the mesnalty is extinct; 232 but insomuch as the tenant held of the mesne by five shillings, and that mesne held but by twelve pence, so that he hath more in advantage by four shillings than he pays to his lord, he shall have the said four shillings as a rent-seck yearly of the lord that purchases the tenancy, &c.

But yet the mesne holds difference, or surplusage of rent; as rent-seck, for where the seignory is gone, the rent is seck.

233 Also, if a man that hath rent-seck be once seised of any parcel of the rent, and if afterwards the tenant will not pay the rent which is in arrear, this is his remedy: he ought to go by himself or by others to the lands or tenements out of which the rent is issuing, and there demand the arrearages of the rent, and if the tenant deny to pay it, this denial is a disseisin of the rent. Also, if the tenant be not then ready to pay it, &c., this is a denial, and a disseisin of rent. Also

Remedy for rent-seck at common law is by a real action; a refusal to pay being a disseisin, § 217, 235, 341.

que serroit inconvenient, et la ley voet pluistost suffrer un mischief que un inconvenientise; et pur ceo le seignourie del mesnalte est extient; 232 *mes entaunt que le tenaunt tenuist del mesne per* v *s. et le mesne tenuist forsque per* xii *d., issint quil avoit pluis en avauntage per* iiii *s. quil paiast a son seignour, il avera les dit* iiii *s. come rent-sekke annuelement de le seignour qui purchasa le tenauncie, &c.*

233 Item, *si home qui ad rent-sekke est un foitz seisi dascun parcel de le rent et apres si le tenaunt ne voit paier le rent que est aderere, ceo est son remedie: il covient daler per luy ou per autre, a les terres ou tenementes dount le rent est issaunt, et la demaunder les arrearages del rent, et si le tenaunt denya ceo de paier, ceo denyer est un disseisin. Auxi si le tenaunt ne soit adonques prest a paier, &c., ceo est un denyer et un*

Machl. or *Roh.* gives this reading. *Lettou & M.* for *seignours*, read *homes*; *Redm.* reads *immediat de divers seignours*, which reading is according to *Berth.*, and followed by *Middl.*, *Sm.*, *Powel*, *Tottyl* 1554. *Rastell's* Translation reads—*immediatlie of divers lords.*

So if premises be deserted.

if the tenant, nor any other man be remaining* upon the lands or tenements, when he demandeth the arrearages, &c., this is a denial in law, and disseisin in fact, and of such disseisins he may have an assise of novel disseisin against the tenant, and recover the seisin of the rent, and the arrearages, and his damages, and the costs of his writ, and of his plea, &c. And if after such recovery the rent be again denied unto him, then he shall have a redisseisin, and shall recover his double damages, &c. 234 And *memorandum* that this name assise is *equivocum*, for sometimes it is taken for a jury; for in the beginning of the record of assise of novel disseisin the record shall begin thus: *Assisa venit recognitura, &c.*, which is the same as *Jurata venit recognitura.* And the reason is, for that by the writ of assise it is commanded to the sheriff,—" Quod faceret duodecim liberos et legales homi-" nes de vicineto, &c., videre tenementum illud, et nomina " illorum imbreviare, et quod summoneat eos per bonos sum-

"Assise" in Lyttleton's sense means a jury.

disseisin. Auxi si le tenaunt ne null autre home soit demurrant sur lez terres ou les tenementes, quant il demaunda les arrerages, &c., ceo est un denyer en ley, et disseisin en fait; et de tielx disseisins il poet aver assise de* novel disseisin *envers le tenaunt, et recovera le seisin de le rent, et les arrerages, et ses damages, et les costages de son brief et de son plee, &c. Et si apres tiel recoverer le rent soit autre foitz luy denye, donques il avera un redisseisin, et recovera sez double damages, &c.* 234 *Et memorandum que cest noun assisa,* est equivocum, *car ascun foitz est pris pur un jurrie, qar ou commencement de le recorde de assise de novel disseisin, le recorde issint commencera:* Assisa venit recognitura &c., quod idem est quod jurata venit recognitura, &c. *Et la cause est, pur ceo que per le brief de assise il est commande a le vicont,* " *Quod " faceret duodecim liberos et legales homines de vicineto, &c., " videre tenementum illud, et nomina illorum imbreviare, et*

* *Rastell's* Translation renders this word—*dwelling*, and so it is rendered by *Sir Edward Coke's* Translation, at § 720.

" monitores, quod sint coram justiciariis, &c., parati inde " facere recognitionem " &c. (*f*). And because, that, by force of such original writ a panel by force of the same writ ought to be returned &c., it is said in the beginning of the record in assise, *Assisa venit recognitura &c.* Also, in a writ of right, it is commonly said, that the tenant may put himself on God and the great assise. And also there is a writ in the Register (*g*), which is called a writ *De magna*

Writ of assise;

" *quod summoneat eos per bonos summonitores, quod sint* " *coram justiciariis, &c., parati inde facere recognitio-* " *nem" &c. Et pur ceo que per force de tiel brief original un panel per force de mesme le brief devoit estre retourne, &c., il est dit en le commencement de recorde en assise,* Assisa venit recognitura, &c. *Auxi en brief de droit il est communement dit, que le tenaunt luy poet metter en Dieu et graund assise. Et auxi il y ad un brief en le Registre que est appel brief* De magna assisa eligenda. *Issint*

(*f*) Albeit the words of the writ be *duodecim;* yet by ancient course the sheriff must return twenty-four, and this is for expedition of justice: for if twelve should only be returned, no man should have a full jury appear, or be sworn in respect of challenges, without a *tales*, which should be a great delay of trials. So in this case usage and ancient course maketh law. And it seemeth to me, that the law in this case delighteth herself in the number of twelve; for there must not only be twelve jurors for the trial of matters of fact, but twelve judges of ancient time for trial of matters in law in the *Exchequer Chamber*. Also for matters of state there were in ancient time *twelve counsellors of state*. He that wageth his law must have *eleven others with him* which think he says true. And that *number of twelve* is much respected in *Holy Writ*, as *twelve apostles*, *twelve stones*, *twelve tribes*, *&c.—Co. Lytt.* 155. *a.*

(*g*) Which book in the stat. of W. 2, c. 24, is called *Registrum de cancellariâ*, because it containeth the forms of writs at the common law that issue out of chancery, as out of the shop [or mint] of justice. —*Co. Lytt.* 159. *a.*

Writs are either original or judicial: The writ that precedes the suit is termed *original*, and those original writs were issued by the chancellor, who directed them, in the king's name, to the sheriff of the county, who *returned* them, (*i. e.* reported what he had done

but the word assise sometimes is taken for the whole

assisa eligenda. So, this is a proof, that this name *assisa* sometimes is taken for a jury, and sometimes it is

est ceo un prove, que cest noun assisa aliquando ponitur pro jurrata: *et ascun foitz il est pris pur tout le brief dassise: et*

---

thereupon), to the Court of common law, who, in pursuance of the suit thus commenced, issued the *mesne* or subsequent processes under its own seal; this latter description of writs were termed *judicial*, to distinguish them from the *original* writ obtained from the Court of Chancery.

This must have been in early times the chief employment of the chancellor, who, in preparing these mandatory letters or writs, followed the ancient formulary known by this name of *Registrum de cancellariâ*, which means no other than the register of *original* writs, for the chancellor issued no other; but as new cases occurred, requiring apt and sufficient remedies, the chancellor had to devise new writs, to give the plaintiffs in those cases a proper and suitable process, and wherein the cause of complaint should be stated in precise terms. And in real actions, at least in that remnant of those antiquated forms yet unrepealed, this practice is used to this day; and in ejectment, as the declaration supposes an *original* writ, it may yet be said to subsist. In personal actions, however, the original writ, until the statute of 2 Will. 4, c. 39, might have been, and in practice was frequently issued; but in ordinary cases the secondary process, or judicial writ, was issued, which *mesne* (middle or subsequent) process was supposed to be warranted by an original *writ;* but for *personal* and *mixed* actions (except in *ejectment*, the substitute for real actions), a new *judicial* process has been framed by the last-mentioned statute of 2 Will. 4, c. 39, and 1 & 2 Vict. c. 110, *viz.* by writ of *summons* and *capias*.

The original writ or *brief*, briefly stated the cause of action, which was, in a somewhat more amplified form repeated in the *count* or *declaration;* so that the abolition of most of the forms of writs in real actions does not supersede the necessity of the student, who wishes to acquire a knowledge of the grounds or principles of the law, being well acquainted with this Book.

However, to return to the *Register*, in very early times it only contained those writs which were applicable to the purposes of rude times; but the chancellor was soon, as we have seen, obliged to devise new forms, to give remedy in cases where none was before administered. And, to quicken the diligence of the clerks in the chancery, who were too much attached to

taken for the whole writ of assise; and, according to that intent, it is most properly and most commonly taken, as assise of *novel disseisin* is taken for the whole writ of assise of *novel disseisin*. And in the same manner an assise of common of pasture is taken for the whole writ of assise of common of pasture, and assise of mortdancestor is taken for

writ of assise, as a writ of assise of novel disseisin and other writs of assise.

solonques cel entent il est pluis proprement et pluis communement pris, sicome assise de novel disseisin *est pris pur tout le brief* dassise de novel disseisin. *Et en mesme le maner, assise de comen de pasture est pris pur tout le brief dassise de comen de pasture, et assise de mortdancestre est pris pur tout*

---

ancient forms, the stat. W. 2, (13 E. 1, c. 24), provides that they should frame new writs, which, if they could not agree upon, should be settled by parliament, so that there should be no deficiency of apt remedies for all causes of complaint. *Sir Edward Coke*, in the Preface to his 8th Report, tells us he had seen a register of our writs original, written in the reign of Hen. 2, and in his Exordium or Preface to the 10th Report, notices this Book as follows :—

"The Register, which containeth the original writs of the common law, is the ancientest book of the law; for the book-case and record of 26 E. 3, lib. Ass. pl. 24, proveth directly that original writs of assise, and other original writs, had been, time out of mind of man (that is, the beginning whereof cannot be known either by remembrance, reading, or record), long before the Conquest; and this book is called *Registrum Cancellariæ*, in the statute of W. 2, c. 24, because that the Chancery is *tanquam officina justitiæ*, all original writs issuing out of that Court."

Bracton informs us, that "*breve formatum est ad similitudinem regulæ juris;*" so that this venerable and ancient formulary of *original* writs contains information of a valuable character; whilst the more modern collection of judicial writs will explain the process of the courts of law in real and personal actions.

A book, from its antiquity, called *The Old Natura Brevium*, subsequently enlarged into *Fitzherbert's Natura Brevium*, is a commentary on the Register.

The word 'Register' is a French word, which seems to denote that the mode of administering justice by these mandatory letters is of Norman origin.

The best edition of the Register is that printed by *Rastell*, fol. Lond. 1531, which is published in two parts, the first containing the *original*, the latter the *judicial* writs.

the whole writ of assise of mortdancestor, and assise of darrein presentment is taken for the whole writ of darrein presentment. But it seems, that the reason why such writs at the beginning were called assises, was, for that by every such writ it is commanded to the sheriff, *That he summon twelve &c.*, which is as much as to say, that he ought to summon a jury. And sometimes assise is taken for an ordinance, to wit, to set certain things into a certain rule and disposition, as an ordinance, which, among the ancient statutes, is called *assisa panis et cervisiæ.*

A severance of the rent from the services makes the rent to be seck. Reason is, because the grantee had not possession.

But on the attornment of tenant, an assise may be had,—seisin of parcel being good for the whole.

235 Also, if there be lord and tenant, and the lord granteth the rent of his tenant by deed to another, saving to him the other services, and the tenant attorneth, this is a rent-seck, as is aforesaid. But if the rent be denied him at the next day of payment, he hath no remedy, because that he had not thereof any possession; but if the tenant, when he attorneth to the grantee, or afterwards, will give a penny or a halfpenny to the grantee, in name of seisin of rent, then if after, at the

le brief dassise de mortdancestre, et assise de darreine presentement est pris pur tout le brief dassise de darreine presentement. Mes il semble que le cause pur que tielx briefes a commencement furent appellez assises, fuist pur ceo que per chescun tiel brief il est commaunde al viscont, quod summoneat xii. &c., *le quel est a tant adire, quil doit somoner un jurrie. Et ascun foitz assise est pris pur un ordeignance, scil. pur mettre certeyn chosez en un certeyn rule et disposicion, sicome ordeignance que est entre les aunciens estatuitz appelle* assisa panis et cervisie.

235 Item, *si soit seignour et tenaunt, et le seignour graunta le rent de son tenaunt per son fait a un autre, savaunt a luy lez autrez services, et le tenaunt attourna, ceo est un rent-sekke, come est dit adevant. Mes si le rent luy soit denye al proschein jour de paiement, il ny ad ascun remedie, pur ceo quil ny avoit de ceo ascun possession; mes si le tenaunt quant il attournast al graunté ou apres, voille doner al graunté un denier ou un maile, en noun de seisin de le rent, donques*

next day of payment, the rent be denied him, he shall have an assise of *novel disseisin*. And so it is if a man grant by his deed a yearly rent, issuing out of his land, to another &c.; if the grantor then or afterwards pay to the grantee a penny or a halfpenny in the name of seisin of the rent, then, if afterwards at the next day of payment the rent be denied, grantee may have an assise, or else not, &c. (*h*).

Remedy for rent-seck.

236 Also, of rent-seck a man may have an assize of *mort-dancestor*, or a writ of *aiel* or *cosinage*, and all other manner of actions real, as the case lieth, as he may have of any other rent.

Three disseisins of rent-service; viz.

Rescous.

237 Also, there be three causes of disseisin of rent-service, *scil.* rescous, replevin, and inclosure. Rescous is, when the lord distraineth in the land holden of him for his rent in arrear, if the distress be rescued from him; or if the lord come

si apres a le proscheyn jour de paiement, le rent a luy soit denye, il avera assise de novel disseisin. Et issint est, si home grauntast per son fait un annuell rent issaunt hors de sa terre a un autre, &c., si le grauntour adonques ou apres paiast al graunté un deniere ou un maile en noun de seisin de le rent, donques si apres a le proscheyn jour de paiement le rent soit denye, le graunté poet aver assise, ou autrement nemye, &c.

236 Item, *de rent-sekke, home poet aver assise de mortdancestre, ou un brief de aiel, ou de cosinage, et toutz autres maners daccions real, sicome le cas gist, sicome il poet aver dascun autre rent.*

237 Item, *trois sont causes de disseisin de rent-service,* scil. *rescous, replevyn, et encloser. Rescous est, quant le seignour en la terre tenus de luy distreigna pur son rent arere, si le distres de luy soit rescousse; ou si le seignour vient sur la*

(*h*) By this (*&c.*) is implied, that the grant and delivery of the deed is no seisin of the rent: and that a seisin in law which the grantee hath by the grant, is not sufficient to maintain an assise, or any other real action, but there must be an actual seisin.—*Co. Lytt.* 160. *a.* In *Rastell's* Translation, this *&c.* does not occur.

upon the land, and willeth to distrain, and the tenant, or another man, will not suffer him &c. Replevin is, when the lord hath distrained, and replevin is made of the distress by writ or by plaint. Inclosure is, if the lands or tenements be so inclosed, that the lord is not able to come within the lands or tenements for to distrain &c. And the reason why such things so done be disseisins made to the lord is, because by such things the lord is disturbed of the mean by which he ought to have come to his rent.

Replevin.

Inclosure.

An additional disseisin of rent-charge is denial.

Disseisins of rent-seck are denial and enclosure.

A mode of disseisin applicable to rent-service, rent-charge, and rent-seck, viz.

238 And four causes there be of disseisin of rent-charge: *viz.* rescous, replevin, inclosure, and denial. For denial is a disseisin of rent-charge, as is before said of rent-seck. 239 And two causes there be of disseisin of rent-seck, *scil.* denial and inclosure. 240 And yet it seemeth that there is another cause of disseisin of all the three services* aforesaid, *scil.* if when the lord is going to the land holden of him to distrain

terre et voilleit distreigner, et le tenaunt ou autre home ne luy voille suffre, &c. Replevyn est, quant le seignour ad distreigne, et replevyn soit fait de le distres per brief ou per pleynt. Encloser est, si lez terres ou les tenementes sont issy enclosez, que le seignour ne poet vener deins les terres ou tenementes pur distreigner, &c. Et la cause pur que tielx choses issint faitz sont disseisins faites al seignour est, pur ceo que per tielx choses le seignour est distourbe de le meane per quel il doit avoir et vener a son rent.

238 *Et quaters sont causes de disseisin de rent-charge,* scil. *rescous, replevyn, encloser, et denyer. Qar denyer est un disseisin de rent-charge, come est avauntdit de rent-sekke.* 239*Et deux causez sont de disseisin de Rent-sekke,* scil. *denyer et encloser.* 240 *Et il semble que il y est un autre cause de disseisin de toutes les trois services* avauntdites;* scil. *quaunt le seignour soit en alant en la terre tenus de luy pur distreigner pur le rent arrere, et le tenaunt, ceo oyant, luy en-*

---

* *Rastell's* Translation renders this word—*rents*.

for the rent behind, and the tenant, hearing this, encountereth him, and forestalleth him (*i. e.* preoccupies) the way with force and arms, or menaceth him in such form, that he dare not come to the land to distrain for his rent behind &c., for doubt of death or bodily hurt, this is a disseisin; because the lord is disturbed of the mean whereby he ought to come to his rent: and so it is, if, by such forestalling or menace, he that hath rent-charge or rent-seck is forestalled, or dare not come to the land to ask for the rent in arrear &c. (*i*).

by forcible prevention of distress, either by menace, threats, or intimidation.

contera, et luy forstalla la voye ovesque force et armes, ou luy manassa en tiel fourme quil ne osast vener a la terre pur distreigner pur son rent arrere, &c., pur doute de mort ou mutilacion de ses membres, ceo est un disseisin, pur ceo que le seignour est distourbe de le meane per quele il doit vener a son rent: et issint est, si per tiel forstallement ou manasse celuy que ad un rent-charge ou rent-sekke est forstalle, ou ne osast vener a le terre a demaunder le rent arrere, &c.

(*i*) These be all the disseisins of a rent that our author speaks of. See hereafter, where a disseisin shall be by way of admittance of the owner of the rent (§ 589.—*Co. Lytt.* 162. *a.*

A disseisin means an unlawful *ouster*, or putting out of possession (§ 279); but it has been considered in a much larger sense by Lyttleton, as in this instance, and in short any possession by another not recognised by law, of the whole, or any part of land and rent issuing out of land, or any obstruction or impediment offered to the possessor or right owner in the enjoyment of it, was deemed a disseisin. Indeed it is apparent, from this paragraph, that disseisins might be either accompanied with violence or be effected without any violent act, and hereafter it will be shewn by Lyttleton (§ 588), that, for the purpose of the owner's entitling himself to certain remedies, one of which Lyttleton here mentions, he might *elect* to be disseised; *i. e.* he was at liberty to feign or suppose himself to be disseised, as the feoffment of the adverse possessor to a stranger was allowed to be disseisin. The reader is, however, referred to *Reeve's Hist.* i. 321. *B. C.* iii. 169. *The annotations of Mr. Hargrave on Co. Lytt.* 306. *b.*, 323. *a.*, *b. Mr. Thomas's Note in his Syst. Arrangement of Co. Lytt.* iii. 5, (E.), *and Booth, On Real Actions, pp.* 285-6, *ed.* 1811. *Plowd.* 537.

CONCLUDING REMARKS.

RENT is the compensation for the possession, and is reserved out of corporeal inheritances; viz. lands and tenements, reversions and remainders; and, regularly, not out of any inheritances incorporeal, or that lie in grant; viz. advowsons, commons, franchises, or the like.

Rent is most commonly rendered in money; but other things, such as corn, seed, oxen, capons, &c., may be rendered; or the rent may consist in matters of pure service, such as to plow such a field, &c. As rent is said to be issuing out of land, &c., it consequently must be a *profit*, not part of the land itself, and can only be reserved, or made payable to the person from whom the land passes, or who has either an immediate or an ultimate reversion.

Lyttleton names only three kinds of rent, viz. rent-service, rent-charge, and rent-seck (*k*).

(*k*) There are also other species of rents, which are reducible to these three. Rents *of assise* are the certain established rents of the freeholders and ancient copyholders of a manor, which cannot be departed from, or varied. Those of the freeholder are frequently called *chief* rents, *reditus capitales;* and both sorts are indifferently denominated *quit* rents, *quieti reditus;* because thereby the tenant goes quit and free of all other services. When these payments were reserved in silver or white money, they were anciently called *white*-rents or *blanch-farms*, *reditus albi;* in contradistinction to rents reserved in work, grain, &c., which were called *reditus nigri*, or *black maile*. *Rack*-rent is only a rent of the full value of the tenement, or near it. A *fee-farm* rent is a rent-charge issuing out of an estate in fee; of at least one-fourth of the value of the lands, at time of its reservation: for a grant of lands, reserving so considerable a rent, is indeed only letting lands to farm in fee-simple, instead of the usual methods for life or years.—*B. C.* ii. 41. [In the old *Termes de la Ley*, *ed.* 1579, the restriction varies, for the words are, "paying to him (the lord) the value of half, or of the third, or of the fourth part, or of other part of the land, by the year:" In the *Olde Tenures* the

Rent-service, or, as it is commonly termed, ***rent,*** was the only rent known at common law, and was payable as a compensation for the services for which the land was liable to the lord of whom the same was holden, who was, in addition, entitled to *fealty* in respect of those services, as incident to his reversion, and as inseparably annexed to tenure.

As distress was the remedy the lord had at common law for compelling the performance of the tenure, it followed as a

---

words are "yielding to the lord the value, or at least the fourth part by the year;" but *Pyns.* and *Berth.* 1531, read for "fourth," *third*, and omit the words "at the least." The Register (*tit. Cessavit*), says "*third or fourth part.*"

The Editor has classed this tenure of fee-farm as a socage tenure, (*ante, p.* 156, *in n.*), considering, perhaps erroneously, that fee-farm rents were originally nothing more than a commutation of, or substitution for a socage tenure, as existing before the statute of *Quia emptores*, 18 E. 1, for the rent was to find certain *estovers* to burn in the winter, &c. Indeed, since the statute of *Quia emptores*, there can be no tenure of fee-farm except of the king; because the grantor, by parting with the fee, is, by the operation of that statute, without a reversion, and without a reversion there cannot be a rent-service according to Lyttleton (§ 216). The old *Termes de la Ley* and the *Olde Tenures* speak of fee-farm as a tenure; though subsequently, and since the statute *Quia emptores*, it assumed the peculiar character of rent-service; for *Plowden*, (132), says that farm and rent are all one, and the Register styles fee-farm *feodi firma*. The reader, however, is referred to F.N.B. 210, A.; to *Mr. Hargrave's Annotation upon Co. Lytt.* 143. *b.;* and the references there cited, whence *Mr. Hargrave* deduces his opinion, that the term *fee-farm* is not properly applicable to any rents except *rent-service;* for grants of the fee reserving a perpetual rent with a clause of distress, are good only as rent-charge.

Rent-charges are of great antiquity, and were probably first adopted for the purpose of providing for younger children. They were considered as contrary to the policy of the common law; for the tenant was less able to perform the military services to which he was bound by his tenure. And the grantee of a rent-charge was under no feudal obligations; for which reason it is said to be against common right.—*Gilb. Rents*, 17, 18, 133; *Walk. Gilb. Ten.* 402.

consequence, that rent, as the substitution or commutation of tenure, was recoverable in like manner; and, as the lord only could distrain for non-performance of the tenure, so it became requisite that he alone should distrain for the rent reserved as compensation for those services, and this was by reason of the fealty due in respect of those services (§ 131, 132). Where there was a rent, but not payable to the lord, or where fealty was not due or not annexed to the grant, distress could not be had (§ 215); therefore, the grantee of a rent out of lands by deed has no right to a distress, but by reason of the clause of distress, which is always inserted in grants of this kind. This second species of rent which is created by act of the parties, and conventional, is styled *rent-charge;* because the land is otherwise than at law or common right, (as Lyttleton terms it), *scil.* by deed, chargeable with a distress (§ 217, 218 (*l*)). In order to support the right of distress, it is necessary that there be a reversion expectant on the determination of the grant or lease (§ 215), so that if the grantor or lessor convey away the estate after the rent become due, the remedy by distress is gone, according to the principle *reversion fait tenure* (*m*); the common case of a lessee parting with all his interest in a lease may be an example to this last proposition, for such lessee cannot distrain for rent due after his assignment, because no reversion is in him, even if he part with all his interest by way of underlease, reserving rent (*n*). Although it always was an undeniable pro-

---

(*l*) Lyttleton at § 253 puts a case of a rent-charge created according to common law, or of common right.

(*m*) It is upon this principle, that rents and services and reservations are incident to, and sometimes may be deemed parcel of, a reversion, § 132, 215, 225, 229, 314, 347, 572, and 590; for the tenure being from the reversioner, and fealty incident to every tenure, it is impossible they should be separated.—*Year-Book*, 5 *H.* 7, 10; *Sulliv. Lect.* x. 97.

(*n*) A tenant from year to year,

position, that, to support a rent-service at common law, the lord must have had a reversion or future estate of the lands after the grantee's or lessee's estate had expired; yet this did not extend to the case where one makes over to another his estate in fee-simple, with a certain rent payable thereout, and (as there is no reversion left in him so as to support a distress), adds to the deed a covenant or proviso, that, if the rent be behind, that it should be lawful for the grantee to distrain; in this case, as Lyttleton informs us, the land is subject to the distress, not of *common right*, but by virtue of the covenant or proviso, which is the act of the parties. This rent is therefore called *rent-charge;* because the land is charged with the payment of the rent by way of distress, according to the intent and act of the parties (§ 217).

The third rent Lyttleton makes mention of is a rent-seck, *i. e.* a dry or barren rent, which *Sir William Blackstone* says, is, in effect, nothing more than a rent reserved by deed, but without any clause of distress. Others more guardedly and more precisely define it as a rent for the recovery of which no power of distress was given either by the rules of common law or by the agreement of the parties, such as rents granted out of a freehold interest *sans* power of distress (§ 217); or rents payable when there is no reversion in the grantor (§ 225); or whenever the remedy by way of charge for the rent is not commensurate to the rent.

The remedy at common law for recovery of rents-seck was by a real action (§ 233), which was applicable to all other rents (§ 236): but rents-seck are now placed upon the same footing in this respect with them; for, by stat. 4 Geo. 2, c. 28, s. 5, the same remedy for distress is given for their recovery.

The grantee of a rent-charge having an election or choice

---

however, has such a reversion as enables him to distrain on a person who rents the premises of him as tenant from year to year.

either to distrain or have a writ of annuity (§ 219), introduces the reader to the doctrine of *election.*

Lyttleton continues the subject by demonstrating how rents may be either extinguished or apportioned (§ 222); and in what cases partially (§ 223), or by changing the nature of the rent (§ 224); and concludes by stating the "causes of," *i. e.* those acts which operate as, a disseisin of rent (§ 237—240).

EXPLICIT LIBER SECUNDUS.

INCIPIT LIBER TERTIUS.

BOOK III.

CHAPTER I.

OF PARCENERS.

OUR Author having treated in his two former Books,—First of estates of lands and tenements, and, in his Second Book, of tenures, whereby the same have been holden: now in his third Book doth teach us divers things concerning both of them; as, 1st. The qualities of their estates. 2ndly. In what cases the entry of him that right hath may be taken away. 3rdly. The remedies, and in what cases the same may be prevented or avoided. 4thly. How a man may be barred of his right for ever, and in what cases the same may be prevented or avoided. For the first, he having spoken of sole estates, divideth the quality of estates into individed and conditional. Individed into coparcenary, joint-tenancy, and tenancy in common: coparcenary, into parceners by the common law, and parceners by the custom; and he beginneth his Third Book with parceners claiming by descent, which, coming by the act of law and right of blood, is the noblest and worthiest means whereby lands do fall from one to another. Conditional, into conditions express or in deed, and conditions in law. Conditions in deed into gages, which he divideth into *vadia mortua* and *vadia viva : vadia mortua*, so called because either money or land may be lost (*a*); and *viva*,

---

(*a*) *Mortuum vadium* or *mortgage*, (a dead pledge), was when the fruits, or rent arising therefrom, did not go towards paying off the demand for which it was pledged.

because neither money nor land can be lost, but both preserved. Then speaketh he of descents, whereby the entry of him that right hath may be taken away.

And next to that the remedy, how to prevent the same, *viz.* by continual claim. Then he teacheth how a man having a defeasible or an imperfect estate, may perfect and establish the same by three means, *viz.* by release, by confirmation, and attornment, where that is requisite. Having spoken of a descent being an action in law which taketh away an entry, he doth then speak of a discontinuance, the act of the party, whereby the entry of them that have that right shall be taken away. And next unto that he teacheth in what case the same may be avoided by remitter. After he had treated of descents and discontinuances, which take away entries, but bar no actions. Lastly, he setteth forth the learning of warranties, (a curious and cunning kind of learning, I assure you), whereby both entry, action, and right may be barred, and the remedies how they may be prevented before they fall; and in what cases they may be avoided after they be fallen. And thus have you an account of the thirteen several chapters of this Third Book. And now this method being understood, let us hear what our Author will say unto us concerning parceners.—*Co. Lytt.* 163.

IN this third Book, something shall be said to thee, my son, concerning parceners, joint-tenants, tenants in common, estates in land and tenements upon condition, descents which toll (*i. e.* take away) entries, continual claim, releases and confirmations, warranties lineal and collateral, and of warranties which commence by disseisin, concerning attornment, surrenders, discontinuance, remitters, tenant by elegit, tenant by statute merchant, and of tenant by statute staple, &c.*

*EN cest tierce liver, ascun chose sera dit a toy, mon fitz, de parceners, de jointenantez, de tenantez en comen, de estatez de terrez et tenementez sur condicion, de discentez que tollount entrez, de continuell clayme, de releissez et confirmacionz, de garrantiez lineall et collaterall et de garrantiez que comensont per disseisin, de attornement, de surrenderons, de discontinuance, de remitterrez, de tenant per elegit, de tenant per estatut merchant, de tenant per estatut de la staple, &c.**

---

* Vell. MS. Sir William Jones, whose notes of readings from the two Cambridge MSS. in an interleaved copy of Lyttleton, (edition 1577), are deposited in the British Museum, therein observes—" It is very remarkable, that, in this argument a chapter is promised concerning *surrenders*, of which Lyttleton has not expressly and separately treated. The word *surrenderons* which is abbreviated by the transcriber, seems completely to have puzzled a former owner of the MS.: he says in the margin, *cest parole est en un auter fragment que jeo ay; quære ceo que il signifie.* Since then *surrenders* are mentioned in two manuscripts, as one of the heads of the third Book; it is not improbable, that the Author intended to have written a distinct chapter concerning them, as he did write concerning tenants by *elegit*, and by *statute merchant* and *staple*. —See § 324, where Lyttleton refers to a chapter on elegits." Also § 291.

Parceners.

241 PARCENERS are in two manners, to wit, parceners according to the course of the common law, and parceners according to the custom.

Parceners at common law defined.

Parceners after the course of the common law are, where a man or woman seised of certain lands or tenements in fee-simple or in tail, hath no issue but daughters, and dieth, and the tenements descend to the daughters*, and the daughters enter into the lands or tenements so to them descended, then they are called parceners, [and although they are daughters, they are parceners†] and make but one heir to their ancestor (*b*). And they are called parceners; because, by the

Are but one heir, for they claim by one title § 398.

241 *Parceners sont en deux maneres, cestassavoir, parceners solonques le cours de comen ley, et parceners solonques le custome.*

Parceners solonques le cours de comen ley sont, lou home ou feme seisi de certeyn terres ou tenementes en fee-simple, ou en fee-taille, et ad issue forsque files et devie, et les tenementes descendont a les files, et les files entrount en les terres ou tenementes issint descendus a eux, donques els sont appellez parceners, [et quanque files els sount, els sount parceners†] et fount que un heire a lour auncestre. Et els sont ap-*

---

* The later copies read *issues* for *files*.

† The ordinary copies read this passage thus:—*et quant a files els sont forsque un heire a lour ancestor:* upon which *Sir Edward Coke* remarks—"This is falsely printed, for the original is—*Et quanque files els sont, els sont parceners, et* sont *forsque un heire a lour auncestor;*" and the three earliest printed copies are, with the exception of *fount, make*, for *sount, are*, in accordance with this corrected reading. *Rastell's* Translation reads—*then they be called parceners, and be but one heir to their ancestor*, which agrees literally with *Redm.* and *Berth.*

Unity of estate.

(*b*) And as they are but one heir, and yet several persons, so have they one entire freehold in the land in respect of strangers, so

writ which is called *breve de participacione facienda***, the law will constrain them, that partition shall be made among them. And if there be two daughters to whom the land descendeth, then they be called two parceners; and if there be three daughters, then they be called three parceners, and if four daughters four parceners, and so forth &c. 242 Also, if a man

Writ of partition.

Female collaterals styled parceners.

pellez parceners, pur ceo que per le brief que est appelle breve de participatione facienda*, *la ley eux voet arter que particion serra fait entre eux. Et si sount deux files as queux la terre descendist, donques els sont appellez deux parceners; et si sount trois files, donques els sont appellez trois parceners; et si quater files, quater parceners, et issint oustre &c.* 242 *Auxi si*

---

* *Sir Edward Coke* notices, that, in "the original" this word is *partitione;* however, in the three earliest editions it is printed *participacione.*

---

long as it remains undivided. But between themselves, to many purposes they have in judgment of law several freeholds; for the one of them may enfeoff the other of her part, and make livery.

And this coparcenry is not severed or divided in law by the death of either of them; for if one die, her part shall descend to her issue. And it is to be observed, that, herein the descent is sometimes *in stirpes*, viz. to stocks or roots; and sometimes *in capita*, to heads. As if a man has issue two daughters and dies, this descent is *in capita*, viz. that each shall inherit alike, as Lyttleton here says. But if a man has issue two daughters, and the eldest daughter has issue three daughters, and the youngest one daughter, all these four shall inherit; but the daughter of the youngest shall have as much as the three daughters of the eldest. Also if a man has issue two daughters, and the eldest has issue divers sons and divers daughters, and the youngest has issue divers daughters, the eldest son of the eldest daughter only shall inherit; for this descent is not *in capita*, but all the daughters of the youngest shall inherit, and the eldest son is coparcener with the daughters of the youngest, and shall have one moiety, viz. his mother's part; so that men descending of daughters may be coparceners as well as women, and in this last case the descent is *in stirpes*.—*Co. Lytt.* 164. *a.*, *b.*

Descent of parceners is either in capita or in stirpes.

seised of tenements in fee-simple or in fee-tail, dieth without issue of his body begotten, and the tenements descend to his sisters, they are parceners, as is aforesaid. And in the same manner, where he hath no sisters, but the lands descend to his aunts, &c. But if a man hath but one daughter, she cannot be called parcener, but she is called daughter and heir, &c. (*c*).

Exceptions in definition.

Partition effected in various ways.

One is, to divide the tenements in severalty and equal value each part by itself.

243 And it is to be understood, that partition between parceners can be made in divers manners. One is, when they agree to make partition, and do make partition of the tenements (*d*); as if there be two parceners, to divide between them the tenements in two parts, each part by itself in severalty, and of equal value. And if there be three parceners, to divide the tenements in three parts *each part* by itself in severalty, &c.

Another mode, by means of third persons.

244 Another partition there is, *viz.* to choose by agreement

home seisi de tenementes en fee-simple ou en fee-taille, devie sauns issue de son corps engendre, et les tenementes descendont a ses soers, els sont parceners, come est avauntdit. En mesme le manere est, lou il nad pas soers, mez les tenementes descendont a ses auntes, &c. Mes si home nad forsque un file, ele ne poet estre dit parcener, mez ele est appelle file et heire, &c.

243 *Et est assavoir, que particion entre parceners poet estre fait en divers maneres. Un est, quant els agreount de faire particion, et font particion de les tenementes; sicome si soient deux parceners a devider entre eux les tenementes en deux parties, chescun partie per soy en severalte, et de egall value. Et si soient trois parceners a devider les tenementes en trois parties per soy en severalte, &c.*

244 *Un autre particion est, deslier per agrement entre eux,*

(*c*) Here by *&c.* is implied sister and heir, aunt and heir, great aunt and heir, and so upward.

(*d*) Partition can be made of a reversion—9 *H.* 7, 17.

between themselves and certain of their friends, to make partition of the lands or tenements in form aforesaid. And in such cases after such partition, the eldest daughter shall first choose one of the parts which she willeth to have for her purparty, and then the second daughter next after her another part, and then the third sister another part, then the fourth another part, &c. (*e*), if so be that there be more sisters, &c., unless it be that they are otherwise agreed between them. For it can be agreed between them, that one shall have such tenements, and another such tenements, &c., without any such first election. 245 And the part which the elder sister hath, is called in Latin *einitia pars*. But if the parceners agree that the elder sister shall make partition of the tenements in manner aforesaid, and if she do this, then it is said, that the eldest sister shall choose last of all her part, after every one of her sisters. 246 Another partition and allotment is, as if there be four parceners; and after partition of the lands be

Elder sister has prior election,

which is termed einitia pars; *but if elder sister make the partition, she shall choose last, for* cujus est divisio, alterius est electio.

By drawing lots.

et certeyn de lour amyes, de faire particion de les terres ou tenementes en le fourme avauntdit. Et en tielx cases apres tiel particion, leisne file primez esliera un des parties quele voet aver pur sa purpartie, et donques la seconde file apres luy autre partie, et donques la tierce soer autre partie, et donques la quarte autre partie, &c., si issint soit que soient plusours soers, &c., si ne soit queles sount autrement agreez entre eux. Qar il poet estre agree entre eux, que une avera tielx tenementes, et une autre tielx tenementes, &c., sauns ascun tiel primer eleccion, &c. 245 *Et la partie que leisne soer ad est appelle en Latin* einecia pars. *Mes si les parceners agreount, que leisne soer ferra particion de les tenementes en la fourme avauntdit, et si ceo ele fait, donques il est dit, que leisne soer esliera pluis darreinement sa partie, apres chescun de sez soers.* 246 *Un autre particion et allottement est, sicome soient quater parceners, et apres la particion de lez terrez fait, chescune*

(*e*) Here the *&c.* implieth the fifth sister, and after her the sixth, and so forth.—*Co. Lytt.* 166. *a.*

made, each part of the land be by itself written in a little scroll, and is covered all in wax in manner of a little ball, so as no one can see the scroll: and then let the four balls of wax be put in a hat kept in the hands of an indifferent man; and then the eldest daughter shall first put her hand into the hat, and take a ball of wax, with the scroll within the same ball for her part; and then the second sister shall put her hand into the hat, and take another; the third sister the third ball, and the fourth sister the fourth ball, &c. And in this case it behoveth each of them to stand to her chance and allotment.

By writ of partition.

247 Also, there is another partition. As if there be four parceners, and they will not agree to a partition to be made between them, then the one can have a writ *de participatione faciendâ* against the other three, or two of them may have a writ *de participatione faciendâ* against the other two, or three of them can have a writ *de participatione faciendâ* against the fourth, at their election. 248 And when judgment shall

Judgment on writ of par-

partie del terre soit per soy soulement escript en un petit escrowet, et soit covert tout en cere, en manere dun petit pile, issint que nul poet veier lescrowet: et donques soient les quaters piles de cere mys en un bonet garde en les mayns dun indifferent home; et donques leisne file primes mettera sa mayn en le bonet, quel prendra un pile de cere ovesque lescrowet deins mesme le pile pur sa purpartie; et donques la seconde soer mettera sa mayn en le bonet et prendra un autre; la tierce soer le tierce pile, et la quarte soer le quater pile, et en ceo cas covient chescun de eux luy tener a sa chaunce et allottement.

247 Item, *un autre particion y ad. Sicome si sont quater parceners, et els ne voillent agreer a particion destre fait entre eux, donques lune poet aver* breve de participacione faciendâ, *envers les autres trois, ou deux de eux poient aver* breve de participacione faciendâ *envers les autres deux, ou trois de eux poient aver* breve de participacione faciendâ *envers le quart, de lour eleccion.* 248 *Et quant juggement serra done sur tiel brief, le*

be given upon this writ, the judgment shall be such, that partition shall be made between the parties, and that the sheriff in his proper person go to the lands and tenements, &c., and that he by the oath of twelve lawful men of his bailiwick, &c., shall make partition between the parties, and that one part of the same lands and tenements be assigned to the plaintiff, or to one of the plaintiffs, and another part to another parcener, &c., not making mention in the judgment of the elder sister more than of the younger; 249 And of the partition which he shall have thus made, he shall give notice to the justices, &c., under his seal, and the seals of the twelve, &c. And so in this case you can see that the eldest sister shall not have the first election, but the sheriff shall assign her the part that she shall have, &c. And it may be that the sheriff will assign first one part to the youngest, &c., and last to the eldest, &c. (*f*). 250 And note, that partition by

tition, and course observed in making partition by writ.

Return to writ of partition.

Partition by parol, good.

juggement serra tiel, que particion serra fait entre les parties, et que le viscount en son propre person alast a les terres et tenementes, &c., et que il per le serrement de xii. *loialx homes de son baillie, &c., ferra particion entre les parties, et que une partie de mesmes terres et tenementes soit assigne al pleintif, ou a un des pleintifs, et une autre partie a un autre parcener, &c., nient fesant mencion en le juggement, de leisne soer pluis que del puisne;* 249 *Et de la particion quil avera issint fait quil ferra notice a les justices, &c., southe son seale, et les seales, de les* xii. *&c. Et issint en ceo cas poies veier que leisne soer navera mye la premier eleccion, &c., mes le viscount luy assignera la partie que ele avera, &c. Et poet estre que le viscount voet assigner premierment une partie a la pluis puisne, &c., et darreynement al eisne, &c.* 250 *Et nota*

(*f*) Since Lyttleton wrote, proceedings on a writ of partition have been greatly facilitated; for, 1. Partition can be effected under the provisions of 8 & 9 Gul. & Mariæ, c. 31, (which extends also to joint-

agreement between parceners can be made by law between them, as well by parol without deed, as by deed.

Rent granted for equality of partition.

251 Also if two meases descend to two parceners, and the one mease is worth twenty shillings *per annum,* and the other but ten shillings *per annum,* in this case partition can be made between them in such form, to wit, that one parcener shall have the one mease, and that the other parcener shall have the other mease: and that she who hath the mease worth twenty shillings *per annum,* and her heirs, shall pay a yearly rent of five shillings issuing out of the same mease to the other parcener, and to her heirs for ever; because each of them should have equality in value: 252 and such partition

que particion per agrément perenter parceners, poet estre fait per la ley entre eux, auxibien per parol sauns fait, come per fait.

251 Item, *si deux meses descendont a deux parceners, et lun mese valuet per an* xx*s. lautre forsque* x*s. per an, en ceo cas particion poet estre fait entre eux en tiel fourme, cestassavoir que un parcener avera lun mese, et que lautre parcener avera lautre mese : et que celuy qui avera la mese que est de le value de* xx*s. et sez heires, paieront un annuell rent de* v*s. issaunt hors de mesme la mese a lautre parcener, et a sez heires a toutz jours per cause que chescun deux averoit owelté en value :* 252 *et tiel particion fait per parole est assetz bone,*

---

tenants and tenants in common). 2. By release or by feoffment; because their seisin to some intents is joint, and to some intents several. 3. By judgment exclusive of that on the writ of *partition* (6 Rep. 12, *b.*) 4. By hotchpot, § 266. 5. By a bill for partition in a court of equity, which is a compulsory process to enforce partition, whereupon, after *decree,* a commission, in the nature of the writ *de partitione faciendâ,* at common law issues, and is executed in the same manner as the writ at common law should be; *scil.* in the presence of the parties.

Before the 12 Car. 2, c. 24, abolishing tenures *in capite* and their incidents, a writ of livery and partition might have been sued out of the chancery, on the behalf of a parcener, or at the instance of the committee of the heir in ward.

made by parol is good enough, and the same parcener who shall have the rent, and her heirs, can distrain of common right for the rent in the said mease worth twenty shillings, if the rent of five shillings be behind at any time, in whose hands soever the same mease shall come, although there never were any writing of this made between them. 253 In the same manner it is of all manner of lands and tenements, &c., where such rent is reserved to one, or to divers, parceners upon such partition, &c. But such rent is not rent-service, but a rent-charge of common right, had and reserved for equality of partition, &c.

Such partition and rent good.

And such rent is a rent-charge of common right.

254 And note well, that, none are called parceners by the common law, but females, or the heirs of females, that come to lands or tenements by descent; for if sisters purchase lands and tenements, of this they are called joint-tenants, and not parceners.

Parceners can only be by descent.

255 Also if two parceners of land in fee simple make partition between themselves, and the part of the one is worth

Unequal partitions bind tenants in fee of full age; but

et mesme la parcener qui avera le rent et ses heires, purront distreigner de comen droit, pur le rent en la dite mese de le value de xx*s, si le rent de* v*s. soit aderere en ascun temps, en queconques mayns que mesme la mese devient, coment que ne fuist unques ascun escripture de ceo fait entre eux.* 253 *En mesme le manere est, de toutes maners de terres et tenementes, &c., lou tiel rent est reserve a un, ou a divers des parceners sur tiel particion, &c. Mes tiel rent nest mye rent-service, mes est rent-charge de comen droit, ewe et reserve pur egalte de la particion, &c.*

254 *Et nota, que nullez sont appellez parceners per la comen ley, mes femelx, ou les heires de femelx qui veignount as terres ou tenementes per discent : qar si soers purchasent terres ou tenementes, de ceo els sont appellez jointenauntes, et nemy parceners.*

255 Item, *si deux parceners de la terre en fee-simple, fount particion entre eux, et la partie de lun vault pluis que la partie*

not the issue in tail, who may enter on his mother's decease.

more than the part of the other, if they were at the time of the partition at full age, *viz.* of twenty-one years, then the partition shall always abide and shall never be defeated. But if the tenements, whereof they make partition, be to them in fee-tail, and the part of the one is better in yearly value than the part of the other, albeit they be excluded during their lives to defeat the partition; yet if the parcener that hath the lesser part in value hath issue and die, the issue may disagree to the partition; and enter and occupy in common the other part which was allotted to his aunt, and so the aunt* may enter and occupy in common the other part allotted to her sister, &c., as if no partition had been made.

Unequal partition does not bind femes-covert.

256 Also, if two parceners of lands in fee take husbands, and they and their husbands make partition between them, if the part of the one be less in value than the part of the other, during the lives of their husbands, the partition shall stand

de lautre, si els furent al temps de la particion de pleyn age, scil. *de* xxi. *ans, donques la particion toutditz demurrera, et ne serra unques defete. Mes si les tenementes, dont els fount particion, soient a eux en fee-taille, et la partie que lun ad est meillour en annuell value, que est la partie de lautre, coment que eux sount excludez duraunt lour vies a defeter la particion; unqore si la parcener qui ad la meindre partie en value ad issue et devie, lissue poet disagreer a la particion, et entrer et occupier en comen lautre partie allotte a sa aunte, et issint launte* poet entrer et occupier en comen lautre partie allotte a sa soer, &c., sicome nul particion ust este fait.*

256 Item, *si deux parceners de tenementes en fee preignont barons, et els et lour barons fount particion entre eux, si la partie lun est meindre en annuell value que la partie lautre, duraunt lez vies lour barons, la particion estoiera en sa force,*

---

* This word, in the later editions, has been strangely corrupted into *lautre—the other.*

in its force, [but albeit it shall stand during the lives of their husbands*], yet after the death of the husband, that woman which hath the lesser part may enter into her sister's part as is aforesaid, and defeat the partition. 257 But if the partition so made between them† were such, that each part at the time of the allotment, was of equal yearly value, then it cannot afterwards be defeated in such cases.

But an equal partition binds them.

258 Also, if two parceners be, and the younger being within the age of twenty-one years, partition is made between them, so as the purparty which is allotted to the younger, is of less value than the purparty of the other; in this case the younger during the time of her nonage, and also when she cometh to full age, *scil.* of twenty-one years, can enter into the purparty to her sister allotted &c., and defeat the partition. But let such parcener take heed, when she comes to her full age, that she take not to her own use all the profits of the lands

An equal partition [by writ] binds infants, [contra, *if made by* prochein amy *or guardian, for they have no authority*]. *If partition unequal, it may be avoided by parcener on her coming of age; but if she then assents, she is bound by the partition.*

[*mes coment que il estoyera duraunt les vies les barons**], *unqore apres la mort le baron, celuy feme qui ad la meindre partie poet entrer en la partie sa soer come est avauntdit, et defeter la particion.* 257 *Mes si la particion icy fait perenter eux*† *fuist tiel, que chescune partie al temps dallottement, fuist de egall annuell value, donques il ne poet apres ceo estre defete en tielx cases.*

258 Item, *si deux parceners y sont, et la puisne esteant deinz lage de* xxi. *ans, particion est fait entre eux, issint que la purpartie que est allotte al puisne est de meindre value que la purpartie lautre, en ceo cas la puisne duraunt le temps de son nonnage, et auxi quant ele vient a pleyn age,* scil. *de* xxi. *ans, poet entrer en la purpartie a sa soer allotte, &c., et defeter la particion. Mes bien soy garde tiel parcener quant ele vient a son pleyn age, que ele ne preigne a son use demesne*

---

* The words within brackets are omitted in *Roh.* and in *Rastell's* Translations.

† The text above given is conformable to *Rastell's* Translation; but *Redm.*, and all the subsequent editions, read *les barons, the husbands.*

or tenements which have been allotted unto her: for then she agrees to the partition at such age, in which case the partition shall stand and remain in its force; but peradventure the profits of the moiety she may take, leaving the profits of the other moiety to her sister, &c.

Disability of infancy § 104, 478, 635.

259 And it is to be understood, that when it is said, that males or females be of full age, this shall be intended of the age of twenty-one years; for if before such age any deed or feoffment, grant, release, confirmation, obligation, or other writing be made by any of them, &c., [or if] any such within such age be bailiff or receiver to any man, &c., all [serveth] for nought, and may be avoided. Also a man before the said age shall not be sworn on inquest*.

toutz les profites des terrez ou tenementes que a luy furent allottes: qar adonques ele soy agrea a la particion a tiel age, en quel cas la particion estoiera et demurrera en sa force; mes peraventure les profites de la moite ele poet prendre, relinquisaunt les profites de lautre moité a sa soer, &c.

259 *Et est assavoir que quant il est dit, que malez ou femelx sont en pleyn age, ceo serra entendus del age de* xxi. *ans; qar si devaunt tiel age, ascun fait ou feoffement, ou graunt, reles, ou confirmacion, obligacion, ou autre escripture soit fait per ascun de eux, &c., [ou si] ascun tiel deins tiel age, soit baillé ou resceyvour dascun home, &c., tout [soit] pur nient, et poet este avoide. Auxi home devaunt le dit age, ne serra mye jurre en enquest*.*

---

* The text of the three earliest copies is very confused here. The reading from *Lettou & M.*, *Machl.*, and *Roh.*, is thus:—en *que ascun tiel deins tiel age soit baillif ou resceyvour dascun home, &c., tout* soit *pur nient et poet estre avoyde: auxi home* devaunt utlage *ne serra my jurre en enquest. Rastell's* Translation renders this passage thus:—*or that any within such age be bailiff or receiver with any man &c., all* serveth *for nought and may be avoided. Also a man before such age shall not be sworn in no jury nor no inquisition. Redm.* says—*tout* serra *pur nient*, and *ne serra mye* jurye *en un enquest &c.*

260 Also, if any tenements be given to a man in the tail, who hath as much of land in fee-simple, and hath issue two daughters, and die, and the two daughters make partition between them, so as the land in fee-simple be allotted to the younger daughter, in allowance for the other tenements entailed in such manner allotted to the elder daughter; if after such partition made, the younger daughter alien the land in fee-simple to another in fee, and hath issue a son or a daughter and die, the issue may well enter into the tenements entailed, and also hold and occupy them in purparty with their aunt. And this is for two causes: the first is, for that the issue can have no remedy for the land aliened by his mother, because the land was to her in fee-simple, insomuch as he (*i. e.* the issue) is one of the heirs in tail*, and hath no recompense of that which to him belongeth of the lands in tail; [and for the same cause it is reason that he have her portion of the lands tailed†]; and also namely, when such partition

Partition, when lands in fee and in tail descend to two daughters, and one takes the fee and the other the tail,—alienation of parcener in fee will not bar her issue of her moiety in the tail.

Recompense.

260 Item, *si ascun tenementes soient donez a un home en le taille, quell ad taunt de terre en fee-simple, et ad issue deux files, et devie, et les deux files fount purpartie entre eux, issint que la terre en fee-simple est allotte a le file puisne en allowance des autres tenementes taillez en tiel manere allottez a la file eisne; si apres tiel particion fait, la file puisne alienast la terre en fee-simple a un autre en fee, et ad issue fitz ou file et devie, lissue poet bien entrer en les tenementes taillez et auxint eux tener et occupier en purpartie ovesque soun aunte. Et ceo est pur deux causes: la premiere cause est, que lissue ne poet aver ascune remedie de la terre aliene per sa mere, pur ceo que la terre fuist a luy en fee-simple entaunt que il est un des heires en taille*, et nad my ascune recompense de ceo que a luy affiert de les tenementes taillez,* [*et pur mesme cestuy cause il est reason que il eit sa purpartie de les tenementes taillez*†] *et auxi nosment quant tiel particion ne*

---

* *Title, Machl.*, and *Roh.*

† The words within brackets do not appear in *Rastell's* Translation.

doth not make any discontinuance in the tail, as shall be said hereafter in the Chapter of Discontinuance*. 261 Another reason is, for that it shall be arrected (*i e.* accounted) the folly of the elder sister that she would suffer or agree to such a partition, where she might, if she would, have had the moiety of the land in fee-simple, and a moiety of lands entailed for her purparty, and so to be sure without loss, &c. 262 Also, if a man be seised in fee of a plough-land of land by just title, and he disseise an infant within age of another plough-land, and hath issue two daughters, and dieth seised of both those plough-lands, the infant being also then within age, and the daughters enter and make partition, so as the one plough-land is allotted for the purparty of the one, as perhaps to the younger in allowance of the other plough-land, which is allotted to the purparty of the other; if afterwards the infant enter into the plough-land whereof he was disseised

Further reason for doctrine contained in § 260. See also § 255.

The eviction of one parcener by elder title, gives to the parcener a right of entry on the other's moiety pro tanto.

fait ascun discontinuance de le taille, sicome serra dit en apres en le Chapitre de Discontinuance. 261 Un aultre cause est, pur ceo que il serra rette la folye del eigne soer quele voet suffrer ou agreer a tiel particion, ou ele puissoit aver, si ele voilleit, la moyté de la terre en fee-simple, et de les tenementes en le taille pur sa purpartie, et issint estre sure sauns damage, &c. 262 Auxi si home soit seisi en fee dun carue de terre per just† title, et disseisist un enfaunt deins age dun autre carue de terre, et ad issue deux files, et morust seisi dambideux carues, lenfaunt auxi adonques esteant deins age, et les files entront et font purpartie, issint que lun carue est allotte al purpartie lun, come per case a la puisne en allowance dautre carue que est allotte a la purpartie de lautre; si puis lenfaunt entra en le carue, dount il fuist disseisi‡ sur le possession la parcener que ad*

---

* In *Redm.* and in *Rastell's* Transl. here follows a cross reference to the Year-Book of *Mich.* 10 *H.* 6, which *Sir E. Coke* informs us is mis-cited, and is also against law, "as appeareth by Lyttleton himself."—*Co. Lytt.* 173. *a.*

† *Injust*, *Lettou & M.*, *Machl.*, and *Roh.*

‡ *Seisi*, *Lettou & M.*, *Machl.*, and *Roh.*

upon the possession of the parcener that hath the same plough-land, then the same parcener may enter into the other plough-land which her sister hath, to hold in parcenry with her: but if the younger sister alien the same plough-land to another in fee-simple before the entry of the infant, and afterwards the infant enter upon the possession of the alienee, then she cannot enter into the other plough-land, because by her alienation she hath utterly dismissed herself to have any part of the tenements as parcener. But if the younger before the entry of the infant make a lease thereof for term of years or for term of life, or in fee-tail, saving the reversion to her, and afterwards the infant enter, there peradventure otherwise it is, because she hath not dismissed herself of all which was in her, but hath reserved to her*self* the reversion and the fee, &c.

Secus, after alienation, for then the privity of the parcener is destroyed: but a lease or reservation of the reversion does not destroy privity.

263 Also, if there be three or four parceners, &c., that make partition, if the part of the one parcener be defeated by such lawful entry, she may enter and occupy the other lands with

On partition thus being defeated by eviction from either purparty, a new partition is to be made.

mesme le carue, donques mesme la parcener poet entre en lautre carue que sa soer ad, a tener en parcenerie ovesque luy : mes si la puisne aliena mesme la carue a un autre en fee-simple devaunt lentre lenfaunt, et puis lenfaunt entra sur le possession lalienê, donques ele ne poet entrer en lautre carue, pur ceo que per son alienacion ele ad luy tout oustrement dismisse daver ascune partie de les tenementes come parcener. Mes si la puisne devaunt lentre lenfaunt fait de ceo un lees pur terme dans, ou pur terme de vie ou en fee-taille†, savaunt la revercion a luy, et puis lenfaunt entra, la, peraventure autrement est, pur ceo que ele ne soy demyst de tout ceo que fuist en luy, mes ad reserve a luy la revercion et le fee, &c.*

263 Item, *si soient trois ou quater parceners, &c., que font particion, si la partie dun parcener soit defete per tiel loiall entre, ele poet entrer et occupier lautres terrez ovesque toutz*

---

* *Reles, Machl.* and *Roh.*

† *Taille,* omitted in *Roh.*; in a copy of that edition *penes Ed.*, this word is supplied by a contemporary hand.

all the other parceners, and compel them to make new partition of the other lands between them, &c. (*g*)

At common law, and when Lyttleton wrote, the husband of one parcener was compellable to make, but he could not compel partition; [but now by stat. 31 H. 8, c. 1, and 32 H. 8, c. 32, he, as well as every description of parcener, is entitled to sue the writ of partition.

264 Also, if there be two parceners, and the one taketh husband, and the husband and wife have issue between them, and the wife dieth, and the husband holdeth himself in the moiety as tenant by the curtesy; in this case the parcener that surviveth, and the tenant by the curtesy may well make partition between them, &c. And if the tenant by the curtesy will not agree to make partition, then the parcener that surviveth may have against the tenant by the curtesy a writ *de participacione faciendâ*, &c., and compel him to make partition. But if the tenant by the curtesy will have partition to be made between them, and the parcener that surviveth will not have this, then the tenant by the curtesy shall have no remedy to have partition, &c. (*h*): for he

lez autres parceners, et eux compeller de faire novel particion de lautrez terrez entre eux, &c.

264 Item, *si sount deux parceners, et lun prent baron, et le baron et sa feme ont issue entre eux, et la feme devie, et le baron soy tient eins en le moite come tenaunt per le curtosye, en ceo cas le parcener qui survesquist, et le tenaunt per le curtosye bien poient faire particion entre eux, &c. Et si le tenaunt per le curtosye ne voet agreer a particion destre fait, donques le parcener qui survesquist poet aver envers le tenaunt per le curtosye, brief* de participacione faciendâ, &c., *et luy compeller de faire particion. Mes si le tenaunt per le curtosye voille aver particion entre eux destre fait et le parcener qui survesquist ne voet ceo aver, donques le tenaunt per le curtosye navera ascun remedye pur aver particion, &c.: qar*

(*g*) This [&c.] implieth, that so it is between the surviving parceners and the heirs of the other, or between the heirs of parceners, all being dead.—*Co. Lytt.* 174. *b.*

(*h*) Here by this (&c). is included all others that be strangers in blood, whether they come to their estates by purchase or by act of law.—*Co. Lytt.* 175. *a.*

cannot have a writ *de participacione faciendâ*, because he is no parcener; for such a writ lieth for parceners only. And so you may see that the writ *de participacione faciendâ** lieth against tenant by the curtesy, and yet he himself cannot have such writ (*i*).

il ne poet aver brief de participacione faciendâ, *pur ceo que il nest parcener ; qar tiel brief gist pur parceners tantsolement. Et issint poies veier que brief* de participacione faciendâ* *gist envers tenaunt per le curtosye, et unqore il mesme ne poet aver tiel brief.*

CONCLUDING REMARKS.

LYTTLETON has, in his two first Books, treated of estates with respect to the quantity or duration of interest a person who is seised of a real estate in tenements hath; but in this Third Book, which may be styled peculiarly his own, he treats of derivative or secondary estates, and of the acts or means by which estates may be either enlarged or limited, confirmed or divested. Estates also are treated of with regard to a plurality of tenants, as distinguished from a sole or several seisin, wherein are considered the unities of title, interest, and possession which such class of *tenants* have; and as to these last named estates with which Lyttleton commences this Book, he treats, first, of parceners who invariably take by descent; secondly,

---

* This is falsely printed, and should be *de partitione faciendâ.—Co. Lytt.* 164. *b.* But notwithstanding this observation of *Sir Edward Coke*, and the writ being so described in the *register*, it is *de participatione faciendâ* in *Lettou & M.*, *Machl.*, and *Roh.*

(*i*) *Houard* derives this writ of partition from the capitulars of the first French kings.—1 *Hou. Lytt.* 318.

of joint tenants who take by purchase; and, thirdly, of tenants in common who acquire their interest in either manner (*k*).

The subject of parcenry is continued in the following and supplementary Chapter, wherein *hotchpot* is noticed as an incident to a species of partition now obsolete; but this doctrine of hotchpot is still applicable to the division of personalty by the customs of London and York (*l*); and in those cases where an intestate's estate is administered by a court of equity, and the question of "advancement" by way of settlement under the statute of distributions intervenes, being the parallel of the case of Lyttleton (*post.* § 266).

(*k*) The estate in coparcenary may be *dissolved*, either by partition, which disunites the possession; by alienation of one parcener, which disunites the title, and may disunite the interest; or by the whole at last descending to and vesting in one single person, which brings it to an estate in severalty.—B. C. ii. 191.

(*l*) The customs of these places, which are according to the ancient or common law, only operate upon two third parts of an intestate's personalty; the other third part was formerly styled the *dead man's* or testamentary part, and is now divisible according to the Statute of Distributions, 22 & 23 Car. 2, c. 10.

In respect to hotchpot. The general rule with regard to the custom of London is, that whatever a freeman gives a child shall be brought into hotchpot: but land or money to be laid out in land is out of the custom. And so is the custom of York.

The *hotchpot*, according to the Statute of Distributions, includes land as well as personalty, the only exception being in favor of the heir at law.—*Post p.* 307. *n.* (*l*).

Where money is expressed to be part of a portion, though of small amount, yet it is an advancement, and must be brought into hotchpot.—1 *Atk.* 403.

CHAPTER II.

OF PARCENERS BY CUSTOM*.

Gavelkind is the name given to a mode of descent, whereby the lands of a deceased proprietor are equally divided amongst the male heirs, and if no male heirs, amongst the female heirs. This mode of descent is peculiar to the county of Kent, and has long been regarded as being the common law of that county, so that all lands in Kent are presumed to be gavelkind; consequently, a man is not to prescribe *in certain*, but to shew the custom *at large*, or *generally*, *viz.* that the land lieth in Kent, and that all the lands there be of the nature of gavelkind. The term *gavelkind* applies to land in Kent only; for in respect of a similar mode of descent and inheritance, which prevails in many parts of the kingdom, and in some manors the term used is " parcenry by custom," or " gavelkind custom," and in these cases, the prescription must be *in certain;* that is, must be pleaded in special terms; *viz.* that the town, borough, or city where the lands be, is an ancient town, borough, or city, and that the custom hath been there, time out of mind, that the lands within the same town, borough, or city, should descend to all the heirs male, &c.

It seems that before the Conquest, all lands were in their nature gavelkind, and descendible to the male heirs equally; and if no male heirs, to the female heirs in like manner: but the introduction of military tenures at the Conquest gradually displaced this partible mode of inheritance; for lands holden by

---

* This does not appear as a separate Chapter in *Lettou & M.*, *Machl.*, *Roh.* and *Pyns.* 1516.

military service, or as *fiefs de Haubert*, (*post*, *p*. 311, *n*. (*p*)), and honorary feuds or dignities were not in their nature partible, according to the custom of Normandy; but lands not holden by such services, but holden by socage tenure, a tenancy analogous to the *heritage roturier*, remained partible long after the Conquest, which may explain the definition that *Rastell*, in his Comment on the Customs, gives of gavelkind, viz. " that all the lands within this shire (Kent), which be of ancient socage tenure, be also of the nature of gavelkind."—*Old Termes de la Ley*, (by *William Rastell*), *p*. 117.

Sir Matthew Hale notices, that by the 70th law of Hen. 1, it seems to appear;—

1. The eldest son, though he had *jus primogenituræ*, the principal fee of his father's land, yet he had not all the land.

2. That for want of children, the father or mother inherited before the brother or sister.

3. That for want of children, and father, mother, brother, and sister, the land descended to the uncles and aunts, to the fifth generation.

4. That in successions collateral, proximity of blood was preferred.

5. That the male was preferred before the female, *i. e.* the father's line was preferred before the mother's, unless the land descended from the mother, and then the mother's line was preferred.

How this law was observed in the interval between Hen. I. and Hen. II., we can give no account of; but the next period that we come to is the time of Hen. II., wherein *Glanville* gives us an account how the law stood at that time: *Vide Glanville, lib*. 7. Wherein notwithstanding it will appear, that there was some uncertainty and unsettledness in the business of descents or hereditary successions, though it was much better polished than formerly; the rules then of succession were either in reference to goods or lands. As to goods, one third part thereof went to the wife, another third part went to the children, and the other third was left to the disposition of the testator, [termed the dead man's part]; but if he had no wife, then a moiety went to the children, and the other moiety was at the deceased's disposal. And the like rule if he had left a wife, but no children.—*Glanv. lib.* 7, *cap.* 5; *et vide lib.* 2, *cap.* 29.

But as to the succession of lands, the rules are these:—

First. If the lands were knights-service, they generally went to the eldest son; and in case of no sons, then to all the daughters; and in case of no children, then to the eldest brother.

Secondly. If the lands were socage, they descended to all the sons to be divided; *Si fuerit soccagium et id antiquitùs divisum;* only the chief house was to be allotted to the purparty of the eldest, and a compensation made to the rest in lieu thereof; *Si vero non fuerit antiquitùs divisum, tunc primogenitus secundum quorundam consuetudinem totam hæreditatem obtinebit, secundum autem quorundam consuetudinem postnatus filius hæres est.*—*Glanville, lib.* 7, *cap.* 3. So that although custom directed the descent variously, either to the eldest or youngest, or to all the sons, yet it seems that at this time, *jus commune,* or common right, spoke for the eldest son to be heir, no custom intervening to the contrary.—*Hale's Hist. C. L. pp.* 225-6.

So that in about two hundred years from the Conquest, a parity of succession obtained, except in Kent, and in some ancient boroughs and places where a contrary custom still prevailed; the owners of such tenements choosing (as *Mr. Robinson* suggests) rather to deprive their younger sons of their customary share of the inheritance, than that their elder sons should not be in a condition to emulate the state and grandeur of the military tenants.

In Scotland, socage lands were anciently partible, and in Wales and Ireland a similar partibility of inheritance prevailed, though in the two last instances they differed in some particulars from gavelkind. The Welsh custom, whereby bastards were permitted to inherit, was, however, made conformable to the Kentish, by the *Statutum Walliæ,* 12

E. 1, and was utterly abolished by 34 & 35 H. 8, c. 26, ss. 91, 128. The Irish custom, which also allowed bastards to inherit, was declared void in law by all the Judges of Ireland, 3 Jac. 1 (*a*).

The chief peculiarities of this mode of inheritance, are: 1st. That the land is partible amongst the heirs-male; 2nd. That the widow of a gavelkind-man has the half of the land for her dower, which she forfeits on a second marriage, or for incontinence; 3rd. That the husband of an inheritrix in gavelkind may be tenant by the curtesy without having issue; but his estate is limited to the half, which he also forfeits on marrying again.

The other customs were formerly deemed important privileges, and were considered of great consequence, as they in fact contained exemptions from the consequences of military tenure, and preserved the laws of King Edward the Confessor and the common law from the innovations introduced at the Conquest. The distribution of a gavelkind-man's personal property was according to the common law, but subsequently became subject to the Statute of Distributions, 22 & 23 Car. 2, c. 10, which, in most particulars, is in affirmance of the ancient law. Indeed, the contentions between the common law and ecclesiastical courts gave rise to its enactment.

(*a*) *Dav. Rep.* 28.—The *Irish gavelkind* was a mode of division—it can scarcely be termed *inheritance*—peculiarly characteristic of that people; it was, that when any one died, all the possessions of the whole family were to be put together (or in hotchpot), and to be anew divided among the survivors, by the *caunfinny* or head of the family, who admitted bastards, but excluded daughters and wives; so that it differed from Kentish gavelkind in five particulars: 1. The Kentish gavelkind admitted only the next of kin, as sons, brothers, &c.; but the Irish admitted the whole race or sept; 2. The Kentish custom excluded bastards; 3. It allowed wives dower; 4. It suffered daughters to inherit for want of males; 5. It divested no man's freehold during his life; whereas the Irish gavelkind deprived the party of his freehold upon every new division.—*Cox's Hist. Ireland, Pref. to pt.* 1, 1689.

These customs being entered in old collections of the statutes before the invention of printing, have—like the *Modus faciendi Homagium et Fidelitatem; Modus levandi Fines,* and the petit Treatise concerning Wards and Reliefs (termed *Statutum de Wardis et Releviis,* 28 *E.* 1), been dignified in the titles of some copies by the name of *Statutum de Consuetudinibus Kançiæ,* though they have no claim to such an appellation. However, the date ascribed to the Custumal is, 21 *E.* 1, it having been allowed in *eire, i. e.* before the *Justiciarii itinerantes,* in that year, as appears by the preamble (*b*) of some copies.

The copies of this Custumal, as appearing to possess any authority, are: 1. A MS. copy, preserved in *Lincoln's Inn Library;* 2. Another MS. in the *Cottonian Library, Claudius, D.* II., *fol.* 122; 3. Another in the custody of the town-clerk of the city of London, *Lib. Horn., fol.* 77. *b.*; 4. Another MS. in the *Harleian MS.,* 667, *fol.* 83. *b.*; 5. Another MS. in the *Arundel MS., No.* 310, *Plut. p.* 94; 6. A printed copy in all the editions of *Lambard's Peramb. of Kent, ed.* 1576, 1596, 1656; which he copied "from an ancient and fair written roll," supposed by him to be of the time of Edward I.; 7. Another printed copy in the *Magna Carta and the Old Statutes,* printed by *Tottyl* 1556; 8. Another printed copy in *The Old Termes de la Ley,* (enlarged by *William Rastell*), *ed.* 1579, *pp.* 100. *b.* 129, with a commentary by *J. Rastell* (*c*). Nos. 5 and 8 have not been noticed by the learned Editor of

(*b*) In those copies, the Custumal commences thus: *viz. These are the usages and customs,* (&c.) *allowed in eire, before John of Berwick and his companions, the justices in eire in Kent, the* xij. *year of King Edward, the son of King Henry. Mr. Robinson* observes, no record is made of these customs, though the *Berwick* roll appears complete.—*Robins. Gavelk.* 279, *n.*

(*c*) This commentary is also used by *Lambard,* in his remarks upon the Customs of Kent; he therein alludes to an old Treatise "that handleth these Customs," and upon which he informs his reader he has enlarged. — *Lamb. Peramb. pp.* 527-588, *ed.* 1596.

the *Statutes of the Realm, fol. Lond.* 1810, *p.* 223, where a concise account is given of *Lambard's* Copy, with different readings from the MS. copies known at the time when that collection of the statutes was printed.

With regard to the copy, now for the first time in print, it appears to have been written in a thick 16mo.-sized book, which formerly belonged to the Monastery of St. Augustin, in Canterbury (*d*), which contains also a collection or rather abridgment of statutes before then promulgated, Customs of the Cinque Ports, the Customs of Romney Marsh, Vocabulary of Law Terms, a Cartulary and Collection of sundry memoranda relating to the county of Kent and the possessions of the Abbey. It was written by *W. Biholt*, a Monk of that Abbey, about the year 1300, 21 Ed. 1 (*e*), or perhaps a little later, being the same book *J. Rastell* alludes to in the before-mentioned edition of the *Old Termes de la Ley*, (*ed.* 1579), *p.* 54, *tit. Cinque Portes.*

Sir Henry Spelman in his *Treatise of Feuds*, *c.* 14, says, that there are such differences between *Tottyl's* and *Lambard's* Copies, that both their authorities may be questioned; an observation that may also be applied to every other copy. However the one now presented to the reader is, according to the Editor's judgment, more clear, and certainly is less inter-

---

(*d*) This book is not to be confounded with another book of the same Abbey of Saint Augustin, Canterbury, and in which a copy of this *Custumal* was also registered, alluded to by *Somner*, *p.* 170, where he gives from that book a clause to the effect that a *felo de se* did not forfeit his land thereby, which is not to be found in other copies. *See Robins. Gavelk.* 285, *n.*

(*e*) The Editor has formed this opinion from a view of the handwriting, and from the circumstance, that the abridgment of the statutes contained in this book does not contain or notice any statute later than Westminster the Second. (7 E. 1.) The *Custumal* itself does not seem to have been in this book considered as a statute, or classed with the statutes therein abridged, but is entered as a separate subject.

polated and corrupted than any other copy. The Editor has given a faithful copy of this ancient *custumal,* omitting only some transposition of the letters by an error of the transcriber, and an evident corruption of some of the Saxon letters in the verses relating to the customs.

The Translation is taken from that given by *J. Rastell* to his Copy, which is *sectioned* by his son, *William Rastell;* a course of division also now adopted for the sake of easier citation and reference. The *custumal* itself is as follows, *viz.*—

(*E Libro membranaceo in Mus. Brit. asservato; Bibl. Arundel.* 310. *Plut.* CLXV. A.)

Consuetudines comit' Kanc'.

Ce sount les usages é les custumes queles la comunalte de Kent cleyment en tenemens de gavelikende é en Gavelikendeis.

Kentishmen free by birth.

1. *Ce est a saver, ke touz les cors de Kenteys seyount francs cum autre franc cors de Engletere:* 2. *é ke ils pussent leur teres e leur tenemens doner et vendre sans conge demaunder a leur seinurage; save a seinurage rentes é services duwes de meme les tenemens.* 3. *E ke il pussent par bref le rei ou par pleynte leur droyt purchacer auxsi bien de leur seigneurs cum de autre gent.*

Liberty of alienation.

4. * *E ke eus ne devient les eschetours le rei elire ne unkes en militems fesoient; mes ki le rei prenge tel cum lui plest, a cel mester por luy servir.*

Ought not to choose escheators.

These are the usages and the customs which the comonalty of Kent claim in tenements of gavelkind, and in gavelkind men.

1. That is to say, that all the bodies of Kentishmen be free as well as the other freemen of England: 2. and that they may their lands and tenements give and sell without asking license of their lord; saving unto the lords the rents and services due from the same tenements. 3. And that they may by writ of the king, or by plaint, their right obtain, as well of their lords as of other men.

4. * And that they ought not the eschetors of the king to choose, nor ever in any time did they; but that the king may take such a one as it shall please him, to serve him in that which shall be needful.

* This passage concerning the escheators is omitted in the printed copy by *Tottyl* in his *Magna Carta, &c.*, 1556, and in the *Lincoln's Inn MS.*: in the copy from which the *custumal* is taken, it does not appear in the order in which it is placed in *W. Rastell's Old Termes de la Ley*, *Tottyl* 1579, *Lambard* and the other copies.

May appear by borsholder and four men, of the borough;

5. And they claim also, that the comonaltye of gavelkind men, which hold none other than tenements of gavelkind nature, ought not to come to the common summons of the eire, but only by the borsholder and four men of the borough, except the towns which ought to answer by twelve men in the eire.

Exception.

Land not forfeit for felony.

6. And they claim also, that if any tenant in gavelkind be attainted of felony, for the which he suffereth judgment* of death; let the king have all his chattels, and let his heir forthwith after his death be enherited of all the lands and tenements which he holds in gavelkind in fee and inheritance: concerning which it is said in Kentish—

The father to the bough,
The son to the plough (*f*).

Wife's dower (§ 21), not forfeit.

7. And if he have a wife, forthwith let her be endowed of the one-half of the heritage, if she be of age to have and to hold in the form aforesaid. And of such lands the king shall neither have the year, or waste, but only as is aforesaid (*g*).

Chattels only forfeit for felony.

5. *E cleiment auxsi ke le commune de gavelikendoys que ne tienent nie de tenement de gavelikende, ne devient venir a la commune sominise del eire, mes per borghesaldre et quatre hommes de la borghe, forspris les viles ki respoynent par* xii. *en eire.* 6. *E cleiment auxsi ke si nul tenaunt de gavelikende soit ateynt de felonie parquex il suffre juise* de mort; eit le roy touz ces chateaus, é soen eir meintenount apres sa mort soyt enerite de tote les teres é tenemens ke il tient du gavelikende en fee, é en eritage: dount est dis en Kenteys—*

The vader to the bou,
The sone to the loghe†.

7. *E si il eit femme, meintenount soit dowe de la moité del eritage, si ele soit de age de aver é de tenir en la forme avaunt diste. E de celes teres ly roy ne avera an ne wast mes tantsoulement si cum est avauntdit.*

---

* In *Rastell's* copy, this word is rendered *judgement*, both in the French and English; the word *juise* is most probably an abbreviation of *justise*, which anciently signified the same thing, by the same metonymy that justice was the term used for a judge.—See *infra*, note (*f*).

† All the other copies (except *MSS. Cott.*) have *ploghe*. In *Lib. Horn.* the word *lowe* is written under *plogh*.

(*f*) But this rule holdeth in case of felony, and of murder only, and not in the case of treason at all; and it holdeth also, in case where the offender is *justised* by order of law, and not where he withdraweth himself after the fault committed, and will not abide his lawful trial. And because that this custom shall not be construed by equity, but by a straight and liberal interpretation: it hath, therefore, been doubted whether the brother or uncle shall have the advantage thereof, because the words do extend to the son only.—See 22 E. 3, abridged by Master *Brooke*, *tit. Custome*, 54. *J. Rastell's Commentary on the Customs of Kent, sub tit. Gavelkind, in the Old Termes de la Ley, enlarged by William Rastell, ed.* 1579, *p.* 104.

(*g*) The wife shall not lose her dower for the default of her husband; but in such case where the heir shall lose his inheritance for the offence of his father.—8 H. 3. *Id.* 104. *b.*

8. *E si nul de gavelikendeis por felonie, ou por reth de felonie se suttret de la peis, é soit en counte demaunde, cum il apent et peus utlage, si il se met en seint eglise é forsjure le reaume, le rei eit le an et le wast des teres et de tous ces tenemens ensemblement, é tuz ces chateaus. Isi ke apres le an é le jur, le plus precheyn seygnours eient lur eschetes de ces teres é de ces tenemens, checun seignour ceo ke de lui est tenuz sauns men.*

8. And if any gavelkind-man either for felony, or for suspicion of felony, withdraw himself out of the country, and be demanded in the county *court* as he ought, and be afterwards outlawed; if he put himself on Holy Church, and abjure the realme, the king shall have the year and the waste of his lands and of all his tenements, all his goods and chattels. So that, after the year and the day, the next lords may have their escheats of his lands and of his tenements, each lord that which is holden of him without mesne (*i. e.* immediately (*h*)).

Flying for felony causes forfeiture.

9. *E cleiment auxsi ke si un tenaunt en gavelikende murt, ke soit enerite de teres é des tenemens en gavelikende, ke touz ces fiz partirunt tel eritage par owel porciun.* 10. *E si nul eir male ne soit, soit la partie fete parentre les femeles si cum parentre les freres.* 11. *E ke mees soit auxsi departi parentre eus, mes ke lastre* demurge a pune.*

9. And they claim also, that if a tenant in gavelkind die, so that he be inherited of lands and of tenements in gavelkind, that all his sons shall part that inheritance by equal portions. 10. And if there be no heir male, let the partition be made between the females, even as between brothers (*i*). 11. And that the messuage also be departed between them; but let the astre* (*see next page n.* (*k*)) remain to the younger.

Gavelkind land partible among sons, if no sons, among females.

The hearth to the younger.

* This word is translated by *Lambard*, "*the hearth for fire*," which in the thirteenth division of this *custumal* he terms the "covert of the *hearth*;" but his interpretation of the word *astre* is by no means conclusive. See *Selden's Notes on Hengham, ad verb.* "*extra astrum*," and the references there cited.

(*h*) So that after the year and the day, the next lord or lords shall have their escheats of those lands and tenements, every lord that which is immediately holden of him. So it is holden in the book, 8 E. 2, abridged by *Fitzh. tit. Prescription*, 50; and 22 E. 3, abridged by *Brooke, tit. Custome*, 54. *Id.* 105.

(*i*) But the statute of *prerogativa regis*, c. 16, sayeth, that the females shall not divide with the males; which is to be understood of such as be in *equal* degree of kindred, as brothers and sisters, as in this ninth and tenth division. For if a man have issue three sons, and the eldest have issue a daughter, and die in the life of his father, and the father dieth: in this case, the daughter shall join with the two other brethren her uncles; for that she is not in equal degree with them as her father was, whose heir nevertheless she must of necessity be.—*Ibid.*

Right of representation.

And be the value thereof delivered to each of the parceners of that heritage, and forty feet from that astre, if the tenant will so suffer (*k*), 12. and then let the elder have the first choice, and the others afterwards according to their degree. 13. Likewise concerning houses which shall be found over and above that messuage, let them be parted amongst the heirs by equal portions, that is, to wit, by feet if need be, saving the covert of the astre, which shall remain to the younger, as is above said. So, nevertheless, that the younger make reasonable amends to his parceners for the part which to them belongeth, by the award of good men. 14. And of the aforesaid tenements, whereof one only suit was wont to be made beforetime, be there not by reason of the partition but one sole suit made, as they were before accustomed; but yet let all the parceners make contribution to him who maketh the suit for them.

Elder has priority of choice.

Houses beyond chief messuage partible.

Sole suit made for partible tenement, and parceners to contribute.

E la value soit de ceo delivere a checun des parciners de cel eritage, é xl. *pees de cel astre si le tenaunt le peust suffrir,* 12. *é dounc le eyne eit la premiere elleccioun, é les autres apres par degre.* 13. *Ensement des meisouns ke serount trovees droit desus cel mes, seient partiz parentre les eirs par owel porciun, ce est a saver par peez cil eist mester, save le covert del astre al pusne si cum il est sourdist. Issi nekedent ke le pusne face renable gre au parciners de la partie ke a eus apent par agard de bone gent.* 14. *E des avauntdis tenemens dount une soule seute soleit estre feete, ne soit par la reyson de la partie fors une soule sute feete, sicum soleient avaunt, mes tuz les parciners fasent contribuciun a celuy ke feet la seute pur eus.*

15. In like sort, let the goods of gavelkind-men be parted into three parts, after the funerals and the debts paid, if there be lawful issue alive. So as the dead *man* have one part, and his lawful sons and

Personal property partible [according to the common law].

15. *Ensement soient les chateaus de gavilikendeis departis en treys apres les exequies é les dettes rendues sil i eit issue muilire en vie. Issi ke le mort eit la une partie é les fis e les filles muiyleres le autre*

(*k*) By this word, *astre*, is meant, as is conjectured, either the hall or chief room of the house, either else the well for water, or the south side of the building, for *astre* being sounded with *s* may come of the Latin word *atrium*, which signifieth a hall; or of *haustrum*, which betokeneth the bucket of a well; or of *austrum*, the south side, every of which have their particular commodities above the rest of the house or tenement. Or otherwise, being sounded with *s*, it may be deduced from the French word, *asister*, by contraction, *astre*, which is as much as a site or situation, and with the article *le* before it, *lester*, a churchyard or court about a house: but at this day there is no such regard made in the partition, but only consideration had, that the parts themselves be equal and indifferent.—*Id.* 106.

partie, et la femme la tierce partie; 16. *é si nul issue muilere ne soit, eit le mort la une moyte é la femme en vie lautre moyte.* 17. *E*

the daughters another part, and the wife the third part (*l*); 16. and if there be no lawful issue *alive*, let the dead *man* have the one half, and the wife, *if* alive, the other half (*m*). 17. And if the heir or the heirs shall

Guardianship in socage of

(*l*) When it is said here, that the dead shall have one part, it is meant for due performance of his legacies by his executors if he make a testament, or by the discretion of the ordinary if he die intestate.—*Id.* 107.

By the common law, two thirds of a deceased's personalty belonged to his wife and children, who had their *partes rationabiles* as is next noticed in n. (*m*). The third part the deceased had the power to dispose of, which was called the *dead man's part.* If he died intestate, the ordinary committed the administration to such administrator as the statutes 31 E. 3, c. 11, and 21 H. 3, c. 5, direct; but now this *pars rationabilis* being abolished, distribution of the whole of an intestate's effects takes place pursuant to the *Statute of Distributions*, 22 & 23 Car. 2, c. 10, whereby it is enacted, "that the surplusage of an intestates' estates, except of femes covert, shall (after the expiration of one full year from the death of the intestate) be distributed in the following manner. One third shall go to the widow of the intestate, and the residue in equal proportions to his children, or if dead, to their representatives; that is, their lineal descendants: if there are no children or legal representatives subsisting, then a moiety shall go to the widow, and a moiety to the next of kindred in equal degree, and their representatives: if no widow, the whole shall go to the children: if neither widow nor children, the whole shall be distributed among the next of kin in equal degree, and their representatives: but no representatives are admitted among collaterals, further than the children of the intestate's brothers and sisters. By this statute, the mother, as well as the father, succeeded to all the personal effects of their children, who died intestate and without wife or issue: in exclusion of the other sons and daughters, the brothers and sisters of the deceased. And so the law still remains with respect to the father; but by statute 1 Jac. 2, c. 17, if the father be dead, and any of the children die intestate without wife or issue, in the lifetime of the mother, she and each of the remaining children, or their representatives, shall divide his effects in equal portions."—B.C. ii. 515.

Hotchpot under Statute of Distributions.

It is also enacted by the Stat. of Distributions, "that no child of the intestate, (except his heir at law) on whom he settled in his lifetime any estate of lands, or pecuniary portion, equal to the distributive shares of the other children, shall have any part of the surplusage with their brothers and sisters; but if the estates so given them, by way of advancement, are not quite equivalent to the other shares, the children so advanced shall now have so much as will make them equal. With regard to goods and chattels, this is part of the ancient custom of London, of the province of York, and of our sister kingdom of Scotland: and with regard to lands descending in coparcenary, that it hath always been, and still is, the common law of England, under the name of *hotchpot*" (§ 267).—*Id.* 516.

Pars rationabilis.

(*m*) The selfsame order that the custom here speaketh of, in the fifteenth and seventeenth division, is at this day observed in the city of London, and the same in effect was long since used throughout the whole realm. For it is evident, both by the law of King *Canutus*, by Master *Glanvil*, by the words of *Magna Charta*, c. 18, by Master *Fitzh.* in his *Natura Brevium*, in the writ *de rationabili parte bonorum*, *fol.* 122, *L.* That the wife and children had their reasonable parts of the goods by the common law of the realm, and that by the common law was so it appeareth also in 33 E. 3, 25 and 21; 30 H. 6. And it was said for law, Mich. 31 H. 8, abridged by Master *Brooke*, *tit. De rationabili parte bonorum*, *pl.* 6, that it hath been often put in

heirs in gavelkind.

be under the age of fifteen years, let the nurture of them be delivered by the lord to the next of blood to whom the inheritance cannot descend; so that the lord take nothing for the committing thereof.

Lord not entitled to marriage.

18. And let him not be married by the lord but by his own will, and by the advice of his friends if he will.

Heir in gavelkind entitled to his land on attaining fifteen.

19. And when such heir, or all the heirs, be of the full age of fifteen years, let their lands and tenements be delivered unto them, together with the chattels and with the profits of those lands, over and beyond their reasonable sustenance: of the which profit and chattels let him be bound to answer who shall have the nurture, or his heirs to whom that nurture was committed.

si leir ou les eirs soit ou soient dedens age de xv. *ans, soit la norëture de eus baile par le seignour a plus preseyn du sonk, a ki eritage ne peust descendre, issi ke le seignour por le bail rien ne prenge.* 18. *E ke il ne soit marieé par le seignour, mes par sa volente demeine, et par conseil de ces amis sil veut.* 19. *E kaunt tel eir, ou teus eirs seyent de plein age de* xv. *ans, soient a eus lur teres et leur tenemens liveres ensemblement oue les chateaus et oue les apruemens de celes teres outre leur renable sustenance, de quel apruement e chateaus soit tenu a respundre a celuy ki avera la noreture, ou as eirs de cel norëture a ki il sera baile.*

Pars rationabilis.

ure as a common law, and never demurred upon; and, therefore, it seemeth, that it is common law: howsoever it came to pass at length that it was admitted for law, but in such countries only, where it was continued by daily usage; and that all the writs in the *Register de rationabili parte bonorum* have mention of the special custom of the shire, in which the party is demanded, and so in the book, 28 H. 6, 4. But as at this day, [*temp. Eliz.*], partition of chattels is not used throughout the whole realm, though in the mean time if it hath not lost the force of common law as many think, and as may be gathered by the opinion aforesaid holden for law, *anno* 31 H. 8. So it is as some think, vanished quite out of all ure within this county of Kent also.—*Id.* 107. *b.*

[This right to the *pars rationabilis* was by the common law, which still holds place as the common law of Scotland]. To which we may add, that, whatever may have been the custom of later years in many parts of the kingdom, or however it was introduced in derogation of the old common law, the ancient method continued in use in the province of York, the principality of Wales, and in the city of London, till very modern times: when, in order to favour the power of bequeathing, and to reduce the whole kingdom to the same standard, three statutes have been provided; the one, 4 & 5 W. & M. c. 2, explained by 2 & 3 Ann. c. 5, for the province of York; another 7 & 8 W. 3, c. 38, for Wales; and a third, 11 Geo. 1, c. 18, for London: whereby it is enacted, that persons within those districts, and liable to those customs, may (if they think proper) dispose of *all* their personal estates by will; and the claims of the widow, children, and other relations, to the contrary, are totally barred. Thus is the old common law now utterly abolished throughout all the kingdom of England, and a man may devise the whole of his chattels as freely as he formerly could his third part or moiety.—B.C. ii. 493.

20. *E feet a saver, ke al oure ke ces eirs de gavelikende unt passe lage de* xv. *auns, list a eus lur teres e leur tenemens doner é vendre a leur volente; sauve les services de seygnurages sicum est avaunt dit.* 21. *E si cel tenaunt mourt, é eit femme ke luy sorvive,*

At fifteen, heir in gavelkind may alien.

20. And this is to be understood, that from such time as those heirs in gavelkind have passed the age of fifteen years, it is lawful for them their lands or tenements to give and sell at their pleasure; saving the services to the chief lords, as is before said (*n*). 21. And if such tenant die, and have a wife that overliveth him, let that

Wife dowable of a moiety;

Alienation by heir in gavelkind.

(*n*) Although that this custom enable the heir to make away his lands and tenements very soon, namely, at the fifteenth year of his age, by means whereof it might be thought unreasonable in giving such scope and liberty to so young years; yet upon the good consideration thereof it may appear, that the custom itself doth reasonably and carefully provide in the behalf of the heir, forsomuch as it licenseth him at that years not to give his lands, for that he might do for nothing, but to give and sell his lands, which it seemeth he should not do without sufficient recompense. Such like interpretation, the common law also seemeth to make of this custom, both by the opinion of *Vavisour* and *Keble*, 5 H. 7, 31 & 41, who said that it was adjudged, that a release made by such an infant was void by the sentence of the book, 21 E. 4, 24, where it is said an infant cannot declare his will upon such a feoffment. And by the judgment of *Hankford*, 11 H. 4, 33, who also held that a warranty or grant of a reversion made at such age, was to no purpose at all, although a lease with release might haply be good by the custom, because it amounteth to a feoffment. And it is not fit that this custom should be construed by equity, forasmuch as it standeth not with any equity, to make an infant of little discretion and less experience, to sell his land, and not to provide withal that he should have *quid pro quo*, and some reasonable recompense for the same; for that were not to defend the pupil and fatherless, but to lay him wide open to every slie deceit and circumvention. In which respect, their opinion is very well to be liked of, who hold, that if an infant in gavelkind at this day [*temp. Eliz.*] will sell at fifteen years of age, these three things ought of necessity to concur, if he will have the sale good and effectual. The first is that he be an heir, and not a purchaser of the land, that he departeth withal; the second, that he have recompense for it; and the third, that he do it with livery of seisin by his own hand, and not by warrant of attorney, nor by any other manner of assurance. And these men for proof of the first and second point of their assertion, do build upon the words of this custom, where it is said, from such time as those heirs in gavelkind be of or have passed the age of fifteen years, it is lawful for them their lands or tenements to give and sell; in which the words, "*those heirs*," do restrain the infant that cometh in by purchase. And, "*give and sell*," in the copulative, do of necessity implie a recompense; forsomuch as selling cannot be without some price or thing given for it. And for maintenance of the third matter, they have of their part besides the common usage of the country, the common law of the realm also, which expoundeth the word, *give*, to mean a feoffment, and which not only disalloweth of any gift made by an infant; but also punisheth the taker in trespass, unless he have it by livery from the infant's own hands, as appeareth in 26 H. 8, 2; 9 H. 7, 24; 18 E. 4, 2; 22 H. 6, 3, and divers other books.—*Id.* 110; *Robins. Gavelk.* 195.

wife forthwith be endowed of the one half of the tenements whereof her husband died* seised, by the heirs if they be of age, or by the lords if they be not of age.

so long as she keep herself single and chaste.

So that she have the one half of those lands and tenements so long as she keepeth her a widow, or be of childbirth attainted, according to the ancient usage, that is to say, that when she is delivered of child, and the child be heard cry, that the hue and cry be raised, and the country assembled, have view of the child and of the mother, then let her lose her dower, and otherwise *not* so long as she keepeth her a widow, whereof it is said in Kentish—

He that doth wend her,
Let him lend her (*o*).

Husband may be tenant by the curtesy without having issue; but it is only of a moiety of the wife's lands, and it ceases if he marries again.

22. And they claim also, that if a man take a wife who hath heritage of gavelkind, and the wife die before him, let the husband have the one half of those lands, so long as he keepeth him a widower, where-

soit cele femme meintenaunt dowe de tenemens dount soen barun murust* seysi, par les eirs sil soient de age, ou par le seignour sil ne soient de age. Issi ke ele eit la moyte de celes teres taunt cum ele tient veve, ou de enfaunt soit ateint par le aunciane usage, cest a saver, ke kaunt ele enfaunt, et lenfaunt soit oi crier, ke heu é cri soit leve, é le pais ensemblee eient vue del enfaunt é de la mere, adunc pert soen dowere, é autrement tount cum ele se tient veve, dount il est dit en Kenteys—

Se thire wende,
Se hire lende.

[And corruptly, for in true Saxon letters it standeth thus ;—

Se that hire wende,
Se hire lende.

Lamb. Per. p. 405, ***ed.*** 1576].

22. ***E cleyment auxsi ke homme ke prent femme ke eit eritaye de gavelikende, et la femme mourge avaunt luy, eit le barun le moyte de ces teres taunt cum il se tient***

---

* The words *vestu e, vested and,* occur at this place in *Lambard's* copy, and in that copy from which *John Rastell* took his *Custumal;* but the other copies do not all give these words. The copy in the *Magna Carta and Old Statutes,* printed by *Tottyl* 1556, in this respect conforms to the copy above given, as does the *Lin. Inn* MSS. *John Rastell* (in his remarks on this part of the *Custumal*), and *Lambard,* both comment on the word *vested,* as indicating a possession in deed or in fact, and not a possession in law only.

(*o*) This expression is explained by *Lambard, viz.*

He that doth turn, or wend her,
Let him also give unto her, or lend her.

It is a doubt, whether that a woman entitled to dower in gavelkind, may waive her dower of the half after this custom, and bring her action to be endowed of the third at the common law, and so exempt herself from all danger of the customary conditions or no. Some have been of opinion, that she is at liberty to take one and refuse the other at her pleasure: and therefore inquire thereof, &c.—*J. Rastell's Commentary in Old Termes de la Ley, by W. Rastell, ed.* 1579, *p.* 113, *b.*

vever, dount ele morust seysi, sauns estrepement ou wast ou exil fere, le quel ke il eit eyr ou nun, e si il prent femme, il pert trestut. 23. *Et si nul tenement de gavelikende enchiece en eschete, soit al seignorage de ky il tient par ffee de hauberk ou par serjauntie, ou ke ceo soit de soen tenaunt, ke avaunt le tynt par quiteclaimaunce de ceo feet, ou soit eschete par la gavelet* cum il est sus dit, remeyne cele tere as eirs nounpartable†.*

of she dieth seised, without committing strippe, or waste, or exile, whether there be heir or no: and if he take another wife, he loses all. 23. And if any tenement of gavelkind fall in escheat, be to the lord of him of whom he holdeth by fee of hauberke or by serjeancie (*p*), or that it be to him of his own tenant, who before held it of him by quit-claim thereof made, or if it be escheated by gavelet* as is hereafter said, let this land remain to the heirs impartible (*q*)†.

Gavelkind land becoming military tenure by escheat, loses its partibility, so if it escheat by gavelet.

* In the copy from which this *custumal* is taken, a blank is left by the transcriber for this word *gavelet;* in all other copies, the word *gavelet* is used.

† *And this is to be understood, where the tenant so rendering, doth retain no service to himself,* [*but saveth nevertheless to the other lords their fees, fermes, and the rents wherewith the aforesaid tenements of gavelkind, so rendered, were before charged by him or them which might charge them.*] All other copies have an interpolation at this place, either of that part of this paragraph which is not within brackets, or of the whole passage.

(*p*) To hold by fee of hawberk, or by serjeancy, (if it be grand serjeancy), is to hold by knight's service. *Heah beony* is in Saxon, a *high defence;* and the customs of Normandy called that fief or ffee, *de haubert,* which oweth to defend the land by full arms; that is, by horse, haubert, target, sword, or helm. And it consisteth of three hundred acres of land, (which is the same, (as some think), that we call a whole knight's fee.—*Id.* 114. *b.; ante, p.* 150, *in n.*

(*q*) Later authorities disprove this article of the customs of Kent. It seems that if gavelkind lands were holden of a seignory which held in knight's-service, the custom was suspended; though many argued that it was destroyed in that instance, as well as in the cases mentioned in the *custumal:* it seems, also, with regard to land in Kent, holden by knight's-service, which were of their nature descendible to the eldest son, if such lands had been *anciently* holden by such a tenure, the partibility was extinguished, otherwise, if such tenure had been created within time of legal memory; for it was not allowed that any *new* creation should alter the old customs. However, in the time of Henry the Sixth, it appears by a statute in the eighteenth year of that reign, that the number of tenants by knight's-service was very small,—not more than thirty or forty at the most,—who held to the value of twenty pounds; and the disgavelling statutes of 31 H. 8, and six private acts not printed, one in 11 H. 7, and others, *viz.* 15 H. 8; 2 & 3 Ed. 6; 1 Eliz; 8 Eliz.; and 21 Jac. 1, have added to their number; but, on the other hand, the presumption of law, *viz.* that all lands in the county of Kent are of the nature of gavelkind, till the contrary be made to appear, throws the burden of proof upon him who claims by the ordinary course of descent, in derogation of the custom, and the difficulty of shewing what lands were *anciently* holden by knight's-service, and what were included in the disgavelling statutes, which specify the lands of some private gentle-

Disgavelled land.

Forfeiture by process of gavelet *or customary* cessavit.

24. And they claim also, that if any tenant in gavelkind withhold his rent and his service of the tenement which he holdeth of his lord, let the lord seek by the award of the court, from three weeks to three weeks, distress upon this tenement, until at his fourth court, it be awarded, that he take that tenement into his hand in the name of a distress, as *if it were* an ox or a cow, and let him keep it a year and a day in his hand without manuring it, (*i. e.* without tilling it), within which term, if the tenant come and pay his arrearages, and make reasonable amends for the detainer, then let him have and enjoy his tenement as his ancestors before held it.

25. And if he do not come before the year and day passed, then let the lord go to the next county court, making suit by testimony of the court, and cause to be proclaimed this process to have witness, and by award of the court after this county court holden, enter and manure in those lands and tenements as he did before in his own demesne. And if the tenant come afterward, and will rehave his tenements, and hold them as he did before, let him make agreement with the lord, as it is anciently said—

24. E cleiment auxsi ke si nul tenaunt reteigne sa rente ou soen servise du tenement kil tient du seignour, quierge le seignour par agard de la curt, de trois simoynes en treys simoynes, destresse sur cel tenement, taunt ke a sa quarte curt soyt agarde, ke il prenge cel tenement en sa meyn, en noun de destresse cum bof ou vache, et le tenge un an é un jour en sa mein sauns meynoverir, dedens quel terme, si le tenaunt vient é rent ces arerages é fet renables amendes de la detenue, dount eit é joie soen tenement si cum ces auncestres avaunt la teneint.

25. E si il ne vient devaunt le an e le jour passe, dount auge le seignour al prechein conte, suaunt par temoinage de la court, é face pronuncier cel proces por temoigne aver et par agard de la court apres cel conte tenue, entre é meinovere en celes teres si cum avaunt cum en soen demeigne. E si le tenaunt vient apres é voile cele tere reaver et tenir si cum avaunt, face gre au seignour si cum il est aunsienement dit—

---

men, to the number of seventy-four, favours the custom; so that it may be stated with certainty, that the disgavelled land is very inconsiderable, especially as it becomes every year more and more difficult to prove what estates the persons comprehended in the disgavelling statutes, were seised of at the time of making those acts. As to the identifying any land in Kent, as having been holden by an ancient knight's-service tenure, that, the Editor takes upon himself to affirm, is nearly impossible, as the proof would be by records, shewing such tenure to have existed at the commencement of the time of what was till lately deemed legal memory, *viz.* the first year of the reign of Richard the First.

Nighe sithes yelde;
And nighe sithes gelde,
And vif pond vor the were,
Ar he be holdere.

Hath he not since any thing given,
Nor hath he not since any thing paid—
Then let him pay five pounds for his were, (*i. e.* a fine),
Before he become *tenant or* holder again.

26. *E cleyment auxsi ke home ne deit serment fere sur le livre, pur destresce ou pur pour de seignour ou de bailif encountre sa volente, sauns bref le roy, sinon pur fealte fere a soen seignour; mes ke devaunt coroners ou devaunt autres ministres le roy ke real poer unt de enquere de trespas fet encuntre la corone.* 27. *E cleiment auxsi ke checun Kentoys peust autre essoner en la court le roy, en conte, en hundred, é en la court soen seignour, auxsi de comune seute cum de commun plai.*

Gavelkind-men not to be sworn save for fealty.

26. Also they claim, that no man ought to make oath upon the book, neither by distress, nor by the power of the lord, nor his bailiff, against his will, without the writ of the king, unless it be to do fealty to his lord; but only before coroners or before other ministers of the king that royal power have, to enquire of trespass committed against the crown. 27. And they claim also, that every Kentishman may essoign another, either in the king's court, in the county, in the hundred, and in the court of his lord, as well of common suit as of common plea.

Essoignes.

28. *Oustre ceo, il cleiment par especial feet le roy Henri, pere le roy ke ore est, ke de tenemens ke sount tenuz en gavelikende, ne soit pris la graunt asise par* xii. *jures, si cum ailurs est pris en le reaume. E ceo est as aver la ou le demaundaunt é le tenaunt tienent en gavelikende, en leu de cel graunt asise, seient eluz* xii. *jures en gavelikende* (*r*). *Issi ke quatre tenauns en gavelikende prengent* xii. *tenauns en gavelikende jures**.

Writ of assise triable by gavelkind-men for jurors.

28. Moreover, they claim by an especial deed of King Henry, the father of the king who now is, that of the tenements which are holden in gavelkind, there shall not be taken the grand assise by jury of twelve, as it is in other places taken in the realm. And it is, to wit, where the demandant and the tenant hold in gavelkind, in place of this grand assise, let there be chosen twelve jurymen in gavelkind (*r*): so that four tenants of gavelkind take twelve tenants of gavelkind to be jurors*.

* In most copies the following conclusion is, with some variations, adopted, *viz.—And the charter of the king of this especialtie is in the custody of Sir John of Norwood, the*

(*r*) By the effect of stat. 3 & 4 W. 4, c. 27, s. 36, which abolished real actions, (except in two instances), this custom and privilege is now lost to Kentishmen, who, till

day of S. Elphey (Alphage) in Canterbury, the twenty-first year of King Edward, the son of King Henry. These be the usages of gavelkind and of gavelkind-men in Kent, which were before the Conquest, and at the Conquest, and ever since till now.

the operation of that act, were accustomed to have their *writs of right* tried by gavelkind men, *i. e.* tenants in gavelkind.

Another custom the Kentishmen formerly enjoyed, it was, that issues on their customs wheresoever taken were to be tried by Kentishmen, "because such issues touched the comunalty of Kent;" and *Robinson* (p. 260) refers to such an award of *venire de corpore comitatûs*. In *Pasch*. 21 E. 4, on judgment being given that the custom, in respect of an infant's alienation, did not extend to a devise, the *Chancellor* is reported as saying; *Ceo covient estre trie per les gentes de Kent coment lour custome est use.* But since the stat. 4 Ann. c. 16, which enacts that all jury process is to be awarded from the body of that county where the issue is triable, has deprived the Kentishmen of their old right.

Expliciunt Consuetud.' Comitis Kanc'.

Gavelkind.

265 PARCENERS by the custom* are, where a man seised in fee-simple or in fee-tail of lands or tenements, which are of the tenure called gavelkind, within the county of Kent, and hath issue divers sons, and dieth; such lands or tenements shall descend to all the sons by the custom; and they shall equally inherit and make partition between them by the custom, as females shall do, and writ *of partition* lieth in this case, as between females; but it behoveth in the declaration to make mention of the custom. Also such custom is in

265 *Parceners per le custome sont lou home seisi en fee-simple ou en fee-taille de terrez ou tenementes, que sont de tenure appelle gavelkynde, deins le conté de Kent, et ad issue divers fitz, et devie, tielx terres ou tenementes descenderont a toutz les fitz per le custome; et ouelment enheriteront et ferront particion entre eux per le custome, sicome femelx ferront, et brief* de participacione faciendâ *gist en ceo cas, sicome entre femelx; mes il covient en la declaracion de faire mencion de*

* In *Lettou & M.*, *Machl.*, *Roh.*, and *Pyns.* 1516. These words form the commencement of a new paragraph, not of a separate chapter.

other places of England. And also such custom is of North Wales, &c.*

266 Also there is another partition, which is of another nature, and of other form than any of the partitions aforesaid be; as if a man seised of certain lands in fee-simple, hath issue two daughters, and the elder is married, and the father giveth part of his lands to the husband with his daughter in frankmarriage, and dieth seised of the remnant, the which remnant is of greater yearly value than the lands given in frankmarriage; 267 in this case, the husband and the wife shall have nothing for their purparty of the said remnant, unless they will put their lands given in frankmarriage in hotchpot with the remnant of the land with her sister. And if they will not do so, then the younger may hold and occupy the same remnant, and take the profits to herself only. And it seemeth that this word "hotchpot" is in English a pudding;

Partition by *hotchpot on a gift in frank-marriage, which* primâ facie *is a sufficient* advancement.

Meaning of the term hotchpot.

*le custome. Auxi tiel custome est en autres lieux dengleterre. Et auxi tiel custome de North Wales, &c.**

266 Item, *il y ad autre particion quele est dautre nature et dautre fourme que ascuns des particions avauntdits sont; sicome home seisi de certeyns terres en fee-simple, ad issue deux files et leisne est marie, et le pere dona parcell de ses terres a le baron ovesque sa file en frank mariage, et morust seisi de le remenaunt, le quel remenaunt est de pluis greindre value per an, que sont les terrez donez en frank mariage ;* 267 *en cel cas le baron et la feme naverount riens pur lour purpartie de le dit remenaunt, sinon quils voillent metter lour terres donez en frank mariage en hochepot ovesque le remenaunt de la terre ovesque sa soer. Et si issint ils ne voillent faire, donques la puisne poet tener et occupier mesme le remenaunt et perner a luy les profites tantsolement. Et il semble que cest parole* hochepot *est en english a puddyng, qar en tiel puddyng nest commenement*

* The concluding words of this section in the two Cambridge MSS. are—*come en Northumberland et North Wales*—*as in Northumberland and North Wales.* The text as above, conforms to *Lettou & M.*, *Machl.*, *Roh.*, and *Rastell's* Translation.

for in this pudding there is not commonly put one thing alone, but one thing with other things: and, therefore, it behoveth, in such case, to put the lands given in frankmarriage, with the other lands in hotchpot, if the husband and his wife will have anything in the other lands; 268 And this term "hotchpot" is but a term similitudinary, and is as much as to say, to put the lands in frankmarriage and the other lands in fee-simple together, and this is for such intent, to know* the value of all the lands, *scil.* the lands given in frankmarriage, and of the remnant which were not given, and then partition shall be made in form following:—As put the case, that a man seised of thirty acres of land in fee-simple, every acre of the value of twelve pence by the year, who hath issue two daughters, and the one is covert baron; and the father gives ten acres of the thirty acres to the husband with his daughter in frankmarriage, and dieth seised of the remnant; then the other sister shall enter into the remnant, *scil.* into

How partition in hotchpot is to be made.

mys un chose tantsolement, mes un chose ovesque autres choses: Et pur ceo il covient en tiel cas de mettre les terrez donez en frank mariage, ovesque les autres terres en hochepot, si le baron et sa feme voillent aver riens en les autres terres; 268 *et cest terme hochepot, est forsque un terme similitudinarie, et est a tant adire, cestassavoir, de mettre les terres donez en frank mariage et les autres terres en fee-simple ensemble, et ceo est a tiel entent conustre* le value de toutz les terres,* scil. *lez terrez donez en frank mariage, et de le remenaunt que ne furent dones, et donques particion serra fait en la fourme que ensuyt: Sicome mettomus que home seisi de* XXX. *acres de terre en fee-simple, chescun acre del value de* xiid. *per an, quel ad issue deux files, et lun est covert de baron, et le pere dona* X. *acres de les* XXX. *acres a le baron, ovesque sa file en frank mariage, et morust seisi de le remenaunt, donques lautre soer entrera en la remenaunt,* scil. *en les* XX. *acres, et*

* In *Lettou & M.*, *Machl.*, and *Roh.*, this word is printed, *encounter, against*, which is evidently erroneous.

the twenty acres, and shall occupy them to her own use, unless the husband and his wife will put the ten acres given in frankmarriage with the twenty acres in hotchpot, that is to say, together; and then when the value of every acre is known, to wit, that every acre valueth by the year [and it is assessed or agreed between them, that every acre is worth by the year*] twelve pence: then the partition shall be made in such manner, *scil.* the husband and the wife shall have, beyond the ten acres given to them in frankmarriage, five acres in severalty of the twenty acres, and the other sister shall have the remnant, *scil.* fifteen acres of the twenty acres for her purparty: so that accounting the ten acres which the husband and wife have by the gift in frankmarriage, and the other five acres of the twenty acres, the husband and wife have as much in yearly value as the other sister hath; 269 and so always upon such partition, the lands given in frankmarriage abide to the donees and to their heirs, according to the form of the gift. For if the other parcener had

The lands given in frankmarriage remain to the donees.

ceo occupiera a son use demesne, sinon que le baron et sa feme voille metter les x. *acres dones en frank mariage ovesque les* xx. *acres en hochepot, cestassavoir, ensemble; et donques quant le value de chescun acre est conus,* scil. *que chescun acre vault per an [et est assesse, ou entre eux agree, que chescun acre vault per an**] xiid.; *donques la particion serra fait en tiel fourme,* scil. *le baron et la feme averont oustre les* x. *acres donez a eux en frank mariage* v. *acres de severalte de les* xx. *acres, et lautre soer avera le remenaunt,* scil. xv. *acres de les* xx. *acres pur sa purpartie: issint que accomptant les* x. *acres que le baron et la feme ount per le done en frank mariage, et les autres* v. *acres de les* xx. *acres, le baron et la feme ount ataunt en annuel value, que lautre soer ad;* 269 *et issint toutzfoitz sur tiel particion, les terres dones en frank mariage demourgent a les donees et a lour heires soloncques la fourme*

* In *Lettou & M.*, *Roh.*, *Redm.*, *Berth.*, and *Rastell's* Translation, the words within brackets do not appear. *Machl.*, and all the copies by *Tottyl* from 1554, retain them.

any of that which is given in frankmarriage, of this would ensue an inconvenience, and a thing against reason, which the law will not suffer. And the reason wherefore lands given in frankmarriage shall be put in hotchpot, is this: that when a man giveth lands or tenements in frankmarriage with his daughter, or with his other cousin, it is intended by the law, that such gift made by such word "frankmarriage" is an advancement [and for advancement*] of his daughter, or of his cousin; and, namely, when the donor and his heirs shall have no rent or service of them; but fealty until the fourth degree be past, &c. And for such cause the law is, that she shall have nothing of the other lands or tenements descended to the other parcener, &c., unless she will put the lands given in frankmarriage in hotchpot, as is said. And if she will not put the lands given in frankmarriage in hotchpot, then she shall have nothing of the remnant, because it shall be intended by the law that she is sufficiently advanced, to

Doctrine of advancement.

de le done, &c. Qar si lautre parcener avoit riens de ceo que est done en frank mariage, de ceo ensueroit inconvenientise, et chose encontre reason, quel la ley ne voet pas suffrer. Et la cause pur que lez terrez donez en frank mariage serront mys en hochepot, est ceo: que quant home dona terrez ou tenementes en frank marriage ovesque sa file, ou ovesque son autre cosin, il est entendus per la ley que tiel done fait per tiel parole "frank mariage" est un avauncement [et pur avauncement,] de sa file, ou de autre cosin, et nosmement quaunt le donour et ses heires naveront ascun rente ne service de eux, sinon que soit fealté, tanques le quart degree soit passe, &c. Et pur tiel cause la ley est, que ele avera riens de les autres terres ou tenementes descendus a lautre parcener, &c., sinon quele voille metter les terres donez en frank mariage en hochepot, come est dit. Et si ele ne voille metter les terrez donez en frank mariage en hochepot, donques ele navera riens del remenaunt, pur ceo que serra en-*

* The words within brackets are omitted in *Roh.*

which advancement she agreeth and holdeth herself content. 270 And the same law is, in this matter, between the donees in frankmarriage and the other parceners, as to putting in hotchpot, &c. The same law is between the heirs of the donees in frankmarriage and the other parceners, &c., if the donees in frankmarriage die before their ancestor, or before such partition, &c. (*r*). 271 As to putting in hotchpot, &c., of tenements given in frankmarriage, this was by the common law before the statute of *Westm.* 2nd, and hath always since been used and continued, &c.*

Right of hotchpot descends to the issue, according to § 313, where the heirs of parceners represent their mother, and are called parceners.

Frankmarriage since Westm. 2, a fee-tail.

tendus per la ley que ele est sufficiantment avaunce, a quel avauncement el soy agrea et luy tient content. 270 *Et mesme la ley est en cest matere perentre les donees en frank mariage et les autres parceners quaunt a metter en hochepot, &c. Mesme la ley est perentre les heirez les doneez en frank mariage et les autres parceners, &c., si les donees en frank mariage deviont devaunt lour auncestre ou devaunt tiel particion, &c.* 271 *Quant a mettre en hochepot, &c., des tenementes dones en frank mariage ceo fuist per la comen ley devaunt le statute de Westm. second, et tout temps puis ad estre use et contynue, &c.**

---

* The common reading which *Sir Edward Coke* literally translates, which also is in accordance with *Redm.* and *Berth.*, is as follows :—

§ 270. *The same law is between the heirs of the donees in frankmarriage, and the other parceners, &c., if the donees in frankmarriage die before their ancestor, or before such partition, &c., as to put in hotchpot, &c.*

§ 271. *And note, that gifts in frankmarriage were by the common law before the statute of Westm. second, and have been always since used and continued, &c.*

The Translation by *Rastell* adopts another reading, (*viz.*)—*And the same lawe is in this matter betwene the donees in frank mariage, and*

(*r*) By these three *&cs.* in this section is implied, that, if either the donees die before the ancestor, or survive the ancestor and die before such partition, or if the donees and all the parceners die before such partition, upon the putting into *hotchpot*, their issues shall have the same benefit to put the lands into *hotchpot*, for that benefit is inheritable and descends to the issues.—*Co. Lytt.* 178. *a.*

Doctrine of hotchpot does not apply, unless descent be from same ancestor.

272 Also such putting in hotchpot, &c., is where lands or tenements other than those which were given in frankmarriage, descend from the donors in frankmarriage only; for if the lands descended to the daughters by the father of the donor, or by the mother of the donor, or by the brother of the donor or other ancestor, and not by the donor, &c., there it is otherwise; for in such case, she to whom such gift in frankmarriage is made, shall have her part, as if no gift in frankmarriage had been made, because that she was not advanced by them, &c., but by another, &c.

Nor can this doctrine attach, where the lands descended are of equal value.

273 Also, if a man be seised of thirty acres of land, every acre of equal annual value, and have issue two daughters as aforesaid, and giveth fifteen acres hereof to the husband with his daughter in frankmarriage, and dies seised of the other fifteen acres; in this case the other sister shall have the fifteen acres so descended to her alone, and the husband and

272 Item, *tiel metter en hochepot, &c., est lou terres ou tenementes autres que furent dones en frank mariage descendont de lez donours en frank mariage tantsolement ; qar si lez terres descendus a les files per le pere le donour, ou per la mere le donour, ou per le frere le donour, ou autre auncestre, et nemye per le donour, &c., la, autrement est ; qar en tiel cas ele a qui tiel done en frank mariage est fait avera sa partie sicome nul tiel done en frank mariage ust este faite, pur ceo que ele ne fuist avaunce per eux, &c., mes per un autre, &c.*

273 Item, *si home seisi de* XXX. *acres de terre chescun acre de owell annuell value, eiant issue deux files come est avauntdit, et dona* XV. *acres de ceo a le baron et sa file ovesque sa file en frank mariage, et morust seisi de les autres* XV. *acres, en ceo cas lautre soer avera les* XV. *acres issint descendus a luy sole,*

---

the other parceners as to put in hotchpot, &c., the same lawe is betwene the heires of the donees in franke mariage, and the parceners, &c., if the donees in franke mariage die before their auncesters, or before such particion, &c., as to put in hotchpot, &c. And note well, that gift in franke marriage was by the common law before the statute of Westminster the second, and alway after hath so been used and continued, &c.

The text as given above is accordant with *Lettou & M.*, *Machl.*, and *Roh.*

his wife shall not in such case put the fifteen acres given to them in frankmarriage in hotchpot; because the tenements given in frankmarriage are of as great and good yearly value as the other lands descended, &c. For if the lands given in frankmarriage be of equal annual value as the remnant, or of more value, in vain and to none intent shall such tenements given in frankmarriage be put in hotchpot, &c., for this that she cannot have any of the other lands descended, &c.; for if she should have any parcel of the lands descended, then she shall have more in yearly value than her sister, &c., which the law willeth not, &c. And as it is [said] in the cases aforesaid of two daughters, or of two parceners, in the same manner and in like case it is, where there are more sisters, according as the case and matter is, &c.

274 And it is to be understood, that lands or tenements given in frankmarriage shall not be put in hotchpot, but with lands descended in fee-simple; for of lands descended in *Or are entailed.*

et le baron et sa feme ne metteront en tiel cas les xv. *acres a eux dones en frank mariage en hochepot; pur ceo que les tenementes donez en frank mariage sont de auxi graund et bon annuell value sicome les autres terres descendus, &c. Qar si les terrez donez en frank mariage sount de egall annuel value que le remenaunt sount, ou de pluis value, en vayn et a null entent tielx tenementes donez en frank mariage serront mys en hochepot, &c.; pur ceo que ele ne poet riens aver de les autres terres descendus, &c.; qar si ele averoit ascun parcel de les tenementes descendus, donques ele avera pluis de annuell value que sa soer, &c., que la ley ne voet, &c. Et sicome est* [*dit*] *en les cases avauntdits de deux files ou de deux parceners, en mesme le manere et en semblable cas est lou sount plusours soers, solonques ceo que le cas et le matere est, &c.*

274 *Et est assavoir, que terres ou tenementes dones en frank mariage ne serrount mys en hochepot, forsque ovesque terres descendus en fee-simple; qar de terres descendus en*

Hotchpot applies only to frankmarriage, consequently it can only take place upon an advancement.

Another mode of partition, scil. *one of three may hold in severalty; and the other two may hold in parcenry: but if partition be made by writ, each parcener must hold in severalty.*

fee-tail, partition shall be made, as if no such gift in frank-marriage had been made. 275 Also, no lands shall be put in hotchpot with other *lands*, but only lands given in frank-marriage: for if any woman have any other lands or tenements by any other gift in the tail, she shall never put such lands so given in hotchpot, but she shall have her purparty of the remnant descended, &c., *scil.* to so much as the other parcener shall have of the same remnant. 276 Also another partition can be made between parceners, that varieth from the partitions aforesaid: as if there be three parceners, and the younger willeth to have partition, and the other two will not; but will to hold in parcenary that which to them belongeth, without partition: in this case, if one part be allotted in severalty to the younger sister, according to that which she ought to have, then the others may hold the remnant in parcenary, and occupy in common without partition if they will; and such partition is good enough. And if afterwards the elder or middle parcener will make partition between them,

fee-taille, particion serra fait, sicome nul tiel done en frank mariage ust este fait. 275 Item, *nulles terres serrount mys en hochepot ovesque autres, sinon terres que sount dones en frank mariage tantsolement: qar si ascun feme ad ascuns autres terres ou tenementes per ascun autre done en taille, ele ne unques mettera tiell terre issint done en hochepot, mes ele avera sa purpartie de le remenaunt descendus, &c., cestassavoir,* scil. *a tant que lautre parcener avera de mesme le remenaunt.* 276 Item, *un autre particion poet estre fait entre parceners, que variast de les particions avauntdites: sicome y sont trois parceners, et la puisne voet aver particion, et les autres deux ne volont, mes voillent tener en parcenerie ceo que a eux affiert sans particion, en ceo cas si une partie soit allotte en severalte al puisne soer solonques ceo que ele doit aver, donques les autres poient tener le remenaunt en parcenerie, et occupier en comen sans particion si eles voillent; et tiel particion est assetes bon. Et si apres leisne et le mulnes parcener voille faire particion entre eux, de ceo que ils teignount,*

of that which they hold, they may well do this when they please. But where partition shall be made by force of a writ *de participacione faciendâ*, there it is otherwise; for there it behoveth that every parcener have her part in severalty, &c.

More shall be said of parceners in the chapter of Joint-tenants, and also in the chapter of Tenants in common.

eles poient ceo bien faire quant a eux pleast. Mes lou particion serra fait per force de brief de participacione faciendâ, *la, autrement est; qar, la, covient que chescun parcener avera sa partie en severalté, &c.*

Pluis serra dit des parceners en le chapitre de jointenauntes, et auxi en le chapitre de tenauntes en comen.

CHAPTER III.

OF JOINT-TENANTS.

Joint-tenancy defined.

277 JOINT-TENANTS are, as if a man *be* seised of certain lands or tenements, &c., and thereof enfeoffeth two, or three, or four, or more, to have and to hold to them [and to their heirs, or letteth to them*] for term of their lives, or for term of an-

277 *Jointenauntes sount, sicome home seisi de certeynes terres ou tenementes, &c., et ent enfeoffe deux, ou trois, ou quatre, ou plusours, a aver et tener a eux [et a lour heires, ou lessa a eux*], pur terme de lour vies, ou pur terme de autre vie, per*

---

* *Sir Edward Coke* has the following note on this section: "This agreeth not with the original, for it should be,"—*Joynt' sont sicome home seisi de certaine terres ou tenements, &c., et* ent *enfeoffe deux, ou trois, ou quater, ou plusors, a aver et tener a eux* et a lour heires, ou lessa a eux *pur terme de lour vies, ou pur terme dauter vie; per force de quel feoffement, ou lease, &c.*

Joint-tenants are, as if a man be seised of certain lands or tenements, &c., and thereof *infeoffeth two, three, four, or more, to have and to hold to them* and to their heirs, or leaseth to them *for the term of their lives, or for term of another's life, by force of which feoffment or lease, &c.*

"The error may easily be perceived by that which is in print, *viz. by force of which feoffment or lease, &c.*" "*Ergo*, there must be feoffment and lease spoken of before."—*Co. Lytt.* 180. *a.* But notwithstanding this censure of the text, it agrees with the print of the three earliest editions; for neither the editions by *Lettou & M.*, *Machl.*, or the *Roh.* edition, have any of the words added by *Sir Edward Coke* except *thereof* before *enfeoff*. Mr. Hargrave in his note on this passage observes, "I think that his (*Sir Edward Coke's*) addition seems requisite to the sense intended to be conveyed by *Lyttleton*, as well for the reason assigned by *Sir Edward Coke*, as because otherwise Lyttleton's descrip-

other's life; by force of which feoffment or lease they are seised, such are joint-tenants.

278 Also, if two or three, &c., disseise another of any lands or tenements to their own use, then the disseisors are joint-tenants. But if they disseise another to the use of one of them, then they are not joint-tenants; but he to whose use the disseisin is made, is sole tenant, and the others have nothing in the tenancy, but are called coadjutors to the disseisin, &c.

Joint disseisors.

Coadjutors to disseisin.

force de quel feoffement ou lees ils sount seisis, tielx sount jointenauntes.

278 Item, *si deux ou trois, &c., disseisont un autre dascuns terres ou tenementes a lour use demesne; donques les disseisours sount jointenauntes. Mes sils disseisont un autre al use dun de eux, donques ils ne sount jointenauntes, mes celuy a que use le disseisin est fait est sole tenaunt, et les autres nont riens en le tenauncie, mes sont appelles coadjutours a le disseisin, &c.*

---

tion of joint-tenancy might be construed to exclude an estate in fee, which certainly could not be his intention. The addition of an estate in fee to Lyttleton's description of joint-tenancy, was first introduced by *Rastell*, in his edition of 1534."

The edition of 1534, referred to by Mr. *Hargrave*, is one of the copies of *Rastell's* Translation, which the Editor conceives to be exceedingly correct; it also seems, that those copies of *Redm.*, which were in *Mr. Hargrave's* possession, were not seen by him when he wrote this note; for the words which import a fee, appear in those copies of *Redm.*, as well as in *Berth.*, *Middl.*, *Powel*, *Sm.*, and *Tottyl* 1554, which four last seem to be reprints of *Berth.* The reading as given by *Berth.* and *Redm.* is as follows—*tenementz, &c., ent enfeoffe deux, trois, quatre, ou plusours a aver et tener a eux en fee, ou pur terme de lour viez, ou a terme dautre vie: par force de quel feffement ou lees, &c. Rastell's* Translation renders this passage thus:—*Joyntenants bee as a man seysed of certayne landes or tenements, &c., and thereof hath enfeoffed two, or three, or foure, or more, to have and to hold to them and to their heires, or to have and to holde to them for terme of their lives or for terme of an other's life, by force of which feoffement they be seysed, such be jointenaunts.*

Disseisin defined. See ante, p. 271, n.

279 And note, that disseisin is properly where a man entereth into any lands or tenements where his entry is not lawful, and putteth out him that hath the freehold, &c.

Survivorship *and when it holds place, distinguished from parceners who take by descent.*

280 And it is to be understood, that the nature of joint-tenancy is, that he that surviveth shall have solely the entire tenancy, according to such estate as he hath, if the jointure be continued, &c. As if three joint-tenants be in fee-simple, and the one hath issue and dieth; yet they that survive shall have the entire tenements, and the issue shall have nothing. And if the second joint-tenant have issue and die, yet the third that surviveth shall have the tenements entire, and those he shall have to him and to his heirs for ever: but otherwise it is of parceners; for if three parceners be, and before any partition made, the one hath issue and dieth, that which to her belongeth shall descend to her issue; and if such parcener die without issue, that which belongeth to her shall descend to her heirs, so as they shall have this by descent, and not by survivor, as joint-tenants shall have, &c. 281 And as the

Survivorship extends to

279 *Et nota, que disseisin est proprement lou un home entra en ascuns terres ou tenementes lou son entre nest pas congeable, et ousta celuy qui ad franktenement, &c.*

280 *Et est assavoir que la nature de jointenauncie est que celuy qui survesquist avera solement lentiere tenauncie solonques tiel estate quil ad, si le jointure soit continue, &c. Sicome si trois jointenauntes sount en fee-simple, et lun ad issue et devie, unqore ceux qui survesquont averont les tenementes entier, et lissue navera riens. Et si le second jointenaunt ad issue et devie, unqore le tierce que survesquist avera les tenementes entier, et eux avera a luy et a ses heires a toutes jours: mes autrement est de parceners; qar si trois parceners sont, et devaunt ascun particion fait, lun ad issue et devie, ceo que a luy affiert descendera a son issue: et si tiel parcener mourust sauns issue, donques ceo que a luy affiert descendera a ses heires, issint que ils averont ceo per discent, et nemy per survivour, come jointenauntes averont, &c.* 281 *Et come le survivour tient lieu entre jointenauntes, en*

survivor holds place between joint-tenants, in the same manner it holdeth place between them that have joint estate or possession with another of chattel real or personal. As if lease of lands or tenements be made to many for term of years, he that survives of the lessees shall have the tenements to him entire, during the term, by force of the same lease. And if a horse or other chattel personal be given to many, he that surviveth shall have the horse solely (*a*).
282 In the same manner, it is of debts and duties, &c. (*b*); for if an obligation be made to many for one debt, he that surviveth shall have all the debt or duty. And so it is of other covenants or contracts, [&c.*]

chattels real and (at law) to chattels personal.

mesme le manere il tient lieu entre eux queux ont joint estate ou possession ovesque autre de chatel reall ou personell. Sicome si lees de terres ou tenementes soit fait a plusours pur terme des ans, celuy qui survesquist de les lessees avera les tenementes a luy entier, durant le terme, per force de mesme le lees. Et si un chival ou un autre chatel personell soit done a plusours, celuy qui survesquist avera le chival solement.
282 *En mesme le manere est de dettes et duytës, &c., qar si un obligacion soit fait a plusours pur une dette, celuy qui survesquist avera tout la dette ou duytë. Et issint est dautres covenantes ou contractes,* [*&c.**]

---

* This &c. not in *Lettou & M.*, *Machl.*, or *Roh.*

(*a*) *Chattel*, or *catel*, whereof cometh the word used in law, *catalla*, and is as *Lyttleton* teacheth, twofold, *viz.* real and personal, and putteth examples of both.

(*b*) Here, by force of this &c. an exception is to be made of two joint-merchants; for the wares, merchandizes, debts, or duties that they have as joint-merchants or parceners, shall not survive, but shall go to the executors of him that deceaseth; and this is *per legem mercatoriam*, which (as hath been said) is part of the laws of this realm for the advancement and continuance of commerce and trade, which is *pro bono publico;* for the rule is, that *jus accrescendi inter mercatores beneficio commercii locum non habet.*

And to the latter &c. in this section, the like exception must be made.—*Co. Lytt.* 182. *a.*

Lands given to two, and to the heirs of their two bodies, they are joint-tenants of the freehold, and have several inheritances in tail, and their issue hold as tenants in common.

283 Also, there some joint-tenants may be who can have joint estate, and be joint-tenants for term of their lives, and yet they have several inheritances. As if lands be given to two men, and to the heirs of their two bodies begotten; in this case, the donees have joint estates for term of their two lives, and yet they have several inheritances; for if the one of the donees hath issue and die, the other that surviveth [shall have all by the survivor for term of his life, and if he that surviveth*] hath also issue and die, then the issue of the one shall have the half, and the issue of the other shall have the other half of the land, and they shall hold the land between them in common; and they are not joint-tenants, but are tenants in common. And the reason why such donees in such case have joint estate for term of their lives, is, for that at the beginning the lands were given to them two; which words, without more saying, make a joint estate to them for term of

Reason why such donees have a joint estate for life is, because the lands were given to them two.

283 Item, *ascun jointenauntes poient estre qui poient aver joint estate, et estre jointenauntes pur terme de lours vies, et unqore ils ount severall enheritaunces. Sicome terres soyent dones a deux homes et a lez heires de lour deux corps engendres, en ceo cas les donees ont joint estates pur terme de lours deux vies, et unqore ils ont severals enheritaunces, qar si lun des donees ad issue, et devy, lautre qui survesquist [avera tout per le survivour pur terme de sa vie, et si celuy qui survesquist*] auxi ad issue, et devy, donques lissue de lun avera la moyte, et issue de lautre avera lautre moyte de la terre, et eux tiendront la terre entre eux en comen, et ne sount pas jointenauntes, mes sount tenauntes en comen. Et la cause pur qui tielx donees en tiel cas ont joint estate pur terme de lour vies est, pur ceo que al commencement les terres furent dones a eux deux; les queux parolx sauns pluis dire font joint estate a eux pur terme de*

* The words within brackets are omitted in *Lettou & M.*, *Machl.*, and *Roh.*

their lives. For if a man will let land to another by deed or without deed, not making mention what estate he shall have, and of this make livery of seisin; in this case, the lessee shall have estate for term of his life; and so inasmuch as the lands were given to them, they have a joint estate for term of their lives: and the reason why they shall have several inheritances is this, insomuch as they cannot by any possibility have an heir between them engendered, as a man and woman may have, &c., then the law willeth that their estate and inheritance be such as is reasonable, according to the form and effect of the words of the gift; and that is to the heirs which the one shall beget of his body, by any of his wives; [and to the heirs which the other shall beget of his body, by any of his wives*], &c.: so it behoveth by necessity of reason, that they shall have several inheritances. And in such case, if [one donee or †] the issue of one of the donees, after the

Reason why such donees shall have several inheritances is, because their estates must consist with reason, according to the form and effect of the gift.

Issue dying, reverter to donor of the moiety—[same rule, § 301.]

lour vies. Qar si home voet lesser terre a un autre per fait ou sauns fait, nient feasaunt mencion quel estate il averoit, et de ceo fait lyvere de seisin, en ceo cas le lessee avera estate pur terme de sa vie; et issint entaunt que les terres furent dones a eux, ils ont joint estate pur terme de lour vies; et la cause pur que ils averont severalx enheritaunces est ceo, entant que ils ne poient aver per nul possibilite un heire entre eux engendre, sicome home et feme poient aver, &c., donques la ley voet que lour estate et lour enheritaunce soit tiel come reason voet, solonques la fourme et effecte dell paroll del done, et ceo est a les heires que lun engendra de son corps per ascun de ses femes, [et a les heires que lautre engendra de son corps per ascun de ses femes], &c.: issint il covient per necessite de reason que ils averont severalx enheritaunces. Et en tiel cas si [lun donee ou†] lissue dun des donees apres la mort des*

---

* The words within brackets are omitted in *Lettou & M., Machl.*, and *Roh.*

† The words within brackets do not appear in any printed copy of

death of the donees, die, so that he hath no issue alive of his body begotten, then the donor or his heirs may enter into the half as in his reversion &c.; although the other of the donees hath issue alive, &c. And the reason is, forasmuch as the inheritances be several, &c., the reversion thereof in law is severed, &c., and the survivor of the issue of the other shall hold no place to have the entirety. 284 And so as it is said of males, in the same manner it is where land is given to two females, and to the heirs of their two bodies begotten.

Reason is, that as the inheritances are several, so is the reversion.

Gift to two women, same as gift to two men.

285 Also, if lands be given to two*, and to the heirs of one of them, this is a good jointure, and the one hath a free-

Gift to two and heirs of one, they are joint-tenants for life, and the fee-simple or fee-tail is in one of them.

donees devie, issint quil nad ascune issue en vie de son corps engendre, donques le donour ou son heire poet entrer en la moyte come en son revercion, &c., coment que lautre des donees ad issue en vie, &c. Et la cause est, que entaunt que les enheritaunces sont severall, &c., la revercion de ceo en ley est severe, &c., et le survivour del issue del autre ne tiendra pas lieu daver lentierte. 284 *Et sicome est dit de males, en mesme le manere est lou terre est done a deux femelx, et a les heires de lour deux corps engendres.*

285 Item, *si terres soyent dones a deux et a les heires de lun de eux, ceo est bone jointure, et lun ad franktenement, et*

Lyttleton, although necessary for the sense. *Sir Edward Coke* remarks on the passage which requires the suppletion of these words—" This is mistaken in the imprinting, and varieth from the *original*, which is, *si lun donee ou lissue* —— &c. For it is evident, that if the one donee himself dieth without issue, the inheritance doth revert for a moiety, and after the decease of the other donee, the donor may enter into that moiety, and whether the issue of the one donee dieth without issue at any time, either in the life of the other donee or after his decease, it is not material; for whensoever no issue is remaining of the one donee, so as the estate tail is spent, the donor may, after the decease of the surviving donee, enter into that moiety."—*Co. Lytt.* 183. *b.* But *Sir Edward Coke's* correction, *Mr. Hargrave* observes, is not in conformity with the earliest printed copies. The Editor has before suggested that this *original* might have been a MS. copy.

* In *Rastell's* Transl. here occurs the word *females*.

hold, and the other a fee-simple (*c*). And if she that hath the fee die, she that has the freehold shall have the entirety by survivor for term of her life. In the same manner it is, where tenements be given to two, and the heirs of the body of one of them engendered, the one hath a freehold and the other a fee-tail, &c. (*d*).

286 Also, if two joint-tenants are seised of lands in fee-simple, and the one grants a rent-charge by his deed to another out of that which to him belongeth: in this case, during* the life of the grantor, the rent-charge is effectual; but after his decease the grant of the rent-charge is void, so as to charge the land, for he that hath the land by the survivor, shall hold all the land discharged. And the cause is, for that he who surviveth, claimeth and hath the land by the survivor, &c., and

Rent-charge granted by one of two joint-tenants in fee, is void as to the survivor, if grantor die —see § 289.

lautre ad fee-simple : et si celuy qui ad le fee devie, celuy que ad le franktenement avera lentierte per le survivour pur terme de sa vie. En mesme le manere est, lou tenementes sount dones a deux et les heires du corps dun de eux engendres, lun ad franktenement, et lautre ad fee-taille, &c.

286 Item, *si deux jointenauntes sount seisis de terres en fee-simple, et lun graunt un rente-charge per son fait a un autre hors de ceo que a luy affiert, en ceo cas duraunt* la vie le grantour le rente-charge est effectuell. Mes apres son decesse le grant de le rente-charge est voide, quant a charger la terre, qar celuy qui ad la terre per le survivour tiendra tout la terre discharge. Et la cause est, pur ceo que celuy qui survesquist clayma et ad la terre per le survivour, &c., et nemy [celuy qui*

---

* This word in *Tottyl* 1585-8 is corrupted to *devaunt, before.*

(*c*) The word "fee-simple" has respect to the inheritance, "freehold" imports a lesser estate; for *fee* in Lyttleton is applied to an inheritable estate. *Frank tenement*, freehold, means an estate in possession or freehold *tantum*.

(*d*) By this section, and the &c. in the end of it, they are joint-tenants for life, and the fee-simple or estate-tail is in one of them, and because it is by one and the same conveyance, they are joint-tenants, and the fee-simple is not executed to all purposes, as hath been said before.—*Co. Lytt.* 184. *a.*

Secus of parceners. *Reason.*

[he that hath the land can] not [claim anything] by descent from his companion, &c*. But otherwise it is of parceners; for if there be two parceners of tenements in fee-simple, and before any partition made, the one chargeth that which to her belongeth, by her deed, with a rent-charge, &c., [and dieth without issue; by which, that which to her belongeth descends to the other parcener: in this case, the other parcener shall hold the land charged, &c.†]; because she cometh to this moiety by descent, as heir, &c.

Will of joint-tenant void; because a devise only takes effect from decease of testa-

287 Also if there be two joint-tenants of land in fee-simple within one borough, where the tenements within the same borough are devisable by testament, and if the one of the said two joint-tenants deviseth that which to him belongeth by his testament &c., and dieth, this devise is void. And the cause is, for that no devise can take effect, but after the

ad la terre, poet de ceo claymer rien] per discent de son compagnion, &c. Mes autrement est de parceners, car si soient deux parceners en fee-simple, et devaunt ascun particion fait, lun chargea ceo que a luy affiert, per son fait, dun rente-charge, &c., [et mourust sauns issue, per ceo que a luy affiert discendist a lautre parcener, en ceo cas lautre parcener tiendra la terre charge, &c.†], pur ceo que il vient a celle moyte per discent come heire, &c.*

287 Item, *si sount deux jointenauntes des terres en fee-simple deins un burgh, lou les tenementes deins mesme le burgh sont devisables per testament, et si lun de les dits deux jointenauntes devisa ceo que a luy affiert per testament, &c., et mourust, ceo devise est voide. Et la cause est pur ceo que nul devise poet prendre effecte, mes apres la mort le devisour, pur*

---

* This passage, although accordant with *Lettou & M.*, *Machl.*, and *Roh.*, is evidentlv corrupted, and should be read with the omission of the words within brackets; in such form it will be conformable with *Rastell's* Transl., *Redm.*, *Berth.*, *Middl.*, *Sm.*, *Powel*, and *Tottyl* 1554, and also agree with the sense and context.

† The words within brackets are omitted in *Roh.*

death of the devisor; and for this, that, by his death, all the land forthwith cometh by the law to his companion that surviveth by the survivor, who doth not claim, nor hath anything in the land by the devisor, but in his own right by the survivor, according to the course of the common law, &c., and for this cause such devise is void. But otherwise it is of parceners seised of tenements devisable in like case of devise, &c. *Causa qua supra.*

tor (§ 168, 174); *but see* § 289, *where things executory shall be executed after decease of joint-tenant.*

288 Also, it is commonly said, that every joint-tenant is seised of the land which he holdeth jointly, &c., *per my et per tout,* (*i. e.* through and by all), and this is as much as to say, he is seised by every parcel and by all, &c.; and this is true, for in each parcel and part, and by all the lands and tenements, he is jointly seised with his companion, &c.

Seisin per my et per tout; *its intent.*

289 Also, if two joint-tenants be seised of certain lands in fee-simple, and the one letteth that to him belongeth to a stranger, for term of forty years, and dieth within the term: in this case, after his decease, the lessee may enter and occupy the moiety unto him letten during the term, &c.; although the

Lease by joint-tenant, *which charges the survivorship, distinguished from a rent-charge which does not.*

ceo que per sa mort tout la terre maintenannt devient per la ley a son compagnion qui survesquist per le survivour, le quell ne clayme, ne ad riens en la terre permye le devisor, mes en son droit demesne per le survivour, solonques le cours de la comen ley, &c., et pur tiel cause tiel devise est voide. Mes autrement est de parceners seisis des tenementes devisables en tiel cas de devise, &c. Causa qua supra.

288 Item, *il est comenement dit, que chescun jointenaunt est seisi de la terre quil tient jointement, &c., per mye et per tout, et ceo est a tant adire quil est seisi per chescun parcell et per tout, &c., et ceo est voire, car en chescun parcell et part, et per toutes les terres et tenementes il est jointement seisi ovesque son compagnion, &c.*

289 Item, *si deux jointenauntes sount seisis de certeyn terres en fee-simple, et lun lessa ceo que a luy affiert a un estraunger pur terme de* xl. *ans, et devie deins le terme, en ceo cas apres son decesse le lessé poet entrer et occupier la moyte a luy lesse duraunt le terme, &c., coment que le lessé navoit*

lessee had never the possession thereof in the life of their lessor, by force of the lease, &c. And the diversity between the case of a grant of a rent-charge [aforesaid, and this case, is this, for in the grant of a rent-charge by*] a joint-tenant, &c., the tenements abide always as they were before, without this that any hath any right to have any parcel of the tenements but they themselves; and the tenements abide in such plight as they were before the charge, &c. But where lease is made by a joint-tenant to another for term of years, &c., forthwith by force of the lease, the lessee hath right in the same land, that is to say, of all that which to the lessor belongeth, and to have by force of the same lease, during his term. And this is the diversity, &c.

See § 286.

Interesse termini, § 66, 459.

Partition, at law, not compulsory. (*As to what shall amount to a partition, see* § 302.)

290 Also, joint-tenants, if they will, may make partition between them, and the partition shall be good enough; but they shall not be compelled to do this by the law (*e*); but if

unques possession de ceo en la vie de lour lessour, per force de le lees, &c. Et le diversite perentre le cas de graunt de le rente-charge [avauntdit, et ceo cas est ceo, qar en graunt de rente-charge per] jointenaunt, &c., les tenementes demorgent toutfoitz come ils furent adevaunt, sauns ceo que ascun ad ascun droit daver ascun parcel de les tenementes forsque eux mesmes, et les tenementes sount en tiel plite, come ils furent devaunt le charge, &c. Mes lou lees est fait per un jointenaunt a un autre pur terme des ans, &c., mayntenaunt per force de lees le lessé ad droit en mesme la terre, cestassavoir de tout ceo que a le lessour affiert, et daver ceo per force de mesme le lees duraunt sa terme. Et ceo est la diversite, &c.*

290 Item, *jointenauntes, sils voillent, poient faire particion, entre eux, et la particion serra assetez bon, mes de ceo faire ils ne serront compelles per la ley. Mes sils voillent faire par-*

* The words within brackets do not appear in *Machl.* or *Roh.*; they are supplied by *Pyns.* 1516, and subsequent editions.

(*e*) Since *Lyttleton* wrote, joint-tenants and tenants in common ge-

they will to make partition of their own proper will and agreement, the partition shall stand in its strength.

291 Also, if a joint estate be made of land to husband and wife, and to a third person: in this case, the husband and wife have not in law in their right but the half; [and the third person shall have as much as the husband and wife, *scil.* the other half*]. And the cause is, for that the husband and wife are but one person in law, and are in like case as if an estate be made to two joint-tenants, where each one hath by force of the jointure the one moiety in law, and the other the other moiety. In the same manner it is, where estate is made to the husband and to his wife, and to two other men; in such case, the husband and wife have but the third part, and the other two men the other two parts, &c. *Causa qua supra.*

Husband and wife being but one person in law (§ 168, 665), *take but one moiety, and their companion the other moiety.*

ticion de lour propre volunte et agrement, la particion estoiera en sa force.

291 Item, *si un joint estate soit fait de terre a le baron et a sa feme et a un tierce persone, en ceo cas le baron et sa feme nount en ley en lour droit forsque la moyte, &c.,* [*et le tierce persone avera taunt come le baron et sa feme ont,* scil. *lautre moyte**]. *Et la cause est, pur ceo que le baron et sa feme ne sount forsque un persone en ley, et sount en semblable cas, sicome estate soit fait a deux jointenauntes, lou lun ad per force de jointure lun moyte en ley, et lautre lautre moyte. En mesme le manere est lou estate est fait a le baron et a sa feme, et as autres deux homes, en tiel cas le baron et sa feme nount forsque la tierce partie, et les autres deux homes les autres deux parties, &c.* Causa qua supra.

---

* The words within brackets first appear in *Pyns.* 1516.

---

nerally, are compellable to make partition by writ framed upon the statutes of 31 & 32 Hen. 8, as before hath been said. And albeit they be now compellable to make partition, yet seeing they are compellable by writ, they must pursue the statutes, and cannot make partition by parol, for that remains at the common law.—*Co. Lytt.* 187.*a.*

More shall be said of the matter touching joint-tenancy in the chapter of Tenants in common (*f*), [tenant by elegit, and tenant by statute-merchant*].

Pluis serra dit de matere touchant jointenauncie en les chapitres de Tenauntes en comen, [tenaunt per elegit, et tenaunt per le statute-marchant].*

---

* Omitted in the Paper MS., which seems to be the latest and most perfect.

(*f*) To holde by elegit is, where a man hath recovered debt or damages by writ against another, or by confession (*conisauns*), or in any other manner, he shall have within the yeare against him a writ judicial called *elegit*, to have execution of the halfe of all his landes and chattels, *exceptis bobus et averius carucæ*, till the debt or damages be utterly levied or paied to him, and during this term he is tenaunt by elegit.

And note well, if he be put out within the terme, he shall have assise of novel disseisin, and afterwards a redisseisin, if neede be, and this is given by the statute of Westm. 2, cap. 18; and also by the equity of the same statute, he that hath his estate, if he bee put out, shall have assise and a redisseisin if neede be; and also if he make his executors and die, and his executors enter and afterwards be put out, they shall have by the equity of the same statute, such action as hee himselfe had as is before saide; but if he be put out, and afterwards make his executors and die, his executors may enter, and if they be estopped of their entry, they shall have a writ of trespass upon their matter and case.

And note well, that if he commit waste in all the land or in parcel, that man to whom the right belongs, shall have against him immediately a writ judicial out of the first recorde, called a *venire facias ad computandum*, by which it shall be enquired, whether he have levyed all the money or parcell, and if hee have not levyed the money, then it shall be enquired to how much the waste amounteth: and if the waste amount but to [the value of†] parcel [of the said monies which are to be levied†], then so much of the money as the waste amounteth to, shall be abridged of the foresaide monies which were to be levyed [†against him who hath the right. And then he shall be in all utterly discharged, and nothing more shall be done, and the other shall hold the lands wasted, and the other lands over, until he hath levied the other

† The words and passages within brackets appear in *Pyns.* and *Berth.* 1531.

CONCLUDING REMARKS.

THE inherent unities of a joint-tenancy are those of interest, title, and possession, to which Sir William Blackstone

---

parcel of the monies aforesaid]. But if he have committed more waste than the aforesaid summe of mony which was to be levied amounteth to, [by twenty pounds beyond], the other shall be discharged immediately of all the said monies, and shall recover the lande, and for the superfluity of the wast made above that which amounteth to the saide summe, he shall recover his single dammages, and the same lawe is of hys executours, and also of him that hath his estate. And note well, that if he alien in fee for terme of lyfe or in taile, all or parcel of the land which he holdeth by elegit, if the alienation be made within the terme or afterwards, he who hath right shall have against him an assize of novell disseisin. And it behoveth that they both be put in the assize, the alienour as well as the alienee; and notwithstandinge that the alienour die presently, yet he who hath right shall have an assize against the alienee alone, as if the alienor had been his simple tenant for terme of yeres, and this is by the equity of the statute of W. 2, c. 25, because he hath not but a chattel in effect, but the same law is of his executours, and of him that hath his estate as is aforesaid. And note well, that in elegit, [that if the party plaintiff demand execution of the lands, that the debtor had the day of the recognisance made, and] the sheriff return that he had nothinge the daye of the recognisance made, but that he purchased lands after the time, then the party plaintiff shall have a newe write to have execution thereof, the same lawe is of a statute-marchant*. [And note well, that if a man sue execution for debt due on a recognizance by a *fieri facias*, and the sheriff return that the recognisor hath nothing of lands or of chattels, he shall have no action of lands or chattels, unless by elegit, *ut dicitur*, to which writ if the sheriff return that he hath nothing of land or chattels the day, &c., the recognisee is without recovery, notwithstanding that after the elegit the recognisor obtain (*happa*) chattels. And note wel, that†] after a

* *Pyns.* and *Berth.* 1531, read this concluding passage thus:—shall have a writ which is called *fieri facias*. But the law of a statute-marchant is otherwise, *ut patet*, *Hillar.* 16.[*E.* 3].

† This sentence in *Pyns.* and *Berth.* 1531, commences, *For after*, and is a continuance of the preceding sentence within brackets, which is not in *Rastell's* copy.

adds, time (*h*), which are apparent from the definition and examples given by Lyttleton. The chief peculiarity of this

---

fieri facias a man may have the elegit, but not *e contra*, forsomuch that the elegit is of higher nature than the *fieri facias*. And note well, that if a man recover by a writ of debt, and sueth a *fieri facias*, and the sherife return that the partye hath nothing whereof he may make gree with the party, then the plaintife shall have a *capias sicut alias* and a *pluries*; and if the sherife return to the *capias mitto vobis corpus*, and he have nothing whereof he may make gree to the partye, he shal be sent to the prison of the Fleete, and there shall abide till he have made agreement with the partye, and if the sherife returne *non est inventus*, then there shall issue an *exigent* against him, *ut dicitur*. And note well, that in a writ of debt brought against a person of Holy Church who hath no lay fee, and the sherife returneth that he hath nought by which he may be summoned, then shall the plaintife sue a writ to the bishoppe, that he make his clerk to come, and the bishop shall make him to come by sequestration of the Church. And note well, that if a man bring a writ of debt and recover, and make his executors and dieth, they shall have execution, notwithstanding that it be within the yeare, by a *fieri facias*.

[And note well, that if a man bring writ of account, and afterwards makes his executors and dieth, they shall have a new action of accompt, as it was adjudged *Anno* xx. *Edwardi tertii*, in a *scire facias*, by which he ought not to accompt, *ut dicitur*.

And in case that any one bring writ of trespass of goods had and received, and make his executors and die, they shall have action, notwithstanding that it be within the year, by a *scire facias*, *ut dicitur**].—*Olde Tenures*, § 22.

To holde by statute-merchant is where a man acknowledgeth to paye certaine money to another at a certaine daye before the maior, bailife, or other warden of any towne, that hath power to make execution

* The words and passages within brackets are not in *Rastell's* copy.

(*h*) That is, that the estate of each joint-tenant should be vested at the same period.—B. C. ii. 180. But this doctrine seems confined to limitations at common law; and not to extend to estates raised by way of use or by devise.—*Thomas's Syst. Arrangement of Co. Lytt.* i. 732, *note* (D.)

estate is the right of survivorship, *i. e.* the right of the survivor of the joint-tenants to the fee or entire interest

---

of the same statute, and if the obligee paye not the debt at the day assigned, and nothinge of his goods, landes, or tenementes can be found within the warde of the maior or warden before saide, but in other places wythout; then the recognizee shall sue the recognizaunce and the obligation with a certification to the Chauncery under the king's seale, and he shal have out of the Chauncery, a *capias* to the sherife of the countie where he is, to take him and to put him in prison, if hee bee not a clarke, tyll he have made greement of the debt. And one quarter of the yeare after that he shall be taken, he shall have his land delivered to himselfe to make gree to the partye of the debte, and he may sel it while he is in prison, and his sale shall be good and sure. And if he do not gree within a quarter of a yere or if it bee returned that he bee not founde, then the recognisee can have a writ of the Chauncery which is called *extendi facias*, directed to the sherife where hee hath landes, to extend his lands and goods, and to deliver the goods, and to seise him in his lands, to hold them to him and to his heires and his assignes till that the debte be levyed or payed ; and for that time he is tenaunt by statute merchant.

[And note well, that if *præcipe quod reddat* be brought against him, and he maketh default after default, and he in the reversion prays to be received, he shall not be received, but seisin of the land shall be awarded immediately, because that the tenant has such a feeble estate that a recovery against him shall be adjudged a disseisin of him in the reversion: upon which he can have a good assise. And the same law is of tenant by elegit, *ut patet.—Hillar.* xvi. *E.* 3.

And note well, if execution upon a statute merchant be awarded to a man by force of an *auditá querelá* : and before that he has fully execution, he appoints his executors and dies, his executors shall not have execution by *scire facias*, but writ on their case out of the Chancery to the justices to hold their plea on their suggestion : and afterwards they shall have the same action as their testator, *ut dicitur**]—*Olde Tenures*, § 23.

And note well, that in a statute merchant the recognisee shall have execution of all the lands which the recognisour had the day of the recognisance made, and any time after by force of the same statute.

And note well, that when any waste or destruction is made by the recognisee, or by him that hath his estate, the reconisour or hys

* The words and sentences within brackets are not in *Rastell's* copy.

on the decease of his companion (*i*). After noticing the joint-tenancy of husband and wife, which, from the unity of

executours shall have the same law as is before saide of the tenant by elegit. And this is by the statute merchant lately made at Westminster.

And note well, if the tenaunt by statute merchant holdeth over his terme, he that hath right may sue against him a *venire facias ad computandum*, or else enter directly [as upon tenant by elegit*].

* But otherwise the law is, with regard to tenant *per elegit, ut dicitur.—Pyns.* and *Berth.* 1531.

(*i*) This is the natural and regular consequence of the union and entirety of their interest. The interest of two joint-tenants is not only equal or similar, but also is one and the same. One has not originally a distinct moiety from the other; but, if by any subsequent act (as by alienation or forfeiture of either) the interest becomes separate and distinct, the joint-tenancy instantly ceases. But, while it continues, each of two joint-tenants has a concurrent interest in the whole; and, therefore, on the death of his companion, the sole interest in the whole remains to the survivor. For the interest, which the survivor originally had, is clearly not divested by the death of his companion; and no other person can now claim to have a *joint* estate with him, for no one can now have an interest in the whole, accruing by the same title, and taking effect at the same time with his own; neither can any one claim a *separate* interest in any part of the tenements; for that would be to deprive the survivor of the right which he has in all, and every part. As therefore the survivor's original interest in the whole still remains; and as no one can now be admitted, either jointly or severally, to any share with him therein; it follows, that his own interest must now be entire and several, and that he shall alone be entitled to the whole estate (whatever it be) that was created by the original grant.

This right of survivorship is called by our ancient authors the *jus accrescendi*, because the right, upon the death of one joint-tenant, accumulates and increases to the survivors; or, as they themselves express it, "*pars illa communis accrescit superstitibus, de persona in personam, usque ad ultimam superstitem.*" And this *jus accrescendi* ought to be mutual; which I apprehend to be one reason why neither the king, nor any corporation, can be a joint-tenant with a private person. For here is no

their persons by marriage, is styled a *tenancy by entireties*, the subject is continued by the cases put concerning joint estates with several inheritances; and this chapter concludes by noticing in what instance, and upon what ground, a joint-tenant is able to charge the survivorship, the mode of *severing the jointure* being a subject necessarily referred to the next Chapter, as a tenancy in common arises upon every severance of a joint-tenancy.

---

mutuality: the private person has not even the remotest chance of being seised of the entirety, by benefit of survivorship; for the king and a corporation can never die.—B. C. ii. 184.

CHAPTER IV.

TENANTS IN COMMON.

LYTTLETON having spoken of parceners, which are only by descent, and of joint-tenants, which are only by purchase and by joint title, speaketh now of tenants in common, which may be by three means, *viz.* by purchase, by descent, or by prescription (§ 310), as hereafter in this chapter shall appear.—*Co. Lytt.* 188. *b.*

The criteria of this estate, are: 1st. Severalty of title; 2nd. An occupation undividedly and in common. Severalty of title is the chief distinction, as is evident from the case put at § 662. The only unity is that of possession: for one tenant in common may hold his part in fee-simple, the other in tail or for life; so that there is no unity of interest. One may hold by descent, the other by purchase; or the one by purchase from one person, and the other by purchase from another; so that there is no unity of title. One's estate may have been vested fifty years, the other's but yesterday; so there is no unity of time.—B.C. ii. 191.

Definition of a tenancy in common.

292 TENANTS in common are they that have lands or tenements in fee-simple, fee-tail, or for term of life, &c., the which

292 *Tenauntes en comen sount ceux, qui ont terres ou tenementes en fee-simple, fee-taille, ou pur terme de vie, &c., les*

have such lands and tenements by several title, and not by joint title, and neither of them knoweth thereof his severalty, but they ought by the law to occupy such lands or tenements in common *pro indiviso*, to take the profits in common. And because that they come to such lands or tenements by several titles, and not by one self-same joint title, and their occupation and possession shall be by law between them in common, they are called tenants in common. As if a man enfeoff two joint-tenants in fee, and the one of them alien that which to him belongeth to another in fee, now the other joint-tenant and the alienee are tenants in common, because they are in such tenements by several titles, for the alienee cometh in the moiety by the feoffment of one of the joint-tenants, and the other joint-tenant hath the other moiety by force of the first feoffment made to him and to his companion: and so they are in by several titles and by several feoffments, &c.

Why so termed.

Example.

Illustration.

Conclusion.

293 And it is to be understood, that when it is said in any

The word fee always in-

queux ount tielx terres ou tenementes per severalx titles, et nemy per joint title, et nul deux savoit de ceo son severall, mes ils doient per la ley occupier tielx terres ou tenementes en comen pur indevise a prendre les profites en comen. Et pur ceo que ils aviendront a tielx terres ou tenementes per severalx titles et nemy per un mesme joint title, et lour occupacion et possession serra per la ley perentere eux en comen, ils sount appelles tenauntes en comen. Sicome un home enfeoffa deux jointenauntes en fee, et lun deux aliena ceo que a luy affiert a un autre en fee, ore lautre jointenaunt et lalienė sount tenauntes en comen, pur ceo que ils sount eins en tielx tenementes per severalx titles, qar lalienė vient en la moyte per le feoffement dun des jointenauntes, et lautre jointenaunt ad lautre moyte per force de le premier feoffement fait a luy et a son compaignon : et issint ils sount eins per severalx titles et per severalx feoffementes.

293 *Et est assavoir, que quant il est dit en ascun lyver,*

tended of a fee-simple.

book, that a man is seised in fee, without more saying, it shall be intended in fee-simple; for it shall not be intended by this word "in fee," that a man is seised in fee-tail, unless there be put there such addition*, *scil.* fee-tail, &c.

If one of three joint-tenants alien, he is tenant in common with the other two.

294 Also, if three joint-tenants be, and one of them alien that which to him belongeth, to another man in fee; in this case, the alienee is tenant in common with the other two joint-tenants: but yet the other two joint-tenants are seised of the two parts jointly, and of these two parts the survivor between them two holdeth place.

So if joint-tenants alien in tail, § 300.

295 Also, if there be two joint-tenants in fee, and the one giveth that which to him belongeth to another in the tail, and the other giveth that which to him belongeth to another in tail, the donee and the other joint-tenant are tenants in common, &c.

Gift to two and the heirs of their bodies,

296 But if lands be given to two men, and to the heirs of their two bodies begotten, the donees have joint estate for term of

que home est seisi en fee, sauns pluis dire, il serra entendus per fee-simple ; qar il ne serra entendus per tiel paroll en fee *que home est seisi en fee-taille, sinon que soit mys a ceo tiel addicion**, scil. *fee-taille, &c.*

294 Item, *si trois jointenauntes sount, et un deux aliena ceo que a luy affiert a un autre home en fee, en ceo cas lalienè est tenaunt en comen ovesque les autres deux jointenauntes : mes unqore les autres deux jointenauntes sont seisis des deux parties jointement, et de ceux deux parties le survivour entre eux deux tient lieu.*

295 Item, *si soient deux jointenauntes en fee, et lun dona ceo que a luy affiert a un autre en le taille, et lautre dona ceo que a luy affiert a un autre en le taille, le donee et lautre jointenaunt sont tenauntes en comen, &c.* 296 *Mes si terres sont dones a deux homes et les heires de lour deux corps engendres, les donees ount joint estate pur terme de lour vies, et*

---

* For *addicion*, *Lettou*, *Machl.*, and *Roh.* read *condicion*.

their lives, and if each of them hath issue and die, their issues shall hold in common &c. But if lands be given to two abbots, as to the abbot of Westminster, and to the abbot of Saint Albans, to have and to hold to them and to their successors; in this case they have forthwith at the beginning, estate in common, and not joint estate. And the reason is, for this that every abbot or other sovereign of a house of religion, before that he was made abbot or sovereign &c., was but as a dead person in law, and when he is made abbot &c., he is as a man or person in law, but only to purchase and have lands or tenements or other things to the use of his house, and not to his own proper use, as another secular man may; and, because at the commencement of their purchase they are tenants in common, if one of them die, the abbot that surviveth shall not have all by the survivor, but the successor of the abbot that dieth, shall hold the moiety in common with the abbot that surviveth &c.

donees are joint-tenants for life, and the issue in tail are tenants in common.

But corporators are tenants in common from the beginning.

Reason. Because their capacities are several.

297 Also, if lands be given to an abbot and to a secular man,

The same reason applies to a

si chescun deux ad issue et devie, lour issues tiendront en comen, &c. Mes si terres sont dones a deux abbes, sicome al abbe de Westminster, *et al abbé de Seynt* Alban, *a aver et tener a eux et a lour successours; en ceo cas ils ount meyntenaunt al commencement, estate en comen, et nemye joint estate. Et la cause est, pur ceo que chescun abbé, ou autre soveraigne de meason de religion, devaunt queil fuist fait abbé, ou soveraigne, &c., il fuist forsque come mort persone en ley, et quant il est fait abbe, &c., il est come un home ou persone en ley tantsolement de purchacer et aver terres ou tenementes, ou autres choses al use de sa meason, et nemye a son propre use, come autre seculer home poet; et pur ceo en commencement de lour purchace ils sount tenauntes en comen, si lun de eux devie, labbe qui survesquist navera mye tout per le survivour, mes le successour de labbé qui mourust, tiendra la moyte en comen ovesque labbé qui survesquist, &c.*

297 Item, *si terres soient donez a un abbé, et a un seculer*

gift made to natural and corporate persons jointly.

to have and to hold to them, *scil.* to the abbot and his successors, and to the secular man, to him and to his heirs, then they have an estate in common, *Causa qua supra.*

Land given to two, habend' *the one moiety to the one, and the other moiety to the other, makes them tenants in common.*

298 Also, if lands be given to two, to have and to hold, *viz.* the one moiety to the one and to his heirs, and the other moiety to the other and to his heirs, they are tenants in common*.

Feoffment by owner of fee of a moiety, creates a tenancy in common.

Assignees of joint-tenants are tenants in common, § 295.

299 Also, if a man seised of certain land enfeoff another of the moiety of the same land without any speech of assignment or limitation of the same moiety in severalty, at the time of the feoffment, then the feoffee and the feoffor shall hold their parts of the land in common, 300 that is to say, that in the same manner as is aforesaid of tenants in common of lands or tenements in fee-simple, or in fee-tail, in the same manner can it be said of tenants for term of life. As if two joint-tenants be in fee, and the one letteth to one man that which

home, a aver et tener a eux, scil. *al abbé, et a ses successours, et al seculer home a luy et a ses heires, donques ils ount estate en comen,* Causa qua supra.

298 Item, *si terres soient dones a deux, a aver et tener, cest-assavoir, lun moyte a lun et a ses heires, et lautre moyte a lautre et a ses heires, ils sont tenauntes en comen*.*

299 Item, *si home seisi de certeyn terre enfeoffa un autre de le moyte de mesme la terre sauns ascun perlaunce dassignment ou limytacion de mesme la moyte en severalte, al temps de le feoffement, donques le feoffé et le feoffour tiendront lour parties de la terre en comen,* 300 *cest assavoir, que en mesme le manere come est avauntdit de tenauntes en comen, de terres ou tenementes en fee-simple, ou en fee-taille, en mesme le manere poet estre dit de tenauntes a terme de vie. Sicome deux jointenauntes sount en fee, et lun lessa a un home ceo que a*

* In *Lettou & M., Machl. & Roh.*, this section is placed immediately after § 300.

to him belongeth for term of life, and the other joint-tenant letteth that which to him belongeth to another for term of life, &c. the two lessees and the other joint-tenant are tenants in common for their lives, &c.

301 Also, if a man let lands to two men for term of their lives, and the one grant all his estate of that which to him belongeth, to another, then the other tenant for term of life, and he to whom the grant is made, are tenants in common during the time that both the lessees be alive.

Assignee of one joint-tenant and his companion are tenants in common.

And *memorandum*, that in all other such *like* cases, although they are not here expressly named or specified, if they be in like reason, they are in the like law.

302 Also, if there be two joint-tenants in fee, and the one letteth that which to him belongeth to another for term of his life, the tenant for term of life during his life, and the other joint-tenant who did not let, are tenants in common.

Lease for life by one joint-tenant a severance of the jointure in the reversion. (As to what acts of a joint-

And upon this case a question may arise, as this: put the

luy affiert pur terme de vie, et lautre jointenaunt lessa ceo que a luy affiert a un 'autre pur terme de vie, &c., les deux lessees et lautre jointenaunt sount tenauntes en comen pur lour vies, &c.

301 Item, *si home lessa terres a deux homes pur terme de lour vies, et lun graunta tout son estate de ceo que a luy affiert, a un autre, donques lautre tenaunt a terme de vie, et celuy a qui le graunt est fait, sont tenauntes en comen duraunt le temps que ambideux lessees sount en vie.*

Et memorandum, *que en toutes autres tielx cases coment que ne sount icy expressement moves ou specifies, si sount en semblable reason, sount en semblable ley.*

302 Item, *si deux jointenauntes en fee sount, et lun lessa ceo que a luy affiert a un autre pur terme de sa vie, le tenaunt a terme de vie duraunt sa vie, et lautre jointenaunt qui ne lessa pas, sount tenauntes en comen.*

Et sur ceo cas une question poet sourdre, come en tiel cas

tenant amount to a severance of the jointure see preceding section).

case that the lessor hath issue and die, living the other joint-tenant his companion, and living the tenant for term of life, the question may be this: Whether the reversion of the moiety, &c. which the lessor hath, shall descend to the issue of the lessor, or that the other joint-tenant shall have this *reversion* by the survivor?

N.B.—*By this a jointure would be severed or destroyed and revived, see* 303, in n.

Some have said in this case, that the other joint-tenant shall have this reversion by the survivor: And their reason is this, *scil.* that when the joint-tenants were jointly seised of fee-simple, &c. although that the one of them made estate of that which to him belongeth for term of life, and although that he hath severed the freehold of that which to him belongeth by the lease, yet he hath not severed the fee-simple, but the fee-simple remains to them jointly as it was before: and so it seemeth to them, that the other joint-tenant, which surviveth, shall have the reversion by the survivor, &c.

Lyttleton's opinion.

And others have said the contrary, and this is their reason, *scil.* when one of the joint-tenants leaseth that to him belongeth,

mettomus, que le lessour ad issue et devie, vivaunt lautre jointenaunt son compaignon, et vivaunt le tenaunt a terme de vie, la question poet estre tiell: Si le revercion de le moyte, &c. que le lessour avoit, descendra al issue le lessour, ou que lautre jointenaunt avera ceo per le survivour?

Ascuns ount dit en ceo cas, que lautre jointenaunt avera cel revercion per le survivour: et lour reason est tiel, scil. *que quant les jointenauntes furent jointement seisis de fee-simple, &c., coment que lun deux fist estate de ceo que a luy affiert pur terme de vie, et coment queil ad severe le franktenement de ceo que a luy affiert per le leese, unquore il nad severe le fee-simple, mes le fee-simple demourt a eux jointenement come il fuist adevaunt: et issint semble a eux, que lautre jointenaunt qui survesquist, avera la revercion per le survivour, &c.*

Et autres ount dit le contrarie, et ceo est lour reason, scil. *quant lun des jointenauntes lessa ceo que a luy affiert*

to another for term of his life, by such lease the freehold is severed from the jointure; and by the same reason, the reversion that is depending upon the same freehold is severed from the jointure. Also if the lessor had reserved to him a yearly rent upon the lease, the lessor solely shall have the rent, &c. the which is a proof, that the reversion is solely in him*, and that the other hath nothing in the reversion, &c. Also if the tenant for term of life were impleaded, and made default after default, then the lessor shall be of this solely received, to defend his right, and his companion in this case shall in no manner be received, which proveth the reversion of the moiety to be only in the lessor: and so by consequence, if the lessor dieth, living the lessee for term of life, the reversion shall descend to the heir of the lessor, and shall not come to the other joint-tenant by the survivor, *Ideo quere*. But in this case, if that joint-tenant who hath the freehold, have issue, and die, living the lessor and the lessee, then it seemeth that the same issue shall have this moiety in demesne, and in fee by

Which is always the better, § 340, 375, 439, 440, 462, 463, 464, 482, 483, 648, 720, 729.

* § 228, 314, 347, 572, 590.

How a rent reserved to a joint-tenant shall enure, (see § 346, where the effect of a reservation of rent to one joint-tenant is stated.)

An estate in freehold or in possession cannot stand in jointure as annexed to a reversion.

a un autre pur terme de sa vie, per tiel lees le franktenement est severe de le jointure; et per mesme le reason, la revercion que est dependant sur mesme le franktenement est severe de le jointure. Auxi si le lessour ust reserve a luy un annuell rente sur le lees, le lessour solement avera le rente, &c., le quel est un prove que la revercion est solement en luy, et que lautre nad riens en la revercion, &c. Auxi si le tenaunt a terme de vie fuist emplede, &c., et fist defaute apres defaute, donques le lessour serroit de ceo solement resceu a defendre son droit, et son compaignion en ceo cas en nul manere serra resceu, le quel prove la revercion de le moyte destre tantsolement en le lessour; et sic per consequens, *si le lessour mourust vivaunt le lessé pur terme de vie, la revercion descendra al heire de le lessour et nemy deviendra a lautre jointenaunt per le survivour,* Ideo quere. *Mes en ceo cas si celuy jointenaunt qui ad le franktenement, ad issue et devie, vivaunt le lessour et le lessé, donques il semble, que mesme lissue avera cest moyte en demesne, et en fee per discent;*

descent; for that freehold cannot by nature of jointure be annexed to a reversion, &c.: and it is certain, that he who leased was seised of the moiety in his demesne as of fee, and none shall have any jointure in his freehold, therefore this shall descend to his issue, &c. *Sed quære.* 303 But if it be so that the law in this case be such, that if the lessor die, living the lessee, and living the other joint-tenant that hath the freehold [*i. e.* an estate in possession] of the other moiety, that the reversion shall descend to the issue of the lessor, then is the joint-holding and the title which any of them can have by the survivor by the right of the jointure, annulled and altogether defeated for ever.

If lease for life by one be in a severance, [as it is] then the survivorship is entirely destroyed.

In the same manner it is, if that joint-tenant who hath the freehold die, living the lessor and the lessee, if the law be such that his freehold and fee which he hath in the moiety shall descend to his issue, then the jointure shall be defeated for ever (*a*).

pur ceo que franktenement ne poet per nature de jointure estre annexe a un revercion, &c., et il est certeyn, que celuy qui lessa fuist seisi de la moyte en son demesne come de fee, et nul avera ascun jointure en son franktenement, ergo *ceo descendera a son issue, &c.* Sed quære. 303 ***Mes si issint soit*** *que la ley en ceo cas est tiel, que si le lessour devie vivaunt le lessé, et vivaunt lautre jointenaunt, qui ad le franktenement de lautre moyte, que la revercion descendera al issue de le lessour, donques est le jointenour et le title que ascun deux poet aver per le survivour per le droit de le jointure, aniente et tout oustrement defete a toutes jours.*

En mesme le manere est, si celuy jointenaunt qui ad le franktenement devie, vivaunt le lessour et le lessé, si la ley soit tiel que son franktenement et fee queil ad en la moyte descendera a son issue, donques le jointure serra defete a toutes jours.

But if lessee dies in both their lifetime, joint-tenancy revives.

(*a*) And the reason is this, for if the jointure be severed at the time of the death of him that was first deceased, the benefit of the survi-

304 (*b*) Also if three joint-tenants be, and the one release by his deed to one of his companions all the right which he hath in the land, then hath he to whom the release is made, the third part of the lands by force of the said release, and he and his companion hold the other two parts jointly. And as to the third part that he hath by force of the release, he holdeth that third part with himself and his companion in common. 305 And it is to be observed, that sometimes deed of release shall take effect and enure to put the estate of him who made the release, in him to whom the release is made, as

Effect of one joint-tenant's releasing to one of his companions, is to create a tenancy in common, as in the preceding cases.

Release mitter l'estate. *Husband, wife, and strangers joint-tenants—by stranger's release to husband he has the moiety.*

304 (*b*) Item, *si trois jointenauntes sount, et lun relessa per son fait a un de ses compaignons tout le droit que il avoit en la terre, donques ad celuy a qui le reles est fait, la tierce partie de les terres per force de le dit reles, et il et son compaignon teignont les autres deux parties jointement. Et quant a la tierce partie queil ad per force de le reles, il tient cel tierce partie ovesque luy mesme et son compaignon en comen.* 305 *Et est assavoir, que ascun foits fait de reles prendra effecte et urera pur metter lestate de celuy qui fist le reles, a celuy a qui le reles est fait, sicome en cas avantdit, et*

---

vor is utterly destroyed for ever, as hath been said afore in the Chapter of joint-tenants (§ 291). But in the case aforesaid, if tenant for life dieth in the life of both the joint-tenants, they are joint-tenants again as they were before.

If two joint-tenants be in fee, and the one letteth his part to another for the life of the lessor, and the lessor dieth, some say that his part shall survive to his companion; for by his death the lease was determined. And others hold the contrary, and their reason is; first, for that at the time of his death the jointure was severed; for so long as he lived the lease continued; and, secondly, that notwithstanding the act of any one of the joint-tenants, there must be equal benefit of survivor as to the freehold. But here if the other joint-tenant had first died, there had been no benefit of survivor to the lessor without question.—*Co. Lytt*, 193. *a.*

Effect of one joint-tenant's lease for his own life.

(*b*) This and the four following sections belong more properly to the Chapter on releases.—*Ritso's Introd. p.* 113.

Effect of stranger's release to wife; viz. the wife takes the moiety, and the husband nothing but jure ux', *because such a release passes estate without words of enlargement,* § 465-6.

in the case aforesaid, and also as if joint estate be made to the husband and to his wife, and to a third person, who releaseth all his right which he hath, &c. to the husband, then hath the husband the moiety which the third person had, and thereof the wife hath nothing. And if in such case the third releaseth, &c. to the wife not naming the husband in the release, then hath the wife the moiety which the third had, &c., and the husband hath nothing thereof but in right of his wife, because that in such case, the release shall enure to make the estate to him to whom the release is made, of all that which belongeth to him who maketh the release, &c. (*c*).

Release mitter le droit.

Release to one of two disseisors, passes the whole estate, § 472, 522.

306 And in some case, a release shall enure to put all the right which he who maketh the release hath, *scil.* to him to whom the release is made: as if a man seised of certain tenements is disseised by two disseisors, (who are thus joint-tenants, § 278), if the disseisee by his deed release all the

auxint sicome joint estate est fait a le baron et a sa feme, et a la tierce persone, qui relessa tout son droit queil ad, &c., a le baron, adonques ad le baron la moyte que le tierce avoit, et la feme de ceo nad riens. Et si en tiel cas le tierce relessa, &c., a la feme nient nosmaunt le baron en le reles, donques ad la feme la moyte que le tierce avoit, &c., et le baron nad riens de ceo forsque en droit sa feme, pur ceo que en tiel cas le reles urera de faire estate a celuy a qui le reles est fait, de tout ceo que affiert a celuy qui fait le reles, &c. 306 *Et en ascun cas un reles urera de metter tout le droit que il ad qui fait le reles,* scil. *a celuy a qui le reles est fait: Sicome home seisi de certeynes tenementes est disseisi per deux disseisours, si le disseisi per son fait relesse tout le droit, &c., a un des*

(*c*) The *&c.* in the end of this section implieth a diversity between a release which enures by way of *mitter l'estate*, (whereof *Lyttleton* here speaketh), and a release that enures by way of extinguishment: for of a lease enuring by way of extinguishment made to the husband, the wife shall take benefit; or to the wife, the husband shall take benefit, as hereafter shall more at large be said.

right, &c. to one of the disseisors, then he to whom the release is made, shall have and hold all the tenements to him solely, and shall oust his companion of every occupation thereof. And the reason is, for that the two disseisors were in the tenements by wrong by them done, against the law, and when one of them happeth (*i. e.* obtains) the release of him that hath right of entry, &c. this right in such case vests in him to whom the release is made, and he is in like plight, as if he who had the right, &c., [had entered and afterwards*] infeoffed him, &c. And the reason is, for that he who before had an estate by wrong, *scil.* by disseisin, &c. hath now by the release a rightful estate, &c. 307 And in some case, a release shall enure by way of extinguishment, and in such case, such release shall aid the joint-tenant to whom the release was not made, as well as him to whom the release be made. As

Release to one joint-tenant enures to both.

disseissours, donques celuy a qui le reles est fait, avera et tiendra toutes les tenementes a luy solement, et oustera son compaignon de chescun occupacion de ceo. Et la cause est, pur ceo que les deux disseisours furent eins en les tenementes per tort per eux fait, encountre la ley, et quant un deux happe le reles de celuy qui ad droit dentre, &c., cest droit en tiel cas veste en celuy a qui le reles est fait, et est en tiel plite, sicome sil qui avoit droit, &c. [avoit entre et puis] luy enfeoffa, &c. Et la cause est, pur ceo queil qui avoit devaunt estate per tort,* scil. *per disseisin, &c., ad ore per le reles un estate droiturel, &c.* 307 *Et en ascun cas un reles urera per voy dextientisement, et en tiel cas tiel reles eidera le jointenant a qui le reles ne fuist fait, auxibien come a celuy a qui le reles soit fait. Sicome si un home soit disseisi, et le dis-*

---

*. The words within brackets first appear in *Redm.* and *Berth.*; these and subsequent editions which retain them, do not have the preceding *&c.*, and in the later editions *puis* is rejected, so that this passage has been hitherto read according to *Rastell's* Transl. *and in such plight as if he that had the right* had entred and *enfeoffed him, &c.*

if a man be disseised, and disseisor makes a feoffment to two men in fee, if the disseisee release by his deed to one of the feoffees, this release shall enure to both the feoffees, for this that the feoffees have estate by the law, *viz.* by feoffment, and not by wrong done to any other, &c.

Release to tenant of the particular estate enures to him in remainder.

308 In the same manner it is, if the disseisor make a lease to a man for term of his life, the remainder over to another in fee, if the disseisee release to the tenant for term of life all his right, &c. this release shall enure as well to him in the remainder, as to the tenant for term of life, [and shall maintain and aid the right of him in the remainder, as well as the right of the tenant for term of life*]. And the reason is, for this that the tenant for life cometh to his estate by course of law, and therefore this release shall enure and taketh effect by way of extinguishment of the right of him who releaseth, &c. And by this release the tenant for term of life hath no more

seisour fait feoffement a deux homes en fee, et le disseisi relesse per son fait a un de les feoffés, donques tiel reles urera a ambideux les feoffés, pur ceo que les feoffés ount estate per la ley, scil. *per feoffement, et nemy per tort fait a nulluy, &c.*

308 *En mesme le manere est si le disseisour fait un lees a un home pur terme de sa vie, le remeyndre oustre a un autre en fee, si le disseisi relessa a le tenaunt a terme de vie tout son droit, &c., cel reles urera auxibien a celuy en le remeyndre come a le tenaunt a terme de vie, [et meynteynera et eidera le droit celuy en le remeyndre, auxibien come le droit de le tenaunt a terme de vie*]. Et la cause est, pur ceo que le tenaunt a terme de vie vient a son estate per cours de ley, et pur ceo cell reles urera et prent effecte per voye dextientisement de droit de celuy qui relessa, &c. Et per tiel reles le*

---

* The words within brackets occur only in *Pyns.* 1516, *Redm.*, *Berth.*, *Middl.*, *Sm.*, *Powell*, and *Tottyl* 1554.

ample or greater estate than he had before the release made to him, and the right of him that releaseth is altogether extinct: and inasmuch as this release cannot inlarge the estate of the tenant for life, it is reason that this release shall enure to him in the remainder, &c.

More shall be said of releases in the Chapter of Releases.

309 Also if there be two parceners, and the one alien that to her belongeth, to another, then the other parcener and the alienee are tenants in common.

Alienation by parcener makes alienee tenant in common with the other parcener.

310 Also tenants in common can be by prescription, as if the one and his ancestors, or those whose estate he hath in one moiety, have holden in common the same moiety with the other tenant who hath the other moiety, and with his ancestors, or with those whose estate he hath, *pro indiviso, &c.*, from time memory runneth not. And divers other manners may make and cause men to be tenants in common, which are not here expressed (*d*).

Tenancy in common by prescription, § 183.

tenaunt a terme de vie nad pluis ample ne greindre estate, que il avoit devaunt le reles fait a luy, et le droit celuy qui relessa est tout oustrement extient : et entaunt que cell reles ne poet enlarger lestate de le tenaunt a terme de vie, il est reason que cel reles urera a celuy en le remeyndre, &c.

Pluis serra dit de relesses en le Chapitre de Relesses.

309 Item, *si soient deux parceners, et lun aliena ceo que a luy affiert, a un autre, donques lautre parcener et lalienė sount tenauntes en comen.*

310 Item, *tenauntes en comen poient estre per prescription, sicome lun et ses auncestres, ou ceux que estate il ad en une moyte, ount tenus en comen mesme la moyte ovesque lautre tenaunt qui ad lautre moyte, et ovesque ses auncestres ou ovesque ceux que estate il ad* pro indiviso, &c., *de temps dount memorie ne court, &c. Et divers autres maneres poient faire et causer homes destre tenauntes en comen, que ne sount icy expresses.*

(*d*) Of this, besides *Lyttleton*, there is as good authority in law,

In real actions, and in actions also that are mixed *with the personalty*, (*viz.* ejectment) *tenants in common shall sever in action, because they have several freeholds, and claim to be in by several titles; and therefore as they shall be severally by others impleaded, so shall they severally implead others in all real and mixt actions, unless for a thing entire.*—Co. Lytt. 195. *b.*

311 Also in some case tenants in common ought to have of their possession several actions, and in some cases they shall join in one action. For if there be two tenants in common and they be disseised, they ought to have against the disseisor two assises, and not one assise; for each of them ought to have one assise of his moiety, &c. And the reason is, for that the tenants in common were seised, &c. by several titles. But otherwise it is of joint tenants; [for if there be twenty joint-tenants, and they are disseised, they shall have in all their names but one assise, because they have but one joint title*].

312 Also if there be three joint-tenants and one release to one of his fellows, all the right which he hath, &c., and afterwards the other two are disseised of the entirety, &c. In this case

311 Item, *en ascun cas tenauntes en comen doient aver de lour possession severalx accions, et en ascun cas ils joindront en un accion. Qar si sount deux tenauntes en comen, et ils sont disseisis, ils doient avoir envers le disseisour deux assises, et nemy une assise, car chescun de eux covient aver une assise de sa moyte, &c. Et la cause est, pur ceo que tenauntes en comen furent seisis, &c., per severalx titles. Mes autrement est de jointenauntes; [qar si soient vint jointenauntes, et ils sont disseisis, ils averount en touts lour nosmes forsque un assise, pur ceo queils nount forsque un joint title*].*

312 Item, *si soient trois jointenauntes, et un relesse a un de ses compaignons tout le droit queil ad, &c., et puis les autres deux sont disseisis de lentierte, &c., en ceo cas les deux autres*

---

as there is, for all his other cases throughout his three books, but joint-tenants cannot be by prescription, beeause there is no survivor between them, but not between tenants in common.—*Co. Lytt.* 195. *b.*

* The words within brackets do not appear in the *Paper MS.*

the two others shall have several assises, &c., in this form, *scil.* they shall have, in both their names, one assise of the two parts, &c., for this that they held the two parts jointly at the time of the disseisin. And as to the third part, he to whom the release was made, ought to have of that one assise in his own name, for that he, as to the same third part, is thereof tenant in common, &c., because he cometh to his third part by force of the release, and not only by force of the jointure.

Example of preceding rule, &c.

313 Also to the sue actions which affect the* realty, there be diversities between parceners that are in by divers Descents, and tenants in common: [for if two parceners seised of certain land in fee, have issue two sons and†] die

If two parceners are to be impleaded, a joint action must be had.

averount severalx assises, &c., en ceo fourme, scil. *ils averount en lour ambideux nouns, une assise de les deux parties, &c., pur ceo que les deux parties ils teignount joyntment al temps de le disseisin. Et quant a la tierce partie, celuy a que la reles fuist fait, covient aver de ceo une assise en son noun demesne, pur ceo que, quaunt a mesme la tierce partie, il est de ceo tenaunt en comen, &c., pur ceo queil vient a cel tierce partie per force de reles, et nemy tantsolement per force de joynture.*

313 Item, *quant a suer daccions que trenchent en* le realte, il est diversite perentre parceners qui sont eins per divers discentes, et tenauntes en comen : [qar si deux parceners seisies de certeyne terre en fee ount issue deux fites, et†] devieront*

---

* *Touchaunt le realte, Pyns.* 1516 : *touchent le realte, Redm., Berth., Middl., Sm., Powell, Tottyl* 1554 : *touchent en le realte, Tottyl* 1557 (both editions), 1567, 1572, 1577 : *touchant le realte, Tottyl* 1581 (by West), 1585-8, which last reading is followed by all subsequent editions.

† The text as above is accordant with the three earliest editions, *Redm., Berth., Middl., Sm., Powell, Tottyl* 1554, and all the editions of *Rastell's* Transl. The more modern or common copies, which may be said to commence with *Tottyl's* two corrected editions in 1557, adopt the following and ordinary reading of this passage, (viz.)—*For if a man*

without partition made between them, by which the one moiety descends to the son of the one parcener, and the other moiety descends to the son of the other parcener, and they enter and occupy in common, and be disseised, in this case they shall have in their two names one assise, and not two assises. And the cause is, that albeit they come in by divers descents, &c.; yet they are parceners, and a writ of partition lieth between them. And they are not parceners, having regard or respect only to the seisin and possession of their mothers; but they are parceners, having respect rather to the estate which descended from their grandfather to their mothers, for they cannot be parceners where their mothers were not parceners before, &c. And so to such respect and consideration, *scil.* as to the first descent, which was to their mothers, they have a title in parcenary, the which makes

For they are them parceners. And also they are but as one heir to their

sauns particion fait entre eux, per que lune moyte descenderoit a les fites dune parcener, et lautre moyte descendist al fitz dautre parcener, et ils entrount et occupiount en comen et sount disseisis, en ceo cas ils averont en lour deux nouns une assise et nemy deux assises. Et la cause est, que coment queils veignount eins per divers discentes, &c., unqore ils sount parceners, et brief de participacione facienda *gist entre eux. Et ils ne sount parceners eiaunt regarde ou respecte tantsolement a le seisin et possession de lour meres, mes ils sount parceners pluis eiaunt respecte de lestate que descendist de lour aiel a lour meres, qar ils ne poient estre parceners ou lour meres ne furent parceners adevaunt. Et issint a tiel respecte et consideracion,* scil. *quant a le premier discent que fuist a lour meres, ils ount un title en parcenerie, le quel fait eux parceners. Et auxi ils ne sount forsque come un heire a lour comen aun-*

---

seised of certain land in fee hath issue two daughters, and dieth, and the daughters enter, &c., and each of them hath issue a son, and die without partition made between them,—&c.

common ancestor, *i. e.* to their grandfather, from whom the land descended to their mothers. And for these causes, before partition between them, &c., they shall have one assise, although they come in by several descents, &c.

but one heir to their ancestor, § 241.

314 Also, if there be two tenants in common of certain land in fee, and they will give this land to a man in tail, or let it to one for term of life, yielding to them yearly a certain rent, and a pound of pepper, and a hawk, or a horse, and they are seised of this service, and afterwards the whole rent is behind, and they distrain for this, and the tenant maketh rescous. In this case, as to the rent and pound of pepper, they shall have two assises, and as to the hawk, or the horse, but one assise. And the reason why they shall have two assises as to the rent and pound of pepper, is this, insomuch as they were tenants in common by several titles, and when they made a gift in the tail or lease for term of life, &c., saving to them the reversion, and yielding to them certain rent, &c., such reservation is incident to their reversion, and for this that

Tenants in common must join when they sue for an entire thing, and of things severable they may have several actions, [*for examples, see* Co. Lytt. 197. *a.*]

§ 228 9, 347, 572, 590.

cestre, scil. *a lour aiel de qui la terre descendist a lour meres. Et pur ceux causes, devaunt particion entre eux, &c., ils averount un assise, coment queils viendrount eins per severalx discentes, &c.*

314 Item, *si sount deux tenauntes en comen de certeyne terre en fee, et ils doneront cell terre a un home en le taille, ou lesseront a un home pur terme de vie, rendaunt a eux annuelment un certeyne rente, et un libre de peper, et un esperver, ou un chivall, et ils sount seisis de cest service, et puis tout le rente est aderere, et ils distreignont pur ceo, et le tenaunt a eux fait rescous. En ceo cas quant a le rente et libre de peper ils averont deux assises, et quaunt a lesperver ou le chival, forsque une assise. Et la cause pur que ils averont deux assises, quant a le rent et libre de peper, est ceo, entaunt que ils furent tenauntes en comen per severalx titles, et quaunt ils fierount un done en le taille ou lees pur terme de vie, &c., savaunt a eux la revercion, et rendant a eux certeyn rente, &c., tiel reservacion est incident a lour*

their reversion is in common, and by several titles, as their possession was before, the rent and other things that can be severed, and were reserved unto them upon the gift or upon the lease, which are incidents by the law to their reversion, such things so reserved* were of the nature of reversion, and entitle† that the reversion is to them in common by several titles, and it behoveth that the rent and the pound of pepper, which may be severed, be to them in common and by several titles, and of this they shall have two assises, and each of them in his assise‡ shall make his plaint of the moiety of the rent, and of the moiety of the pound of pepper: but of the hawk, or of the horse, which cannot be severed, they shall have but one assise; for a man cannot make a plaint in assise

revercion, et pur ceo que lour revercion est en comen et per severalx titles, sicome lour possession fuist devaunt, le rente et autres choses que poient estre severes, et furent a eux reserves sur le done, ou sur le lees, queux sont incidentz per la ley a lour revercion, tielx choses issint reserves furent de la nature de revercion, et entitlount† que la revercion est a eux en comen per severalx titles, et il covient que le rente, et le libre de peper, queux poient estre severes, soient a eux en comen, per severalx titles, et de ceo ils averont deux assises, et chescun deux en son assise‡ ferra sa pleint de la moyte de le rente, et de le libre de peper : mes de lesperver, ou de chivall que ne poient estre severes, ils averont forsque une assise, qar home ne poet*

---

* *Rastell's* Translation reads *severed* in ed. 1581, 1586, 1597, but not in *Powell* 1551.

† This word *entitlount*, has been corrupted to *entant*, *inasmuch*, so that in the corrupted copies this reads as the commencement of a new sentence, *Et entant—and inasmuch.* This passage is corrected in an edition of *Lyns.* 1516, (which reads as in the text), by a contemporary hand, viz. *de reversion, quel reversion* est ; and all the editions of *Rastell's* Transl. read accordingly, *of the reversion, which reversion is to them — &c.*

‡ *Poss. Lettou & M., possession, Machl. & Roh.*

of the moiety of a hawk, or of a horse, &c. (*e*). In the same manner it is of other rents and of other services, which tenants in common have in gross by divers titles (*f*).

315 Also as to actions personal, tenants in common ought to have such actions personals (*g*) jointly in all their names, that is to say, of trespass, or of offences which concern their tenements in common; as of breaking their houses, breaking of their closes, feeding, wasting, and defouling of their grass, cutting their wood, of fishing in their piscary, and such like. In this case tenants in common shall have one action jointly, and shall recover jointly their damages, because the action is in the personalty, and not in the realty.

Reason why tenants should join in personal actions, is, that of personal actions they are joint-tenants, for such actions survive.

[Real actions did not, for if one plaintiff died after suit commenced, the action was gone].

faire une pleint en assise de la moyte dun esperver, ou dun chivall, &c. En mesme le manere est dautres rentes et dautres services que tenauntes en comen ount en grosse per divers titles.

315 Item, *quant a accions personelx, tenauntes en comen deveroùnt aver tielx accions personelx jointement en toutes lour nouns, cestassavoir, de trespas, ou offence que touche lour tenementes en comen, sicome debruser de lour measons, denfreindre de lour closes, depaster, degaster, et defouler de lour herbes, de couper lour boys, de pescher en lour pescherie,* et hujusmodi. *Et ceo cas tenauntes en comen averont une accion jointement, et recoveront jointement lour damages, pur ceo que laccion est en le personalte, et nemy en le realte.*

(*e*) Here is implied, or any other entire rent or service.

(*f*) That is, by several titles, and not by one joint title, as hath been said.

(*g*) By this it appeareth, that tenants in common shall have personal actions jointly. And it is to be observed, that where damages are to be recovered for a wrong done to tenants in common, or parceners on a personal action, and one of them die, the survivor of them shall have the action; for albeit the property or estate be several between them, yet, (as it appeareth by *Lyttleton*) the personal action is joint.—*Co. Lytt.* 198. *a.*

The same.

316 Also, if two tenants in common make a lease of their tenements to another for term of years, yielding unto them yearly certain rent during the term, if the rent be behind, &c., the tenants in common shall have one action of debt against the lessee, and not divers actions, for that the action is in personalty*.

Partition not compulsory at law; [*but partition at this day is compellable by stat.* 31 *H.* 8, *c.* 1, *&* 32 *H.* 8, *c.* 32]. § 247, 259, 264, 290.

318 Also, tenants in common can well make partition between them if they will, though they shall not be compelled to make partition by the law; but if they make partition between themselves by their agreement and consent, such partition is good enough, as is adjudged in the book of assises. [*Pasch.* 3 *E.* 4 (*h*).]

Tenancy in

319 Also, as there be tenants in common of lands and tene-

316 Item, *si deux tenauntes en comen fount un lees de lour tenementes a un autre pur terme des ans, rendaunt a eux annuelement certeyn rente duraunt le terme, si le rente soit aderere, &c., les tenauntes en comen averont une accion de dette envers le lessé, et nemy divers accions, pur ceo que luccion est en personalte**.

318 Item, *tenauntes en comen poient bien faire particion enter eux sils voillent, coment que ils ne serront compelles de faire particion per la ley; mes sils fount entre eux particion per lour agrement et consent, tiel particion est assetes bon, come est ajugge en le lyver dassises.*

319 Item, *sicome y sont tenauntes en comen de terres et te-*

---

* Here follows in all the copies since *Redm.* (the editions of *Rastell's* Translation excepted), an addition to Lyttleton which forms the 317th section or subdivision of the text by *West.* 1581. As it is consonant to law, it may be noticed, *viz.* " But in avowry for the said rent, they ought to sever; for this is in the realty, as the assise is above." In *Redm.* this addition forms the conclusion to the 315th section.

(*h*) This book is of great authority in law, and is so called, because it principally containeth the proceedings upon writs of assise of

ments, &c., as aforesaid; *so* in the same manner there be possessions and properties* of chattels real and personal: as if a lease be made of certain lands to two men for term of twenty years, and when they be thereof possessed, the one of the lessees granteth that which to him belongeth, to another during the term, then he to whom the grant is made, and the other, shall hold and occupy in common (*i*).

common of chattels real. Example. 1. A lease.

320 Also, if two joint-tenants have the wardship of the body and lands of an infant within age, and one of them grant to another that which to himself belongeth of the same ward, then the grantee, and the other who did not grant, shall have and hold this in common, &c. (*k*).

2. A ward-ship, (*which is a chattel real entire*).

nementes, &c., come est avauntdit: en mesme le manere y sont possessions et propretees de chatelx realx et personelx: sicome si lees soit fait de certeynes terres a deux homes pur terme de* xx. *ans et quaunt ils sount de ceo possessiones, lun de les lessees graunta ceo que a luy affiert duraunt le terme, a un autre, donques mesme celuy a qui le graunt est fait, et lautre tiendra et occupiera en comen.*

320 Item, *si deux jointenauntes ont la garde de corps et de terres dun enfaunt deins age, et lun deux graunta a un autre ceo que a luy affiert de mesme la garde, donques le graunté et lautre que ne graunta pas, averont et tiendront ceo en comen, &c.*

---

* *Possessourz et proprieturez—possessors and proprietors, Camb.* MSS., *Rastell's* Transl. accords with the text as above given from the three earliest editions.

---

novel disseisin, which in those days was *festinum et frequens remedium.—Co. Lytt.* 198. *b.* The reference to the Year-Book appears in *Redm.* and in *Rastell's* Transl.

(*i*) The same law it is, if the one lessee in this case make a lease for part of the term, the second lessee and the other are tenants in common, as hath been said in the Chapter of Joint-tenants. The *&c.* in this section implieth other hereditaments, whereof men may be tenants in common, whereof sufficient hath been said before.—*Co. Lytt.* 199. *a.*

(*k*) Here *&c.* implieth any other entire chattel.

Tenancy in common of chattels personal.

321 In the same manner it is of chattels personals. As if two have joint estate by gift, or by buying a horse or an ox, &c., and the one grant that which to him belongeth to another, then the grantee and the other that did not grant shall have and possess such chattels personal in common, &c.: and in such cases where divers persons have chattels real or personal in common, and by divers titles, if the one of them dieth, the other who survives shall not have this by the survivor, but the executors of him that dieth shall hold and occupy that with him who surviveth, as their testator did or ought in his life, because their titles and rights in this case were several, &c.

No survivorship existing in either, where tenants hold by several titles.

Action by one tenant in common against his companion—in respect of a term, ejectment.

322 Also, in the case aforesaid, as if two have an estate in common for term of years, and the one occupy all, and putteth the other out of possession and occupation, he that is put out of occupation shall have against the other a writ of *ejectione firmæ*, of the moiety, &c. 323 In the same manner it is where two hold the wardship of lands or tenements during

Remedies by one tenant in common

321 *En mesme le manere est de chateux personelx: sicome deux ount joint estate per done ou per achate dun chivall ou boef, &c., et lun graunte ceo que a luy affiert a un autre: donques le graunté et lautre qui ne graunta pas, averount et posiderount tielx chateux personelx en comen, &c. Et en tielx cases, ou divers persones ount chateux realx ou personelx en comen et per divers titles, si lun deux mourust les autres que survesqount, naverount ceo per le survivour, mes les executours celuy qui mourust tiendrount et occupierount ceo ovesque luy qui survesquist, sicome lour testatour fist ou devoit en sa vie, pur ceo que lour titles et droitz en ceo cas furent severalx, &c.*

322 Item, *en le cas avauntdit, sicome deux ount estate en comen pur terme dans, et lun occupia tout, et myst lautre hors de possession et occupacion, &c., donques celuy, qui est mys hors doccupacion avera envers lautre brief* de ejectione firmæ, *de la moyte, &c.* 323 *Et mesme le manere est lou deux teignount la garde des terres ou tenementes duraunt le*

the nonage of an infant, if the one oust the other of his possession, he that is ousted shall have a writ of *ejectment de gard* of the moiety, &c., because these things are but chattels real, and can be apportioned and severed, &c., but no such action, that is to say, *Quare clausum suum fregit, et herbam suam, &c., conculcavit et consumpsit, &c.*, and such like actions, the one cannot have against the other; for this that each of them may enter and occupy in common, &c., through and by all the lands and tenements which they hold in common. But if two be possessed of chattels personals in common by divers titles, as of a horse, an ox, or a cow, &c., if the one take this all to himself out of the possession of the other, the other hath no other remedy but to take it from him who hath done to him the wrong, to occupy in common, &c., when he can see his time, &c.

against the other in respect of chattels real and personal, and with regard to their being either apportionable and severable, or entire.

In the same manner it is of chattel real, which cannot be severed, as in the case aforesaid, where two be possessioners of a wardship of the body of an infant within age, if the one

nonage dun enfaunt, si lun ousta lautre de sa possession, il qui est ouste avera briefe dengettement de garde de la moyte, &c., pur ceo que ceux choses sont chateux realx, et poient estre apporciones et severes, &c. Mes nul tiel accion, cestassavoir, Quare clausum suum fregit et herbam suam, &c., conculcavit et consumpsit, &c., et hujusmodi actiones, &c., *lun ne poet aver envers lautre, pur ceo que chescun deux poet entrer et occupier en comen, &c. per my et per toutz les terrez et tenementes queux ils teignount en comen. Mes si deux sont possessiones de chatelx personelx en comen per divers titles, sicome dun chivall, ou boef, ou vache, &c., si lun prent ceo tout a luy hors de possession dautre, lautre nad nul autre remedye mes de prendre ceo de luy qui ad fait luy le tort, pur occupier en comen, &c., quant il poet veier son temps, &c.*

En mesme le manere est de chatell reall, que ne poet estre severe, sicome en le cas avauntdit, que deux sount possessiones dun garde de corps dun enfaunt deins age, si lun prent len-

taketh the infant out of the possession of the other, the other hath no remedy by any action by the law, but to take the infant, out of the possession of the other when he seeth his time, &c.

Seisin *and* possession *distinguished.*

324 Also, when a man in pleading will shew a feoffment made unto him, or a gift in tail, or a lease for life, of any lands or tenements, there he shall say, by force of which feoffment, gift, or lease, he was seised, &c., but where one will plead a lease or grant made to him of chattel real or personal, there he shall say, by force of which he was possessed, &c.

More shall be said of tenants in common in the Chapters of Releases and Confirmations, and Tenant by *Elegit**.

faunt hors de possessione dautre, lautre nad ascune remedye per ascun accion per la ley, mes de prendre lenfaunt hors de le possession dautre quaunt il veiet son temps, &c.

324 Item, *quaunt un home en pleder voille monstrer un feoffement fait a luy ou un done en le taille, ou un lees pur terme de vie dascunes terres ou tenementes, la il dirra per force de quell feoffement, done, ou lees il fuist seisi, &c., mes lou un voille pleder un lees ou graunt fait a luy de chatel reall ou personell, la il dirra, per force de quel il fuit possessione, &c.*

Pluis serra dit de tenementes en comen en les Chapitres de Relesses et Confirmacions, et tenaunt per Elegit*.

---

* See *ante*, § 291, *ad fin.* The later copies in French do not refer to the Chapter on Confirmation, nor does *Sir Edward's Coke's* Copy and Translation do so. The above text accords with *Rastell's* Transl.

CHAPTER V.

ESTATES UPON CONDITIONS.

A CONDITION is a kind of law or bridle annexed to one's act, staying or suspending the same, and making it uncertain whether it shall take effect or not;—it is also sometimes annexed to, and depending upon, estates; and sometimes annexed to, and depending upon, recognizances, obligations, contracts, and other things. Conditions also are contained in acts of parliament and records. But of these we speak not here in the ensuing matters, which are especially to be applied to such conditions as are usually contained in deeds, and annexed to the realty, *i. e.* to estates in fee-simple, fee-tail, for life or years.—*Touchst.* 117.

Estates upon condition, or rather those qualifications that are annexed to real estates by donors or grantors, are classed by Lyttleton as conditions in deed (*i. e.* expressed), and conditions in law (*i. e.* implied).

Conditions expressed, he informs us, are when the words of the gift or grant operate as a restraint upon the estate granted or intended to be passed; or, to use his own significant language, the estate of the feoffee is defeasible, if the condition be not performed (§ 325). With regard to this kind of conditions, they are divided into conditions *precedent* and conditions *subsequent;* and here it may be noticed, with regard to these conditions, that although their primary object is to operate as a restraint, yet they may subsist to create and enlarge, as well as to defeat an estate; for the quantity of estate which may pass from the grantor, may be granted with such condition annexed to it as he may think fit to create. So, where a condition is to be performed before the estate can commence or vest, it is called a condition *precedent;* but where the effect of a condition is either to enlarge or defeat an estate already commenced, it is called a condition *subsequent*.

With respect to conditions precedent, which are defeasible upon condition, or restrained, or do not vest until the condition be performed, Lyttleton instructs his reader by examples, *viz*. of a condition precedent to enlarge an estate (§ 349, 350); of a restraint against alienation to particular persons (§ 361); of an estate defeasible on condition (§ 364); of a mortgage (§ 332); all which cases involve the collateral learning of tender (§ 341); satisfaction and performance, to which last the doctrine of *cy pres* (§ 352) is referred.

With respect to the remedy the donor, feoffor, or grantor has on breach of the condition, Lyttleton tells us he is at liberty to enter (*a*) for the condition broken; in which case he is said to be *in* (*i. e.* again seised) of his former estate (*b*): as conditions are in legal language said to "enure in privity," so that none but privies shall take advantage of them, no one can enter for a condition broken, except the feoffor, donor, or grantor and lessor, or their heirs (§ 347), the conclusion or consequence is, that as none but privies shall avoid an estate previously made for the breach of a condition, so none but privies shall take a new estate by the performance of a condition.—*Plowd.* 24 (*c*). The same doctrine applies to reservations (§ 346).

(*a*) *Entry* by a legal owner is a notorious act of ownership, and equivalent to a feodal investiture by the lord, and gives the owner seisin, and makes him complete owner of the estate and capable of conveying it from himself, either by descent or purchase. As to the nature of making entry and claim, *post*, § 417, 419, 422, 423. B.C. iii. 175; iv. 147.

(*b*) Regularly this is true, but to this rule there are many exceptions.—*Co. Lytt.* 202. *a.* And the *Abridgments, tit. Condition.*

(*c*) But now by stat. 32 Hen. 8, c. 34, the grantees or assignees of a reversion may take advantage of re-entries and forfeitures for conditions broken.—See *Co. Lytt.* 215.

Estates upon condition expressed, are not determined, *ipso facto*, on the breach of the condition, but only upon the donor, &c., entering or bringing his ejectment upon a real or supposed entry to recover the possession, and this is the chief test of the distinction between this class of conditions and that of conditions implied, which will next attract the reader's attention.

The conditions in law (§ 378) or implied, are either by common law or by statute laws. The first sort are, some of them, founded on skill, as where an office is granted, there is a condition *tacitè* implied, that if the grantee doth not execute it faithfully according to the trust, the grantor may put him out. And some are without skill, as where an estate is made for life or years of land, there is this condition implied, that if the lessee do waste, he shall forfeit the place wasted; or if the lessee make a feoffment of the land he shall forfeit his estate, and the lessor shall enter. And where an estate is made in fee of land; this condition is implied, that the feoffee shall not alien it in mortmain. [And to every estate of tenant by the curtesy, in dower, for life, &c., there is a condition in law secretly annexed to their estates, that if they alien in fee, &c., that he in the reversion or remainder may enter.—*Co. Lytt.* 233. *b*.] And these conditions do sometimes give a recovery, and no entry, as in the case of waste, and sometimes they give an entry and no recovery, as in the case of alienation in mortmain. In the case of exchange also there is a condition in law, [*viz*. that if, after an exchange of lands, either party be evicted of those which were taken by him in exchange, through defect in the other's title, he shall return back to his own, by virtue of the implied warranty contained in all exchanges.—B. C. ii. 323. *Touchst*. 118, 290].

Lyttleton next mentions another species of condition in law, which shortly after his time was termed a *limitation*, because the cases put as examples of this estate (§ 380, 382), are but times of limitations, *i. e*. the estate shall cease on the happening of the events mentioned in those two sections, the practical effect, in those two cases being, that the freehold in law is cast upon the feoffor or lessor, so that he has the possession in law before entry: as if land is given to a man in tail so long as J. S. shall have issue of his body, or until J. S. shall die without issue of his body, there, if J. S. dies without issue, the land shall revert, and the same effect takes place as in the cases last named; for the words *so long as* and *until,* or similar expressions denoting duration of time, are words which mark the boundary and the uttermost continuance of the estate granted, while, on the other hand, a *condition* marks some event which if it happen, is to defeat the estate.

The circumstance of the utmost time of continuance being marked by this species of condition in law, *scil.* a limitation, distinguishes it from conditions generally so termed; for when an estate is granted to A. B., upon condition that he does not do a particular act, the estate is said to be *limited* until such an act is done. So if land is granted to a man until out of the rents and profits he shall have made one hundred pounds. In these cases, the estate determines so soon as such a particular act is done by A. B., or so soon as he has received the one hundred pounds, and the next subsequent estate which depends upon such determination, becomes immediately vested, without any act to be done by him in expectancy, or the land reverts to the grantor, as it may chance to happen in either case: " so that," as the author of the *Touchstone* expresses himself, " howsoever a limitation hath much affinity and agreement with a condition, and therefore it is sometimes called a condition in law, both of them do determine an estate in being before; and a limitation cannot make an estate to be void as to one person, and good as to another; as if a gift be made in tail to one and his heirs-male, until he do such a thing, and then his estate to cease and go to another: yet herein they differ; 1. A stranger may take advantage of an estate determined by limitation, and so he cannot upon a condition; 2. A limitation doth always determine the estate without entry or claim, and so doth not a condition."—*Touchst.* 121.

Conditions in devises which are expressed in terms where the sense amounts to a limitation, are generally so taken, for the intent only is regarded in such instruments, and the words although they are not apt in law for the subject-matter, yet will be drawn to the intent; for devisors are, by a favourable construction of law, deemed *inopes consilii:* so also in cases of wills and devises, it is fully settled, that a condition is to be construed to be precedent or subsequent, as the intent of the testator may require. The question always is, whether the thing is to happen before or after the estate is to vest; if before, the condition is precedent; if after, it is subsequent.

There are various words and phrases which of themselves make an estate conditional, without expressly giving power of entry. Lyttleton enumerates some of these (§ 328, 329), although it may be observed, that no precise form of words is necessary to raise a condition; it being sufficient if it appears that the words used are intended to have the effect of creating it, and the exception *Lyttleton* makes with respect to the words *si contingat,* which to be efficacious as a condition, require to be coupled with words expressly giving a power of entry (§ 331), justify the rule. It may be also remarked, that the words "*Proviso semper,*" may constitute both a condition and a covenant, and sometimes a covenant only, and the same remark applies in most cases to the *ita quod,* indeed, the interpretation of these words depends chiefly on the context and their relation to another sentence (*d*).

(*d*) The same remarks will apply equally to a limitation. The word *si* also, doth not always make a condition, for sometimes it makes a limitation; as where a lease is made for years if J. S. shall live so long.—*Touchst.* 123.

The most apt and proper words to make a limitation of an estate, are, *quamdiu, dummodo, dum, quousque, si,* and such like, (*Id.* 125); indeed any words that have reference to the extent of an estate as measured by duration of time, and whether or not dependent or determinable upon any event, may be construed as words of limitation, and make such an estate limited, but not conditional.

With respect to *provisos with powers of revocation,* which operate by means of the Statute of Uses. See *Co. Lytt.* 237. *a.*

Estates on condition are either express *or* implied.

325 ESTATES [on condition*] which men have in lands or tenements, are of two sorts, that is to say, they have estates upon condition in deed, or upon condition in law.

Example of an express condition.

Upon condition in deed is, as if a man by deed indented enfeoffs another in fee, reserving to him and his heirs yearly, a certain rent payable at one feast or at divers feasts by the year, upon condition that if the rent be behind, &c., that it may be lawful for the feoffor and his heirs into the same lands or tenements to enter, &c., [or if land be aliened to another man in fee, rendering unto him certain rent, &c.†],

325 *Estates [sur condicion*]que homes ount en terres ou tenementes sount en deux maners, cestassavoir, ils ount estate sur condicion en fait, ou sur condicion en ley.*

Sur condicion en fait est, sicome un home per fait endente enfeoffa un autre en fee, reservaunt a luy et a ses heires annuelement un certeyn rente paiable a un feste, ou a divers festes per an, sur condicion que si le rente soit aderere, &c., que bien list a le feoffour et a ses heires en mesmes les terres ou tenementes dentrer, &c., ou si terre soit aliene a un autre home en fee rendaunt a luy certeyn rente, &c., et sil happast

---

* This Chapter is intituled by *Brook*, in his *Abr. tit. Condition*, 33, " Chapter of Estates," from the initial words of this Chapter, which omit *on condition*, if we are to depend upon the oldest printed copies and *Rastell's* Transl. The common copies commence this Chapter thus, " *Estates which men have in lands or tenements upon condition —— &c. Astates*, also is placed for *estates*, which mode of spelling this word was not uncommon when *Lyttleton* wrote, and, indeed, not unfrequently occurs in the first printed editions of the year-books, as well as in the three earliest editions of the *Tenures*. In this instance, the Illuminator has placed a capital Gothic A in the editions by *Lettou & M.*, and *Machl.*: the printer of the latter, for the direction of the Illuminator, also putting the same letter in a small character.

† The words within brackets are omitted in all the copies of *Sir Ed-*

and if it happen that the rent be behind by a week after any day of payment thereof, or by a month after any day of payment thereof, or by half a year, &c., that then it shall be lawful to that same feoffor and to his heirs to enter, &c. In these cases, if the rent be not paid at such time, or before such time limited and specified within the condition comprised in the indenture, then can the feoffor or his heirs enter into such lands or tenements, and them in his first estate to have and hold, and the feoffee quite to oust thereof. And it is called estate upon condition, because that the estate of the feoffee is defeasible* if the condition be not performed, &c.

Illustration.

Conclusion.

326 In the same manner it is, if lands be given to a man in the tail, or let for term of life or of years, upon such condition, &c. 327 But where feoffment is made of certain lands reserving certain rent, upon such condition, that if the rent be behind, that it shall be lawful to the feoffor and his heirs

The same.

But where feoffment on condition to pay rent is made with power of distress and entry, and rent

que le rente soit aderere per une semaigne apres ascun jour de paiement de ceo, ou per une moys apres ascun jour de paiement de ceo, ou per un demy an, &c., que adonques bien lirroit a mesme cestuy feoffour et a ses heires dentrer, &c. En ceux cases si le rente ne soit paie a tiel temps ou devaunt tiel temps limite et specifie deins le condition comprise en lendenture, donques poet le feoffour ou ses heires entrer en tielx terres ou tenementes, et eux en son premier estate aver et tener, et de ceo ouster le feoffee tout net. Et est appelle estate sur condicion, pur ceo que lestate le feoffee est defeasible si le condicion ne soit perfourme, &c.*

326 *En mesme le manere est, si terres sount dones a un home en le taille, ou lesses a terme de vie ou des ans, sur tiel condicion, &c.* 327 *Mes lou feoffement est fait de certeynes terres reservant certeyn rente, sur tiel condicion que si le rente soit aderere, queil bien lirroit al feoffour et ses heires dentrer en*

---

ward Coke's Translation, as well as in the Translation adopted in the English and French edition of 1671.

* This word appears as *defensible* in the three earliest copies.

is behind, the feoffor is not quite excluded, although the feoffee shall have the land till satisfied by the profits.

to enter into the land holden of them, until they be satisfied or paid the rent behind, &c. In this case, if the rent be behind, and the feoffor or his heirs enter, the feoffee is not altogether excluded from this, but the feoffor shall have and hold the land, and thereof take the profits until that he be satisfied of the rent behind; and when he is satisfied, then may the feoffee re-enter into the same land, and hold it as he held it before. For in such case the feoffor shall have it but in manner as for a distress, until that he be satisfied of the rent, &c., though he take the profits in the mean time, [to his own use*], &c.

Words of condition.

Sub conditione.

328 Also, divers words among others there be, which by virtue of themselves make estates upon condition, one is the word, "condition†:" as if A. enfeoff B. of certain land, "To have and to hold to the same B. and his heirs, upon "condition that the same B. and his heirs, do pay or cause

la terre tenus de eux, tanques ils soient satisfies ou paies de le rente aderere, &c. En ceo cas si le rente soit aderere, et le feoffour ou ses heires entra, le feoffé nest pas exclude de ceo tout de nette, mes le feoffour avera et tiendra la terre, et prendra ent les profites, tanques que il soit satisfie de le rente aderere; et quant il est satisfie, donques poet le feoffé entrer en mesme la terre, et ceo tener coment il tient adevaunt. Qar en tiel cas le feoffour ceo avera forsque en manere come pur un distresse, tanques que il soit satisfie de rente, &c., coment que il prendra les profites en le meane temps [a son use demesne], &c.*

328 Item, *divers parolx entre les autres y sount, que per vertue deux mesmes fount estates sur condicion, un est le paroll de condicion† : sicome A. enfeoffa B. de certeyne terre, "Habendum et tenendum eidem B. et hæredibus "suis, sub condicione, quod idem B. et heredes sui solvant*

---

* The words within brackets are not in the three earliest editions.

† The text as above is conformable to *Lettou & M.*, *Machl.* and *Roh.*, and *Rastell's* Transl. The subsequent editions give the words *sub conditione*. The *Camb. MSS.* read *condicion mesme.*

" to be paid to the aforesaid A. and to his heirs, yearly, such " a rent &c." In this case, without any more saying, the feoffee hath estate upon condition.

329 Also, if the conditions* were such, " *Provided always,* " that the aforesaid B. do pay or cause to be paid to the " aforesaid A., such a rent, &c.; " or were thus, " *So that* " the said B. do pay or cause to be paid to the said A., " such a rent, &c," [or such†, *so as.*] In these cases, without more saying, the feoffee hath not estate but upon condition: so that if he doth not perform the condition, the feoffor and his heirs can enter, &c. **Proviso.** **Ita quod.**

330 Also, there be other words in a deed which cause the tenements to be conditional: as if upon such feoffment, a rent is reserved to the feoffor, &c., and afterwards it be put in the deed, " That *if it happen* the aforesaid rent to be " behind in part or in all, &c., that then it shall be lawful for " the feoffor and his heirs to enter," &c., this is a deed upon **Si contingat.**

" *seu solvi faciant præfato A. et heredibus suis annuatim* " *talem redditum, &c.*" *En ceo cas sans ascun pluis dire le feoffé ad estate sur condicion.*

329 *Auxy si les condicions* furent tielx,* " Proviso *quod,* " semper *prædictus B. solvat, seu solvi faciat præfato A.* " *talem redditum, &c.,*" *ou furent tielx,* " Ita quod *prædict'* " *B. solvat, seu solvi faciat præfato A. talem redditum, &c.*" [*ou tielx*†, sic quod]. *En ceux cases sauns pluis dire, le feoffé nad estate forsque sur condicion: issint que sil ne performast le condicion, le feoffour et ses heires poient entrer, &c.*

330 Item, *autres parolx sount en un fait que causont les tenementes estre condicionels: sicome sur tiel feoffement un rente est reserve al feoffour, &c., et puis soit mette en le fait,* " *Quod* si contingat *redditum prædictum aretro fore in parte* " *vel in toto, &c., quod tunc bene liceat, a le feoffour et a ses*

---

* The ordinary copies read for *conditions*, *words*. *Rastell's* Transl. reads the passage thus; *Also if the condition were such* —— *&c.*

† The words within brackets occur only in the *Camb. MSS.*, and they may be deemed an interpolation.

Si contingat, unless prefixed to clause of re-entry, useless in the last case; but in the other cases the words there used import a condition of re-entry.

condition. 331 But there is a diversity between these words, *si contingat, &c.*, and the words next aforesaid. For these words, *si contingat, &c.*, are nought worth to such condition, unless it hath these words following, " that it shall be lawful for the feoffor and his heirs to enter," &c. But in the cases aforesaid, it is not necessary by the law to put such clause, that is to say, that the same feoffor and his heirs may enter, &c., because they can do this by force of the words aforesaid, for that they import in themselves in the law a condition, *scil.* that the same feoffor and his heirs may enter, &c,; yet it is commonly used in all such cases aforesaid, to put such clauses in the deeds, *scil.* if the rent be behind, &c., that it shall be lawful to the same feoffor and his heirs to enter, &c. And this is well done, to this intent, to declare and express to laymen who are not learned in the law, the matter and condition of the feoffment*, &c. As if a man seised of land as

To satisfy the ignorant scruples of the unlearned, more clauses are commonly introduced in deeds.

" *heires dentrer," &c., ceo est un fait sur condicion.* 331 *Mes il est diversite perentre cest paroll* si contingat, &c., *et les parolx proscheyn avauntdites. Qar cest paroll* si contingat, &c., *ne vaut riens a tiel condicion, si non que il ad ceux parolx subsequentes, que bien list a lavauntdit feoffour et a ses heires dentrer, &c. Mes en les cases avauntditez, il ne besoigne per la ley de mettre tiel clause, cestassavoir, que mesme cestuy feoffour, et ses heires poient entrer, &c., pur ceo que ils poient faire ceo per force des parolx avauntdites, pur ceo queils empreignent en eux mesmes en la ley une condicion,* scil. *que le mesme cestuy feoffour et ses heires poient entrer, &c., unqore il est communement use en touts tielx cases avauntdites de mettre tielx clauses en les faitz,* scil. *si le rente soit aderere, &c., que bien lirroit a mesme le feoffour et a ses heires dentrer, &c. Et ceo est bon fait, a cel entent, pur declarer et expresser a les laies gentes que ne sount appris de la ley, la matere et la condicion de le feoffement*, &c. Si-*

---

* *Feoffour.—Roh.* and *Pyns.* 1516.

Que ne sount expert de la ley en la mater et de la ley en tiel cas—

of freehold, let the same land to another by deed indented, for term of years, rendering to him certain rent, it is used to put into the deed, that if the rent be behind at the day of payment, either by a week or a month, &c., that then it shall be lawful to the lessor to distrain, &c., yet the lessor may distrain of common right for the rent being in arrear, &c., though such words were never put into the deed, &c.

332 Also, if feoffment be made upon such condition, that if the feoffor pay to the feoffee at a certain day, &c., forty pounds of money, that then the feoffor may re-enter, &c., in this case the feoffee is called tenant in mortgage, which is as much as to say in French, as *mort gage*, and in Latin, *mortuum vadium*. And it seemeth, that the cause wherefore it is called mortgage, is, for that it standeth in doubt whether the feoffor can* pay at the day limited such sum or **Mortgage.**

come home seisi de terre, come de franktenement lessa mesme la terre a un autre per fait endente, pur terme des ans, rendaunt a luy certeyn rente, il est use de mettre en le fait, que si le rente soit aderere al jour de paiement, ou per un semaigne, ou per un moys, &c., que adonques bien lirroit al lessour a distreygner, &c., unqore le lessour poet distreygner de comen droit pur le rent esteaunt arere, &c., coment que tielx parolx ne unques furent myses en le fait, &c.

332 Item, *si feoffement soit fait a ascun home sur tiel condicion, que si le feoffour paia al feoffé a certeyn jour, &c.* xl. *lib. dargent, que adonques le feoffour poet reentrer, &c., en ceo cas le feoffé est appelle tenaunt en morgage, que est autant a dire en Fraunceys come mort gage, et en Latin* Mortuum vadium. *Et il semble, que la cause pur quell il est appelle morgage, est, pur ceo que il estoit en awerouste si le feoffour poyet* payer al jour lymite tiel somme, ou non : et sil*

---

who are not learned in the law in the matter and of the law in such case.—Redm., Berth., Middl., Sm., Powell, and *Tottyl* 1554.

* *Voet—will.—Pyns.* 1516, and all subsequent editions.

See ante, *p.* 277, *in n.*

not: and if he doth not pay, then the land which he puts in pledge upon condition for the payment of the money is gone from him for ever, and so dead as to the tenant, &c.* (*e*).

*ne paia pas, donques la terre queil metta en gage sur condicion de paiement de le money, est ale de luy a toutes jours, et issint mort quant a le tenaunt, &c.**

---

* In all the copies since *Roh.* this passage concludes thus—*et issint* mort a luy sur condition, &c., et sil paya le money, donques est le gaige *mort quaunt a le tenaunt, &c.—and so* dead to him upon condition, &c. And if he doth pay the money, then the pledge is *dead as to the* tenant, *&c. Rastell's* Transl. is in conformity with the text of the three earliest editions.

(*e*) To hold in morgage is to hold for a certain term, upon condition that if the lessor pay so much money at such a day, that he may enter, and if not, that the other shall have a fee-simple or fee-tail or freehold. And in every case where lands or tenements be given to a man for a certain term, upon condition on the part of the lessor, to make the lessee to have more long time or term, if the other do not as the condition is, the landes and tenementes until the day that the condition shoulde be performed, be holden in morgage as in a dead gage.

And note well, that if land be let to a man in morgage in fee-simple, or in fee-taile upon condition that if the first lessor, as is beforesaid, pay so much money at such a day, that he may enter, and if not, that the lessee have the same estate in the lands that the lessor did him graunt at the beginning. And if before the day assigned, the lessee be disseised, he shall have assize of *novel disseisin.* And in case that if the lessee take a wife and die seised before the day assigned, the woman shall be endowed.

And note well, that if the lessor after the death of the lessee, pay not the money at the day assigned, then the woman shall hold her dower and the issue his heritage. And in case the lessor at the day assigned, pay the money to the heir of the lessee, then he may put out the woman and the heir also of all the land first let. And if a man give lands to another in the taile, yielding to him a certain rent by the year, and one enter for default of payment, the donee taketh a wife, and dieth seised, the woman shall be endowed. And in case that after the rent be behind, the

333 Also, as a man can make feoffment in fee in mortgage*, and a lease for term of life, or for term of years in mortgage, all such tenants are called tenants in mortgage according to the estates which they have in the land, &c. *May be either for life or years.*

334 Also, if feoffment be made in mortgage upon condition that the feoffor shall pay such a sum at such a day, &c., as is between them by their deed indented, accorded and limited, although the feoffor dieth before the day of payment, &c., yet if the heir of the feoffor pay the same sum of money at the same day to the feoffee, or shall tender to him the money, and the feoffee refuse to receive it, then can the heir enter into the land, and yet the condition is, that the feoffor do pay such a sum at such a day, &c., not making mention in *Heir of mortgagor may redeem, although not named; secus of a stranger.*

333 Item, *sicome home poet faire feoffement en fee en morgage*, et un lees pur terme de vie, ou pur terme des ans en morgage, toutes tielx tenauntes sount appelles tenauntes en morgage, solonques les estates queils ount en la terre, &c.*

334 Item, *si feoffement soit fait en morgage sur condicion que le feoffour paiera tiel somme a tiel jour, &c., come est parentre eux per lour fait endente accorde et lymite, coment que le feoffour morust devaunt le jour de paiement, &c., unqore si leire de le feoffour paia mesme la somme de money a mesme le jour a le feoffé, ou tendra a luy les deneres, et le feoffé ceo refusa de resceyver, donques poet leire entrer en la terre, et unqore la condicion est, que le feoffour paia tiel somme a tiel jour, &c., nient fesaunt mencion en la condicion*

---

* All the copies since *Roh.* insert at this place as follows, viz.—*issint home poet faire donc en tail en mortgage—so a man may make a gift in tail in mortgage.*

---

donour may enter and put out the woman and the heir also.

And note well, that if lands be let to a man in morgage in fee, upon condition, the lessee doth alien, the lessor shall be charged to pay the money to the alienee, and not to the feoffee as it is saide, &c. [12 *Ass.* 2].—*Olde Tenures*, § 11.

For the heir has interesse de droit *in the condition.*

the condition of any payment to be made by his heir, because that the heir hath interest of right in the condition, &c., and the intent was but that the money should be paid at the day appointed, &c., and the feoffee hath no more loss if he be paid by the heir, than though he were paid by the father, &c. And for this reason if the heir pay the money, at the day appointed, &c., and the other refuse it, he may enter, &c. But if a stranger of his own head, who hath not any interest, &c., will tender the aforesaid money to the feoffee at the day appointed, the feoffee is not bound to receive it.

After tender and refusal, the mortgagee has no remedy at law.

335 And be it remembered that in such case, where such tender of the sum of money is made, &c., and the feoffee refuse to receive it, whereupon the feoffor or his heirs enter, &c., then the aforesaid feoffee hath not any remedy by the common law to have this money, because it shall be rected (*i. e.* accounted) his folly that he should refuse the money, when a lawful tender of it was made unto him.

If a feoffment

336 Also, if a feoffment be made on such condition, that if the

dascun paiement destre fait per son heire, mes pur ceo que leire ad interesse de droit en la condicion, &c., et lentent fuist forsque que les deneres serront paies al jour assesse, &c., et le feoffé nad pluis damage, sil soit paie per leire que sil fuit paie per le pere, &c. Et pur cest cause, si leire paiast les deneres, a le jour assesse, &c., et lautre ceo refusa, il poit entrer, &c. Mes si un estrange de son teste demesne, qui nad ascun interesse, &c., voille tendre les avauntdites deneres al feoffé a le jour assesse, le feoffé nest pas tenus de ceo resceyver.

335 *Et memorandum que en tiel cas, lou tiel tender de la somme de la money est fait, &c., et le feoffé de resceyver ceo refusast, per que le feoffour ou ses heirs entrount, &c., donques lavauntdit feoffé nad ascun remedye daver la somme de money per la comen ley, pur ceo que il serra rette sa folye que il refusast la somme de money quant un loial tender de ceo fuist fait a luy.*

336 Item, *si feoffement soit fait sur tiel condicion, que si le*

feoffee pay to the feoffor at such a day between them limited, twenty pounds, that then the feoffee shall have the land to him and to his heirs; and if he fail (*f*) to pay the money at the day appointed, that then it shall be lawful for the same feoffor or his heirs to enter, &c., and afterwards before the day appointed, the feoffee sell the land to another, and thereof maketh a feoffment to him; in this case, if the second feoffor will tender the sum of money at the day appointed, to the feoffor, and the feoffor refuse it, &c., then hath the second feoffee estate in the land clearly without condition. And the reason is, for that the second feoffee hath interest in the condition for the preservation of the tenancy: and in this case it seems that if the first feoffee after such sale of the land will tender the money at the day appointed, &c., to the

be made upon condition that if the feoffee does not pay the feoffor such a sum at such a day, then the feoffor shall enter there if the feoffee before the day make a feoffment over, and at the day does not pay the sum, the second feoffee at the day may tender the sum, although the agreement reached no further than that the first feoffee should pay it, because he is privy in

feoffé paia al feoffour, a tiel jour entre eux lymite, xx. *lib. que adonques le feoffé avera la terre a luy et a ses heires ; et sil faille de paier les deneres a le jour assesse, que adonques bien list a mesme le feoffour ou a ses heires dentrer, &c., et puis devaunt le jour assesse, le feoffé venda la terre a un autre, et de ceo fait feoffement a luy, en ceo cas si le second feoffé voille tendre la somme de les deneres a le jour assesse a le feoffour, et le feoffour ceo refusa, &c., donques ad le second feoffé estate en la terre clerement sauns condicion. Et la cause est pur ceo que le second feoffé avoit interesse en la condicion pur salvacion de le tenauncie : et en ceo cas il semble que si le premier feoffé apres tiel vender de la terre voille tender la money a le jour assesse, &c. a le feoffour, ceo serra*

(*f*) If a man make a feoffment of lands, to have and to hold to him and to his heirs, upon condition, that if the feoffee pay to the feoffor at such a day twenty pounds, that then the feoffee shall have the lands to him and his heirs : if the condition had not proceeded further it had been void ; for that the feoffee had a fee-simple by the first words ; and therefore the words subsequent are materially added. (And if he fail to pay the money, &c.)—*Co. Lytt.* 207. *b.*

law, and hath an interest in the condition for the salvation of his tenancy.

feoffor, this shall be good enough for the preservation of the estate of the second feoffee, because the first feoffee was privy to the condition, and so the tender of either of them two is good enough, &c.

Heir of mortgagor cannot perform condition, nor can he tender, unless he is mentioned or a day be named for payment; for where no day of payment is appointed, the mortgagor may pay it when he pleases during his life, for he is to have the benefit, scil. his land again.

337 Also, if feoffment be made upon condition, that if the feoffor pay a certain sum of money to the feoffee, then it shall be lawful to the feoffor and to his heirs to enter, &c. In this case if the feoffor die before the payment made, and the heir will tender to the feoffee the money, such tender is void, because the time within which this ought to be done, is past; for when the condition is, that if the feoffor pay the money to the feoffee, this is as much as to say, that if the feoffor during his life pay the money to the feoffee, &c., and when the feoffor dieth, then the time of the tender is past. But otherwise it is where a day of payment is limited, and the feoffor die before the day, then may the heir tender the money, as is aforesaid, for this that the time of the tender had not elapsed by the death of the feoffor. Also it seemeth, in such case

In this case

assetz bon pur salvacion de lestate de le second feoffé, pur ceo que le premier feoffé fuist privë a le condicion, et issint le tender de ascun de eux deux est assetz bon, &c.

337 Item, *si feoffement soit fait sur condicion, que si le feoffour paiast certeyn somme dargent al feoffé, que adonques bien lirroit al feoffour, et a ses heires dentrer, &c., en ceo cas si le feoffour devie devaunt le paiement fait, et leire voet tendre al feoffé les deneres, tiel tender est voide, pur ceo que le temps deins quel ceo doit estre fait est passe; qar quaunt la condicion est, que si le feoffour paia les deneres al feoffé, ceo est tant a dire, que si le feoffour duraunt sa vie paia les deneres al feoffé, &c., et quaunt le feoffour morust, donques le temps de le tender est passe. Mes autrement est lou un jour de paiement est lymite, et le feoffour devie devaunt le jour, donques poet leire tender les deneres, come est avauntdit, pur ceo que le temps de le tender ne fuist passe per la mort del feoffour. Auxi il semble, en tiel cas lou le feoffour*

where the feoffor dieth before the day of payment, if the executors of the feoffor shall tender the money to the feoffee at the day of payment, this tender is good enough; and if the feoffee refuse it, then can the heirs of the feoffor enter, &c. And the reason is, for that the executors represent the person of their testator, &c.

also, if day named, the executors may tender, for executors represent their testator, § 192.

338 And note, that in all cases of condition for payment of a certain sum in gross, touching lands or tenements, if lawful tender be once refused, he that ought to tender the money is of this assoiled (*i. e.* quit) and clearly discharged for ever after.

Refusal of tender of a sum in gross touching lands, discharges the land, for the condition is gone, [*but the debt remains*].

339 Also, if the feoffee in mortgage, before the day of payment which should be made to him, appoint his executors and die, and his heir entereth into the land as he ought, &c. It seemeth in this case, that the feoffor ought to pay the money at the day appointed to the executors, and not to the heir of the feoffee, because the money at the beginning belonged to the feoffee in manner as a duty, and it shall be in-

Mortgagees' executors entitled to the money and not the heir, and tender should be made to them, unless heir be specially named.

devie devaunt le jour de paiement, si les executours de le feoffour tenderont les deneres al feoffé al jour de paiement, cel tender est assetz bon. Et si le feoffé ceo refusa donques les heires del feoffour poient entrer, &c. Et la cause est, pur ceo que les executours representont la persone lour testatour, &c.

338 *Et nota, que en touts les cases de condicion de paiement de certeyn somme en gros, touchaunt terres ou tenementes, si loyal tender soit une foits refuse, celuy qui duissoit tendre la money est de ceo assouth, et nettement discharge pur touts temps apres.*

339 Item, *si le feoffé en morgage, devaunt le jour de paiement que serroit fait a luy, face ses executours et devie, et son heire entra en la terre come il devoit, &c., il semble en ceo cas que le feoffour doit paier le money al jour assesse as executours, et nemy al heire le feoffé, pur ceo que la money al commencement trenchast al feoffé en manere come un duyte, et*

tended that the estate was made by reason of the loan of the money of the feoffee, or by reason of another duty; and therefore the payment shall not be made to the heir, [as it seemeth; but the words of the condition may be such, that the payment shall be made to the heir*], as if the condition were, that if the feoffor pay to the feoffee, or to his heirs, such a sum of money at such a day, &c., there after the death of the feoffee, if he dieth before the day limited, the payment ought to be made to the heir at the day appointed, &c.

As to tender, whether it should be made to the party or on the land.

Lyttleton's opinion (which is always the latter and the best) in this case is, that

340 Also, in such case of feoffment in mortgage, a question hath been asked, in what place is the feoffor bound to tender the money to the feoffee at the day appointed, &c.? And some have said, upon the land so holden in mortgage, because the condition is depending upon the land. And they have said, that if the feoffor be [upon the land there†] ready

serra entendus que lestate fuist fait pur cause de le prompt de la money de le feoffé, ou pur cause dautre duytë; et pur ceo le paiement ne serra fait a leire, [*come il semble. Mes les parols del condicion poyent estre tiels, que le paiement serra fait al heire**], *come si le condicion fuist, que si le feoffour paia al feoffé, ou a ses heires, tiel somme de money a tiel jour, &c., là apres la mort le feoffé, sil moutust devaunt le jour lymite, donques le paiement doit estre fait al heire al jour assesse, &c.*

340 Item, *en tiel cas de feoffement en morgage, question ad este demaundee en quel lieu le feoffour est tenus de tendre les deneres a le feoffé al jour assesse, &c.? Et ascuns ount dit, que sur la terre issint tenus en morgage, pur ceo que le condicion est dependaunt sur la terre. Et ount dit, que si le feoffour* [*sur le terre là*†] *prist a paier lavauntdit money al fe-*

---

* The words within brackets are neither in *Lettou & M.*, *Machl.*, *Roh.*, *Pyns.* 1516, *Redm.* or *Berth.* But they appear in *Rastell's* Transl.

† The words within brackets do not appear in *Lettou & M.*, *Machl.*, or *Roh.*; but they are given in *Redm.* and in *Rastell's* Transl.

to pay the money to the feoffee at the day set, and the feoffee be not there at the day appointed, then the feoffor is assoiled and excused of the payment of the money, for that no default is in him. But it seemeth to others that the law is contrary, and that default is in him; for he is bound to seek the feoffee, if he be then in any other place within the realm of England; as if a man be bound in an obligation of twenty pounds upon condition endorsed upon the same obligation, that if he pay to him to whom the obligation is made at such a day, ten pounds, then the obligation of twenty pounds shall lose its force, and be holden for nought: in this case it behoveth him that made the obligation to seek him to whom the obligation is made, if he be in England, and at the day appointed to tender unto him the said ten pounds, otherwise he shall forfeit the sum of twenty pounds comprised within the obligation. And so it seemeth in the other case, &c. And albeit that some have said that the condition is depending upon the land, yet this proves not that the making of the condition to be performed, ought to be made upon the land,

seeing that the money is a sum in gross, and collateral to the land, the mortgagor must tender to the mortgagee personally, if he be in England; [in cases of debt or obligation, if time *of performance or payment be uncertain, notice must be given of obligor's attendance to perform or pay.—* Co. Lytt. 210, *a. b.;] If no* place *is named for payment, the obligor or debtor must seek the obligee, &c., wheresoever he be within the realm.*

offé a le jour assesse, et le dit feoffé adonques ne soit pas la a le jour assesse, que adonques mesme le feoffour est assouth et excuse de paiement de la dit money, pur ceo que nul defaut est en luy. Mes il semble a ascuns que la ley est contrarie, et que defaut est en luy qar il est tenus de querer le feoffé sil soit adonques en ascun autre lieu deins le roialme dengleterre; come si home soit oblige en un obligacion de xx. *lib. sur condicion endorce sur mesme lobligacion, que sil paiast a celuy a qui lobligacion est fait a tiel jour* x. *lib. que adonques lobligacion de* xx. *lib. perdra sa force, et serra tenus pur null: en ceo cas il covient a celuy qui fist obligacion de querer celuy a qui lobligacion est fait, sil soit deins Engleterre, et al jour assesse de tendre a luy les dits* x. *lib., autrement il forfetera la somme de* xx. *lib. compris deins lobligacion. Et issint il semble en lautre cas, &c. Et coment que ascuns ount dit, que la condicion est dependant sur la terre, unqore ceo ne prove que le fesaunce del condicion destre per-*

&c., no more than if the condition were that the feoffor at such a day shall do some special corporal service to the feoffee, not naming the place where such corporal service shall be done; in this case, the feoffor ought to do such corporal service at the day limited to the feoffee in what place soever of England that the feoffee be, if he willeth to have advantage of the condition, &c., so it seemeth in the other case. And it seems to them, that it shall be more properly said, that the estate of the land is depending upon the condition, than to say that the condition is depending upon the land, &c. *Sed quære, &c.*

Tender of rent must be on the land, [rent at common law being payable there].

341 But if a feoffment in fee be made, reserving to the feoffor a yearly rent, and for default of payment a re-entry, &c., in this case it needeth not for the tenant to tender the rent when it is behind, but upon the land, because this is a rent issuing out of the land, for this is rent-seck. For if the feoffor be once seised of this rent, and afterwards he cometh upon the land, &c., and the rent is denied him, he may have an assise of novel disseisin: for albeit he may enter by reason

§ 217, 233, 325.

Party having

fourme, covient estre fait sur la terre, &c., nient pluis que si condicion fuist que le feoffour ferroit a tiel jour, &c., un especial corporal service al feoffé nient nosmaunt le lieu ou tiel corporal service serra fait; en cel cas le feoffour doit faire tiel corporal service al jour lymite al feoffé en queconques lieu dengleterre que le feoffé est, sil voet aver avauntage de la condicion, &c. Issint semble en lautre cas. Et il semble a eux que il serrait pluis proprement dit, que lestate de la terre est dependant sur la condition, que est a taunt adire, que la condition est dependant sur la terre, &c. Sed quære, &c.

341 *Mes si feoffement en fee soit fait reservaunt al feoffour un annuel rente, et per defaut de paiement un reentre, &c., en ceo cas il ne bosoigne a le tenant a tender le rente, quant il est arere forsque sur la terre, pur ceo que ceo est rent issaunt hors de la terre, qar ceo est rent seck: qar si le feoffour soit seisi un foitz de cest rente, et puis il vient sur la terre, &c., et le rente luy soit denie, il poet aver assise de no. dis.: qar coment queil poet entrer per cause de la condicion*

of the condition broken, &c. Yet he may choose either to relinquish his entry or to have an assise, &c. And so there is a diversity as to the tender of a rent which is issuing out of his land, and of the tender of another sum in gross, which is not issuing out of any land; [342] And therefore it will be a good and sure thing for him that will make such feoffment in mortgage, to appoint an especial place where the money shall be paid, and the more especial that it be put, the better it is for the feoffor. As if A. enfeoff B. to have to him and to his heirs, upon such condition, that if A. pay to B. on the feast of Saint Michael, the archangel next coming, in the cathedral church of Saint Paul's in London, within four hours next before the hour of noon of the same feast, at the rood-loft of the north door within the same church*, or at the tomb of St. Erkenwald, or at the door of such a chapel, or at such a pillar within the same church, that then it shall be

right of entry, may either enter on the land, or bring action against the person.

Place should be appointed in mortgage condition.

Example of such a condition.

enfreynt, &c., unqore il poet ellier, cestassavoir, de relinquiser son entre, ou daver un assise, &c. Et issint est diversite quaunt al tender de le rente que est issaunt hors de sa terre, et del tender dautre somme en gros que nest pas issaunt hors dascun terre; [342] *et pur ceo il serra bon et sure chose pur celuy qui voet faire tiel feoffment en morgage, de mettre un especial lieu lou les deneres serront paies, et le pluis especial que est mys, le meliour est pur le feoffour. Sicome A. enfeoffa B. a aver a luy et a ses heires, sur tiel condicion, que si A. paiast a B. en le feste de Seynt Michell larchangell procheyn advenyr, en lesglise cathedrall de Powels en Loundres, deins quatre heures proschein devant le heure de none de mesme le feste a le rode lofte de le North dore, deins mesme lesglise*, ou al tombe de Seynt Erkenwalde, ou al huys de tiel chappell, ou a tiel piller deins mesme lesglise que adonques*

---

* *Rastell's* Transl. renders the conclusion of this sentence more concisely, omitting all mention of the tomb of *Erkenwald*, *viz. or any other certain place within the same church. Poules, Redm.*, and later copies: *Paules*, editions 1621, 1639, and the copy prefixed to *Co. Lytt.*

Where a certain place is appointed for payment, the one party is not bound to pay, nor the other to accept payment in any other place, for the place is parcel of the condition or covenant.

lawful to the aforesaid A. and his heirs to enter, &c. In this case it needeth not to seek the feoffee in another place, nor to be in any other place, but in the place comprised in the indenture; nor to be there longer than the time specified in the same indenture, for to tender or pay the money to the feoffee, &c. 343 Also, in such case where the place is limited, the feoffee is not bound to receive the payment in any other place but in the same place so limited: but yet if he receive the payment in another place, this is good enough, and as strong for the feoffor, as if the receipt had been in the same place so limited, &c.

Acceptance by mortgagee at another place *[or before the time] is a good performance of the condition, for the value is the substance, and the place but a circumstance.*

So if another thing (though of less value) is accepted in satisfaction.

344 Also, in such case of feoffment in mortgage, if the feoffor pay to the feoffee a horse, or a cup of silver, or a ring of gold, or other thing in full satisfaction of the money, and the other receiveth it, this is good enough, and as strong as if he had received the sum of money, though the horse or the other thing were not of the twentieth part of the value of the sum of money, because that the other hath accepted it in full satisfaction, &c.

bien lyst al avauntdit A. et a ses heires dentrer, &c., en tiel case il ne besoigne de querer le feoffé en autre lieu, ne destre en autre lieu, forsque en lieu compris en lendenture ; ne destre là pluis long temps, que le temps specifie en mesme lendenture, pur tender ou paier la money a le feoffé, &c. 343 Item, *en tiel cas lou le lieu est lymite, le feoffé nest pas oblige de resceyver le paiement en null autre lieu forsque en mesme le lieu issint lymite : mes unqore si il resceust le paiement en autre lieu, ceo est assetz bon et auxi fort pur le feoffour, sicome le receyst ust este en mesme le lieu issint lymite, &c.*

344 Item, *en tiel cas de feoffement en morgage, si le feoffour paia al feoffé un chival, ou un hanap dargent, ou un annule dor, ou autre chose en plein satisfaccion del money, et lautre ceo receust, ceo est assetz bon et auxi fort sicome il ust resceu la somme del money, coment que le chival, ou lautre chose ne fuist de vintisme part del value a la somme de la money, pur ceo que lautre avoit ceo accepte en pleine satisfaccion, &c.*

345 Also, if a man infeoff another in fee upon condition, that he and his heirs shall render to a stranger and to his heirs a yearly rent of twenty shillings, &c., and if he or his heirs fail of payment thereof, that then it shall be lawful to the feoffor and his heirs to enter, this is a good condition; and yet in this case, albeit* such annual payment be called in the indenture, a yearly rent, this is not properly a rent: for if it were rent, it ought to be rent-service, rent-charge, or rent-seck, and it is not any of these; for if the stranger were seised of this, and afterwards it was to him denied, he shall never have an assise of this, because that it is not issuing out of any tenements; and so the stranger hath not any remedy if such yearly rent be behind in this case, but that the feoffor, or his heirs can enter, &c. And yet if the feoffor, or his heirs, enter for default of payment†: then such rent is gone for ever: and so such a rent is but as a penalty set upon the te-

Condition for payment of rent to a stranger, good as a condition, but bad as a reservation, as being made to a stranger; therefore "annual rent" is taken for a sum in gross, and not as a rent issuing out of the land.

† (*For being but a sum in gross, there needs no demand*).

345 Item, *si home enfeoffa un autre sur condicion, que il et ses heires renderont a un estraunge home et a ses heires un annuell rent de* xxs., *&c., et si il ou ses heires faillont del paiement de ceo, que adonques bien lirroit al feoffour et a ses heires dentrer, cest bon condicion, et unqore en ceo cas, coment* que tiel annuell paiement est appelle en lendenture un annuell rente, ceo nest pas proprement rente: qar sil serroit rente, il covient estre rente-service, ou rente-charge, ou rente-sekke, et il nest ascun deux; qar si lestraunge fuist seisi de ceo, et puis il fuit a luy denie, il navera unques assise de ceo, pur ceo que il nest issaunt dascuns tenementes; et issint lestraunge nad ascun remedye si tiel annuell rente soit aderere en ceo cas, mes que le feoffour ou ses heires poient entrer, &c., et unqore si le feoffour ou ses heires entrount pur defaute de paiement, donques tiel rente est ale a toutz jours: et issint tiel rente*

* This word is printed *covient, it behoveth*, in *Lettou & M.*, *Machl.*, and *Roh.*

Conclusion to be drawn is, that words in a condition may be taken out of their proper or literal sense, ut res magis valeat quam pereat.—*Co. Lytt.* 213. *a.*

nant and his heirs, that if they will not pay this according to the form of the indenture, that they shall lose their land by the entry of the feoffor, or his heirs, for default of payment: and it being but a sum in gross, there needeth no demand to be made. And in this case it seemeth that the feoffee, and his heirs ought to seek the stranger, and his heirs, if they be within England, because [there is no place limited where the payment shall be made, and for that*] such rent is not issuing out of any land, &c.

Two rules of law, viz. 1. *Reservation can only be to the grantor and his heirs.*

346 And here note two things, one is, that no rent, that is properly called a rent, can be reserved upon any feoffment, gift, or lease, but only to the feoffor, or to the donor, or to the lessor, or to their heirs (*f*); and in no other manner can

est forsque un peyne assys a le tenaunt et a ses heires, que sils ne voillent paier ceo solonques la fourme del endenture, que ils perderont loür terre per lentre del feoffour ou ses heires pur defaute de paiement, et en ceo cas il semble que le feoffé et ses heires doient querer lestraunge et ses heires sils sont deins Engleterre, pur ceo [que nul lieu est limit lou le paiement serra fait, et pur ceo] que tiel rente nest pas issaunt dascun terre, &c.*

346 Et hic nota *deux choses, un est, que nul rente proprement dit rente, poet estre reserve sur ascun feoffement, done, ou lees, forsque tantsolement al feoffour, ou a le donour, ou a le lessour, ou a lour heires ; et en nul autre manere il poet estre*

* The words within brackets do not appear in *Lettou & M.*, *Machl.*, or *Roh.* They first occur in *Pyns.* 1516.

(*g*) Although *Lyttleton* says that a man cannot reserve rent but to the lessor or to his heirs, yet if a man makes a lease, rendering to his heir, it is void, for if it should be good, then his heir should take it as a purchaser, and a stranger too.—[*Co. Lytt.* 99. *b.*] But *Lyttleton* is not so to be understood, but the disjunctive shall there

it be reserved to any strange person. But if two joint-tenants make a lease by deed indented, reserving to one of them a certain yearly rent, this is good enough to him to whom the rent is reserved, for that he is privy to the lease, and not a stranger to the lease, &c.

Exception by reason of privity.

347 The second thing is, that no entry or re-entry, which is all one, can be reserved or given to any person, except only to the feoffor, or to the donor, or to the lessor, or to their heirs (*g*): and such re-entry* cannot be granted to another

2. And that a stranger cannot enter for condition broken, for none (at law) can enter for

reserve a ascun estraunge person. Mes si deux jointenauntes font un lees per fait endente reservaunt a un deux un certeyne annuell rente, ceo est assetes bon a luy a qui le rente est reserve, pur ceo que il est privë a le lees, et nemy estraunge al lees, &c.

347 *Le second chose est, que nul entre ou re-entre, que est tout un, ne poet estre reserve, ne done a ascun persone forsque tantsolement al feoffour, ou al donour, ou al lessour, ou a lourheires : et tiel reentre* ne poet estre graunt a un autre persone : qar*

---

* In *Lettou & M.*, *Machl.*, and *Roh.*, this word is given *rent.*

---

be taken as a copulative. [See § 141, p. 176, where *or* has the sense of *and.*] For if a man enfeoffs one upon condition to re-enfeoff him or his heirs before Easter, and before Easter the feoffor dies, now the feoffee ought to make the feoffment before request, because the heir is a stranger, for that the condition was in the disjunctive. So the words of *Lyttleton* are not to be understood literally as above, for then they would be contrary to law. But the difference between the principal case and the other is this—the rent is not a condition, nor can it be reserved to the devisor, because the devise does not take effect until after his death, but where the rent is reserved to the heir, it ought to be reserved to the lessor himself, and if it is not, it shall be void.—*Plowd. Quæres,* 107. *Co. Lytt.* 213. *b.*

(*g*) The principle which gave rise to this rule is, that rent is considered as a retribution for the land, and is therefore payable to those who otherwise would have had the land.—*Hargr. in n. Co. Lytt.* 214. *n.*

condition broken, save the feoffor, &c., and his heirs; for entry on condition is but a title to enter.

Grantee may distrain, but cannot enter, for conditions always enure in privity.

person: for if a man let land to another for term of life by indenture, rendering to the lessor and to his heirs a certain rent, and for default of payment, a re-entry, &c., if afterwards the lessor by a deed grant the reversion of the land to another in fee, and the tenant for term of life attorn, &c., if the rent be afterwards in arrear, the grantee of the reversion may distrain for the rent, because that the rent is incident to the reversion (§ 229, 572, 590); but he may not enter into the land and oust the tenant, as the lessor might have done, or his heirs, if the reversion had been continued in them, &c. And in this case the entry is taken away for ever, for the grantee of the reversion cannot enter, *causa qua supra.* And neither the lessor or his heirs can enter; for if the lessor might enter, then he ought to be in as of his former estate, &c.; and this cannot be, because he hath aliened from him the reversion (*h*).

si home lessa terre a un autre pur terme de vie per endenture, rendaunt al lessour, et a ses heires certeyn rente, et pur defaute de paiement un reentre, &c., si apres le lessour per un fait graunta la revercion de la terre a un autre en fee, et le tenaunt a terme de vie attourna, &c., si le rente apres soit aderere, le graunté de la revercion poet distreyner pur le rente, pur ceo que le rente est incident a la revercion; mes il ne poit entrer en la terre, et ouster le tenaunt, sicome le lessour puissoit, ou ses heires, si la revercion ust este continue en eux, &c. Et en ceo cas lentre est tolle a touts temps, qar le graunté de la revercion ne poet entrer, causa qua supra. *Et le lessour, ne ses heires poient entrer; qar si le lessour poet entrer, donques il covient quil serroit a son premier estate, &c.; et ceo ne poet estre, pur ceo que il ad aliene de luy la revercion.*

(*h*) For none shall enter for a condition broken except privies, *i. e.* the feoffor, donor, and lessor, or their heirs, and the preamble of the stat. 32 Hen. 8, c. 34, declares the common law to be so, *scil.* that

348 Also, if there be lord and tenant, and the tenant make such a lease for term of life, rendering to the lessor and to his heirs such annual rent, and for default of payment, a re-entry, &c.; and afterwards the lessor dieth without heir during the life of the tenant for life, whereby the reversion cometh to the lord by way of escheat, and afterwards the rent of the tenant for life, is in arrear, the lord can distrain the tenant for the rent: but he can not enter into the land by force of the condition, &c., because that he is not heir to the feoffor, &c.

Lord in by escheat, may distrain for rent, but cannot enter for breach of condition. The same doctrine applies to a disseisee's entry, § 389.

349 Also, if land be granted to one for term of two years, upon such condition, that if he shall pay to the grantor within the said two years forty marks, that then he shall have the land

Example of a condition precedent. Tenant for years to have fee on

348 Item, *si soit seignour et tenaunt, et le tenaunt fait un tiel lees pur terme de vie, rendaunt al lessour et a ses heires tiel annuell rente, et pur defaute de paiement un reentre, &c.; et apres le lessour morust sauns heire duraunt la vie, le tenaunt a terme de vie, per que la revercion devient al seignour per voye deschete, et puis le rente de le tenaunt a terme de vie, soit aderere, le seignour poet distreyner le tenaunt pur le rente : mes il ne poet entrer en la terre per force del condicion, &c., pur ceo que il nest pas heire al feoffour, &c.*

349 Item, *si terre soit graunte a un pur terme de deux ans sur tiel condicion, que sil paieroit al grauntour deins les dites deux ans* xl. *marcs, que adonques il averoit la terre a luy et*

---

no grantee or assignee of the reversion could take advantage of a re-entry by force of any condition. For at the common law, if a man had made a lease for life reserving a rent, &c., and if the rent be behind a re-entry, and the lessor grant the reversion over, the grantee should take no benefit of the condition for the cause before rehearsed. But by the said statute, the grantee may take advantage thereof, and upon demand of the rent, and non-payment, re-enter. And by this statute all grantees or assignees, &c., and their heirs, executors, successors, and assignees, have the same remedy against the lessees, &c., by entry for non-payment of the rent, for doing of waste, or other forfeiture, &c., as the lessors or grantors themselves have.—*Plowd.* 24. *Co. Lytt.* 215. *a.*

payment of a sum, good, if with livery and before entry, for livery to tenant in possession, bad, § 60.

to him and to his heirs, &c., in this case if the grantee enter by force of the grant, without any livery of seisin made unto him by the grantor, and afterwards he payeth the grantor the forty marks within the two years, yet he hath nothing in the land but for term of two years, because no livery of seisin was made to him at the beginning; for if he should have freehold and fee in this case, because he hath performed the condition, then he should have a freehold by force of the first grant, where no livery of seisin was made thereof, which would be against reason, &c.; but if the grantor had made livery of seisin to the grantee by force of the grant, then should the grantee have the freehold and the fee upon the same condition; [because he is privy to the condition, and therefore he shall take benefit by it.—*Plowd.* 26.]

[*See* § 59. 60, 62, *that a freehold in possession does not pass without livery, except as to those things which do not lie in livery as a rent, &c.*]

Another example of condition precedent, scil. *of a defeasible estate,* scil. *an estate granted* on condition, *is subject to be*

350 Also, if land be granted to a man for term of five years, upon condition, that if he pay to the grantor within the two first years forty marks, that then he shall have fee, or otherwise but for term of the five years, and livery of seisin is made to him by force of the grant, now he hath

a ses heires, &c., en ceo cas si le graunté entra per force de le graunt sans ascun lyverë de seisin fait a luy per le grauntour, et puis il paia al grauntour les xl. *marcs deins les deux ans, unqore il nad riens en la terre forsque pur terme de deux ans, pur ceo que nul lyverë de seisin a luy fuist fait au commencement; qar si il averoit fraunktenement et fee en ceo cas, pur ceo que il ad performe la condicion, donques il averoit fraunktenement per force del premier graunt, lou nul lyverë de seisin de ceo fuist fait, que serroit encountre reason, &c.; mes si le grauntour ust fait lyverë de seisin al graunté per force de le graunt, donques averoit le graunté le fraunktenement et le fee sur mesme la condicion.*

350 Item, *si terre soit graunt a un home pur term de* v. *ans sur condicion, que sil paia al grauntour deins les deux premiers ans,* xl. *marcs, que adonques il averoit fee, ou autrement forsque pur terme de les* v. *ans, et lyverë de seisin est fait a luy per force de le graunt, ore il ad fee-simple condicionel,*

a fee-simple conditional, &c. And if in this case the grantee do not pay to the grantor the forty marks within the first two years, then immediately after the said two years past, the fee and the freehold is, and shall be adjudged, in the grantor; because that the grantor cannot after the said two years forthwith enter upon the grantee, for that the grantee hath yet title for three years to have and occupy the land by force of the same grant. And so because that the condition of the part of the grantee is broken, and the grantor cannot enter, the law shall put the fee and the freehold in the grantor: for if the grantee in this case make waste, then after the breach of the condition, &c., and after the two years, the grantor shall have his writ of waste. And this is good proof then, that the reversion is in him, &c. 351 But in such cases of feoffment upon condition, where the feoffor may lawfully enter for the condition broken, &c., there the feoffor hath not* the freehold before his entry, &c.

devested on non-performance of the condition.

Lyttleton's opinion being, that where livery of seisin is made upon a conveyance the fee passes immediately, and the grantee has fee-simple on condition.

Entry must be made before freehold can vest in feoffor for the condition broken.

352 Also if a feoffment be made upon such condition, that

Performance

&c. Et si en ceo cas le graunté ne paia mye al grauntour les xl. *marcs deins les premiers deux ans, donques immediate apres mesmes les deux ans passes, le fee et le fraunktenement est, et serra ajugge, en le grauntour; pur ceo que le grauntour ne poet apres les dites deux ans meyntenaunt entrer sur le graunté, pur ceo que le graunté ad unqore title pur trois ans daver et occupier la terre per force de mesme le graunt. Et issint pur ceo que la condicion del part le graunté est enfreynt, et le grauntour ne poet entrer, la ley mettera le fee et le fraunktenement en le grauntour: qar si le graunté en cel cas fait wast, donques apres lenfreindre de la condicion, &c., et apres les deux ans, le grauntour avera son brief de wast. Et ceo est bon prove que adonques la revercion est en luy, &c.* 351 *Mes en tielx cases de feoffement sur condicion lou le feoffour poet loyalment entrer pur la condicion enfreynt, &c., là le feoffour nad le franktenement devaunt son entre, &c.*

352 Item, *si feoffement soit fait sur tiel condicion, que le*

---

* In most of the copies of *Rastell's* Translation this word is omitted.

of condition cy pres.

Feoffment upon condition that the feoffee shall make an estate in special tail to the feoffor and to his wife, and to the heirs of their two bodies, there if the husband dies before the estate made, it shall be made so near (cy pres) *the condition as may be*, i. e. *he shall make an*

the feoffee shall give the land to the feoffor, and to the wife of the feoffor, to have and to hold to them and to the heirs of their two bodies engendered, and for default of such issue, the remainder to the right heirs of the feoffor: in this case if the husband die, living the wife, before any estate in tail made to them, [&c.*] (*i*), then ought the feoffee by the law to make estate to the wife so near the condition, and also so near† to the intent of the condition as he can make it; *scil.* to let the land to the wife for term of life without impeachment of waste, the remainder after her‡ decease, to the heirs of the body of her husband and her§ begotten, and for default

feoffé donera la terre al feoffour, et a la feme del feoffour, a aver et tener a eux, et a les heires de lour deux corps engendres, et pur defaut de tiel issue, le remeyndre as droit heires le feoffour : en ceo cas si le baron devie vivaunt la feme devant ascun estateen le taille fait a eux, [*&c.**], *donques doit le feoffé per la ley faire estate a la feme si apres† la condicion, et auxi apres† lentent de la condicion que il poet faire ;* scil. *de lesser la terre al feme pur terme de vie sans empeschement de wast, le remeyndre apres son‡ decesse, a les heires de les corps de son baron et§ luy engendres, et pur de-*

* This *&c.* between the brackets is not in *Lettou & M.*, *Machl.*, and *Roh.*, *Redm.*, and *Berth.*

† These words are read *cy pres* in all the editions subsequent to *Roh.*, except in *Pyns.* 1516, who reads *apres*, *after*, but in the copy of that edition which is deposited in the *Brit. Museum*, as also in that copy of *Roh. penes ed.*, the word *apres* is altered by a contemporary hand to *sipres*, and doubtless it was originally so written.

‡ These words *apres* son *decease*, are rendered by *Sir Edward Coke*, *after* his *decease*, which is erroneous and also is contrary to *Rastell's* Translation, *son* evidently relating to the last antecedent.

§ The later and corrupted copies give this passage, *a les heires de corps sa baron* de *luy engendres*, *to the heirs of the body of her husband on her begotten*, the word *et* being omitted. *Rastell's* Transl. more correctly renders the words of this passage, *to the heirs engendered*

(*i*) Here the *&c.* implieth according to the condition with the remainder over.—*Co. Lytt.* 219. *a.*

of such issue the remainder to the right heirs of the husband. And the reason why the lease shall be in this case to the wife alone without impeachment of waste, is, because the condition is, that the estate should be made to the husband and to his wife in the tail: and if such estate had been made in the life of the husband, then after the death of the husband she should have had sole estate in the tail; which estate is without impeachment of waste. And therefore it is reason, that if afterwards* a man can make estate to the intent of the condition, &c., that he shall make it, albeit she cannot have estate in tail, as she might have had if the gift in tail had been made to her husband and her in the lifetime of her husband (*k*).

estate to the wife for life sans waste, remainder to the issue in tail, and if no issue remainder to the right heirs, of the husband.—2 H. 4, 5. 1 Vent. 381.

faut de tiel issue, le remeyndre as droit heires le baron. Et la cause pur que la lees serra en ceo cas a la feme sole sans empeschement de wast, est, pur ceo que la condicion est, que lestate serroit fait a le baron et a sa feme en le taille : et si tiel estate ust este fait en le vie le baron, donques apres la mort le baron el ad ewe estate sole en le taille; quel estate est sauns empeschement de wast. Et issint il est reason, que si apres* que home poet faire estate a lentent de la condicion, &c., que il ferroit, &c., coment quele ne poet aver estate en taille sicome ele puissoit aver si le done en le taille ust este fait a son baron et luy en la vie son baron.

---

of the body of her husband and hers. This misreading of the common copies has been frequently noticed, *vide infra*, (*k*).

* As *sipres* has been corrupted to *si apres* in the three earliest editions, so these words *si apres*, *if afterwards*, have in the later copies been corrupted to *cy pres*, *so near as*.

(*k*) See 2 *Bl. Rep.* 728, (*Frogmorton*, dem. *Robinson* v. *Wharrey*), which was a special case on which *Wilmot*, C. J., delivered his own as well as the opinion of *Bathurst*, *Gould*, and *Blackstone*, Js. thereby ruling that an estate made by A. to B. (whom A. intends to marry) and the heirs of their two bodies begotten, is not an estate tail; but is an estate for life to B., with a contingent remainder to the issue. The words of that judgment which refer particularly to this case of Lyttleton, are as follows, viz.:—

If husband and wife die before the day and before the gift is made, leaving issue,

353 Also, in this case if the husband and the wife have issue, and die before the gift in the tail made to them, &c., then ought the feoffee to make estate to the issue, and to the

353 Item, *en ceo cas si le baron et la feme ount issue, et devieront devaunt le done en le taille fait a eux, &c., donques le feoffé doit faire estate al issue, et a les heires de corps son*

" For no estate tail can be made to one only, and the heirs of the body of that person and another. This appears from *Lytt.* § 352, according to the true reading collected from the original editions. The common editions made the estate *cy pres*, therein mentioned to be, to the widow and " *les heirs de corps sa baron* de *luy engendres*," which is not so near as might be to the original estate intended, if the husband had lived, *viz.* to the husband and wife, and the heirs of their two bodies. But the original edition by *Lettou* and *Machlinia*, in *Lyttleton's* lifetime, and the *Roan* edition which is the next (both which my brother *Blackstone* has) read it thus, " *Les heirs de les corps de son baron* et *luy engendres*," which is quite consonant to the original estate. And this estate to the widow for life, and the heirs of the body of her husband and herself begotten, *Lyttleton* in the same section declares not be an estate tail.

The same is held in *Dyer*, 1 *Ma.* 99; in *Lane* v. *Pannel*, 1 *Roll. Rep.* 438; and in *Gossage* v. *Taylor*, *Styles*, 325., which from a MS. of *Lord Hale* in possession of my brother *Bathurst*, appears to have been first determined in *Hil.* 1651, which accounts for some expressions of Chief Justice *Rolle* in *Styles's case*, which was *Pasch.* 1652. There it was expressly held that this was a contingent remainder to the heirs of both their bodies.'—*Co. Lytt.* 219. *a. n.*

This case of *Lyttleton* is also referred to in the former part of the same report of *Lane* v. *Pannel*, for *Davenport*, Serjeant, *arguendo*, is there reported as saying, ' *Jeo aie un auntient Lyttleton imprimee* 33 *Hen.* 6, *per Lettou;* " to which *Sir Edward Coke* replies, " *Jeo aie le primer impression que fuit in temps E.* 4;' and *Davenport* in continuing his argument, says, " there the case of *Lyttleton* of the performance of the condition is, that the estate shall be made to the wife for life without impeachment of waste, the remainder to the heirs of the body of the husband and wife, so that by this it appears that this remainder is not executed, but continueth in contingency. *Coke;* This case of *Lyttleton* is grounded upon 2 *Hen.* 4, for there the case is according to *Lyttleton.*'—1 *Roll. Rep.* 317.

The opinion of *Fenner*, J., in *Chudleigh's case*, 1 *Rep.* 137, supplies *et.* The reader is also referred to *Plowd.* 7, (*n*). *Id.* 291. (*b*).

heirs of the body of his father and mother begotten, and for default of such issue, the remainder to the right heirs of the husband, &c. And the same law is in other like cases: and if such feoffee will not make such estate, &c., when he is reasonably required by them that ought to have estate by force of the condition, &c., then can the feoffor or his heirs enter, &c.

then if feoffee make a gift to the issue and to the heirs of his father and mother begotten, the condition is performed.

354 Also, if a feoffment be made upon condition, that [if*] the feoffee shall enfeoff† many men, to have and to hold to them and to their heirs for ever, and all they that ought to have estate die before any estate made to them, then ought the feoffee to make the estate to the heir of him that surviveth of them, to have and to hold to him and to the heirs of him that surviveth, &c. (*l*).

The same doctrine exemplified as in the two preceding cases, viz. that the performance of the condition may be to the intent, although condition be not literally performed.

pere et son mere engendres, et pur defaut de tiel issue, le remeyndre a les droit heires le baron, &c. Et mesme la ley est en autres cases semblables : et si tiel feoffé ne voet faire tiel estate, &c., quant il est resonablement requis per eux qui devoient aver estate per la condicion, &c., donques poet le feoffour ou ses heires entrer, &c.

354 Item, *si feoffement soit fait sur condicion que [si*] le feoffé enfeoffera† plusours homes a aver et tener a eux et a lour heires a toutz jours, et toutz ceux qui devoient aver estate murreront devaunt ascun estate fait a eux, donques doit le feoffé faire estate al heire celuy qui survesquist de eux, aver et tener a luy et a les heires celuy qui survesquist, &c.* (*l*).

---

* This word within brackets, *si*, *if*, as here placed is unintelligible, it certainly should be rejected, although it has the authority of the three oldest editions ; *Pyns.* 1516, *Redm.* and all subsequent editions, including *Rastell's* Transl., read this passage without *if*, but *Sir Edward Coke*, from his adherence to the text of *Roh.* has retained this word in his *Transl.*

† This word in the copies prefixed to *Co. Lytt.* is printed *re-enfeoffera*, *shall re-enfeoff*; and *Sir Edward Coke* in his comment ascribes a pecu-

---

(*l*) Hereupon questions have been made, wherefore the *habendum* is not to the heirs of the heir, and for what reason it is by *Lyttleton* limited to the heirs of the survivor? And the cause is, for that

Condition broken by a disability to perform: which may exist either by act of the party or by act of law.

355 Also, if a feoffment be made upon condition, to enfeoff another, or to make a gift in tail to another, &c., if the feoffee before the performance of the condition enfeoff a stranger, or make a lease for term of life, then may the feoffor and his heirs enter, &c., because he hath disabled himself to perform the condition, insomuch as he made estate to another, &c.: 356 In the same manner it is, if the feoffee before the condition performed letteth the same land to a stranger for term of years; in this case the feoffor and his

Condition broken by a disability to perform, i. e. make an estate in the same

355 Item, *si feoffement soit fait sur condicion, de enfeoffer un autre, ou doner en le taille a un autre, &c., si le feoffé devaunt le performer de la condicion enfeoffa un estraunge persone, ou fist un lees pur terme de vie, donques poet le feoffour et ses heires entrer, &c., pur ceo que il ad luy mesme disable de performer la condicion, entaunt quil fist estate a autre, &c.:* 356 *En mesme le manere est, si le feoffé devaunt la condicion performe lessa mesme la terre a un estraunge pur terme des ans; en ceo cas le feoffour et ses*

---

liar significance to this word *re-enfeoff. Rastell's* Translation, as well as the later French editions, follow the three earliest printed copies. The only edition the editor has seen or can find with this reading, is the ed. 1671, which gives *re-enfeoff* as well in the French as in the English.

---

if it were made to the heirs of the heir, then some persons by possibility would be inheritable to the land who would not have inherited if the estate had been made to the survivor and his heirs, and consequently the condition broken.

For example; if the survivor took to wife Alice Fairefield, in this case if the limitation were to the son and his heirs, then if the son should die without heirs of his father, the blood of the Fairefields (being the blood of his mother) would inherit. But if the limitation be to the right heirs of the father, then should not the blood of the Fairefields by any possibility inherit; for then it is as if the estate had been made to the survivor and his heirs: and therefore these words *et a les heires celuy que survesquist* which many have thought superfluous, are very material. Note well this kind of fee-simple, for it is worthy the observation: but sufficient has been said to open the meaning of *Lyttleton,* and therefore I will dive no deeper into this point, but leave it to the further consideration of the learned reader.—*Co. Lytt.* 220. *b.*

heirs can enter, &c., because the feoffee hath disabled himself to make estate of the tenements according to that which was in the tenements when the estate thereof was made unto him; for if he will make an estate of the tenements according to the conditions, &c., then may the feoffee for term of years enter and oust him to whom the estate is made, &c., and occupy this during his term, &c. 357 And many have said, that if such feoffment be made to a single man upon the same condition, and before that he hath performed the same condition, he taketh wife, then the feoffor and his heirs forthwith may enter, because if he hath made an estate according to the condition, and afterwards dieth, then the wife shall be endowed, and can recover her dower by a writ of dower, &c., and so by the taking of a wife, the tenements be put in other plight (*m*) than they were at the time of the

plight, which is a disability by act in præsenti.

Example of a disability to perform condition both by act in law, and in futuro.

heires poient entrer, &c., pur ceo que le feoffé ad luy disable de faire estate de les tenementes accordant a ceo que estoit en les tenements, quant estate ent fuist fait a luy; qar sil voet faire estate de les tenementes accordant a les condicions, &c., donques poet le feoffé pur terme des ans entrer et ouster mesme celuy a qui lestate est fait, &c., et occupier ceo duraunt son terme, &c. 357 Et plusours ount dit, que si tiel feoffement soit fait a un home sole sur mesme la condicion, et devaunt que il ad perfourme mesme la condicion, il prent feme, donques que le feoffour et ses heires meyntenant poient entrer, pur ceo que sil fesoit estate accordant a la condicion, et puis mourust, donques sa feme serra endowe, et poet recoverer son dower per brief de dower, &c., et issint per le presell del feme les tenementes sont mys en un autre plite que ne furent a

(*m*) *Plight* is an old English word, and here signifieth not only the estate, but the habit and quality of the land, and extendeth to rent-charges, and to a possibility of dower. *Vide* § 289, where plight is taken for an estate or interest of and in the land itself, and extendeth not to a rent-charge out of the land.—*Co. Lytt.* 221. *b.*

feoffment upon condition, because at that time no such woman was dowable, nor should be endowed by the law, &c. 358 In the same manner it is if the feoffee charge the land by his deed with a rent-charge before the performing of the condition, or be bound in a statute-staple or statute-merchant; that in such cases the feoffor and his heirs may enter, &c. *Causa qua supra:* for whosoever cometh to the tenements by the feoffment of the feoffee, then the tenements must be liable, and be put in execution by force of the statute-merchant, or of the statute-staple, &c.* But when the feoffor or his heirs, for the causes aforesaid, have entered, as it seems they ought, &c., then all such things that before such entry might trouble or incumber the land so given upon condition, &c., so far as concerns the same tenements, are utterly defeated.

The former doctrine of a disability in presenti *to perform condition, continued and illustrated by another example.*

Livery of sei-

359 Also, if a man make a deed of feoffment to another,

temps del feoffement sur condicion, pur ceo que adonques nul tiel feme fuist dowable, ne serroit dowe per la ley, &c. 358 *En mesme le manere est si le feoffé charge la terre per son fait dun rente-charge devaunt le perfourmer del condicion, ou soit oblige en un estatute del staple ou de statute marchaunt; que en tielx cases le feoffour et ses heires poient entrer, &c.* Causa qua supra: *qar quiconques que venust a les tenementes per le feoffement de le feoffé, donques les tenementes covient estre lyables, et estre mys en execucion per force destatute marchaunt, ou destatute del staple, &c.* Mes quant le feoffour ou ses heires, pur les causes avauntdits, avont entre, come ils devont come il semble, &c., donques toutz tielx choses que devaunt tiel entre puissont troubler ou encombrer les tenementes issint dones sur condicion, &c., quant a mesmes les tenementes, sont oustrement defetes.*

359 Item, *si un home fist un fait de feoffement a un autre,*

* At this place, a *quære* is interpolated in all the French copies after *Pyns.* 1516. It does not however occur in any copy of *Rastell's* Translation.

and in the deed is no condition, &c., and when the feoffor will make to him livery of seisin by force of the same deed, he makes livery of seisin unto him upon certain condition, &c.; in this case nothing of the tenements* passeth by the deed, for this that the condition is not comprised within the deed, and the feoffment is of such force as if no such deed had been made.

sin upon condition made in pursuance of a feoffment, wherein there is no condition, bad [at common law, before Statute of Frauds, 29 Car. 2, c. 3].

360 Also, if a feoffment be made upon such condition, that the feoffee do not alien the land to any one, this condition is void; because when a man is enfeoffed of lands or tenements, he hath power to alien them to any person by the law: for if such condition should be good, then the condition should oust him of all the power which the law gives him, which should be against reason; and for this such condition is void (*n*). 361 But if the condition be such, that the feoffee

Condition against alienation void; for it is a repugnant condition; but

Condition not

et en le fait est null condicion, &c., et quant le feoffour a luy voille faire lyverë de seisin per force de mesme le fait, il fist le lyverë de seisin sur certeyn condicion, &c.; en ceo cas riens de les tenementes passa per le fait, pur ceo que la condicion nest compris deins le fait, et le feoffement est en tiel force sicome nul tiel fait ust este fait.*

360 Item, *si feoffement soit fait sur tiel condicion, que le feoffé ne aliena la terre a nulluy, ceo condicion est voide; pur ceo que quaunt home est enfeoffe de terres ou tenementes, il ad poiar de eux aliener a ascun person per la ley: qar si tiel condicion serroit bon, donques la condicion luy osteroit de tout le poiar que la ley luy dona, quel serroit encontre reason; et pur ceo tiel condicion est voyde.* 361 *Mes si la condicion soit*

* For *de les tenementes* which is the true reading, *Lettou & M.*, *Machl.*, and *Roh.*, give *la condicion.*

(*n*) Before the statute of *Quia Emptores*, the feoffor might have enfeoffed upon condition that the feoffee should not alien, because he had a possibility of *reverter*, and this is a consequence of privity of

to alien to a particular person, good.

do not alien to such a one, naming his name, or to any of his heirs, or of the issues of such a one, &c., or the like, the which conditions do not take away all the power of alienation of the feoffee, &c., then such condition is good.

Condition that tenant in tail shall not alien except for his own life, good; [for he may be restrained by condition against alienation].

Reason because his alienation is a discontinuance.

Alienation beyond tenant's life, a discon-

362 Also, if tenements be given in the tail, upon such condition, that neither the tenant in the tail or his heirs, &c., shall alien in fee, or in tail, or for term of another's life, but only for their own lives, &c., such condition is good. And the reason is, for this when he maketh such alienation and discontinuance of the tail, he doeth contrary to the intent [of the donor*], for which the statute of Westm. second was made, by which statute estates in the tail are ordained; 363 for it is proved by the words comprised in the same statute, that the intent of the making the same statute was,

tiel, que le feoffé ne aliena a un tiel, nosmant son noun, ou a ascun de ses heires, ou des issues dun tiel, &c., ou hujusmodi, *les queux condicions ne tollont tout la poiar dalienacion del feoffé, &c., donques tiel condicion est bon.*

362 Item, *si tenementes soient dones en le taille, sur tiel condicion, que le tenaunt en le taille ne ses heires, &c., ne alieneront en fee, ou en le taille, ne pur terme dautre vie, forsque pur lour vies demesne, &c., tiel condicion est bon. Et la cause est, pur ceo que quant il fist tiel alienacion et discontinuance de le taille, il fait le contrarie a lentent [le donour*], pur que lestatute de Westm. seconde fuist fait, per quel estatut les estates en le taille sont ordeignes;* 363 *qar il est prove per les parolx compris en mesme lestatut, que fuist al entent*

---

* The words within brackets do not appear in any copies of *Rastell's* Transl.

---

tenure, for the king may grant upon such a condition, because of the tenure to himself, there being a possibility of *reverter* in him as lord paramount.

that the will of the donor in such case should be observed, and when the tenant in the tail maketh such discontinuance, he acts contrary thereto, &c. And also in estates in the tail of any tenements, when the reversion of the fee-simple [or remainder in fee-simple*] is in other person, when such discontinuance is made, then the fee-simple in the reversion or the fee-simple in the remainder is discontinued. And because tenant in tail shall do no such thing against the profit [of his issues†] and good right, such condition is good, as is aforesaid.

tinuance of remainder, and bad, consequently restrainable by condition.

de le fesaunce de mesme lestatut, que la volunte del donour en tiel case serroit observe, et quaunt le tenaunt en le taille fait une discontinuaunce, il fait le contrarie a ceo, &c. Et auxi en les estates en le taille dascuns tenementes, quant la revercion de fee-simple [ou remeyndre en fee-simple] est en autre person, quant tiel discontinuance est fait, donques le fee-simple en la revercion ou le fee-simple en le remeyndre est discontinue. Et pur ceo que tenaunt en le taille ne ferra tiel chose encontre profit [de ses issues†] et bon droit, tiel condicion est bon, come est avauntdit.*

---

* The words within brackets, which are in the later and common copies, do not occur in *Lettou & M.*, *Machl.*, *Roh.*, or *Rastell's* Transl. but *Redm.*, *Berth.*, *Middl.*, *Powel*, *Sm.*, and *Tottyl* 1554, read this passage thus :—*Et auxi en les estates en le tayle dascun tenementes, la revercion* est en le donour, sinon que il done le rem' oustre, ou puis le doné graunt la revercion a un autre, &c. *Et quant tiel discontinuance est fait, donques le fee-simple* del donour ou de cesty *en la revercion ou en le rem' est discontinue. And also in estates in the tail of any tenements, the reversion* is in the donor, unless that he give the remainder over, or afterwards the donee grant the reversion to another, &c. *And when such discontinuance is made, then the fee-simple* of the donor, or of him *in the reversion or in the remainder is discontinued.*

† This passage, excluding the words within brackets, is according to the three earliest editions, with the exception, that in *Lettou & M.*, *Machl.*, and *Roh.*, for *et pur ceo*, is printed *et pur* oustre, which same error must have appeared in the copy from which *Rastell* made his

Condition to re-enter on discontinuance of tail and *death of issue, good.*

364 Also, a man can give lands in the tail upon such condition, that if the tenant in the tail or his heirs alien in fee or in tail, or for term of another's life, &c., and also that if all the issue coming of the tenant in tail be dead without issue, that then it shall be lawful for the donor and for his heirs to enter, &c. And by such way the right of the tail may be saved after discontinuance to the issue in the tail, if any issue there be: so that by way of entry of the donor or of his heirs, the tail shall not be defeated by such condition*: and yet if the tenant in tail in this case, or his heirs, make any discontinuance, &c., he in the reversion or his heirs, after this that the tail is determined for default of issue, can enter into the land by force of the same condition, and shall not be compelled to sue a writ of formedon in the reversion, &c.

[*This case is not much unlike to* § 350.—Anon. Commentator on Lytt.]

364 Item, *home poet doner terres en le taille sur tiel condicion, que si le tenaunt en le taille ou ses heires alienount en fee ou en le taille, ou pur terme dautre vie, &c., et auxi que si tout lissue venant de le tenaunt en le taille soient mortz sauns issue, que adonques bien lirroit al donour et a ses heires dentrer, &c. Et per tiel voye le droit en le taille poet estre salve apres tiel discontinuaunce al issue en le taille, si ascun issue y soit : issint que per voye dentrer del donour, ou de ses heires, le taille ne serra mye defete per tiel condicion* : et unqore si le tenaunt en le taille en ceo cas, ou ses heires font ascun discontinuaunce, &c., celuy en la revercion ou ses heires, apres ceo que le taille est determine, pur defaut dissue, poient entrer en la terre per force de mesme la condicion, et ne serra my arte de suer brief de formedon en la revercion, &c.*

Transl., for his reading is, *And for* to put out (*oustre*) *that the tenant shall doe no such thing against right, such conditions are good as it is aforesaid.* In the copy of *Roh.* edition *penes ed., oustre* is altered to *ceo* by a contemporary hand, and a similar error in that copy of *Pyns.* 1516, which is in the *Brit. Museum*, is altered in the same manner.

* A *quære hoc*, which first appeared in *Redm.*, occurs at this place in all subsequent editions except *Tottyl* 1557 (both editions) and the copies of *Rastell's* Translation.

365 Also, a man cannot plead in any action, that estate was made in fee, or in the tail, or for term of life upon condition, unless he vouch a record thereof, or shew a writing under seal, proving the same condition; for it is a common learning, that a man by pleading shall not defeat any estate of freehold by force of any such condition, unless he shew the proof of the condition in writing, &c., except it be in some especial case, &c.† But of chattels real, as of a lease for years, or of grants of wards made by guardians in chivalry, and such like, &c., a man may plead that such leases or grants were made upon condition, &c., without shewing any writing of the condition. So in the same manner a man may do of gifts and grants of chattels personal, and of contracts personal, &c.

Condition annexed to a freehold and inheritance, shall not be pleaded unless it be by deed; for in pleading a condition to defeat an estate of freehold, the party must make profert *of the deed under seal:* [*and this holds good in personal actions as well as in real*].

† Co. Lytt. 225. b.; 226. a.

366 Also, albeit a man in some action cannot plead a condition that toucheth and concerneth freehold without shewing a writing thereof, as is aforesaid, yet a man may be aided upon such a condition by the verdict of twelve men taken at large

But a condition annexed to a lease for years or other chattel real, may be pleaded, though the

365 Item, *home ne poet pleder en ascun accion, que estate fuist fait en fee, ou en le taille, ou pur terme de vie sur condicion, que sil ne voucha un recorde de ceo, ou monstrera un escripte south seale, provant mesme la condicion; qar il est un comen erudicion, que home per pleder ne defetera ascun estate de franktenement per force dascun tiel condicion, sinon quil monstera la prove de la condicion en escripte, &c., sinon que ceo soit en ascun especial cas, &c. Mes de chatel real, sicome de lees fait a terme dans, ou de grauntes de gardes faits per gardeins en chivalrie et hujusmodi, &c., home poet pleder que tielx lesses ou grauntes fueront faites sur condicion, &c., sans monstrer ascun escripte de la condicion. Issint en mesme le manere home poet faire de dones et grauntz de chatelx personelx et de contractes personelx, &c.*

366 Item, *coment que home en ascun accion ne poet pleder un condicion que toucha et concerna franktenement sauns monstrer escripte de ceo, come est avauntdit, unqore home poet estre eide sur tiel condicion per verdit de* xii. *homes pris*

lease or grant were made without deed, and the jury upon a general issue pleaded in any cause of freehold, may find the condition, which verdict at large, i. e. special verdict, *shall aid the defendant; [for in real or personal actions, the jury may give a special verdict, finding the matter at large, pertinent to the point in issue.*—Plowd. 92].

in an assise of novel disseisin, or in some other action where the justices will take the verdict of twelve jurors at large. As put the case, that a man seised of certain land in fee, letteth the same land to another man for term of life without deed, upon condition to render to the lessor a certain rent, and for default of payment, a re-entry, &c., by force whereof the lessee is seised, as of freehold, and afterwards the rent is behind, by which the lessor entereth into the land, and afterwards the lessee arraign an assise of novel disseisin of the land against the lessor, who pleads that he did no wrong nor no disseisin, and upon this the assise is taken: in this case the recognitors of the assise may say and render to the justices their verdict at large upon the whole matter, as to say that the defendant was seised of the land in his demesne as of fee, and being so seised let the same land to the plaintiff for term of his life, rendering to the lessor such yearly rent payable at such a feast, &c., upon such condition, that if the rent were behind at any such feast that it ought to be paid, then

a large en assise de novel disseisin, ou en ascune autre accion, lou les justices voillent prendre per verdit de xii. *jurrors a large. Sicome mettomus, que home seisi de certeyn terre en fee, lessa mesme la terre a un autre home pur terme de vie sauns fait, sur condicion de rendre al lessour un certeyn rente, et pur defaut de paiement, un reentre, &c., per force de quel le lessé est seisi, come de franktenement, et puis le rent est aderere, per que le lessour entre en la terre, et puis le lessé arraigne un assise de novel disseisin de la terre envers le lessour, le quel plede quil ne fist nul tort ne nul disseisin, et sur ceo lassise soit pris: en ceo cas les recognitours del assise poient dire et rendre a les justices lour verdit a large sur tout le matere, come adire que le defendant fuist seisi de la terre en son demesne come de fee, et issint seisi mesme la terre lessast al pleintif pur terme de sa vie, rendant al lessour tiel annuel rent paiable a tiel feste, &c., sur tiel condicion, que si le rente fuist aderere a ascun tiel feste que doit estre paie,*

it should be lawful for the lessor to enter, &c., by force of which lease the plaintiff was seised in his demesne as of freehold, and that afterwards the rent was behind at such feast or year, &c.; for which the lessor entered into the land upon the possession of the lessee; and pray the discretion of the justices, whether this be a disseisin done to the plaintiff or not; and then for this that it appeareth to the justices that this was no disseisin done to the plaintiff, insomuch as the entry of the lessor was lawful on him; the justices ought to give judgment that the plaintiff shall take nothing by his writ of assise: and so in such case the lessor shall be aided, and yet no writing was ever made of the condition; for as well as the jurors may have knowledge [of the lease, they also as well may have conusance*] of the condition which was

donques bien lirroit al lessour dentrer, &c., per force de quel lees le pleintif fuist seisi en son demesne come de franktenement, et que puis apres le rente fuist aderere a tiel feste ou an, &c.; pur que le lessour entra en la terre sur la possession le lessé; et prier la discrecion de les justices, si ceo soit un disseisin fait al pleintif ou nemy; et donques pur ceo que appiert a les justices que ceo fuist nul disseisin fait al pleintif, entaunt que lentre de le lessour fuist congeable sur luy; les justices doient doner juggement que le pleintif ne prendera riens per son brief dassise: et issint en tiel cas le lessour serra eide, et unqore nul escripture ne unques fuist fait del condicion; qar auxi bien que les jurrors poient aver conusaunce [de le lees, auxi bien ils poient aver conusaunce] de la condicion*

* The words within brackets do not appear in *Lettou & M.*, *Machl.*, *Roh.*, or in any of the copies of *Rastell's* Transl. *Redm.*, *Berth.*, *Middl.*, *Sm.*, *Powel*, and *Tottyl* 1554, omit the words *auxi bien que*, and read this sentence as follows:—*car les jurrours poient en ceo cas aver conusaunce de la condition que fuist declare et reherce sur le lees. For the jurors can in this case have conusance, &c.* It is suggested that if this paragraph be read, omitting the words within brackets, then § 367 will appear to be an illustration by antithesis.

So of a feoffment or gift in tail upon condition.

A general verdict may be given in real as well as in personal actions.

declared and rehearsed upon the lease; 367 so in the same manner is it of feoffment in fee, or gift in the tail upon condition, although no writing were ever made thereof, &c. And as it is said of a verdict at large in assise, &c., in the same manner it is of a writ of entry founded upon disseisin, and in all other actions where the justices will take the verdict at large (*o*), whereby such verdict at large maketh the nature of the matter put in the issue*.

que fuist declare et reherce sur le lees ; 367 *en mesme le manere est de feoffement en fee, ou done en le taille sur condicion, coment que nul escripture unques fuist fait de ceo, &c. Et sicome est dit de verdit a large en assise, &c., en mesme le manere est en brief dentre fondu sur disseisin, et en toutes autres accions ou les justices voillent prendre le verdit a large, par la ou tiel verdit a large fait la nature de matere mis en lissue**.

---

* All editions after the three first read this passage thus :—*et en toutes autres accions ou les justices doient prendre le verdit a large, par la ou tiel verdit a large est fait*, la maner del entre entier *est mys en issue*, [or, *lissue*], &c., which is thus translated by *Sir Edward Coke*, "*and in all other actions where the justices will take the verdict at large, there where such verdict at large is made, the* manner of the whole entry *is put in the issue, &c.*" *Rastell's* Transl. renders the passage thus :—*and in all other actions where the justices will take a verdict at large, there where the verdict at large maketh the nature of the matter put in the issue.* The ordinary reading is *evidently* adopted by *Booth on Real Actions, infra, n.*

(*o*) It is called a verdict at large, because it findeth the matter at large, and leaves it to the judgment of the court: or it is called a special verdict, because it findeth the special matter, &c.—*Co. Lytt.* 228. *a.* To take the assise at large, is to take a special verdict of the recognitors of the assise, finding not only the seisin but the special manner of the entry, and so leaving it to the judgment of the court, whether there be any disseisin or not. The peculiarities here alluded to, with respect to an assise, (for, as *Lyttleton* informs

368 Also, in such case where the inquest may say their verdict at large, if they will take upon them the knowledge of the law upon the matter, they may say their verdict generally as it is put in their charge, as in the case aforesaid they may well say, that the lessor did not disseise the lessee, if they will, &c. (*p*).

As well as in such cases where the jury will take upon themselves the knowledge of the law.

369 Also, in the same case, if the case were such, that after the lessor had entered for default of payment, &c., that the lessee had entered upon the lessor, and him disseised: in this case, if the lessor arraign an assise against the lessee, the lessee may bar him of the assise; for he may plead against him in bar, how the lessor that is plaintiff, made a lease to the defendant for term of his life, saving the reversion to the plaintiff, which is a good plea in bar, insomuch as

But if lessee re-enter, and in bar to an action by lessor, pleads the lease made by plaintiff, and the reversion in him, lessor is without remedy. The conclusion is, that albeit the condition was executed by re-entry, yet the

368 Item, *en tiel cas lou lenquest poet dire lour verdit a large, sils voillent prendre sur eux la conusaunce de la ley sur le matere, ils poient dire lour verdit generalement come est mys en lour charge, come en le cas avauntdit, ils poient bien dire, que le lessour ne disseisist pas le lessé, sils voillent, &c.*

369 Item, *en mesme le cas, si le cas fuist tiel, que apres ceo que le lessour avoit entré pur defaut de paiement, &c., que le lessé ust entre sur le lessour, et luy disseisist : en ceo cas, si le lessour arraigne un assise envers le lessé, le lessé luy poet barrer dassise ; qar il poet pleder envers luy en barre, coment le lessour qui est pleyntif, fist un lees al defendant pur terme de sa vie, savaunt la revercion al pleintif, lequel est bon plee en*

---

us, to take a special verdict is common to other actions), are, where the recognitors are bound to find and inquire of other matters besides the seisin and disseisin.—*See Booth on Real Actions*, 213, *Ed.* 1811.

(*p*) Although the jury, if they will take upon them (as *Lyttleton* here saith) the knowledge of the law, may give a general verdict; yet it is dangerous for them so to do; therefore to find the special matter is the safest way, where the case is doubtful.—*Co. Lytt.* 228. *a.*

lessor cannot plead it, without shewing of a deed.—Co. Lytt. 228. b.

he acknowledges the reversion to be to the plaintiff: in this case the plaintiff hath no matter to aid himself, but the condition made upon the lease, and this he cannot plead, because he hath not any writing of this; and insomuch as he cannot answer to the bar, he shall be barred; and so in this case you may see that a man is disseised, and yet he shall not have assise; and yet if the lessee be plaintiff, and the lessor defendant, he shall bar the lessee by verdict of the assise, &c.; but in this case where the lessee is defendant, if he will not plead the said plea in bar, but plead, no wrong no disseisin, then the lessor shall recover by assise, &c. *Causa qua supra.*

Concerning indentures and deeds poll containing condition.

370 Also, that such conditions are most commonly put and specified in deeds indented, some little thing shall here be said, to thee my son, of indentures and of a deed-poll containing* condition.

barre, entaunt que il conust la revercion estre al pleyntif: en ceo cas le pleyntif nad matere de luy aider forsque la condicion fait sur le lees, et ceo il ne poet pleder, pur ceo que il nad ascun escripture de ceo ; et entaunt que il ne poet respondre al barre, il serra barre ; et issint en ceo cas poyes veyer que home est disseisi, et unqore il navera assise ; et unqore si le lessé soit pleintif, et le lessour defendant, il barrera le lessé per verdit dassise, &c. ; mes en ceo cas lou le lessé est defendant, si il ne voet pleder le dit plee en barre, mes pleda, nul tort nul disseisin, donques le lessour recovera per assise, &c., Causa qua supra.

370 Item, *pur ceo que tielx condicions sount pluis communement mys et specifies en faitez endentez, ascun petit chose serra icy dit, a toy mon fits, de endenturez et de fait polle conteignant* condicion.*

---

* The later and corrupted copies read *concernants—concerning*. *Rastell's* Transl. is according to the text of the earliest editions, which give *containing*.

And it is to be understood, that if the indenture be bipartite, or tripartite, or quadripartite, the parts of the indenture are but one deed in law, and every part of the indenture is of as great force and effect as all the parts together.

371 And the making of indentures is in two manners. One is to make them in the third person. Another is to make them in the first person. The making in the third person is as in such form:—

Indentures are either in the third person or first person.

" This indenture made between A. of B. of the one part, " and C. of D. of the other part, witnesseth, that the afore- " said A. of B. hath given, granted, and by this present " charter [or deed] indented hath confirmed, to the aforesaid " C. of D., such land, &c. To have and to hold upon con- " dition, &c. In witness whereof the parties aforesaid in- " terchangeably have put their seals." *Or thus*:—" In " witness whereof to the one part of this indenture, re- " maining with the said C. of D., the said A. of B. hath put " his seal; and to the other part of the same indenture re-

Forms of indenture in the third person.

Et est assavoir, que si lendenture soit bipertite, ou tripertite, ou quadripertite, les parties de lendenture ne sount que un fait en ley, et chescun partie de lendenture est de auxi graunde force et effecte sicome toutez les parties ensemble.

371 *Et la fesaunce des endentures est en deux maneres. Une est de faire eux en la tierce persone. Un autre est de faire eux en la premier persone. Le fesance en la tierce persone est come en tiel fourme*:—

" *Hec indentura facta inter A. de B. ex una parte, et C.* " *de D. ex altera parte, testatur, quod prædictus A. de B.* " *dedit, concessit, et hac præsenti carta indentata confir-* " *mavit, præfato C. de D. talem terram, &c. Habendum et* " *tenendum sub condicione, &c. In cujus rei testimonium* " *partes prædicte sigilla sua alternatim apposuerunt.*" Vel sic:—" *In cujus rei testimonium uni parti hujus indentũre,* " *penes præfatum C. de D. remanenti, prædictus A. de* " *B. sigillum suum apposuit; alteri verò parti ejusdem inden-*

" maining with him the said A. of B., the said C. of D. hath " put his seal. Dated," &c.

Such indenture is called an indenture made in the third person, because the verbs, &c., are in the third person. And this form of indentures is the most sure making, because it is most commonly used, &c.

Forms of indenture in the first person.

372 The making of indentures in the first person, is in such form:—" To all Christian people to whom these present " writing indented shall come, A. of B. sends greeting in " our Lord God everlasting. Know ye, me to have given, " granted, and by this my present deed indented, confirmed " to C. of D., such land, &c." *Or thus:*—" Know all men " present and to come, that I, A. of B., have given, granted, " and by this my present deed indented, confirmed to C. of " D., such land, &c. To have, &c., upon condition following, " &c. In witness whereof, as well I, the said A. of B., as the " aforesaid C. of D., to these indentures have interchangeably " put our seals." *Or thus:*—In witness whereof to the one

" *ture penes ipsum A. de B. remanenti, idem C. de D. sigil-* " *lum suum apposuit. Dat.' &c.*"

Tiel endenture est appelle endenture fait en la tierce persone, pur ceo que les verbes, &c., sount en la tierce persone. Et tiel fourme dendentures est de pluis sure fesaunce, pur ceo que est pluis communement use, &c.

372 *La fesaunce dendentures en la premier persone est en tiel fourme :*—" *Omnibus Christi fidelibus ad quos presentes litere* " *indentate pervenerint, A. de B. salutem in Domino sempi-* " *ternam. Sciatis me dedisse, concessisse, et hac præsenti* " *carta mea indentata confirmasse C. de D. talem terram,* " *&c.*" Vel sic:—" *Sciant præsentes et futuri, quod ego A.* " *de B. dedi, concessi, et hac præsenti carta mea indentata* " *confirmavi C. de D. talem terram, &c. Habendum, &c.,* " *sub condicione sequenti, &c. In cujus rei testimonium tam* " *ego predictus A. de B., quam predictus C. de D., his inden-* " *turis sigilla nostra alternatim apposuimus.*" Vel sic:—

" part of this indenture have I put my seal, and to the other " part of the same indenture the said C. of D. hath put his " seal, &c." 373 And it seemeth that such indenture made in the first person is as good in law as the indenture made in the third person, when both parties have thereto put their seals; for in the indenture made in the third person, or in the first person, if mention be made that the grantor hath set his seal only, and not the grantee, then is the indenture the deed of the grantor only. But where mention is made that the grantee hath set his seal to the indenture, &c., then is the indenture as well the deed of the grantee as the deed of the grantor: and so it is the deed of them both; and also each part of the indenture is the deed of both parties in such case, &c.

Indenture in the first person is as good as in the third person, and if the party to whom deed is made, put his seal, it is the deed of them both.

374 Also, if estate be made by indenture to a man for term of his life, the remainder to another in fee, on certain condition, &c., and if the tenant for term of life hath set his seal to the part of the indenture, and afterwards dieth, and he in

Although the remainder-man do not seal deed, for he is no party to the deed, yet is he

" *In cujus rei testimonium uni parti hujus indenture sigillum* " *meum apposui, alteri verò parti ejusdem indenture præ-* " *dictus C. de D. sigillum suum apposuit, &c.*" 373 *Et il semble que tiel endenture fait en la premier persone est auxi bon en ley come en lendenture fait en la tierce persone, quant ambideux parties ount a ceo mys lour seales; qar en lendenture fait en la tierce persone, ou en la premier persone, si mencion soit fait que le grauntour avoit mys solement son seale, et nemy le graunté, donques est lendenture tauntsolement le fait le grantour. Mes lou mencion est fait que le graunté ad mys son seale a lendenture, &c., donques est lendenture auxibien le fait le graunté come le fait le grauntour: et issint il est le fait dambideux, et auxi chescune partie de lendenture est le fait dambideux parties en tiel cas, &c.*

374 Item, *si estate soit fait per endenture a un home pur terme de sa vie, le remeyndre a un autre en fee, sur certeyn condicion, &c., et si le tenaunt a terme de vie avoit mys son seale a partie de lendenture, et puis morust, et cestuy en le re-*

bound by the condition.

the remainder entereth into the land by force of his remainder, &c., in this case he is holden to perform all the conditions comprised in the indenture, as the tenant for life ought to do in his life, and yet he in the remainder never sealed any part of the indenture; but the cause is, that insomuch as he entered and agreed to have the lands by force of the indenture, he is holden (*i. e.* bound) to perform the conditions within the same indenture, if he will have the land, &c.

The reason is, he must take the land with its burthens.

Where the feoffor may plead a condition contained in a deed-poll.

375 Also if a feoffment be made by deed-poll upon condition, &c., and because the condition is not performed, the feoffor entereth and happeth (*i. e.* gets) the possession of the deed-poll, if the feoffee bring an action of that entry against the feoffor, it hath been a question, whether the feoffor can plead the condition by the said deed-poll against the feoffee; and some have said nay, insomuch as it seemeth to them that a deed-poll and the property of the same deed belongeth to him to whom the deed is made, and not to him that made the deed; and insomuch as such a deed doth not belong to

meyndre entra en la terre per force de son remeyndre, &c., en ceo cas il est tenus de perfourmer toutes les condicions compris en lendenture, sicome le tenaunt a terme de vie devoit faire en sa vie, et unqore cestuy en le remeyndre ne unques enseala ascune partie del endenture ; mes la cause est, que entaunt que il entre et agrea daver les terres per force del endenture, il est tenus de perfourmer les condicions deins mesme lendenture, sil voille aver la terre, &c.

375 Item, *si feoffement soit fait per fait polle sur condicion, &c., pur ceo que la condicion nest pas perfourme, le feoffour entra et happa la possession de le fait polle, si le feoffé porta un accion de cel entre envers le feoffour, il ad este question, si le feoffour poet pleder la condicion per le dit fait polle encountre le feoffé. Et ascuns ount dit que non, entant que semble a eux que un fait polle a le propreté de mesme le fait appertient a celuy a qui le fait est fait, et nemy a celuy qui fist le fait ; et entaunt que tiel fait ne atteigne al feoffour, il*

the feoffor, it seemeth unto them that he cannot plead this, &c. And others have said the contrary, and have shewed divers reasons.

One is, if the case were such, that in the action between them, if the feoffee plead the same deed, and shew it to the court: in this case, insomuch as the deed is in court, the feoffor can shew to the court how in the deed there are divers conditions to be performed, [on the part of the feoffee, &c., and because they were not performed*], he entered, &c., and thereto he shall be received. By the same reason when the feoffor hath the deed in hand, and sheweth it to the court, he shall well be received to plead it, &c., and namely, when the feoffor is privy to the deed, for he ought to be privy to the deed when he made the deed, &c. 376 Also, if two men do a trespass to another, who releases to one of them by his deed all actions personal, and notwithstanding he sueth an action of trespass against the other, the defendant

Lyttleton's opinion, [which is always the better and the last, § 170, 302, 340].

Profert *of deed; see* § 376, 377, 573, 748.

When divers do a trespass, the same is joint or several at the will of him to whom the wrong is

semble a eux que il ne poet pas ceo pleder, &c. Et autres ont dit le contrarie, et ount monstre divers causes.

Une est, si le cas fuist tiel, que en accion entre eux, si le feoffé pledast mesme le fait, et monstre ceo al court: en ceo cas, entaunt que le fait est en court, le feoffour poet monstrer al court coment en le fait sount divers condicions destre perfourmes [de le part le feoffé, &c., et pur ceo que ils ne furent perfourmes], il entrast, &c., et a ceo il serra resceu. Per mesme le reason quant le feoffour ad le fait en poigne, et ceo monstra a le court, il serra bien resceu de ceo pleder, &c., et nosment, quant le feoffour est privé al fait, qar il covient destre privé al fait quant il fist le fait, &c.* 376 *Auxi, si deux homes font un trespas a un autre, le quel relessa a un deux per son fait toutes accions personelx, et nient obstant il suist accion de trespas envers lautre, le defendant bien poet monstrer que le*

* The words within brackets are omitted in *Lettou & M.*, *Machl.*, and *Roh.*, but they appear in every other edition, *French* as well as *English.*

done; yet if he release to one of them, all are discharged, because his own deed shall be taken most strongly against himself.—Co. Lytt. 232. a.

may well shew that the trespass was done by him, and by another his fellow, and that the plaintiff by his deed, which he sheweth forth, releaseth to his fellow all actions personal, [judgment if action, &c.*]; and yet such deed belongeth to his fellow, and not to him, but because he may have advantage by the deed if he will shew the deed to the court, he therefore can well plead it, &c. By the same reason *is it* in the other case, when the feoffor ought to have advantage by the condition in the deed-poll. 377 Also, if the feoffee gave and† granted the deed-poll to the feoffor, such grant shall be good, and then the deed and the property thereof belongeth to the feoffor, &c.‡ And when the feoffor hath the deed in hand, and pleadeth it to the court, it shall be rather intended that he cometh to the deed by a lawful mean, than by a wrongful mean: and so it seemeth, that the feoffor may well plead such a deed-poll that compriseth condition, &c., if he hath the deed in hand, &c.

The property of a deed grantable, and rightful possession of a deed presumed.

trespas fuist fait per luy, et pur un autre son compaignon, et que le pleintif per son fait quil monstre avaunt, relessa a son compaignon toutez accions personelx, [juggement si accion, &c.]; et unqore tiel fait appertient a son compaignon, et nemye a luy, mes pur ceo que il poet aver-avantage per le fait sil voet monstrer le fait al court, il poet pur ceo bien pleder, &c. Per mesme le reason en lautre cas, quaunt le feoffour doit aver avantage per le condicion deinz le fait polle, &c.* 377 *Auxi, si le feoffé donast et† grauntast le fait-polle al feoffour, tiel graunte serra bon, et donques le fait et le propreté del fait appertient al feoffour, &c.‡ Et quaunt le feoffour ad le fait en poigne, et ceo pleda al court, il serra pluis tost entendus quil vient al fait per loial mesne, que per torcious mesne : et issint a eux semble, que le feoffour poet bien pleder tiel fait-polle que comprent condicion, &c., sil ad le fait en poigne, &c.*

---

* The words within brackets do not appear in *Rastell's* Transl.

† In *Rastell's* Transl. *or*, which is followed by the later copies, and by *Sir Edward Coke's* Translation.

‡ This *&c.* does not appear in *Rastell's* Transl.

*" Ideo semper quære de dubiis, quia per rationes pervenitur " ad legitimam rationem, &c."**

Conditions in law or implied conditions. ***Examples of such conditions, viz. of an office which is forfeitable for nonfeasance.***

378 Estates that men have upon condition in law, are such estates that have a condition by the law to them annexed, though it be not specified in writing. As if a man grant by his deed to another the office of parkership of a park, to have and occupy the same office for term of his life, the estate which he hath in the office is upon condition in law, to wit, that the parker shall well and lawfully keep the park, and do that which to such office appertaineth to do, or otherwise that it shall be lawful to the grantor and to his heirs to oust him, and to grant it to another if he will, &c. And such condition that is intended by the law to be annexed to any thing, is as strong as if the condition were set or put in writing. 379 In the same manner it is of grants of the offices of stewardship, constableship, bedelary, bailiwick, or other officers, &c. But

Offices not exerciseable by deputy except so granted.

*" Ideo semper quære de dubiis, quia per rationes pervenitur " ad legitimam rationem, &c."**

378 *Estates que homes ount sur condicion en ley, sont tielx estates que ount un condicion per la ley a eux annexe, coment que ne soit especifie en escripture. Sicome home graunta per son fait a un autre loffice de parkership de un parke, a aver et occupier mesme loffice pur terme de sa vie, lestate quil ad en office est sur condicion en ley, cestassavoir, que le parker bien et loialement gardera le parke, et ferra ceo que a tiel office appent a faire, ou autrement que bien lirroit al grauntour et a ses heires de luy ouster, et de graunter ceo a un autre sil voet, &c. Et tiel condicion que est entendus per la ley estre annexe a ascun chose, est auxy fort sicome la condicion fuist mis ou monstre en escripte.* 379 *En mesme le manere est de grauntez doffices de seneschalcie, constabularie, bedelarie, baylliwik, ou autres officers, &c. Mes si tiel office soit*

* This &c. does not appear in *Rastell's* Transl.

if such office be granted to a man, to have and to occupy by himself or by his deputy, then if the office be occupied by him or his deputy, as it ought by the law to be occupied, this sufficeth for him, or else the grantor and his heirs may oust him, as afore is said (*q*).

Limitations. *Land given to husband and wife during coverture, or so long as A. is abbot of B., the estate shall end if the husband or wife die in the one case, or the abbot die, resign, or be deposed in the other case: as these are times of limitations, the words of the text are not properly a con-*

380 Also, estates of lands or tenements may be upon condition in law, albeit upon the estate made there was not any mention or rehearsal made of the condition: as put the case that a lease be made to the husband and to his wife, to have

graunte a un home, a aver et occupier per luy ou per son deputé, donques si loffice soit occupie pur luy, ou per son deputé, sicome il devoit per la ley estre occupie, ceo suffist pur luy, ou autrement le grauntour et ses heires luy poient ouster, come avaunt est dit.

380 Item, *estates de terres ou tenementes purrount estre sur condicion en ley, coment que sur lestate fait ne fuist ascun mencion ou rehersel fait de la condicion: sicome mettomus que un lees soit fait a le baron, et a sa feme a aver et tener a*

(*q*) Offices, which are a right to exercise a public or private employment, and to take the fees and emoluments thereunto belonging, are incorporeal hereditaments: whether public, as those of magistrates; or private, as of bailiffs, receivers, and the like. For a man may have an estate in them, either to him and his heirs, or for life, or for a term of years, or during pleasure only: save only that offices of public trust cannot be granted for a term of years, especiall if they concern the administration of justice, for then they might perhaps vest in executors or administrators. Neither can any *judicial* office be granted in reversion; because though the grantee may be able to perform it at the time of the grant, yet before the office falls he may become unable and insufficient: but *ministerial* offices may be so granted: for those may be executed by deputy. Also, by statute 5 & 6 Edw. VI. c. 16, no public office shall be sold, under pain of disability to dispose of or hold it. For the law presumes that he who buys an office, will by bribery, extortion, or other unlawful means, make his purchase good, to the manifest detriment of the public.—B. C. ii. 36.

and to hold to them during the coverture between them; in this case they have an estate for term of their two lives upon condition in law, that is to say, if one one of them die, or if divorce be made between them, that then it shall be lawful for the lessor and his heirs to enter, &c.; 381 and that they have estate for term of their two lives, it is proved thus; every man that hath an estate of freehold in any lands or tenements, either he hath estate in fee, or in fee-tail, or for term of his own life, or for term of another's life, and by such a lease they have a freehold, but they have not by that grant, fee, or fee-tail, or for term of another's life, *ergo* they have an estate for their own* lives; but this is upon condition in the law in form aforesaid; and in this case, if they commit waste, the lessor shall have a writ of waste against them, supposing by his writ, *Quod tenent ad terminum vite sue, &c.;* but in his count he shall declare how, and in what manner the lease was made [*ante*, § 67]. 382 In the same man-

dition, but a limitation; for in the first case it is a condition, which is the boundary of the estate: and in the second case of the abbot [which applies to a bishop, archdeacon, ecclesiastical or temporal body politic or corporate, or to any officer, &c.], it is not a condition defeating the estate before its natural determination, but more properly a limitation.
§ 381 is a parenthesis containing the proof by argument, that the husband and wife are tenants by entireties without

eux duraunt la coverture entre eux; en ceo cas ils ount estate pur terme de lour deux vies sur condicion en ley, cestassavoir, si un deux devie, ou que devorce soit fait entre eux, que adonques bien lirroit al lessour et a ses heires dentrer, &c.; 381 *et quils ount estate pur terme de lour deux vies,* probatur sic; *chescun home qui ad estate de franktenement en ascunes terres ou tenementes, ou il ad estate en fee, ou en fee-taille, ou pur terme de sa vie demesne, ou pur terme dautre vie, et per tiel lees ils ount franktenement, mes ils nount per ceo graunt, fee, ne fee-taille, ne pur terme dautre vie,* ergo *ils ount estate pur terme de lour* vies; mes ceo est sur condicion en ley en la fourme avauntdit; et en ceo cas, sils fieront wast, le lessour avera envers eux brief de wast, supposant per son brief,* Quod tenent ad terminum vite sue, &c.; *et en son count il declara coment et en quel manere le lees fuist fait.* 382 *En mesme la*

---

* *Two, Rastell's* Transl.

survivorship, so long as both lives jointly continue.

ner it is, if an abbot make a lease to a man, to have and to hold to him during the time that the lessor is abbot; in this case the lessee hath an estate for term of his own life: but this is upon condition in law, that is to say, that if the abbot resign or be deposed*, that it shall be lawful for his successor to enter, &c.

Devise of land to be sold by executor; if he does not sell within reasonable time, heir may recover.

383 Also, one may see in the book of assises, *anno* 38 *E.* 3, a plea of assise in this form following:—assise *de no. diss.* was sometime brought against A. who pleaded to the assise, and it was found by verdict, that the ancestor of the plaintiff devised his lands to be sold by the defendant who was his executor, and to make distribution of the money for his soul, [*ante*, § 169]: and it was found, that presently† after the death of the testator, one tendered to him a certain sum of money for the tenements, but not to the value, and that the executor afterwards held the tenements in his own hand two

manere est, si un abbe fait un lees a un home, a aver et tener a luy duraunt le temps que le lessour est abbe; en ceo cas le lessé ad estate pur terme de sa vie demesne: mes ceo est sur condicion en ley, cestassavoir, que si labbe resigna, ou soit depose, que bien lirroit a son successour dentrer, &c.*

383 Item, *home poet veyer en le lyver dassise,* viz. anno xxxviij. E. 3, *un plee dassise en cest fourme que ensuist :— un assise* de no. diss. *autrefoitz fuist porte vers un A. qui pleda al assise, et trove fuist per verdit, que launcestre le pleyntif devisa les tenementes a vendre per le defendaunt qui fuist son executour, et de faire distribucion des deneres pur son alme: et fuist trouve, que meyntenant† apres la mort le testatour, un home luy tendist certeyn somme de deneres pur les tenementes, mes non pas al value, et que lexecutour puis avoit tenus les tenementes en sa main demesne per deux ans, al en-*

---

* *Rastell's* Transl. reads this passage—*that if the abbot* die or *resign, or be deposed* —— *&c.*

† *Rastell's* Translation does not give this word.

years, to the intent to sell the same dearer to some other; and it was found that he had all the while taken the profits of the tenements to his own use, without doing any thing for the soul of the deceased, &c. *Mowbray;* The executor in such case is holden by the law to make the sale so soon as he can after the death of the testator, and it is found that he had refused to make the sale, and so the default was in him, and also by force of the devise he was bound to put all the profits coming of the lands to the use of the dead, and it is found that he took them to his own use, and so another default is in him; wherefore it was adjudged, that the plaintiff should recover, &c. And so it appeareth by the said judgment, that by force of the said devise the executor had no estate nor power in the tenements, but upon condition in law (*r*):

John Mowbray *was a reverend judge of the Court of Common Pleas* [*made C. J. 11th July, 1360*], *and descended of a noble family.*—Co. Lytt. 236. a.

For such devise is a condition in law.

tent de les vendre pluis chier a ascun autre; et trove fuit que il avoit tout temps pris le profit de les tenementes a son use demesne, sauns rien faire pur lalme le mort, &c. Mowbray; *Lexecutour en tiel cas est tenus per la ley a faire le vende a pluis tost queil purroit apres la mort son testatour, et trove est queil est refuse de faire le vende, et issint avoit il un defaut en luy, et issint per force del devise il fuist tenus daver mys toutz les profites provenantes de les tenementes al use le mort, et trove est queil les ad pris a son use demesne, et issint autre default est en luy; per que fuist ajugge que le pleintif recovera, &c. Et issint appiert per le dit juggement, que per force del dit devise, que lexecutour navoit estate ne poiar en les tenementes, forsque sur condicion en ley:*

(*r*) In this section is implied a diversity, viz. when a man devises that his executor shall sell the land, there the land descends in the mean time to the heir, and until the sale be made, the heir may enter and take the profits. But when the land is devised to his executor to be sold, there the devise takes away the descent, and vests the estate of the land in the executor, and he may enter and take the profits and make sale according to the devise. And here it appears, by our author, that when a man devises his tenements to be sold by his executors,

Devise to executor to sell, and devise that executor shall sell, distinguished. [*See* 1 *Jac. & W.* 189; 4 *Mad.* 44, 142; 2 *S. & S.* 238.]

Limitations (which Lyttleton *termeth conditions in law) may be pleaded without a deed.*— Co. Lytt. 236. b.

384 In* such case there needeth not to have shewed any deed, rehearsing the condition, [for that the law itself purporteth the condition, &c.†]

" *Ex paucis dictis intendere plurima potes.*"

More shall be said of Conditions in the Chapter of Descents which toll Entries, [in the Chapter of Releases, and in the Chapter of Discontinuances‡].

384 *En* tiel cas il ne besoigne daver monstre ascun fait, rehersant la condition, [pur ceo que la ley en luy mesme purport la condicion, &c.†]*

" Ex paucis dictis intendere plurima potes."

Pluis serra dit de Condicions en le Chapitre de Discentez que tollount Entrees, [en le Chapitre de Relesses, et en le Chapitre de Discontinuaunces‡].

---

* *And many other things and cases there are of estates upon condition in the law, and in such cases, &c., Redm., Berth., Middl., Sm., Powell,* and *Tottyl* 1554.

† The words within brackets do not appear in *Rastell's* Transl.

‡ These concluding words within brackets are not given in the *Camb. MSS.*

---

it is all one as if he had devised his tenements to his executors to be sold; and the reason is, because he devises the tenements, whereby he breaks the descent. — *Co. Lytt.* 236. a.

CHAPTER VI.

DESCENTS WHICH TOLL ENTRIES.

An entry is the taking peaceable possession by the legal owner of a corporeal estate or freehold, which being a notorious act of ownership, is equivalent to seisin or feudal investiture; but if the legal owner had been ousted by a wrong doer, and, after his decease, the heir of such party had entered, then, because the heir of such party came to the land by act of law, *scil.* the descent, the law would not permit his possession to be divested, until the legal owner or claimant had proved a better right; and, therefore, such person was driven to his real action, *i. e.* the bringing of a writ of entry, which at common law was the proper remedy till the abolition of real actions, and as no such writ could be brought unless by such claimant who had either been in possession or made entry, or had made continual claim in lieu of an entry (§ 414), such seisin, entry, or claim, as the case might be, was the qualification for bringing the writ.

However, as real actions fell into disuse, and in fact were superseded by the action of *ejectment*, for in such form of action the claimant was allowed *to lay his demise*, *i. e.* suggest the entry to have been made at any time within twenty years, which fact the defendant being bound by rule of court to admit, the necessity of a claimant's making an actual entry was evaded in almost all cases, except where rendered absolutely necessary, as to avoid a fine with proclamations, or on a vacant possession.

A right of entry also could have been kept alive by making continual claim, a subject hereafter treated upon by Lyttleton (§ 414), so that a right of entry may be deemed to have been synonymous with right of title or action.

The act 3 & 4 Will. 4, c. 27, has abolished *real* actions, with the exception of *dower* and *quare impedit*, and has substituted the *mixed* action of *ejectment* in their place (s. 36), and has also enacted, that no person shall be deemed to have been in possession of any land merely by reason of having made an entry thereon (s. 10); and further, that no *descent cast*, *discontinuance* (§ 592), or *warranty* (§ 697), which may happen to be made after the 31st Dec. 1833, shall *toll* or defeat any right of entry or action for the recovery of land (s. 39). But this Chapter nevertheless must be studied for its illustration of many doctrines which, though obsolete, are yet collateral to other points of learning in Lyttleton's Treatise, and tend to shew its consistency.

The doctrine of *bastard eisne* and *mulier puisne* (§ 399), a special case, in which the ancient law allowed the *mulier* or legitimate heir to be barred by the heir of his bastard elder brother (by the same mother), has been by some persons adduced as an example of the allowance of the law of legitimation by subsequent marriage; a doctrine which never formed part of the English common law, and to which this case is not to be referred, it being deducible from feudal principles, and indeed is not applicable to the bastard himself, who was liable to eviction himself at any period of his life, but only to his issue, and therefore this case is to be considered as an argument of incapacity, rather than a favourable exception of the position—that a child, born out of wedlock, has never been by our law legitimated by the subsequent marriage of the parents (*a*).

(*a*) Robertson's Law of Legitimation by subsequent Marriage. Lond. 8vo. 1829, pp. 44, 45.

385 DESCENTS which toll (*i. e.* take away) entries, are in two manners, that is to say, where the descent is in fee, or in fee-tail.

Descents which take away entry are either in fee or in fee tail; in fee, when the entry of a disseisee is taken away by the descent to the issue of the disseisor in fee.

Descents in fee which toll entries are, as if a man seised of certain lands or tenements, is by another disseised, and the disseisor hath issue, and dieth of such estate seised, now the lands descend to the issue of the disseisor by course of law, as heir unto him: and because the law putteth the lands or tenements upon the issue by force of the descent, so as the issue cometh to the lands by course of the law, and not by his own act, the entry of the disseisee is taken away, and he is thereof put to sue a writ of *entrie sur disseisin* against the heir of the disseisor, to recover the land, &c.

386 Descents in tail which take away entries are, as if a man be disseised, and the disseisor giveth the same land to another in tail, and the tenant in tail hath issue, and dieth seised of such estate, and the issue enter; in this case the

And in like manner the dying seised of an estate tail, takes away the entry of disseisee.

385 *Discents que tollount entrees sount en deux maneres, cestassavoir, ou le discent est en fee, ou en fee-taille.*

Discents en fee que tollount entrees sont, sicome home seisi de certeyn terres ou tenementes, est pur un autre disseisi et le disseisour ad issue et morust de tiel estate seisi, ore les tenementes descendount al issue del disseisour per cours de la ley come heire a luy: et pur ceo que la ley myst les terres ou tenementes sur lissue per force del discent, issint que lissue vient a les tenementes per cours de la ley, et nemy per son fait demesne, lentré le disseisi est tolle, et il est ent mys de suer un brief dentre sur disseisin envers leire le disseisour, de recoverer la terre, &c.

386 *Discents en le taille que tollount entrees sount, sicome home est disseisi, et le disseisour dona mesme la terre a un autre en le taille, et le tenaunt en le taille ad issue, et morust de tiel estate seisi, et lissue entrast; en ceo cas lentré le disseisi est*

entry of the disseisee is taken away, and he is thereof put to sue against the issue of the tenant in tail a writ of *entrie sur disseisin.*

There must be a dying seised in fee, not of a less estate.

387 And note, that in such descents which take away entries, it behoveth that a man die seised in his demesne as of fee, or in his demesne as in fee-tail; for a dying seised for term of life, or for term of another man's life, doth never take away an entry, &c.

And the descent of a reversion or remainder is not sufficient.

388 Also, a descent of a reversion, or of a remainder, doth never take away an entry, &c.*: so that in such cases which

tolle, et il est ent mys de suer envers lissue de le tenaunt en le taille un brief dentre sur disseisin, &c.

387 *Et nota, que en tielx discentes que tollount entrees, il covient que home morust seisi en son demesne come de fee, ou en son demesne come en fee-taille ; qar un murrant seisi pur terme de vie, ne pur terme dautre vie, ne unques tollount entre, &c.*

388 Item, *un discent de revercion, ou de remeyndre, ne unques tollount entre, &c.*: issint que en tielx cases que tollount*

---

* In the editions by *Redm.*, *Berth.*, *Middl.*, *Sm.*, *Powel*, and *Tottyl* 1554, is the following case inserted, which as it seems put by way of illustration, may, perhaps, have been part of the original, the conclusion of this paragraph or division of the text—*issint que en tielx cases; so that in such cases*—seems to refer to some illustration as having preceded it. The case is thus:—*Come si home moy disseisist, et le disseisour lessa les tenementes a un home pur terme de vie, le remeyndre en fee, si cesty en le remeyndre ad issue et morust, et puis le tenaunt a terme de vie devie, lissue de cesti en le remeyndre entra, en ceo cas lentré le disseisi nest pas tolle: As if a man disseises me, and the disseisour leases the tenements to a man for term of life, the remainder in fee, if he in the remainder has issue and dies, and afterwards the tenant for term of life die, the issue of him in the remainder enters, in this case the entry of the disseisee is not tolled:* So that *in such cases*—not, as *Sir E. Coke's* Transl. renders it, As *in such cases* ——.

The *&c.* does not appear in the more modern copies.

take away entries by force of descent, it behoveth that he that dieth seised have fee and freehold at the time of his decease*; or else such descent doth not take away entry.

389 Also, as it is said of descents which descend to the issue of those who die seised, &c. (*b*), the same law is where they have not any issue, but the tenements descend to the brother, or to the sister, or to the uncle, or to some other cousin of him that dieth seised, &c.

A descent in the collateral line takes away an entry, as well as in the lineal.

390 Also, if there be lord and tenant, and the tenant be disseised, and the disseisor alien to another in fee, and the alienee die without heir, and the lord enter as in his escheat: in this case the disseisee may enter upon the lord, because the lord cometh not to the land by descent, but by way of escheat.

The issue of a disseisor dying sans *heir, and the lord in by escheat, does not take away the disseisee's entry,* [*by the same rule that the lord cannot enter for the condition broken,* § 348].

391 Also, if a man be seised of certain land in fee, or in fee-tail, upon condition to render certain rent, or upon other

So entry for condition

entrees per force de discent, il covient que celuy qui morust seisi ad fee et franktenement al temps de son murrant ; ou au-trement tiel discent ne tolle entree.*

389 Item, *come est dit de discentes que discendount al issue de ceux qui murront seisis, &c., mesme la ley est lou ils nount ascun issue, mes les tenementes descendount al frere, ou soer, ou uncle, ou a autre cosyn de cely qui morust seisi, &c.*

390 Item, *si soit seignour et tenaunt, et le tenaunt soit dis-seisi, et le disseisour aliena a un autre en fee, et lalienè devie sauns heire, et le seignour entra come en son eschete : en ceo cas le disseisi poet entrer sur le seignour, pur ceo que le seignour ne vient a la terre per discent, mes per voie des-chete.*

391 Item, *si home seisi de certeyn terre en fee, ou en fee-taille, sur condicion de rendre certeyn rent, ou sur autre con-*

---

* All copies since *Roh.* add here, *or of fee-tail and freehold at the time of his death ;* or else —— &c.

(*b*) Here &c. implieth fee-simple or fee tail.—*Co. Lytt.* 239. b.

broken is not taken away by death of tenant in possession.

condition, albeit such tenant seised in fee, or in fee-tail, die seised, yet if the condition be broken in their lives, or after their decease, this shall not take away the entry of the feoffor or of the donor, or of their heirs, for this that the tenancy is charged with the condition, and the estate of the tenant is conditional, in whose hands soever that the tenancy shall come, &c.

A descent cast will not take away a condition.

392 Also, if such tenant upon condition be disseised, and the disseisor die thereof seised, and the land descend to the heir of the disseisor, now the entry of the tenant upon condition that was disseised, is taken away. [Yet if the condition be broken, then can the feoffor or the donor that made the estate upon condition, or their heirs, enter, *Causa qua supra**].

Disseisee may enter upon disseisor's wife's dower, for the wife is in by

393 Also, if a disseisor die seised, &c., and his heir enter, &c., who endoweth the wife of the disseisor of the third part of the tenements, &c. In this case, as to this third part

dicion, coment que tiel tenaunt seisi en fee, ou en fee-taille, morust seisi, unqore si la condicion soit enfreint en lour vies, ou apres lour decesse, ceo ne tollera pas lentre del feoffour, ou del donour, ou de lour heires, pur ceo que le tenauncie est charge ovesque la condicion, et lestate de le tenaunt est condicionel, en queconques mayns que la tenauncie avient, &c.

392 Item, *si tiel tenaunt sur condicion est disseisi, et le disseisour devia ent seisi, et la terre descendist al heire le disseisour, ore lentré le tenaunt sur condicion, qui fuist disseisi, est tolle. [Mes unqore si la condicion soit enfreint, donques poet le feoffour ou le donour que firent estate sur condicion, ou lour heires, entrer,* Causa qua supra*].

393 Item, *si un disseisour devie seisi, &c., et son heire entra, &c., le quel endowa la feme le disseisour de la tierce partie de lez tenementes, &c. En ceo cas, quant a ceste tierce*

---

* This passage is not in the text of the Vell. MS., but is added in the margin.

which is assigned to the wife in dower, forthwith after the wife entereth, and she hath the possession of the same third part, the disseisee may lawfully enter upon the possession of the wife into the same third part. And the reason is, for this, that when the wife hath her dower, she shall be adjudged in immediately by her husband, and not by the heir; and so as to the freehold of the same third part, the descent is defeated, &c.: and so you may see that before the endowment the disseisee can not enter into any part, &c., and after the endowment he can enter, &c.*; but yet he cannot enter upon the other two parts which the heir of the disseisor hath by the descent, &c.

her husband, not by his heir or by descent, and the possession of the heir is thus avoided by relation.

394 Also, if a woman be seised of land in fee, whereof I have right and title to enter, if the woman take husband and have issue between them, and afterwards the wife die seised, and afterwards the husband die, and the issue enter, &c.,

Disseisee may enter on tenant by curtesy, [upon the principle of § 390].

partie que est assigne a la feme en dower, meyntenaunt apres ceo que la feme entra, et el ad le possession de mesme la tierce partie, le disseisi poet loialement entrer sur la possession la feme en mesme la tierce partie. Et la cause est, pur ceo, que quant la feme ad son dower, el serra ajugge eins imediate per son baron, et nemy per leire; et issint quant a le franktenement de mesme la tierce partie, le discent est defete, &c.: et issint poies veyer, que devant le dowment, le disseisi ne poet entrer en ascune partie, &c., et apres le dowement il poet entrer, &c.; mes unqore il ne poet entrer sur les autres deux parties que leire le dissessour ad per le discent, &c.*

394 Item, *si une feme soit seisie de terre en fee, dont jeo aye droit et title dentrer, si la feme prent baron, et ount issue entre eux, et puis la feme devie seisie, et apres le baron devie, et lissue entra, &c., en ceo cas jeo poy entrer sur la possession*

* In *Pyns.* 1516, and *Redm.*, and in most, if not all, of the subsequent editions, the words *sur la feme, upon the wife*, are inserted; these words supply what the *&c.* is meant to infer; but in this, as well as in other instances, the words inferred and the *&c.* have been both given.

in this case I may enter upon the possession of the issue, for this that the issue cometh not to the tenements immediately by descent after the death of his mother, &c.*

If disseisor infeoff his father so as to come in by descent, the entry of disseisee is not taken away.

395 Also, if a disseisor infeoff his father in fee, and the father dieth of such estate seised, by which the tenements descend to the disseisor as son and heir: in this case the disseisee may well enter upon the disseisor, notwithstanding the descent, for this that as to the disseisin, the disseisor shall be adjudged in but as a disseisor, notwithstanding the descent. &c.†

The descent of the younger brother or his issue does not take away the entry of the elder or his issue.

396 Also, if a man seised of certain land in fee have issue two sons, and die seised, and the younger son enter by abatement in the land, who hath issue, and dieth seised thereof, and the tenements descend to the issue, and the issue enter

*lissue, pur ceo que lissue ne vient a les tenementes imediate per discent apres la mort sa mere, &c.**

395 Item, *si un disseisour enfeoffa son pere en fee, et le pere ent morust de tiel estate seisi, per que les tenementes descendount a le disseisor come fitz et heire : en ceo cas le disseisi bien poet entrer sur le disseisour, nient obstant le discent, pur ceo que quaunt a le disseisin, le disseisour serra ajugge eins forsque come disseisour, nient obstant le discent, &c.*†

396 Item, *si home seisi de certeyne terre en fee ad issue deux fitz, et morust seisi, et le puisne fitz entra per abatement en la terre, quel ad issue, et de ceo morust seisi, et les tenementes descendount al issue, et lissue entra en la terre;*

---

* This &c. is supplied in *Pyns.* 1516, *Redm.*, and subsequent editions, by the following termination of this paragraph—*but by the death of the father.* An addition of two references to the Year-Books also occur here in those and other corrupted editions, *viz. Contrarium tenetur P.* 9 *H.* 7, *per tout le court, & M.* 37 *H.* 6; upon which *Sir Edward Coke* remarks, "at this day this case of *Lyttleton* is holden for clear law."

† In *Redm.* and later editions, the words *quia particeps criminis* appear as a conclusion to this paragraph. The &c. only appears in the three earliest editions.

into the land; in this case the eldest son or his heir may enter by the law upon the issue of the younger son, notwithstanding the descent; because that when the younger son abated in the land after the death of his father, before any entry of the elder, the law will intend that he entereth in claiming as heir unto his father, and for this that the elder son claims by the same title, *scil.* as heir to his father, he and his heirs can enter upon the issue of the younger brother, notwithstanding the descent, &c., for this that they claim by self-same title. And in the same manner it shall be, if there were more descents from one issue to another issue of the younger son: 397 but in such case if the father were seised of certain land in fee, and hath issue two sons, and die, and the elder brother enter, and is seised, &c., and afterwards the younger brother disseiseth him, and by disseisin he is seised in fee, and hath issue, and of such estate dieth seised, then the elder brother cannot enter, but is put to his writ of *entre sur disseisin,* to recover the land. And the cause is, for this that the youngest brother cometh to the lands by wrongful disseisin done to

Otherwise if elder brother were seised.

en ceo cas le fitz eisne ou son heire poet entrer per la ley sur lissue del fitz puisne, nient contristeant le discent; pur ceo que quaunt le fitz puisne abatist en la terre apres la mort son pere, devaunt ascun entre per le fitz eisne, la ley entendera queil entra enclaymant come heire a son pere, et pur ceo que leisne fits clayma per mesme le title, scil. *come heire a son pere, il et ses heires poiont entrer sur lissue del puisne frere, nient obstant le discent, &c., pur ceo que ils claymont per un mesme title. Et en mesme le manere il serra, si furent plusours discentz dun issue a un autre issue del puisne fitz :*
397 *mes en tiel cas si le pere fuit seisi de certeyn terre en fee, et ad issue deux fitz, et devie, et leisne frere entra, et est seisi, &c., et puis le puisne frere luy disseisist, et per disseisin il est seisi en fee, et ad issue, et de tiel estate morust seisi, donques leisne frere ne poet entrer, mes est mys a son brief dentre sur disseisin, de recoverer la terre. Et la cause est, pur ceo que le puisne frere vient a les tenements per torcious*

his elder brother; and for this wrong the law cannot intend that he claimeth as heir to his father, no more than a stranger who had disseised the elder brother, who had* not any title, &c. And so you may see the diversity, where the younger brother entereth after the death of the father, before any entry made by the elder brother in such case, &c., and where the elder brother enters after the death of his father, and is disseised by the younger brother, where the younger afterwards dieth seised, &c.: 398 In the same manner it is, if a man seised of certain land in fee, hath issue two daughters, and dieth, and the elder daughter enter into the land, claiming all the land to herself, and thereof solely taketh the profits, and hath issue, and dies seised, by which her issue enter, which issue hath issue and dieth seised; and the second issue enter, &c., [*et sic ultra*†]; yet the younger daughter or her issue, as to the moiety, may enter upon any issue whatsoever of the elder daughter, notwithstanding such descent, for this that they claim by one selfsame title, &c. (§ 241); but in this

Privity of blood.
One coparcener dying seised of entirety, does not take away the entry of the other.

disseisin fait a son eisne frere ; et pur cell tort la ley ne poet entendre queil clayme come heire a son pere, nient pluis que un estraunge persone qui ust disseisi leisne, qui navoet ascun title, &c. Et issint poies veyer la diversite, lou le puisne frere entre apres la mort le pere, devaunt ascun entre fait per leisne frere en tiel cas, &c., et lou leisne frere entre apres la mort son pere, et est disseisi per le puisne frere, lou le puisne frere puis morust seisi, &c. :* 398 *En mesme le manere est, si home seisi de certeyn terre en fee, ad issue, deux filles, et devie, et leisne fille entra en la terre, claymant tout la terre a luy, et ent solement prent les profites, et ad issue et morust seisie, per que son issue entre, quel issue ad issue et devie seisi ; et le seconde issue entre, &c.,* [et sic ultra†]; *unqore la puisne fille ou son issue, quant a le moyte, poiont entrer sur queconques issue de leisne fille, nient obstant tiel discent, pur ceo que els claymont per un mesme title, &c. ; mes en cell*

* The three earliest editious read, *qui avoet ascun title, who had some title.*

† These words within the brackets do not appear in the Paper MS.

case if both sisters had entered after the death of their father, and thereof were seised, and afterwards the elder sister had disseised the younger of that which to her belonged, and was thereof seised in fee, and hath issue, and of such estate dieth seised, whereby the lands descend to the issue of the elder sister, then neither the younger sister nor her heirs can enter, &c. *Causa qua supra.*

If the bastard eisne *abate into fee simple after the death of the father, and die seised without interruption, and his issue enter, he shall hold it, and the right of the* mulier puisne *and of his heirs is bound for ever.*

399 Also, if a man seised of certain lands in fee, hath issue two sons, and the elder son is a bastard, and the younger brother is mulier, and the father dieth, and the bastard entereth in claiming as heir to his father, and occupieth the land all his life, without any entry made upon him by the mulier, and the bastard hath issue and dieth seised of such estate in fee, and the land descendeth to his issue, and his issue entereth, &c. In this case the mulier is without remedy; for he cannot enter, nor have any action to recover the land, because there is an ancient law in such case used (*c*).

cas, si ambideux soers avoient entrés apres la mort lour pere, et ent fuerent seisies, et puis leisne soer ust disseisie la puisne soer de ceo que a luy affiert, et ent fuit seisie en fee, et ad issue, et de tiel estate morust seisie, per que les tenementes descendont al issue del eisne soer, donques la puisne soer, ne ses heires poient entrer, &c. Causa qua supra.

399 Item, *si home seisi de certeyn terre en fee, ad issue deux fitz, et leisne fitz est bastarde, et le puisne frere est mulere, et le pere devie, et le bastarde entre enclaymant come heire a son pere, et occupia la terre tout sa vie sans ascun entre fait sur lui per le mulere, et le bastarde ad issue et morust seisi de tiel estate en fee, et la terre descendist a son issue, et son issue entre, &c. En ceo cas le mulere est sauns remedye ; qar il ne poet entrer, ne aver ascun accion pur recoverer la terre, pur ceo que est un auncien ley en tiel cas use.*

(c) The reasons assigned for this by *Blackstone*, (ii. 248), and by *Sir Edward Coke*, (*Co. Lytt.* 244. a.), are conceived too general by *Mr. Robertson*, the author of a *Treatise on the Law of Legitima-*

Bastard eisne *must be by same mother as* mulier puisne.

400 But it hath been the opinion of some, that this ought to be intended where the father hath a son bastard by a woman, and afterwards he marrieth the same woman, and after the espousals he hath issue by the same woman a son or a daughter mulier, and afterwards the father dieth, &c., if such bastard entereth, &c., and hath issue and die seised, &c., then shall the issue of such bastard have the land clearly to him, as it is said before, &c., and not any other bastard of the mother, who was never married to his father: and this seemeth to be a good and reasonable opinion, for such bastard born before marriage celebrated between them, to wit, the father and his mother, by the law of holy church is mulier, albeit by the law of the land he is bastard, and so he hath a colour to enter as heir to his father, for that he is by one law mulier, &c., *scil.* by law of holy church: but otherwise it is of a bastard that hath no colour to enter as heir, insomuch as he can by no law be said to be mulier; for such a bastard son is said

400 *Mes il ad este opinion dascuns, covient que ceo serra entendus lou le pere ad un fitz bastarde per un feme, et puis il espousa mesme la feme, et apres lespousell il ad issue per mesme la feme un fitz, ou une fille mulere, et puis le pere morust, &c., si tiel bastarde entra, &c., et ad issue et devie seisi, &c., donques avera lissue de tiel bastarde la terre clerement a luy, come avaunt est dit, &c., et nemy ascun autre bastarde la mere, que ne fuist unques espouse a son pere : et ceo semble bone et resonable opinion ; qar tiel bastarde nee devant espousells celebres perentre eux, cestassavoir, le pere et sa mere, per la ley de seynt esglise est mulere, coment que per la ley de la terre il est bastarde, et issint il ad un colour dentrer come heire a son pere, pur ceo que il est per une ley mulere, &c.,* scil. *per la ley de seynt esglise : mes autrement est de bastarde qui nad ascun colour dentrer come heire, entaunt que il ne poet per null ley estre dit mulere, qar tiel bastarde fitz est dit en la ley,* Quasi nullius

tion by subsequent Marriage. 8vo. Lond. 1829, *8vo. p. 44, et seq.*, to which learned tract the curious reader is referred.

in the law to be, *Quasi nullius filius, &c.* (§ 188). 401 But in the case aforesaid, where the bastard enters after the death of the father, and the mulier ousts him, and afterwards the bastard disseises the mulier, and hath issue and dieth seised, and the issue enters, then the mulier may have a writ of *entrie sur disseisin* against the issue of the bastard, and shall recover the land, &c. And so you may see the diversity where such bastard continues his possession all his life without interruption, and where the mulier entereth and interrupteth the possession of such bastard, &c.

But where bastard is ousted, and he subsequently disseises mulier, *the mulier shall recover.*

402 Also, if an infant within age have such cause to enter into any lands or tenements upon another, who is seised in fee, or in fee-tail of the same lands or tenements, if such man who is so seised, dieth of such estate seised, and the tenements descend to his issue, during the time that the infant is within age, such descent shall not take away the entry of the infant, but that he may enter upon the issue which is in by descent, &c., for that no laches shall be adjudged in an infant within age in such a case.

Infant. *A descent does not take away the entry of him who was under age at the time of the descent cast.*

filius, &c. 401 *Mes en le cas avauntdit, lou le bastarde entre apres la mort le pere, et le mulere luy ousta, et puis le bastarde disseisist le mulere, et ad issue et devie seisi, et lissue entre, donques le mulere poet aver brief dentre sur disseisin envers issue del bastarde, et recovera la terre, &c. Et issint poies veyer le diversité lou tiel bastarde continue sa possession tout sa vie sans interrupcion, et lou le mulere entra et interrupte la possession de tiel bastarde, &c.*

402 Item, *si un enfaunt deins age ad tiel cause dentrer en ascuns terres ou tenementes sur un autre, qui est seisi en fee, ou en fee-taille, de mesmes les terres ou tenementes, si tiel home qui est tielment seisi, morust de tiel estate seisi, et les tenementes descendount a son issue duraunt le temps que lenfaunt est deins age, tiel discent ne tollera lentré lenfant, mes quil poet entrer sur lissue que est eins per discent, &c., pur ceo que nul lachesse serra ajugge en un enfaunt deins age en tiel cas.*

Feme covert and her heirs not prejudiced by a descent during coverture.

403 Also, if the husband and his wife, as in right of the wife, have title and right to enter in tenements which another hath in fee, or in fee-tail, and such tenant dieth seised, &c. In such case the entry of the husband upon the heir who is in by descent is taken away: but if the husband die, then the wife can well enter upon the issue who is in by descent, for this that no laches of the husband shall turn to the prejudice or damage of the wife or her heirs in such case, but that the wife and her heirs may well enter [where such descent is fallen during the coverture*].

See § 436, 437, 440, cases upon the same reason.

Descent cast is of no effect against heir of non compos.

405 Also, if a man that is of non-sane memory, that is to say in Latin, *Qui non est compos mentis*, hath cause to enter into any such tenements, if such descent, *ut supra*, be

403 Item, *si le baron et sa feme, come en droit la feme, ount title et droit dentrer en tenementes que un autre ad en fee, ou en fee-taille, et tiel tenaunt morust seisi, &c. En tiel cas lentré le baron est tolle sur leire qui est eins per discent : mes si le baron devie, donques la feme bien poet entrer sur lissue que est eins per discent, pur ceo que lachesse le baron ne tournera la feme ne ses heires en prejudice nen damage en tiel cas, mes que la feme et ses heires bien poiont entrer, [lou tiel discent est eschue durant le coverture*].*

405 Item, *si home que est de non sane memorie, que est adire en Latin,* Qui non est compos mentis, *ad cause dentrer en ascuns tielx tenementes, si tiel discent,* ut supra, *soit ewe en*

As to what is "folly" or laches *of feme covert; see § 666—of heir; § 664, 665, 726.*

* The words within brackets do not appear in *Pyns.* 1516, and here follows in all the copies since *Redm.*, (the editions of *Rastell's* Transl. excepted), an addition to *Lyttleton*, which forms the 404th subdivision of his text, by *West*, 1581, *viz.:—But the court holdeth, where such title is given to a feme sole [of full age], who after taketh husband, which doth not enter, but suffers a descent, &c., there otherwise it is, for it shall be said the folly of the wife to take such a husband which entered not in time, &c.—[Pasch. 9 Hen. 7, pl. 24]*, on which *Sir E. Coke* remarks, "This is added, and therefore, as formerly I have done, I meddle not withal; howbeit the opinion is holden for law, as it appeareth in the section next precedent."

had in his life during the time he was of non-sane memory, and afterwards die, his heir may well enter upon him that is in by descent. And in this case you may see a case where the heir can enter, and yet his ancestor that had the same title could not enter; for he that was out of his mind at the time of such descent, if he willeth to enter after such a descent, if an action upon this be sued against him, he hath nothing for himself to plead or to help him, but to say, that he was not of sane memory at the time of such descent, &c.; and he shall not be received to say this, because that no man of full age shall be received in any plea by the law to stultify and disable* his own person; but the heir may well disable the person of his ancestor for the advantage of the heir in such case; for this that no laches can be adjudged by the law in him who hath no discretion in such case. 406 And if such man of non-sane memory make feoff- *As to feoffment*

sa vie, durant le temps que il fuist de non sane memorie, et puis devia, son heire bien poet entrer sur luy qui est eins per discent. Et en ceo cas poies veyer un cas que leire poet entrer, et unqore son auncestre qui avoit mesme le title ne puissoit entrer; qar celuy qui fuist hors de sa memorie al temps de tiel discent, sil voille entrer apres tiel discent, si accion sur ceo soit sue denvers luy, il nad riens pur luy a pleder, ou eider, mes adire, quil fuist de non sane memorie a temps de tiel discent, &c.; et a ceo ne serra il resceu a dire, pur ceo que nul home de plein age serra resceu en ascun plee per la ley a destultiser et disabler son mesme persone; mes leire bien poet disabler le persone son auncestre, pur lavantage del heire en tiel cas; pur ceo que nulle lachesse poet estre ajugge per la ley en celuy qui ad nul discrecion en tiel cas.* 406 *Et si tiel home de non sane memorie fait feoffment, &c.,*

* *A defalsesser et disabler; Pyns.* 1516. *A defalser et disabler; Redm. To falsify and disable.*

by non compos or infant.

ment, &c. (*d*), he cannot enter nor have a writ called *Dum non fuit compos mentis, &c., causa qua supra:* but after his death his heir may well enter, or have the said writ of *Dum non fuit compos mentis,* at his election, &c.*

Disseisin by infant takes away entry;

407 Also, if I be disseised by an infant within age, who alieneth to another in fee, and the alienee die seised, and the tenements descend to his heir, the infant still being within age†, my entry is taken away; 408 but if the infant within age enter upon the heir that is in‡ by descent, as he well may, for

but if infant enter on heir of his alienee,

il ne poet entrer ne aver brief appelle Dum non fuit compos mentis, &c., causa qua supra: *mes apres sa mort son heire bien poit entrer, ou aver le dit brief* Dum non fuit compos mentis, *a son eleccion, &c.**

407 Item, *si jeo sue disseisi per un enfaunt deins age, le quel aliena a un autre en fee, et lalienê devie seisie, et les tenementes descendount a son heire, et esteant lenfaunt deins age*†, *mon entrê est tolle;* 408 *mes si lenfaunt deins age entra sur leire qui est eins*‡ *per discent, come il poet bien, pur ceo que*

---

* Here follows an interpolation which first occurs in *Pyns.* 1516, translated by *Sir Edward Coke*, with whom it passed unnoticed, thus.—"The same law is where an infant within age maketh a feoffment and dieth, his heir may enter, or have a writ of *Dum fuit infra ætatem.*" The comment of *Sir E Coke* on this passage is thus:—"This is true, as to the bringing of a *Dum fuit infra ætatem, &c.*, but without question the infant in that case might have entered, as it appeareth in the next section."—*Co. Lytt.* 247. b.

† The Translation by *Sir Edward Coke*, renders this passage, *being an infant within age*, which error has been noticed by *Hargrave* and *Butler*, in their annotations upon *Coke's* Commentary.

‡ In the three earliest editions this word is printed *heire*, but erroneously.

(*d*) Or any other like conveyances *in pais;* but fines and other assurances of record are not implied in this *&c.*—*Co. Lytt.* 247. b.

this that the same descent was during his nonage, then I may well enter upon the disseisor, because by his entry he hath defeated and annulled the descent: 409 In the same manner it is where I am disseised, and the disseisor makes a feoffment in fee upon condition, and the feoffee dies of such estate seised, &c., I cannot enter upon the heir* of the feoffee: but if the condition be broken, so that for this cause the feoffor entereth upon the heir, now I may well enter; for this that when the feoffor or his heirs entereth for the condition broken, the descent is utterly defeated.

his entry is not taken away.

So if disseisor make feoffment on condition, entry cannot be made on feoffee's heir, until feoffor enter on him.

410 Also, if I be disseised, and the disseisor hath issue and entereth into religion, by force whereof the lands descend to his issue; in this case I may well enter upon the issue, and yet there was a descent; but for this that such descent cometh to the issue by the act of the father, *scil.* for that he entereth into religion, &c., and the descent came not unto

Descent not cast by profession, § 200.

mesme le discent fuist durant son nonnage, donques jeo bien puis entrer sur le disseisour, pur ceo que per son entré il ad defete et aniente le discent : 409 *En mesme le manere est lou jeo sue disseisi, et le disseisour fait feoffement en fee sur condicion, et le feoffé morust de tiel estate seisi, &c., jeo ne purroye my entrer sur leire* le feoffé : mes si la condicion soit enfreynt, icy que pur cel cause le feoffour entre sur leire, ore jeo bien puis entrer ; pur ceo que quaunt le feoffour ou ses heires entra pur la condicion enfreynt, le discent est oustrement defete.*

410 Item, *si jeo sue disseisi, et le disseisour ad issue et entra en religion, per force de quel les tenementes descendount a son issue ; en ceo cas jeo bien puis entrer sur lissue, et ungore la fuist un discent ; mes pur ceo que tiel discent vient al issue per fait le pere,* scil. *pur ceo que il entre en re-*

* This word is misprinted in the three earliest copies, *la terre, the land*, but subsequent copies rectify the error, and *Rastell's* Transl. also renders this word according to the true sense.

him by the act of God*, that is to say, by death, &c., my entry is lawful: for if I arraign an assise of novel disseisin against my disseisor, albeit he after enter into religion, this shall not abate my writ, but my writ, this notwithstanding, shall stand in its force, and against him shall be good. And by the same reason the descent which cometh to his issue by his own act, shall not take from me my entry, &c.

A descent cast will not prejudice the lessee for years.

411 Also, if I let unto a man certain lands for term of twenty years, and another disseiseth me, and ousts the termor, and dieth seised, and the lands descend to his heir, I cannot enter; and yet the lessee for years may well enter, because he by his entry doth not oust the heir who is in by descent of the freehold which is to him descended, but only to have the tenements for term of years, which is no expulsion from the freehold of the heir who is in by descent. But otherwise it is where my tenant for term of life is disseised: *Causa patet.*

Secus *of lessee for life.*

ligion, &c., et le discent ne vient a luy per fait de Dieu, cestassavoir, per mort, &c., mon entré est congeable: qar si jeo arrayne un assise* de novel disseisin *envers mon disseisour, coment que il puis entra en religion, ceo ne abarera mye mon brief, mes mon brief, ceo non obstant, estoiera en sa force, et envers luy serra bon. Per mesme le reason le discent que aveigne a son issue per son fait demesne, ne moy tollera de mon entré, &c.*

411 Item, *si jeo lesse a un home certeynes terres pur terme de* xx. *ans, et un autre moy disseisist, et ousta le termor, et devie seisi, et les tenementes descendount a son heire, jeo ne purroye entrer; et unqore le lessé pur terme dans bien poet entrer, pur ceo que il per son entré ne ousta leire que est eins per discent de le franktenement que est a luy descendus, mes solement daver les tenementes pur terme dans, le quel nest expulsement de le franktenement del heire que est eins per discent. Mes autrement est ou mon tenaunt a terme de vie est disseisi :* Causa patet.

* These words are in the three earliest copies misprinted *dedit.*

412 Also, it is said that if a man be seised of tenements in fee by occupation in time of *civil* war, and thereof dieth seised in the time of war, and the tenements descend to his heir, such descent shall not oust any man of his entry; and of this a man may see in a plea upon a writ of aiel, *anno 7 E. 2.*

Dying seised in time of [civil] war casts no descent.

413 Also, that no dying seised, where the tenements shall come to another by succession, shall take away the entry of any person, &c. For as to prelates, abbots, priors, deans, or of parsons of churches*, &c., albeit there were twenty dyings seised, and twenty successions, this shall not toll from any man his entry, &c.†

The doctrine of descent-cast does not apply to corporations.

More shall be said of Descents in the Chapter of Continual Claim.

412 Item, *il est dit que si home est seisi de tenementes en fee per occupacion en temps de guerre, et ent morust seisi en temps de guerre, et les tenementes descendount a son heire, tiel discent ne ousta ascun home de son entré, et de ceo home poet veyer en un plee sur un brief de aiel,* Anno vii. E. ii..

413 Item, *nul murrant seisi, lou les tenementes viendront a un autre per succession, ne tollera lentré dascun persone, &c. Qar de prelatz, abbés, priours, deanes, ou persones desglises, &c.**, coment que furent* xx. *murrantes seisis, et* xx. *successions, ceo ne tollera jammes ascun home de son entré, &c.*†

Pluis serra dit de discentez en le chapitre de continuell clayme.

---

* This *&c.* may perhaps be supplied by the words which appear in all the editions since *Roh., viz. ou de autres corps politiques, or of other bodies politick.*

† In *Redm., Berth., Middl., Sm., Powel,* and *Tottyl* 1554, appear the following words—*car ceo nest proprement dit discent, &c., for this is not properly termed a descent, &c.*

CHAPTER VII.

CONTINUAL CLAIM.

CONTINUAL claim was, where a man who had right and title to enter into any lands or tenements, whereof another was seised in fee or in tail, made continual claim to them before the disseisor or party in possession died seised thereof: the effect of which was, that notwithstanding the dying seised of such party, thereby " casting a descent," yet he who made such *continual claim* might enter, because he had done all that, perhaps, he could or durst do, to regain possession; and, therefore, as no laches could be said to be in him, his right of entry, (which in a full sense means "right of title,") remained as it was before, notwithstanding such descent or dying in possession of the adverse party or party holding adverse possession; the doctrine of law being, that a continual claim was, as being an entry in law, as good and as efficacious as an entry " in deed " or in fact (§ 414). Thus, if tenant for life aliened in fee, he in reversion or remainder might enter on the alienee, or make continual claim on the land before the dying seised of the alienee, and then he might have entered at any time after his death, though a descent had been cast in the manner above related (§ 415).

The effect of continual claim in relation to such adverse possessions, and the mode by which its efficacy became dispensed with, may be briefly noticed.

Any person having right to the possession of tenements, might enter upon such tenements; and as such entry was deemed equivalent to feodal investiture, he was then able to prosecute any possessory action to try his right or title thereto at any period of time, as having been himself seised thereof. However, as it became expedient that certain periods should be fixed within which real actions should be commenced, and to which they were *limited*, certain historical events were from time to time selected for that purpose, as the accession of Richard the First, the return of King John from Ireland, and the coronation of Henry the Third: ultimately the stat. 32 Hen. 8, c. 2, limited the periods or *limitation* within which no person should maintain any writ of right, or make any prescription, title, or claim to or for any *manors, lands, tenements, rents, annuities, commons, pensions, portions, corodies*, or *other hereditaments*, either upon his own or ancestor's possession; also by stat. 4 Hen. 7, c. 24, a fine with proclamations was made a bar to all persons having present rights of entry, and not being under any disabilities, if they did not claim within five years after the proclamations made, to all persons under disabilities if they did not claim within five years after their disabilities were removed, and to all persons not having present rights, if they did not claim within five years after their rights of entry accrued, unless under disabilities, and then within five years after the removal of their disabilities (*a*). The stat. 21 Jac. 1, c. 16, limited the period for all writs of *formedon* to twenty years, and enacted, that no persons should at any time thereafter make any entry into any lands, tenements, or hereditaments, but within twenty years next after his title should first descend or accrue to the same, and in default thereof, such persons so not entering, and their heirs, should be disabled from such entry after to be made. By the stat. 4 & 5 Ann, c. 16, s. 14, it was enacted, that no entry upon lands should be of force to satisfy the last-mentioned statute, or to avoid a fine levied of lands, unless an action were thereupon commenced within one year after, and prosecuted with effect.

These statutes of *limitation*, it will have been observed, did not, otherwise than by restriction as to the time within

---

(*a*) By the abolition of fines, the practice of gaining a title by a fine and non-claim has been prevented.—See stat. 3 & 4 Gul. 4, c. 74, s 2.

which real actions should have been brought, or an entry made, interfere with the doctrine of *descents, continual claim,* and *discontinuance;* and therefore *limitation of actions* which also involved, as those doctrines did, the cases of *adverse possession,* may be said to have been merely collateral to that species of learning which depended on *disseisin* and *ouster;* but at length this statutory doctrine of *limitation of actions* has, like the serpent of Aaron, swallowed up its brethren, and for many purposes has rendered the learning of Lyttleton contained in these chapters more an object of curious inquiry than professed utility: yet it must not be forgotten, that every word of Lyttleton is material, the principles of his arguments and illustrations either as elucidating the reason of the common or ancient law, or as applied to the construction of modern cases, still remaining unchanged.

The acts passed in the late reign, especially the stat. 3 & 4 Gul. 4, c. 27, "for the Limitation of Actions and Suits relating to Real Property," have, in simplifying the ancient law, created a revolution in this branch of our jurisprudence; for by s. 2 of that act, "no person shall make an entry or distress, or bring an action to recover any land or rent," but within twenty years next after the times therein mentioned, and the efficacy of an entry, so far as concerns the doctrine of continual claim, is annihilated; for by s. 10, "no person shall be deemed to have been in possession of any land within the meaning of that act, merely by reason of having made an entry thereon:" and with regard to the subject of this Chapter, it is enacted, "that no continual or other claim upon or near any land, shall preserve any right of making an entry or distress, or of bringing an action (*b*)."

However, to return to Lyttleton, he proceeds, after defini-

(*b*) This clause in the act shortens the period within which an ejectment can be brought; for under the stat. of Anne, a party might enter just before the expiration of the twenty years, and commence his action within one year afterwards.

tion and illustration, to state how continual claim (which must have been made within a year and a day before the descent cast (*c*) (§ 422)), should have been made (§ 417—421), wherein he considers the relation of principal and agent, so far as concerns the validity of an act, where less is executed than is delegated by the authority or *power*, or where a servant does less than is expressly committed to him (§ 434, 435): the practical effect of continual claim is next stated, which was, if made upon a tenant in tail, to defeat such estate tail, and thereby to create a disseisin by the party in possession; and so *toties quoties* upon every claim (§ 429). As a consequence of or immediately referring to the doctrine of claim, the excuses or *disabilities* which the disseisee or claimant might urge for not making continual claim, and yet preserve his right of entry, are next noticed, two of which Lyttleton describes, as imprisonment (*d*) (§ 436), and being abroad (§ 439) (*e*), and the subject of this Chapter is concluded by Lyttleton's putting a case where it is inquired, whether a descent cast during the vacancy of an abbacy, which equally applies to the case of a bishop, parson, vicar, prebendary, or any sole corporation, was a bar to the successor's entry, nowithstanding the want of continual claim (§ 443), which *quære* Lyttleton

---

(*c*) By stat. 32 Hen. 8, c. 33, no dying seised, &c., of a disseisor tolled an entry, unless he had been in quiet possession for five years after the disseisin; but it is said, that the statute extended not to abators or intruders, nor to the disseisor's feoffee, but to all disseisins with or without force, and to successors whose predecessors were disseised, though it only speaks of the disseisee and his heirs; after the five years, continual claim was required to have been made every year and day.

(*d*) Imprisonment is not a *disability* under the new Statute of Limitations. The only disabilities therein mentioned are *infancy*, *lunacy*, *coverture*, and *absence beyond seas*. See stat. 3 & 4 Gul. 4, c. 27, s. 16.

(*e*) The disabilities of infancy, lunacy, and coverture are noticed in the preceding Chapter, of which, in fact, the present is a continuation, § 402, 403, 405.

resolves in the affirmative of the proposition. The chapter itself concludes with two monkish verses in the praise of *quæres* (*g*), the authenticity of these not perfectly Augustan lines, like many of the *quæres* ascribed to Lyttleton, may be doubted, excepting perhaps those which, in the language of an anonymous commentary on Lyttleton lately published, appear to be noted (as the last case in this Chapter seems to be), "not for the difficulty of the case, but to incite the student to a diligent search of the reasons thereof."

If a disseisee make continual claim unto lands, whereof the disseisor or his donee or feoffee

414 CONTINUAL claim is where a man hath right and title to enter in any lands or tenements whereof another is seised in fee, or in fee-tail, if he that hath title to enter make continual claim to the lands or tenements before the dying seised

414 *Continuell clayme est par là ou home ad droit et title dentrer en ascuns terres ou tenementes dount un autre est seisi en fee, ou en fee-taille, si cestuy qui ad title dentrer fait continuell clayme a les terres ou tenementes devaunt le mur-*

(*g*) The *quæres* of *Lyttleton* occur at §§ [35], 42, [55], 96, 108, 124, 170, 302, 340, [358], 375, 435, 442, 443, 499, [509], 527, 530, 636, 677, 739. Many of these are of questionable origin, those included within *brackets* are only to be met with in the corrupted copies, and are noticed by *Sir Edward Coke* as additions. One of these *quæres*, (§ 124), *Sir Ed. Coke* remarks, "came not out of *Lyttleton's* quiver."—*Co Lytt.* 90. a., *ante*, p. 161. *Mr. Houard* considers, for reasons he does not state, all the *quæres* spurious. The *verses* do not appear in either of the Camb. MSS., and they also vary in the earlier editions, a sign of their having been interpolated. *Sir William Jones* in his notes of readings from the Camb. MS. remarks, that "these barbarous verses are not in the MS., they are unworthy of being cited by Lyttleton."

of him that holdeth the tenements, then albeit that such tenant dies thereof seised, and the lands or the tenements descend to his heir; yet can he that hath made such continual claim, or his heir, enter into the lands or tenements so descended, by reason of the continual claim made, notwithstanding such descent. As in case that a man be disseised, and the disseisee make continual claim to the tenements in the life of the disseisor, although that the disseisor dieth seised in fee, and the land descend to his heir, yet can the disseisee enter upon the possession of the heir, notwithstanding the descent, &c. 415 In the same manner it is, if tenant for term of life alien in fee, he in the reversion, or he in the remainder, can enter upon the alienee: and if such alienee die seised of such estate without continual claim made to the tenements before the dying seised of the alienee, and the tenements by reason of the dying seised of the alienee descend to the heir of the alienee, then neither can he in the reversion, or he in the remainder enter; but if he in the reversion, or he in

is seised, or if he in reversion or remainder make continual claim upon the alienee of a particular tenant guilty of a forfeiture, before a descent cast, they save their entry thereby, notwithstanding the descent.

[*A distinction taken between* a right *of entry which was bound by a descent, as in this case; and* a title *of entry which was not bound by descent, as in the case*, § 409.]

rant seisi de celuy qui tient les tenementes, donques coment que tiel tenaunt morust ent seisi, et les terres ou les tenementes descendount a son heire; unqore poet celuy qui avoit fait tiel clayme, ou son heire, entrer en les terres ou tenementes issint discendus, per cause de continuel clayme fait, nient contristeant tiel discent. Sicome en cas que home est disseisi, et le disseisi fait continuel clayme a les tenementes en la vie le disseisour, coment que le disseisour devie seisi en fee, et la terre descendist a son heire, unqore poet le disseisi entrer sur la possession leire, nient obstant le discent, &c. 415 *En mesme le manere est, si tenaunt a terme de vie aliena en fee, celuy en la revercion, ou celuy en le remeyndre, poet entrer sur lalienć: et si tiel alienć devia seisi de tiel estate sauns continuel clayme fait a les tenementes devaunt le murrant seisi del alienć, et les tenementes per cause del murrant seisi del alienć descendount al heire del alienć, donques ne poet celuy en la revercion, ou celuy en le remeyndre entrer; mes si celuy en la revercion, ou celuy en le remeyndre, qui ad cause*

the remainder, who hath cause to enter upon the alienee, make continual claim to the tenements before the dying seised of the alienee, then such man can enter after the death of the alienee, as well as he could in his lifetime, &c.

Continual claim must be made by him who has a right of entry.

416 Also, if land be let to a man for term of his life, the remainder to another for term of his life, the remainder to the third in fee, if the tenant for term of life alien to another in fee, and he in the remainder for term of life make continual claim to the land before the dying seised of the alienee, and afterwards the alienee dieth seised, &c., and afterwards, he in the remainder for term of life die before any entry made by him; in this case he in the remainder in fee can enter &c. upon the heir of the alienee, by reason of the continual claim made by him that had the remainder for term of his life, because that such right as he shall have of entry, shall go* and remain to him in the remainder after him, insomuch that he in the remainder in fee† could not enter

dentrer sur lalienė, fait continuel clayme a les tenementes devaunt le murrant seisi del alienė, donques tiel home poet entrer apres la mort dalienė, auxibien come il poet a sa vie, &c.

416 Item, *si terre soit lesse a un home pur terme de sa vie, le remeyndre a un autre pur terme de sa vie, le remeyndre a le tierce en fee, si le tenaunt a terme de vie aliena a un autre en fee, et celuy en le remeyndre pur terme de vie fait continuel clayme a la terre devaunt le murrant seisi dalienė, et puis lalienė morust seisi, &c., et puis apres, celuy en le remeyndre pur terme de vie morust, devaunt ascun entre fait per luy; en ceo cas celuy en le remeyndre en fee poet entrer &c. sur leire lalienė, per cause de continuel clayme fait per luy qui avoit le remeyndre pur terme de sa vie, pur ceo que tiel droit quil avera dentre, alera* et remeyndra a celuy en le remeyndre apres luy, entant que celuy en le remeyndre en fee† ne puissoit pas en-*

* This is printed in the three earliest editions, ne *alera*, *shall* not *go*; all other editions read as above.

† In the three earliest editions, a misprint occurs here, by inserting the word *qui*, *who*.

upon the alienee in fee, during the life of him in the remainder for term of life, and because he could not then make continual claim, [for none can make continual claim*] but when he hath title to enter, &c.

How continual claim is to be made, and three rules propounded by Lyttleton.

417 But it is to be seen of thee, my son, how and in what manner such continual claim shall be made; and to learn this well, three things are to be understood.

1. Entry into part of lands in the name of the whole, is good for lands in the county wherein the claim is made.

The first thing is, if a man have cause to enter in any lands or tenements in divers towns within one shire, if he enter into one parcel of the lands or tenements which are in one town, in the name of all the lands or tenements to the which he hath right to enter, within all the towns of the same shire, by such entry he hath as good possession and seisin of such lands and tenements whereof he hath title to enter, as if he had entered indeed into every parcel; and this seemeth great reason. 418 For if a man will enfeoff another

trer sur lalienê en fee, duraunt la vie celuy en le remeyndre pur terme de vie, et pur ceo il ne puissoit adonques faire continuel clayme, [qar nul poet faire continuel clayme] mes quaunt il ad title dentrer, &c.*

417 *Mes est a veyer a toy, mon fitz, coment et en quel manere tiel continuel clayme serra fait ; et ceo bien apprendre, trois choses sount entendus.*

Le premier chose est, si home ad cause dentrer en ascunes terres ou tenementes en divers villes deins un mesme countee, sil entra en un parcell de les terres ou tenementes que sount en un ville, en noun de toutes les terres ou tenementes as queux il ad droit dentrer, deins toutes les villes de mesme le countee, per tiel entre il avoet auxi bon possession et seisin de tielx terres ou tenementes dont il ad title dentre, sicome il avoet entre en chescun parcel ; et ceo semble graund reason.
418 *Qar si home voille enfeoffer un autre sauns fait de cer-*

---

* These words do not appear in these three earliest editions, but they are given in all subsequent copies and in *Rastell's* Transl.

§ 61, 177. without deed of certain lands or tenements, which he hath in many towns within one shire, and he willeth to deliver seisin to the feoffee of parcel of the tenements within one town in the name of all the lands or tenements which he hath in the same town, and in all the other towns, &c., all the said tenements, &c., pass by force of the said livery of seisin to him to whom such feoffment in such manner is made: and yet he, to whom such livery of seisin was made, hath not right to all the lands or tenements in all the towns, but by reason of the livery of seisin made of parcel of the lands or tenements in one town: *A multo fortiori* it seemeth good reason, that when a man hath title to enter into the lands or tenements in divers towns in one same shire, before any entry by him made, that by the entry by him made in parcel of the lands in one town in the name of all the lands and tenements whereto he hath title to enter within the same shire, this is a seisin of all in him; and by such entry he hath possession and seisin in deed, as if he had entered into every parcel, &c.

[Title *of entry is here taken for* right *of entry as well at the commencement of this chapter* (§ 414), *as at* § 417, 419. 426, 428, *and* 432.]

teynes terres ou tenementes, que il ad deins plusours villes en un countee, et il voille lyverer seisin al feoffé de parcell des tenementes deins un ville en noun de toutes les terres ou tenementes queil ad en mesme la ville, et en les autres villes, &c., toutz les ditz tenementes, &c., passont per force de le dit lyverë de seisin a celuy a qui tiel feoffement en tiel manere est fait: et unqore celuy a qui tiel lyverë de seisin fuist fait, navoit droit a toutes les terres ou tenementes en toutes les villes, mes per la cause de la lyverë de seisin fait de parcell de les terres ou tenementes en un ville: A multo fortiori *il semble bon reason, que quaunt home ad title dentrer en les terres ou tenementes en divers villes deins un mesme countee, devaunt ascun entré per luy fait, que per lentré per luy fait en parcell de les terres en un ville en le noun de toutes les terres et tenementes as queux il ad title dentrer deins mesme le countee, ceo est un seisin de toutes en luy; et per tiel entré il ad possession et seisin en fait, si come il avoit entre en chescun parcell, &c.*

419 The second thing is, to understand, that if a man hath title to enter into any lands or tenements, if he dare not enter into the same lands or tenements, or into any parcel thereof, for doubt of beating, or for doubt of maiming, or for doubt of death, if he go and approach so near to the tenements as he dare for such doubt, and claim by word the tenements to be his own, forthwith by such claim he hath a possession and seisin in the tenements, as well as if he had entered in fact, although he never had possession or seisin of the same tenements before the said claim; 420 and that the law is such, it is well proved by a plea of an assise, in the book of assise, *anno* 38 *E.* 3, [*pl.* 23], the tenor whereof ensueth in such form:—In the county of Dorset, before the same justices, it was found by verdict of assise, that the plaintiff that had right by descent of heritage to have the tenements put in plaint, at the time of the decease of his ancestor, was dwelling in the town where the tenements were, and by word claimeth the tenements amongst his neighbours, but for fear of death

2. If party having right of entry, make continual claim so near the land as he durst go, it is sufficient.

Which principle is vouched by a book-case, 38 *Ass.* placito 23.

419 *Le seconde chose est, a entendre, que si home ad title dentrer en ascuns terres ou tenementes, sil ne osast entrer en mesmes les terres ou tenementes, ne en ascun parcell de ceo, pur doute de baterie, ou pur doute de maheyme, ou pur doute de mort, sil alast et approche auxi pres a les tenementes come il osast pur tiel doute, et clayma per parolle les tenementes estre les soens, meyntenaunt per tiel clayme il ad un possession et seisin en les tenementes, auxy bien come sil ust entre en fait, coment quil navoit unques possession ou seisin de mesmes les tenementes devaunt le dit clayme;* 420 *et que la ley est tiel, il est bien prove per un plee dun assise, en le lyver dassise* anno xxxviij. E. 3, *le tenure de quel ensuyst en tiel fourme:—En le countee de Dorset, devaunt mesmes les justices, trove fuist per verdit dassise, que le pleintif qui avoit droit per discent deritage daver les tenementes mys en pleynt, al temps del murrant son auncestre, fuist demurrant en la ville ou les tenementes furent, et per parolle clayme les tenementes entre ses viceyns, mes pur doute*

he durst not approach the tenements, but bringeth his assise; and upon the matter found, it was awarded that he should recover, &c.

3. Within what time continual claim should be made, (which should be made at the land, or as near thereto as disseisee can possibly go),

421 The third thing is, to understand, within what time the claim which is styled continual claim, shall serve and aid him that made the claim, and his heirs: as to this, it is to be understood, that he that hath title to enter, when he will make his claim, if he dare approach the land, then it behoveth him to go to the land, or to parcel of it, and make his claim, and if he dare not approach the land for doubt or fear of beating or maiming, or death, then it behoveth him to go and approach as near as he dares towards the land, or parcel of it, and make his claim; 422 and if his adversary who occupieth the land, die seised in fee, or in fee-tail within the year and a day after such claim, whereby the tenements descend to his son as heir to him, yet can he that makes the claim enter upon the possession of the heir (*h*):

viz. within a year and a day after the claim made upon the adversary or his heir.

de mort il nosa approcher les tenementes, mes port lassise, et sur ceo matere trove, agarde fuit queil recovera, &c.

421 *La tierce chose est, a entendre, deins quel temps le clayme que est dit continuel clayme, servera et eidera celuy qui fist le clayme, et ses heires : quant a ceo, est assavoir, que celuy qui ad title dentrer, quaunt il voet faire son clayme, sil osast approcher la terre, donques il covient aler a la terre, ou a parcell de ceo, et faire son clayme, et sil nosast approcher la terre pur doute ou pavour de baterie, ou maheyme, ou mort, donques a luy covient daler et approcher auxi pres come il osast vers la terre, ou a parcell de ceo, et faire son clayme ;* 422 *et si son adversaire qui occupia la terre, morust seisi en fee, ou en fee taille deins lan et le jour apres tiel clayme, per que les tenementes descendount a son fits come leire a luy, unqore poet celuy qui fist le clayme entrer sur la possession leire :*

(*h*) It is to be observed that the law in many cases hath limited a year and a day to be a legal and convenient time for many purposes.

423 But in this case after the year and the day that such claim was made, if no other claim were made, if the father then died seised the morrow the next after the year and the day, or any other day afterwards, &c., then cannot he that made the claim enter: and therefore if he that made the claim will be sure at all times that his entry shall not be taken away by such descent, &c., it behoveth him, within the year and the day after the first claim, to make another claim in the form aforesaid, and within the year and the day after the second claim, to make the third claim in the same manner, and within the year and the day after the third claim, to make another claim, and so on; that is

But insomuch as after the year and day the claim cannot be made, a new claim should be made from year to year, within the year and day from the previous claim made, so that whenever the adversary dies, the right of entry is preserved,

423 *Mes en ceo cas apres lan et le jour que tiel clayme fuist fait, si null autre clayme fuist fait, si le pere donques morust seisi lendemayn proscheyn apres lan et le jour, ou a un autre jour apres, &c., donques ne poet celuy qui fist le clayme entrer : et pur ceo si celuy qui fist le clayme voet estre sure a tout temps que son entre ne serra tolle per tiel discent, &c., il covient a celuy, que deins lan et le jour apres le premier clayme, de faire un autre clayme en la fourme avantdit, et deins lan et le jour apres le seconde clayme, de faire le tierce clayme en mesme le manere, et deins lan et le jour de le tierce clayme, de faire un autre clayme, et issint oustre ; cest-*

As at the common law upon a fine or final judgment given in a writ of right, the party grieved had a year and a day to make his claim. So the wife or heir hath a year and a day to bring an appeal of death. If a villein remained in ancient demesne a year and a day, he was privileged. If a man be wounded or poisoned, &c., and dieth thereof within the year and the day, it is felony. By the ancient law, if the feoffee of a disseisor had continued a year and a day, the entry of the disseisee for his negligence had been taken away. After judgment given in a real action, the plaintiff within the year and the day may have an *habere facias seisinam*, and in an action of debt, &c., a *capias*, *fieri facias*, or a *levari facias*. A protection shall be allowed but for a year and a day, and no longer, and in many other cases.—*Co. Lytt.* 245. b.

to say, to make another claim within every year and day next after every claim made during the life of his adversary; and then at what time soever that his adversary die seised, his entry shall not be taken away by any such descent; and such claim in such manner to be made is most commonly taken and styled the continual claim of him that maketh the claim; 424 but yet in the case aforesaid, where his adversary dieth within the year and the day next after the claim, this is in law a continual claim, insomuch that his adversary within the year and the day next after the same claim died. For there is no need for him that hath made his claim, to make any other claim, but at what time he will within the same year and day, &c.

whether the adversary, (i. e. the disseisor or the party claiming from him in adverse possession to the claimant), live or die.

And this continual claim extends to any other disseisor who may die seised.

425 Also, if the adversary be disseised within the year and the day after such claim, and the disseisor thereof dieth seised within the year and the day, &c., such dying seised shall not hurt him that made the claim, but that he may enter, &c. For whosoever he be that dieth seised within the year and the day after such claim made, this shall not hurt

assavoir, de faire un autre clayme deins chescun an et jour proscheyn apres chescun clayme fait duraunt la vie son adversarie; et donques, a quecunques temps que son adversarie morust seisi, son entré ne serra tolle per nul tiel discent; et tiel clayme en tiel manere destre fait, est pluis communement prise et nosme continuel clayme de luy qui fist le clayme; 424 *mes unqore en cas avauntdit, lou son adversarie morust deins lan et le jour proscheyn apres le clayme, ceo est en ley un continuel clayme, entaunt que ladversarie deins lan et le jour proscheyn apres mesme le clayme morust. Qar il ne bosoigne a celuy que fist son clayme, de faire ascun autre clayme, mes a quel temps que il voet deins mesme lan et le jour, &c.*

425 Item, *si ladversarie soit disseisi deins lan et le jour apres tiel clayme, et le disseisour ent morust seisi deins lan et le jour, &c., tiel murrant seisi ne grevera my celuy qui fist le clayme, mes queil poet entrer, &c. Qar quiconques qui soit qui morust seisi deins lan et le jour proscheyn apres tiel clayme, ceo ne grevera my celuy qui fist le clayme, mes quil*

him that made the claim, but that he may enter, &c., albeit there were many dyings seised, and many descents within the year and day, &c.

426 Also, if a man be disseised, and the disseisor die seised within the year and day next after the disseisin committed, whereby the tenements descend to his heir, in this case the entry of the disseisee is taken away; for the year and the day which should aid the disseisee in such case, &c., shall not be taken from the time of title of entry accrued to him, but only from the time of the claim made by him in manner aforesaid: and for this cause it shall be good for such disseisee to make his claim, &c., in as short time as he can after the disseisin, &c. (*i*).

As death of disseisor within the year and day casts a descent, which takes away entry.

Lyttleton recommends disseisee to make claim so soon as he can after the disseisin.

poet entrer, &c., coment que furent plusours murrantes seisi, et plusours discentes deins lan et le jour, &c.

426 Item, *si home soit disseisi, et le disseisour morust seisi deins lan et le jour proscheyn apres le disseisin fait, per que les tenementes descendount a son heire, en ceo cas lentré le disseisi est tolle; qar lan et le jour que eiderount le disseisi en tiel cas, &c., ne serra pris de temps de title dentré a luy accrue, mes tantsolement de temps del clayme per luy fait en le manere avauntdit: et pur cel cause il serroit bon pur tiel disseisi pur faire son clayme, &c., en auxi brief temps que il puissoit apres le disseisin, &c.*

(*i*) A dying seised and descent within a year and a day after claim made, takes not away the entry of him that claimed, though there be never so many disseisins, alienations, or descents within that time, and though it were not made till many years after the disseisin; but at law, a descent cast within a year and a day after the disseisin, barred the disseisee not making continual claim; but this has been altered by 32 Hen. 8, c. 33. Since which statute no dying seised within five years after the disseisin takes away an entry, and consequently the tenant's dying seised within five years after the continual claim takes not away an entry, because the tenant's continuing in possession after the continual claim amounts to a new disseisin.—*Hawk. Abr. Co. Lytt.* 342.

Claim made at any time during life of disseisor, good.

427 Also, if such disseisor occupy the land forty years, or for many more years, without any claim made by the disseisee, &c., and the disseisee a short time before the death of the disseisor, make a claim in the form aforesaid, if so it fortune, that, within the year and the day after such claim, the disseisor die, &c., the entry of the disseisee is congeable, &c. And therefore it shall be good for such a man that hath not made claim, and that hath good title of entry &c., when he heareth that his adversary lieth languishing, to make his claim, &c.

The right may accrue by disseisin or by any other title.

428 Also, as it is said in the cases *before* put, where a man hath title to enter by cause of a disseisin, &c., the same law is where a man hath right to enter by cause of any other title, &c.

First corollary to third proposition or rule of Lyttleton, (§ 421), viz. a continual claim, which is an entry in law, is as

429 Also, of the said precedents may ye know, my son, two things. The one is, where a man hath title to enter upon a tenant in tail, if he make any such claim to the land, then is the estate-tail defeated; for this claim is as an entry made by him, and is of the same effect in law as if he were upon the

427 Item, *si tiel disseisour occupiast la terre per* xl. *ans, ou pur pluis plusours ans, sans ascun clayme fait per le disseisi, &c., et le disseisi per petit space devaunt le murrant del disseisor, fait un clayme en le fourme avauntdit, si issint fortunast, que, deins lan et le jour apres tiel clayme, le disseisour morust, &c., lentre le disseisi est congeable, &c. Et pur ceo il serroit bon pur tiel home qui ne fist clayme, qui ad un title dentrer &c., quaunt il oye que son adversarie gist languissaunt, faire son clayme, &c.*

428 Item, *si come est dit en les cases myses, lou home ad title dentrer per cause dun disseisin, &c., mesme la ley est lou home ad droit dentrer per cause dascun autre title, &c.*

429 Item, *de les dits precedentes poies saver, mon fitz, deux choses. Lun est, lou home ad title dentrer sur un tenaunt en le taille, sil fist un tiel clayme a la terre, donques est lestate de le taille defete ; qar cel clayme est come un entré fait per luy, et est de mesme effect en ley sicome il fuissoit sur mesmes*

same tenements, and had entered in the same tenements as is aforesaid: thereupon when the tenant in tail immediately after such claim continueth his occupation in the tenements, this is a disseisin made of the same tenements unto him that made the claim, *et sic per consequens*, the tenant then hath fee-simple.

strong as an entry in deed, [i. e. in fact]. Co. Lytt. 256. b.; and if made on a tenant in tail, shall defeat estate tail, and if tenant in tail continue in possession, it is a disseisin.

430 The second thing is, that so often as he that hath right to enter maketh such claim, &c., notwithstanding his adversary continue his occupation, &c., so often doeth the adversary wrong and disseisin to him that made the claim; and for this cause so often may he that made the same claim, for every such wrong and disseisin done unto him, have a writ of trespass*, 431 upon the statute of R. 2, made in the fifth year of his reign, supposing by his writ that his adversary

Second corollary to third proposition or rule of Lyttleton (§ 421), viz. that the adversary's staying in possession after continual claim, amounts to a new disseisin for which the dis-

les tenementes, et ust entré en mesmes les tenementes come devaunt est dit : donques quant le tenaunt en le taille immediate puis tiel clayme continua son occupation en les tenementes, ceo est un disseisin fait de mesmes les tenementes, a celuy que fist le clayme, et sic per consequens, *le tenaunt adonques ad fee-simple.*

430 *Le seconde chose est, que auxi sovent quil qui ad droit dentrer fait tiel clayme, &c., nient contristeant son adversarie continua son occupacion, &c., auxi sovent ladversarie fait tort et disseisin a celuy qui fist le clayme; et pur cell cause auxi sovent poet celuy que fist mesme le clayme, pur chescun tiel tort et disseisin fait a luy, aver un brief de trespas**, 431 *sur lestatuit le roy Ric. le second, fait lan de son reigne quint, supposant per son brief que son adversarie*

---

* The later copies including the copies of *Rastell's* Transl. read this passage thus, viz. *Or* have a writ of trespass, *Quare clausum fregit, &c., and recover his damages, &c.* (§ 431). *Or he may have a writ* upon the statute —— *&c.*, independent of a variation which demonstrates their suspicious origin, the interpolated words do not appear in the Camb. MSS.

seisee may bring trespass, or an action on the 5 Ric. 2, c. 7, and suppose that his adversary entered where his entry was not given by law, and therein recover damages, but not mesne profits; and if his adversary occupied with force and arms, or with a multitude, he might have a writ of forcible entry and recover treble damages.

has entered into the lands or tenements of him that made the claim, where his entry was not given by the law, &c., and by such action he shall recover his damages, &c.; and if the case be such that the adversary occupy the tenements with force and arms, or with a multitude of people at the time of such claim, &c., then may he that made the claim, for every such time have a writ of forcible entry, and recover his treble damages, &c.

432 Also, here it is to be seen, whether the servant of a man, who hath title to enter, can, by commandment of his master, make continual claim for his master or not*.

433 And it seemeth that in some cases he can do this, for

avoit entre en les terres ou tenementes celuy qui fist le clayme, lou son entré ne fuist pas done per la ley, &c., et per tiel accion il recovera ses damages, &c.; et si le cas fuist tiel, que ladversarie occupiast les tenementes ovesque force et arms ou ovesque multitude de gentz a temps de tiel clayme, &c., donques poet celuy qui fist le clayme, pur chescun tiel foitz aver un brief de forcible entry, et recovera ses treble damages, &c.

432 Item, *icy est a veyer, si le servaunt dun home qui ad title dentrer, poet, per commandement son maistre, faire continuel clayme pur son maistre, ou non**.

433 *Et il semble que en ascuns cases il poet ceo faire, qar*

---

* The two last words in this section or paragraph appear to the Editor to be a corruption of the words, *en son noun, in his name*, which words indeed, appear in all the copies of *Rastell's* Transl.; independent of the context requiring such suppletion or correction, the words in the 435th section *in the name of his master*, evidently point to such a construction; besides the words *ou non*, are not to be construed *or not*, regard being had to the idiom of the French adopted by *Lyttleton*, of which an instance occurs in the 435th section, where *or not* is rendered by the words *ou nemy*. However, as this reading is given by all the *French* copies and by *Coke's* Transl., the above text is given accordingly, leaving it to the reader's own judgment whether to adopt or reject this amended reading.

if he by his commandment come to any parcel of the land, and there make claim, &c., in the name of his master, this claim is good enough for his master, for this that he doeth all that which his master ought to do in such case, &c. But if the master say to his servant, that he dare not come to the land, nor to any parcel of the land to make his claim, &c., and that he dare not approach nearer to the land than to such a place called Dale, and command his servant to go to the same place of Dale, and there make a claim for him, &c., if the servant so doeth, &c., this seemeth also as good claim for his master, as if his master had been there in his own person, for that the servant did all that which his master durst, and ought by the law to do in such case, &c. 434 Also, if a man be so languishing, or so decrepit, that he cannot by any means come to the land or to any parcel of the same, or if he be a recluse which may not by reason of his order go out of his house, if such manner of person command his servant to go and make claim for him,

Continual claim may be made by a servant, at the land, for his master, in some cases, i. e. *if he enter into a part and claim, or if the master say that he dares not go to any part of the land, nor approach nearer than to Dale, and command his servant to go there and the servant do so, it is sufficient, though the servant had no fear, for he does as much as he was commanded to do, and all that his master durst or ought to do.*

If the master be sick or a recluse, so that

sil per son commandement vient a ascun parcell de la terre, et là fait clayme, &c., en le noun son maistre, cest clayme est assetes bon pur son maistre, pur ceo queil fait tout ceo que son maistre devoit faire en tiel cas, &c. Si le maistre dit a son servaunt, que il ne osast vener a la terre, ne ascun parcell de la terre, pur faire son clayme, &c., et que il ne osast approcher pluis procheyn a la terre forsque a tiel lieu appelle Dale, et commaunda son servant daler a mesme le lieu de Dale, et là faire un clayme pur luy, &c., si le servaunt issint fait, &c., ceo semble auxi bone clayme pur son maistre, sicome son maistre là fuist en son propre persone, pur ceo que le servaunt fist tout ceo que son maistre osast et devoit faire per la ley en tiel cas, &c. 434 Auxy, si home soit cy languissaunt, ou cy decrepyte, quil ne poet pur nul manere vener a la terre, ne a ascun parcell dicell, ou si un recluse soit qui ne poet per cause de son ordre aler hors de sa meason, &c., si tiel manere de persone commaunda son servaunt daler et faire clayme pur luy, et tiel servaunt ne osast aler a la terre, ou a

by reason of his profession he cannot go, and he command his servant to go and claim for him, and the servant goes so near as he dare, this is sufficient, though the command were to go to the land.

and such servant dare not go to the land, or to any parcel of it, for doubt of beating, maim, or death, and for that cause the servant cometh so near to the land as he dare for such dread, and maketh such claim, &c. for his master, it seemeth that such claim for his master is sufficiently strong and good in the law (*k*): for otherwise his master should be in a very great mischief; for it may well be that such person that is sick, decrepit, or recluse, cannot find any servant who dare go to the land, or to any parcel of the same, to make the claim for him, &c. 435 But if the master of such servant be in good health, and well dare go to the tenements, or to parcel thereof, to make his claim, &c., if such master command his servant to go to any parcel of the land to make claim for him, and when the servant is in going to do the commandment of his master,

But if the master be in health and command his servant to go to the land and claim, in this case a claim made by the servant so

ascun parcell de ceo, pur doute de baterie, maheyme, ou mort, et pur cel cause tiel servaunt vient auxi pres a la terre come il osast pur tiel pavour, et fait tiel clayme, &c. pur son maistre, il semble que tiel clayme pur son maistre est assetes fort et bon en la ley: qar autrement son maistre serroit en tres graund myschief; qar il bien poet estre que tiel persone qui est languissaunt, decrepite, ou recluse, ne poet trover ascun servaunt qui osast aler a la terre, ne a ascun parcell dicell, de faire le clayme pur luy, &c. 435 *Mes si le maistre de tiel servaunt soit en bone santé, et poet et osast bien aler a les tenementes, ou a parcell de ceo, de faire son clayme, &c., si tiel maistre commaunda son servaunt daler a ascun parcell de la terre a faire clayme pur luy, et quant le servaunt est en alant de faire le commande-*

(*k*) And yet regularly, when a servant does less than the command, his act is void; *for where a man is forced to make use of a servant, he is more favoured than one who is able to do his own business; and if the servant do as much as it may be presumed his master would have done himself, it is sufficient*, for *impotentia excusat legem;* when a servant exceeds his master's command, it is void only so far as he hath exceeded.—*Hawk. Abr. Co. Lytt.* 345.

he heareth by the way such things that he dare not go to any parcel of the land to make the claim for his master, and for that reason he goeth so near to the land as he dare for doubt of death, and there maketh claim for his master, and in the name of his master, &c., it seemeth that the doubt in law in such case should be, whether such claim shall avail his master, or not, for this that the servant did not all which his master at the time of his commandment durst have done, &c. *Quære* (*l*).

near as he dares is void; for he does not do all that is commanded, nor so much as the master durst have done.

436 Also, some have said that where a man is in prison and is disseised, and the disseisor dieth seised during the time that the disseisee is imprisoned, whereby the tenements descend to the heir of the disseisor; they have said, that this shall not hurt the disseisee who is imprisoned, but that he well may enter, notwithstanding such descent, because he could not

Entry not tolled by descent whilst disseisee be in prison.

ment de son maistre, il oye per le voye tielx choses que il ne osast vener a ascun parcel del terre pur faire le clayme pur son maistre, et pur cell cause il vient auxi pres de la terre come il osast pur doute de mort, et là fait clayme pur son maistre, et en le noun de son maistre, &c., il semble que le doute en ley en tiel case serroit, si tiel clayme availlera a son maistre, ou nemy, pur ceo que le servaunt ne fist tout ceo que son maistre a temps de son commaundement osast faire, &c. Quære.

436 Item, *ascuns ount dit que lou home est emprisone et est disseisi, et le disseisour morust seisi duraunt le temps que le disseisi est emprisone, per que les tenementes descendont al heire le disseisour; ils ount dit, que ceo ne noyera mye le disseisi qui est emprisone, mes que il bien poet entrer, nient obstaunt tiel discent, pur ceo que il ne puissoit faire continuel*

(*l*) This continual claim is void, for that the servant doth less than that which is expressly commanded, and there is no impotency or fear in the master.—*Co. Lytt.* 259. a.

If one in prison be outlawed, he shall reverse the outlawry by writ of error.

make continual claim when he was imprisoned: 437* and also if he that is in prison be outlawed in an action of debt, or trespass, or in an appeal of robbery, &c., he shall reverse such outlawry by writ of error &c., because he was in prison at the time of the outlawry against him pronounced, &c. 438 Also, if a recovery be had by default against such a one as is in prison, he shall avoid the judgment by writ of error, because he was in prison at the time of such default made, &c. And for this that such matters of record shall not hurt him that is in prison, but that they shall be reversed, &c., *a multo fortiori* it seemeth, that a matter in deed (*i. e.* in fact), *scil.* such a descent had when he was in prison, shall not hurt him, &c., specially for this that he could not go out of prison

Also if one in prison lose his land by default in a real action, he can avoid it by writ of error; therefore a descent cast shall not prejudice such person for he was not able to make continual claim.

clayme, quaunt il fuist emprisone: 437* *et auxi si tiel qui est en prison soit utlage in accion de dette, ou trespas, ou en appelle de robberye, &c., il reversera tiel utlagarie per brief derrour &c., pur ceo que il fuist in prison al temps de utlagarie envers luy prononce, &c.* 438 *Auxy, si une recoverie soit ewe per defaut vers tiel qui est en prison, il avoydera le juggement per brief derrour, pur ceo que il fuist en prison al temps de tiel defaut fait, &c. Et pur ceo que tielx maters de recorde ne noyeront celuy qui est en prison, mes que ils serront reverses, &c.,* a multo fortiori *il semble, que un matere en fait,* scil., *tiel discent ewe quaunt il fuist en prison, ne luy noyera, &c. especialment pur ceo que il ne puissoit aler hors de prison pur*

* Here follows in *Redm.* and all the *French* editions from 1581, a reference to the *Year-Book*, 9 *Hen.* 7, *fol.* 24. *b.*, to the effect that a disseisin before the disseisee's imprisonment tolled his entry, although the disseisor's dying seised took place whilst the disseisee was in prison. This reference appears as a side-note in *Berth.*, *Middl.*, *Sm.*, *Powel*, and *Tottyl* 1554, and is embodied in the text in *ed.* 1581, by *West*, and forms the commencement of § 437. It is, however, there placed between two *flowers*.

to make continual claim, &c. 439 In the same manner it seemeth to them, where a man is out of the realm, in the king's service, for business of the realm, if such man be disseised when he is in service of the king*, that such descent shall not hurt the disseisee, but for this that he could not make continual claim, &c., it seemeth to them, that when he cometh again into England, he can enter upon the heir of the disseisor, &c.; for such a man shall reverse an outlawry which is pronounced against him during the time that he is in the king's service, &c. Therefore, *a multo fortiori* he shall have aid [and indemnity†] by law in the other case, &c.

If a man out of the realm be disseised, his entry is not barred by a descent cast.

440 Also, others have said, that if a man be out of the realm, although he be not in the king's service; if such man being out of the realm, be disseised of lands or tenements within the realm, and the disseisor die seised, &c., the disseisee being out of the realm, it seemeth unto them, that

Whether he was in the king's service or not.

faire continuell clayme, &c. 439 *En mesme le manere ils semblont, lou home est hors du roialme, en service le roy, pur besoignier du roialme, si tiel home soit disseisi quaunt il est en service le roy*, que tiel discent ne grevera le disseisi, mes pur ceo que il ne puissoit faire continuell clayme, &c., il semble a eux, que quaunt il revient en Engleterre, il poet entrer sur leire le disseisour, &c.; qar tiel home reversera un utlagarie que est pronounce envers luy duraunt le temps que il est en le service le roy, &c.* Ergo, a multo fortiori *il avera ayde [et indemnité†] per la ley en lautre cas, &c.*

440 Item, *autres ount dit, que si ascun soit hors du roialme, coment quil ne soit en service le roy; si tiel home esteant hors du roialme, est disseisi de terres ou tenementes deins le roialme, et le disseisour devie seisi, &c., le disseisi esteant hors du roialme, il semble a eux, que quaunt le disseisi vient*

---

* *Et le disseisour morust seisi, &c., le disseisi esteant en le service le roy; And the disseisor die seised, &c., the disseisee being in the service of the king: Redm.* and all later editions except *Rastell's* Transl.

† These words do not appear in *Rastell's* Transl.

when the disseisee cometh into the realm, that he can well enter upon the heir of the disseisor, &c.; and this seemeth unto them for two causes: one is, that he that is out of the realm cannot have knowledge of disseisin done unto him, by intendment (*i. e.* understanding) of law (*m*), no more than that a thing done out of the realm can be tried within the same realm by the oath of twelve, &c., and to compel such man by the law to make continual claim, who by the understanding of the law cannot have any knowledge or conusance of such disseisin, this shall be inconvenient, and namely, when such a disseisin is done unto him when he is out of the realm, and also the dying seised was when he was out of the realm; for in such case he cannot by any possibility according to common presumption make continual claim: but otherwise it should be if such disseisee were within the realm at the time of the disseisin, or at the time of the dying of the disseisor.

But if he were disseised before he went beyond sea, or during his stay within the realm, his entry is taken away.

441 Another matter they allege for proof, [*scil.* of the allegation contained in the preceding section, that a disseisin and descent shall not bind the disseisee who is out of the realm at

deins le roialme, queil poet bien entrer sur leire le disseisour, &c.; et ceo semble a eux pur deux causes: une est, que celuy que est hors du roialme ne poet aver conusauns de disseisin fait a luy, per entendement de ley, nient pluis que chose fait hors du roialme poet estre trie deins mesme le roialme per le serement de xii., *&c., et de compeller tiel home per la ley de faire continuell clayme, le quel per lentendement de la ley ne poet aver ascun notice ou conusauns de tiel disseisin, ceo serra inconvenient, et nosmement, quaunt tiel disseisin est fait a luy quaunt il est hors du roialme, et auxi le murrant seisi fuist quaunt il fuist hors du roialme; qar en tiel cas il ne poet per nul possibilite solonques le comen presumpcion faire continuell clayme: mes autrement serroit si tiel disseisi fuist deins le roialme a temps de le disseisin, ou al temps del murrant de le disseisour.* 441 *Un*

(*m*) *Vide* for intendment of law, 406, 439, 462, 463, 467.—*Co.* § 99, 100, 110, 293, 377, 393, *Lytt*, 261. b.

the time, &c.—*Ritso's Introd.* p. 109], that before the statute of King Ed. 3, made in the 34th year of his reign [*s.* 15], by which statute non-claim is ousted, &c., the law was such, that if a fine were levied of certain lands or tenements, if any one that was stranger to the fine had right to have and recover the same lands or tenements, if he came not and made his claim thereof within the year and the day next after the fine levied, he should be barred for ever, *Quia dicebatur, finis finem litibus imponebat.* [But if he were out of the realm at the time of the fine levied, &c., or in prison, or not of full age, he was not barred, although he made not his claim*]. And that the law was such it is proved by the statute of Westminster 2, *De donis conditionalibus*, where it speaketh, if the fine be levied of tenements given in the tail, &c. That "the fine shall be void in the law; neither shall the "heirs, or such as the reversion belongeth unto, though they "be of full age, within England, and out of prison, need to

A party out of the realm could never be barred by non-claim on a fine.

autre matere ils allegeont pur prouve, que devaunt lestatuit fait en temps le roy Ed. le tierce, lan de son reigne xxxiiij., *per quel estatuit non-clayme est ouste, &c., la ley fuist tiel, que si un fyn fuist levé de certeyn terres ou tenementes, si ascun qui fuist estraunge al fyn avoit droit daver et recoverer mesmes les terres ou tenementes, sil ne venust et fist son clayme de ceo deins lan et le jour proscheyn apres le fyn leve, il serra barre a toutz jours,* Quia dicebatur, finis finem litibus imponebat. *Et que la ley fuist tiel il est prove per le estatuit de Westminster seconde,* De donis conditionalibus, *lou il est parle si le fyn soit levé des tenementes dones en le taille, &c. Quod "finis ipso jure fit nullus; nec habeant heredes, aut "illi ad quos spectat reversio, licet plenæ sint ætatis, in "Anglia, et extra prisonam, necesse apponere clameum suum."*

* This is a suppletion by *Mr. Ritso*, of words necessary to convey the true sense of this passage, and which words, he says, we may presume to have been originally written by Lyttleton, as he observes, that without such words, this § of Lyttleton is plainly contradictory and unintelligible according to the present reading.—*Ritso's Introduction*, pp. 108, 109.

"make their claim." So this is proved, that if a stranger that hath right unto the tenements, if he were out of the realm at the time of the fine levied, &c., should have no damage, though* that such fine was matter of record: by greater reason it seemeth unto them, that a disseisin and descent that is matter in fact, shall not so hurt him that was disseised, when he was out of the realm at the time of disseisin, and also at the time that the disseisor died seised, &c., but that he can well enter notwithstanding such descent, &c.

If a disseisee bring an assise, and the jury find for him, and the justices will be advised till the next assise, and in the mean time the disseisor die, it seems that the entry of the disseisee is not taken away; for the suit amounted to a continual claim.

442 Also, inquire if a man be disseised, and he arraign an assise against the disseisor, and the recognitors of the assise chant (*i.e.* find†) for the plaintiff, and the justices of assise will be advised of their judgments until the next assise, &c., and in the mean season the disseisor dieth seised, &c., whether the said suit of the assise shall be *taken* in law for the said disseisee a continual claim? insomuch that no default was in him, &c.

Issint ceo est prove, que si un estraunge home qui avoet droit a les tenementes, sil fuist hors du roialme al temps de fyn leve, &c., naveroit damage, coment que tiel fyn fuist matere de recorde: per greyndre reason il semble a eux, que un disseisin et discent que est matere en fait, ne issint trops grevera celuy qui fuist disseisi, quaunt il fuist hors du roialme al temps de disseisin, et auxi al temps que le disseisour morust seisi, &c., mes quil bien poet entrer nient contristeant tiel discent, &c.*

442 Item, quære *si home soit disseisi, et il arraine un assise envers le disseisour, et les recognitours del assise chanterount† pur le pleintif, et les justices dassise voillont estre avises de lour juggement, tanques al procheyne assise, &c., et en dementiers le disseisour morust seisi, &c., si le dit suyte del assise serra en ley pur le dit disseisi un continuell clayme? entaunt que nul defaut fuist en luy.*

---

* The words *que il ne fist son claime, &c., coment—that he made not his claim, &c., though*—occur at this place in *Pyns.* 1516, and in all the copies since, *Rastell's* Transl. excepted; but they may be deemed a corruption, as indeed almost all of the variations which have their origin in the faulty edition of *Pyns.* 1516.

† *Rastell's* Transl. renders this word, *challenge.*

443 Also, inquire if an abbot of a monastery die, and during the time of vacation, a man wrongfully enter in certain parcel of land of the monastery, claiming the land unto him and his heirs, and of such estate die seised, and the land descend unto his heirs, and after that an abbot is chosen and made abbot of the same monastery, *a question is,* whether the abbot can enter upon the heir, or not? And it seemeth to some, that the abbot can well enter in this case; because the convent in time of vacation was not a person able to make continual claim: for no more than they be personable to [sue*] an action, no more be they able to make continual claim; for the convent is but a dead body without head, for in time of vacation a grant made unto them†, is void: and in this case an abbot cannot have a writ of entry upon dis-

And if an abbot or mayor of a corporation or parson die, and before there can be a successor, a stranger enter into the land, and a descent be cast, yet the successor may enter; for it was an unavoidable fact that no claim could be made; and for the same reason the successor may present, notwithstanding an usurpation of a church in time of vacation.

443 Item, quære *si un abbé dun monasterie morust, et duraunt le temps de vacacion, un home torciousement entra en certeyn parcel de terre del monasterie, claymant la terre a luy et a ses heires, et de tiel estate morust seisi, et la terre descendist a son heire, et puis apres un abbé est eslieu et fait abbé de mesme le monasterie, si labbé poet entrer sur leire, ou nemy? Et il semble a ascuns, que labbé bien poet entrer en ceo cas; pur ceo que le covent en temps de vacacion ne fuist ascun persone able de faire continuell clayme: qar nient pluis que ils soient personables de [faire*] une accion, nient pluis ils sount ables de faire continuell clayme; qar le covent est forsque come un mort corps sauns teste, qar en temps de vacacion un graunt fait a eux†, est voyd: et en ceo cas labbé ne poet aver*

---

* *Faire accion—Pyns.* 1516. *Suer accion—Redm., Berth.*, and all subsequent editions; *Rastell's* Transl. reads—*to sue an action.*

† In all the French copies from *Pyns.* 1516, there occurs at this place a corruption and interpolation of *ou per eux, or by them,* which has kept its ground to this day, and has been included in those parts of this section commented upon by *Sir Edward Coke.* In an edition of Lyttleton with MS. Notes, *penes Ed.*, the Annotator who wrote, *temps Car.* 1, notices these words, viz. "*ceo nest en le olde edition.*" *Pyns.* 1516, reads, *fait* per *eux, est voide.*

seisin against the heir, for this, that he was never disseised; and if the abbot may not enter in this case, then he shall be put unto his writ of right, which shall be very hard for the house: by which it seemeth to them, that the abbot can well enter, &c. (*n*).

"Quæras de dubiis, legem bene discere si vis:
"Quærere dat sapere quæ sunt legitima vere*."

brief dentre sur disseisin *envers leire, pur ceo, que il ne fuist unques disseisi; et si labbé ne puissoit entrer en ceo cas, donques il serra mys a son brief de droit, le quel serra trop dure pur la meason: per que semble a eux, que labbé bien poet entrer, &c.*

"Quæras de dubiis, legem bene discere si vis:
"Quærere dat sapere quæ sunt legitima vere."*

* See *ante*, p. 448 (*g*).

(*n*) Here by this *&c.* is implied, or make his continual claim in such sort as hath been before expressed. —*Co. Lytt.* 264. a.

CHAPTER VIII.

RELEASES.

The reader is now introduced to those instruments and acts which are termed secondary, as pre-supposing in the party executing or performing them, some title precedent, and these ordinarily serve to perfect, establish, or enlarge some estate or interest in the party in whose favour they are made, and which estate or interest, but for such subsequent acts, would be imperfect, defeasible, or restrained; of this class are releases and confirmations, to which was formerly added attornment, which last, when necessary or efficacious, was commensurate in effect with livery of seisin and actual entry.

With respect to releases, Lyttleton divides them into releases of lands and tenements, and releases of actions and other things.

A release has been generally defined as the giving or discharging of the right or action that any one hath or may have or claim against another or his land (*New Termes de la Ley*): and with respect to land, it is the conveyance of an interest or right which any one has therein, to another who has obtained possession thereof or some lawful estate therein; and, according to the circumstances under which it is given, may operate either to transfer or extinguish, abridge or enlarge the estate and interest of the relessee, *i. e.* the person in possession.

It is contrary to the nature of a release to give possession; for such instrument can only operate upon some estate, interest, or right in the relessor: the principles upon which this conveyance is founded are concisely stated by Lord

Chief Baron Gilbert, whose Treatise on Tenures particularly explains the doctrine of releases, viz.—"When a disseisin is committed, the possession and the right are separated; but they may by a lawful conveyance be again united. Now when a man has the right and possession in him, he must convey by feoffment, which made a notoriety among the tenants, by the feoffment *coram paribus*. When a man was out of possession, he might convey by release only; for the disseisor had the possession, which of itself made the notoriety, and the release transferred the right; so that a release is a conveyance of right to a person in possession: and this comes instead of a feoffment; for a man cannot be put in possession, which is the operation of the feoffment, when he is in possession before."

Lyttleton commences his first division or classification of releases, viz. releases of rights in lands or tenements, by stating the *formula* of such an instrument (§ 445); and distinguishes them with regard to their operation, as—

1. Releases *mettre et vester le droit,* which enure to pass the right of the relessor, as from disseisee to disseisor (§ 466).

2. Releases *extinguisher le droit,* which enure to extinguish the right of the relessor, as from disseisee to lessee of disseisor (§ 449, and in the cases put in § 470, 472).

3. Releases *extinguisher lestate,* which enure to extinguish the estate of the relessor, as from the grantee of a rent-charge to the owner of the land, or a release of the services from the lord to the tenant, or a release of common of pasture, &c. (§ 479, 480).

4. Releases *denlargir lestate,* which enure by way of enlargement of the estate as from the remainder-man or reversioner to tenant of the particular estate (§ 465, 470). *Sir Edward Coke* states it as a certain rule, that in this species of release, there should be privity of estate between the relessor and relessee, as lessor and lessee, donor and donee, or that they should stand in the relation of particular tenant and remainder-man, &c.

5. Releases *mettre lestate,* which enure by passing the

estate of the relessor, as when two or more persons are seised of the same estate by joint title, either as joint-tenants or co-parceners, and one of them releases his right to the other; this species of release has one peculiarity, it does not always require words of inheritance to pass the estate, contrary to the rule, *Sir Edward Coke* states, (§ 465), viz. " that when a release doth enure by way of enlargement of an estate, no inheritance either in fee-simple or fee-tail, can pass without words of inheritance: " the reason of the exception is, that insomuch as the relessee is not *in* by such release *mettre le droit,* but by some other act or conveyance which passed an inheritance, this release only discharges the claim of one of the parties (§ 304): otherwise it is with regard to tenants in common who having each a freehold created by different acts, there such inheritance being distinct and disunited, must pass by different liveries of seisin, or tantamount conveyances. Privity of estate existing at the time of the release, is also requisite to support this kind of release.

6. Releases *by way of entry and feoffment,* which enure to pass the right of the relessor who is disseised, to the relessee-disseisor, in the same manner as if the relessor-disseisee had actually revested his former estate by his entry, and afterwards had made a feoffment with livery of seisin to the relessee, the operation whereof in legal language, is, " he shall now hold out every other; "—but this release may be deemed in fact to be a species of release *mettre et vester le droit,* differing but in circumstances, for such a release though it may operate by way of entry and feoffment, yet equally operates to pass and vest the right of the disseisee, who releases to one or both of his disseisors (§ 477).—See *Ritso's Introd.* pp. 39—42.

In pursuing his second division of this Chapter, viz. releases of actions and other things, Lyttleton discourses of the nature of actions real, personal, and mixed, and some of their incidents (§ 492); and after noticing some now obsolete, but then important, peculiarities in the form of real actions, he concludes the Chapter.

Releases are either of rights or of actions.

444 RELEASES are in divers manners, *scil.* releases of all the right that a man hath in lands or tenements, &c., and releases of actions personal and real, and other things (*a*). Release of all the right that a man hath in lands or tenements, &c., is commonly made in such form, or to such effect.

Form of a release of rights.

445 " Know all men by these presents, that I, A., of B., have " remised, released, and altogether from me and my heirs " quiet claimed," [*or thus,* " for me and my heirs quiet " claimed* (*b*)], to C. ,of D., all the right, title, and claim " which I had, have, or by any means may have, of and in " one messuage, with the appurtenances in F." &c.

444 *Relesses sount en divers maneres,* scil. *relesses de tout le droit que home ad en terres ou tenementes, &c., et relesses daccions personelx et realx, et dautres choses. Reles de tout le droit que home ad en terres ou tenementes, &c., est commenement fait en tiel fourme, ou a tiel effecte.* 445 " *Noverint " universi per presentes, me, A., de B., remisisse, relaxasse, " et omnino de me et heredibus meis quietum clamasse,* " [vel sic, " *pro me et hæredibus meis quietum clamasse**], *C., de D., " totum jus, titulum, et clameum quæ habui, habeo, vel quo- " vismodo in futurum habere potero, de et in uno mesuagio, " cum pertinentiis in F." &c.*

---

* The words within brackets are not given in *Rastell's* Translation.

(*a*) These words must be referred thus :—Releases are of two sorts, viz. a release of all the right which a man hath either in lands and tenements, or in goods and chattels : or there is a release of actions real, of or in lands or tenements : or personal, of or in goods or chattels : or mixed, partly in the realty and partly in the personalty. *Co. Lytt.* 264. a. b.

(*b*) Here *Lyttleton* sheweth, that there be three proper words of release, and be much of one effect : besides there is *renunciare, acquietare* ; and there be many other words of release : as if the lessor grants to the lessee for life, that he shall be discharged of the rent, this is a good release.—*Vide Sect.* 532. *Ibid.*

And it is to be understood, that these words *remisisse, et quietum clamasse,* are of the like effect as these words, *relaxasse, &c.**

446 Also, these words which are commonly put in such deeds of releases, &c., *quæ quovismodo in futurum habere potero,* are as words void in the law; for no right passeth by a release but the right that the relessor hath at the time of the release made. For if there be father and son, and the father be disseised, and the son, living his father, releaseth by his deed *to the disseisor,* all the right that he hath, or may have, in the same tenements, without clause of warranty, &c., and afterwards the father dieth, [&c.†], the son may lawfully enter upon the possession of the disseisor, for this, that he had no right in the land at the time he released, *scil.* in the lifetime of his father, but the right descended to him by descent after the release made, by the death of his father, [&c.†].

A release does not extinguish a possibility or future right.

447 Also, in releases of all the right that a man hath in certain lands, &c., it behoveth him to whom the release is

In release mettre le droit. *Relessee must have the freehold, either in fact or in law* [i. e. *by*

Et est assavoir, que ceux verbes, remisisse et quietum clamasse, *sont dautiel effecte sicome tiel verbe,* relaxasse, &c.*

446 Item, *ceux parolx que sount commenement mettz en tielx faitz de relesses, &c.,* quæ quovismodo in futurum habere potero, *sount come voydes en la ley; qar nul droit passa per un reles, forsque le droit que le relessour ad al temps de le reles fait. Qar si soient pere et fitz, et le pere soit disseisi, et le fitz, vivaunt son pere, relessa per son fait, tout le droit que il ad, ou aver puissoit, en mesmes les tenementes, sauns clause de garrantie, &c., et puis le pere morust,* [*&c.*†], *le fitz poet loialment entrer sur la possession le disseisour, pur ceo, quil navoit droit en la terre quaunt il relessast,* scil. *en la vie son pere, mes le droit descendist a luy per discent apres le reles fait, per la mort son pere,* [*&c.*†]

447 Item, *en relesses de tout le droit que home ad en certeyn terres, &c., il covient a celuy a que le reles soit fait en tiel*

---

* *Rastell's* Translation, as well as *Sir Edward Coke's* Translation, concludes, *are of such effect as these words, 'relaxasse,' &c.*

† The *&c.* within brackets does not occur in *Rastell's* Transl.

surrender to the reversioner by fine, or by means of uses raised on good considerations, and operating by the Statute of Uses].

made in such case, that he have freehold in the lands, &c., in deed, or in law, at the time of the release made; for in every case where he to whom the release is made hath freehold in deed, or freehold in law, at the time of the release made, &c., the release is good.

Freehold in law defined with respect to operation of law as distinguished from the act of parties.

448 Freehold in law is, as if a man disseiseth another, and thereof dieth seised, whereby the tenements descend to his son, howbeit that his son enter not into the tenements, yet he hath a freehold in law, which by force of the descent is cast upon him, and therefore a release made to him so being seised of freehold in law* is good enough, and if he take wife so being seised in law, although he never enter in deed, and dieth, his wife shall be endowed, &c.

Wife dowable sans seisin of the husband; a similar case, § 681.

In some cases a release mettre le droit made to one who has neither freehold in deed or in law, is good *by way of* extinguisher le droit; *a release of all the right to him in the reversion, being*

449 Also, in some case of releases of all the right, howbeit that he to whom the release is made, hath nothing in the freehold in deed, or in law, yet the release is good enough: as if the disseisor let the land which he hath by disseisin,

cas, que il ad franktenement en les terres, &c., en fait, ou en ley, al temps de reles fait, qar en chescun cas lou celuy a qui le reles est fait ad franktenement en fait, ou franktenement en ley, al temps del reles fait, &c., le reles est bon.

448 *Franktenement en ley est, sicome un home disseisist un autre, et ent mourust seisi, per que les tenementes descendount a son fitz, coment que son fitz nentra pas en les tenementes, unqore il ad un franktenement en ley, quell per force de discent est jette sur luy, et pur ceo un reles fait a luy issint esteant seisi de franktenement en ley, est assetez bon, et sil prent feme issint esteant seisie en ley, coment quil ne unques entra pas en fait, et mourust, sa feme serra endowe, &c.*

449 Item, *en ascun case de relesses de tout le droit, coment que celuy a qui le reles est fait, nad riens en le franktenement en fait, ne en ley, unqore le reles est assetez bon : sicome le disseisour lessa la terre quil ad per disseisin, a un autre pur*

---

* *Rastell's* Transl. reads—*and therefore the release made is good enough.*

to another for term of his life, saving the reversion to him, if the disseisee or his heir release to the disseisor all the right, &c., this release is good; because he to whom the release is made, had in him a reversion at the time of the release made. 450 In the same manner it is, where a lease is made to one man for term of life, the remainder to another for term of life, the remainder to the third in tail, the remainder to the fourth in fee; if a stranger that right hath to the land, release all his right to any of them in the remainder, such release is good; because every of them hath a remainder [in deed*] vested in himself. 451 Yet if the tenant for term of life be disseised, and afterwards he that hath right, the possession being in the disseisor, release to one of them to whom the remainder was made, all the right, &c., that release is void; because he had not in him a remainder in deed at the time of the release made, but only a right of a remainder (*c*), [at the time of the release made†].

good; for although he has nothing in the freehold, yet he has an estate, and the land is comprised in the reversion.

And release to one remainder-man enures to all.

But a release to one who has no more than a right is void.—[See Touchst. 325.]

terme de sa vie, savant la revercion a luy, si le disseisi ou son heire relessa al disseisour tout le droit, &c., cell reles est bon; pur ceo que celuy a qui le reles est fait, avoit en luy un revercion al temps del reles fait. 450 *En mesme le manere est, lou un lees est fait a un home pur terme de vie, le remeyndre a un autre pur terme de vie, le remeyndre a le tierce en le taille, le remeyndre a le quart en fee; si un estraunge qui droit ad a la terre, relessa tout son droit a ascun deux en le remeyndre, tiel reles est bon; pur ceo que chescun deux ad un remeyndre [en fait*] vestu en luy.* 451 *Mes si tenaunt a terme de vie soit disseisi, et puis celuy qui ad droit, esteant le possession en le disseisour, relessa a un de eux a qui le remeyndre fuist fait, tout le droit, &c., cell reles est voyde; pur ceo quil navoit en luy un remeyndre en fait al temps de le reles fait†, forsque tantsolement un droit del remeyndre.*

---

* These words do not occur in *Rastell's* Transl.

† These words do not appear in any other copies than *Rastell's* Transl.

(*c*) For a release of a right to one that hath but a bare right, re-

Release mettre le droit *to one, shall sometimes enure to another, so release to reversioner enures to tenant of particular estate.* Profert *pleaded.*

And e converso, *as seisin of the particular tenant is the seisin of the reversioner,* (§ 452, 453, 470, 471). (*d*)

Release by extinguishment. *Release of seigniory to one having only a right, is good, by reason of* privity, *for the lord shall be compelled to*

452 And note, that every release made to him that hath a reversion or a remainder in deed, shall serve and aid him who hath the freehold, as well as him to whom the release was made, if the tenant have the release in his hand*. 453 In the same manner a release made to the tenant for life, or to the tenant in tail, shall enure to them in the reversion, or to them in the remainder, as well as to the tenant of the freehold; and they shall have as great advantage of that, if they can shew it, &c.

454 Also, if there be lord and tenant, and the tenant be disseised, and the lord releaseth to the disseisee all the right that he hath in the seigniory or in the land, this release is good, and the seigniory is extinct: and [this is by reason of the

452 *Et nota, que chescun reles fait a celuy qui ad une revercion ou un remeyndre en fait, servera et aidera celuy qui ad le franktenement, auxibien come a celuy a qui le reles fuist fait, si le tenaunt avoit le reles en son poigne*.* 453 *En mesme le manere un reles fait al tenaunt pur terme de vie, ou al tenaunt en le taille, urera a eux en la revercion, ou a eux en le remeyndre, auxibien come al tenaunt de franktenement; et averount auxi graund avantage de cell, sils ceo poient monstrer, &c.*

454 Item, *si soient seignour et tenaunt, et le tenaunt soit disseisi, et le seignour relessa al disseisi tout le droit quil avoet en le seignourie ou en la terre, cel reles est bon, et le sei-*

---

* *Rastell's* Transl., and the earliest printed copies conclude as in the text above, but an *&c.* is added, which *&c.* is supplied by the words, *de pleder, to plead,* in the common copies.

---

gularly is void; for as *Lyttleton* hath before said, he to whom a release is made of a bare right in lands and tenements, must have either a freehold in deed or in law in possession, or an estate in remainder, or reversion in fee, or fee-tail, or for life.—*Vide Sect.* 454. *Co. Lytt.* 267. a.

(*d*) See also § 673, where the same doctrine applies to a remitter of the *particular* tenant.

privity (§461), which is between the lord and the disseisee: for*] if the beasts of the disseisee be taken, and of them the disseisee sue a replevin against the lord, he shall compel the lord to avow upon him (*e*); for if he should avow upon the disseisor, then upon the matter shewn, the avowry shall abate, for the disseisee is tenant to him in right and in law.

avow on the disseisee, if his cattle be distrained, the disseisee being his tenant.

Gilb. Ten. 58.

455 Also, if land be given to a man in tail, reserving to the donor and to his heirs certain rent, if the donee be disseised, and afterwards the donor release to the donee and his heirs all the right that he hath in the land, and afterwards the donee enter into the land upon the disseisor, in this case the rent is gone; for this that the disseisee at the time of the release made, was tenant in right and in law unto the donor, and avowry, of fine force (*i. e.* of ne-

Extinguishment. ***Release of right extinguishes rent or seigniory, but it does not extend to the land itself.***

gnourie est extient : et ceo est pur cause del privetë, que est perentre le seignour et le disseisi : qar si les avers le disseisi soient pris, et de eux le disseisi suist un replegiare envers le seignour, il compellera le seignour davower sur luy; qar il avoweroit sur le disseisour, donques sur le matere monstre, lavower abatera, qar le disseisi est tenaunt a luy en droit et en la ley.*

455 Item, *si terre soit done a un home en le taille, reservaunt al donour et a ses heires certeyn rente, si le doné soit disseisi, et puis le donour relessa al doné et a ses heires tout le droit qil avoet en la terre, et puis le doné entra en la terre sur le disseisour, en ceo cas le rente est ale ; pur ceo que le disseisi al temps de le reles fait, fuist tenaunt en droit et en la ley al donour, et avowerë, a fyn force, covient destre fait sur luy*

* The passage between brackets does not appear in *Rastell's* Transl.

(*e*) This is regularly true; but if the lord hath accepted services of the disseisor, then the disseisee cannot enforce the lord to avow upon him, though his beasts be taken, &c.—*Co. Lytt.* 268. a.

cessity), ought to be made upon him by the donor for the rent behind, &c.: but yet nothing of the right of the land, *scil.* of the reversion, shall then pass by such release; for this that the donee to whom the release was made, then had nothing in the land, but only a right, and so the right of the land could not pass to the donee by such release. 456 In the same manner it is, if a lease be made to one for term of life, reserving to the lessor and to his heirs certain rent, if the lessee be disseised, and afterwards the lessor release to the lessee, and to his heirs, all the right which he hath in the land, and afterwards the lessee entereth; howbeit in this case the rent be extinct, yet nothing of the right [of the reversion*] passeth, *Causa qua supra.* 457 But if there be very lord and very (*g*) tenant, and the tenant make a feoffment in fee, the which feoffee doth never become tenant to the lord, &c., if the lord release to the feoffor all his right,

The same of a release to lessee for life; there being a distinction between a release of a rent-service out of land, and release of a right to land.—Co. Lytt. 269. a.

Release of right of seigniory by very lord *to* very tenant *after feoffment in fee by him, void.*

per le donour pur le rente aderere, &c.: mes unqore rien del droit de la terre, scil. *de droit de la revercion, adonques ne passera per tiel reles; pur ceo que le doné a qui le reles fuist fait, adonques navoit riens en la terre, forsque tantsolement un droit, et issint droit del terre ne puissoit passer al doné per tiel reles.* 456 *En mesme le manere est, si lees soit fait a un pur terme de vie, reservant al lessour et a ses heires certeyn rente, si le lessé soit disseisi, et puis le lessour relessa al lessé, et a ses heires, tout le droit quil ad en la terre, et apres le lessé entra; coment que en ceo cas le rente soit extient, unqore rien del droit de la revercion passa,* Causa qua supra. 457 *Mes si soit verray seignour et verray tenaunt, et le tenaunt fait un feoffement en fee, le quel feoffé ne unques devient tenaunt al seignour, &c., si le seignour relessa al feoffour*

* The words within brackets do not appear in *Rastell's* Transl.

(*g*) This is to be understood of a lord in fee-simple, and of a tenant of like estate.—*Co. Lytt.* 268. a.

&c., that release is altogether void, because the feoffor* hath no right in the land, and he is no tenant in right to the lord, but only tenant as for the avowry to be made, and he shall never compel the lord to avow upon him, for the lord shall avow upon the feoffee if he will. 458 Otherwise it is where the very tenant is disseised, as in the case aforesaid; for if the very tenant who is disseised, hold of the lord by knight's service, and dieth, his heir being within age, the lord shall have and seize the wardship of the heir; and so he shall not have the ward of the feoffor that made the feoffment in fee, and so there is a great diversity between these two cases, &c.

Distinction between this case and the last, which is of a very tenant being disseised as to wardship of heir.

459† Also, if a man let his land to another for term of years, if the lessor release to the lessee all his right, &c., before that the lessee had entered into the same land by force of the same lease, such release is void, for this that the lessee

Release denlarger lestate. *A right of entry or* interesse termini (§ 66, 289), *is not sufficient to*

tout son droit, &c., cell reles est en tout voyde, pur ceo que le feoffour nad nul droit en la terre, et il nest tenaunt en droit al seignour, mes tantsolement tenaunt quaunt al avowrë faire, et il ne unques compellera le seignour davower sur luy, qar le seignour poet avower sur le feoffé sil voille.* 458 *Autrement est lou le verray tenaunt est disseisi, sicome en le cas avaunt-dit; qar si le verray tenaunt qui est disseisi, teigne del seignour per service de chivaler, et mourust, son heire esteant deins age, le seignour avera et seisera le garde del heire; et issint il navera mye le garde del feoffour qui fist le feoffement en fee, et issint il est graunde diversité entre les deux cases, &c.*

459† Item, *si home lessa sa terre a un autre pur terme dans, si le lessour relessa al lessé tout son droit, &c., devaunt que le lessé avoit entre en mesme la terre per force de mesme le lees, tiel reles est voyde, pur ceo que le lessé navoit possession en la*

---

* *Feoffé; Lettou & M., Machl., Roh.,* and *Pyns.* 1516.

† This section does not appear in *Rastell's* Translation.

support a release to enlarge *the estate,* [*for such release cannot operate without a possession joined with an estate.*—*Touchst.* 324]: *and before possession had, there can be no reversion,* § 517.

had not possession in the land at the time of the release made, but only a right to have the same land by force of the lease. But if the lessee had entered into the same land, and had possession thereof by force of the same lease, then such release made to him by the feoffor, or by his heir, is sufficient to him, by reason of the privity which by force of the lease is between them, &c. 460* In the same manner it is, as it seemeth, where a lease is made to a man to hold of the lessor at his will, by force of which lease the lessee hath possession; if the lessor in this case make a release to the lessee of all his right, &c., this release is good enough for the privity which is between them; for it shall be in vain to make an estate by a livery of seisin to another, where he hath possession of the same tenements by the lease of the

Release to tenant at will, is good; but release to a tenant at sufferance, is bad, (the words "of his own head" not applying to

terre al temps del reles fait, mes tauntsolement un droit daver mesme la terre per force de mesme le lees. Mes si le lessé ust entre en mesme la terre, et ent eit possession per force de mesme le lees, donques tiel reles fait a luy per le feoffour, ou per son heire, est bon est sufficiant a luy, per cause de le privité que per force del lees est perentre eux, &c. 460* *En mesme le manere est, come il semble, ou lees est fait a un home a tener de le lessour a sa volunté, per force de quell lees le lessé eit possession ; si le lessour en ceo cas fait un reles al lessé de tout son droit, &c., ceo reles est assetez bon pur le privité que est parentre eux ; car en veyn serroit de faire estate per un liverë de seisin a un autre, lou il ad possession de mesmes les tenementes per le lees de mesme celuy devaunt, &c.*

---

* This section does not appear in *Rastell's* Transl. Its tenor appears to have been misunderstood if we are to judge from the cross reference which in almost all the common copies concludes this section.

† In almost all the copies from the four earliest editions, there occurs the following interpolation—*Sed contrarium tenetur, Pasch.* 2 *Ed.* 4, *per toutes les justices; But the contrary is holden, Easter* 2 *Ed.* 4, *by all the justices;* upon which *Sir Edward Coke* remarks, "This is of a new addition, and the book here cited ill understood, for it

same man before, &c. 461* But where a man of his own head shall occupy lands or tenements at the will of him that hath the freehold thereof, and such occupier claimeth nothing but at will, &c., if he that hath the freehold will release all his right to the occupier, &c., this release is void, because there is no privity between them by lease made to the occupier, nor by other manner, &c.

a disseisin); [*for albeit he have a possession, yet hath he no estate, and besides in this case there is* no privity, *which is the third thing required in these releases.—Touchst.* 325].

462 Also, if a man enfeoff other men of his land, upon confidence (*i. e.* trust), and to the intent to perform his last will, and the feoffor occupy the same land at the will of his feoffees, and afterwards the feoffees release by their deed to

A cestuy que trust *holding at the will of the trustees, is capable of a release by enlargement.*

461* *Mes lou home de sa teste demesne occupia terres ou tenementes a la volunté celuy qui ad ent le franktenement, et tiel occupiour ne clayma riens forsque a volunté, &c., si celuy qui ad le franktenement voille relesser tout son droit al occupiour, &c., tiel reles est voyde, pur ceo que nulle privitë est perentre eux per lees fait al occupiour, ne per autre manere, &c.*

462 Item, *si home enfeoffa autres homes de sa terre, sur confidence, et al entent de perfourmer sa darreyn volunté, et le feoffour occupia mesme la terre a volunté de ses feoffés, et puis les feoffés relessount per lour fait a lour feoffour tout*

---

is to be understood of a tenant at sufferance."—*Co. Lytt.* 270. b. In *Redm.* these words appear as a side-note, and are also incorporated into the text of that edition.

* This section does not appear in *Rastell's* Transl. Independent of this circumstance, it may be questionable, whether this section is any part of *Lyttleton's* Treatise. It has been observed by *Mr. Preston,* in his *Treatise of Conveyancing*, that the case put in this section is the general authority that a mere trespasser, or a mere occupier, though he may claim to hold at will has no estate; and that without an estate creating the relative situation of tenant, or *quasi* tenant, and lord or reversioner, there cannot be an effectual release by way of enlargement. In modern practice, however, *Mr. Preston* concludes the law would consider the occupier by sufferance, under the circumstances stated in the text, as tenant at will. 2 *Prest. Conv.* 303, 304. See the case of *Rees* dem. *Chamberlain* v. *Lloyd*, Wightw. 123, in which it was held that mere permission to occupy was a lease.—*Id.* 305, 309.

their feoffor all their right, &c., this hath been a question, whether such release be good or not? And some have said, that such release is void*; because there was no privity between the feoffees and their feoffor, insomuch that no lease was made after such feoffment by the [feoffees to the feoffor†], to hold at their will: and some have said the contrary, and that for two causes.

463 One is, that when such feoffment is made upon confidence to perform the will of the feoffor, that it shall be intended (*i. e.* understood) by the law, that the feoffor ought straightway to occupy the land at the will of his feoffees; and so there is such manner of privity between them, as if a man make a feoffment to others, and they immediately upon the feoffment, will and grant that their feoffor shall occupy the land at their will, &c.

464 Another cause they allege, that if such land be worth

lour droit, &c., ceo ad este un question, si tiel reles soit bon ou non? Et ascuns ount dit que tiel reles est voyde; pur ceo que nulle privité fuist perentre les feoffés et lour feoffour, entaunt que nul lees fuist fait apres tiel feoffement per les [feoffés al feoffour†], a tener a lour voluntees: et ascuns ount dit le contrarie, et ceo pur deux causes.*

463 *Une est, que quaunt tiel feoffement est fait sur confidence a perfourmer la volunté del feoffour, que il serra entenduz per la ley, que le feoffour doit meyntenaunt occupier la terre a la volunté de ses feoffés; et issint il est tiel manere de priveté entre eux, sicome home fait un feoffement as autres, et ils incontinent sur le feoffement, voillent et grantent que lour feoffour occupia la terre a lour volunté, &c.*

464 *Un autre cause ils allegiount, que si tiel terre vault*

* Some copies of *Rastell's* Translation by a misprint read this word, *good.*

† The four earliest editions read these words, *feoffours al feoffé;* but this seems an erroneous reading, all the later copies with *Rastell's* Transl. read as in the text, and in that copy of *Roh. penes Ed.*, these words are corrected according to the above text by a cotemporary hand.

forty shillings a year, &c., then such feoffor shall be sworn in assise and other inquests in pleas real, and also in pleas personal, of what great sum soever the plaintiffs will count (*i. e.* declare). And this is by the common law of the land (*h*): *ergo*, this is for a great cause: and the cause is, for that the law willeth that such feoffors and their heirs ought to occupy, &c., and take and enjoy all manner of profits, issues, and revenues, &c., as if the lands were their own, without interruption of the feoffees, notwithstanding such feoffment: *ergo*, the same law giveth a privity between such feoffors (*i*) and the feoffees

xl*s. per an, &c., donques tiel feoffour serra jurre en assise et en autres enquestes en plees realx, et auxi en plees personelx de quel graund somme que les pleintifs voillent counter. Et ceo est per la comen ley de la terre :* ergo, *ceo est pur un graund cause : et la cause est, que la ley voet que tielx feoffours et lour heires doient occupier, &c., et prendre et enjoyer toutes maners profites, issuez, et revenus, &c., sicome les tenementes furent ses mesmes, sauns interrupcion de les feoffés, nient obstant tiel feoffement :* ergo, *mesme la ley done un priveté perentre tielx feoffours et les feoffés sur confidence, &c., pur queux*

(*h*) Here three things are to be observed :—First, that the surest construction of a statute is by the rule and reason of the common law. Secondly, that uses were at the common law. Thirdly, that now seeing the statute of 27 H. 8, c. 10, which hath been enacted since *Lyttleton* wrote, hath transferred the possession of the use, this case holdeth not at this day; but this latter opinion before that statute was good law, as *Lyttleton* here taketh it.—*Co. Lytt.* 272. b.

(*i*) Hereof it followeth, that when the law gives to any man any estate or possession, the law giveth also a privity and other necessaries to the same: and *Lyttleton* concludeth it with an illative ; ergo, *mesme la ley done privité*, which is very observable for a conclusion in other cases. *Nota*—A use is a trust or confidence reposed in some other, which is not issuing out of the land, but as a thing collateral annexed in privity to the estate of the land, and to the person touching the land, *scil.* that *cestuy que use* shall take the profit, and that the terre-tenant shall make an estate according to his direction. So as *cestuy que use* had neither *jus in re*, nor *jus ad rem*, but only

upon confidence, &c., for which causes they have said, that such releases made by such feoffees upon confidence to their feoffor or to his heirs, &c., so occupying the land, &c., shall be good enough; and this is the better opinion, as it seemeth*.

Release enlarger estate, *how it shall enure; A release that gives an estate requires words of enlargement,* i. e. *words expressing the quantum, or extent of interest to be passed by such a release.*

465 Also, releases according to the matter in fact, sometimes have their effect by force to enlarge the estate of him to whom the release is made. As if I let certain land to one for term of years, by force whereof he had possession, and afterwards I release to him all the right that I have in the land, without more words put in the deed, and deliver to him the deed; then he hath estate but for term of his life. And the reason is, for that when the reversion or remainder is in a

causes ils ount dit, que tielx relesses faites per tielx feoffés sur confidence a lour feoffour ou a ses heires, &c., issint occupiant la terre, &c., serra assetez bon; et cest le meliour opinion, come il semble, &c.*

465 Item, *relesses solonques le matere en fait, ascun foitz ount lour effecte per force denlarger le estate celuy a qui le reles est fait. Sicome jeo lessa certeyn terre a un home pur terme des ans, per force de quel il eit possession, et puis jeo relessa a luy tout le droit que jeo ay en la terre, sans pluis perolx motes en le fait, et delivera a luy le fait; donques il ad estate forsque pur terme de sa vie. Et la cause est, pur ceo que quaunt la revercion ou le remeyndre est en un home le*

---

* In all the corrupted editions, commencing at *Redm.*, here follows:—*Quære, for this seemeth no law at this day*, which *quære Sir Edward Coke* remarks, "is not in the original, but added by some other, and therefore to be rejected."

---

a confidence and trust, for which he had no remedy by the common law; but for breach of trust his remedy was only by *subpœna* in Chancery: and yet the judges, for the cause aforesaid, made the said construction upon the said statute.—*Co. Lytt.* 272. b.

man who willeth by his release to enlarge the estate of the tenant, &c., he shall have no greater estate, but in such manner and form as if such relessor were seised in fee, and by his deed willeth to make estate to one in a certain form, and deliver unto him seisin by force of the same deed; if in such deed of feoffment there be not any word of inheritance, &c., then he hath but estate for term of life, and so it is in such releases § 1.
made *by them* in the reversion or in the remainder. For if I let land to a man for term of his life, and afterwards I release to him all my right (*k*), without saying more in the release, § 469.
his estate is not enlarged: but if I release to him and to his heirs, then he hath fee-simple; and if I release to him and § 468.
to his heirs of his body begotten, then he hath fee-tail, &c. And so it behoveth to specify in the deed what estate he to whom the release is made shall have.

466 Also, sometimes releases shall enure to put and vest the Release mettre

quel voile enlarger per son reles lestate de le tenaunt, &c., il navera plus greyndre estate mes en tiel manere et fourme sicome tiel relessour fuist seisi en fee, et voilleit per son fait faire estate a un en certeyn fourme, et deliverer a luy seisin per force de mesme le fait; si en tiel fait de feoffement ne soit ascun parol denheritaunce, &c., donques il ad forsque estate pur terme de vie, et issint il est en tielx relesses faitz en la revercion, ou en le remeyndre. Qar si jeo lessa terre a un home pur terme de sa vie, et puis jeo relessa a luy tout mon droit, sauns pluis dire en le reles, son estate nest my enlarge: mes si jeo relessa a luy et a ses heires, donques il ad fee-simple; et si jeo relessa a luy et ses heires de son corps engendres, donques il ad fee-taille, &c. Et issint il covient de specifier en le fait quel estate celuy a qui le reles est fait avera.

466 Item, *ascuns foitz relesses ureront de mettre et vester le*

(*k*) *Sir Edward Coke* in his Commentary here refers to § 650. See *post*, § 650.

et vester le droit how it shall enure; Effect of such release by disseisee to disseisor. (This case puts the distinction between § 465 and this).

Distinction between a release mettre le droit and release denlarger.

Release for the shortest space of time, as effectual as a release to releasee and his heirs. [So it is of a confirmation in both cases, 519, 520].

Release to him who has the fee, good, without words of enlargement.

right of him that maketh the release, to him to whom the release is made. As if a man be disseised, and he release to his disseisor all the right that he hath; in this case the disseisor hath his right, so that whereas his estate before was wrongful, now by this release it is made lawful and right (§ 473).

467 But here note, that when a man is seised in fee-simple of any lands or tenements, and another will release to him all the right that he hath in the same tenements, it needeth not to speak of the heirs of him to whom the release is made, for this that he had fee-simple at the time of the release made: for if the release was made to him [and to his heirs*] for one day or for one hour, this shall be as strong unto him in law, as if he had released to him and his heirs: for when his right was gone from him once (*i. e.* at one time) by his release without any condition, &c., to him that hath fee-simple, it is gone for ever. 468 But where a man hath a reversion in fee-simple, or

droit celuy qui fait le reles, a celuy a qui le reles est fait. Sicome un home est disseisi, et il relessa a son disseisour tout le droit que il ad; en ceo cas le disseisour ad son droit, issint que lou son estate adevaunt fuist torcious, ore per cell reles il est fait loiall et droiturell.

467 *Mes* hic nota, *que quaunt home est seisi en fee-simple dascuns terres ou tenementes, et un autre voille relesser a luy tout le droit quil ad en mesmes les terres, il ne besoigne de parler de les heires cestuy a qui le reles est fait, pur ceo quil eit fee-simple al temps de le reles fait : qar si reles fuist fait a luy [et a ses heires*] pur un jour, ou pur une heure, ceo serroit auxi fort a luy en ley, sicome il ust relesse a luy et a ses heires : qar quaunt son droit fuist ale de luy a un foitz per son reles sauns ascun condicion, &c., a celuy qui ad fee-simple, il est ale e toutes jours.* 468 *Mes lou home ad une re-*

---

* The words do not appear in any edition subsequent to *Pyns.* 1516, save the copies of *Rastell's* Transl. which retain them.

a remainder in fee-simple, at the time of the release made, there if he will release to the tenant for term of years, or for term of life, or to the tenant in the tail, it behoveth to determine the estate, which he to whom the release is made shall have by force of the same release; for this that such release goeth* to enlarge the estate of him to whom the release is made, &c. 469 But otherwise it is where a man hath but a right to the land, and hath nothing in the reversion nor in the remainder in deed; for if such a man release all his right to one that is tenant of the freehold, all his right is gone, albeit no mention be made of the heirs of him to whom the release is made. For if I let lands or tenements to a man for term of his life, if I afterwards release unto him for to enlarge his estate, it behoveth that I release to him and to his heirs of his body begotten, or to him and his heirs, or by such words: "To have and to hold to him and to the heirs males of his

And for words to raise the estate, it is usual and most safe to specify in the deed what estate he to whom the release is made shall have; (see ante, § 465).

And in most cases this is needful, (the exception being [viz. this present case], that where a mere right is released to the tenant of the freehold), for it is generally true, that when a release enures by way of enlargement of estate, no inheritance in fee or fee tail can pass without apt words of inheritance.—[Touchst. 327].

vercion en fee-simple, ou un remeyndre en fee-simple, al temps del reles fait, là sil voille relesser al tenaunt pur terme dans, ou pur terme de vie, ou al tenaunt en le taille, il covient a determiner lestate, que celuy a qui le reles est fait avera per force de mesme le reles; pur ceo que tiel reles va pur enlarger lestate, de celuy a qui le reles est fait &c.* 469 *Mes autrement est lou home ad forsque droit a la terre, et nad riens en la revercion ne en le remeyndre en fait; qar si tiel home relessa tout son droit a un que est tenaunt de le franktenement, tout son droit est ale, coment que nul mencion soit fait de les heires celuy a qui le reles est fait. Qar si jeo lessa terres ou tenementes a un home pur terme de sa vie, si jeo puis relesser a luy pur enlarger son estate, il covient que jeo relessa a luy et a ses heires de son corps engendres, ou a luy et a ses heires, ou per tielx parolx: "A aver et tener a luy et a les heires*

---

* The common copies read this word *enurera, shall enure.*

Release per extinguisher le droit. *If tenant for life make lease for life of the lessee, the remainder over in fee, and the first lessor release all his right to him to whom the tenant made the lease for life, this is good, although not expressed to be made to him "and his heirs," it enuring in respect of privity* (*l*).

body begotten," or by such like estates; or otherwise he hath no greater estate than he had before. 470 But if my tenant for term of life let the same land over to another for term of the life of his lessee, the remainder to another in fee, now if I release unto him to whom my tenant leased for term of life, I shall be barred for ever, albeit that no mention be made of his heirs; for this that at the time of the release made, I had no reversion, but only a right to have the reversion. For by such lease, and (*i. e.* with) the remainder over which my tenant made in this case, my reversion is discontinued (*i. e.* divested); and such release shall enure to him in the remainder, to have advantage thereof as well as to the tenant for term of life, 471 For to that intent the tenant for term of life, and he in the remainder, are as one tenant in law, and are as if one tenant were sole seised in his demesne as of fee at the time of such release made unto him, &c.

§ 453.

Particular estate and remainder constitute but one tenancy in fee, and therefore release of right to tenant of particular estate enures to him in remainder, § 60, 452, 453, 470, 557, 590.

males de son corps engendres," ou per tielx semblable sestates; ou autrement il nad pluis greindre estate que il avoit adevaunt. 470 *Mes si mon tenaunt a terme de vie lessa mesme la terre oustre a un autre pur terme de vie de son lessé, le remeyndre a un autre en fee, ore si jeo relessa a celuy a qui mon tenaunt lessast pur terme de vie, jeo serray barre a toutes jours, coment que nul mencion soit fait de ses heires; pur ceo que al temps de reles fait jeo avoye nul revercion, mes tantsolement droit daver la revercion. Qar per tiel lees, et le remeyndre oustre que mon tenaunt fist en ceo cas, mon revercion est discontinue, et tiel reles urera a celuy en le remeyndre, daver avantage de ceo auxibien a tenaunt a terme de vie,* 471 *Qar a cel intent le tenaunt a terme de vie, et celuy en le remeyndre, sount sicome un tenaunt en ley, et sount sicome un tenaunt fuist sole seisi en son demesne come de fee al temps de tiel reles fait a luy, &c.*

(*l*) But in all the cases of a release of a bare right to him that hath an estate of a freehold in deed or in law, generally there needs no privity to make the release good.—*Touchst.* 330.

472 Also, if a man be disseised by two, if he release to one of them, he shall hold his companion out of the land, and by such release shall have sole possession and estate in the land (*m*): but if one disseisor enfeoff two in fee, and the disseisee release to one of the feoffees, this shall enure to both of the feoffees; and the cause of the diversity between these two cases is pregnant enough* (*n*).

Release mettre le droit *how it shall enure; If made to one of two disseisors, it enures to him alone,* (§ 306, 522), *and if made to one of two feoffees of a disseisor, it enures to both* (§ 307).

472 Item, *si home soit disseisi per deux, sil relessa a un deux, il tiendra son compaignion hors del terre, et per tiel reles avera sole possession et estate en la terre : mes si un disseisour enfeoffa deux en fee, et le disseisi relessa a lun des feoffés, ceo urera a ambideux de les feoffés ; et la cause de diversité entre ceux deux cases est assetez pregnant**.

---

* In *Redm.* and in every edition since, appears the following addition, "For that they come in by feoffment, (*i. e.* by right), and the others by wrong, (*i. e.* by disseisin), &c." which *Sir Edward Coke* remarks, is "a new addition, and not in the original, and therefore I pass it over."—*Co. Lytt.* 276. a.—*Pugnant, Roh.*, but errroneously, some also read, *preignant, pugnant,* and *repugnant.*

(*m*) If heir and a stranger disseise the father, and he dies, the heir is remitted to the whole, because a descent is a release in law, (*i. e.* he comes in by right), and he shall hold his companion out.—*Year-Book, Mich.* 11 *H.* 7, *pl.* 38.

(*n*) The reason appears to be, because in the one case he is in by the feoffment, and in the other case by the release, for there is a distinction where a disseisee releases to one who is in by title, (for there the first possession continues), and in a release to one who is in by wrong, as in the case of a release made to one of two disseisors, he shall be adjudged *in* by him who releases the entirety, and shall hold his companion out: *contra*, where the disseisor enfeoffs, and the disseisee releases to one feoffee, this shall enure to both; because this is an extinguishment, and the other release is the creation of an estate.—*Anon. Comm. on Lytt. penes Ed.*

The different operation of a release, when made to one of two disseisors, and to one of two feoffees of a disseisor, is to be explained by the distinction which the law takes between a defective title and no title at all. For when

Distinction between the two cases Lyttleton puts of release made to one who is in by wrong, *enuring by way of entry and feoffment,* (§ 473), *and the case where the releasee is in by* title (§ 474, 475).

Release enuring by entry and feoffment; *If one be disseised and afterwards another disseise him, and the disseisee release to the last disseisor, this is a good release* (§ 466).

473 Also, if I be disseised, and my disseisor is disseised, if I release to the disseisor of my disseisor, I never shall have assise nor shall I enter upon his disseisor, because his disseisor hath my right by my release, &c.; so it seemeth in such case, if there be twenty disseisors one after another, and I release to the last disseisor, he shall bar all the others of their actions and their titles. And the cause is, for this that in many cases when a man hath lawful title of entry, and entereth not*,

473 Item, *si jeo sue disseisi, et mon disseisour est disseisi, si jeo relesse a le disseisour de mon disseisour, jeo naveray unques assise ne entray sur son disseisour, pur ceo que son disseisour ad mon droit per mon reles, &c.; issint il semble en tiel cas, si soient* xx. *disseisours chescun apres autre, et jeo relessa a le darreyn disseisour, il barrera toutes les autres de lour accions et lour titles. Et la cause est, pur ceo que en moltes cases, quaunt home ad loial title dentré, et nentre*, il*

---

the party has a defective title, (not having possession by his own wrong), the law protects him in the possession until he is evicted by the rightful claimant. But with respect to those who have no title at all, it is otherwise. Thus, if A. is disseised by B. and C., the disseisors have only a naked possession, unaccompanied with even the shadow of the right of possession; and, consequently, if A. releases to one of them, it operates as a feoffment to the relessee, precisely in the same manner as if A. had actually revested his former estate by his entry, and then granted, with livery of seisin, to the relessee. See *Co. Lytt.* 275. b. and *note.* But where there are joint feoffees, and the disseisee releases to one of them, it operates for the benefit of each feoffee indifferently, because the feoffees have colour of title. *Co. Lytt.* 194. b., 275. a. and *note.* For, originally, no tenant could make a feoffment without the lord's license, and when the lord consented to the alienation, the only form of conveyance was by livery of seisin, which was a public act, and to which the ceremonies of homage and fealty were also necessary. There was, consequently, in this case, a colourable title or presumption of right, but in the other case there was no pretence of any right or title at all.—*Co. Lytt.* 264. a. and *note.*—*Ritso's Introd. p.* 40, *n.*

---

* This is printed in *Letlou & M.*, *Machl.*, and *Roh.*, *et entre, and entereth*, evidently a misprint for *nentre.*

he shall defeat all mesne titles by his release, &c. But this holds not in every case, as shall be said hereafter.

474* Also, if my disseisor let the tenements whereof he disseised me, to a man for term of life, and afterwards the tenant for term of life alieneth in fee, and I release to the alienee, &c., then my disseisor cannot enter, *Causa qua supra*, albeit that at one time the alienation was to his disinheritance.

Release extinguisher le droit.
So if my disseisor lease for life, and the lessee for life alien in fee, and I release to the alienee all my right, &c., this is a good release.

475 Also, if a man be disseised, who hath a son within age and dieth, and the son being within age, the disseisor dieth seised, and the land descendeth to his heir, and a stranger abateth, and afterwards the son of the disseisee when he cometh to his full age, releaseth all his right to the abator; in this case the heir of the disseisor shall not have assise of mortdancestor against the abator, but shall be barred of the assise, because the abator hath the right of the son of the disseisee by his release, and the entry of the son was lawful, &c., for this that he was within age at the time of the

If one who hath a son within age, be disseised and die, and the disseisor die seised, and the land descend to his heir, and a stranger abate, and the son releases to him on his attaining age, this is a good release mettre le droit.

defetera toutes mesnes titles per son reles, &c. Mes ceo nest en chescun cas, come serra dit apres.

474* Item, *si mon disseisour lessa les tenementes dount il moy disseisist, a un home pur terme de vie, et puis le tenaunt a terme de vie aliena en fee, et jeo relessa al aliené, &c., donques mon disseisour ne poet entrer,* Causa qua supra, *coment que a un foitz lalienacion fuist a son disheritaunce.*

475 Item, *si home soit disseisi, le quel ad fitz deins age et morust, et esteant le fitz deins age, le disseisour morust seisi, et la terre descendist a son heire, et un estraunge abate, et puis le fitz le disseisi quaunt il vient a son pleyn age, relessa tout son droit al abatour; en ceo cas leire le disseisour navera assise de mortdancestre envers labatour, mes serra barre dassise, pur ceo que labatour ad le droit de fitz le disseisi per son reles, et lentré le fitz fuist congeable, &c., pur ceo qil*

---

* This section does not appear in *Rastell's* Transl.

On such release to disseisor's feoffee on condition, the condition is not avoided.

descent, &c. 476 But if any man be disseised, and the disseisor maketh a feoffment upon condition, *scil.* to render to him certain rent, and for default of payment a re-entry, &c., if the disseisee release to the feoffee upon condition, yet this shall not abate* the estate of the feoffee upon condition; [for notwithstanding such release, yet his estate is upon condition†] as it was before‡. 477 In the same manner it is where a man is disseised of certain land, and the disseisor grant a rent-charge out of the same land, &c., albeit that afterwards the disseisee doth release to the disseisor, &c., yet the rent-charge abideth in its force. And the reason in these two cases is, that a man shall not have advantage by such release, which shall be against his own proper accept-

And on such release to disseisor, rent-charges, &c., previously granted by him, are not avoided; because he shall not avoid his own grant by a release he himself hath ac-

fuist deins age al temps del discent, &c. 476 *Mes si ascun home soit disseisi et le disseisour fait feoffement sur condicion,* scil. *de rendre a luy certeyn rente, et pur defaut de paiement un re-entre, &c., si le disseisi relessa al feoffé sur condicion, unqore ceo ne abatera* lestate le feoffé sur condicion; [qar nient obstant tiel reles, unqore son estate est sur condicion†], come il fuist adevaunt‡.* 477 *En mesme le manere est lou home soit disseisi de certeyn terre, et le disseisour graunta un rent-charge hors de mesme la terre, &c., coment que apres le disseisi relessa al disseisour, &c., unqore le rente-charge demurt en sa force. Et la cause est en ceux deux cases, que home navera avantage per tiel reles, que serra encontre son propre acceptance, et encontre son graunt demesne : et coment*

* *Ne alterast, altereth not, Paper MS.* and *Rastell's* Transl.: *navoidera, shall not avoid,* Vell. MSS.: *nabatera, Pyns.* 1516, *namendra, shall not amend, Redm.*, and subsequent copies.

† The words within brackets do not appear in some copies of *Rastell's* Transl.

‡ Here follows the following reference which occurs in *Redm.* and in later copies, viz. *And with this agreeth the opinion of all the justices. Pasch.* 9 *H.* 7, *pl.* 51. The Editor of the 11th Edition of *Co. Lytt.* remarks, that this addition appeared first in *Pyns.* 1528, and was copied by subsequent publishers as part of Lyttleton.

ance, and against his own grant: and albeit that some have said, that where the entry of a man is lawful upon a tenant, if he release to the same tenant, that this shall avail the tenant, just as if he had entered upon the tenant, and afterwards enfeoffed him, &c., this is not true in every case: for in the first case of these two cases aforesaid, if the disseisee had entered upon the feoffee upon condition, and afterwards enfeoffed him, then should the condition be wholly defeated and avoided. And so in the second case, if the disseisee enter and enfeoff him that granted the rent-charge, then is the rent-charge annulled and avoided; but it is not avoided by any such release without entry made, &c.

quired since the grant.—Co. Lytt. 278. a.

§ 466.

Another kind of release, viz. *a release which enureth by way of* entry and feoffment; *for if a disseisee release to one of the disseisors, to some purpose this shall enure by way of entry and feoffment*, viz. *as to hold out his companion.*—Ibid.

478 Also, if a man be disseised by an infant, who aliens in fee, and the alienee dieth seised, and his heir entereth, the alienor* being within age, now is it in the election of the alienor to have a writ *Dum fuit infra ætatem*, or a writ of right against the heir of the alienee; and whichever writ of

Release per mettre et vester, *enuring by way of* extinguisher le droit.

A. disseised by B. an infant, who aliens in

que ascuns ount dit que lou lentre de home est congeable sur un tenaunt, sil relessast a mesme le tenaunt, que ceo availleroit a le tenaunt, sicome il ust entre sur le tenaunt, et puis luy enfeoffa, &c., ceo nest pas veray en chescun cas: qar en le premier cas de les deux avantditz cases, si le disseisi ust entre sur le feoffé sur condicion, et puis luy enfeoffa, donques serroit la condicion tout defete et avoyde. Et issint en le seconde case, si le disseisi entrast et enfeoffast celuy qui graunta le rent-charge, donques serroit le rente-charge anientie et avoyde; mes il nest pas avoyde per ascun tiel reles sauns entré fait, &c.

478 Item, *si home soit disseisi per un enfaunt, le quel aliena en fee, et lalienê devie seisi, et son heire entra, esteant lalienour* deins age, ore est en eleccion dalienour daver un brief* Dum fuit infra ætatem, *ou brief de droit, envers leire dalienê;*

---

* The word *alienor* is printed *disseisor* in all other copies than the three earliest editions.

fee to C., and C. die seised, and D. his heir enter, B. the disseisor being within age, if A. the disseisee release to D., (the heir of C., the alienee); this is a good release, for A.'s entry was taken away by the descent; but B. the infant might either enter, or have a writ of right. Therefore if D. obtain a release from A., and afterwards B. bring a writ of right, he shall be barred by the release from A. to D.

the two he will choose, he ought thereby to recover by law. And also he can enter into the land without any recovery; and in this case the entry of the disseisee is taken away, &c.: but in this case if the disseisee release his right to the heir of the alienee, and afterwards the disseisor bringeth a writ of right against the heir of the alienee, and he join the mise upon the mere* right, &c., the grand assise ought by the law to find, that the tenant hath more mere right, &c., than hath the disseisor, for this that the tenant hath the right of the disseisor by his release, the which is the most ancient and mere right. For by such release all the right of the disseisee passeth to the tenant, and is in the tenant. And to this some have said, that in such case where a man hath right to lands or tenements, but his entry is not lawful, if he release to the tenant, &c., [all his right, &c.†], that such release shall enure by way of extinguishment: so far as concerns this it may be

et quel brief deux il esliera, il doit recoverer per la ley. Et auxi il poet entrer en la terre sauns ascun recoverer; et en ceo cas lentre le disseisi est tolle, &c.: mes en ceo cas si le disseisi relessa son droit a leire daliené, et puis le disseisour porta brief de droit envers leire daliené, et il joyndra le myse sur le mere droit, &c., le graunde assise doit trouver per la ley, que le tenaunt ad pluis mere droit, &c., que ad le disseisour, pur ceo que le tenaunt ad le droit del disseisi per son reles, le quel est pluis auncien et pluis mere droit. Qar per tiel reles tout le droit del disseisi passa a le tenaunt, et est en le tenaunt. Et a ceo ascuns ount dit, que en tiel cas lou home ad droit a terres ou tenementes, mes son entré nest pas congeable, sil relessast al tenaunt, &c., [tout son droit, &c.†], que tiel reles urera per voye dextientisement: quaunt a ceo poet estre dit, que ceo*

---

* The word *mere* is in all the copies of *Rastell's* Transl. printed *clere*.

† The words within brackets do not appear in *Rastell's* Transl., the previous *&c.* evidently supplies these words.

said, that this is truth, as to him that releaseth: for by his release he hath dismissed himself completely* of all his right, as to his person; but yet the right which he hath, can well pass to the tenant by his release. For it should be inconvenient that such ancient right should be extinct altogether, &c. For it is commonly said, that right cannot die. 479 But release which goeth by way of extinguishment against all persons (*m*), is where he to whom the release is made, cannot have that which to him is released, &c. As if there be lord and tenant, and the lord release to the tenant all the right that he hath in the seignory†, or all the right that he hath in the

Release per extinguisher lestate *against* all persons *defined and illustrated, viz.* 1. *Lord and tenant; lord releases to tenant all his right in the seignory or in the land, this operates as an extinguishment, because*

est verité, quant a celuy qui relessast: qar per son reles il ad luy dismisse nettement de tout son droit, quaunt a sa persone; mes unqore le droit queil avoet, bien poet passer a le tenaunt per son reles. Qar inconvenient serroit que tiel auncien droit serroit extient tout ousterment, &c. Qar il est communement dit que droit ne poet pas murier.* 479 *Mes relesse que va per voye dextientisement envers toutes persones, est lou celuy a qui le reles est fait, ne poet aver ceo que a luy est relesse, &c. Sicome si soient seignour et tenaunt, et le seignour relessa al tenaunt tout le droit qil ad en la seignourie†, ou tout le droit*

---

* This word does not occur in *Lettou & M.*, *Machl.*, or *Roh.*, but it is given in the Camb. MSS., later copies read *quitement* which has the same meaning.

† *Services*, Camb. MSS.

(*m*) Here *Lyttleton* putteth a diversity between releases which enure by way of extinguishment against all persons, and whereof all persons may take advantage, and releases which in respect of some persons enure by way of extinguishment, and of other persons by way of *mitter le droit*. Or between releases which in deed enure by extinguishment; for that he to whom the release is made, cannot have the thing released; and releases which having some quality of such releases are said to enure by way of extinguishment, but in troth do not; for that he to whom the release is made may receive and take the thing released. And here *Lyttleton* putteth cases where releases do absolutely enure by extinguishment without exception, having respect to all persons, and first, of the lord and tenant; secondly, of the rent-charge; thirdly, of the common of pasture.—*Co. Lytt.* 279. *b.*

tenant cannot receive service of himself.

land, &c., such release goeth by way of extinguishment against all persons, because that the tenant cannot have this of himself. [480] In the same manner it is of a release made to the tenant of the land of a rent-charge or common of pasture, &c., because the tenant cannot have that which to him is released, &c., so such releases shall enure by way of extinguishment against all persons (*n*)*.

2. The same case of a release from the grantee of rent-charge to the owner of the land, or a release of common of pasture or profit a prendre.

[481] Also to prove that the grand assise ought to pass for the tenant† in the case aforesaid, I have often heard in the reading of the statute of West. 2, which began thus:—" In " casu quando vir amiserit per defaltam tenementum quod fuit

Lease for life, remainder in fee, if tenant for life had suffered a recovery, re-

qil ad en la terre, &c., tiel reles va per voy de extientisement envers toutes persones, pur ceo que le tenaunt ne poet aver ceo de luy mesme. [480] *En mesme le manere est de reles fait al tenaunt del terre dun rente-charge ou comen de pasture, &c., pur ceo que le tenaunt ne poet aver ceo que a luy est relesse, &c., issint tielx relesses ureront toutz foitz per voye dextientisement envers toutes persones*.*

[481] Item, *de prover que le graunde assise doit passer pur le tenaunt† en le cas avauntdit, jeo ay oye sovent en la lecture de lestatuit de Westminster seconde, que commence, " In casu " quando vir amiserit per defaltam tenementum quod fuit jus*

* The reading of the text is conformable to the three earliest editions and the *Paper MS.* The reading of all subsequent editions concludes this section—*by way of extinguishment in all ways.*

† This appears *demandaunt* in every copy of *Lytt.* In that copy of *Roh. penes ed.*, the word *tenant* is substituted by a cotemporary hand; and in other copies of *Lytt. penes ed.*, this alteration appears to have been made by the first possessors, so that this misprint has been long known to be an error. *Sir Edward Coke*, however, passed it over.

(*n*) If the lord sell the freehold of the inheritance of the copyhold to another, and afterwards the copyholder release to a purchaser, this also is a release *per extinguisher lestate*, and the copyhold interest becomes extinct. 1 *Leon.* 102. (*Wakeford's case*).

jus uxoris suæ, &c.", that at common law before the said statute, if lease were made to the tenant for term of life, the remainder over in fee, and a stranger by feigned action recovered against the tenant for life by default, and afterwards the tenant dieth, he in the remainder had no remedy before the statute, because he had not any possession of the land. 482 But if he in the remainder had entered upon the tenant for life, and him disseised, and afterwards the tenant enter upon him, and afterwards the tenant for life lose by such recovery, that is to say, by default, and die, now he in the remainder may well have a writ of right against him that recovered, because the mise shall be joined solely upon the mere right, &c. Yet in this case the seisin of him in the remainder was defeated by the entry of the tenant for term of life. But peradventure some will argue and say, that he shall not have writ of right in this case, for that when the mise is joined, it is joined in such manner, *scil.* if (*i. e.* whether) the tenant hath more mere right to the land in the manner as he

mainder-man was without remedy till West. 2, c. 3.

A disseisin gotten by wrong, and defeated by the entry of him that right hath, is sufficient to maintain a writ of right against the recoveror in this case.— Co. Lytt. 280. b ; *for in a writ of right, the question is of the mere right, and the words* modo et forma *are words of form only.*

" *uxoris suæ, &c.," que a le comen ley devant lestatuit, si lees soit fait a le tenaunt pur terme de vie, le remeyndre oustre en fee, et un estraunge per feynt accion recoverast envers le tenaunt a terme de vie per defaut, et puis le tenaunt morust, celuy en le remeyndre navoit ascune remedie devant lestatuit, pur ceo quil navoit ascun possession del terre.* 482 *Mes si celuy en le remeyndre ust entre sur le tenaunt a terme de vie, et luy disseisist, et apres le tenaunt entra sur luy, et apres le tenaunt a terme de vie perda per tiel recoverer, cestassavoir, per defaut, et morust, ore celuy en le remeyndre bien poet aver brief de droit envers celuy qui recoverast, pur ceo que le myse serra joynt solement sur le mere droit, &c. Unqore en ceo cas, le seisin de celuy en le remeyndre fuist defete per lentré del tenaunt a terme de vie. Mes peraventure ascuns voillont arguer et dire, que il navera brief de droit en ceo cas, pur ceo que quant le myse est joynt, il est joynt en tiel manere,* scil. *si le tenaunt ad pluis mere droit a la terre en le manere come*

holdeth, than the demandant hath in the manner as he demandeth; and for that the seisin of the demandant was defeated by the entry of the tenant for term of life, &c., then he hath no right in the manner as he hath demanded (*o*):

Modo et forma *in many cases words of form in pleading and not words of substance.*

483 To this it may be said, that these words, *modo et forma prout, &c.*, in many cases are words of form of pleading, and not words of substance: for if a man bring a writ of entry *in casu proviso,* of the alienation made by the tenant in dower to his disinheritance, and counteth of the alienation made in fee, and the tenant saith, that he did not alien in manner as the demandant hath declared, and upon this they are at issue, and it is found by verdict, that the tenant had aliened in tail, or for term of another's life, the demandant shall recover, and yet the alienation was not in manner as the demandant had declared.

Case where

484 Also if there be lord and tenant, and the tenant hold of

il tient, que le demaundant ad en le manere come il ad demaunde; et pur ceo que le seisin del demaundant fuist defete per lentre de le tenaunt a terme de vie, &c., donques il nad nul droit en le manere come il ad demaunde: 483 *A ceo poet estre dit, que ceux parolx,* modo et forma prout, &c., *in moltes des cases sount parolx de fourme de pleder, et nemy parolx de substance: qar si home porta brief dentre* in casu proviso, *del alienacion fait per le tenaunt en dower a son disheritaunce, et counta del alienacion fait en fee, et le tenaunt dit, qil naliena pas en le manere come le demaundant ad declare, et sur ceo sount a issue, et trove est per verdit, que le tenaunt alienast en le taille, ou pur terme dautre vie, le demandaunt recovera; unqore lalienacion ne fuist en le manere come lc demaundant avoit declare.*

484 *Auxi si soient seignour et tenaunt, et le tenaunt tient*

(*o*) And thus the original disseisee, having more mere right than the demandant, may grant a release which shall enure *per mettre et vestre* that right in the relessee, notwithstanding he has no longer a right of entry.—*Co. Lytt.* 278. b. *Ritso's Introd.* p. 41, *n.*

the lord by fealty only, and the lord distrain the tenant for rent, and the tenant bring writ of trespass against his lord for his cattle so taken, and the lord plead that the tenant holds of him by fealty and certain rent, and for the rent behind he came and distrained, &c., and demand judgment of the writ brought against him, *quare vi et armis, &c.;* and the other saith, that he doth not hold of him in the manner he supposes, and upon this they are at issue, and it is found by verdict that he holdeth of him by fealty only, in this case the writ shall abate, and yet he doth not hold of him in the manner as the lord hath said, for the matter of the issue is, whether the tenant holdeth of him or no? For if he holdeth of him, although that the lord distrain the tenant for other services which he ought not to have, yet such writ of trespass, *quare vi et armis, &c.*, doth not lie against the lord, but shall be abated.

modo et forma *are but words of form,* (ante, § 482).

485 Also in writ of trespass for battery, or for goods carried away, if the defendant plead, not guilty, in manner as the plaintiff supposes, and it is found that the defendant is guilty

Transitory actions.

del seignour per fealté solement, et le seignour distreigna le tenaunt pur rente, et le tenaunt porta brief de trespas envers le seignour pur ses avers issint prisez, et le seignour pleda que le tenaunt tient de luy per fealté et certeyn rente, et pur le rente arere il vient et distreigna, &c., et demaunde juggement de brief porte envers luy, quare vi et armis, &c.; *et lautre dit que il ne tient de luy en le manere come il supposa, et sur ceo sount a issue, et trove est per verdit quil tient de luy per fealté tantum, en ceo cas le brief abatera, et unqore il ne tient de luy en le manere come le seignour avoet dit, qar le matere del issue est, le quel le tenaunt tient de luy ou nemy? Qar sil tient de luy, coment que le seignour distreigna le tenaunt pur autres services que ne doit aver, unqore tiel brief de trespas,* quare vi et armis, &c., *ne gist envers le seignour, mes serra abate.*

485 *Auxi en brief de trespas de baterie, ou des biens emportes, si le defendant plede, riens culpable, en le manere come le pleintif ad suppose, et trove est que le defendant est culpa-*

in another town, or at another day than the plaintiff hath supposed, yet he shall recover. And in many other cases these words, *scil.* "in the manner as the demandant or the plaintiff hath supposed," are* not any matter of the substance of the issue: for in writ of right, where the mise is joined upon the mere right, it is as much as to say, and to such effect, *scil.* who hath the more mere right, the tenant or the demandant, to the thing in demand?

Distinction taken as to when the possession should draw the right of the land to it and when not.—Co. Lytt. 283. b.

486 Also, if a man be disseised, and the disseisor die seised, &c., and his son and heir is in by descent, and the disseisee enter upon the heir of the disseisor, the which entry is a disseisin, &c., if the heir bring assise or writ [of entry in nature of assise, he shall recover (*p*); but if the heir bring writ†] of

ble en autre ville, ou a autre jour que le pleintif ad suppose, unqore il recovera. Et en moltes plusours autres cases ceulx parolx, scil. "*en le manere come le demaundant ou le pleintif ad suppose,*" *ne sont* ascun matere del substance del issue: qar en brief de droit, lou le myse est joint sur le mere droit, il est a tant udire, et a tiel effecte,* scil. *le quel ad le pluis mere droit, le tenaunt ou le demaundant, al chose en demande?*

486 Item, *si home soit disseisi, et le disseisour devie seisi, &c., et son fitz et heire est eins per discent, et le disseisi entra sur leire le disseisour, lequel entré est un disseisin, &c., si leire porta assise ou brief [dentre en nature de assise, il recovera; mes si leire porta brief†] de droit envers le dis-*

---

* *Lettou & M., Machl., Roh., Pyns.* 1516, and *Redm.*, read this passage, *ne font ascun* manere *del substance*—which has been translated by *Sir E. Coke—do not* make —— &c. The first misreading of the passage is the placing the (f) for the long (ſ). The second misreading, *manner* for *matter*, has been corrected by the later copies, and by *Rastell's* Translation, with the words in the text.

† The words within brackets do not appear in the three earliest editions or in *Rastell's* Translation, but they are given in the Camb. MSS.

(*p*) And the reason hereof is, for that in the writ of right mentioned

right against the disseisee, he shall be barred; for that when the grand assise is sworn, their oath is upon the mere right, and not upon the possession: for if the heir of the disseisor had brought an assise of novel disseisin, or writ of entry in nature of assise, and recovered against the disseisee, and sued execution, yet can the disseisee have writ of entry in the *per* against him, of the disseisin done to him by his father, or he can have against the heir writ of right; 488 but if the heir ought to recover against the disseisee in the case aforesaid, by writ of right, then all his right should be clearly gone, for this that final judgment would be given against him, which should be against reason where the disseisee hath the more mere right. 489 And know ye, my son, that in a writ of right, after that the four knights have chosen in the

seisi, il serra barre; pur ceo, que quant le graund assise est jurre, lour serement est sur le mere droit, et nemy sur la possession: qar si leire le disseisour portast un assise de no. diss. ou brief dentre en nature dassise, et recoverast vers le disseisi, et suist execucion, unqore poet le disseisi aver brief dentre en le per *envers luy, de le disseisin fait a luy per son pere, ou il poet aver envers leire brief de droit;* 488 *mes si leire doit recoverer envers le disseisi en le cas avauntdit, per brief de droit, donques tout son droit serroit clerement ale, pur ceo que juggement finall serroit done envers luy, que serroit encontre reason lou le disseisi ad le pluis mere droit, &c.* 489 *Et sachez, mon fitz, que en brief de droit, apres ceo que les quater chivaliers ont eslues en le graund assise, donques il*

---

and in all other copies. *Sir Edward Coke* has commented upon these words, see n. (*p*), In *Rastell's* Translation, *clere* (clear) *right*, is given for *mere right.*

in the next section, the charge of the grand assise upon their oaths is upon the mere right, and not upon the possession.—*Co. Lytt.* 283. b.

grand assise, then there is no greater delay than in a writ of formedon, after that the parties be at issue, &c. (*i. e.* or demurrer). And if the mise be joined upon battle, then there is less delay.

Release de metter le droit to one not having the freehold, sometimes good; *viz. if tenant alien, pending writ, and demandant release to him, release is good; because the demandant is estopped to say that the tenant is not tenant as supposed by the suit.*

490 Also, release of all the right, &c., in some case is good, *when* made to him that is supposed tenant in law, albeit he hath nothing in the tenements. As in *præcipe quod reddat*, if the tenant alien the land pending the writ, and afterwards the demandant release to him all his right, &c., that release is good, because he is supposed to be tenant by the suit of the demandant, and yet he hath nothing in the land at the time of the release made.

And so if demandant release to vouchee; in both cases the tenancy is in law. § 448.

491 In the same manner it is, if in *præcipe quod reddat* the tenant vouch, and the vouchee enter into the warranty, if afterwards the demandant release to the vouchee all his right, &c., this is good enough, for this that the vouchee, after that he hath entered into the warranty, is tenant in law to the demandant, &c.

Release of

492 Also, as to releases of actions real and personal, it is thus,

nad pluis greindre delaye que en un-brief de formedon, apres ceo que le parties sount a issue, &c. Et si le myse soit joynt sur le batell, donques il ad meyndre delaye.

490 Item, *relesse de tout le droit, &c., en ascun cas est bon, fait a celuy qui est suppose tenaunt en ley, coment quil nad riens en les tenementes. Sicome en* præcipe quod reddat, *si le tenaunt aliena la terre pendant le brief, et puis le demaundant relessa a luy tout son droit, cel reles est bon, pur ceo que il est suppose destre tenaunt per le suyt del demaundant, et unqore il ny ad riens en la terre al temps del reles fait.*

491 *En mesme le manere est, si en* præcipe quod reddat *le tenaunt vouche, et le vouché entra en la garrantie, si apres le demaundant relessa al vouché tout son droit, &c., ceo est assetes bone, pur ceo que le vouché, apres ceo que il avoet entre en la garrantie, est tenaunt en ley al demaundant, &c.*

492 Item, *quant a relesses daccions realx et personelx, il*

that some actions are mixed in the realty and in the personalty; as if an action of waste be sued against the tenant for term of life, this action is in the realty, because the place wasted shall be recovered; and also is in the personalty, because the treble damages shall be recovered for the wrong and waste done by the tenant; howsoever, in this action a release of actions real is a good plea in bar; and so is a release of actions personal*.

actions real and personal. ***Release of real actions bar to a mixed action.***

494 In the same manner it is in assise of novel disseisin, for this that it is mixed in the realty and in the personalty. But if such assise be arraigned against† the disseisor and the te-

In assise of novel disseisin against disseisor and the tenant, disseisor may plead a re-

est issint, que ascuns accions sont mixtes en le realte et en le personalte; sicome un accion de waste sue envers le tenaunt a terme de vie, cest accion est en le realté, pur ceo que le lieu waste serra recovere; auxi est en le personalte, pur ceo que les trebles damages serront recoveres pur le tort et wast fait per le tenaunt; et pur taunt en cest accion, un reles daccions realx est bon plee en barre; et issint est un reles daccions personelx*.

494 ***En mesme le manere est en assise de no. diss., pur ceo quil est mixte en le realte et en le personalte. Mes si un tiel assise soit arraigne envers† le disseisour et le tenaunt, le***

---

* At this place in *Redm.* and in the later copies, occurs the following interpolation, which forms the 493rd section of *Lyttleton*, as subdivided by *West*, 1581 :—And in a *quare impedit*, a release of actions personal is a good plea, and so is a release of actions real; *per Martin*, *Quod fuit concessum*. *Hil.* 9 *H.* 6, *fo.* 57, upon which *Sir E. Coke* remarks—"This is an addition to *Lyttleton*, which although it be law, and the book truly cited, yet I pass it over."—*Co. Lytt.* 285. b. In *Berth.*, *Middl.*, *Sm.*, *Powell*, and *Tottyl* 1554, this interpolation appears as a side-note, but *Redm.* gives it as a side-note and also as portion of the text.

† The word *envers*, *against*, has been corrupted by the later copies into *enter*, *between*. *Rastell's* Transl. renders this passage as follows :—*But if such assise be arraigned against the disseisor*, the tenant of the dis-

lease of actions personal, but not of actions real.

nant, the disseisor can well plead a release of actions personal to bar the assise; but not a release of actions real; for no one shall plead release of actions real in assise, but the tenant.

Release of all actions real must be made to him that is tenant of the land.

495 Also, in such actions real which ought to be sued against the tenant of the freehold, if the tenant have a release of actions real of the demandant made unto him before the writ purchased, and he plead this, it is a good plea for the demandant to say, that he who pleaded the plea had nothing in the freehold at the time of the release made; for then he had no cause to have any action real against him.

Remedies not barred by release; *viz. where one may enter, a release of all actions doth not bar him of his right, because he hath another remedy, viz. to enter.* Secus, *where his entry is not lawful.*—Co. Lytt. 266. a.

496 Also, in such case where a man can enter into lands or tenements, and also can have an action real thereof, which is given to him by the law, against the tenant, &c., if in this case the demandant release to the tenant all manner of actions real; yet this shall not bar the demandant of his

disseisour bien poet pleder un reles daccions personelx pur barrer lassise; mes nemye un reles daccions realx; qar nul pledera reles daccions realx en assise, forsque le tenaunt.

495 Item, *en tielx accions realx que covient destre sues envers tenaunt del franktenement, si le tenaunt ad un reles daccions realx del demaundant fait a luy devant le brief purchase, et il pleda ceo, il est bon plee pur le demaundant a dire, que celuy qui pleda le plee navoit rien en le franktenement al temps de reles fait; qar adonques il navoit cause daver ascun accion real envers luy.*

496 Item, *en tiel cas ou home poet entrer en terres ou tenementes, et auxi poet aver un accion real de ceo, que est done per la ley, envers le tenaunt, &c., si en ceo cas le demandaunt relessa al tenaunt toutes maneres de accions realx; unqore ceo ne tollera le demaundant de son entré, mes le demaundant*

---

seisor *may plead a release of all actions personal to bar the assise; but not release of actions real, for none shall plead a release of all actions real in assise, but the tenants, &c.*

entry, but the demandant can well enter notwithstanding such release, because nothing is released but the action. 497 In the same manner is it of things personal; as if a man by wrong take my goods, if I release unto him all actions personal, yet I am able by law to take my goods out of his possession.

[But release of all demands bars an entry. § 509].

So goods may be retaken after release of action.

498 Also, if I have cause to have a writ of detinue of my goods against another, albeit that I release to him all actions personal, yet I can take my goods out of his possession; because no right of the goods is released to him, but only the action, &c.

The reason is, because no right is released, but only the action.

499 Also, if a man be disseised, and the disseisor make feoffment to divers persons to his use, &c., and the disseisor continually taketh the profits, &c., and the disseisee release unto him all actions real, and afterwards he sue against him a writ of entry in nature of assise by reason of the statute, [4 H. 4, c. 7, and 11 H. 6, c. 4], because he taketh the profits, &c. *Quære*, how shall the disseisor be aided by the said release? For if he will plead the release generally, then the

When the statute had given the action real against the pernor of the profits, it enabled him to plead a release of all actions real; now by the statute of 27 H. 8, c. 10, (the Stat. of Uses), those statutes have lost their force.—Co. Lytt. 287. a.

bien poet entrer nient contristeant tiel reles, pur ceo que nul chose est relesse forsque laccion. 497 *En mesme le manere est de choses personelx; sicome home a tort prent mes biens, si jeo relessa a luy toutes accions personelx, unqore jeo puisse per la ley de prendre mes biens hors de sa possession.*

498 *Auxi, si jeo ay cause daver brief de detenue de mes biens vers un autre, coment que jeo relessa a luy toutes accions personelx, unqore jeo puisse prendre mes biens hors de sa possession; pur ceo que nul droit des biens est relesse a luy, mes solement laccion, &c.*

499 Item, *si home soit disseisi, et le disseisour fait feoffement a divers persones a son use, &c., et le disseisour continuelment prent les profites, &c., et le disseisi relessa a luy toutes accions realx, et puis il suist vers luy brief dentre en nature dassise per cause de lestatuit, pur ceo que il prent les profites, &c.* Quære, *coment le disseisour serra eide per le dit reles? Qar sil voille pleder le reles generalement, donques le*

demandant can say that he had nothing in the freehold at the time of the release made; and if he plead the release specially, then he must acknowledge a disseisin, and then can the demandant enter into the land, &c., by his acknowledgment of the disseisin, &c.; but peradventure by special pleading he may bar him of action, albeit the demandant can enter, &c.*

Release of all manner of actions better than a release of all manner of actions real and personal.

500 Also, if a man sue appeal of felony of the death of his ancestor against another, albeit the appellant release to the defendant all manner of actions real and personal, this shall not aid the defendant, for that this appeal is not action real, insomuch as the appellant shall not recover any realty in such appeal; neither is such appeal an action personal, insomuch as the wrong was done to his ancestor, and not unto him. But if he release to the defendant all manner of actions, then it shall be a good bar in appeal. And so it

*demaundant poet dire quil navoit riens en le franktenement al temps de le reles fait; et sil pleda le reles specialement, donques il covient conustre un disseisin, et donques poet le demaundant entrer en le terre, &c., per son conusaunce de le disseisin, &c.; mes peradventure per especial pleder il luy poet barrer de laccion, coment que le demaundant poet entrer, &c.**

500 Item, *si home suist appelle de felonye del mort son ancestre envers un autre, coment que lappellant relessa al defendant toutes maneres daccions realx et personelx, ceo neidera my le defendant, pur ceo que cest appelle nest pas accion real, entaunt que lappellant ne recovera ascun realte en lappelle; ne tiel appell nest pas accion personell, entaunt que tort fuist fait a son auncestre, et nemye a luy. Mes sil relessa a le defendant toutes maneres accions, donques ceo serra bon barre en*

---

* *Rastell's* Transl. renders this passage thus:—*But peradventure by special pleading he may* be barred *of the action* that he sueth, &c., *though the demandant may enter, &c.*

may be seen that a release of all manner of actions is better than a release of all manner of actions real and personal, &c.

501 Also, in an appeal of robbery, if the defendant will plead release of the appellant of all actions personal, this seemeth no plea; for action of appeal, where the appellee* shall have judgment of death, &c. (*q*), is higher than any action personal is, and is not properly personal: and therefore, if the defendant will have a release of the appellant to bar him of appeal, in this case it behoveth him to have a release of all manners of appeal, or all manner of actions, as it seemeth, &c. 502 But in appeal of mayhem, a release of all manner of

Release of actions personal will not bar appeals or actions criminal, but release of all actions will.

Secus *in appeal of mayhem.*

appelle. Et issint home poet veier que reles de toutes maneres daccions est meliour que reles de toutes maneres daccions realx et personelx, &c.

501 Item, *en une appelle de robberie, si le defendant voille pleder un reles del appellant de toutes accions personelx, ceo semble null plee; qar accion del appellé, lou appelle* avera juggement de mort, &c., est pluis haute que accion personell est, et nest pas proprement personell: et pur ceo, si le defendant voille aver un reles del appellant de luy barrer dappelle, en cell cas il covient daver un reles de toute maneres daccions dappelle, ou toutes maneres daccions, come il semble, &c.*
502 *Mes en appelle de mayheme, un reles de toutes maneres*

---

* This word is printed *appellant* in the four earliest copies, and in *Rastell's* Translation, but evidently is erroneous: in a copy of *Roh. penes Ed.*, and in that copy of *Pyns.* 1516, in the *British Museum*, this word is altered to *defendant* by a contemporary hand; the defendant in these appeals was termed the "appellee."

(*q*) By this &c. is implied appeals of rape, of arson or burning, of felony or larceny; for therein also is judgment of death, and are within our author's reason.—*Co. Lytt.* 288. a. These appeals have been abolished, see *ante*, p. 223, (*h*). In appeals from inferior to superior courts, the defendant in appeal is termed "respondent."

actions personal is a good plea in bar (*r*), for that in such an action he shall recover nothing but damages.

§ 194.

Outlaw-plaintiff "in error," can only be barred by a release of the writ of error.

503 Also, if a man be outlawed in action personal by process upon the original, and bring a writ of error, if he at whose suit he was outlawed, will plead against him a release of all manner of actions personal, this seemeth no plea; for by the said action he shall not recover anything in the personalty, but only to reverse the outlawry: but a release of the writ of error would be a good plea (*s*).

Distinction between release of an action *and an* execution, *for release of actions is no bar to an execution.* Secus *if it be*

504 Also, if a man recover debt or damages, and he release to the defendant all manner of actions, yet he may lawfully sue execution* by *capias ad satisfaciendum*, or by *elegit*, or by *fieri facias*: for execution by such a writ cannot be termed an action; 505 but if after the year and the day the plaintiff will

dacciens personelx est bon plee en barre, pur ceo que en tiel accion il ne recovera forsque damages, &c.

503 Item, *si home soit utlage en accion personell per proces sur loriginal, et porta brief derror, si celuy a que suyte il fuist utlage, voille pleder envers luy un reles de toutes maneres daccions personelx, ceo semble null plee; car per le dit accion il ne recovera rien en le personalte, forsque tantsolement de reverser le utlagarie: mes un reles de brief derrour serroit bon plee.*

504 Item, *si home recovera dette ou damages, et il relessa al defendant toutes maneres daccions, unqore il poet loyalement suer execucion* per* capias ad satisfaciendum, *ou per* elegit, *ou per* fieri facias: *qar execucion per tiel brief ne poet estre dit accion;* 505 *mes si apres lan et le jour le pleintif*

* In *Machl.*, *Roh.*, and *Pyns.* 1516, this word is printed *accion*; but erroneously.

(*r*) And the reason is, for that every action wherein damages only are recovered by the plaintiff, is in law taken for an action personal.—*Co. Lytt.* 288. a.

(*s*) *Vide* Sect. 197, where it appeareth by *Lyttleton*, that the plaintiff cannot be disabled by outlawry, unless it appeareth of record.—*Co. Lytt.* 288. b.

sue a *scire facias*, [to have*] execution, then it seemeth that a release of all actions should be a good plea in bar: but some have thought the contrary, insomuch as the writ of *scire facias* is a writ of execution, and is to have execution, &c. But yet insomuch as upon the same writ the defendant may plead divers matters after the judgment given to oust him of execution, as outlawry, and divers other matters, therefore this may well be termed an action, &c. (*t*). 506 And I trow, that in a *scire facias* out of a fine, a release of all manner of actions is a good plea in bar. 507 But where a man recovereth debt or damages, and it is agreed between them that the plaintiff shall be ousted of action†, then it behoveth that the plaintiff make a release to him of all manner of executions, &c.

pleaded to a sci. fa. on the judgment.

Or on a fine.

Execution should be released by express words.

voille suer un scire facias, [*daver**] *execucion, donques il semble que un reles de toutes accions serroit bon plee en barre: mes ascuns ount semble le contrarie, entant que le brief de* scire facias *est un brief dexecucion, et est daver execucion, &c. Mes unqore entant que sur mesme le brief le defendant poet pleder divers materes puis le juggement rendu de luy ouster dexecucion, come utlagarie, et divers autres materes, et pur ceo bien poet estre dit accion, &c.* 506 *Et jeo creye, que en un* scire facias *hors dun fyn, un reles de toutes maneres daccions est bon plee en barre.* 507 *Mes lou home recovera dette on damages, et est accorde perentre eux que le pleintif serroit ouste daccion†, donques il covient que le pleintif fait un reles a luy de toutes maneres dexecucions, &c.*

---

* Instead of the words within brackets, all French copies from *Pyns.* 1516, have—*a sacher si le defendant poet rien dire pur que le pleintiff navera—to know if the defendant can any thing say why the plaintiff should not have. Rastell's* Transl. reads as above.

† This passage is rendered in all French copies, except *Lettou & M.*, *Machl.*, and *Roh.*, *que le pleintif ne suera execucion, that the plaintiff*

(*t*) Here is to be observed, that every writ whereunto the defendant may plead, be it original or judicial, is in law an action.—*Co. Lytt.* 291. a.

Release of all demands ***bars all actions, appeals, and executions,***

508 Also, if a man release to another all manner of demands, this is the best release that he to whom the release is made can have, and shall enure most to his advantage; for by such release of all manner of demands, all manner of actions real, and personal, and actions of appeal are gone and extinct, [and all manner of executions are gone and extinct*]. 509 And if a man hath title to enter in any lands or tenements, by such release his title is gone†.

and title of entry,

also rents and profits **a prendre.**

510 And if a man have rent-service or rent-charge, or common of pasture, &c., by such release of all manner of demands made to the tenants of the land whereout the service or the rent is issuing, or wherein the common is, the service

508 Item, *si home relessa a un autre toutes maneres demandes, ceo est le pluis meliour reles que celuy a qui le reles est poet aver, et pluis urera a son avantage; qar per tiel reles de toutes maneres demandes, toutes maneres daccions realx, et personelx, et accions dappell sont ales et extientez,* [*et toutz maneres dexecucions sont ales et extientez**]. 509 *Et si home ad title dentrer en ascuns terres ou tenementes, per tiel reles son title est ale*†.

510 *Et si home ad rente-service ou rente-charge, ou comen de pasture, &c., per tiel reles de toutes maneres demandes fait al tenauntes de la terre dount le service ou le rente est issaunt,*

---

shall not sue execution; Rastell's Transl., *Tottyl* 1556, and subsequent editions so far agree with the text, but conclude this section thus:—*of all manner of* actions.

* This concluding passage concerning executions does not appear in *Rastell's* Transl., *Tottyl* 1556, and subsequent editions.

† Here follows in *Redm.* and all subsequent French editions (except *Tottyl* 1557, both editions,) the following interpolation, viz.—*Sed quære de hoc;* for *Fitzjames*, Chief Justice of England, holdeth the contrary, because an entry cannot be properly said a demand, 19 *H.* 8, upon which *Sir E. Coke* remarks—"This is an addition, and no part of *Lyttleton*, and the opinion here cited clearly against law."—*Co. Lytt.* 292. a. In *Berth.*, *Middl.*, *Sm.*, *Powell*, and *Tottyl* 1554, this interpolated passage appears as a side-note only; but *Redm.* gives it as a side-note as well as a portion of the text.

and the rent, and the common is gone and extinct, &c. 511 Also, if a man release to another all manner of quarrels, or all controversies or debates between them, &c., *Quære*, to what matter and to what effect such words extend themselves.

Quære; extent of release of quarrels, &c.

512 Also, if a man by his deed be bound to another in a certain sum of money, to pay at the feast of Saint Michael next ensuing, &c.; if the obligee before the said feast release to the obligor all actions, he shall be barred of the duty for ever, and yet he could not have action at the time of the release made. 513 But if a man let land to another for term of a year, to yield to him at the feast of Saint Michael next ensuing, forty shillings, and afterwards before the same feast he releaseth to the lessee all actions, yet after the same feast he shall have an action of debt for non-payment of the forty shillings, notwithstanding the said release. [*Stude causam diversitatis* between the two cases*.]

Distinction between a release of all actions to obligee before day of payment, and to lessee before rent payable.

ou en quell terre le comen est, le service, et le rent, et le comen est ale et extient, &c. 511 Item, *si home relessa a un autre toutez maneres querelx, ou toutes contraversies ou debates entre eux, &c.*, Quære, *a quell matere et a quell effecte tielx parolx soy extiendont.*

512 Item, *si home per son fait soit oblige a un autre en certeyn somme de money, a paier al feste de Seint Michel procheyn ensuant, &c. ; et si lobligé devaunt le dit feste relessa al obligour toutez accions, il serra barre del duytẽ a tout temps, et unqore il ne puissoit aver accion al temps del reles fait.* 513 *Mes si home lessa terre a un autre pur terme dun an, rendant a luy al feste de Seint Michel proscheyn ensuant,* xl *s., et puis devaunt mesme le feste il relessa al lessé toutez accions, unqore apres mesme le feste il avera accion de dette pur le nonpaiement de les* xl *s. nient obstant le dit reles.* [Stude causam diversitatis *entre les deux cases**.]

* *Sir Edward Coke* in his 8th Report, 304, says, these words within

If the seisin of the demandant or his ancestor be not in the time of the king in whose reign he has alleged in his count, the tenant may tender a demy mark to the king to have the seisin inquired of by the grand assise; and then if the grand assise find not the seisin, as it is alleged, they ought not to inquire any

514 Also, where a man will sue a writ of right, it behoveth that he count of the seisin of himself, or of his ancestors, and also that the seisin was in the time of the same king, as he pleadeth in his plea (*u*); for this is an ancient law used, as appeareth by the report of a plea in the eyre of Nottingham* in such form as ensueth:—*Sir* John Barrey brought his writ of right against Raynold Ashlington, and demanded certain tenements &c.; the mise was joined in bank, and the original and the process were sent before the justices errants, whither the parties came, and the [twelve†] knights were sworn without challenge of the parties to be allowed, because the choice was made by

514 Item, *lou home voille suer brief de droit, il covient quil counta del seisin de luy, ou de ses auncestres, et auxi que le seisin fuist en temps de mesme le roy, come il counta en son count; qar cest un auncien ley use, come appiert per le report dun plee en le eire de Nottingham* en tiel fourme que ensuyst:—John Barri porta son brief de droit envers Reynold de Aslyngton, et demanda certeyn tenementes, &c.; le myse fuist joint en le bank, et loriginal et le proces furent demandes devaunt justices errantes, ou les parties viendront, et les* [xii.†] *chivalers fisteront lour serement sans chalange des parties destre allowes, pur ceo que la eleccion fuist fait per assent des parties,*

---

brackets form no part of *Lyttleton;* they occur however in the three earliest editions, and are not excluded in the two expurgated editions of *Tottyl* 1557, or from *Rastell's* Translation.

* This should be *Northampton*, according to the original.—*Co. Lytt.* 293. b.

† This word is not given in the three earliest editions, but it appears in *Rastell's* Transl. and every other copy.

(*u*) Or if neither he nor any of the ancestors were seised of the land, &c., within the time of limitation, he cannot maintain a writ of right, for the seisin of him of whom the demandant himself purchased the land, &c., availeth not.

And so it is in a writ of advowson.—*Co. Lytt.* 293. a.

assent of the parties, with the four knights; and the oath was such:—That I shall say truth, &c., whether R. of A. have more meer* right to hold the tenements which John Barrey demandeth against him by his writ of right, or John to have them, as he demandeth, and for nothing to let to say the truth, so help me God, &c., without saying to their knowledge†. And such oath shall be made in attaint, and in battail, and in wager of law, for these set every thing to an end. But John Barrey counted (*or* pleaded) of the seisin‡ of one Ralfe his ancestor, in the time of King Henry, and Raynold upon the mise joined, tendered half a mark for the time, &c. And hereupon *Herle,* Justice, said to the grand assise after that they were charged upon the meer right:— You good men, Raynold gave half a mark to the king for the

further of the right.—Booth on Real Actions, edit. 1811, p. 98.

ove les quatre chivalers; et le serement fuist tiel:—Que jeo verité dirray, &c., le quel R. de A. ad pluis mere droit a tener les tenementes que Johan Barri demanda vers luy per son brief de droit, ou Johan de aver les, sicome il demanda, et pur rien lirray que le verité jeo dirray, sicome moy aide Dieu, &c., sauns dire a lour escient†. Et tiel serement serra fait en atteynt, et en batell, et en la ley gager, car ceux mettont chescun chose a fyn. Mes Johan Barri counta del seisin‡ dun Rauf son auncestre, en temps le roy Henry, et Reynold sur le mys joint, tendist demy marc pur le temps, &c. Et sur ceo dit* Herle, *Justice, al graund assise, apres ceo quils furent charges sur le mere droit:—Vous gentes, Reynold donast demy marc al roy pur le temps, &c., et ceo*

---

* This word does not appear in *Rastell's* Translation.

† This word is printed ext*ient* in the three earliest editions. The words also *sauns dire a lour escient*, appear to be a comment or note, which has been embodied in the text: in some ancient editions which the Editor has observed, they are struck out with the pen.

‡ This word is printed dis*seisin* in the three earliest editions and in *Rastell's* Translation.

time, &c., to the intent that if ye find that the ancestor of John was not seised in the time that the demandant hath counted, it shall not be enquired further upon the right, and therefore ye shall say, whether the ancestor of John, Ralph by name, was seised in the time of King Henry, as he hath counted (*i. e.* pleaded), or not. And if you find that he was not seised in that time, you shall enquire no more; and if ye find that he was seised, then enquire further of the right. And afterwards the grand assise came in with their verdict, and said, that Ralfe was not seised in the time of King Henry; whereby it was awarded, that Raynold should hold the tenements against him demanded, to him and his heirs quit of John Barrey and his heirs from thenceforth. And John in mercy, &c. *And the reason why I have here shewed to thee, my son, this plea, is to prove the matter precedent which is stated in the writ of

*sert que si home trove que launcestre Johan ne fuist pas seisi en le temps que le demaundant ad counté, home nenquerra pluis avaunt del droit, et pur ceo vous nous dirrez, le quel launcestre Johan, Rauf per noun, fuist seisi en temps le roy Henry, come il ad counté, ou non. Et si vous trovez que il ne fuist seisi en cel temps, vous nenquerrez nient pluis; et si vous troves que il fuist seisi, donques enquires ouster del droit. Et puis le graund assise reviendront ove lour verdit, et disont, que Rauf ne fuist pas seisi en temps le roy Henry; per que agarde fuist, que Reynold tiendroit les tenementes vers luy demandes, a luy et a ses heires quites de Johan Barri et ses heires a remenaunt. Et Johan en le mercy, &c. *Et la cause pur ceo que jeo ay monstre icy a toy, mon fitz, ceo plee, est pur prover la matere precedent que est dit en brief de*

---

* This concluding part of the paragraph and chapter does not appear in the copies of *Rastell's* Translation, *Tottyl* 1556, 1581, 1586, *J. Yetsweirt* 1597, and subsequent editions to 1656, although it appears in *Powell* 1551, and *Marshe* 1556.

right, &c.; for it seemeth by this plea*, that if Reynold had not tendered the demy mark for to enquire of the time, &c., then the grand assise ought to have been charged only *to enquire* of the mere† right, and not of the possession, &c. So that always in writ of right, if the possession whereof the demandant pleadeth, be in the time of the king, as he hath pleaded, then the charge of the grand assise shall be only upon the meer‡ right, although that the possession were against the law, as it is said before in this Chapter, &c.||

droit, &c.; qar il semble per ceo plee, que si Reynold navoit pas tendu demy marc pur enquerrer del temps, &c., donques le graund assise duissoit estre charge tauntsolement del mere† droit, et nemy del possession, &c. Issint touts foitz en brief de droit, si le possession dount le demaundant counta, soit en temps le roy, come il avoit counté, donques le charge del graund assise serra fait tauntsolement sur le mere‡ droit, coment que le possession fuist encontre la ley, come il est dit adevaunt en ceo Chapitre, &c.*||

CONCLUDING REMARKS.

All the leading cases put by Lyttleton of releases which enure by way of *mettre le droit*, and some others, turn upon the relative status of disseisor and disseisee: indeed, the fundamental principle with which Lyttleton first sets out, is, that when a disseisin is committed, the possession and right is

* *By this* writ.—*Powell* 1551.

† *Charged only of the* clere *right.*—*Id.*

‡ *Clere*, (clear).—*Id.*

|| *Rastell's* Transl. does not give this *&c.*—*Powell* 1551.

separated; but that they may by a lawful conveyance be again united (*Gilb. Ten.* 48); and as the right of possession is by no means conclusive as to the right of property, some important distinctions have always prevailed with respect to what are termed *estates*, and what *droits* or rights; it therefore necessarily follows, that those distinctions should pervade the whole of the past Chapter, especially those cases which depend upon the doctrine of disseisin, wherein, and for the fully understanding of Lyttleton, it is material that the student should apprehend the precise meaning conveyed by these terms, which, with reference to the subject-matter of this Chapter, have a peculiar effect (*r*). The release of an estate

---

(*r*) State or estate signifieth such inheritance, freehold, term for years, tenancy by statute-merchant, staple, *elegit*, or the like, as any man hath in lands or tenements, &c. And by the grant of his estate, &c., as much as he can grant shall pass, as here by *Lyttleton's* case appeareth. Tenant for life, the remainder in tail, the remainder to the right heirs of tenant for life; tenant for life grants *totum statum suum* to a man and his heirs; both estates do pass.

Right.—Jus sive rectum (which *Lyttleton* often useth) signifieth properly, and specially in writs and pleadings, when an estate is turned to a right, as by discontinuance, disseisin, &c., where it shall be said, *Quod jus descendit et non terra.* But (right) doth also include the estate *in esse* in conveyances; and therefore if tenant in fee-simple make a lease for years, and release all his right in the land to the lessee and his heirs, the whole estate in fee-simple passeth.

And so commonly in fines, the right of the land includeth and passeth the state of the land, as *A. cognovit tenementa prædicta esse jus ipsius B. &c.* And the statute W. 2, cap. 3, saith, *Jus suum defendere* (which is) *statum suum.* And note that there is *Jus recuperandi, jus intrandi, jus habendi, jus retinendi, jus percipiendi, jus possidendi.*

Title properly (as some say) is when a man hath a lawful cause of entry into lands whereof another is seised, for the which he can have no action; as title of condition, title of mortmain, &c. But legally, this word title includeth a right also, as you shall perceive in many places in *Lyttleton* (§ 429, 509, 659); and title is the more general word, for every right is a title, but every title is not such a right for which an action lieth; and there-

is, where there is already a vested estate at the time of the release made both in the relessor and the relessee; and also privity should exist between the parties, *i. e.* to say the relessee's estate must be *immediately* derived out of the relessor's estate, so that the two estates should together make but one and the same estate in law, as donor and donee, lessor and lessee: but the release of a *droit* is where the relessor's estate has been previously divested or turned to a right, as in the case of abatement, intrusion, disseisin, discontinuance, or deforcement; and, consequently, where no privity is required, nor indeed can, from the nature of the case, exist between them.—*Ritso's Introd.* 190.

There is also a further distinction to be observed between releases of *estates* and of *droits,* viz. that the release of an *estate* admits of being qualified at the will of the relessor. Thus the lord may release his seignory to the tenant of the land, whether in fee, or in fee-tail, or for life, or for term of years. But the release of a *droit* admits of no such qualifi-

---

fore *Titulus est justa causa possidendi quod nostrum est,* and signifieth the means whereby a man cometh to land, as his title is by fine, or by feoffment, &c. And when the plaintiff in assise maketh himself a title, the tenant may say, *Veniat assisa super titulum,* which is as much as to say, as upon the title which the plaintiff hath made by that particular conveyance; *Et dicitur titulus à tuendo,* because by it he holdeth and defendeth his land; and as by a release of right a title is released, so by release of a title a right is released also.

Interest.—Interesse is vulgarly taken for a term or chattel real, and more particularly for a future term; in which case it is said in pleading, that he is possessed *De interesse termini.* But *ex vi termini,* in legal understanding, it extendeth to estates, rights, and titles, that a man hath of, in, to, or out of lands; for he is truly said to have an interest in them: and by the grant of *totum interesse suum* in such lands, as well reversions as possessions in fee-simple shall pass. And all these words singularly spoken are *nomina collectiva;* for by the grant of *totum statum suum* in lands, all his estates therein pass; *et sic de cæteris.—Co. Lytt.* 345. a. b.

cation; for if one release but for an hour, it is extinguished for ever.—*Id.* 192.

The forms of action also which till lately could be adopted in contesting the right to real property, were either *droitural* or *possessory*, terms which have relation to the right of *property* as distinguished from the right of *possession* (*s*); for by a droitural action, the *mere right* was tried, by a possessory action, the *right of possession:* but now by the abolition (except in two instances) of real actions, and by the effect of the Statute of Limitations, the *mixed* action of ejectment (*t*), purely a *possessory* remedy, is the only process by which real property can be recovered; and, therefore, this distinction of *mere right* and *right of possession* is practically abolished, and

---

(*s*) See B. C. ii. c. xiii. p. 195, where these distinctions and their practical application before the stat. 3 & 4 Gul. 4, c. 27, s. 36, are fully explained.

(*t*) An ejectment is a *possessory* action (*i. e.* an action brought upon the claimant's own possession) wherein the title to lands and tenements may be tried, and the *possession* recovered, [in a writ of right the possession was not recovered, but the *right* only was tried], in all cases where the party claiming title has a *right of entry*, whether such title be to an estate in fee, fee-tail, for life, or for years. In order to maintain an ejectment, the party at whose suit it is brought must have been in possession, or at least clothed with the right of possession, at the time of the actual or supposed ouster (*Keilw.* 130. a.); hence this action is termed a possessory action. The party who has the legal estate in the lands in question must prevail; hence a party who claims under an *elegit*, (*Doe* d. *Da Costa* v. *Wharton*, 3 *T. R.* 2), subsequent to a lease granted to a tenant in possession, cannot recover, although he give notice to the tenant that he does not intend to disturb the possession, and only means to get into the receipt of the rents and profits of the estate, (*Selw. N. P. Ejectment, s.* 1.) It will be observed that the 39th section of the act 3 & 4 Gul. 4, c. 27, by enacting that no descent cast, discontinuance, or warranty, which may be made after the 31st of December, 1833, shall toll or defeat any *right of entry* or action for the recovery of land, has extended the remedy by ejectment to cases in which it was not before applicable.

the doctrine of *estates* and *droits,* by the abolition of *descents which toll* (*i. e.* bar) *entries,* and *discontinuance,* is very much circumscribed in its operation.

The student will bear in mind that the releases which Lyttleton treats of, are releases at common law; for the Statute of Uses, which transmuted or transferred the use into possession, was not passed till the 27 H. 8; and *uses* as they existed in Lyttleton's time, were then what *trusts* are now, an example whereof is presented at § 462 (*u*).

(*u*) The most common example of the distinction between releases at common law, and those operating by the Statute of Uses, is the conveyance by *lease and release,* now the most usual mode of passing freehold estates. This is a common-law conveyance, requiring privity of estate between the relessor and relessee, the release operating by way of enlargement of an estate already created (§ 459). This mode of conveyance is referred to in the *Year-Book,* 21 *E.* 4, *pl.* 24, but the actual entry of the lessee was requisite, and then this conveyance obtained the effect of a feoffment, as the seisin was completed by the entry of the relessee.

The mode by which actual entry has been superseded, is, by a *bargain and sale* being made for *one* year, (which does not require inrolment) upon pecuniary consideration, (5*s.*) and this vests in the bargainee, by operation of the statute, *scil.* by *transmutation of or transferring the use into possession,* the legal estate: the effect is, that the bargainee is thus made capable of receiving a release of the reversion without either entry made, deed inrolled, or livery of seisin given.—B. C. ii. 339; *Sand. Uses,* ii. 60, (*ed.* 1824). With regard to conveyances taking effect by the Statute of Uses the reader is referred to *Mr. Sanders' Treatise on Uses, Sir E. Sugden's Introduction to his edition of Gilb. Tenures, and the late Mr. Butler's Note, Co. Lytt.* 271. b.

The actual execution of the *bargain and sale* or "lease for a year" is dispensed with by 4 Vict. c. 21, provided the stamp duty which would otherwise have been payable thereon is impressed upon the deed of release.

CHAPTER IX.

OF CONFIRMATION.

A CONFIRMATION is defined by *Sir Edward Coke* to be a conveyance (*a*) of an estate or right *in esse*, whereby a voidable estate is made sure and unavoidable, or whereby a *particular* estate is increased, *Co. Lytt.* 295. b.: but although the effect of a confirmation is to impart validity to a voidable or defeasible estate, it cannot operate upon an estate which is either absolutely void (§ 541), or where the confirmor has no right (§ 548); for the operation of a confirmation extends only to the right existing in the confirmor (§ 528).

Lyttleton does not appear to have considered a specific definition of this conveyance necessary for his reader, nor in fact is it, when the technical words of the *formula* with which he opens this Chapter are attentively considered: the subject of this Chapter is divided into confirmations expressed or *in deed*, and confirmations implied or *in law*, whereof examples are given (§ 515; 531). And in treating of the operation of a confirmation, which is a peculiar conveyance (*b*), *Lyttleton* puts cases and shews eight instances

---

(*a*) A confirmation though it perfect the estate of the confirmee, does not alter the quality of the estate confirmed (§ 519); and yet the quantity of the estate can be altered by express words (§ 523). Also, upon the same principle services cannot be increased by a confirmation, though they can be abridged (§ 538, 539); and by various cases depending upon the doctrine contained in these *sections*, the tenure can be changed, although no new services are reserved.

(*b*) But a release, confirmation,

wherein a confirmation and release differ, and he also states as many cases wherein they agree; in most of which, the *quantum* of estate which passes to the confirmee, seems to be regulated by the terms of the *habendum*.

As in a release, the existence of that relative status between the parties which the law terms *privity*, is essentially necessary (§ 459, 547): so in a confirmation, possession in the confirmee is also requisite (§ 516, 541); and moreover it is to be borne in mind, that when it is intended that the confirmation is to operate by way of *enlargir lestate* of the confirmee, privity should hold place between the parties: upon this principle, therefore, he who has no reversion in him, cannot by a confirmation enlarge the estate of the particular tenant (§ 548, 549): on the other hand, a release is concluded by *Sir Edward Coke* to be more forcible in law than a confirmation (§ 522); and after stating cases where a grant to two or more, shall enure as a confirmation to one (§ 534), and where the same words which have effect as a confirmation in law, can also operate by way of extinguishment (§ 543), *Lyttleton* himself further informs us, that there are " divers great diversities between releases and confirmations " (§ 546).

---

515 A DEED of confirmation is commonly in such form, or to such effect:—" Know all men, &c., that I, A. of B., have

***Confirmation defined. Formula of* confirmation in deed.**

515 *Fait de confirmacion est en communement en tiel fourme, ou a tiel effecte :—" Noverint universi, &c., me, A. de B., ratifi-*

---

or surrender, &c., cannot amount to a grant, &c., nor a surrender to a confirmation, or to a release, &c., because these be proper and peculiar manner of conveyances, and are destined to a special end.—*Co. Lytt.* 302. a.

" ratified, approved, and confirmed to C. of D., the estate " and possession which I have, of and in one messuage, &c., " with the appurtenances in F." &c.

First case wherein release and confirmation differ.
Confirmation by owner to the lessee for years of his tenant for life, is good;

though a release would be void, there being no privity.

516 And in some case a deed of confirmation is good and available, where in the same case a deed of release is neither good nor available. As if I let land to a man for term of his life, who letteth the same land to another for term of forty years, by force of which he is possessed. If I by my deed confirm the estate of the tenant for term of years, and afterwards the tenant for life dieth during the term of forty years, I cannot enter into the land during the said term: 517 Yet if I by my deed of release had released to the tenant for years in the lifetime of the tenant for term of life, that release shall be void, for this that then there was no privity between him and myself; for a release is not available to the tenant for years, but when there is a privity between him and him that releaseth*.

" *casse, approbasse, et confirmasse C. de D., statum et posses-* " *sionem quos ego habeo, de et in uno messuagio, &c., cum per-* " *tinentiis in F." &c.*

516 *Et en ascun cas un fait de confirmacion est bon et availlable, lou en tiel cas un fait de reless nest pas bon ne availlable. Sicome jeo lessa terre a un home pur terme de sa vie, le quel lessa mesme la terre a un autre pur terme de* xl. *ans, per force de quel il est possessione. Si jeo per mon fait confirma lestate del tenaunt a terme dans, et puis le tenaunt a terme de vie morust durant le terme de* xl. *ans, jeo ne puisse entrer en la terre durant le dit terme:* 517 *Unqore si jeo per mon fait de reles avoy relesse al tenaunt a terme dans en la vie le tenaunt a terme de vie, cel reles serra voide, pur ceo que adonques nul priveté fuist perentre luy et moy; qar reles nest availlable al tenaunt a terme dans, mes lou y est un privete perentre luy et celuy qui relessast*.*

---

* *Et ceo est destre entendus lou home relessa le droit dun franktene-*

518 In the same manner it is, if I be disseised, and the disseisor make a lease to another for term of years, if I release to the termor, this is void; but if I confirm the estate of the termor, this is good and effectual.

Second distinction between release and confirmation.
Release to lessee of disseisor is void, but his confirmation is good.

519 Also, if I be disseised, and I confirm the estate of the disseisor, then he hath good and rightful estate in fee-simple, albeit in the deed of confirmation no mention be made of his heirs, because he had fee-simple at the time of the confirmation; for in such case, if the disseisee confirm the estate of

First case where release and confirmation agree.
Confirmation to him who has the fee, good

518 *En mesme le manere est, si jeo soy disseisi, et le disseisour fait un lees a un autre pur terme dans, si jeo relessa al termour, cest voide; mes si jeo confirma son estate, ceo est bon et effectuell.*

519 Item, *si jeo soy disseisi, et jeo confirma lestate le disseisour, donques il ad bon et droiturel estate en fee-simple, coment que en le fait de confirmacion nul mencion soit fait de ses heires, pur ceo quil avoit fee-simple al temps de confirmacion; qar en tiel cas, si le disseisi confirma lestate le dissei-*

---

ment ou enheritaunce. Mes en cas que cestuy qui relessast nad droit forsque dun terme, autrement serra; come si le tenaunt a terme dans soie engette per un estraunge qui ent fait lees a un autre pur terme dans, si cesty qui fuist engette relesse al second tenaunt pur terme dans, ceo est bon reles, causa qua supra; *et unqore nul privetè est entre eux.*— And this is to be understood where a man releases the right of a freehold or inheritance. But otherwise it shall be in the case where he who releases has right but for a term; as if the tenant for term of years be ejected by a stranger who makes lease thereof to another for term of years, if he who was ejected release to the second tenant for term of years, this is a good release, *causa qua supra;* and yet there is no privity between them.—This *case* only occurs in the editions by *Redm.*, *Berth.*, *Middl.*, *Sm.*, *Powell*, and *Tottyl* 1554. An asterisk in the two expurgated editions by *Tottyl* 1557, which denotes the place of an expunged addition, is perhaps sufficient to question this case ever having formed part of the text of *Lyttleton;* although the Year-Book, 9 H. 6, *pl.* 44, is cited as an authority in its support, in *Tottyl* 1554. The French edition by *Jane Yetsweirt* (*circa*) 1597, which professes to be " revieu et corrige en divers lieux," does not give this case.

without the word "heirs."

the disseisor, to have and to hold to him [and his heirs of his body engendered; or to have and to hold to him*] for term of his life, yet the disseisor hath a fee-simple, and is seised in his demesne as of fee, because when his estate was confirmed, then he had fee-simple, and such deed cannot change his estate, without entry made upon him, &c. 520 In the same manner it is, if his estate be confirmed for term of a day, or for term of an hour, he hath good estate in fee-simple, for this, that estate in fee-simple was once confirmed; *Quia confirmare idem est, quod firmum facere, &c.*

Second case wherein the release and confirmation agree. *Confirmation to him who has fee, for an hour is good for ever.*

Third case where release and confirmation differ; *confirmation to the tenant for life does not enure to him in the remainder.* [*but otherwise it is of a release*].

521† Also, if my disseisor make a lease for life, the remainder over in fee, if I release to the tenant for life, this shall enure to him in the remainder; but if I confirm the estate of the tenant for term of life, yet after his decease I can well enter, because nothing is confirmed but the estate of the tenant for life, so that after his decease I can well enter.

sour, a aver et tener a luy [et a ses heires de son corps engendres ; ou a aver et tener a luy] pur terme de sa vie, unqore le disseisour ad fee-simple, et est seisi en son demesne come de fee, pur ceo que quaunt son estate fuist confirme, donques il avoit fee-simple, et tiel fait ne poet chaunger son estate, sauns entré sur luy, &c.* 520 *En mesme le manere est, si son estate soit confirme pur terme dun jour, ou pur terme dun heure, il ad bon estate en fee-simple, pur ceo que estate en fee-simple fuist un foitz confirme ;* Quia confirmare idem est, quod firmum facere, &c.

521† Item, *si mon disseisour fait un lees a terme de vie, le remeyndre oustre en fee, si jeo relessa al tenaunt a terme de vie, ceo urera a celuy en le remeyndre ; mes si jeo confirma lestate de le tenaunt a terme de vie, unqore apres son decesse jeo puis bien entrer, pur ceo que nul riens est confirme forsque lestate le tenaunt a terme de vie, issint que apres son decesse*

* The words within brackets do not appear in *Rastell's* Transl., *Tottyl* 1556, and subsequent editions.

† This section does not appear in *Rastell's* Transl., *Tottyl* 1556, and subsequent editions.

But when I release all my right to the tenant for life, this shall enure to him in the remainder or in the reversion, because all my right is gone by such release. But in this case, if the disseisee confirm the estate and the title of him in the remainder, without any confirmation made to tenant for term of life, the disseisee cannot enter upon the tenant for term of life; because the remainder is depending upon the estate of the tenant for term of life; and if his estate should be defeated, the remainder should be defeated by the entry of the disseisee, and that is no reason that he by his entry should defeat the remainder against his confirmation, &c.

Third case wherein release and confirmation agree. ***But confirmation of the estate of the remainder man or reversioner, enures to the particular tenant.***

522 Also, if two be disseisors, and the disseisee releases to one of them, he shall hold his companion out of the land; but if the disseisee confirm the estate of the one without saying more in the deed, some say that he shall not hold his companion out, but shall hold jointly with him, for that nothing was confirmed but his estate which was joint, &c.; 523 and for this some have said, that if two joint-tenants be,

Fourth case wherein the release and confirmation seem to differ, being made unto one of two disseisors. ***For confirmation to one of them enures not to the other, but*** **secus** ***of a release, § 306, 472.***

jeo puis bien entrer. Mes quant jeo relessa tout mon droit al tenaunt a terme de vie, ceo urera a celuy en le remeyndre ou en la revercion, pur ceo que tout mon droit est ale per tiel reles. Mes en ceo cas, si le disseisi confirma lestate et le title celuy en le remeyndre, sauns ascun confirmement fait al tenaunt a terme de vie, le disseisi ne poet entrer sur le tenaunt a terme de vie; pur ceo que le remeyndre est dependant sur lestate le tenaunt a terme de vie; et si son estate serroit defete, le remeyndre serroit defete per lentré le disseisi, et ceo ne serra reason que il per son entré defeteroit le remeyndre encontre sa confirmacion, &c.

522 Item, *si sount deux disseisours, et le disseisi relessa a un deux, il tiendra son compaignon hors de la terre; mes si le disseisi confirma lestate de lun sans plus parlance en le fait, ascuns diont que il ne tiendra son compaignon dehors, mes tiendra jointement ovesque luy, pur ceo que nul riens fuist confirme forsque son estate que fuist joint, &c.;* 523 *et pur ceo*

Confirmation by one joint-tenant to his companion with "heirs," passes the fee. Secus *if* habendum *to heirs.*

and the one confirm the estate of the other, that he hath but a joint estate, as he had before: but if he have such words in the deed of confirmation, "to have and to hold to him and to his heirs" all the tenements whereof mention is made in the confirmation, then he hath sole estate in the tenements (*c*); and therefore it is a good and sure thing in every confirmation to have these words, "to have and to hold the tenements, &c., in fee, or in fee-tail, or for term of life, or for term of years," according as the case or the matter lieth:

Confirmation of life estate does not pass fee even with "heirs;" but if habendum *be to heirs it is good, for* habendum *operates by way of enlargement.*

524 for to the intent of some, if a man letteth land to another for term of life, and afterwards confirm his estate which he hath in the same land, "to have and to hold his estate to him and to his heirs;" this confirmation so far as concerns his heirs is void; for his heirs cannot have his estate, which was but for term of his life (§ 650). But if he confirm his estate by these words, "to have the same land to him

ascuns ount dit, que si deux jointenauntes sount, et lun confirma lestate lautre, que il nad forsque joint estate, sicome il avoit adevaunt : mes sil ad tielx parolx en le fait de confirmacion, "a aver et tener a luy et a ses heires" toutes les tenementes dont mencion est fait en le confirmacion, donques il ad estate sole en les tenementes; et pur ceo il est bon et sure chose en chescune confirmacion daver ceulx parolx, "a aver et tener les tenementes, &c., en fee, ou en fee-taille, ou per terme de vie, ou pur terme dans," solonques ceo que le cas, ou le matere gist : 524 *qar al entent dascuns, si home lessa terre a un autre pur terme de vie, et puis il confirma son estate quil ad en mesme la terre, "a aver et tener son estate a luy et a ses heires;" cest confirmacion quant a ses heires, est voyde; qar ses heires ne poient aver son estate, que fuist forsque pur terme de sa vie. Mes sil confirma son estate per ceux parolx, "a aver*

(*c*) And this confirmation leaveth the state as it was, and doth not amount to any severance of the jointure, as some have said.—*Co. Lytt.* 298. b.

and to his heirs," this confirmation maketh fee-simple in this case to him in the land, for that the "to have and to hold," &c., goeth to the land, and not to the estate which he hath.

525 Also, if I let certain land to a feme sole for term of her life, who taketh husband, and afterwards I confirm the estate of the husband and the wife, to have and to hold the land for term of their two lives, in this case the husband holdeth not jointly with his wife, but holdeth in right of his wife for term of her life. But this confirmation shall enure to the husband by way of remainder for term of his life if he survive his wife. 526 But if I let land to a feme sole for term of years, who taketh husband, and afterwards I confirm the estate of the husband and the wife, to have and to hold the land for term of their two lives*: in this case they have joint estate in the freehold of the land, for this that the wife had not freehold before (*b*).

The fourth case wherein release and confirmation agree. *Woman, lessee for life, takes husband; lessor confirms* habendum *for term of their two lives: confirmation enures to husband by way of remainder for life, if he survive*, § 573.

The fifth case wherein release and confirmation agree. *Confirmation to the husband and wife for their lives of lease granted to feme for years, maketh them joint tenants for life.*

mesme la terre a luy et a ses heires," ceo confirmacion fait fee-simple en ceo cas a luy en la terre, pur ceo que le "aver et tener," &c., va a le terre, et nemy al estate quil ad.

525 Item, *si jeo lessa certeyn terre a une feme sole pur terme de sa vie, laquele prent baron, et puis jeo confirme lestate le baron et la feme, a aver et tener la terre pur terme de lour deux vies, en ceo cas le baron ne tient jointement ovesque sa feme, mes tient en droit de sa feme pur terme de sa vie. Mes ceo confirmacion urera a le baron per voye de remeyndre pur terme de sa vie sil survesquist sa feme.* 526 *Mes si jeo lessa al feme sole terre pur terme dans, laquele prent baron, et puis jeo confirme lestate le baron et la feme, a aver et tener la terre pur terme de lour deux vies: en ceo cas ils ount joint estate en le franktenement de la terre, pur ceo que la feme navoit franktenement adevaunt.*

---

* *Rastell's* Transl. renders this passage thus, *and afterwards I con-*

(*b*) Note a diversity between a lease for life, and a lease for years

The fifth case wherein release and confirmation differ. Quære *if rent charge be avoided if estate be defeated by entry of confirmor? a release in this case being void.*

527* Also, if my disseisor grant a rent-charge out of the land whereof he disseised me, and I rehearsing the said grant, confirm the same grant, and all that which is comprised within the same grant, and afterwards I enter upon the disseisor, *quære* in this case, whether the land be discharged of the rent or no, &c.† (*c*)?

At common law confirmation by patron of parson's grant (the ordinary concur-

528 Also, if a parson of a church charge the glebe *land* of his church [by his deed‡], and afterwards the patron and ordinary confirm the same grant, then the grant shall stand in its force, according to the purport of the same grant. But in such

527* Item, *si mon disseisour graunta un rente-charge hors de la terre dount il moy disseisist, et jeo rehersant le dit graunt, confirma mesme le graunt, et tout ceo que est compris deins mesme le graunt, et puis jeo entra sur le disseisour,* quære, *en ceo cas, si la terre soit discharge de le rente ou nemy, &c.* †?

528 Item, *si un person dun esglise charge un glebe de son esglise, et puis le patron et lordinarie confirmont mesme le graunt. donques le graunt estera en sa force, soloncques le purport de mesme le graunt. Mes en tiel cas il covient, que le*

---

firm the estate to the husband and the wife for term of both *their lives.*

* This section does not appear in *Rastell's* Translation, *Tottyl* 1556, and subsequent editions.

† This *&c.* does not appear in *Rastell's* Transl., *Powell* 1548, 1551, *Marshe* 1556.

‡ The words within brackets, although necessary to supply the full sense, appear only in *Rastell's* Transl.

---

made to a feme-covert, for her estate of freehold, cannot be altered by the confirmation made to her husband and her, as the term for years may, whereof her husband may make disposition at his pleasure.—*Co. Lytt.* 300. a.

(*c*) It is holden by some authority since *Lyttleton* wrote, that the disseisee after his re-entry shall not avoid the rent-charge against his own confirmation; and there a general rule is taken, that such a thing as I may defeat by my entry, I may make good by my confirmation.—*Ibid.*—See § 529.

case it behoveth, that the patron have fee-simple in the advowson; for if he have estate in the advowson but for term of life or in the tail, then the grant shall stand but during his life, and the life of the parson that granted it, &c. (*d*).

ring), was good, if patron had the fee, § 648.

529 Also, if a man let land for term of life, the which tenant for term of life charges the land with a rent in fee, and he in the reversion confirm the same grant, the charge is good enough and effectual.

Reversioner's *confirmation of rent created by his tenant for life, good,* § 527.

[**Secus** *where confirmor has no reversion,* § 548.]

530 Also, if there be a perpetual chauntry, wherewith the ordinary hath nothing to do or meddle, (*i. e.* a chantry donative), [*quære** if] the patron of the chauntry, and the chaplain of the same chauntry can charge the chauntry with a rent-charge in perpetuity.

The same of a chantry, all parties concurring. § 648.

531 Also, in some case this verb *dedi*, or this verb *concessi*,

Confirmation

patron eit fee-simple en lavoweson; qar sil ad estate en lavoweson forsque pur terme de vie ou en le taille, donques le graunt estera forsque duraunt sa vie, et la vie le person qui grauntast, &c. 529 Item, *si home lessa terre pur terme de vie, le quel tenaunt a terme de vie charge la terre ovesque un rente en fee, et celuy en la revercion confirma mesme le graunt, le charge est assetes bon et effectuell.*

530 Item, *si soit un perpetuell chaunterie, dont lordinarie nad riens a medler ne a faire,* [quære* *si*] *le patron del chaunterie, et le chapeleyn de mesme le chaunterie poient charge le chaunterie ovesque un rente-charge en perpetuitê.*

531 Item, *en ascun cas cest verbe* dedi, *et cest verbe* con-

* The word *quære* is printed in *Machl.*, *Roh.* and *Pyns.* 1516, *q̄r.* The two words within brackets, *quære si*, do not appear in *Rastell's* Transl. So that this *quære* seems questionable, and indeed by omitting these words, the sense as well as the law when *Lyttleton* wrote will be complete. In that copy of *Pyns.* 1516 which is in the *Brit. Museum*, a contemporary hand has altered *qar si* to *là*, so that the amended passage reads, *there the patron* ——. *Q̄r.* appears sometimes in *Lettou & M.*, and also in *Machl.*, as an abbreviation for *quere*, though it is mostly used to express *qar*, *for*.

(*d*) As to conveyances by ecclesiastical corporations which have been restrained since *Lyttleton* wrote, see *ante*, pp. 84, 85 (*m*).

in law dedi et concessi *amount to a confirmation*, § 543.
[*A grant also enures sometimes as a confirmation*, § 534.]

hath the same effect in substance, and shall enure to the same intent, as this verb *confirmavi*. As if I be disseised of a plough-land, and I afterwards make such a deed *as this*, *sciant præsentes, &c., quod dedi* to the disseisor the said plough-land, &c., and I deliver only the deed to him without any livery of seisin of the land, this is a good confirmation, and as strong in law, as if he had in the deed this verb *confirmavi, &c.*

The sixth case wherein confirmation and release agree. *Confirmation to lessee for years, for life, enures for his life; and so to* heirs of his body *gives an estate tail, and to* his heirs *a fee-simple.*

532 Also, if I let land to a man for a term of years, by force whereof he is possessed, and afterwards I make a deed to him, &c., *quod dedi et concessi, &c.*, the said land to have for term of his life, and deliver to him the deed, &c., then forthwith he hath an estate in the land for term of life; 533 and if I say in the deed, to have and to hold to him and to his heirs of his body engendred, then he hath estate in the tail. And if I say in the deed, to have and to hold to him and to his heirs, then he hath estate in fee-simple; for this shall enure to him by force of confirmation to enlarge his estate (*e*).

cessi, *ad mesme le effecte en substaunce, et urera a mesme lentent, come cest verbe* confirmavi. *Sicome jeo suy disseisi dun carue de terre, et puis jeo face tiel fait,* sciant præsentes, &c., quod dedi *a le disseisour le dit carue de terre, &c., et jeo delyvera tantsolement le fait a luy sauns ascun lyverë de seisin del terre, ceo un bon confirmacion, et auxi fort en ley, sicome il avoet en le fait cest verbe* confirmavi, &c.

532 Item, *si jeo lessa terre a un home pur terme dans, per force de quel il est possessione, et puis jeo face un fait a luy, &c.*, quod dedi et concessi, &c., *la dit terre a aver pur terme de sa vie, et delyvera a luy le fait, &c., donques meyntenant il ad estate en la terre pur terme de vie;* 533 *et si jeo die en le fait, a aver et tener a luy et a les heires de son corps engendres, donques il ad estate en le taille. Et si jeo die en le fait, a aver et tener a luy et a ses heires, donques il ad estate en fee-simple; qar ceo urera a luy per force de confirmement denlarger son estate.*

(*e*) Whensoever a confirmation doth enlarge and give an estate of

534 Also, if a man be disseised, and the disseisor die seised, and his heir is in by descent, and afterwards the disseisee and the heir *of the disseisor* make jointly a deed to another in fee, and livery of seisin thereupon is made; as to the heir of the disseisor that sealeth the deed, the tenements pass by the same deed by way of feoffment, and as to the disseisee who sealeth the same deed, this shall not enure but by way of confirmation. But if the disseisee in this case bring writ of entry in the *per* and *cui* against the alienee of the heir of the disseisor: *quære* how shall he plead that deed against the demandant by way of confirmation.

Joint feoffment by disseisee and disseisor's heir, operates as to the disseisee as a confirmation.

AND KNOW YE THIS, MY SON, that it is one of the most honourable, laudable, and profitable things in our law, to have the science of well pleading in actions real and personal; and therefore I counsel thee especially to set all thy courage and care to learn that, &c.*

Good pleading commended.

534 Item, *si home soit disseisi, et le disseisour devie seisi, et son heire est eins per discent, et puis le disseisi et leire fount jointement un fait de feoffement a un autre en fee, et lyverë del seisin sur ceo est fait; quant al heire le disseisour qui ensealast le fait, les tenementes passont per mesme le fait per voie de feoffement, et quant al disseisi qui ensealast mesme le fait, ceo ne urera mes per voie de confirmacion. Mes si le disseisi en ceo cas porta brief dentre en le* per *et* cui *envers lalienė leire le disseisour:* quære *coment il pledera cel fait envers le demaundant per voye de confirmacion.*

ET SACHEZ, MON FITZ, que est un de pluis honorables, et laudables et profitables choses en nostre ley, daver le science de bien pleder en accions realx et personelx; et pur ceo jeo toy counseyla especialement de mettre tout ton courage et cure de ceo apprendre, &c.*

* This &c. is not given in *Rastell's* Transl., *Tottyl* 1556, and subsequent editions, although it is given in *Marshe* 1556, and earlier editions; nor does it occur in the later French copies.

inheritance, there ought to be apt words (as *Lyttleton* here expresseth them) used for the same.—*Co. Lytt.* 302. a.

The sixth case wherein release and confirmation differ.
If lord confirm the estate of his tenant in the tenements; or if one that has a profit à prendre, confirm to terre-tenant his estate, the seigniory or profit are not extinguished as in a release, for confirmation does not give distinct rights.

No service of another can be reserved upon confirmation.

535 Also, if there be lord and tenant, and the lord confirm the estate which the tenant hath in the tenements, yet the seigniory wholly abideth to the lord as it was before. 536* In the same manner is it, if a man hath rent-charge out of certain land, and he confirm the estate which the tenant hath in the land, yet abideth to the confirmor the rent-charge. 537 In the same manner it is, if a man hath common of pasture in† the land of another, if he confirm the estate of the tenant of the land, nothing shall depart (*i. e.* pass) from him of his common; but this, notwithstanding, the common abideth to him as it was before. 538 But if there be lord and tenant, which tenant holdeth of his lord by the service of fealty, and twenty shillings of rent, if the lord by his deed confirm the estate of the tenant, to hold by twelve pence, or by a penny, or by a half-penny: in this case the tenant is discharged of all the

535 Item, *si soient seignour et tenaunt, et le seignour confirma lestate que le tenaunt ad en les tenementes, unqore le seignourie entierement demourt al seignour come il fuist adevaunt.* 536* *En mesme le manere est, si home ad rente-charge hors de certeyne terre, et il confirma lestate que le tenaunt ad en la terre, unqore demourt a le confirmour le rente-charge.* 537 *En mesme le manere est, si un home ad comen de pasture en*† *autre terre, sil confirma lestate le tenaunt de la terre, rien departera de luy de son comen, mes ceo nient obstant le comen demourt a luy come fuist adevaunt.* 538 *Mes si soient seignour et tenaunt, le quel tenaunt tient de son seignour per le service de fealté, et* xx*s. de rente, si le seignour per son fait confirma lestate le tenaunt, a tener per* xii*d. ou per un denere, ou per un mayle: en ceo cas le tenaunt est discharge*

* This section is given thus in *Redm.*, *Berth.*, *Middl.*, *Sm.*, *Powell*, and *Tottyl* 1554, (which copies also, do not give § 537), *viz. En mesme le manere est, si home ad rent-charge* ou comen de pasture *hors de certeyn terre, et il confirma lestate que le tenaunt ad en la terre; unqore demourt a le confirmour le rente-charge* ou [en *Berth.*] le comen come il fuist adevaunt.

† In *Lettou & M.*, *Machl.*, and *Roh.*, this word is printed *ou*, *or*.

other services, and shall render nothing to the lord, but that which is comprised within the same confirmation.

539 But* if the lord willeth by deed of confirmation, that the tenant in this case ought to yield to him a hawk or a rose yearly at such a feast, &c., this reservation† is void; because he reserveth to him a new thing which was not parcel of the services before the confirmation: and so the lord can well abridge the services by such confirmation, but he cannot reserve to him new services.

Lord can abridge the services of his tenant, but cannot reserve a new service.

540 Also, if there be lord, mesne, and tenant, and the tenant is an abbot that holdeth of the mesne by certain service yearly, who hath no cause to have acquittance against his mesne for to bring a writ of mesne [against his mesne‡], in this case, if the mesne confirm the estate that the abbot hath

Illustration of preceding doctrine by case of lord, mesne, and tenant, who being an abbot receives confirmation in frankal-

de toutes les autres services, et ne rendra rien al seignour, forsque ceo que est compris deins mesme le confirmacion.

539 *Mes* si le seignour voille per fait de confirmacion, que le tenaunt en ceo cas doit rendre a luy un esperver ou un rose annuelement a tiel feste, &c., ceo reservation† est voide ; pur ceo que il reserva a luy un novel chose que ne fuist parcel de les services devaunt le confirmacion : et issint le seignour poet bien abregger les services per tiel confirmation, mes il ne poet reserver a luy novel services.*

540 Item, *si soit seignour, mesne, et tenaunt, et le tenaunt est un abbé qui tient de mesne per certeyn service annuelement, le quel nad ascun cause per case daver acquitaunce pur porter brief de mesne [envers son mesne‡], en ceo cas, si le*

* *Yet*, *Rastell's* Translation.

† This word has been corrupted to *confirmacion*, in *Pyns*. 1516, and in all the French copies since *Pyns*. 1516, and so it appears in *Sir E. Coke's* Transl. *Rastell's* Transl., *Tottyl* 1556, and subsequent editions, which seem in many respects to follow the three earliest copies, have *reservation*; but *Marshe* 1556, and previous editions, have *confirmation*.

‡ These words within brackets are not given in *Rastell's* Transl., they appear to be supplied by an *&c.* which appears in the common copies at this place, but it very often occurs, that the words inferred by the *&c.*, and the *&c.* itself, are both given.

moign, which confirmation, for the reasons Lyttleton gives, is good.

in the land, to have and to hold the land unto him and his successors in frankalmoigne, &c., in this case confirmation is good, and then the abbot shall hold of the mesne in frankalmoigne: and the reason is, because no new service is reserved, for all the services specially specified are extinct, and nothing is reserved *to the mesne*, but the abbot holdeth of him the land, and this was to him before the confirmation; for he that holdeth in frankalmoigne ought not to do any
§ 135. corporal service; so by such confirmation it appeareth the mesne doth not reserve unto him any new service, but that the land shall be holden of him as it was before, and in this case the abbot shall have a writ of mesne if he be distrained in his default, by force of the said confirmation, where percase he might not have such writ before,&c.

Dispossession of a villein in gross; confirmation to party taking him, bad.

541 Also, if I be seised of a villein as of a villein in gross, and another taketh him out of my possession, claiming him to be his villein [whereas he has no right to have him as his villein*], and afterwards I confirm to him the estate which he

mesne confirma lestate que labbé ad en la terre, a aver et tener la terre a luy et a ses successours en frankalmoigne, &c., en ceo cas confirmacion est bon, et adonques labbé tiendra del mesne en frankalmoigne : et la cause est, pur ceo que nul novel service est reserve, qar toutz les services especialement specifiez sont extientez, et nul rien est reserve, forsque labbé tient de luy la terre, et ceo fuist a luy devant la confirmacion ; qar celuy qui tient en frankalmoigne ne doit faire ascun corporel service ; issint per tiel confirmacion il appiert que le mesne ne reserva a luy ascun novel service, mes que les tenementes serront tenus de luy come ceo fuist adevaunt, et en ceo cas labbé avera un brief de mesne sil soit distreigne en son defaute, per force del dit confirmacion, lou per cas il ne puissoit aver tiel brief adevaunt, &c.

541 Item, *si jeo suy seisi dun villeyn come de villeyn en gros, et un autre luy prent hors de ma possession, enclaymant luy estre son villeyn [là ou il navoet ascun droit daver luy come son villeyn*], et puis jeo confirma a luy lestate quil ad en*

* These words within brackets do not appear in the three earliest

hath in my villein, this confirmation seemeth to be void, for that no one can have possession of a man as of a villein in gross, save he that hath right to have him as his villein in gross; and so inasmuch as he to whom the confirmation was made, was not seised of him as of his villein at the time of the confirmation made, such confirmation is void: 542 but in this case, if such words were in the deed, *Sciatis me dedisse et concessisse, &c., talem villanum meum,* this is good; but this shall enure by force and way of grant, and not by way of confirmation, &c.

Reason.

[§ 516—*confirmation should be made to one in possession*].

Inheritance in a villein.

§ 531.

543 Also, sometimes these verbs *dedi et concessi* shall enure by way of extinguishment of the thing given or granted; as if a tenant hold of the lord by certain rent, and the lord by his deed granteth to the tenant and his heirs the rent, &c., this shall enure to the tenant by way of extinguishment; for by that grant the rent is extinct (*f*).

Dedi et concessi *may enure by way of extinguishment.*

mon villeyn, cest confirmacion semble estre voide, pur ceo que nul poet aver possession dun home come de villeyn en gros, sinon celuy qui ad droit de luy aver come son villeyn en gros; et issint entaunt que celuy a qui le confirmacion fuist fait, ne fuist seisi de luy come de son villeyn a le temps del confirmacion fait, tiel confirmacion est voide : 542 *mes en ceo cas, si tielx parolx, furent en le fait,* Sciatis me dedisse et concessisse, &c., talem villanum meum, *cest bon ; mes ceo urera per force et voye de graunt, et nemy per voye de confirmacion, &c.*

543 Item, *ascun foitz ceux verbes* dedi et concessi *ureront per voye dextientisement del chose done ou graunte ; sicome un tenaunt tient de son seignour per certeyn rente, et le seignour per son fait graunta a le tenaunt et a ses heires le rente, &c., ceo urera a le tenaunt per voye dextientisement ; qar per cell graunt le rente est extient.*

---

editions, they, however, are given in *Rastell's* Transl., and in all other editions.

(*f*) And this grant of the rent shall enure by way of release.

Grant of rent-charge to terre-tenant is extinguishment of such rent.

544 In the same manner it is, where a man hath a rent-charge out of certain land, and he grant to the tenant of the land the rent-charge, &c.; and the reason is, because it appeareth by the words of the grant, that the will of the donor is, that the tenant shall have the rent, &c., and insomuch as he cannot have or perceive rent out of his own land, therefore the deed shall be intended and taken for the most advantage and avail for the tenant that it can be taken, and this is by way of extinguishment (*g*).

The seventh case wherein a release and confirmation differ.
The different effects of a simple confirmation of a termor's estate, and of my right in the land, distinguished.

545 Also, if I let land to a man for term of years, and afterwards I confirm his estate without more words put in the deed, by this, he hath no greater estate than for term of years, as he had before: 546 but if I release to him my right which I have in the land, without putting more in the deed, he hath estate of freehold. And so mayst thou, my son, understand divers great diversities between releases and confirmations.

544 *En mesme le manere est, lou home ad un rente-charge hors de certeyn terre, et il graunta al tenaunt del terre le rente-charge, &c.; et la cause est, pur ceo quil appiert per les parolx del graunt, que le volunté le donor est, que le tenaunt avera le rente, &c., et entaunt quil ne poet aver ne percever rente hors de sa terre demesne, pur ceo le fait serra entendue et pris pur le pluis avantage et availle pur le tenaunt que poet estre pris, et ceo est per voye dextientisement.*

545 Item, *si jeo lessa terre a un home per terme dans, et puis jeo confirme son estate sauns pluis parolx mettez en le fait, per cel, il nad pluis greyndre estate que pur terme dans, sicome il avoit adevaunt :* 546 *mes si jeo relessa a luy mon droit que jeo ay en la terre, sans pluis mettre en le fait, il ad estate de franktenement. Et issint poiez entendre, mon fits, divers graundes diversitees perentre relesses et confirmacions.*

(*g*) But if the grantee of the rent-charge granted it to the te-

547 Also, if I being within age, let land to another for term of twenty years, and afterwards he grant the land to another for term of ten years, so that he grant but parcel of his term; in this case when I am of full age, if I release to the grantee of my lessee, &c., this release is void, because there is no privity between him and me; but if I confirm his estate, then this confirmation is good (*h*). But if my lessee grant all his estate to another, then my release made to the grantee is good and effectual.

The eighth case wherein a release and confirmation differ.
Infant grants lease for years, lessee sub-lets, infant on attaining age confirms sub-lease, good as a confirmation, bad as a release.

548 Also, if a man grant a rent-charge issuing out of his land to another for term of his life, and afterwards he confirmeth his estate in the said rent, to have and to hold to him in fee-tail or in fee-simple; this confirmation is void so as to enlarge his estate, because he that confirmeth had not any reversion in the rent (*i*): 549 but if a man be seised in fee of

Distinction between rent newly created, and a rent in esse.
He who has no reversion cannot by confirmation enlarge estate of particular tenant.
[If tenant for life grant rent in fee, and he in reversion confirm, this is good, for he has reversion at the time of confirmation, § 529.]

547 Item, *si jeo esteaunt deins age, lessa terre a un autre pur terme de* xx. *ans, et puis il graunte la terre a un autre pur terme de* x. *ans, issint quil graunta forsque parcel de son terme ; en ceo cas quant jeo suy de pleyn age, si jeo relessa al graunté de mon lessé, &c., ceo reles est voide, pur ceo que il nest ascun privete parentre luy et moy ; mes si jeo confirme son estate, donques ceo confirmacion est bon. Mes si mon lessé graunta tout son estate a un autre, donques mon reles fait al graunté est bon et effectuel.*

543 Item, *si home graunte un rente-charge issaunt hors de sa terre a un autre pur terme de sa vie, et puis il confirma son estate en le dit rente, a aver et tener a luy en fee-taille ou en fee-simple ; ceo confirmacion est voyde quant a enlarger son estate, pur ceo que celuy qui confirmast navoit ascun reversion en le rente :* 549 *mes si home soit seisi en fee de rente-*

---

nant of the land and a stranger, it shall be extinguished but for the moiety: and so it is of a seigniory.—*Co. Lytt.* 307. b.

(*h*) For it is a rule, that which I may defeat by my entry, I may confirm by my deed.

(*i*) Here the diversity is appa-

The eighth case wherein release and confirmation agree. *Rule of law, viz. that confirmor must have right at the time of the grant.* § 548.

a rent-service or rent-charge, and he grant the rent to another for term of life, and the tenant attorneth, and afterwards he confirm the estate of the grantee in fee-tail or in fee-simple, this confirmation is good, so as to enlarge his estate, according to the words of confirmation; because he that confirmed the estate at the time of confirmation had the reversion of the rent (*k*).

Confirmation of rent newly created should be by fresh deed.

550 But in the case aforesaid, where a man grants a rent-charge to another for term of life, if he will that the grantee should have an estate in the tail, or in fee, it behoveth that the deed of the grant of the rent-charge for term of life be surrendered (*l*) or cancelled, and then to make a new deed of

service ou de rente-charge, et il graunta le rente a un autre pur terme de vie, et le tenaunt attourna, et puis il confirma lestate de le graunté en fee-taille ou en fee-simple, cest confirmacion est bon, quant a enlarger son estate, soloncques les parolx de confirmacion ; pur ceo que cestuy qui confirmast lestate al temps del confirmacion avoit la revercion del rente.

550 *Mes en le cas avauntdit, lou home graunta un rente-charge a un autre pur terme de vie, sil voille que le graunté averoit estate en le taille, ou en fee, il covient que le fait del graunt del rente-charge pur terme de vie soit surrendu ou*

---

rent between a rent newly created and a rent *in esse*, which needeth no explication. Only this is to be observed, that *Lyttleton* intendeth his deed of confirmation not to contain any clause of distress; for otherwise, as to the confirmation the deed is void, but the clause of distress doth amount to a new grant, as in the chapter of rents hath been said.—*Co. Lytt.* 308. a.

(*k*) It is here to be observed, that to the grant of the estate for life, *Lyttleton* doth put an attornment, because it is requisite: but to the confirmation to the grantee of the rent to enlarge his estate, there is none necessary; and therefore he putteth none. But of this more shall be said in the chapter of attornment, § 556, 575.—*Co. Lytt.* 308. b.

(*l*) A surrender, *sursumredditio*, or rendering up, is of a nature directly opposite to a release; for, as that operates by the greater

the like rent-charge, to have and to take to the grantee in the tail, or in fee, &c. *Ex paucis dictis intendere plurima potes, &c**.

cancelle, et donques de faire un novel fait dautiel rente-charge, a aver et percever a le graunté en le taille, ou en fee, &c. Ex paucis dictis intendere plurima potes, &c.*

---

* This concluding apophthegm appears in some copies as *ex paucis dictis plurima* concipit ingenium. *Lettou & M.* reads *Ex paucis dictis, &c.* See *ante*, p. 448 (*g*).

---

estate's descending upon the less, a surrender is the falling of a less estate into a greater by deed. It is defined (*Co. Lytt.* 337), a yielding up of an estate for life or years to him that hath the immediate reversion or remainder, wherein the particular estate may merge or drown, by mutual agreement between them. It is done by these words, "hath surrendered, granted, and yielded up." The surrenderor must be in possession (*Id.* 338); and the surrenderee must have a higher estate, in which the estate surrendered may merge: therefore tenant for life cannot surrender to him in remainder for years. In a surrender there is no occasion for livery of seisin (*Id.* 50); for there is a privity of estate between the surrenderor, and the surrenderee; the one's particular estate, and the other's remainder, are one and the same estate; and livery having been once made at the creation of it, there is no necessity for having it afterwards. And, for the same reason, no livery is required on a release or confirmation in fee to tenant for years or at will, though a freehold thereby passes: since the reversion of the relessor, or confirmor, and the particular estate of the relessee, or confirmee, are one and the same estate; and where there is already a possession, derived from such a privity of estate, any farther delivery of possession would be vain and nugatory (§ 460).—B. C. ii. 326. Also see *Co. Lytt.* 338. a.

Surrender *distinguished from a confirmation.*

CHAPTER X.

ATTORNMENT.

ATTORNMENT is an agreement of the tenant to the grant of the seignory, or of a rent, or of the donee in tail, or tenant for life or years, to a *grant* of a reversion or remainder made to another.—*Co. Lytt.* 309. *a.* It has been already noticed, (p. 17), that of hereditaments, some are corporeal and some incorporeal, a distinction that applied itself to the mode by which either were transferred or conveyed, for at law the conveyance of corporeal hereditaments was by livery of seisin, (since the Statute of Frauds *necessarily* accompanied by a deed of feoffment), whilst incorporeal hereditaments, whereof livery of seisin cannot be had, could only pass by deed of grant, whereto attornment of the tenant of the land was requisite; and as such acts involved matter of equal notoriety with livery of seisin, they were deemed tantamount thereto and equivalent to feudal investiture, so that corporeal hereditaments, and those things which consist in manual occupation, are said to *lie in livery,* whilst incorporeal hereditaments, though perhaps of equal duration, as flowing from the land, or as in the case of reversions and remainders, as parcel of the land itself, but which cannot, from their very nature, be the subject of such manual occupation, are said to *lie in grant.*

Inheritances that "*lie in grant*" are advowsons, services, rents, commons, reversions, and such like.—*Co. Lytt.* 172. *a.*

It is to be observed to what kind of inheritances being granted, an attornment is requisite. And in this chapter, Lyttleton speaketh of five: first, of a seignory, rent-service, &c. (§ 553-5); secondly, of a rent-charge (§ 556); thirdly, of a rent-seck (§ 572). And hereafter in this chapter of two more, viz. of a reversion and remainder of lands (§ 557), for the tenant shall never need to attorn, but where there is tenure, attendance, remainder, or payment of a rent out of land.—*Co. Lytt.* 312. *a.*

The doctrine of attornment, as it is derived from feudal principles, and is perfectly analogous to that of livery, had for its object three purposes: first, that the tenant in possession might not be subjected to a stranger, or a new lord, without his own approbation and consent; secondly, that he might know to whom he was to render his services, and distinguish the lawful distress from the tortious taking of his cattle: and this reason was so prevalent, that when the statute *Quia emptores* gave a free alienation, in respect of the superior lord, yet the tenant's right of attornment continued unaltered; thirdly, that by such attornment, the grantee of the reversion or seignory might be put into the possession of it, and that others might be apprised and informed of the transfer.—See *Gilb. Ten.* 81. And these objects are kept in view by Lyttleton, who in a series of cases details the principles and the distinctions governing and applicable to this obsolete, but not useless learning: these cases are classed as attornments in deed or *expressed,* and attornments in law or *implied,* resolving themselves into rules which declare where attornment was deemed necessary or unnecessary. With regard to the general rule as to the necessity of attornment by the tenant of the freehold, who was obliged to attorn when the freehold was charged, it is expressly laid down by Lyttleton, that attornment must have been made during the life of the grantor (§ 551); that it should be in conformity to the grant (§ 552); that services did not pass without it (§ 553); that attornment to a grant of a reversion should be made by the tenant of the particular estate (§ 571), and to a grant of rent, attornment ought to be made by the tenant of the freehold, or according to the language of the Books, by the "tenants to the avowry," *viz.* the terre-tenants (§ 556), wherein the remainder-man was not deemed tenant to the lord (§ 557), though the reversioner was (§ 554—562); from which it may be concluded, that no one should attorn upon the grant of any seignory, rent-service, reversion, or remainder, but he who was *immediately* privy to the grantor.

The cases in which attornment was not necessary, were chiefly in the cases where the tenant was not *attendant* upon the lord for performance of services, as in the case of tenant by *elegit;* where privity of estate, (which is always *immediate*), existed between the grantor and the grantee before the attornment, as in the case of joint-tenants (§ 574); or where the party came to the land by act of law or by title paramount, *i. e.* by descent, forfeiture, &c. (§ 583, 584).

The necessity of attornment was partly avoided by the method of conveying to uses under the stat. 27 Hen. 8, c. 10, by which the possession is immediately executed to the use; by the Statute of Wills, 32 Hen. 8, c. 2, explained by 34 Hen. 8, c. 5, by which the legal estate is vested in the devisee (as in the case of devises by the custom (§ 585); and the statutes 4 & 5 Anne, c. 16, and 11 Geo. 2, c. 19, have so restrained the doctrine of attornment, that, except in the cases excepted by the latter statute (see 2 *Bingh.* 59; 1 *Powell, Mortg.* 174. *n.*), it is seldom heard of, except in the case where tenants attorn after recovery by an elder title, to save the expense of bringing ejectment or enforcing writ of possession. Attornment, where necessary, can be made either by word or writing, and by payment of a small coin where no rent is due, or by payment of rent (in part or *in toto*) where rent is payable. Attornment does not pass any interest of him who attorns, but only perfects a *grant* made by another.

Attornment defined, and in what cases ne-

551 Attornment is, if there be lord and tenant, and the lord will grant by his deed the services of his tenant to ano-

551 *Attournement est, si soit seignour et tenaunt, et le seignour voille graunter per son fait les services de son tenaunt*

ther for term of years, or for term of life, or in the tail, or in fee, it behoveth that the tenant attorn to the grantee in the life of the grantor, by force and virtue of the grant, or otherwise the grant is void. And attornment is none other in effect, but when the tenant hath heard of the grant made by his lord, that the same tenant do agree by word to the said grant, as to say to the grantee, I am agreeable to the grant made to you, or, I am content with the grant made to you ; but the more common attornment is, to say, &c., Sir, I attorn to you by force of the said grant; or, I become your tenant, &c., or to deliver to the grantee a penny, or a half-penny, or a farthing by way of attornment, &c.

cessary. It must be made in the lifetime of the grantor.

Is in effect an agreement to the grant;

form of attornment stated.

552* Also, if the lord grant the service of his tenant to one man, and after by a deed bearing a later date he grant the same services to another, and the tenant attorn to the second grantee, now the second grantee hath the services; and albeit

In the case of two grants made of the same service, the grantee who obtains the first attornment is preferred; [for where the equities are equal, he who has the law shall prevail].

a un autre pur terme dans, ou pur terme de vie, ou en le taille, ou en fee, il covient que le tenaunt attourna al granté en la vie le grantour, per force et vertue del graunt, ou autrement le graunt est voide. Et attournement est nul autre en effecte, forsque quaunt le tenaunt ad oye de le graunt fait per son seignour, que mesme le tenaunt agrea per parol a le dit graunt, sicome adire a le graunté, jeo moy agrea a le graunt fait a vous, ou, jeo sue contente de le graunt fait a vous ; mes le pluis comen attornement est, adire, &c., Sir, jeo attourna a vous per force del dit graunt ; ou, jeo deveigne vostre tenaunt, &c., ou a deliverer al graunté un denere, ou un mayle, ou un ferlyng per voye dattournement, &c.

552* Item, *si le seignour graunte le service de son tenaunt a un home, et puis per un fait portant darrein date il graunta mesmes les services a un autre, et le tenaunt attourna a le seconde graunté, ore le seconde graunté ad les services ; et*

* This and the following sections to, and inclusive of, section 559, do not appear in *Rastell's* Transl., *Tottyl* 1556, and subsequent editions by him, *Jane Yetsweirt* 1597, *Wight* 1604, and the *Stationers* to 1661, but they appear in the older editions of *Rastell's* Transl., and in *Marshe* 1556.

By whom attornment must be made.

afterwards the tenant willeth to attorn to the first grantee, this is clearly void, &c.

On feoffment of a manor, the services do not pass, but remain in the feoffor until the tenants attorn.

553 Also, if a man be seised of a manor, which manor is parcel in demesne, and parcel in service, if he willeth to alien this manor to another, it behoveth that by force of the alienation, all the tenants that hold of the alienor as of his manor, &c., do attorn to the alienee, or otherwise the services abide (*i. e.* remain) continually in the alienor, except tenants at will, &c.; for it needeth not that tenants at will do attorn upon such alienation, &c.; for this that the same lands and tenements which they hold at will do pass to the alienee by force of such alienation.

Tenants at will need not attorn.

No one can attorn but he who is privy to the grantor; therefore reversioner, not the undertenant, must attorn to grantee.

554* Also, if there be lord and tenant, and the tenant letteth the land to another for term of life, or giveth the land in the tail, saving the reversion to himself, &c., if the lord in such case grant his seigniory to another, it behoveth that he in the

coment que apres le tenaunt voille attourner a le premier grаunté, cest clerement voide, &c.

553 Item, *si home soit seisi dun manor, quel manor est parcel en demesne, et parcel en service, sil voille aliener cel manor a un autre, il covient que per force del alienacion, que touts lez tenauntes qui teignont del alienour come de son manor, &c., attournerent al alienė, ou autrement les services demourront continuellement en lalienour, forpris tenauntes a volunté, &c.; qar il ne besoigne que tenauntes a volunté attournent sur tiel alienacion, &c.; pur ceo que mesmes les terres et tenementes quils teignont a volunté passont al alienė per force detiel alienacion.*

554* Item, *si soient seignour et tenaunt, et le tenaunt lessa la terre a un autre pur terme de vie, ou dona la terre en le taille, savaunt la revercion a luy, &c., si le seignour en tiel cas graunta a un autre sa seignourie, il covient que celuy en*

* At this place occurs in those editions of *Rastell's* Transl. previous to *Tottyl* 1556, with a slight variation, the same case that forms § 560, 561, which therefore, in those editions and in *Marshe* 1556, appears twice; and with respect to this section it does not appear in *Rastell's* Transl., *Tottyl* 1556, and subsequent editions to 1661.

reversion attorn to the grantee, and not the tenant for term of life, or the tenant in the tail, because that in this case he in the reversion is tenant to the lord, and not the tenant for term of life, nor the tenant in the tail. 555* In the same manner it is where there are lord, mesne, and tenant, if the lord will grant the services of the mesne, albeit he make no mention in his grant of the mesne, yet it behoveth that the mesne attorn, and not the tenant paravail, &c., because the mesne is tenant unto him, &c. 556* But otherwise it is where certain land is charged with a rent-charge or rent-seck, for in such case, if he that hath the rent-charge grant this to another, it behoveth that the tenant of the freehold attorn to the grantee, for this that the freehold is charged with the rent, &c. And in rent-charge no avowry ought to be made upon any person for the distress taken, &c., but he shall avow the prisel (*i. e.* the taking) to be good and rightful, as in lands or tenements so charged with his distress, &c.

Lord, mesne, and tenant: if lord grant the seignory, the mesne must attorn.

But in grant of a rent-seck or rent-charge the under tenant must attorn.

557* Also, if there be lord and tenant, and the tenant letteth

Tenant for

la revercion attourna al graunté, et nemy le tenaunt a terme de vie, ou le tenaunt en le taille, pur ceo que en ceo cas celuy en la revercion est tenaunt al seignour, et nemye le tenaunt a terme de vie, ne le tenaunt en le taille. 555* *En mesme le manere est lou sount seignour, mesne, et tenaunt, si le seignour voille graunter les services del mesne, coment que il ne fait ascun mencion en son graunt del mesne, unqore il covient que le mesne attourna, et nemy le tenaunt peravaile, &c., pur ceo que le mesne est tenaunt a luy, &c.* 556* *Mes autrement est lou certeyn terre est charge dun rente-charge ou rente-sekke, qar en tiel cas, si celuy qui ad le rente-charge ceo graunta a un autre, il covient que le tenaunt del franktenement attourna al graunté, pur ceo que le franktenement est charge del rente, &c. Et en rente-charge nul avowerë doit estre fait sur ascun person pur le distres pris, &c., mes il avowera le pris bon et droiturel, come en terres ou tenementes issint charges a sa distres, &c.*

557* Item, *si soit seignour et tenaunt, et le tenaunt lessa son*

* See p. 546 (*).

life, remainder in fee, if the reversioner grant to a stranger, the tenant for life is the only person to attorn.

his tenement to another for term of life, the remainder to another in fee, and afterwards the lord grant the services, &c., to another, and the tenant for term of life attorn, this is good enough, for this that the tenant for life is tenant in this case to the lord, &c., and he in the remainder cannot be said to be tenant to the lord, as to that intent, until after the death of the tenant for life; yet in this case, if he in the remainder dieth without heir, the lord hath the remainder by way of escheat, because it behoveth the lord in such case to avow upon the tenant for term of life, &c., yet the whole entire tenement, as to all the estates of the freehold or of fee-simple, or otherwise, &c., in such case are altogether holden of the lord, &c.*

Attornments in law. *Husband's acceptance of grant of service will bind the wife,*

558† Also, if there be lord and tenant, and the tenant let the tenements to a woman for term of life, the remainder over in fee, and the woman taketh husband, and afterwards the lord grant

*tenement a un autre pur terme de vie, le remeyndre a un autre en fee, et puis le seignour graunta les services, &c., a un autre, et le tenaunt a terme de vie attourna, ceo est assetes bon, pur ceo que le tenaunt a terme de vie est tenaunt en ceo cas al seignour, &c., et celuy en le remeyndre ne poet estre dit tenaunt al seignour, quaunt a cell entent, forsque apres la mort le tenaunt a terme de vie; unqore en ceo cas, si celuy en le remeyndre morust sauns heire, le seignour ad le remeyndre per voye deschete, pur ceo que covient que le seignour en tiel cas davower sur le tenaunt a terme de vie, &c., unqore tout lentier tenement, quaunt a toutes les estates de franktenement ou de fee-simple, ou autrement, &c., en tiel cas sont ensembles tenus de le seignour, &c.**

558† Item, *si soient seignour et tenaunt, et le tenaunt lessa les tenementes a une feme pur terme de vie, le remeyndre oustre en fee, et la feme prent baron, et puis le seignour*

* Here follows in all the French copies from *Redm.* and *Berth.*, the following reference, which *Sir Edward Coke* remarks (312 b.) "is added to *Lyttleton*, but it is consonant to law, and the authority truly cited:" viz.—*Mes nemy de faire avowry sur eux toutz ensemble*—But not to make avowry upon them altogether.—*M.* 3, *H.* 6. 1.

† See p. 546 (*).

the services, &c., to the husband and to his heirs, in that case the service is put in suspense during the coverture. But if the wife die, living the husband, the husband and his heirs shall have the rent of them in the remainder, &c. And in this case there needeth no attornment by parol, &c., for that the husband, who ought to attorn, accepted the deed of the grant of the services, &c., the which acceptance is an attornment in the law.

acceptance of the grant being an attornment in law.

559* In the same manner is it, if there be lord and tenant, and the tenant take wife, and afterwards the lord grant his services to the wife and her heirs, and the husband accept the deed, in this case, after the death of the husband, the wife and her heirs shall have the services, &c.; for by the acceptance of the husband, this is a good attornment, &c., albeit during the coverture the services are put in suspense, &c.

Second example of an attornment in law. *So if the grant was made to the wife of the tenant, and he accepted the grant.*

560 Also, if there be lord and tenant, and the tenant grant the tenements to a man for term of his life, the remainder to another in fee, if the lord grant the services to the tenant for

Third example of attornment in law; *viz. to a grant of services suspended for life, ac-*

graunta les services, &c., a le baron et a sez heires, en celle cas le service est mys in suspence duraunt la coverture. Mes si la feme devie, vivant le baron, le baron et ses heires averount le rente de ceux en le remeyndre, &c. Et en ceo cas il ne besoigne ascun attournement per parol, &c., pur ceo que le baron, qui doit attourner, accepta le fait del graunt de les services, &c., le quel acceptaunce est un attournement en la ley.

559* *En mesme le manere est, si soient seignour et tenaunt, et le tenaunt prent feme, et puis le seignour graunta les services a la feme et ses heires, et le baron accepta le fait, en ceo cas, apres la mort de le baron, la feme et ses heires averount les services, &c.; qar per lacceptance le baron, ceo est bon attournement, &c., coment que duraunt la coverture les services sont mys en suspence, &c.*

560 Item, *si soient seignour et tenaunt, et le tenaunt graunta les tenementes a un home pur terme de sa vie, le remeyndre a un autre en fee, si le seignour graunta les services a le tenaunt*

* See p. 546 (*).

ceptance by lessee for life being an attornment.

term of life; in this case the tenant for term of life hath fee in the services: but the services are put in suspense during his life. But his heirs shall have the services after his decease: and in this case there needeth no attornment, for by the acceptance of the deed by him that ought to attorn, &c., this is attornment of itself, &c.

But where grantee holds in fee simple, a grant to him operates as an extinguishment.

561 But where the tenant hath as great and as high estate in the tenements, as the lord hath in the seigniory; in such case, if the lord grant the services to the tenant in fee, this shall enure by way of extinguishment. *Causa patet.*

During suspense of seigniory, reversioner must attorn,

because he is tenant to the lord.

562 Also, if there be lord and tenant, and the tenant make a lease to a man for term of his life, saving the reversion to himself, if the lord grant the seigniory to the tenant for life in fee, in this case it behoveth that he in the reversion attorn to the tenant for term of life by force of that grant, or otherwise the grant is void; for this that he in the reversion is tenant to the lord, &c.*

a terme de vie; en ceo cas le tenaunt a terme de vie ad fee en les services: mes les services sont mys en suspence duraunt sa vie. Mes ses heires averont les services apres son decesse: et en ceo cas il ne besoigne ascun attournement, qar per lacceptance del fait de celuy qui doit attourner, &c., ceo est attournement de luy mesme, &c. 561 *Mes lou le tenaunt ad cy graund et haute estate en les tenementes, sicome le seignour ad en le seignourie; en tiel cas, si le seignour graunta les services al tenaunt en fee, ceo urera per voye dextientisement,* Causa patet.

562 Item, *si soient seignour et tenaunt, et le tenaunt fait un lees a un home pur terme de sa vie, savaunt la revercion a luy, si le seignour graunta la seignourie al tenaunt a terme de vie en fee, en ceo cas il covient que celuy en la revercion attourna al tenaunt a terme de vie per force de cel graunt, ou autrement le graunt est voide; pur ceo que celuy en la revercion est tenaunt al seignour, &c.**

---

* The final &c. does not appear in *Rastell's* Transl., and there also

563 Also, if there be lord and tenant, and the tenant holdeth of the lord by twenty manner of services, and the lord grant his seigniory to another, if the tenant pay [in deed*] any parcel of any of the services to the grantee, this is good attornment of and for all the services, albeit the intent of the tenant was to attorn but for that parcel, because the seigniory is but one and entire, although there be divers manner of services which the tenant ought to do, &c.

The fourth example of attornment in law, *viz. attornment made for parcel, is good for the whole.*

564 Also, if there be lord and tenant, and the tenant holdeth of the lord by many manners of services, and the lord grant the services to another by fine, if the grantee sue a *scire facias* out of the same fine for any parcel of the services, and hath judgment to recover, that judgment is a good attornment in law for all the services, &c.

Conusee of a fine of services, suing a* sci. fa. *good attornment.

563 Item, *si soient seignour et tenaunt, et le tenaunt tient del seignour per* XX *maneres des services, et le seignour graunta sa seignourie a un autre, si le tenaunt paia [en fait*] ascun parcel dascun de les services al graunté, ceo est bon attournement de et pur toutes les services, coment que lentent de le tenaunt fuist dattourner forsque de cel parcel, pur ceo que le seignourie est forsque un et entier, coment quils sont divers maneres des services que le tenaunt doit faire, &c.*

564 Item, *si soit seignour et tenaunt, et le tenaunt tient del seignour per plusours maneres des services, et le seignour graunta les services a un autre per fyn, si le graunté sua un* scire facias *hors de mesme le fyn pur ascun parcel de les services, et ad juggement de recoverer, cel juggement est bon attournement en ley pur toutes les services, &c.*

---

follows in *Redm.* and *Berth.*, and in all subsequent French editions, except the expurgated editions of *Tottyl* 1557, an addition which *Sir Edward Coke* notices, "is not in the original, and is against law, and therefore to be rejected."

* *Or do*, (*i. e.* perform) *Rastell's* Translation; which seems most correct, for the words, *en fait*, were probably written, *ou fait*. See p. 534*, where a similar error occurs.

Payment of the rent before-hand is an attornment and consequently a seisin.

565 Also, if the lord of a rent-service grant the services to another, and the tenant attorn by a penny, and afterwards the grantee distrain for the rent behind, and the tenant make rescous: in this case the grantee shall not have assise for the rent, but writ of rescous, because the gift of the penny by the tenant was not but by way of attornment, &c. But if the tenant had given to the grantee the said penny as parcel of the rent, or half a penny, or a farthing by way of seisin of the rent, then this is a good attornment, and also it is a good seisin to the grantee of the rent, and then upon such rescous the grantee shall have assise, &c.

Distinction between payment by way of attornment to grant of a rent, and payment by way of seisin.

What tenants shall attorn to the grant: *Attornment by one joint tenant good for the others.*

566* Also, if there be many jointenants that hold by certain services, and the lord grant to another the services, and one of the jointenants attorn to the grantee, this is as good as if all had attorned, because the seigniory is entire, &c.

565 Item, *si le seignour dun rente-service graunta les services a un autre, et le tenaunt attorna per une denere, et puis le graunté distreigna pur le rente arere, et le tenaunt a luy fait rescous : en ceo cas le graunté navera assise del rente, forsque brief de rescous, pur ceo que le done del deniere per le tenaunt ne fuist forsque per voye dattournement, &c. Mes si le tenaunt avoit done a le graunté le dit denere come parcel de le rente, ou un maile, ou un ferlyng per voye de seisin del rente, donques ceo est bon attournement, et auxi est bon seisin al graunté del rente, et donques sur tiel rescous le graunté avera assise, &c.*

566* Item, *si sont plusours jointenauntes qui teignont per certeyn services, et le seignour graunta a un autre les services, et un de les jointenauntes attourna al graunté, ceo est auxi bon sicome toutz attornerent, pur ceo que la seignourie est entier, &c.*

---

* This section does not appear in *Rastell's* Translation, *Tottyl* 1556, and subsequent editions to 1661, but it is given in previous editions, and in *Marshe* 1556; and to these editions a *quære* is added.

567 Also, if a man let tenements for term of years, by force of which lease the lessee is seised, and afterwards the lessor by his deed grant the reversion to another for term of life, or in the tail, or in fee; it behoveth in such case that the tenant for term of years attorn, or otherwise nothing passeth to such grantee by such deed. And if in this case the tenant for term of years attorn to the grantee, then forthwith the freehold passeth to the grantee by such attornment without any livery of seisin, &c.; because if any livery of seisin, &c., should be or were needful to be made in that case, then the tenant for years should be at the time of the livery of seisin ousted of his possession, which should be against reason, &c.*

On grants of reversion.
Tenant of particular estate must attorn.

568† Also, if tenements be letten to a man for term of life, or given in the tail, saving the reversion, &c., if he in the reversion in this case grant the reversion to another by his

567 Item, *si home lessa tenementes a terme dans, per force de quel lees le lessee est seisi, et puis le lessour per son fait graunta la revercion a autre pur terme de vie, ou en le taille, ou en fee; il covient en tiel cas que le tenaunt a terme dans attourna, ou autrement rien passa a tiel graunté per tiel fait. Et si en ceo cas le tenaunt a terme dans attourna al graunté, donques meyntenaunt passa le franktenement al graunté per tiel attournement sans ascun liverë de seisin, &c.; pur ceo que si ascun liverë de seisin, &c., serroit ou besoigneroit destre fait en cel cas, donques le tenaunt a terme dans serroit al temps de liverë de seisin ouste de sa possession, que serroit encontre reason, &c.**

568† Item, *si tenementes soient lessés a un home pur terme de vie, ou donez en le taille, savaunt la revercion, &c., si celuy en la revercion en ceo cas graunta la revercion a un autre per*

---

* This final *&c.* does not appear in *Rastell's* Translation.

† This and the following section, 569, do not appear in *Rastell's* Translation, *Tottyl* 1566, and subsequent editions to 1661, but it is given in previous editions, and in *Marshe* 1556.

deed, it behoveth that the tenant of the land do attorn to the grantee in the life of the grantor, or otherwise the grant is void, &c.

On grant of remainder, expectant on determination of an estate of freehold, the tenant for life should attorn in the life of the grantor.

569* In the same manner is it, if land be [given in the tail or†] let to a man for term of life, the remainder to another [&c.‡], if he in the remainder willeth to grant the (*his*) remainder to another &c., if the tenant of the land attorn in the life of the grantor, then the grant of such remainder is good, or otherwise not§.

son fait, il covient que le tenaunt de la terre attourna al graunté en la vie le grauntour, ou autrement le graunt est voyde, &c.

569* *En mesme le manere est, si terre soit [done en le taille ou†] lesse a un home pur terme de vie, le remeyndre a un autre [&c.‡], si celuy en le remeyndre voille graunter le remeyndre a un autre, &c., si le tenaunt de la terre attourna en la vie le grantour, donques le graunt de tiel remeyndre est bon, ou autrement nemye§.*

---

* This section is not given in any edition of *Rastell's* Transl. since *Powell* 1551, except *Marshe* 1556, *ante*, p. 553 (†).

† The words within brackets not in *Lettou & M.*, *Machl.*, or *Roh.*—"These words [*done en tail ou*], which visibly corrupt the sense of our author, though they are inserted in all the editions of this book, and the old edition of *Lyttleton's* Tenures printed at London by *Richard Pynson* (1528), are however to be omitted, for they are not in the original edition that was printed at *Rohan.*"—*Note of Editor to* 11*th and* 12*th edition, Co. Lytt.* Some of *Tottyl's* editions previous to the first sectioned edition, 1581, say, *lesse en tail ou lesse*, which is also erroneous. The editions of *Rastell's* Translation which retain this section, (*viz.* all before, and inclusive of, *Powell* 1548, 1551, and *Marshe* 1556), read as above, and as *Sir Edward Coke* does not notice these words, but comments upon them, the Editor has not thought fit to expunge them. The whole section may be deemed questionable, as the copies vary. The case seems vouched by 12 *E.* 4. 3, 4.

‡ In all editions subsequent to the three earliest, this *&c.* is supplied by the words, *in fee*.

§ Here follows in every other French copy after the four earliest editions,

571 Also, if land be let to a man for years, the remainder to another for term of life, reserving to the lessor a certain rent by year, and livery of seisin thereupon is made to the tenant for term of years, if he in the reversion in this case grant the reversion to another, and the tenant that is in the remainder after the term of years, attorn; this is a good attornment, and he to whom this reversion is granted by force of such attornment may distrain the tenant for term of years for the rent due after such attornment, although the tenant for years never attorned unto him. And the reason is for this that where the reversion is dependant upon the estate of freehold, it sufficeth that the tenant of the freehold attorn upon such grant of the reversion, &c.

Lease for years, remainder for life, grant by lessor of his reversion, either tenant for life or years may attorn to grantee of the reversion.

572 And it is to be understood, that where a lease for term

Lease or gift

571 Item, *si terre soit lessé a un home pur terme dans, le remeyndre a un autre pur terme de vie, reservaunt al lessour un certeyn rente per an, et liverë de seisin sur ceo est fait al tenaunt pur terme dans, si cestuy en la revercion en ceo cas graunta la revercion a un autre, et le tenaunt qui est en le remeyndre apres le terme dans, attourna ; ceo est bon attournement, et celuy a qui cest revercion est graunte per force de tiel attournement distreynera le tenaunt a terme dans pur le rente due apres tiel attournement, coment que le tenaunt a terme dans ne unques attournast a luy. Et la cause est pur ceo que lou la revercion est dependant sur lestate del franktenement, suffist que le tenaunt del franktenement attourna sur tiel graunt del revercion, &c.*

572 *Et est assavoir, que lou un lees a terme dans, ou a*

---

the following reference which forms the 570th subdivision of the text by *West* 1581, *viz. Pasch.* 12 *Edw.* 4, 3, 4. *It is there holden by the whole court, that tenant in tail shall not be compelled to attorn ; but if he will attorn* gratis, *it is good enough :* upon which *Sir E. Coke* remarks, " This is added to *Lyttleton;* and therefore though it be good law, and the book truly cited, yet I pass it over." This reference appears as a side-note in *Redm.*, and is also incorporated with the text. *Rastell's* Transl. does not give this addition.

Attornment by tenant in tail.

reserving rent, on the grant of the reversion in fee reserving rent, the attornment of terre-tenant vests the reversion, although rent not named, it being incident to the reversion, § 225, 229, 347.

of years, or for term of life, or a gift in the tail, is made to any man, reserving to such lessor, or donor, a certain rent, &c., if such lessor, or donor, grant his reversion to another, and the tenant of the land attorn, the rent passeth to the grantee, although in the deed of the grant of the reversion no mention be made of the rent, for that the rent is incident to the reversion in such case, and not *è converso*. For if a man willeth to grant the rent in such case to another, reserving to him the reversion of the land; although the tenant attorn to the grantee, this shall be but a rent-seck, &c.

The sixth example of an attornment in law, *viz. case of a remainder whereunto attornment is requisite.*

573 Also, if a man let land to another for his life, and afterwards he confirm by his deed the estate of the tenant for life, the remainder to another in fee, and the tenant for term of life accept the deed, then is the remainder in deed to him to whom the remainder was given or limited by the same deed, [for] by acceptance of the tenant for life [of the same deed*], this is an [agreement†] of him (*i. e.* to attorn), and so

Acceptance by tenant of particular estate is an attornment.

terme de vie, ou done en le taille, est fait a ascun home, reservaunt a tiel lessour, ou donour, un certeyn rente, &c., si tiel lessour, ou donour, graunta sa revercion a un autre, et le tenaunt del terre attourna, le rente passa al graunté, coment que en le fait del graunt del revercion nul mencion soit fait de le rente, pur ceo que le rente est incident al revercion en tiel cas, et nemye è converso. *Qar si home voille graunter le rente en tiel cas a un autre, reservaunt a luy la revercion del terre; coment que le tenaunt attourna al graunté, ceo serra forsque un rente-sekke, &c.*

573 Item, *si home lessa terre a un autre pur terme de sa vie, et puis il conferma per son fait lestate del tenaunt a terme de vie, le remeyndre a un autre en fee, et le tenaunt a terme de vie accepta le fait, donques est le remeyndre en fait a celuy a qui le remeyndre fuist done ou lymite per mesme le fait, [qar] per acceptaunce del tenaunt a terme de vie [del mesme le fait*], ceo est un [agreement†] de luy, et issint un attourne-*

* The words within brackets are given in all the copies of *Rastell's*

† The editions of *Rastell's* Transl. since *Powell* 1551, except *Marshe*,

an attornment in law. But yet he in the remainder shall have no action of waste nor other benefit by such remainder, unless that he hath the said deed in hand, whereby the remainder was entailed or granted unto him. And because that in such case the tenant for life peradventure will retain* to him the deed, to the intent that he in the remainder should have not† any action of waste against him, so that he cannot come to have the deed in his possession, &c., it shall be good in such case for him in the remainder, that a deed indented be made by him that will make such confirmation and the remainder over, &c., and that he that maketh such confirmation deliver one part of the indenture to the tenant for term of life, and the other part to him that shall have the remainder. And then he by shewing of the part of the indenture is able to have action of waste against the tenant for term of life, and all

Profert of deed of grant.

Counterparts of indentures are the same as originals.

ment en ley. Mes unqore celuy en le remeyndre navera ascun accion de wast ne autre benefice per tiel remeyndre, sinon queil avoet le dit fait en poigne, per que le remeyndre fuist taillé ou graunte a luy. Et pur ceo que en tiel cas le tenaunt a terme de vie voille per cas reteigner le fait a luy, a cel entent que celuy en le remeyndre naveroit ascun accion de wast envers luy, pur ceo que il ne poet vener davèr le fait en sa possession, &c., il serra bon en tiel cas pur celuy en le remeyndre, que un fait endente soit fait per celuy qui voille faire tiel confirmacion et le remeyndre ouster, &c., et que celuy qui fait tiel confirmacion delivera une parte del endenture al tenaunt a terme de vie, et le autre parte a celuy qui avera le remeyndre. Et donques il per monstrance de le parte del endenture, poet aver accion de wast envers le te-*

Translation, as well as in most of the French copies, but they do not occur in the three earliest editions.

1556, read this word *grant;* all the other editions, French as well as English, in this instance, accord with the text.

* This word in *Lettou & M.*, *Machl.*, and *Roh.* is printed *resceyver*, *receive; Rastell's* Transl. gives *retain.*

† Some editions of *Rastell's* Transl. since *Tottyl*, 1556, omit this word, but erroneously.

other advantages that he in the remainder can have in such case, &c.

In what cases attornment unnecessary. *If joint-tenants make a lease for life, rendering rent, and one of them release to the other, attornment not necessary.*

574 Also, if two joint-tenants be, the which let the land to another for term of life, rendering to them and to their heirs a certain rent by the year: in this case, if one of the joint-tenants in the reversion release to the other joint-tenant in the same reversion, this release is good; and he to whom the release is made shall have solely the rent of the tenant for term of life, and shall solely have a writ of waste against him, although he never attorned by force of such release. And the reason is, on account of the privity which at one time was between the tenant for life and them in reversion. 575 In the same manner, and for the same cause is it, where a man letteth land to another for term of life, the remainder to another for term of life, reserving the reversion to him; in this case, if he in the reversion release to him in the remainder and to his heirs all his right, &c., then he in the remainder hath a fee, &c., and shall have writ of waste against the tenant for term of life, without any attornment of him, &c.

Lease for life, remainder for life, lessor releases to remainder-man for life, attornment of lessee for life not necessary.

naunt a terme de vie, et toutes autres avauntages que celuy en le remeyndre poet aver en tiel cas, &c.

574 Item, *si deux jointenauntes soient, les queux lessont la terre a un autre pur terme de vie, rendant a eux et a lour heires certeyn rente per an: en ceo cas, si un des jointenauntes en la revercion relessa a lautre jointenaunt en mesme la revercion, cest reles est bon; et celuy a qui le reles est fait avera solement le rente del tenaunt a terme de vie, et avera solement un brief de wast envers luy, coment que il ne unques attourneroit per force de tiel reles. Et la cause est, pur le privité que a un foitz fuist perentre le tenaunt a terme de vie et eux en la revercion.* 575 *En mesme le manere, et pur mesme la cause est, lou home lessa terre a un autre pur terme de vie, le remeyndre a un autre pur terme de vie, reservaunt la revercion al luy; en ceo cas, si celuy en la revercion relessa a celuy en le remeyndre et a ses heires tout son droit, &c., donques celuy en le remeyndre ad un fee, &c., et avera un brief de wast envers le tenaunt a terme de vie, sauns ascun attournement de luy, &c.*

576* Also, if a man let lands or tenements to another for term of years, and afterwards he oust his termor, and thereof enfeoff another in fee, and afterwards the tenant for years enter upon the feoffee, in claiming his term, &c., and afterwards commits waste; in this case the feoffee shall have by law a writ of waste against him, and yet he did not attorn. And the reason is, as I suppose, because he that hath right to have lands or tenements for years, [or otherwise†], should not by law be misconusant of the feoffments which were made of and upon the same lands, &c., and insomuch as by such feoffment the tenant for years was [put out of his possession, and by his entry he caused the reversion to be to him to whom the feoffment was†] made, this is a good attornment; for he to whom the feoffment was made had no reversion before the tenant for years had entered upon him, because he was seised in his demesne as of fee, and by the entry of the tenant for

Doctrine of notice in law. *Case of attornment by re-entry. The sum of this and the two preceding sections, is, that where privity exists before the grant, there needs no attornment upon the grant.*

576* Item, *si home lessa terres ou tenementes a un autre pur terme des ans, et puis il ousta son termour, et ent enfeoffa un autre en fee, et puis le tenaunt a terme dans entra sur le feoffé, enclaymant son terme, &c., et puis fait wast; en ceo cas le feoffé avera per la ley un brief de wast envers luy, et unqore il nattornerast pas. Et la cause est, cōme jeo suppose, pur ceo que celuy qui ad droit daver terres ou tenementes pur terme dans, [ou autrement†], ne serroit per la ley misconusaunt de les feoffementes que furent faitz de et sur mesmes les terres, &c., et entaunt que per tiel feoffement le tenaunt a terme dans fuist [mys hors de sa possession, et per son entré il causast la revercion destre a celuy a qui le feoffement fuist†] fait, ceo est bon attournement; qar celuy a qui le feoffement fuist fait avoit nulle revercion devaunt que le tenaunt a terme dans avoit entré sur luy, pur ceo queil fuist seisi en son demesne come de fee, et per lentré del tenaunt*

---

* This section does not appear in any edition of *Rastell's* Translation.

† The words within brackets do not appear in *Lettou & M., Machl.*, or *Roh.*

years he hath but a reversion, the which is by the act of the tenant for term of years, *scil.* by his entry, &c. 577* The same law is, as it seemeth, where a lease is made for term of life, saving the reversion to the lessor, if the lessor disseise the lessee, and make a feoffment in fee, if the tenant for term of life enter and make waste, the feoffee† shall have a writ of waste without any other attornment, *Causa qua supra.*

Lease for life, remainder in tail, remainder to the right heirs of tenant for life, who grants his remainder in fee, attornment of tenant in tail not necessary.

§ 194, 273.

578 Also, if lease be made for term of life, the remainder unto another in the tail, the remainder over to the right heirs of the tenant for term of life; in this case if the tenant for term of life grant his remainder in fee to another by his deed, that remainder forthwith passeth by the deed without any attornment. For if any one ought to attorn in this case, it should be the tenant for term of life; and in vain it would be that he should attorn upon his own grant (*a*).

a terme dans il y ad forsque une revercion, lequele est per le fait le tenaunt a terme dans, scil. *per son entré, &c.* 577* *Mesme la ley est, come il semble, lou un lees est fait pur terme de vie, savaunt la revercion al lessour, si le lessour disseisist le lessé, et fait feoffement en fee, si le tenaunt a terme de vie entra et fait wast, le feoffé† avera brief de wast sans ascun autre attournement,* Causa qua supra.

578 Item, *si lees soit fait pur terme de vie, le remeyndre a un autre en le taille, le remeyndre oustre a les droit heires le tenaunt a terme de vie ; en ceo cas si le tenaunt a terme de vie graunta son remeyndre en fee a autre per son fait, cel remeyndre meyntenant passa per le fait sauns ascun attournement. Qar si ascun doit attourner en ceo cas, ceo serroit le tenaunt a terme de vie; et en vayn serroit quil attourneroit sur son graunt demesne.*

---

* This section does not appear in any edition of *Rastell's* Translation.

† This word is misprinted *lessé, lessee,* in *Lettou & M., Machl.,* and *Roh.*

(*a*) Here it appeareth, that where the ancestor taketh an estate of

579 Also, if there be lord and tenant, and the tenant hold of the lord by certain rent and knight's service, if the lord grant the services of his tenant by fine, the services are forthwith in the grantee by force of the fine; but yet the lord can not distrain for any parcel of the services without attornment: but if the tenant die, his heir being within age, the lord shall have the wardship of the body of the heir, and of the lands, &c., albeit he never attorned, because the seignory was in the grantee forthwith by force of the fine. And also in such case, if the tenant die without heir, the lord shall have the tenancy* by way of escheat.†

Grant by fine good for many purposes before attornment.

Some advantages the conusee of a fine might have before attornment; but yet he could not distrain;

† *For before attornment the seignory is fully settled in the grantee by the fine, see* § 583.

579 Item, *si soit seignour et tenaunt, et le tenaunt tient del seignour per certeyn rente et service de chivaler, si le seignour graunta les services de son tenaunt per fyn, les services sount meyntenaunt en le graunté per force del fyn; mes unqore le seignour ne poet pas distreyner pur ascun parcel de les services sauns attournement: mes si le tenaunt devia, son heire esteant deins age, le seignour avera le garde del corps del heire, et de les terres, &c., coment quil ne unques attournast, pur ceo que la seignourie fuist en le graunté meyntenaunt per force del fyn. Et auxi en tiel cas, si le tenaunt morust sauns heire, le seignour avera la tenauncie* per voye deschete.*

* *Redm.*, *Berth.*, *Middl.*, *Sm.*, *Powell*, and *Tottyl* 1554, read, *te-*

freehold, and after a remainder is limited to his right heirs, that the fee-simple vesteth in himself as well as if it had been limited to him and to his heirs; for *his right heirs* are in this case words of limitation of estate, and not of purchase. Otherwise it is, where the ancestor taketh but an estate for years; as if a lease for years be made to A., the remainder to B. in tail, the remainder to the right heirs of A., there the remainder vesteth not in A., but the right heirs shall take by purchase, if A. die during the estate-tail; for as the ancestor and the heir are *correlativa* of inheritances, so are the testator and executor, or the intestate and administrator of chattels. And so it is, if A. make a feoffment in fee to the use of B. for life, and after to the use of C. for life, or in tail, and after to the use of the right heirs of B., B. hath the fee-simple in him as well when it is by way of limitation of use, as when it is by act executed. *Co. Lytt.* 319. b.

or have action of waste.

580 In the same manner it is, if a man grant the reversion of his tenant for life to another by fine, the reversion forthwith passeth* to the grantee by force of the fine, but the grantee shall never have an action of waste without attornment, &c.: 581 but yet if the tenant for term of life alien in fee, the grantee can enter, &c., because the reversion was in him by force of the fine, and such alienation was to his disheritance. 582 But in this case where the lord granteth the services of his tenant by fine, if the tenant die, his heir being of full age, the grantee by the fine shall not have relief, nor shall ever distrain for relief, unless there had been attornment of the tenant that died, &c.; for of such thing that lieth in distress, whereupon the writ of replevin is sued, &c., a man should and ought to avow the taking good and rightful, &c., and there ought to be an attornment of the tenant, although

Yet on alienation in fee of tenant for life, grantee of reversion might enter.

The same distinction, § 579.

580 *En mesme le manere est, si home graunta la revercion de son tenaunt a terme de vie a un autre per fyn, la revercion passa meyntenaunt al grauntê per force del fyn, mes le grauntê jammes navera accion de wast sauns attournement, &c.:* 581 *mes unqore si le tenaunt a terme de vie alienast en fee, le grauntê poet entrer, &c., pur ceo que la revercion fuist en luy per force del fyn, et tiel alienacion fuist a son disheritaunce.* 582 *Mes en ceo cas lou le seignour graunta les services de son tenaunt per fyn, si le tenaunt devie, son heire esteant de pleyn age, le grauntê per le fyn navera relief, ne unques distreynera pur relief, si non que fusoit attournement del tenaunt qui morust, &c.; qar de tiel chose que gist en distresse, sur que le brief de replevin est suy, &c., home doit et covient davower le pris bon et droiturel, &c., et là covient estre attournement del*

---

nancy, and so do all the editions of *Rastell's* Transl. *Sir Ed. Coke's* Translation also renders *tenancy*, though all the later French editions read *tenements*.

* The editions of *Rastell's* Transl. previous to, and inclusive of, *Marshe* 1556, read, *passeth anon*, which, in some subsequent editions by *Tottyl*, is corrupted to, *passeth not*. *Jane Yetsweirt*, 1597, reads, *passeth presently*.

the grant of such things* be by fine; but to have the wardship of the lands or tenements so holden during the nonage of the heir, or to have them by way of escheat, there needeth not any distress, &c., but an entry into the land by force of the right of the seignory which the grantee hath by force of the fine, &c.† *Et sic vide diversitatem, &c.*

583‡ Also, if there be lord, mesne, and tenant, and the mesne grant by fine the services of his tenant to another in fee, and afterwards the grantee die without heir, now the services of the mesnalty shall come to, and shall escheat to, the lord paramount by way of escheat; if afterwards the services of the mesnalty be in arrear, in this case he that was lord paramount can distrain the tenant, notwithstanding that the tenant did never attorn; and the reason is, because the mesnalty was in deed in

Escheat of mesnalty before attornment and avowry on mesne before attornment: ***where any one comes in by title paramount as by escheat [or by surrender, forfeiture, or by descent], attornment of tenant is useless.***

tenaunt, coment que le graunt de tielx choses soit per fyn; mes daver le garde de les terres ou tenementes issint tenus duraunt le nonnage leire, ou de eux aver per voye deschete, là ne besoigne ascun distresse, &c., mes un entré en la terre per force de le droit del seignourie que le graunté ad per force del fyn, &c.*† Et sic vide diversitatem, &c.

583‡ Item, *si soit seignour, mesne, et tenaunt, et le mesne graunta per fyn les services de son tenaunt a un autre en fee, et puis le graunté morust sauns heire, ore les services del mesnaltë deviendront et escheteront al seignour paramont per voye deschete; si apres les services del mesnaltë sont aderere, en ceo cas celuy qui fuist seignour paramont poet distreyner le tenaunt, nient obstant que le tenaunt ne unques attournast; et la cause est, pur ceo que le mesnaltë fuist en fait en le*

---

* *Services; Rastell's* Translation.

† This *&c.* and the concluding words are not given in those editions of *Rastell's* Translation since *Powell* 1551, and *Marshe* 1556, viz. by *Tottyl* 1556, and subsequently to 1661.

‡ This section does not appear in those editions of *Rastell's* Translation by *Tottyl* 1556, and subsequent editions to 1661; but it is given in previous editions, and in *Marshe* 1556.

Attornment not necessary where a man comes to the seignory or reversion by act of law.

the grantee by force of the fine, and the lord paramount could avow upon the grantee, because he was his tenant in deed, although he should not be thereto compelled, &c. But if the grantor in this case had died without heir in the life of the grantee, then he should be compelled to avow upon the grantee, and also insomuch as the lord paramount doth not claim the mesnalty by force of the grant made by fine levied by the mesne, &c., but by virtue of his seignory paramount, by way of escheat, he shall avow upon the tenant for the services which the mesne had, &c., albeit that the tenant did never attorn. 584* In the same manner it is, where the reversion of a tenant for term of life is granted by fine to another in fee, and the grantee afterwards dieth without heir, now the lord hath the reversion by way of escheat; and if afterwards the tenant commit waste, the lord shall have a writ of waste against him, notwithstanding that he never attorned, *Causa qua supra.*† But where a man claimeth by force of the

(By stat. 21 Hen. 8, c. 19, avowry for rent-service is to be made upon the land and not upon the person), § 457.

graunté per force de le fyn, et le seignour paramont puissoit avower sur le graunté, pur ceo que il fuist son tenaunt en fait, coment que il ne serroit a ceo compelle, &c. Mes si le grauntour en ceo cas deviast sauns heire en la vie le graunté, donques il serroit compelle davower sur le graunté, et auxi entant que le seignour paramont ne clayma le mesnaltë per force del graunt fait per fyn levé per le mesne, &c., mes per vertue de son seignourie paramont, per voye deschete, il avowera sur le tenaunt pur les services que le mesne avoit, &c., coment que le tenaunt ne unques attournast pas. 584* *En mesme le manere est, lou la revercion dun tenaunt a terme de vie soit graunte per fyn a un autre en fee, et le graunté apres morust sauns heire, ore le seignour ad la revercion per voye deschete; et si apres le tenaunt fait wast, le seignour avera brief de wast envers luy, nient contristeant quil ne unques attournast,* Causa qua supra.† *Mes lou un home clayma per force del*

* See p. 563, (‡).

† In *Tottyl*, 1588, a small *asterisk* is placed over this word, to denote, it is presumed, that this *causa qua supra* is questionable.

grant made by the fine, &c., *scil.* as heir, or as assignee, &c., there he shall not distrain or have action of waste, &c., without attornment.

585 Also, in ancient boroughs and cities, where lands and tenements within the same boroughs and cities are devisable by testament, by custom and the use, &c., if in such borough or city a man be seised of rent-service, or of rent-charge, and he devise such rent or service to another by his testament, and die, in this case he to whom such devise is made may distrain the tenant for the rent or service being arrear, although the tenant did never attorn (*b*). 586 In the same manner is it,

Attornment not necessary in the case of a devise of rents; for devisee may distrain.

In the case of a

graunt fait per le fyn, &c., scil. *come heire, ou come assigné, &c., là il ne distreynera ne avera accion de wast, &c., sauns attournement.*

585 Item, *en aunciens boroghes et citees, lou terres et tenementes deins mesme les boroghes et citees sount devisables per testament, per custome et le use, &c., si en tiel boroghe ou citee home soit seisi de rent-service, ou de rent-charge, et il devisa tiel rente ou service a un autre per son testament, et morust, en ceo cas celuy a qui tiel devise est fait poet distreyner le tenaunt pur le rente ou service esteant aderere, coment que le tenaunt nattournast pas.* 586 *En mesme le ma-*

(*b*) By the common law of England since the Conquest, no estate, greater than for term of years, could be disposed of by testament; except only in Kent, and in some ancient burghs, and a few particular manors, where their Saxon immunities by special indulgence subsisted (§ 167). And though the feudal restraint on alienations by deed vanished very early, yet this on wills continued for some centuries after, from an apprehension of infirmity and imposition on the testator *in extremis*, which made such devises suspicious. Besides, in devises there was wanting that general notoriety, and public designation of the successor, which in descents is apparent to the neighbourhood, and which the simplicity of the common law always required in every transfer and new acquisition of property.

But when ecclesiastical ingenuity had invented the doctrine of uses, as a thing distinct from the land, uses began to be devised very fre-

devise of the reversion, devisee may have action of waste.

where a man letteth such tenements devisable, to another for term of life or for term of years, and deviseth the reversion by his testament to another in fee, or in fee-tail, and dieth, and afterwards the tenant commits waste, he to whom the devise

nere est, lou home lessa tielx tenementes devisables, a un autre pur terme de vie ou pur terme dans, et devisa la reversion per son testament a un autre en fee, ou en fee-taille, et morust, et puis le tenaunt fait wast, celuy a qui le devise fuist fait avera

---

quently, and the devisee of the use could in chancery compel its execution. But when the statute of uses had annexed the possession to the use, these uses, being now the very land itself, became no longer devisable; which might have occasioned a great revolution in the law of devises, had not the statute of wills been made about five years after, viz. 32 Hen. 8, c. 1. explained by 34 Hen. 8, c. 5., which enacted that all persons being seised in fee-simple (except feme-coverts, infants, idiots, and persons of nonsane memory) might by will and testament in writing devise to any other person, but not to bodies corporate, two thirds of their lands, tenements and hereditaments, held in chivalry, and the whole of those held in socage; which now, through the alteration of tenures by the statute of Charles the Second, amounts to the whole of their landed property, except their copyhold tenements. [And these last by the statutory fiction which presumes a surrender *to the use of the will* are at last placed on the same footing with other real property.—B.C. ii. 375.]

The custom of the city of London, *viz.* that the freemen as well as the inhabitants of that city, may devise their tenements by will, and if freemen, in mortmain, (*Dyer*, 255), appears to be a consequence of their burgage tenure, (for a city is but a borough incorporated, *Co. Lytt.* 109. b.), which tenure is frank-burgage of the city (not of the king), and was always as such, deemed a socage tenure, (*Dalison*, 6 *Eliz.*, and *Bendloes*, 20 *Eliz.* (*Ashe's Table*)), consequently not altered by the Statute of Wills. However by the custom such devise should be inrolled in the hustings, and within a convenient time, (*Cro. Car.* 669); which is a proof *per testes.*—See *Bohun's Priv. Lond.* 208-11, *ed.* 1723.

It is said, that by the ancient custom of London, where reversions of rents are devised by a will inrolled in the hustings, such reversions are so executed, that, after the testator's death, the devisee may distrain and make avowry, or sue a writ of waste, without any attornment of the tenants, &c.—*Ibid.*

was made shall have writ of waste, although the tenant doth never attorn. And the reason is, because the will of the devisor made by his testament shall be performed according to the intent of the devisor; and if the effect of this should lie upon the attornment of the tenant, &c., then perchance the tenant would never attorn, and then the will of the devisor should never be performed, and therefore the devisee shall distrain, &c., or shall have an action of waste, &c., without attornment. For if a man devise such tenements to another by his testament, *Habendum sibi in perpetuum,* and dieth, and the devisee enter, he hath fee-simple, *Causa qua supra:* and yet if* deed of feoffment had been made to him by the devisor, of the same tenements, *Habendum sibi in perpetuum,* and livery of seisin were made thereupon, he shall have estate but for term of his life.

Voluntas testatoris observetur.

brief de wast, coment que le tenaunt ne unques attournast. Et la cause est, pur ceo que la volunté le devisour fait per son testament serroit perfourme solonques lentent del devisour; et si leffecte de ceo girroit sur lattournement del tenaunt, &c., donques percas le tenaunt ne voille unques attourner, et donques la volunté del devisour ne serroit unques perfourme, et pur ceo le devisé distreynera, &c., ou avera accion de wast, &c., sauns attournement. Qar si home devisa tielx tenementes a un autre per son testament, Habendum sibi in perpetuum, *et morust, et le devisé entra, il ad fee-simple,* Causa qua supra: *et unqore si* fait de feoffement ust estre fait a luy per le devisour, de mesmes les tenementes,* Habendum sibi in perpetuum, *et lyverë de seisin sur ceo fuist fait, il navera estate forsque pur terme de sa vie.*

---

* This word is printed *le, the,* in *Lettou & M., Machl., Roh.,* and *Rastell's* Transl. *Rastell's* Translation reads the concluding passage of this section thus, but erroneously, *viz. if livery and seisin were* never *thereupon made upon this* ——.

An estate of a seignory cannot be gained by a disseisin, abatement, or intrusion, without an attornment.

587 Also, if a man seised of a manor which is parcel in demesne and parcel in service, and thereof be disseised, but the tenants that hold of the manor do never attorn to the disseisor: in this case, albeit the disseisor die seised, and his heir is in by descent, &c., yet can the disseisee distrain for the rent behind, and have the services, &c. But if the tenants come to the disseisor, and say, we become your tenants, &c., or other attornment to him make, &c., and afterwards the disseisor die seised, then the disseisee cannot distrain for the rent, &c., for that all the manor descendeth to the heir of the disseisor, &c. 588 But if one hold of me by rent-service, which is a service in gross, and another that no right hath, claimeth the same rent to receive, and taketh the same rent of my tenant by coercion of distress, or by other form, and disseiseth me by such taking of the rent, albeit such disseisor dieth so seised in receiving of the rent, yet after his death I can well distrain the tenant for the rent

And therefore if one disseise another of a manor which is part in demesne and part in services, the services are not gained until the tenants attorn.

587 Item, *si home seisi dun manor quel est parcel en demesne et parcel en service, et ent soit disseisi, mes les tenauntes qui teignount del manor ne unques attournent al disseisour: en ceo cas, coment que le disseisour morust seisi, et son heire soit eins per discent, &c., unqore poet le disseisi distreyner pur le rente arere, et aver les services, &c. Mes si les tenauntes viendront al disseisour, et diont, nous deveignomus vostre tenauntes, &c., ou autre attournement a luy fesoient, &c., et puis le disseisour morust seisi, donques le disseisi ne poet distreyner pur le rente, &c., pur ceo que tout le manor descendist al heire le disseisour, &c.* 588 *Mes si un tient de moy per rente-service, le quele est un service en gros, et un autre que nul droit ad, claymast mesme le rente a resceiver, et prent mesme le rente de mon tenaunt per cohercion de distresse, ou per autre forme, et disseisist moy per tiel prendre del rente, coment que tiel disseisour morust issint seisi en pernant de rente, unqore apres sa mort jeo poy bien distreyner le*

which was behind before the distress* of the disseisor, and also after his decease. And the cause is, for that such disseisor is not my disseisor, but at my election and my will. For albeit that he take the rent of my tenant, &c., yet I can at all times distrain my tenant for the rent behind, &c., so that it is to me but as if I am willing to suffer the tenant to be so long time behind payment of the same rent unto me, &c. 589 For the payment of my tenant to another, to whom he ought not to pay, is no disseisin to me, nor ousteth me of my rent, without my will or without my election; for although I may have an assise against such pernor, yet this is at my election, whether I will take him as my disseisor, or not. So that such descents of rents in gross shall not oust the lords of their distress, but at each time they† can well distrain for the rent behind, &c. And

Disseisin at election.

A man shall not be disseised of rent-service in gross, rent-charge or rent-seck by attornment made to a stranger, but at his election or pleasure.

tenaunt pur le rente que fuist aderere devaunt le distresse del disseisour, et auxi apres son decesse. Et la cause est, pur ceo que tiel disseisour nest pas mon disseisour, forsque a ma eleccion et ma volunté. Qar coment quil prent le rente de mon tenaunt, &c., unquore jeo puissoy a toutez foitz distreyner mon tenaunt pur le rente arere, &c., issint que il est a moy forsque sicome jeo voille suffrer le tenaunt estre per tant de temps arere de paier a moy mesme le rente, &c.* 589 *Qar le paiement de mon tenaunt a un autre, a quil ne doit pas paier, nest pas disseisin a moy, ne ousta moy pas de mon rente, sauns ma volunté ou sauns mon eleccion; qar coment que jeo puissoy aver assise envers tiel pernor, unqore cest a mon eleccion, si jeo voille prendre luy come mon disseisour, ou non. Issint tielx discentz de rentes en gros ne ousteront pas les seignours de distreyner, mes a chescun temps ils† poient bien distreyner pur le rente arere, &c. Et en ceo cas, si apres*

* In all other than the three earliest editions, French as well as English, this word is printed *decease*, and *death*.

† *Roh.* reads, but erroneously—ils *ne* poient.

in this case, if after the distress* of him that so wrongfully took the rent, I grant by my deed the service to another, and the tenant attorn, this is good enough, and the services by the grant and attornment are forthwith in the grantee, &c. But otherwise it is, where the rent is parcel of the manor, and the disseisor dieth seised of the whole manor, as in the case next aforesaid, &c.

Secus *where the rent is parcel of a manor and a descent is cast.*

590† Also, if I be seised‡ of a manor, parcel in demesne, and parcel in service, and I give certain acres of the land, parcel of the demesne of the same manor, to another in the tail yielding to me and to my heirs a certain rent, &c., if in this case I be disseised of the manor, and all the tenants attorn and pay their rents to the disseisor, and also the said

A man shall not be disseised of rent incident to the reversion, but at his election, so long as the lessee is in possession.

le distresse de luy que issint torciousement prist le rente, jeo graunta per mon fait le service a un autre, et le tenaunt attourna, cest assetes bon, et les services per le graunt et attournement meyntenaunt sount en le graunté, &c. Mes autrement est, lou le rente est parcel del manor, et le disseisour morust seisi del manor entier, come en le cas proscheyn avaunt dit, &c.*

590† Item, *si jeo suy seisi‡ dun manor, parcel en demesne, et parcel en service, et jeo done certeyn acres del terre, parcel del demesne de mesme le manor, a un autre en le taille rendaunt a moy et a mes heires un certeyn rente, &c., si en ceo cas jeo suy disseisi de le manor, et toutes les tenauntes attournont et paiont lour rentes al disseisour, et auxi le dit tenaunt en*

---

* In *Lettou & M.*, *Machl.*, *Roh.*, *Redm.*, *Berth.*, and in every other French edition, except the edition by *Charles Yetsweirt* (*circa*) 1594, and that of *Jane Yetsweirt* (*circa*) 1597, this word is read as in the text; but these two editions, as well as all the editions of *Rastell's* Translation, read *decease*. The French edition by *Jane Yetsweirt* places the word *decease* between two *asterisks*, as denoting a new correction of the text.

† See § 563, (‡).

‡ This word is printed *disseisi*, in *Roh.*

tenant in tail pay the rent by me reserved to the disseisor, and afterwards the disseisor die seised, &c.,* and his heir enter, and is in by descent, yet in this case I can well distrain the tenant in the tail, and his heirs, for the rent by me reserved upon the gift, *scil.* as well for the rent being in arrear before the descent to the heir of the disseisor, as also for the rent which happeneth to be in arrear after the same descent, notwithstanding such dying seised of the disseisor, &c. And the reason is, for that when a man giveth tenements to another in the tail, saving the reversion to him*self*, and he upon the said gift reserveth to him*self* a rent or other services, all the rent and the services are incident to the reversion; and when a man hath a reversion, he cannot be ousted of his reversion by the act of a stranger, unless that the tenant be ousted of his estate and possession, &c. For so long in this case as

For seisin and possession of the particular tenant, is seisin of him in the reversion.

le taille paie le rente per moy reserve al disseisour, et puis le disseisour morust seisi, &c., et son heire entra, et est einz per discent, unqore en ceo cas jeo puis bien distreyner le tenaunt en le taille, et ses heires, pur le rente per moy reserve sur le done,* scil. *auxi bien pur le rente esteant aderere devaunt le discent al heire le disseisour, et auxi pur le rente que happa estre aderere apres mesme le discent, nient obstant tiel murrant seisi del disseisour, &c. Et la cause est, pur ceo que quaunt home dona tenementes a un autre en le taille, savaunt la revercion a luy, et il sur le dit done reserva a luy un rente ou autres services, tout le rente et les services sount incidentes a la revercion ; et quaunt un home ad une revercion, il ne puissoit estre ouste de sa revercion per le fait dun estraunge home, si non que le tenaunt soit ouste de son estate et possession, &c. Qar si longement en ceo cas que le*

* This *&c.* does not occur in *Machl.* or *Roh.*, but it is given in *Rastell's* Transl., *Powell* 1548, 1551, and *Marshe* 1556, *Tottyl* 1556, and subsequent editions, do not retain this section.

the tenant in tail and his heirs continue their possession by force of my gift, so long is the reversion in me and in my heirs: and insomuch as the rent and services reserved upon the gift be incident and dependant upon the reversion, whosoever hath the reversion shall have the same rent and the services, &c.

Distinction between rents and services parcel of a manor, and rents and services incident to a reversion parcel of a manor.

591* In the same manner it is, where I let parcel of the demesne of the manor to another for term of life, or for term of years, rendering to me a certain rent, &c., albeit I be disseised of the manor, &c., and the disseisor die seised, and his heir be in by descent, yet I can distrain for the rent arrear, notwithstanding such descent, *ut supra:* for when a man hath made such gift in tail, or such lease for life, or for term of years, of parcel of the demesnes of a manor, &c., saving the reversion to such donor or lessor, &c., and afterwards he is disseised of the manor, &c., such reversion after such disseisin is severed from the manor in deed, though it

tenaunt en le taille et ses heires continuont lour possession per force de mon done, si longement est la revercion en moy et en mes heires: et entaunt que le rente et les services reserves sur le done sont incidentes et dependantes al revercion, quiconques qui ad la revercion avera mesme le rente et les services, &c.

591* *En mesme le manere est, lou jeo lessa parcel del demesne del manor a un autre pur terme de vie, ou pur terme dans, rendaunt a moy certeyn rente, &c., coment que jeo suy disseisi del manor, &c., et le disseisour morust seisi, et son heire esteant einz per discent, unqore jeo distreynera pur le rente arere, nient obstant tiel discent,* ut supra: *qar quaunt home ad fait tiel done en le taille, ou tiel lees pur terme de vie, ou pur terme dans, del parcel de les demesnes dun manor, &c., savaunt la revercion a tiel donour ou lessour, &c., et puis il soit disseisi de le manor, &c., tiel revercion apres tiel disseisin est severe del manor en fait, coment que ne soit severe en*

* See p. 563, (‡).

be not severed in right, &c.* And so thou mayst see, my son, a diversity where there is a manor parcel in demesne and parcel in services, the which services are parcel of the same manor not incident to any reversion, &c., and where they are incident to the reversion, &c.

droit, &c. Et issint poies veier, mon fitz, diversité lou il y ad un manor parcel en demesne et parcel en services, les queux services sont parcel de mesme le manor nient incidentes a ascun revercion, &c., et lou ils sount incidentes al revercion, &c.*

---

* This *&c.* does not occur in *Machl.* or *Roh.*, or in *Rastell's* Translation, *Powell* 1548, 1551, *Marshe* 1556. This section also does not appear in *Tottyl* 1556, and subsequent English editions to 1661.

CHAPTER XI.

DISCONTINUANCE.

The doctrine of discontinuance is a consequence of tenure (*a*). It is defined to be such an alienation of things which lie in livery, *scil.* corporeal hereditaments, as takes away the right of entry of the person entitled after the death of the alienor, and puts such person to his action. A consequence also, from one of the principles of tenure, is, that a prior estate in possession, and the remainders over, constitute but one estate (§ 60, 471); and that the residue of the fee is *supported* by the seisin of the party entitled to this prior or (as it is termed) *particular* estate. Therefore, if the particular estate be disrupted or disconnected from the remainders which depend upon it, the estate must be "discontinued," the link in the chain of interests which are carved out of the fee being broken.

By a discontinuance, the estate under the ancient title ceases, and another estate in fee-simple arises (§ 599), which, though it be not "legitimum" (§ 1), as being gained by wrong, and as being liable to be devested by a recovery on action brought, yet, till the rightful owner of the inheritance recover the seisin, the discontinuance remains in force. And he cannot make any disposition of the estate by deed or will, for the estate in the language of the law is *turned to*

(*a*) Therefore, the doctrine of discontinuance is, it is apprehended, confined to *legal* estates, and is not applicable to *equitable* estates. As to discontinuance generally, and its operation, see *Doe* d. —— v. *Finch*, 1 Nev. & M. 130, in n.; and Blackst. iii. 175.

a right, i. e. exists only in right as distinguished from possession.

Discontinuances, at the time Lyttleton wrote, could only be committed by three classes of tenants of the freehold. 1. Ecclesiastical persons. 2. Husbands seised in right of their wives. 3. Tenants in tail. With respect to the *first*, an alienation made by a *sole* corporation, as a bishop or dean, without consent of the chapter, was a discontinuance at common law; but the disabling statutes of 1 Eliz. c. 19, and 13 Eliz. c. 10, have declared all such alienations void *ab initio*. With regard to the *second*, the alienation of husbands seised in right of their wives operated as, or "worked," a discontinuance at common law, till the stat. 32 Hen. 8, c. 28, provided that no act *by the husband alone* should work a discontinuance of, or prejudice the inheritance of the wife; but that after his death, she, or her heirs, might enter on the lands aliened. The *third* instance in which a discontinuance could be worked, was by tenant in tail, when he made a larger estate of the land than by law he was entitled to do; in which case the estate was only good so far as the power of him who made it extended, or during the continuance of the estate tail or till avoidance, but no further (*b*).

Lyttleton commences the subject, in his usual manner, by definition and example, and then proceeds to explain what alienations work a discontinuance; and incidentally demonstrates the distinction which prevails between rightful or innocent, and tortious or wrongful conveyances, and the effects of each (§ 598—600). Discontinuances, he shews by different cases, could be worked either by feoffment, (which included its equivalents—fine, or feigned recovery), or by release or confirmation with warranty, such warranty descending on the heir or rightful owner (§ 601). These

---

(*b*) With regard to discontinuances, by women, of estates tail *ex provisione viri*, see § 595, in n.

conveyances operated to the prejudice of wives, heirs, successors, reversioners, and remainder-men. And Lyttleton concludes by stating the cases in which a discontinuance may be temporary, and ultimately *purged* (§ 630, 636), defeated, or otherwise rendered inoperative (§ 632). With regard to the doctrine of discontinuance in tail, the knowledge of this part of the subject may be practically useful for some years; but the operation of the 3 & 4 Gul. 4, c. 27, § 39, will shortly make this learning, indeed the doctrine of discontinuances altogether, obsolete; for it is by this statute enacted, that no discontinuance made after the 31st December, 1833, shall *toll* (*i. e.* bar) or defeat any right of entry on action for the recovery of land (*c*).

Discontinuance *defined.*

592 DISCONTINUANCE is an ancient word in the law, and hath divers significations (*d*), &c. But as to one intent it hath such signification, that is to say, where one man hath aliened to another certain lands or tenements, and dieth, and

592 Discontinuaunce est un auncien parole en la ley, et ad diverses significacions, &c. Mes quaunt a un entent il ad tiel significacion, cestassavoir, lou un home ad aliene a un autre certeyn terres ou tenementes, et morust, et un autre ad

(*c*) By § 38 of this statute, real actions cannot be brought after twenty years from 1st June, 1835, during which time real actions may be brought by those whose right of entry has been taken away, but only within the period during which (according to the provisions of this Act) an entry might have been made, had not the right been so taken away. See *ante*, p. 446.

(*d*) Discontinuance is used by *Lytt.* § 470, for a devesting or displacing of a reversion, though the entry be not taken away; he also alludes to discontinuance of process. See also § 147, p. 183.

another (*or* third party) hath right to have the same lands or tenements, but he cannot enter into them, by reason of such alienation, &c. 593 As if an abbot seised of certain lands or tenements in fee, alien the same lands or tenements to another in fee, or in fee tail, or for term of life, and the abbot dieth, his successor cannot enter into the said lands or tenements, albeit he hath right to have them as in the right of his house; but is put to his action to recover the same lands or tenements, which is called *a writ de ingressu sine assensu capituli.*

Examples. 1. *Discontinuance by* ecclesiastical corporation.

[*This branch of the subject is continued at* § 651 *to* 657].

594 Also, if a man be seised of land as in the right of his wife, and thereof enfeoff another, and dieth, the wife cannot enter, but is put to her action, the which is called *Cui in vita*, &c.

2. *Discontinuance of husband seised* jure uxoris.

595 Also, if tenant in the tail (*e*) of certain land thereof

3. *Discontinu-*

droit daver mesmes les terres ou tenementes, mes il ne poet entrer en eux, per cause de tiel alienacion, &c. 593 *Sicome un abbé seisi de certeyn terres ou tenementes en fee, alienast mesmes les terres ou tenementes a un autre en fee, ou en fee-taille, ou pur terme de vie, et labbé morust, son successour ne poet entrer en les ditz terres ou tenementes, coment quil ad droit de eux aver come en droit de son meason; mes est mys a son accion de recoverer mesmes les terres ou tenementes, quel est appelle* Brief de ingressu sine assensu capituli.

594 Item, *si home soit seisi de terre come en droit de sa feme, et ent enfeoffa un autre, et morust, la feme ne poet entrer, mes est mys a son accion, le quele est appelle* Cui in vita, &c.

595 Item, *si tenaunt en le tuille de certeyn terre ent en-*

(*e*) This extended to a woman as well as a man, and was good law when *Lyttleton* wrote, consequently a woman, who had an estate-tail jointly with her husband, of lands of his, or relations', purchase, inheritance, or provision, could, after his decease, discontinue the same to the prejudice of his issue after her husband's decease.

ance by a tenant in tail, whose alienation discontinues the tail to the prejudice of his issue,

enfeoff another, &c., and hath issue, and dieth, his issue cannot enter into the land, albeit he hath title and right thereto, but is put to his action, which is called a *Formedon en le descendre, &c.*

the reversioner,

596 Also, if there be tenant in tail and the reversion is to the donor and his heirs, if the tenant make feoffment, and die without issue, he in the reversion cannot enter, but is put to his action of *Formedon en le reverter, &c.* 597 In the same manner is it, where tenant in tail seised of certain land, whereof the remainder is to another in the tail, or to another in fee: if the tenant in the tail alien in fee, or in fee-

and remainder-man.

feoffa un autre, &c., et ad issue, et morust, son issue ne poet pas entrer en la terre, coment quil ad title et droit a ceo, mes est mys a son accion, que est appelle Formedon en le descendre, &c.

596 Item, *si soit tenaunt en le taille et le revercion est al donour et a sez heires, si le tenaunt fait feoffement, et morust sauns issue, celuy en la revercion ne poet entrer, mes est mys a son accion de* Formedon en le reverter, &c. 597 *En mesme le manere est, lou tenaunt en le taille seisi de certeyne terre, dount le remeyndre est a un autre en le taille, ou a un autre en fee: si le tenaunt en le taille alienast en fee, ou en fee-*

But the stat. 11 Hen. 7, c. 20, provides that *every* alienation by "a woman having any estate in dower, or for life, or in tail jointly with her husband, or only to herself, or to her use in any manors, &c., the inheritance or purchase of her husband, or given to the husband and wife in tail, or for life by any of the ancestors of the husband, or by any other person seised to the use of the husband, or of his ancestors, shall be void and of no effect; and it shall be lawful for the person in remainder or reversion, to enter immediately."—This act was confirmed by stat. 32 Hen. 8, c. 36, s. 2, which provides that no fine levied by any woman of any such estate as is mentioned in the stat. 11 Hen. 7, shall be of any effect. After the death of the husband the wife may alien with concurrence of the issue in tail, or those having a prior estate in remainder or reversion (*Cro. Eliz.* 524); but such consent must appear on record.

tail, &c., and afterwards die without issue, those in the remainder cannot enter, but shall be put to their writ of *Formedon* in the remainder, &c., and for this that by force of such feoffments and alienations in the cases aforesaid, and in other like cases, those that have title and right after the death of such feoffor or alienor cannot enter, but are put to their actions, *ut supra;* and for this reason such feoffments and alienations are called discontinuances.

598 Also, if tenant in the tail be disseised, and he release by his deed to the disseisor and to his heirs all the right which he hath in the same tenements, this is not discontinuance, because nothing of the right passeth to the disseisor but for term of the life of tenant in the tail, that made the release, &c.

Release of right not a discontinuance, that being a rightful estate: i. e. *no more passes than what the relessor may rightfully convey:* contra *of feoffment which passes a fee-simple in possession and is tortious, turning the estate of the reversioner or remainder-man*

599 But by feoffment of the tenant in the tail, fee-simple passeth by the same feoffment by force of the livery of seisin, &c. 600 But by force of a release nothing passeth but the right which he can lawfully and rightfully release, without hurt or damage to other persons who shall have

taille, &c., et puis deviast sauns issue, ceux en le remeyndre ne poient entrer, mes serront mys a lour brief de Formedon *en le remeyndre, &c., et pur ceo que per force de tielx feoffementes et alienacions en les cases avauntdites, et en semblables autres cases, ceux queux ount title et droit apres la mort de tiel feoffour ou alienour ne poient pas entrer, mes sount mys a lour accions,* ut supra; *et pur ceo cause tielx feoffementes et alienacions sount appelles discontinuaunces.*

598 Item, *si tenaunt en le taille soit disseisi, et il relessa per son fait a le disseisour et a ses heires tout le droit le quel il ad en mesmes les tenementes, ceo nest pas discontinuaunce, pur ceo que riens de droit passa al disseisour forsque pur terme de vie le tenaunt en le taille, qui fist le reles, &c.*

599 *Mes per feoffement del tenaunt en le taille, fee-simple passa per mesme le feoffement per force de le lyverë de seisin, &c.* 600 *Mes per force dun reles rien passa forsque le droit que il poet loyalement et droiturelement relesser, sauns leede ou damage a autres persons queux ent averont droit apres*

to a mere right of action, so that a discontinuance cannot operate unless by livery or by a warranty descending on him that hath the right,

or on the issue inheritable.

right therein after his decease, &c. So there is a great diversity between a feoffment of the tenant in tail, and a release made by tenant in the tail. 601 But it is said, that if the tenant in the tail in this case release to his disseisor, and bind him and his heirs to warranty, &c., and die, and this warranty descend to (*i. e.* upon) his issue, then this is a discontinuance by reason of the warranty, &c. 602 But if a man hath issue a son by his wife, and his wife dieth, and afterwards he taketh another wife, and tenements are given to him and to his second wife, and to the heirs of their two bodies engendered, and they have issue another son, and the second wife dieth, and afterwards the tenant in the tail is disseised, and he release to the disseisor all his right, &c., and bind himself and his heirs to warranty, &c., and die, this is not discontinuance to the issue in the tail by the second wife, but he can well enter, &c., for this that the warranty descendeth upon his elder brother that his father had by the first wife. 603 In the same manner is it, where tenements are descendible to the youngest son after the custom of Borough-English which

§ 718. 735. 736, *where it is shewn, that warranty shall not be a bar unless it descends on the person who has right to the land.*

Conclusion, *that when the land descends*

son decesse, &c. Issint il est graund diversité perentre un feoffement del tenaunt en le taille, et un reles fait per tenaunt en le taille. 601 *Mes il est dit, que si tenaunt en le taille en ceo cas relessa a son disseisour, et obligea luy et ses heires a la garrauntie, &c., et morust, et cest garrauntie descendist a son issue, donques ceo est discontinuaunce per cause dela garrauntie, &c.* 602 *Mes si un home ad issue fitz per sa feme, et sa feme morust, et puis il prent autre feme, et tenementes sount dones a luy et a sa seconde feme, et a les heires de lour deux corps engendres, et ils ount issue un autre fitz, et la seconde feme morust, et puis le tenaunt en le taille est disseisi, et il relessa al disseisour tout son droit, &c., et obligea luy et ses heires a la garrauntie, &c., et devia, ceo nest pas discontinuaunce al issue en le taille per la seconde feme, mes il poet bien entrer, &c., pur ceo que la garrauntie descendist a son eisne frere que son pere avoit per la premier feme.* 603 *En mesme le manere est, lou tenementes sount descendables a le fitz puisne solonques*

are entailed, &c., and the tenant in the tail hath two sons, and is disseised, and he releaseth to his disseisor all his right with warranty, &c., and dieth, the younger son can enter upon the disseisor notwithstanding the warranty, for this that the warranty descended to the elder son; for always the warranty shall descend upon him who is heir by the common law.

one way and the warranty another, no discontinuance is worked. See § 604, 605. § 718, 735—7.

604 Also, if any abbot be disseised, and he releaseth to the disseisor with warranty, this is not discontinuance to his successor, because nothing passeth by that release but the right which he hath during the time that he is abbot, and the warranty is expired by his deprivation, or by his death.

Release with warranty, *no discontinuance to successor of a corporation sole.*

605* Also, if a man seised in the right of his wife be disseised, and he releaseth, &c., with warranty, this is not discontinuance to the wife, if she survive her husband, but she can enter, &c. *Causa patet.*

***The same with regard to husband and wife, [unless wife be his heir.]* § 726.**

606 Also, if tenant in the tail of certain land let the same

Tenant in

le custome de Burgh-English queux sount entaillés, &c., et le tenaunt en le taille ad deux fitz, et est disseisi, et il relessa a son disseisour tout son droit ovesque garrauntie, &c., et morust, le fitz puisne poet entrer sur le disseisour nient obstant la garrauntie, pur ceo que la garrauntie descendist a leisne fitz; qar toutes foitz la garrauntie descendera a celuy qui est heire per le comen ley.

604 Item, *si ascun abbé soit disseisi, et il relessa a le disseisour ovesque garrauntie, ceo nest pas discontinuaunce a son successour, pur ceo que riens passa per cel reles forsque le droit quil ad duraunt le temps que il est abbé, et la garrauntie est expiré per son privacion, ou per sa mort.*

605* Item, *si home seisi en droit sa feme est disseisi, et il relessa, &c., ovesque garrauntie, ceo nest discontinuaunce a la feme, si ele survesquist son baron, mes ele poet entrer, &c.* Causa patet.

606 Item, *si tenaunt en le taille de certeyn terre lessa mesme*

---

* This section does not appear in those editions of *Rastell's* Translation, by *Tottyl* 1556, and subsequent years.

tail's lease and release no discontinuance, § 465.

land to another for term of years, by force whereof the lessee is possessed, in whose possession the tenant in the tail by his deed releaseth all the right that he hath in the same land, to have and to hold to the lessee and to his heirs for ever; this is not discontinuance: but after the decease of the tenant in tail his issue can well enter, because by such release nothing passeth but for term of the life of the tenant in the tail. 607 In the same manner it is, if the tenant in tail confirm the estate of the lessee for term of years, to have and to hold to him and to his heirs; this is not discontinuance, for this that nothing passeth by such confirmation but the estate which the tenant in tail hath for term of his life, &c.

Because only the right that the releasor has, passes, § 598—600.

Neither is his confirmation, because nothing but an estate created by livery works a discontinuance. § 528, 610.

So his grant of the reversion to a stranger

608* Also, if tenant in tail after such lease, grant the reversion in fee, by his deed to another, and willeth that after the

la terre a un autre pur terme des ans, per force de quel le lessé est possessione, en quel possession le tenaunt en le taille per son fait relesse tout le droit quil il avoet en mesme la terre, a aver et tener a le lessé et a ses heires a toutes jours; ceo nest pas discontinuaunce: mes apres le decesse le tenaunt en le taille son issue poet bien entrer, pur ceo que per tiel reles riens passa forsque pur terme de la vie de le tenaunt en le taille. 607 *En mesme le manere est, si le tenaunt en le taille confirma lestate le lessé pur terme des ans, a aver et tener a luy et a ses heires; ceo nest pas discontinuaunce, pur ceo que riens passa per tiel confirmacion forsque lestate que le tenaunt en le taille avoet pur terme de sa vie, &c.*

608* Item, *si tenaunt en le taille apres tiel lees, graunta la revercion en fee, per son fait a un autre, et voille que apres le*

---

* This and the consecutive sections to § 612, inclusive, do not appear in those editions of *Rastell's* Translation by *Tottyl* 1556, and by others to 1661. They are given in *Powell* 1551, and *Marshe* 1556, and the previous editions commencing at 1534.

term finished the same land remain to the grantee and his heirs for ever, and the tenant for term of years attorn; this is not discontinuance. For such things which pass in such cases of tenant in tail solely by way of grant, or by confirmation, or by release, nothing can pass to make an estate to him to whom the grant, or confirmation, or release is made, save what the tenant in tail can rightfully make, and this is but for term of his life, &c.

in fee with attornment, does not discontinue the estate-tail, for no grant shall work a discontinuance, but is void by the death of the grantor.

[*This doctrine continued to* § 619].

609* For if I let land to a man for term of his life, &c., and the tenant for term of life let the same land to another for term of years, &c., and afterwards my tenant for term of life grant the reversion to another in fee, and the tenant for term of years attorn, in this case the grantee hath not in the freehold, estate but for term of the life of his grantor, &c.; and I that am in the reversion of the fee-simple can not enter by force of this grant of the reversion made by my

Grant *works no discontinuance or forfeiture, but is void by the death of the grantor.*

[See § 615, *where grant by tenant in tail of a remainder does not work a discontinuance,* and § 616, 617, *as to a grant of ad-*

terme fyny mesme la terre remeyndroit a le graunté et a ses heires a toutes jours, et le tenaunt a terme dans attourna; ceo nest pas discontinuaunce. Qar tielx choses queux passont en tielx cases de tenaunt en le taille tantsolement per voye de graunt, ou per confirmacion, ou per reles, riens poet passer pur faire estate a celuy a qui le graunt, ou confirmacion, ou reles est fait, forsque ceo que le tenaunt en le taille poet droiturelement faire, et ceo est forsque pur terme de sa vie, &c.

609* *Qar si jeo lesse terre a un home pur terme de sa vie, &c., et le tenaunt a terme de vie lessa mesme la terre a un autre pur terme des ans, &c., et puis mon tenaunt a terme de vie graunta la revercion a un autre en fee, et le tenaunt a terme des ans attourna, en ceo cas le graunté nad en le franktenement, estate forsque pur terme de vie son grantour, &c.; et jeo que sue en la revercion en fee-simple ne puisse entrer per force de cel graunt del revercion fait per mon tenaunt*

---

* See *ante*, p. 582 (*).

vowson or profit a prendre, *and* § 627, 628, *as to a grant by an ecclesiastical corporation.*]

tenant for life, for this that by such grant my reversion is not discontinued, but always it abideth (*i. e.* remains) to me as it was before, notwithstanding such grant of the reversion made to the grantee, to him and to his heirs, &c., because nothing passeth by force of such grant, but the estate which the grantor hath, &c. 610* In the same manner it is, if tenant for term of life by his deed confirm the estate of his lessee for term of years, to have and to hold to him and to his heirs, or release to his lessee and his heirs, yet the lessee for years hath estate but for term of the life of the tenant for term of life, &c. 611* But otherwise it is when tenant for term of life maketh a feoffment in fee, for by such a feoffment the fee-simple passeth; for tenant for years can make feoffment in fee, and by his feoffment fee-simple shall pass, and yet he had not at the time of the feoffment made, but estate for term of years, &c.

[*This is the same doctrine as that contained in* § 607.]

Land is discharged by the death of grantors, who have only power to grant but for their lives, although they have granted in fee.

If tenant for life or years enfeoff, a fee passes.

As to such feoffments with warranty, § 698.

No discontinu-

612* Also, if tenant in tail grant his land to another for

a terme de vie, pur ceo que per tiel graunt mon revercion nest pas discontinue, mes touts temps demourt a moy sicome il fuist adevaunt, nient obstaunt tiel graunt del revercion fait al graunté, a luy et a ses heires, &c., pur ceo que riens passa per force de tiel graunt, forsque lestate que le grantour avoet, &c. 610* *En mesme le manere est, si le tenaunt a terme de vie per son fait confirma lestate son lessé pur terme des ans, a aver et tener a luy et a ses heires, ou relessa a son lessé et a ses heires, unqore le lessé a terme dans nad estate forsque pur terme de vie de le tenaunt a terme de vie, &c.* 611* *Mes autrement est quaunt tenaunt a terme de vie fait un feoffement en fee, qar per tiel feoffement le fee-simple passa ; qar tenaunt a terme dans poet faire feoffement en fee, et per son feoffement fee-simple passera, et unqore il navoit al temps del feoffement fait, forsque estate pur terme dans, &c.*

612* Item, *si tenaunt en le taille graunta sa terre a un*

---

* See *ante*, p. 582 (*).

term of the life of the same tenant in the tail, and deliver to him seisin, &c., and afterwards by his deed he release to the tenant and to his heirs all the right which he hath in the same land; in this case the estate of the tenant of the land is not enlarged by force of such release, because when the tenant had the estate in the land for term of the life of the tenant in the tail, then had he all the right which the tenant in the tail could rightfully grant or release, &c. So that by such release no right passeth, insomuch as his right was gone already.

ance is caused by tenant in tail releasing all his right to his lessee for life. § 600, 606.

613 Also, if tenant in the tail by his deed grant to another all his estate which he hath in the tenements to him intailed, to have and to hold all his estate to the other and to his heirs for ever, and deliver seisin accordingly; in this case the tenant to whom the alienation was made, hath no other estate but for term of life of the tenant in the tail; and so it can be well proved, that the tenant in the tail can neither grant, or alien, or make any rightful estate of the free-

According to this case, an estate pur autre vie, *and no more, passes to grantee of tenant in tail. See* § 650. [*No authority for this case, note* (*f*), p. 586.

autre pur terme de vie de mesme le tenaunt en le taille, et lyvera a luy seisin, &c., et apres per son fait il relessa a le tenaunt et a ses heires tout le droit quil avoet en mesme la terre; en ceo cas lestate del tenaunt de la terre nest pas enlarge per force de tiel reles, pur ceo que quaunt le tenaunt avoit lestate en la terre pur terme de vie de le tenaunt en le taille, donques il avoit tout le droit que le tenaunt en le taille puissoit droiturelement graunter ou relesser, &c. Issint que per tiel reles nul droit passa, entant que son droit fuist ale adevant.

613 Item, *si tenaunt en le taille per son fait graunta a un autre tout son estate que il avoet en les tenementes a luy taillés, a aver et tener tout son estate a lautre et a ses heires a toutes jours, et delivera seisin accordaunt; en ceo cas le tenaunt a qui lalienacion fuist fait, nad autre estate forsque pur terme de vie del tenaunt en le taille; et issint il poet bien estre prove, que le tenaunt en le taille ne poet pas graunter, aliener, ne faire ascun droiturel estate del frankte-*

hold to another person, but for term of his own life, &c. (*f*).

Resumption of argument in § 612.

614 For if I give land to a man in the tail, saving the reversion to myself, and afterwards the tenant in the tail enfeoff

nement a autre person, forsque pur terme de sa vie demesne, &c. 614 *Qar si jeo dona terre a un home en le taille, savaunt la revercion a moy, et puis le tenaunt en le taille enfeoffa un*

(*f*) The doctrine of this case, *viz.* that a tenant in tail is for all purposes of alienation, a tenant for life, and that the grantee of a tenant in tail has merely an estate of freehold, has been frequently denied; and it has long been clearly settled, that every conveyance by a tenant in tail, either by grant, bargain and sale, or release, gives a *base fee* commensurate with the estate tail; in other words, an estate which continues until actual entry by the issue in tail.—3 *Rep.* 84. *b.*; 10 *Rep.* 96; 2 *Salk.* 619; *Farresley*, 18; *Comb.* 119; *Hobart*, 338, 339; 2 *Raym.* 778—782; 3 *Burr.* 1703. In 3 *Rep.* 84, this *case* of *Lyttleton* was considered; and there it is holden, that the words ought not to be understood in their literal sense; but in another sense, *viz.* that it is no discontinuance, but will drive the issue in tail to enter to avoid it. See also *Bedingfield's case*, *Cro. Eliz.* 895.

Sir Edward Coke, in his Commentary, refers to § 650, and in the case put in that section, the doctrine is, that by such grant the estate-tail is in abeyance; but that doctrine is questioned in *Plowd.* 556, 561—563; for there the case therein ascribed to *Lyttleton* is overruled, it being "agreed, that the diversity of *Lyttleton* (§ 650) is not law, for when a tenant in tail grants over all his estate to another, and when he makes a lease for his own life, it is one and the same thing, for the lessee has but the land for the life of the tenant in tail, and the intail is not out of the tenant in tail in the one case more than in the other, but it remains in him equally in both the cases; and there is no ancient book which warrants the said opinion of *Lyttleton*, *viz.* that the intail shall be in abeyance by the grant of his estate; nor is there any reason why it should be in abeyance in that case any more than when the tenant in tail makes a lease for his own life, and afterwards releases all his right to the lessee." And *Hobart*, 339, says, that *Lyttleton* was confounded in himself when he held, that a grant of *totus suus status* by tenant in tail put the estate in abeyance, and also, that the law abhors abeyance; therefore the inheritance must be rather in the relessee than in abeyance: so that it seems very questionable, whether this doctrine ought ever to have

another in fee, the feoffee hath not rightful estate in the tenements, for two reasons: one is, because by such feoffment my reversion is discontinued, the which is a wrongful act, and not a rightful act. Another reason is, if the tenant in the tail dieth, and his issue sue writ of *Formedon* against the feoffee, the writ shall say, and so shall the count (*i. e.* the declaration), &c., that the feoffee by wrong him deforced, &c. *Ergo*, if he by wrong him deforced, &c., he hath not rightful estate.

Feoffment by tenant in tail is a discontinuance, and divests reversion, and drives issue in tail to an action.

615 Also, if land be let to a man for term of his life, the remainder to another in the tail, if he in the remainder willeth to grant his remainder to another in fee by his deed, and the tenant for term of life attorn, this is not discontinuance of the remainder, &c.

What acts do not work discontinuance. Grant in fee by remainderman in tail no discontinuance.

autre en fee, le feoffé nad pas droiturel estate en les tenementes, pur deux causes : une est, pur ceo que per tiel feoffement ma revercion est discontinue, le quel est a tort fait, et nemye a droit fait. Une autre cause est, si le tenaunt en le taille morust, et son issue suist brief de Formedon *envers le feoffé, le brief dirra, et auxy le count, &c., que le feoffé a tort luy deforce, &c.* Ergo, *sil a tort luy deforce, &c., il nad pas droiturel estate.*

615 Item, *si terre soit lesse a un home pur terme de sa vie, le remeyndre a un autre en le taille, si celuy en le remeyndre voille graunter son remeyndre a un autre en fee per son fait, et le tenaunt a terme de vie attourna, ceo nest pas discontinuaunce de le remeyndre, &c.*

---

been charged upon *Lyttleton;* and in addition to this, that section is not to be found in *Rastell's* Transl., *Tottyl* 1556, and subsequent editions by him, *Jane Yetsweirt* 1597, *Wight* 1604, and the *Stationers* to 1661; *Powell* 1548, 1551, and *Marshe* 1556, certainly retain this section in their editions of *Rastell's* Transl., but then those copies contain as much spurious matter as their *French* contemporaries. Lastly, that same section, 650, is repugnant to § 606 and § 612.

Grant in fee by tenant in tail of rent, no discontinuance.

§ 627, *as to corporation, S. C.*

The like of an advowson or profit a prendre.

§ 628, *as to corporation, S. C.*

616* Also, if a man hath rent-service or rent-charge in the tail, and he grant the said rent to another in fee, and the tenant attorn, &c., this is no discontinuance, &c.

617 Also, if a man be tenant in the tail of an advowson in gross, or of a common in gross, if he by his deed willeth to grant the advowson or common to another in fee, this is not discontinuance: for in such cases the grantees have not estate but for term of the life of the tenant in tail that made the grant, &c.

Fine of things lying in grant no discontinuance: the rule being that there can be no discontinuance of things lying in grant, unless by fine.—See § 627.

618 And note, that of such things which pass by way of grant, by deed made in *pais*, &c., and without livery; there such grant maketh not discontinuance, as in the cases aforesaid, or other like cases, &c., albeit such things be granted in fee by fine levied in the king's court, &c., yet this maketh not discontinuance, &c.

Neither lease

619† Also, if I give land to another in tail, and he letteth the

616* Item, *si home ad rent-service ou rent-charge en le taille, et il graunta le dit rent a un autre en fee, et le tenaunt attourna, &c., ceo nest pas discontinuaunce, &c.*

617 Item, *si home soit tenaunt en le taille dun avoweson en gros, ou dun comen en gros, sil per son fait voille graunter lavoweson ou le comen a un autre en fee, ceo nest pas discontinuance: qar en tielx cases les grauntés nount estate forsque pur terme de vie de le tenaunt en le taille qui fist le graunt, &c.*

618 *Et nota, que de tielx choses que passont per voye de graunt, per fait fet en pays, &c., et sauns lyverë; là, tiel graunt ne fait pas discontinuaunce, come en les cases avauntdites, ou autres cases semblables, &c., coment que tielx choses sont grauntes en fee per fyn levé en le court le roy, &c., unqore ceo ne fait discontinuaunce, &c.*

619† Item, *si jeo dona terre a un autre en taille, et il lessa*

---

* This section does not appear in those editions of *Rastell's* Transl. commencing *Tottyl* 1556, and continued by him and others to 1661; although it is given in *Marshe* 1556, and previous editions.

† *Sir Edward Coke* remarks, in his commentary upon this section, that " this is added to *Lyttleton*, and not in the *original*: yet is the case

same land to another for term [of years, and afterwards the lessor granteth the reversion to another in fee, and the tenant for years attorn to the grantee, and the term is expired during the life of the tenant in the tail, whereby the grantee enters, and afterwards the tenant in tail hath issue and die: in this case this is not discontinuance, notwithstanding the grant be executed in the life of the tenant in the tail, for this that at the time of the lease made for term of years, no new fee-simple was reserved in the lessor, but the reversion abides to him in the tail, as it was before the lease made. 620 But if the tenant in the tail make lease for term*] of the life of the lessee, &c.: in this case the tenant in the tail hath thereof made a new reversion in fee-simple, because when he made lease for term

for years or grant of reversion devests any estate so as to work a discontinuance or cause a forfeiture: [for discontinuance cannot be worked but by livery or warranty.]

But tenant in tail's lease for life and grant of reversion works a discontinuance if reversion upon

mesme la terre a un autre pur terme [dans, et puis le lessour graunta la reversion a un autre en fee, et le tenaunt a terme dans attourna al grauntê, et le terme est expire duraunt la vie le tenaunt en le taille, per que le grauntê entra, et puis le tenaunt en le taille ad issue et devia: en cest cas ceo nest discontinuaunce, nient obstant que le graunt soit execute en la vie le tenaunt en le taille, pur ceo que al temps de lees fait a terme dans, nul novel fee-simple fuit reserve en le lessour, mes la revercion demourt a luy en le taille, sicome il fuist devaunt le lees fait. 620 Mes si le tenaunt en le taille fait lees a terme] de vie le lessê, &c.: en ceo cas le tenaunt en le taille ad ent fait un novel revercion en fee simple, pur ceo que quant il fist lees pur terme de vie, &c., il discontinua [le*

---

good in law, because neither the lease for years, nor the grant of the reversion devesteth any estate." But the fact is, that part of this section, as introductory to the case of § 621, does appear in the three earliest editions; and the interpolated text is here placed within brackets, to shew the difference between those editions and the commonly-received text. In addition it may be observed that this and the next section do not appear in the editions of *Rastell's* Translation by *Tottyl*, commencing 1556, and by others in subsequent years, to 1656 and 1661; although the previous editions by *Powell* 1548, 1551, and *Marshe* 1556, give the text as hitherto read.

* The words within brackets do not appear in *Lettou & M.*, *Machl.*, and *Roh.*, see *ante*, p. 588 (†).

the lease be executed, or if reversion falls in his life-time, [for to work a discontinuance the alienation must be for an estate enduring beyond the life of tenant in tail.]

of life, &c., he discontinued [the tail, by force of the same lease, and also he discontinued*] my reversion, &c. And it behoveth that the reversion of fee-simple be in some person in such case, and it cannot be in me that am the donor, insomuch as my reversion is discontinued. *Ergo* it behoveth that the reversion of fee be in the tenant in the tail, that discontinued my reversion by such lease, &c. But† if in this case the tenant in tail grant by his deed this reversion in fee to another, and the tenant for term of life attorn, &c., and afterwards the tenant for term of life dieth, living the tenant in the tail, and the grantee of the reversion enter, &c., in the life of the tenant in tail, then this is a discontinuance in fee; and if afterwards the tenant in tail dieth, his issue cannot enter, but is put to his writ of *Formedon*. And the reason is, because he that hath the grant of such reversion in fee-simple, hath the seisin and execution of the same lands or tenements,

taille, per force de mesme le lees, et auxi il discontinua] ma revercion, &c. Et il covient que la revercion de fee-simple soit en ascun person en tiel cas, et il ne poet estre en moy que suy donour, entant que ma revercion est discontinue.* Ergo *il covient que la revercion de fee soit en le tenaunt en le taille, qui discontinua ma revercion per tiel lees, &c. Mes† si en ceo cas le tenaunt en le taille graunta per son fait cest revercion en fee a un autre, et le tenaunt a terme de vie attourna, &c., et puis le tenaunt a terme de vie morust, vivaunt le tenaunt en le taille, et le graunté de revercion entra, &c., en la vie le tenaunt en le taille, donques ceo est un discontinuaunce en fee; et si apres le tenaunt en le taille morust, son issue ne poet entrer, mes est mys a son brief de* Formedon. *Et la cause est, pur ceo que cestuy qui avoet le graunt de tiel revercion in fee-simple, avoet le seisin et execucion de mesmes les terres ou*

---

* The words within brackets do not appear in *Lettou & M.*, *Machl.*, or *Roh.*, see p. 588 (†).

† *Machl.* and *Roh.* read *Et*, *And*, in which they are followed by all the subsequent French copies.

to have to him and to his heirs in his demesne as of fee, in the life of the tenant in the tail, [and this is by force of the grant of the said tenant in the tail*].

§ 642.

[621† In the same manner shall it be, in the case aforesaid, if the tenant for term of life after the attornment to the grantee, had aliened in fee, and the grantee had entered for forfeiture of his estate, and afterwards the tenant in tail had died; this is a discontinuance: *Causa qua supra.*] 622‡ But in

Or by entry for cause of forfeiture.—See § 629, S. C.

Distinction between tenant

tenementes, daver a luy et a ses heires en son demesne come de fee, en la vie le tenaunt en le taille, [et ceo est per force de graunt de mesme le tenaunt en le taille].*

[621† *En mesme le manere serra, en le cas avauntdit, si le tenaunt a terme de vie apres lattournement al graunté, ust aliene en fee, et le grauntè ust entre pur forfayture de son estate, et puis le tenaunt en le taille ust devie; cest un discontinuaunce:* Causa qua supra.] 622‡ *Mes en ceo cas, si te-*

---

* The words between the brackets do not appear in *Lettou & M.*, *Machl.*, or *Roh.*, but they are given in the *Camb. MSS.*, and in all other French copies, as well as those copies of *Rastell's* Transl. previous to *Tottyl* 1556. *Sir Edward Coke* also comments upon them as being *Lyttleton's* opinion, 15 *E.* 4. See *Co. Lytt.* 333. b.

† *Sir Edward Coke* remarks on this *section:* "This is added in this place, but in the *original* it cometh in after this chapter;" and *Mr. Hargrave,* adopting *Sir William Jones's* remarks on the different readings in the *Camb. MSS.*, states that this section does not appear in this chapter in *Lettou & M.*, *Roh.*, or the *Camb. MSS.*, and it may be added that it is not in *Machl.* The case is simply a breviate of the case put at § 629, and for the reasons already mentioned may be deemed spurious. When *Sir E. Coke* says that "it cometh in afterwards," he evidently means to state that the case is repeated, *scil.* at § 629. *Tottyl* 1557 (both editions), and all the subsequent editions that profess to note the *additions*, include this section within *flowers* or *asterisks.* The French editions by *Charles Yetsweirt* (*circa*) 1594, and *Jane Yetsweirt* (*circa*) 1597, add *puis* 38, referring thereby to that section of the chapter according to their subdivision, which corresponds to § 629 of *West's* sectioning, 1581.

‡ This section does not appear in those editions of *Rastell's* Transl. commencing *Tottyl* 1556, and continued by him and others to 1661; although it is given in *Marshe* 1556, and previous editions.

in tail's lease for years and his lease for life.

this case, if tenant in the tail that grants the reversion, &c., die, living the tenant for life, and afterwards the tenant for term of life die, and afterwards he to whom the reversion was granted enter, &c., then this is not discontinuance, but that the issue of the tenant in tail can well enter upon the grantee of the reversion; because the reversion which the grantee had, &c., was not executed, &c., in the life of the tenant in the tail, &c. And so there is a great diversity when tenant in the tail maketh a lease for years, and where he maketh a lease for life; for in the one case he hath a reversion in the tail, and in the other case he hath reversion in fee. 623* For if [the reversion of†] land be given to a man and to his heirs males of his body engendered, who hath issue two sons, and the eldest son hath issue of a daughter and dieth, [and

Continuation of preceding argument by example.

naunt en le taille qui graunta la revercion, &c., morust, vivaunt le tenaunt a terme de vie, et puis le tenaunt a terme de vie morust, et puis celuy a qui la revercion fuist graunte entra, &c., donques ceo nest pas discontinuaunce, mes que lissue del tenaunt en le taille poet bien entrer sur le graunté del revercion; pur ceo que la revercion que le graunté avoit, &c., ne fuist execute, &c., en la vie del tenaunt en le taille, &c. Et issint il est graund diversite quant tenaunt en le taille fait un lees pur terme des ans, et lou il fait lees pur terme de vie; qar en lun cas il ad revercion en le taille, et en lautre cas il ad revercion en fee. 623* *Qar si [la revercion del†] terre soit done a un home et a ses heires males de son corps engendres, le quel ad issue deux fitz, et leisne fitz ad issue file et devie, [et le tenaunt en le taille fait un lees pur terme des ans,*

---

* This section does not appear in those editions of *Rastell's* Transl. commencing *Tottyl* 1556, and continued by him and others to 1661; although it is given in *Marshe* 1556, and previous editions.

† In that copy of *Roh. penes Ed.* these words within brackets are inserted by a contemporary hand; in fact, they seem to supply the matter next comprehended within the brackets, and which does not appear in the three earliest editions.

the tenant in tail maketh a lease for years and die*;] now the reversion descendeth to the younger son, for this that the reversion was but in the tail, and the younger son is heir male, &c. But if the tenant† *in tail* had made a lease for term of life, &c., and afterwards died, now the reversion descendeth to the daughter of the elder son, because the reversion is in fee-simple, and the daughter is heir general, &c.

624 Also, if a man be seised in the tail of lands devisable by testament, &c., and he deviseth this to another in fee, and dieth, and the other enter, &c., this is not discontinuance, because no discontinuance was made in the life of the tenant in the tail, &c.

Devise no discontinuance, because no livery made thereupon.

625‡ Also, if land be given in the tail, saving the reversion to the donor, and afterwards the tenant in the tail by his deed

Tenant in tail's feoffment to him in

et devie;] ore la revercion descendist a le fitz puisne, pur ceo que la revercion fuit forsque en le taille, et le fitz puisne est heire male, &c. Mes si le tenaunt† ust fait un lees pur terme de vie, &c., et puis morust, ore la revercion descendist a la file del eisne fitz, pur ceo que la revercion est en fee simple, et la file est heire generall, &c.*

624 Item, *si home soit seisi en le taille de terres devisables per testament, &c., et il ceo devisa a un autre en fee, et morust, et lautre entra, &c., ceo nest pas discontinuaunce, pur ceo que nul discontinuaunce fuist fait en la vie del tenaunt en le taille, &c.*

625‡ Item, *si terre soit done en le taille, savaunt la revercion al donour, et puis le tenaunt en le taille per son fait enfeoffa*

---

* The words within brackets do not appear in the three earliest editions.

† This should be either *tenant in tail* or *donee*, to render the sense perfect. In those editions of *Rastell's* Transl., which retain this section, the words *in tail* are supplied. In the copy of *Roh. penes Ed.*, the word *donee* is substituted for *tenaunt* by a contemporary hand.

‡ This section does not appear in those editions of *Rastell's* Transl. commencing *Tottyl* 1556, and continued by him and others to 1661; although it is given in *Marshe* 1556, and previous editions.

remainder, the donor's reversion being immediately expectant on the gift in tail, is no discontinuance; [for if the reversion in fee is not taken away or discontinued, the estate tail cannot be taken away or discontinued —Per Lytt. Trin. 9 *E.* 4, 24. *b.* Plowd. 562. Id. Quæres, §342.]

enfeoff the donor to have and to hold to him and to his heirs for ever, and deliver to him seisin accordingly, &c., this is not discontinuance, because no one can discontinue the estate in the tail, unless he discontinue the reversion of him who hath in reversion, &c., or in the remainder, if any hath in the remainder, &c., and insomuch as by such feoffment made to the donor, reversion then being in him, his reversion was neither discontinued or altered, &c., this feoffment is not discontinuance, &c. 626* In the same manner is it where lands are given to a man in the tail, the remainder to another in fee, and the tenant in the tail enfeoff him that is in the remainder, to have and to hold to him and to his heirs, this is not discontinuance, *Causa qua supra.* 627 Also, if an abbot hath a reversion, or rent-service, or rent-charge, and willeth to grant one of these to another in fee, and the tenant attorn, &c., this is not discontinuance. 628 In the same

No discontinuance can be worked of inheritances lying in grant. —*See* § 609, 616, 617, 618.

le donour a aver et tener a luy et a ses heires a toutz jours, et lyvera a luy seisin accordant, &c., ceo nest pas discontinuaunce, pur ceo que nul poet discontinuer lestate en le taille, si non queil discontinua la revercion celuy qui ad en revercion, &c., ou en le remeyndre, si ascun ad en le remeyndre, &c., et entant que per tiel feoffement fait a le donour, revercion adonques esteant en luy, sa revercion ne fuist discontinue ne alterate, &c., cest feoffement nest pas discontinuaunce, &c. 626* *En mesme le manere est lou terres sont dones a un home en le taille, le remeyndre a un autre en fee, et le tenaunt en le taille enfeoffa celuy qui est en le remeyndre, a aver et tener a luy et a ses heires, ceo nest pas discontinuaunce,* Causa qua supra. 627 Item, *si un abbé ad une revercion, ou rent-service, ou rent-charge, et voille graunter un deux a un autre en fee, et le tenaunt attourna, &c., ceo nest discontinuaunce.* 628 *En mesme le manere est, lou abbé*

---

* This section does not appear in those editions of *Rastell's* Transl. commencing *Tottyl* 1556, and continued by him and others to 1661; although it is given in *Marshe* 1556, and previous editions.

manner is it, where an abbot is seised of an advowson, or of such things which pass by way of grant without livery of seisin, &c. (*g*) *.

629† Also, if tenant in the tail letteth his land to another for term of life, and afterwards he granteth in fee the reversion to another, and the tenant doth attorn, and afterwards the tenant for term of life alieneth in fee, and the grantee of the reversion entereth, &c., in the life of the tenant in tail, and afterwards the tenant in tail dieth, his issue cannot enter, but is put to his writ of *Formedon*, because the reversion in fee-

S. C. § 621. *Execution of a reversion in possession is a discontinuance, because issue in tail is put to his action.*

*est seisi dun avoweson, ou de tielx choses que passont per voye de graunt sans lyverë de seisin, &c.**

629† Item, *si tenaunt en le taille lessa sa terre a un autre pur terme de vie, et puis il graunta en fee la revercion a un autre, et le tenaunt attourna, et puis le tenaunt a terme de vie aliena en fee, et le graunté de revercion entra, &c., en la vie le tenaunt en le taille, et puis le tenaunt en le taille morust, son issue ne poet entrer, mes est mys a son brief de* Formedon,

---

* In all the copies of *Rastell's* Transl. the case of the grandfather, father, and son, § 637, is placed here; and in *Marshe* 1556, and the editions previous to *Tottyl* 1556, it is given again in its place with the spurious introduction. See p. 597 (†).

† This and the following sections to, and inclusive of, § 632, do not appear in those editions of *Rastell's* Transl. commencing *Tottyl* 1556, and continued by him and others to 1661; although these sections are given in *Marshe* 1556, and previous English editions.

(*g*) *Lyttleton* here would appear to say broadly that *all* advowsons are incorporeal hereditaments, and, consequently, lie in grant; but this is to be understood of an advowson in gross, which, being an incorporeal inheritance, and not lying in manual occupation, was not passed by livery, but might have been granted by deed of grant without livery. He who has an advowson or a right of patronage in fee, can by deed alien the same either in fee for life or for years, or he can grant the next presentation, or any future number of presentations.

What alienations do or do not work a discontinuance: *Some discontinuances are temporary, viz. during life of a tenant in tail.*—§ 636, 637;

Otherwise if made with livery. [*As to rightful conveyances, see* § 598-600.]

simple, which the grantee* had by the grant of the tenant in the tail, was executed in the life of the same tenant in the tail, and for that reason it is a discontinuance in fee, &c. 630† And note, that some are discontinuances for term of life. As if tenant in the tail make a lease for term of life, saving the reversion to himself, so long as the reversion is to the tenant in the tail, or to his heirs, this is not discontinuance, but during the life of tenant for term of life, &c. And if such tenant in the tail give the lands to another in the tail, saving the reversion, then this is discontinuance during the second tail, &c. 631† But where the tenant in the tail maketh a lease for term of years, or for term of life, the remainder to another in fee, and delivereth livery of seisin accordingly, this is discontinuance in fee, because the fee-simple passeth by force of the livery of seisin, &c.

pur ceo que la revercion en fee-simple, que le grаunté avoit per le graunt del tenaunt en le taille, fuist execute en la vie de mesme le tenaunt en le taille, et pur celle cause ceo est un discontinuaunce en fee, &c.* 630† *Et nota, que ascuns sount discontinuaunces pur terme de vie. Sicome tenaunt en le taille fait un lees pur terme de vie, savaunt la revercion a luy, auxi longement que la revercion est a le tenaunt en le taille, ou a ses heires, ceo nest discontinuaunce, forsque duraunt la vie le tenaunt a terme de vie, &c. Et si tiel tenaunt en le taille dona les tenementes a un autre en le taille, savaunt la revercion, donques ceo est discontinuaunce duraunt le seconde taille, &c.* 631† *Mes lou le tenaunt en le taille fait un lees pur terme des ans, ou pur terme de vie, le remeyndre a un autre en fee, et delivera lyverë de seisin accordant, ceo est discontinuaunce en fee, pur ceo que le fee-simple passa per force de lyverë de seisin, &c.*

---

* This word has been corrupted to *grant*or in some copies of *Coke's* Transl. in *Co. Lytt.* See *Ritso's* Introd. p. 113.

† See *ante*, p. 595 (†).

632* And it is to be understood, that some such discontinuances are made upon condition, &c., and for this that the conditions be broken, &c., or for other causes, according to the course of the law, such estates are defeated, then are discontinuances defeated, and do not by force of them bar any man of his entry, &c.†

Discontinuance may be defeated by entry for condition broken. Example of husband's feoffment on condition.

633 Also, if a woman inherited who hath a husband, which husband is within age, and he being within age make a feoff-

A stranger shall have benefit of infancy;

632* *Et est assavoir, que ascuns tielx discontinuaunces sount faites sur condicion, &c., et pur ceo que les condicions sount enfreintes, &c., ou pur autres causes, solonques le cours de la ley, tielx estates sount defetes, donques sount discontinuaunces defetes, et ne tollont ascun home, per force deux, de son entré, &c.*†

633 Item, *si feme enherite qui ad un baron, quel baron est deins age, et il esteant deins age fait un feoffement de les*

---

* See *ante*, p. 595 (†).

† Here follows, in *Lettou & M.*, *Machl.*, *Roh.*, *Pyns.* 1516, and the *Camb. MSS.*, that portion of the text distinguished as § 637 ; but in all subsequent editions commencing with *Redm.* and *Berth.*, is substituted the following text or *example*, to illustrate the preceding part of the paragraph, *viz.*:—*Come si le baron soit seisi de certeyn terre en droit sa feme, et fait feoffement en fee sur condicion, et devie, si leire apres entra sur le feoffee pur la condicion enfreint, lentré la feme est congeable sur leire, pur ceo que per lentré del heire le discontinuaunce est defete, come est ajugge.*—As if the husband be seised of certain land in right of his wife, and maketh a feoffment in fee upon condition, and dieth, if the heir afterwards enter upon the feoffee for the condition broken, the entry of the wife is congeable upon the heir, for that by the entry of the heir the discontinuance is defeated, as is adjudged.

This portion of doubtful text is not noticed as an addition by *Sir Edward Coke*, nor is it included between the *flowers* or *asterisks* of *West's* edition, and subsequent copies ; but is commented upon by *Sir Edward Coke*, and its obscurity explained. The circumstance of this *example* not appearing in *Lettou & M.*, *Machl.*, *Roh.*, *Pyns.* 1516, or either of the *Camb. MSS.*, and the fact of its place being filled by the *case* of § 637, with considerable variations in the latter, coupled with the circumstance that the whole of this section does not appear in *Rastell's* Transl., *Tottyl* 1556, and subsequent editions to 1661, render both *case* and *example* very questionable.

Feoffment by minor seised jure uxoris, *works no discontinuance.*

ment of the tenements of his wife in fee, and die, it hath been a question, whether the wife can enter or not, &c. And it seemeth to some, that the entry of the wife after the death of her husband is lawful in this case: for when her husband made such feoffment, &c., he could well enter, notwithstanding such feoffment, &c., during the coverture, and he could not enter in his own right, but in the right of his wife. *Ergo* such right as he hath to enter in the right of his wife, &c., this right of entry remaineth to the wife after his decease (*h*). 634 And it hath been said, that if two joint-tenants being within age make a feoffment in fee, and one of the infants die, and the other survive, insomuch as both the infants might enter jointly in their lifetime, this right of entry accrueth all to him that surviveth, and therefore he that surviveth may be able to enter into the whole, &c.* And also

tenementes sa feme en fee, et morust, il ad este question, si la feme poet entrer ou non, &c. Et il semble a ascuns, que lentré la feme apres la mort son baron est congeable en ceo cas: qar quant son baron fesoit tiel feoffement, &c., il puissoit bien entrer, nient contristeant tiel feoffement, &c., duraunt la coverture, et il ne puissoit entrer en son droit demesne, mes en la droit sa feme. Ergo *tiel droit quil avoet dentre en droit sa feme, &c., cest droit dentre demourt a la feme apres son decesse.* 634 *Et il y ad este dit, que si deux jointenauntes esteantes deins age font un feoffement en fee, et lun de les enfantes devie, et lautre survesquist, entant que lambideux enfantes puissont entrer jointement en lour vies, cest droit dentré accrust tout a celuy qui survesquist, et pur ceo celuy qui survesquist purroit entrer en lentierte, &c.* Et auxi leire*

---

* *Mr. Ritso* observes that these concluding words of this section should be read after the preceding section (§ 633); the editor suggests the *dictum*

(*h*) The reason here rendered by *Lyttleton* is, for that the husband cannot enter in his own right, but in the right of his wife; and the

the heir of the husband that made the feoffment within age cannot enter, &c., because no right descendeth to such heir in the case aforesaid, for this that the husband had nothing but in right of his wife, &c. 635 And also when an infant makes a feoffment being within age, this shall neither prejudice or hurt him, but that he can well enter, &c., for it would be against reason, that such feoffment made by him that was not able to make such feoffment, should prejudice or hurt others, to bar them of their entry, &c. And for these reasons it seemeth to some, that after the death of such husband so being within age at the time of the feoffment, &c., that his wife can well enter, &c.

Same doctrine continued, Example of minors joint-tenants. § 259, 478.

636 Also, if a woman inherited taketh husband, and they have issue a son, and the husband dieth, and she takes another husband, and the second husband letteth the land which

Discontinuance can be temporary, and then subsequently purged.

le baron qui fist le feoffement deins age ne poet entrer, &c., pur ceo que nul droit discendist a tiel heire en le cas avaunt-dit, pur ceo que le baron navoit unques riens forsque en droit de sa femme, &c. 635 *Et auxi quant un enfant fait un feoffement esteant deins age, ceo ne luy grevera ne ledera, mesque il poet bien entrer, &c., qar ceo serroit encontre reason, que tiel feoffement fait per celuy qui ne fuist able de faire tiel feoffement, grevera ou ledera autres, de toller eux de lour entré, &c. Et pur ceux causes il semble a ascuns, que apres la mort de tiel baron issint esteant deins age a temps de le feoffement, &c., que sa femme bien poit entrer, &c.*

636 Item, *si femme enherite prent baron, et ils ount issue fitz, et le baron morust, et ele prent autre baron, et le second baron lessa la terre quil ad en droit sa feme a un autre pur*

---

immediately preceding this passage to be an interpolation made while the treatise was published in MS. See *Ritso's* Introd., p. 115.

---

heir of the husband cannot enter, for no right or title descends unto him; and the wife in this case shall take benefit of the nonage of her husband, and enter into the land.—*Co. Lytt.* 336. *b.*

he hath in right of his wife to another for term of his life, and afterwards the wife dieth, and afterwards the tenant for term of life surrendereth his estate to the second husband, &c.; *Quære* (*i*) whether the son of the wife can enter in this case upon the second husband during the life of the tenant for term of life; but it is clear law, that, after the death of the tenant for term of life, the son of the wife can enter, because the discontinuance, which was only for term of life, is determined, &c., by the death of the same tenant for life, &c.

§ 550. *n.*

Quære *whether discontinuance is purged by surrender, as in the case here of death of lessee for life.*

No discontinuance in tail can be worked of estate whereof discontinuor was never seised in tail; [even though reversion executed in the life-time of the

637 Also, if there be grandfather, father and son, [and the grandfather is tenant in tail, and is disseised by the father, who is his son*,] and the father make feoffment in fee without warranty, and die, and afterwards the grandfather die, the son can well enter upon the feoffee, because this was not discontinuance, insomuch as the father was not seised by force

terme de sa vie, et puis la feme morust, et puis le tenaunt a terme de vie surrendist son estate a le second baron, &c.; Quære *si le fitz la feme poet entrer en ceo cas sur le second baron duraunt la vie le tenaunt a terme de vie; mes il est clere ley, que, apres la mort le tenaunt a terme de vie, le fitz la feme poet entrer, pur ceo que la discontinuaunce, que fuit tantsolement pur terme de vie, est determyne, &c., per la mort de mesme le tenaunt a terme de vie, &c.*

637 Item, *si soit aiel, pere, et fitz, [et laiel soit tenaunt en le taille, et est disseisi per le pere, qui est son fitz,*] et le pere fait feoffement en fee sauns garrauntie, et devia, et puis laiel devia, le fitz bien poet entrer sur le feoffé, pur ceo que ceo ne fuist pas discontinuaunce, entant que le pere ne fuist seisi per*

* The words within brackets first appear in *Pyns.* 1516: with some slight variations they appear in all subsequent editions.

(*i*) Here *Lyttleton* maketh a *quære.* So, as grave and learned men may doubt without any imputation to them: for the most learned doubteth most, and the more ignorant, for the most part, are the more bold and peremptory.—*Co. Lytt.* 338. *a.*

of the entail at the time of the feoffment, &c., but was seised in fee by the disseisin done to the grandfather, &c.*

grantor.—Plowd. 233;] unless by warranty, this discontinuance being but for life.
§ 640—641.
[This subject continued to § 643.]

638† Also, if tenant in the tail make a lease to another for term of life, and the tenant in the tail have issue and die, and the reversion descendeth to his issue, and after the issue granteth the reversion to him descended to another in fee, and the tenant for term of life attorn, &c., and afterwards the tenant for term of life die, and he in the reversion enter, &c.,

*force de le taille a temps del feoffement, &c., mes fuist seisi en fee per le disseisin fait al aiel, &c.**

638† Item, *si tenaunt en le taille fait un lees a un autre pur terme de vie, et le tenaunt en le taille ad issue et devie, et la revercion descendist a son issue, et puis lissue graunta la revercion a luy descendus a un autre en fee, et le tenaunt a terme de vie attourna, &c., et puis le tenaunt a terme de vie morust, et celuy en la revercion entra, &c., et est seisi en fee*

---

* This section in all the *French* copies, commencing with *Redm.*, begins thus:—

[§ 637.] Note, that an estate tail cannot be discontinued, but there where he that makes the discontinuance was once seised by force of the tail, unless it be by reason of warranty, &c. As—

This introduction to this case is not given in those editions of *Rastell's* Transl., which commence with *Tottyl* 1556, which place this case between § 628 and § 629 (its proper place being the concluding paragraph of § 632); but this introduction appears in *Marshe* 1556, and previous editions. In such editions, however, this case of the grandfather, father, and son, is also given without the introduction between § 628 and § 629; so in those copies it appears twice, whilst in the later English editions it appears but once, *viz.*, between § 628 and § 629. The case itself, divested of the introduction as before noticed (p. 597(†),) is in the four earliest editions and the *Camb. MSS.*, inserted at that place where in the later copies a substitution of spurious text is given. The words within brackets do not appear in *Lettou & M.*, *Machl.*, and *Roh.*—See preceding page (*).

† This and the following sections to § 642, inclusive, do not appear in those editions of *Rastell's* Transl. commencing *Tottyl*, 1556, and continued by him and others to 1656 and 1661; although they are given in *Marshe* 1556, and previous editions.

and is seised in fee in the life of the issue, and afterwards the issue in tail hath issue a son and dieth, it seems that this is not discontinuance to the son, but that the son may enter, &c., for this that his father, to whom the reversion of fee-simple descended, &c., had never anything in the land by force of the entail, &c. 639* For if a man seised in right of his wife, let the same land to another for term of life, now is the reversion of the fee-simple to the husband, &c., and if the husband dieth, living his wife and the tenant for life, the reversion descendeth to the heir of the husband, if the heir of the husband grant the reversion to another in fee, and the tenant, &c., attorn, and afterwards the tenant for life dies, and the grantee of the reversion in this case enter: this is not discontinuance to the wife, but the wife can enter upon the grantee, &c., because the grantor had nothing at the time of the grant in the right of the wife, at the time when he made the grant of the reversion; 640* and so it seem-

Similar doctrine of grant of a reversion by heir of husband seised jure uxoris.

Feoffment made without

en la vie del issue, et puis lissue en le taille ad issue fitz et devie, il semble que ceo nest pas discontinuaunce a le fitz, mes que le fitz poet entrer, &c., pur ceo que son pere a qui la revercion de fee-simple descendist, &c., navoit unques riens en la terre per force de le taille, &c. 639* *Qar si home seisi en droit sa feme, lessa mesme la terre a un autre pur terme de vie, ore est la revercion de fee-simple a le baron, &c., et si le baron morust, vyvant sa feme et le tenaunt a terme de vie, la revercion descendist al heire le baron, si leire le baron graunte la revercion a un autre en fee, et le tenaunt, &c., attourna, et puis le tenaunt a terme de vie morust, et le graunté del revercion en ceo cas entra: ceo nest pas discontinuaunce a la feme, mes la feme poet entrer sur le graunté, &c., pur ceo que le grauntour navoit riens al temps de le graunt en le droit la feme, quant il fist le graunt del revercion;* 640* *et issint il semble, coment que homes queux sount enheritables*

* See *ante*, p. 601 (†).

eth, though that men which are inheritable by force of the entail, and they never were seised by force of the same tail, that such feoffments or grants by them made without clause of warranty, is not discontinuance to their issues after their decease, but that their issues may well enter, &c., albeit they that made such grants in their lives were forebarred to enter by their own act, &c. 641* And if tenant in the tail hath issue two sons, and the eldest disseise his father, and thereof make a feoffment in fee, without clause of warranty, and die without issue, and afterwards the father die, the younger son can well enter upon the feoffee, for that the feoffment of his elder brother cannot be discontinuance, because he was never seised by force of the tail. For it seemeth *to be* against reason, that by matter in fact, &c., without clause of warranty, that a man can discontinue a tail†, &c., who was never seised by force of the same tail, &c.‡

warranty, is no discontinuance, although a warranty [notwithstanding feoffor were never seised under the entail,] worked a discontinuance, § 592, 596, 597, 601, 637, 658.

§ 637, S. C.

per force de le taille, et ils ne furent unques seisis per force de mesme le taille, que tielx feoffementes ou grauntes per eux faitz sauns clause de garrauntie, nest pas discontinuaunce a lour issues apres lour decesse, mes que lour issues poient bien entrer, &c., coment que ceux queux firent tielx grauntes en lour vies furent forbarrez dentrer per lour fait demesne, &c. 641* *Et si tenaunt en le taille ad issue deux fits, et leisne disseisist son pere, et ent fait feoffement en fee, sauns clause de garrauntie, et devia sauns issue, et puis le pere devie, le puisne fits poet bien entrer sur le feoffé, pur ceo que le feoffement son eisne frere ne poet estre discontinuaunce, pur ceo que il ne fuist unques seisi per force de le taille. Qar il semble encontre reason, que per matere en fait, &c., sauns clause de garrauntie, que home poet discontinuer un taille*†, *&c., qui ne fuist unques seisi per force de mesme le taille, &c.*‡

---

* See *ante*, p. 601 (†).

† This word *taille, tail,* has been misprinted *fait, deed;* so that in

‡ Here follows in *Redm., Berth., Middl., Sm., Powell,* and *Tottyl*

The lord by escheat cannot receive benefit from a warranty by tenant in tail, because as the reversion is not

642* Also, if there be lord and tenant, and the tenant give his tenements to another in fee tail†, and afterwards the tenant in the tail make a lease to a man for term of life, &c., saving the reversion, &c., and afterwards grant the reversion to

642* Item, *si soit seignour et tenaunt, et le tenaunt dona sez tenementes a un autre en fee taille*†, *et puis le tenaunt en le taille fait un lees a un home pur terme de vie, &c., savaunt la revercion, &c., et puis graunta la revercion a un autre en*

---

some later copies the text has been rendered *discontinue a* deed. This misprint first appeared in *Tottyl* 1585.—See also *Co. Lytt.* 340. *a.*, and 1 *Roll.* 632.

1554, the following case, which is thus rendered by *Powell* 1548, 1551, and *Marshe* 1556, in those editions of *Rastell's* Transl. :—*In the same manner it is, if a man make a lease for term of life, the remainder to another in tail, and he in the remainder disseises the tenant for term of life, and maketh a feoffment to another in fee, and dieth, and afterwards the tenant for term of life dieth: it seemeth in this case that he in the reversion may well enter upon the feoffee, for this that he in the remainder that made the feoffment was never seised in the tail by force of the same remainder, &c.*—This paragraph, however, does not appear in those editions of *Rastell's* Transl., commencing *Tottyl* 1556, and continued to 1656 and 1661; although given in preceding editions.

* This and the preceding sections from § 638, inclusive, seem questionable for the reasons stated at p. 601 (*). These sections, also, the studious reader will observe, mostly consist of cases which *Lyttleton* has already put.

† This word *taille* is not in *Lettou & M.*, *Machl.*, or *Roh.*, but it is necessary to complete the sense; and indeed *Redm.*, *Berth.*, and other ancient copies read *taille*, and that copy of *Roh. penes Ed.* has been altered by a contemporary hand to *fee taille*; but all the *French* editions commencing with *Tottyl* 1557 (both editions), read—*a un autre en tail*, le remaindre a un autre en fee, *et puis*:—*to another in tail*, the remainder to another in fee, *and afterwards*;—and so the text has ever since been given. Those editions of *Rastell's* Transl., previous to *Tottyl* 1556, and including *Marshe* 1556, which retain this section, read as in the text; but the editions of *Rastell's* Transl. subsequent to *Tottyl* 1556, reject the whole section.

another in fee, and the tenant for term of life attorn, &c., and afterwards the grantee of the reversion die without heir, now the same reversion cometh to the lord by way of escheat: if in this case the tenant for life die, and the lord by force of his escheat enter in the life of the tenant in the tail, and afterwards the tenant in the tail die, it seemeth in this case that this is not discontinuance to the issue in the tail, nor to him in the remainder, but that he can well enter, because the lord is in by way of escheat, and not by the tenant in the tail: but otherwise it should be, if the reversion had been executed in the grantee, in the life of the tenant in the tail, for then had the grantee been in in the tenements by the tenant in the tail, &c.*

***executed in possession (the lord being in by escheat, not by tenant in tail;) contra if reversion be executed in possession, in the life of tenant in tail.* § 520.**

643 Also, if a parson of a church, or a vicar of a church, alien certain lands or tenements, parcel of his glebe, &c., to another in fee, and die, or resign, &c., his successor can well enter,

Alienation by parson no discontinuance of his successor.

fee, et le tenaunt a terme de vie attourna, &c., et puis le graunté del revercion morust sans heire, ore mesme la revercion devient al seignour per voye deschete: si en ceo cas le tenaunt a terme de vie devia, et le seignour per force de son eschete entra en la vie le tenaunt en le taille, et puis le tenaunt en le taille morust, il semble en ceo cas que ceo nest pas discontinuaunce al issue en le taille, ne a celuy en le remeyndre, mes que il poet bien entrer, pur ceo que le seignour est eins per voye deschete, et nemy per le tenaunt en le taille: mes secus esset, *si la reversion ust estre execute en le graunté, en la vie le tenaunt en le taille, qar adonques ust le graunté estre eins en les tenementes per le tenaunt en le taille, &c.**

643 Item, *si un parsone dun eglise, ou un viker dun esglise, aliene certeyn terres, ou tenementes, parcel de son glebe, &c., a un autre en fee, et morust, ou resigna, &c., son successour*

* This final *&c.* is stated in all the editions of *Hargr. & Butl. Co. Lytt.* 340. *b.*, not to appear in *Lettou & M.*, or *Roh.;* but this is an oversight, for this *&c.* appears in those editions as well as in *Machl.*

notwithstanding such alienation, as is said in a *Nota*, 2 *H*. 4. *Termino Mich.*, which beginneth thus:—644 *Nota, quod dictum fuit pro lege* in a writ of account brought by a master of a college against a chaplain*, that if a parson or vicar grant certain land†, which is of the right of his church, to another, and die, or changeth, that the successor can enter, &c. And I trow (*i. e.* I take it) the reason is, because the parson or vicar that is seised, &c., as in right of his church, hath not right of fee-simple in the tenements, nor doth‡ the right of the fee-simple abide in any other person; and for this cause his successor can well enter, notwithstanding such alienation,

Secus *in the case of sole corporations hav-*

&c. 645 For a bishop can have writ of right of [tenements of the right of his church, for this that the right is in his chap-

poet bien entrer nient contristeant tiel alienacion, come est dit en un Nota, Anno ii. H. iiii. Termino Michīs. quod sic incipit:—644 Nota, quod dictum fuit pro lege *en un brief daccompt port per un maistre dun college vers un chapleyn* dun chappell, que si un parsone ou viker graunta certeyn terre†, quelle est de droit de son esglise, a un autre, et devie, ou permute, que le successour poet entrer, &c. Et jeo crey que la cause est, pur ceo que le parsone ou viker qui est seisi, &c., come en droit de son esglise, nad pas droit de fee-simple en les tenementes, ne‡ le droit de fee-simple de ceo demourt en ascun autre persone; et pur cele cause son successour poet bien entrer nient contristeant tiel alienacion, &c.* 645 *Qar un evesque poet aver brief de droit de [tenementes de droit de son esglise, pur ceo que le droit est en son chapitre, et*

---

* The words *vers un chapleyn, against a chaplain,* are omitted in the three earliest editions.

† This word is misprinted *rent* in *Roh.*

‡ This word *ne* has been corrupted to *et* in *Redm.* and subsequent editions. All the editions of *Rastell's* Transl. translate this passage, *and the right—;* but *Sir Edward Coke's* Transl. continues this mis-reading; and in the faulty English edition by *H. Butterworth*, 1825, this corruption is unnoticed.

ter, and the*] fee-simple *is* abiding in him and in his chapter. And a dean can have a writ of right, because the right remains in him, [and an abbot can have a writ of right, for that the right remains in him*], and in the convent. And a master of an hospital may have a writ of right, because the right remaineth in him and in his confreres, &c. *And so of others in like cases,* &c. But a parson or vicar cannot have a writ of right, &c. (*k*) 646 But the highest writ that they can have is the writ of *juris utrum,* which is a great proof that the right of fee is not in them, nor in any other; but the right of the fee-simple is in abeyance, that is to say, that it

ing a sole seisin.—[*See* Co. Lytt. 341. *b. as to the learning concerning the sole corporations named in this section.*]

Argument deduced from the remedy, viz. *that fee of glebe is in abeyance.*

*le**] *fee-simple demurrant en luy et en son chapitre. Et un dean poet aver brief de droit, pur ceo que le droit demourt en luy,* [*et un abbé poet aver brief de droit, pur ceo que le droit demourt en luy**,] *et en le covent. Et un maistre dun hospitail poet aver brief de droit, pur ceo que le droit demourt en luy et en ses confreres, &c.* Et sic de aliis in casibus consimilibus, &c. *Mes un parsone ou un viker ne poet aver brief de droit, &c.* 646 *Mes le puis haute brief que ils poient aver est le brief de* juris utrum, *le quel est graund prove que le droit de fee nest en eux, ne en nul autre; mes le droit de fee-simple est en abyance, cest adire, quil est tantsolement en le remem-*

* The words within brackets do not appear in *Lettou & M., Machl.,* and *Roh. Rastell's* Translation renders this section thus:—" For a bishop may have a writ of right of tenements in right of his bishoprick; for this that the right of fee-simple abideth in him and in his chapter; and a dean may have a writ of right, &c., for this that the right abideth in him and in his chapter; and an abbot may have a writ of right, for this that the right abideth in him and in his convent: *et sic de aliis casibus consimilibus, &c.;* but a parson or vicar may not have a writ of right, &c."

(*k*) As to conveyances by ecclesiastical corporations, which have been restrained since *Lyttleton* wrote, see *ante*, pp. 84, 85 (*m*).

is only in the remembrance, intendment, and consideration of the law, &c., for it me seemeth that such thing, and such right, which is said in divers books to be in abeyance (*l*), is as much as to say in Latin (*sc.*):—" Talis res, vel tale rectum, quæ, vel quod, non est in homine adtunc superstite, sed tantummodo est, et consistit in consideratione et intelligentiâ legis, &c., et quidam alii dixerunt talem rem, aut tale rectum fore in nubibus, &c." [But I suppose, that they mean by these words, *in nubibus, &c.**] as I have said before, &c.

During vacancy, the freehold of glebe is in abeyance.

647 Also, if a parson of a church die, now the freehold of the glebe of the parsonage is in no one during the time that the parsonage is void, but is in abeyance, *scil.* in consideration

brance, entendement, et consideracion de la ley, &c., qar il moy semble que tiel chose, et tiel droit, que est dit en divers lyvers estre en abyance, &c., est a tant adire en Latin (scil.) " *Talis res, vel tale rectum, quæ, vel quod, non est in homine adtunc superstite, sed tantummodo est, et consistit in consideratione et intelligentiâ legis, &c., et quidam alii dixerunt talem rem, aut tale rectum fore in nubibus, &c.*" [*Mes jeo suppose que ils entenderont per ceux parols,* in nubibus, &c.*] *come jeo ay dit adevaunt, &c.*

647 Item, *si un parsone dun esglise devie, ore le franktenement del glebe del parsonage est en nulluy duraunt le temps que le parsonage est voyde, mes est en abyance,* scil. *in*

---

* These words within brackets do not appear either in *Lettou & M., Machl., Roh.*, or in the *Camb. MSS.:* they are given in *Pyns.*, 1516, and *Redm.*, and in subsequent editions, and in all the editions of *Rastell's* Transl., but in these last without the *&cas.*

(*l*) That is in expectation, of the French word *bayer*, to expect. For when a parson dieth, we say that the freehold is in abeyance, because a successor is in expectation to take it; and here note the necessity of the true interpretation of words.—*Co. Lytt.* 342. *b.*

and in intelligence (*i. e.* understanding) of the law, until another be made parson of the same church; and immediately when another is *made* parson, the freehold in deed is in him as successor, &c.

Induction is a seisin.

648 Also, peradventure, some will argue and say, that insomuch as a parson, with the assent of the patron and ordinary, can grant a rent-charge out of the glebe of the parsonage in fee, and so charge the glebe of the parsonage perpetually, *Ergo*, they have fee-simple, or *either* two, or one of them hath fee-simple at the least, &c. To this may be answered, that it is a principle in the law, that of every land there is a fee-simple, &c., in some one, or *else* the fee-simple is in abeyance, &c. And another principle *there is*, that every land of fee-simple can be charged with a rent-charge in fee by one way or by other, &c. And when such rent is granted by the deed of the parson, and the patron, and ordinary, &c., in fee, no one shall have prejudice or loss by force of such grant, but the grantors* in their lives, and the heirs of the patron,

At common law, before the disabling statutes, the parson might have charged the glebe in perpetuity with the consent of the patron and ordinary.

consideracion et en intelligence de la ley, tanques un autre soit fait parsone de mesme lesglise; et immediate quant un autre est parsone, le franktenement en fait est en luy come successour, &c.

648 Item, *ascuns peraventure voillent arguer et dire, que entant que un parsone, ovesque lassent de patron et ordinarie, poet graunter un rente-charge hors del glebe del parsonage en fee, et issint charger le glebe del parsonage perpetuelment,* Ergo, *ils avoient fee-simple, ou deux, ou un deux avoit fee-simple au meyns, &c. A ceo poet estre respondu, quil est un principal en la ley, que de chescun terre il y ad fee-simple, &c., en ascun home, ou le fee-simple est en abyance, &c. Et un autre principal est, que chescun terre de fee-simple poet estre charge dun rente-charge en fee per un voye ou per autre, &c. Et quant tiel rente est graunte per le fait le parsone, et le patron, et lordinarie, &c., en fee, nul avera prejudice ou perde per force de tiel graunt, forsque les grauntours* en lour*

* This word is misprinted *grantees* in *Lettou & M.*, *Machl.*, and *Roh.*

Reason is, that all parties having interest consent.

and the successors of the ordinary after their decease (*i. e.* after the decease of those who had consented to the charge). And after such charge, if the parson die, his successor cannot come to the said church to be parson of the same church by the law, but by presentment of the patron, and admission and institution of the ordinary, &c. And for that reason it behoveth the successor that he hold himself content, and agree to that which the patron and the ordinary lawfully should have done before, &c.; but this is no proof that the fee-simple, &c., is in the patron and the ordinary, or in either of them, &c., but the reason why such grant of rent-charge, &c., is good is because they who had interest, &c., in the said church, *scil.* the patron according to the law temporal, and the ordinary according to the law spiritual, had assented, or *were* parties to such charge, &c. And this seemeth to be the true cause why such glebe can be charged in perpetuity.

Tenant in tail

649* Also, if tenant in the tail hath issue and be disseised,

vies, et les heires le patron, et les successours dordinarie apres lour decesses. Et apres tiel charge, si le parsone devie, son successour ne poet vener a le dit esglise destre parsone de mesme lesglise per la ley, forsque per presentement del patron, et admission et institucion del ordinarie, &c. Et pur celle cause il covient que le successour soy teigne contente, et agrea de ceo que le patron et lordinarie loialement fesoient adevant, &c.; mes ceo nest prove que le fee-simple, &c., est en le patron et lordinarie, ou en ascun de eux, &c., mes la cause que tiel graunt de rente-charge, &c., est bon est pur ceo que ceux queux averount interesse, &c., a la dit esglise, scil. *le patron solonques la ley temporell, et lordinarie solonques la ley spirituell, furent assentus ou parties a tiel charge, &c. Et ceo semble estre la veray cause que tiel glebe poet estre charge en perpetuité.*

649* Item, *si tenaunt en le taille ad issue et soit disseisi, et*

---

* This and the next section (§ 650) do not appear in those editions of

and afterwards he release by his deed all his right to the disseisor: in this case no right of the entail can be in the tenant in the tail, because he hath released all his right; and no right can be in the issue in the tail during the life of his father; and such right of the inheritance in the tail is not altogether utterly expired by force of such release, &c., *ergo*, it must needs be, that such right abide (*i. e.* remain) in abeyance, &c., *ut supra*, during the life of the tenant in tail that releaseth, &c., and after his decease, then is such right forthwith in his issue in fact, &c. (*m*).

having issue is disseised, if he release to the disseisor, the estate-tail is in abeyance during his life, [but this doctrine is not law (m)].

650* In the same manner is it, where tenant in the tail grants all his estate to another; in this case the grantee

If tenant in tail grant all his estate to

puis il relessa per son fait tout son droit al disseisour: en ceo cas nul droit del taille poet estre en le tenaunt en le taille, pur ceo queil avoit relesse tout son droit; et nul droit poet estre en lissue en le taille duraunt la vie son pere; et tiel droit del enheritaunce en le taille nest pas tout oustrement expire per force de tiel reles, &c., ergo, *il covient, que tiel droit demurt en abyance, &c.,* ut supra, *duraunt la vie le tenaunt en le taille qui relessast, &c., et apres son decesse, donques est tiel droit meyntenaunt en son issue en fait, &c.*

650* *En mesme le manere est, lou tenaunt en le taille graunta tout son estate a un autre; en ceo cas le graunte*

Rastell's Transl. commencing *Tottyl* 1556, and continued by him and others to 1661, although they are given in *Marshe* 1556, and previous editions. See *ante*, (§ 613), p. 585.

* See preceding section, p. 610, (*).

(*m*) This *case* ascribed to *Lyttleton* is evidently against law, as well as the following *case* in § 650, which depends upon the same doctrine, for the right of the tail shall not be in abeyance, but remains always in the tenant in tail: and therefore his release in this instance shall operate just as if he had released to the disseisor his estate, which is only for his own life.—*Plowd.* 556. See *ante*, (§ 613), p. 585.

another, the reversion in tail is not in the tenant in tail, nor shall he have an action of waste, for the reversion is not in him, [*but this doctrine is not law*, ante, § 613, n.: Plowd. 556—563, *and is inconsistent with* § 606, 612].

hath not estate but for term of life of the tenant in tail, and the reversion of the tail is not in the tenant in the tail, because he hath granted all his estate and his right, &c.: and if the tenant to whom the grant was made, commit waste, the tenant in tail shall never have writ of waste, because no reversion is in him. But the reversion and inheritance of the entail, during the life of the tenant in the tail, is in abeyance, *scil.* only in the remembrance, consideration, and in intelligence of the law, &c. (*n*).

Alienation by bishop a discontinuance, § 593.

651 Also, if a bishop alien lands which are parcel of his bishoprick, and die, this is a discontinuance to his successor, because he cannot enter, but is put to his writ *De ingressu sine assensu capituli.*

Secus *of a dean unless he be solely seised.*

652 Also, if a dean alien lands parcel of his deanery, and die, his successor cannot enter, but can have writ *De ingressu*

nad estate forsque pur terme de vie del tenaunt en le taille, et la revercion de le taille nest pas en le tenaunt en le taille, pur ceo queil avoet graunte tout son estate et son droit, &c.: et si le tenaunt a qui le graunt fuist fait, fist wast, le tenaunt en le taille ne unques avera brief de wast, pur ceo que null revercion est en luy. Mes la revercion et lenheritaunce de le taille, duraunt la vie le tenaunt en le taille, est en abyance, scil. *tantsolement en le remembrance, consideracion, et en intelligence de la ley, &c.*

651 Item, *si un evesque aliena terres que sont parcell de son evescherie, et devia, ceo est un discontinuaunce a son successour, pur ceo que il ne poet entrer, mes est mys a son brief* De ingressu sine assensu capituli.

652 Item, *si un dean aliena terres parcell de sa deanrie, et morust, son successour ne poet entrer, mes poet aver brief* De

(*n*) This case is against law and cannot be considered as any part of *Lyttleton*, although it appears in the most ancient editions. See *ante*, (§ 613), p. 585.

*sine assensu episcopi et capituli, &c.** But if the dean be sole seised as in right of his deanery, then his alienation is discontinuance to his successor, as is said before.

653 Also, peradventure, some will argue and say, that if an abbot and his convent be seised in their demesne as of fee, of certain lands to them and to their successors, &c., and the abbot without assent of his convent alien the same lands to another, and die, this is a discontinuance to his successor, &c. 654 By the same reason they will say, that where a dean and chapter are seised of certain lands to them and their successors, if the dean alien the same lands, &c., this shall be a discontinuance to his successor, so that his successor cannot enter, &c. To this it can be answered, that there is a great

Distinction between abbot and convent, and dean and chapter, as to the acts of the abbot, who is a dead person in law.

ingressu sine assensu episcopi et capituli, &c.* *Mes si le dean est sole seisi come en droit de sa deanrie, donques son alienacion est discontinuaunce a son successour, come est dit adevaunt.*

653 Item, *peraventure ascuns voillont arguer et dire, que si un abbé et son covent sount seisis en lour demesne come de fee, de certeyn terres a eux et a lour successours, &c., et labbé sauns assent de son covent aliena mesmes les terres a un autre, et devia, ceo est un discontinuance a son successour, &c.* 654 *Per mesme le reason ils voillont dire, que lou un dean et le chapitre sont seisis de certeyn terres a eux et a lour successours, si le dean aliena mesmes les terres, &c., ceo serroit un discontinuaunce a son successour, issint que son successour ne poet entrer, &c. A ceo poet estre respondu quil y ad graund*

---

* *Rastell's* Transl. at this place interposes a sentence, which with a slight variation, as to commencement and location, is also given in *Redm.*, *Berth.*, *Middl.*, *Sm.*, *Powell*, and *Tottyl* 1554, *viz.—But if the dean and the chapter have land to them and to their successors in common, &c., howbeit that the dean alien such lands, his successors may well enter, for this, that the franktenement, at the time of the alienation, was as well in the chapter as in the dean.* But where *the dean is sole seised as in right* ——.

For abbot shall have a real action in his own name solely.

diversity between the said two cases: 655 For when an abbot and the convent are seised, yet if they be disseised, the abbot shall have assise in his own name, without naming the convent, &c. And if any will sue a *Præcipe quod reddat, &c.*, of the same lands whilst they were in the hands of the abbot and convent, it behoveth that such action real be sued against the abbot only, without naming the convent, &c., because they are all dead persons in law, except the abbot who is the sovereign, &c.: and this is by reason of the sovereignty; for otherwise he should be but as *one* of the other monks of the convent, &c. 656 But a dean and the chapter are not dead persons in law, &c., for each of them can have action by himself in divers cases. And of such lands or tenements which the dean and the chapter have in common, &c., if they be disseised, the dean and the chapter shall have one assise, and not the dean alone. And if another willeth to have action real for such lands or tenements against the

But dean and chapter are not dead in law, and therefore action must be brought by or against dean and chapter.

diversite perentre les dites deux cases: 655 *Qar quant un abbé et le covent sount seisis, unqore sils sount disseisis, labbé avera assise en son nosme* demesne, sans nosmer le covent, &c. Et si ascun voille suer* Præcipe quod reddat, &c., *de mesmes les terres quant ils furent en le main labbé et le covent, il covient que tiel accion reall soit sue envers labbé solement, sans nosmer le covent, &c., pur ceo que toutes sont mortez persones en la ley, forsque labbé que est le soverain, &c: et ceo est per cause del soveraintë; qar autrement il serroit forsque come de les autres moignes de le covent, &c.* 656 *Mes un dean et le chapitre ne sount mortes persones en la ley, &c., qar chescun deux poet aver accion per soy en divers cases. Et de tielx terres ou tenementes que le dean et le chapitre ount en comen, &c., sils soient disseisis, le dean et le chapitre averont un assise, et nemy le dean soul. Et si autre voille aver accion reall de tielx terres ou tenementes envers le dean, &c., il*

* In *Lettou & M.*, this word is *noun*, which has the same meaning.

dean, &c., it behoveth *him* to sue against the dean and the chapter, and not against the dean alone, &c., and so there appeareth a great diversity between the two cases, &c.

657 Also, if the master of an hospital discontinue certain land of his hospital, his successor cannot enter, but he is put to his writ of *De ingressu sine assensu confratrum et sororum, &c.* And all such writs fully appear in the register, &c.

If a master of an hospital discontinue, his successor is put to his action.

658* Also, if land be let to a man for term of his life, the

Tenant in tail

covient de suer envers le dean et le chapitre, et nemy envers le dean soul, &c., et issint il appiert graund diversité perentre les deux cases, &c.

657 Item, *si le maistre dun hospitall discontinue certeyn terre de son hospitall, son successour ne poet entrer, mes il est mys a son brief* De ingressu sine assensu confratrum et sororum, &c. *Et toutes tielx briefs pleinement appeiront en le registre, &c.*

658* Item, *si terre soit lesse a un home pur terme de sa vie,*

---

* This section is not given in *Redm.*, *Middl.*, *Sm.*, *Powell*, and *Tottyl* 1554, nor does it appear in *Rastell's* Transl., *Tottyl* 1556, and subsequent editions by him and others to 1656 and 1661; but the edition of *Rastell's* Transl. by *Marshe* 1556, (which is a reprint of *Powell* 1548, 1551), and other previous editions, retain this portion of text.

With respect to those sections which do not appear in *Rastell's* Transl., *Tottyl* 1556—1586, *Jane Yetsweirt* 1597, *Wight* 1604, and subsequent editions by the *Stationers* to 1661, it may be observed, that although those sections are given in the earliest *French* editions, yet that they vary in numerous instances from other copies, a circumstance which the Editor has previously noticed as an argument against the legitimacy of such text; and also, that although these sections appear in the earliest *English* editions of *Rastell's* Transl., yet that those editions contain quite as much spurious matter as the French copies: finally, so far as regards the fact of two, at least, of these sections containing *cases* not only against law, but in absolute conflict with the doctrine of previously stated cases, together with the fact which is also apparent, that many of these cases are mere repetitions of cases already put, the Editor suggests, that, on the first impression of this Book, the then latest copy in MS. was probably selected for publication, which in that indiscriminating age might be deemed an argument of correctness, and held out as an induce-

in remainder disseises tenant for life, and infeoffs a stranger, this is not a discontinuance, for reversioner can enter upon the stranger, because the remainder-man was never seised under the entail, § 592, 596, 597, 601, 637, 640, 641.

remainder to another in the tail, saving the reversion to the lessor, and afterwards he in the remainder disseise the tenant for term of life, and maketh a feoffment to another in fee, and afterwards dieth without issue, and the tenant for life dieth; it seemeth in this case, that he in the reversion can well enter upon the feoffee, because he in the remainder that made the feoffment was never seised in the tail by force of the same remainder, &c.

le remeyndre a un autre en le taille, savaunt la revercion a le lessor, et puis celuy en le remeyndre disseisist le tenaunt a terme de vie, et fait un feoffement a un autre en fee, et puis morust sauns issue, et le tenaunt a terme de vie morust; il semble en ceo cas, que celuy en la revercion bien poet entrer sur le feoffé, pur ceo que celuy en le remeyndre qui fist le feoffement ne fuist unques seisi en le taille per force de mesme le remeyndre, &c.

---

ment to purchasers: this indeed seems evident from a careful inspection of *Redm.*, which, from the circumstance of a peculiar *sign* being used for reference in one instance, the Editor conceives was printed from a MS. copy, for that edition abounds with additions and interpolations, which are copied by *Powell* 1548, 1551, and *Marshe* 1556, in their editions of *Rastell's* Transl.

CHAPTER XII.

REMITTER.

Lyttleton having treated of descents which take away entries, an act of law whereby the entry of a party was taken away; of continual claim, a remedy by act of the party for preserving entry where otherwise it would have been lost; and of discontinuance, an act of the party whereby entry was taken away (*a*), now discourses of remitter, a means whereby the party is remedied and restored to his right by mere operation of law.

Sir Edward Coke defines remitter to be an operation in law upon the meeting of an ancient right remediable, and a later estate, in one person, where there is no "folly" in him, whereby the ancient right is restored and set up again, and the now defeasible estate ceased and vanished away.—*Co. Lytt.* 347. b.

As unity of right and possession effect a remitter, there must be to every remitter these two incidents: 1st, an ancient right; and, 2ndly, a new defeasible estate of freehold in possession (in fact or in law), uniting in one and the same person, and this new and defeasible estate must be cast upon the party by act of law, and not be the result of his own act, acquiescence, or purchase, which the law terms "folly," as thereby the party is estopped or precluded from insisting

(*a*) There are three modes of barring entry, 1st, by descent, which is an act of law; 2nd, by discontinuance, which is an act of the party; 3rd, by the statutes of limitation. The two former modes are now so far as regards descents and discontinuances, after 31st December, 1833, abolished, so that the only mode by which title of entry is barred, is by the statutory doctrine of limitations.

upon his elder and more sure title. Therefore, this conjunction of ancient right remediable, and the new estate in lawful possession, but defeasible, cannot take place but where the party, to use *Lyttleton's* expression, " cometh to the land without folly," as by descent (§ 659); or by remainder (§ 682, 683); or by acceptance of an estate during minority (§ 660); or by marriage during minority; and in the case of a feme-covert, where her husband takes back the estate (§ 666); or where such feme-covert takes back the estate (§ 677), so that such taking back the estate be without covin (§ 678); or if he come to the land by survivorship without his privity (§ 684); or by disclaimer of the discontinuee (§ 691); or by falsifier of recovery (§ 688); or by acceptance of the estate from the disseisor, and under circumstances not forming matter of estoppel (§ 693): in all these cases, the party is remitted or seated in his former or ancient right, just as if he had recovered the land by judgment of law (§ 661). But where the party comes to the land being of full age, or in any case where " folly " can be imputed, remitter does not have place; for if the party re-obtain the possession of the land by agreement, he must hold it under the agreement, and take the right of possession according to the terms by which it has been conveyed—in plain English, keep to the terms of his bargain, leaving in the person from whom he takes his new estate, all the right he has not contracted for, so that it is said to be " his folly " that he would make the subject of his right a matter of contract, and take a less estate, instead of asserting his right of possession by an action.

That class of tenants of the fee to whom remitters are wrought, and whom *Lyttleton* particularly mentions, are, issue in tail (§ 659—662); femes-covert and their heirs (§ 666—669); reversioners and remainder-men and their heirs (§ 682); and corporations sole (§ 686): the consequence of a remitter (which when it enures to the tenant of the particular estate, also enures to them in reversion or remainder (§ 673)), was the avoidance of feigned recoveries by a feme-covert (§ 674), and the defeating of all mesne charges effected by those who had the previous wrongful estate (§ 660, 686).

Sir Edward Coke infers from *Lyttleton*, who mentions *title* in the largest sense including rights, (§ 659), that remitter is not wrought but to those who have precedent *right*, not *bare title* of entry, as in the case of a condition for which no action is given before entry; and he also observes, that *Lyttleton* puts all his cases concerning remitters to rights remediable.

With regard to the operation of "remitter to the *feme*," which only took place upon the husband's discontinuance, this learning will be shortly obsolete, as discontinuances are prospectively abolished; and in the case where the husband makes a feoffment of the land of his wife to the use of himself and his wife, the *feme* has her election of taking, by the Statute of Uses, 27 Hen. 8, c. 10, or of entering by the 32 Hen. 8, c. 28, (*ante*, p. 575), upon which latter statute she is *de facto* remitted.

Remitters do not take effect in estates created by conveyances operating by the Statute of Uses, for there the statute settles the possession according to the limitations of the use; and as there can be no remitter by the use, so there can be none by the possession.

---

659 REMITTER is an ancient term in the law, and is where a man hath two titles to lands or tenements, *scil.* one a more ancient (*i. e.* elder) title, and another a later title, and he cometh to the land by the later title; yet the law will adjudge him in by force of the elder title, because the elder title is the more sure and the more worthy title. And then when a

Definition of remitter.

Illustration.

659 *Remitter est un auncien terme en la ley, et est lou home ad deux titles a terres ou tenementes,* scil. *un pluis auncien title, et un autre title pluis darrein, et il vient a la terre per le pluis darrein title; unqore la ley luy ajuggera eins per force del pluis eisne title, pur ceo que le pluis eisne title est le pluis sure title et le pluis digne title. Et donques quant home est*

man is adjudged in by force of his elder title, this is termed a remitter to him, for that the law doth admit him to be in the land by the elder and surer title. As if tenant in the tail discontinue the tail, and afterwards he disseise his discontinuee, and so dieth seised, whereby the tenements descend to his issue or cousin, inheritable by force of the tail: in this case this is to him to whom the tenements descend, who hath right by force of the tail, a remitter in the tail, because the law shall put and adjudge him to be in by force of the tail, which is his elder title; for if he should be in by force of the descent, then the discontinuee might have writ of entry *sur disseisin* in the *per* against him, and recover the tenements and his damages. But insomuch as he is in in his remitter* by force of the tail, the title and the interest of the discontinuee is utterly annulled and defeated.

Example.

Remitter by descent; *to issue in tail.*

ajugge eins per force de son eisne title, ceo est a luy dit un remitter, pur ceo que la ley luy mette destre eins en la terre per le pluis eisne et sure title. Sicome tenaunt en le taille discontinua le taille, et puis il disseisist son discontinué, et issint morust seisi, per que les tenementes descendount a son issue ou cosyn, enheritable per force de le taille: en ceo cas, ceo est a luy a qui les tenementes descendount, qui ad droit per force de le taille, un remitter en le taille, pur ceo que la ley luy mettera et ajuggera destre eins per force de le taille, que est son eisne title; qar sil serroit eins per force de le discent, donques le discontinué puissoit aver brief dentré sur disseisin *en le* per *envers luy, et recoverer les tenementes et ses damages. Mes entant que il est eins en son remitter* per force de le taille, le title et le interesse le discontinué est tout oustrement aniente et defete.*

---

* The word *eins* is not in *Lettou & M.*, *Machl.*, or *Roh.*; and the words, *en son remitter*, are not given in those editions of *Rastell's* Transl. since *Powell* 1551, and *Marshe* 1556, *viz.* by *Tottyl* 1556, and subsequently to 1661. The common French copies read *eins en son remitter*, which has been corrupted to *en*.

660 Also, if the tenant in the tail infeoff in fee his son, or his cousin inheritable by force of the tail, the which son or cousin at the time of the feoffment is within age, and afterwards the tenant in the tail die, and he to whom the feoffment was made is his heir by force of the tail, in the tail; this is a remitter to the heir in the tail to whom the feoffment was made: for albeit that during the life of the tenant in the tail who made the feoffment, such heir shall be adjudged in by force of the feoffment, yet after the death of the tenant in tail, the heir shall be adjudged in by force of the tail, and not by force of the feoffment. For* although that such heir were of full age at the time of the death of the tenant in the tail who made the feoffment, this maketh no matter, if the heir were within age at the time of the feoffment made to him. And if such heir, being within age at the time of such feoffment, cometh to full age, living the tenant in tail that made the feoffment,

The feoffment of tenant in tail to his issue within age avoided by remitter.

Remitter avoids charge or lease.—See § 286.

660 Item, *si le tenaunt en le taille enfeoffa en fee son fitz ou son cosyn enheritable per force de le taille, le quel fitz ou cosyn al temps del feoffement est deins age, et puis le tenaunt en le taille devia, et celuy a qui le feoffement fuist fait est son heire per force de le taille, en le taille; ceo est un remitter al heire en le taille a qui le feoffement fuist fait: qar coment que duraunt la vie le tenaunt en le taille qui fist le feoffement, tiel heire serra ajugge eins per force de le feoffement, unqore apres la mort le tenaunt en le taille, leire serra ajugge eins per force de le taille, et nemy per force de le feoffement. Qar* coment que tiel heire fuist de pleyn age al temps de le murrant de le tenaunt en le taille qui fist le feoffement, ceo ne fait ascun matere, si leire fuist deins age al temps del feoffement fait a luy. Et si tiel heire, esteaunt deins age al temps de tiel feoffement, vient a pleyn age, vivaunt le tenaunt*

---

* This word *For*, *Mr. Ritso* observes, would have been more accurately written *And;* for this is rather an amplification than a conclusion. —*Ritso's* Introd. 113.

and so being of full age, he chargeth by his deed the same land with a common of pasture, or with a rent-charge, and afterwards the tenant in tail dieth; now it seemeth that the land is discharged of the common, and of the rent, for this that the heir is in by another estate in the land than he was at the time of the charge made, insomuch as he is in his remitter by force of the tail, and so the estate, which he had at the time of the charge, is utterly defeated.

The reason of the doctrine of remitter is, that no one can be both agent and patient, i. e. the heir cannot sue himself.

661 Also, a principal cause why such heir in the cases aforesaid, and other like cases, shall be said *to be in* in his remitter, is, for this that there is not any person against whom he can sue his writ of *Formedon:* for against himself he cannot sue, and he cannot sue against any other, for none other is tenant of the freehold; and for that reason the law adjudgeth him in in his remitter, *scil.* in such plight, as if he had lawfully recovered the same land against another, &c.

662 Also, if land be entailed to a man and to his wife, and to the heirs of their two bodies begotten, who have issue

en le taille qui fist le feoffement, et issint esteaunt de pleyn age, il chargea per son fait mesme la terre ove un comen de pasture, ou ove un rente-charge, et puis le tenaunt en le taille morust ; ore il semble que la terre est discharge de le comen, et de le rente, pur ceo que leire est eins dautre estate en la terre que il fuist al temps de la charge fait, entant que il est en son remitter per force de le taille, et issint lestate, que il avoit al temps de le charge, est oustrement defete.

661 Item, *un principal cause est pur que tiel heire en les cases avauntdites, et autres causes semblables, serra dit en son remitter, est, pur ceo que il ny ad ascun persone envers qui il poet suer son brief de* Formedon: *qar envers luy mesme il ne poet suer, et il ne poet suer envers nul autre, qar nul autre est tenaunt del franktenement ; et pur celle cause la ley luy ajugge eins en son remitter,* scil. *en tiel plite, sicome il avoit loialement recovere mesme la terre envers un autre, &c.*

662 Item, *si terre soit taillé a un home et a sa feme, et a les heires de lour deux corps engendres, les queux ount issue*

a daughter, and the wife die, and the husband take another wife, and hath issue another daughter, and discontinue the tail, and afterwards he disseise the discontinuee, and so die seised, now the land descendeth to the two daughters; in this case, as to the elder daughter, that is inheritable by force of the tail, this is a remitter but of the moiety; and as to the other moiety, she is put to sue her action of *Formedon* against her sister: for in this case the two sisters are not tenants in parcenry, but are tenants in common, for that they be in by divers titles; for the one sister is in in her remitter by force of the entail, as to that which to her belongeth; and the other sister is in, as to that which to her belongeth in fee-simple, by the descent *from* her father. 663 In the same manner it is, if tenant in tail infeoff his heir apparent in the tail, the heir being within age, and another jointly* in fee, and the tenant in the tail dieth; now the heir in the tail is in his remitter as to the

Remitter to a moiety.

Tenants in common.

[See § 696, where a joint-tenant is remitted to one moiety and not to the other.]

file, et la feme devia, et le baron prent autre feme, et ad issue une autre file, et discontinua le taille, et puis il disseisist le discontinué, et issint morust seisie, ore la terre descendist a les deux files; en ceo case, quaunt al eisne file, que est enheritable per force de le taille, ceo est un remitter forsque de le moyté; et quaunt a lautre moyté, ele est mys a suer son accion de Formedon *envers sa soer: qar en ceo cas les deux soers ne sount pas tenauntes en percenerie, mes sount tenauntes en comen, pur ceo que els sount eins per divers titles; qar lun soer est eins en son remitter per force de le taille, quaunt a ceo que a luy affiert; et lautre soer est eins, quaunt a ceo que a luy affiert en fee-simple, per le discent son pere.* 663 *En mesme le manere est, si tenaunt en le taille enfeoffa son heire apparaunt en le taille, esteaunt leire deins age, et un autre jointement* en fee, et le tenaunt en le taille morust; ore leire en le taille*

---

* All the copies of *Rastell's* Transl., and the later French copies, read this word *joint-tenant.*

one moiety, and as to the other moiety he is put to his writ of *Formedon.*

No remitter where there is "folly" in the party. § 660.

664 Also, if tenant in the tail infeoff his heir apparent, the heir being of full age at the time of the feoffment, and afterwards the tenant in the tail die; this is not remitter to the heir, because it was his folly, that he being of full age would take such feoffment, &c. But such folly cannot be adjudged in the heir being within age, &c., at the time of the feoffment.

Remitter by marriage of infant issue in tail with feme discontinuee.

665 Also, if tenant in the tail infeoff a woman in fee, and die, and his issue within age taketh the same woman *to wife;* this is a remitter to the infant, and the wife then hath nothing, because the husband and his wife are but as one person in law. And in that case the husband cannot sue a writ of *Formedon,* unless he willeth to sue against himself, the which should be inconvenient; and for that cause the law adjudgeth the heir in his remitter, for this that no folly can be arrected (*i. e.* judged) in him, being within age at the time of the espousals, &c. And if the heir be in his remitter by force of

est en son remitter quaunt a le moyté, et quaunt a lautre moyté il est mys a son brief de Formedon.

664 Item, *si tenaunt en le taille enfeoffa son heire apparaunt, leire esteaunt de pleyn age al temps de le feoffement, et puis le tenaunt en le taille morust; ceo nest remitter al heire, pur ceo que il fuist sa folie, que il estaunt de pleyn age voille prendre tiel feoffement, &c. Mes tiel folie ne poet estre ajugge en leire esteaunt deins age, &c., al temps de le feoffement.*

665 Item, *si tenaunt en le taille enfeoffa un feme en fee, et morust, et son issue deins age prent mesme la feme; cest un remitter al enfaunt, et la feme donques nad rien, pur ceo que le baron et sa feme sont forsque un persone en ley. Et en cel cas le baron ne poet suer brief de* Formedon, *sinon queil voleit suer envers luy mesme, le quel serroit inconvenient; et pur celle cause la ley ajuggera leire en son remitter, pur ceo que nulle folie poet estre arrette a luy esteaunt deins age al temps despouselx, &c. Et si leire soit en son remitter per*

the entail, it followeth by reason that the wife hath nothing, &c., for insomuch as the husband and wife be but as one person, § 291. the land cannot be severed by moieties, and for that cause § 672. the husband is in his remitter of the whole: but otherwise it is if such heir had been of full age at the time of the espousals, for then the heir hath nothing but in right of his wife.

Remitter to feme covert, *on alienee of husband letting to husband and wife for life.*

666 Also, if a woman seised of certain land in fee taketh husband, who alieneth the same land to another in fee, and the alienee letteth the same land to the husband and wife for term of their two lives, saving the reversion to the lessor and to his heirs; in this case the wife is in in her remitter, and she is seised in deed in her demesne as of fee, as she was before, § 671, 672. because the taking back of the estate shall be adjudged in law the deed of the husband, and not the deed of the wife; so no folly can be adjudged in the wife, who is covert, in such case, and in this case the lessor hath nothing in the reversion, because the wife is seised in fee: 667 but in this case if the lessor will sue action of waste against the husband

But husband is estopped, although wife is remitted.

force de le taille, il ensuyst per reason que la feme nad riens, &c., qar entant que le baron et la feme sount come une persone, la terre ne poet estre severe per moytees, et pur celle cause le baron est en son remitter de lentierté : mes autrement est si tiel heire fuist de pleyn age al temps de les espouselx, qar adonques leire nad riens forsque en droit sa feme.

666 Item, *si feme seisie de certeyn terre en fee prent baron, le quel aliena mesme la terre a un autre en fee, et lalienê lessa mesme la terre al baron et a sa feme pur terme de lour deux vies, savaunt la revercion al lessour et a ses heires ; en ceo cas la feme est eins en son remitter, et ele est seisie en fait en son demesne come de fee, sicome ele fuist adevaunt, pur ceo que le reprisel del estate serra ajugge en ley le fait le baron, et nemye le fait la feme ; issint nulle folie poet estre ajugge en la feme, que est covert, en tiel cas, et en ceo cas le lessour nad ascun rien en la revercion, pur ceo que la feme est seisie en fee :* 667 *mes en ceo cas si le lessour voilleit suer accion de*

Doctrine of estoppel, § 58, 693.

Estoppel by matter in fact.

Feme covert received in a real action, to plead as a feme sole, and in aid of her husband, he otherwise being without remedy.

and his wife, because the husband hath committed waste, the husband cannot bar the lessor by shewing this, that the taking back of the estate made to him and to his wife makes* a remitter to his wife, because the husband is estopped to say this against his own feoffment and his own taking back of the estate for term of life to him and to his wife, and yet the lessor hath no reversion, for this that the fee-simple is in the wife. And so a man may see one thing in this case, that a man shall be estopped by a matter in deed, although no writing by deed indented, or otherwise, be thereof made. 668 But if in the action of waste the husband make default at the grand distress, and the wife pray to be received, and is received, she shall well shew the whole matter, and how she is in her remitter, and she shall bar the lessor of his action. 669 For in every instance that the wife is received for default of her husband, she shall plead and have the same advantage in pleading, as

*wast envers le baron et sa feme, pur ceo que le baron avoet fait wast, le baron ne poet barrer le lessour per monstrer ceo, que le reprisel del estate fait a luy et a sa feme fait** *un remitter a sa feme, pur ceo que le baron est estoppe a dire ceo encontre son feoffement et son reprisel demesne del estate pur terme de vie a luy et a sa feme, et unqore le lessour nad nulle revercion, pur ceo que le fee-simple est en la feme. Et issint home poet veir un matere en ceo cas, que home serra estoppe per un matere en fait, coment que nulle escripture per fait endente, ou autrement, ent soit fait.* 668 *Mes si en laccion de wast le baron fait defaut a le graund distres, et la feme pria destre resceu, et soit resceu, ele monstrera bien tout le matere, et coment ele est en son remitter, et ele barrera le lessour de son accion.* 669 *Qar en chescun cas que la feme est resceu pur defaut son baron, ele pledera et avera mesme lavantage en pleder,*

---

* This word has been corrupted in the later copies to *fuist, was*. *Redm.* reads, *quel fait, which makes.*

if she were a feme sole, &c., and although that the alienee made the lease to the husband and to his wife by deed indented, yet this is a remitter to the wife: and also although the alienee yielded the same land to the husband and to his wife by fine for term of their lives, yet this is a remitter to the wife, because feme covert that taketh an estate by fine shall not be examined by the justices.

Feme covert concluded by fine as to estates given to her and her husband, but not as to estates taken by them.

670 And here note well, that when any thing shall pass from the wife that is covert of husband by force of a fine, as if the husband and his wife make a conusance of right to another, &c., or make a grant to yield to another, or release by fine unto another, *et sic de similibus*, where the right of the wife shall pass from the wife by force of the same fine; in all such cases the wife shall be examined before that the fine be taken, because such fines shall conclude such femes covert for ever. But where nothing is moved in the fine but only that the husband and wife do take estate by force of the said fine;

come si ele fuist feme sole, &c., et coment que lalienė fist le lees al baron et a sa feme per fait endente, uncore ceo est un remitter a la feme: et auxi coment que lalienė rendist mesme la terre al baron et a sa feme per fyn pur terme de lour vies, unqore ceo est un remitter a la feme, pur ceo que feme covert qui prent estate per fyn ne serra mye examine per les justices.

670 Et hìc nota, *que quand ascun chose passera de la feme qui est covert de baron per force dun fyn, sicome que le baron et la feme fesont un conusance de droit a un autre, &c., ou fesoient un graunt et rendre a un autre,* et sic de similibus, *lou le droit del feme passeroit de la feme per force de mesme le fyn; en toutes tielx cases la feme serra examine devaunt que le fyn soit accepte, pur ceo tielx fyns concluderont tielx femes covertes a toutes jours. Mes lou riens est moete en le fyn forsque tantsolement que le baron et sa feme preignont estate per force de mesme le fyn; ceo ne concludera la*

this shall not conclude the wife, for this that in such case she shall never be examined.

Husband of feme issue in tail taking back from the discontinuee estate for their lives works a remitter. See § 666 672.

671 Also, if tenant in the tail discontinue the tail, and hath issue a daughter, and dieth, and the daughter being of full age take husband, and the discontinuee make a lease* of this to the husband and to his wife for term of their lives; this is a remitter [in deed†] to the wife, and the wife is in by force of the tail, *Causa qua supra.*

Remitter maugre le baron. *If husband alien in fee, and take back estate to himself and wife for life, a remitter to both.*

672 Also, if land be given to the husband and to his wife, to have and to hold to them and to the heirs of their two bodies begotten, and afterwards the husband alien the land in fee, and take back an estate to him and to his wife for term of their two lives; in this case this is a remitter in deed to the husband and to his wife, maugre the husband; for it cannot be a remitter in this case to the wife unless it be a remitter to the husband, because the husband and wife be but one

feme, pur ceo que en tiel cas ele jammes ne serra mye examine.

671 Item, *si tenaunt en le taille discontinua le taille, et ad issue file, et morust, et la file esteaunt de pleyn age prent baron, et le discontinué fait un lees* de ceo al baron et a sa feme pur terme de lour vies; ceo est un remitter al feme, et la feme est eins per force de la taille,* Causa qua supra.

672 Item, *si terre soit done a le baron et a sa feme, a aver et tener a eux et a les heires de lour deux corps engendres, et puis le baron aliena la terre en fee, et reprent estate a luy et a sa feme pur terme de lour deux vies; en ceo cas ceo est un remitter en fait a le baron et a sa feme, maugre le baron; qar il ne poet estre un remitter en ceo cas a la feme sinon que soit un remitter a le baron, pur ceo que le baron et sa feme sount*

---

* This word has been corrupted to *release* in the later copies.

† These words do not appear in any French copy, but are given in all the copies of *Rastell's* Transl.

person in law (§ 665), though the husband be estopped to claim this to be a remitter in him against his alienation and his own reprisal, as is said before.

Discontinuance of particular tenant is a discontinuance of all the remainders, so a remitter to the particular tenant is a remitter to the remainder-men, upon the principle in § 452, 453, 471, *where a release to the tenant of the particular estate enures to him in the remainder.*

673 Also, if land be given to a woman in the tail, the remainder to another in the tail, the remainder to the third in the tail, the remainder to the fourth in fee, and the woman taketh husband, and the husband discontinue the land in fee, by this discontinuance all the remainders are discontinued. For if the wife die without issue, they in the remainder shall have no other remedy than to sue their writs of *Formedon* in the remainder, when it comes to their time, &c. But if after such discontinuance estate be made to the husband and his wife for term of their two lives, or for term of another's life, or other estate, &c., for that this is a remitter to the wife, this is also a remitter to all them in the remainder; for after this that the wife that is in her remitter dieth without issue, they in the remainder can enter, &c., without suing any action, &c. In the same manner

tout un mesme persone en ley, coment que le baron est estoppe de claymer ceo estre un remitter en luy encountre son alienation et son reprisel demesne, come est dit adevaunt.

673 Item, *si terre soit done a un feme en le taille, le remeyndre a un autre en le taille, le remeyndre a la tierce en le taille, le remeyndre al quarte en fee, et la feme prent baron, et le baron discontinua la terre en fee, per celle discontinuaunce toutes les remeyndres sont discontinués. Qar si la feme deviast sauns issue, ceux en le remeyndre naveront ascun remedie forsque de suer lour briefs de* Formedon *en le remeyndre, quant avient a lour temps, &c. Mes si apres tiel discontinuaunce estate soit fait a le baron et a sa feme pur terme de lour deux vies, ou pur terme dautre vie, ou autre estate, &c., pur ceo que ceo est un remitter al feme, ceo est auxi un remitter a touts ceux en le remeyndre; qar apres ceo que la feme qui est en son remitter morust sauns issue, ceux en le remeyndre poient entrer, &c., sauns ascun accion suer, &c. En*

is it of those that have the reversion after such entail, &c.

Recovery had against feme-sole tenant for life devests the reversion, but if feme sole be covert, and recover or let to her and her husband for their lives, remitter is wrought to the wife.

674 Also, if a man let a house to a woman for term of her life, saving the reversion to the lessor, and afterwards one sueth a feigned and false action against the woman, and recovereth the house against her by default, so that the woman can have against him a *Quod ei deforceat*, according to the statute of Westm. 2, now is the reversion of the lessor discontinued, so that he cannot have any action of waste. But in this case, if the woman take husband, and he that recovereth let the house to the husband and his wife for term of their two lives, the wife is in in her remitter by force of the first lease; 675 And if the husband and the wife commit waste, the first lessor shall have against them writ of waste, for this that insomuch as the wife is in in her remitter, he is remitted to his reversion. But it seemeth in this case, if he that recovereth by the false action willeth to bring another writ of waste against the husband and his wife,

And this remitter to the wife operates as a remitter to the reversioner.

mesme le manere est de ceux que ount la revercion apres tiel taille, &c.

674 Item, *si home lessa un mese a un feme pur terme de sa vie, savaunt la revercion al lessour, et puis un suist un feint et faux accion envers la feme, et recoverast le mese envers luy per defaute, issint que la feme poet aver envers luy un* Quod ei deforceat, *solonques lestatuit de Westm. seconde, ore est la revercion le lessour discontinue, issint que il ne poet aver ascun accion de wast. Mes en ceo cas si la feme prent baron, et celuy qui recoverast lessa le mese al baron et a sa feme pur terme de lour deux vies, la feme est eins en son remitter per force del premier lees;* 675 *Et si le baron et la feme fount wast, le premier lessour avera envers eux brief de wast, pur ceo que entaunt que la feme est eins en son remitter, il est remys a sa revercion. Mes il semble en ceo cas, si celuy qui recoverast per la faux accion voille porter autre brief de wast envers le baron et sa feme, le baron nad autre remedie envers luy, mes*

the husband hath no other remedy against him, but to make default at the grand distress, &c., and cause his wife to be received, and plead the matter against the second lessor, and shew how the action, whereby he recovered, was false and feigned in law, &c., so the wife can bar him, &c.

Baron's discontinuance and taking back estate of freehold to baron, feme, and a third person, is remitter to the wife but for a moiety. § 663.

676 Also, if the husband discontinue the land of his wife, and afterwards take back an estate to him and to his wife, and to a third man, for term of their lives, or in fee, this is a remitter to the wife, but as to the moiety; and for the other moiety it behoveth her after the death of her husband to sue a writ of *Cui in vitâ, &c.*

Baron discontinues land of the feme, and goes beyond sea, the discontinuee lets the land to the feme for life, a remitter to the wife.

677 Also, if the husband discontinue the land of his wife, and go beyond sea, and the discontinuee let the same land to the wife for term of her life, and deliver to her seisin, and afterwards the husband cometh* and agreeth to that livery of seisin, this is a remitter to the wife; and yet, if the wife had

de faire defaute a la graund distres, &c., et causer sa feme destre resceu, et pleder le matere envers le seconde lessour, et monstrer coment laccion, per quel il recoverast, fuist faux et feynt en ley, &c., issint la feme poet luy barrer, &c.

676 Item, *si le baron discontinua la terre sa feme, et puis reprent estate a luy et a sa feme, et a tierce home, pur terme de lour vies, ou en fee, ceo est un remitter a la feme, forsque quant a la moyté; et pur lautre moyté ele covient apres la mort son baron de suer un brief de* Cui in vitâ, &c.

677 Item, *si le baron discontinua la terre de sa feme, et ala oustre le mear, et le discontinué lessa mesme la terre al feme pur terme de sa vie, et lyvera a luy seisin, et puis le baron vient*, et agrea a cel lyverë de seisin, ceo est un remitter a*

---

* The later French copies give this word, *revient*; which *Sir Edward Coke* translates *cometh back*, but this is at variance with the four earliest editions, *Redm.*, and *Berth.*, as well as *Rastell's* Transl.

been sole at the time of the lease made to her, this should not be to her a remitter; but insomuch as she was covert baron at the time of the lease and of the livery of seisin made unto her, albeit she take solely the livery of seisin, this was a remitter to her, because a feme covert shall be adjudged as an infant within age in such case, &c. *Quære**, in this case, if the husband when he cometh back willeth to disagree to the lease and livery of seisin made to his wife in his absence, whether this shall oust the wife of her remitter?

Quære *whether disagreement of husband on his return devests the remitter?* [Semble que nemy.—*See* Co. Lytt. 357. *a.*]

678 Also, if the husband discontinue the tenements of his wife, and the discontinuee is disseised, and afterwards the disseisor let the same lands to the husband and his wife for term of life, this is a remitter to the wife. But if the husband and his wife were of covin or consent that the disseisin should be made, then it is no remitter to the wife, because she is a disseisoress: but if the husband were

Covin by husband and wife in order to effect a remitter to the wife, will not be allowed to operate, secus, *if wife not privy to the fraud.*

la feme; et unqore, si la feme fusoit sole al temps del lees fait a luy, ceo ne serroit a luy un remitter; mes entaunt que ele fuist covert de baron a temps de le lees et de le lyverë de seisin fait a luy, coment que ele prist solement le lyverë de seisin, ceo fuist un remitter a luy, pur ceo que feme covert serra ajugge sicome enfaunt deins age en tiel cas, &c. Quære*, *en ceo cas, si le baron quant il revient voille disagreer a le lees et lyverë de seisin fait a sa feme en son absence, si ceo oustera la feme de son remitter?*

678 Item, *si le baron discontinua les tenementes sa feme, et le discontinué est disseisi, et puis le disseisour lessa mesmes les tenementes a le baron et a sa feme pur terme de vie, ceo est un remitter a la feme. Mes si le baron et sa feme furent de covin ou consent que le disseisin doit estre fait, donques il nest remitter a la feme, pur ceo que ele est disseiseresse:*

---

* This *quære*, although it is given in every copy of *Lyttleton*, may be questioned, as the copies vary, although the variations are not material.

of covin and consent to the disseisin, and not the wife, then such lease made to the wife is a remitter, because no default was in the wife.

679 Also, if such discontinuee had made estate of freehold to the husband and to his wife by deed indented, upon condition, *scil.* reserving to the discontinuee a certain rent, and for default of payment a re-entry, and because the rent is behind, the discontinuee entereth, of this entry the wife shall have assise of *novel disseisin,* after the death of her husband, against the discontinuee, because the condition was wholly annulled, insomuch as the wife was in in her remitter, yet the husband with his wife cannot have an assise, because the husband is estopped, &c.

The effect of a remitter is to defeat conditions, and rents annexed to or reserved upon defeated estate.

680 Also, if the husband discontinue the tenements of his wife, and take back an estate to him for term of his life, the remainder after his decease to his wife for term of her life, in this case this is no remitter to the wife during the life of the

Remitter maugre le feme. *Husband discontinues his wife's estate, and takes back estate for life,*

mes si le baron fuist de covin et consent a le disseisin, et nemye la feme, donques tiel lees fait al feme est un remitter, pur ceo que nul defaute fuist en la feme.

679 Item, *si tiel discontinué fesoit estate de franktenement al baron et a sa feme per fait endente, sur condicion,* scil. *reservant al discontinué un certeyn rente, et pur defaute de paiement un re-entré, et pur ceo que le rente est aderere, le discontinué entre, de cel entré la feme avera un assise de* no. diss., *apres la mort son baron, envers le discontinué, pur ceo que la condicion fuist tout oustrement aniente, entant que la feme fuist en son remitter, unqore le baron ovesque sa feme ne poient aver assise, pur ceo que le baron est estoppe, &c.*

680 Item, *si le baron discontinua les tenementes sa feme, et reprist estate a luy pur terme de sa vie, le remeyndre apres son decesse a sa feme pur terme de sa vie, en ceo cas ceo nest* remitter a la feme duraunt la vie le baron,*

* In *Lettou & M.*, *Machl.*, and *Roh.*, this word is printed *est.*

remainder to wife for life, no remitter to the wife, till the husband's decease.

husband (*b*), because during the life of the husband the wife hath nothing in the freehold. But if in this case the wife survive the husband, this is a remitter to the wife, because a freehold in law is cast upon him, maugre the wife (*i. e.* against her will); and insomuch as she cannot have action against any other person, and against herself she cannot have action, therefore she is in her remitter: for in this case, although the wife doth not enter into the tenements, yet a stranger that hath cause to have action may sue his action against the wife for the same tenements, because she is tenant in law, though she be not tenant in deed (*c*); 681 for tenant of freehold in deed is he, who, if he be disseised of the freehold, may have assise, but tenant in law before his entry shall not

Remitter cannot be waived. *See* § 672, remitter maugre le baron.

Tenancy in deed and tenancy in law, § 447, 448.

pur ceo que duraunt la vie le baron la feme nad riens en le franktenement. Mes si en ceo cas la feme survesquist le baron, ceo est un remitter a la feme, pur ceo que un franktenement en ley est gette sur luy, maugre la feme ; et entant que ele ne poet aver accion envers nul autre persone, et envers luy mesme ele ne poet aver accion, pur ceo que ele est en son remitter : qar en ceo cas, coment que la feme nentra pas en les tenementes, unqore un estraunge qui ad cause daver accion poet suer son accion envers la feme de mesmes les tenementes, pur ceo que ele est tenaunt en ley, coment que ele ne soit tenaunt en fait ;* 681 *qar tenaunt de franktenement en fait est celuy, qui sil soit disseisi de franktenement poet aver assise, mes tenaunt en ley devaunt son entré navera*

* This word has been misprinted *soen* in *Lettou & M.*, *Machl.*, *Roh.*, and all subsequent editions. The text is according to *Pap. MS.*

(*b*) For it is a settled principle that there can be no remitter without unity of right and possession, *scil.* possession in deed or in law; and here there is neither in the wife, who has but a remainder.

(*c*) By the same reason, the husband cannot by his dissent devest the remitter of his wife. See § 677 (in the *quære*).

have assise*. And if a man seised in fee of certain land, hath issue a son, who taketh wife, and the father dieth seised, and afterwards the son dieth before any entry made by him into the land, the wife of the son shall be endowed in the land, and yet he had no freehold in deed, but he had a fee and freehold in law. And so note well, that a *Præcipe quod reddat* may as well be maintained against him that hath the freehold in law, as against him that hath the freehold in deed. 682 Also, if tenant in the tail hath issue two sons of full age, and he let the land entailed to the elder son for term of his life, the remainder to the younger son for term of his life, and after the tenant in the tail die; in this case the eldest son is not in in his remitter, because he took estate of his father. But if the elder die without issue of his body, then this a remitter to the younger brother, because he is heir in the tail, and a freehold in law is

See a similar case, § 681, where wife is dowable sans seisin of husband.

Tenant in tail leases to his eldest son for life, remainder to his second son—no remitter to the eldest, because he takes estate; but on the eldest son dying sans issue, a remitter is wrought to the youngest, because he is heir in tail, and has estate of freehold cast upon him.

mye assise. Et si home seisi de certeyn terre, ad issue fitz quel prent feme, et le pere devie seisi, et puis le fitz devie devaunt ascun entré fait per luy en la terre, la feme le fitz serra endowe en la terre, et unqore il navoit nul franktenement en fait, mes il avoit un fee et franktenement en ley. Et issint nota, quod* Præcipe quod reddat *poet auxibien estre maintenue envers celuy qui ad franktenement en ley, sicome envers celuy qui ad franktenement en fait.* 682 Item, *si tenaunt en le taille ad issue deux fits de pleyn age, et il lessa la terre taillé al eisne fitz pur terme de sa vie, le remeyndre al fitz puisne pur terme de sa vie, et puis le tenaunt en le taille morust ; en ceo cas leisne fitz nest pas en son remitter, pur ceo queil prist estate de son pere. Mes si leisne fitz morust sauns issue de son corps, donques ceo est un remitter al puisne frere, pur ceo queil est heire en le taille, et un*

---

* All copies since the three earliest read this passage thus, *viz.—Mes tenaunt* de franktenement *en ley devaunt son entré* en fait, *navera mye assise. Rastell's* Transl. accords with the text.

fallen to* and cast upon him by force of the remainder, and there is none against whom he can sue his action, &c. 683 In the same manner it is, where a man is disseised, and the disseisor dieth thereof seised, and the tenements descend to his heir, and the heir of the disseisor make a lease to a man of the same tenements for term of his life, the remainder to the disseisee for term of life, or in the tail, or in fee, and the tenant for term of life die, now this is a remitter to the disseisee, &c. *Causa qua supra.*

Further examples in illustration of two preceding sections.

684† Also, if tenant in the tail infeoff his son and another, by his deed, of the land entailed, in fee, and livery of seisin

Waiver of estate a cause of remitter.

franktenement en le ley est eschue et yette sur luy per force de le remeyndre, et il y ad nul envers qui il poet suer son accion, &c.* 683 *En mesme le manere est, lou home soit disseisi, et le disseisour ent morust seisi, et les tenementes descendont a son heire, et leire le disseisour fait un lees a un home de mesmes les tenementes pur terme de sa vie, le remeyndre a le disseisi pur terme de vie, ou en le taille, ou en fee, et le tenaunt a terme de vie morust, ore ceo est un remitter al disseisi, &c.* Causa qua supra.

684† Item, *si tenaunt en le taille enfeoffa son fitz et un autre, per son fait, de la terre taillé, en fee, et lyverë de*

---

* In the editions by *Tottyl* 1557, 1567, 1572, 1577, and all the subsequent editions, and in the edition of 1671 (French and English), this word is erroneously printed *eschete, escheated. Sir Edward Coke's* Transl. follows this corrupted reading.

† This section was deemed an addition by *West*, who includes it in a *flower*, in his first sectioned edition of 1581 ; but in *Tottyl's* expurgated editions of 1557, this section is given, and it also appears in all previous editions, *Rastell's* Transl., and the *Camb. MSS.* In the later editions, this section commences with *Nota. Sir Edward Coke* remarks upon the *sign* which denotes this to be an addition thus, *viz.*—It should seem by this mark, that this was an addition to *Lyttleton*, but it is of *Lyttleton's* own words, and agreeth with the origninal, saving the original began this section thus, *Item si, &c.—Co. Lytt.* 359. *a.*

is made to the other according to the deed, the son neither knowing thereof, nor* agreeing to the feoffment, and afterwards he that took the livery of seisin dieth, and the son neither occupieth the land, nor taketh any profit of the land during the life of the father, and afterwards the father dieth, now this is a remitter to the son, because the freehold is cast upon him by the survivor: and no default was in him, because he never agreed, &c., in the life of his father, and there is none against whom he may sue his writ of *Formedon, &c.* 685 For if a man be disseised of certain land, and the disseisor make a deed of feoffment, whereby he infeoffeth B., C., and D., and the livery of seisin is made to B. and C., but D. was not *present* at the livery of seisin, nor ever agreed to the feoffment, nor ever willed to take the profits, &c., and afterwards B. and C. die, and D. survive them, and the disseisee bring his writ upon disseisin

Tenant in tail infeoffs another and his son, who is neither cognizant of the deed, nor occupies the land, remitter to the son.

Case where by waiver or dissent to estate, c. 1. damages under stat. of Gloucester not recoverable.

seisin est fait a lautre accordant al fait, le fitz nient conusant de ceo, ne agreant a le feoffement, et puis celuy qui prist le lyverë de seisin devia, et le fitz ne occupia la terre, ne prent ascun profit del terre duraunt la vie le pere, et puis le pere morust, ore ceo est un remitter a le fitz, pur ceo que le franktenement est gette sur luy per le survivour : et nul defaute fuist en luy, pur ceo quil ne unques agrea, &c., en la vie son pere, et il ad nul envers qui il poet pursuer son brief de* Formedon, &c. 685 *Qar si home soit disseisi de certeyn terre, et le disseisour fait un fait de feoffement, per quel enfeoffa B., C., et D., et le lyverë de seisin est fait a B. et C., mes D. ne fuist al lyverë de seisin, ne unques agrea a le feoffement, ne unques voille prendre les profites, &c., et puis B. et C. devieront, et D. eux survesquist, et le disseisi porta son brief sur disseisin en le* per *envers D., mesme celuy*

---

* This word, *ne*, is omitted in *Tottyl* 1585, 1588, 1591, and in the edition 1671 (French and English).

in the *per* against D., this same D. shall shew all the matter, and how that he never agreed to the feoffment, and so he shall discharge himself of damages, so that the demandant shall recover no damages against him, although he be tenant of the freehold of the land. And yet the statute of Gloucester (cap. 1) directs, that the disseisee recover damages in a writ of entry founded upon the novel disseisin against him that is found tenant; and this is a proof in the other case, that insomuch as the issue in the tail cometh to the freehold, and this not by his act, nor by his agreement, that after the death of his father this is a remitter to him, insomuch as he cannot sue action of *Formedon* against any other person, &c.

This is a special case, and see § 691, 692, where damages are to be recovered if the tenant disclaim, the plaintiff can aver him to be tenant.

Successor of an abbot or dean remitted by reprisal of the estate by his predecessors.

686 Also, if an abbot alien the land of his house to another in fee, and the alienee by his deed charge the land with a rent-charge in fee, and afterwards the alienee infeoff the abbot with licence, to have and to hold to the abbot and to his successors for ever, and afterwards the abbot die, and another is chosen, and made abbot; in this case the abbot

D. monstrera tout le matere, et coment que il ne unques agrea a le feoffement, et issint il dischargera luy de damages, issint que le demaundant ne recovera ascuns damages envers luy, coment quil soit tenaunt del franktenement del terre. Et unqore lestatuit de Gloucest' voet, que le disseisi recovera damages en brief de entre foundu sur le novel disseisin vers celuy qui est trove tenaunt; et ceo est un prove en lautre cas, que entaunt que lissue en le taille avient a le franktenement, et ceo nemy per son fait, ne per son agreement, que apres la mort son pere ceo est un remitter a luy, entaunt que il ne poet suer accion de Formedon *envers nul autre persone, &c.*

686 Item, *si un abbé aliena la terre de son meason a un autre en fee, et lalienё per son fait chargea la terre ovesque un rent-charge en fee, et puis lalienё enfeoffa labbé ovesque licence, a aver et tener al abbé et a ses successours a toutz jours, et puis labbé morust, et un autre est eslieu, et fait abbé; en ceo cas labbé qui est le successour, et son covent,*

that is the successor, and his convent, are in their remitter, and shall hold the land discharged, because the same abbot cannot have any action, or a writ of entry *sine assensu capituli*, of the same land against any other person: 687 In the same manner it is, where a bishop or a dean, or other such persons alien, &c., without assent, &c., and the alienee charge the land, &c., and afterwards the bishop take back estate of the same land by licence (*d*), to him and to his successors, and afterwards the bishop dieth; his successor is in his remitter, as in right of his church, and shall defeat the charge, &c. *Causa qua supra.*

688 Also, if a man sue false action against tenant in tail, as if a man willeth to sue against him a writ of entry in the *Post*, supposing by this writ that the tenant in tail had not his entry, but by A. of B., who disseised the grandfather of the demandant, and this *suggestion* is false, and he reco-

Falsifier of recovery by issue in tail; (*the rule being that remitter cannot be in conflict with matter of record; but where a recovery has*

sount en lour remitter, et tiendront la terre discharge, pur ceo que mesme labbé ne poet aver ascun accion, ne brief dentre sine assensu capituli, *de mesme la terre envers nul autre persone:* 687 *En mesme le manere est, lou un evesque ou un dean, ou autres tielx persones alienount, &c., sauns assent, &c., et lalienė chargea la terre, &c., et puis levesque reprent estate de mesme la terre per licence, a luy et a ses successours, et puis levesque devie; son successour est en son remitter, come en droit de son esglise, et defetera le charge, &c.* Causa qua supra.

688 Item, *si home suist faux accion envers le tenaunt en le taille, sicome home voille suer envers luy un brief dentre en le* Post, *supposaunt per son brief que le tenaunt en le taille nad pas son entré, sinon per A. de B., qui disseisist laiel le demaundant, et ceo est faux, et il recovera envers le tenaunt en*

(*d*) That is, of the king and of the lords immediate and mediate, to dispense with the statutes of mortmain, whereof see more before, *Sect.* 140.—*Co. Lytt.* 360. b.

been had by default, or by false pleading, there it is otherwise).

vereth against the tenant in the tail by default, and sues execution, and afterwards the tenant in tail dieth, his issue can have a writ of *Formedon* against him that recovereth; and if he willeth to plead the recovery against the tenant in tail, the issue can say, that the said A. of B. did not disseise the grandfather of him that recovered in manner as his writ supposeth, and so he shall falsify his recovery. Also suppose this were true, that the said A. of B. did disseise the grandfather of the demandant that recovered, and that after the disseisin, the demandant, or his father, or his grandfather by a deed had released to the tenant in the tail all the right which he had in the land, &c., and this, notwithstanding he sueth a writ of entry in the *post* against the tenant in the tail, in the manner as is aforesaid, and the tenant in tail plead *in answer* to him, that the said A. of B. did not disseise his grandfather in such manner as his writ supposeth, and upon this they are at issue, and the issue is found for the demandant, whereby he hath judgment to recover, and sueth execution, and afterwards the tenant in tail dieth, his issue

le taille per defaute, et suist execucion, et puis le tenaunt en le taille morust, son issue poet aver brief de Formedon *envers celuy qui recovera ; et sil voille pleder le recoverë envers le tenaunt en le taille, lissue poet dire, que le dit A. de B. ne disseisist point laiel celuy qui recoverast, en le manere come son brief supposa, et issint il fauxera son recoverë. Auxi* posito, *que ceo fuist voire, que le dit A. de B. disseisist laiel le demaundant qui recoverast, et que apres le disseisin, le demaundant, ou son pere, ou son aiel per un fait avoit relesse al tenaunt en le taille tout le droit quil avoet en la terre, &c., et ceo nient contristeaunt il suist un brief dentre en le* post *envers le tenaunt en le taille, en le manere come est avauntdit, et le tenaunt en le taille pleda a luy, que le dit A. de B. ne disseisist pas son aiel en le manere come son brief supposa, et sur ceo sount a issue, et lissue est trove pur le demaundant, per que il ad juggement de recoverer, et suist execucion, et puis le tenaunt en le taille morust, son issue poet*

can have a writ of *Formedon* against him that recovered, and if he will plead the recovery by the action tried against his father, tenant in tail, then he can shew and plead the release made to his father, and so the action which was sued, feint in law, &c.

689 And it seemeth that a feint action is as much as to say in English, *a feyned action, scil.* such action that although the words of the writ be true, yet for certain causes he hath neither cause or title by the law to recover by the same action. And false action is where the words of the writ be false. And in these two cases aforesaid, if the case were such, that after such recovery, and execution thereof made, the tenant in tail had disseised him that recovered, and thereof died seised, whereby the land descended to his issue, this is a remitter to the issue, and the issue is in by force of the tail; and for that reason I have put the two cases preceding, to inform thee, my son, that the issue in the tail by force of a descent made unto him after a recovery and execu-

Feigned and false action distinguished.

[*See* ante, § 674, *where feme is remitted against her own recovery.*]

aver un brief de Formedon *envers celuy qui recovera, et sil voet pleder le recoverë per le accion trié envers son pere, tenaunt en taille, donques il poet monstrer et pleder le reles fait a son pere, et issint laccion que fuist sue, feynt en ley, &c.*

689 *Et il semble que feynt accion est ataunt adire en English,* feyned action, scil. *tiel accion que coment que les parolx de le brief sont voires, unqore pur certeyn causes il nad cause ne title per la ley de recoverer per mesme laccion. Et faux accion est, lou les parolx de le brief sount faux. Et en les deux cases avauntdites, si le cas fuist tiel, que apres tiel recoverë et execucion ent fait, le tenaunt en le taille ust disseisi celuy qui recovera, et ent morust seisi, per que la terre descendist a son issue, ceo est un remitter al issue, et lissue est eins per force de le taille; et pur celle cause jeo ay mys les deux cases precedentes, pur enfourmer toy, mon fits, que lissue en le taille per force dun discent fait a luy apres un recoverë et execucion ent fait envers son auncestre, poet*

tion thereof made against his ancestor, can be also well in in his remitter, just as he should be by the descent made to him after a discontinuance made by his ancestor of the entailed lands by feoffment in the country, or otherwise, &c.

The effect of a recovery or fine upon the issue in tail: *If tenant in tail suffer recovery by default, and die before execution had, the issue is remitted, and shall avoid execution by falsifier of the recovery.*

690 Also, in the cases aforesaid, if the case were such, that after that the demandant had judgment to recover against the tenant in the tail, and the same tenant in the tail die before any execution had against him, whereby the tenements descend to his issue, and he who recovereth sueth a *scire facias* out of the judgment, to have execution of the judgment against the issue in the tail, the issue shall plead the matter as afore is said; and so shall prove that the said recovery* was false or feint in law, and so shall bar him to have execution of (*i. e.* upon) the judgment, &c.

Upon plea of non-tenure, or disclaimer of

691 Also, if tenant in the tail discontinue the tail, and die, and his issue bring his writ of *Formedon* against the discon-

estre auxi bien en son remitter, sicome il serroit per le discent fait a luy apres un discontinuaunce fait per son auncestre de les terres taillés per feoffement en pais, ou autrement, &c.

690 Item, *en les cases avantdites, si le cas fuist tiel, que apres ceo que le demaundant avoit juggement de recoverer envers le tenaunt en le taille, et mesme le tenaunt en le taille morust devaunt ascun execucion ewe envers luy, per que les tenementes descendont a son issue, et celuy qui recovera suist un* scire facias *hors de le juggement, daver execucion de le juggement envers lissue en le taille, lissue pledera le matere come avaunt est dit : et issint provera que le dit recoverie* fuist faux ou feynt en ley, et issint luy barrera daver execucion de le juggement, &c.*

691 Item, *si tenaunt en le taille discontinua le taille, et morust, et son issue porta son brief de* Formedon *envers*

* This word is misprinted *revercion* in *Roh.*; in that copy *penes Ed.*, a contemporary hand has struck out *revercion*, and substituted *laccion, the action.*

tinuee, being tenant of the freehold of the land, and the discontinuee plead that he is not tenant, but otherwise* disclaimeth from the tenancy in the land; in this case the judgment shall be that the tenant go without day, and after such judgment the issue in the tail that is demandant may enter into the land, notwithstanding the discontinuance; and by such entry he shall be adjudged in in his remitter. And the reason is, for that if any man sue a *Præcipe quod reddat* against any tenant of freehold, in which action the demandant shall not recover damages, and the tenant plead† non-tenure, or otherwise disclaim in the tenancy, the demandant cannot aver his writ‡, that he is tenant as the writ supposeth. And for that cause the demandant, after that the judgment is given that the tenant go without day, can

tenant in Formedon, *albeit the judgment be that the tenant go without day; yet in judgment of law the demandant may enter according to the title of his writ, and be seised in tail, notwithstanding the discontinuance, and shall be adjudged in his remitter, remitter being taken in a large sense.*— Co. Lytt. 362. a.

le discontinué, esteant tenaunt de franktenement del terre, et le discontinué pleda que il nest tenaunt, mes autrement disclayma de la tenauncie en la terre; en ceo cas le juggement serra que le tenaunt alast sauns jour, et apres tiel juggement lissue en le taille qui est demaundant poet entrer en la terre, nient contristeant le discontinuaunce; et per tiel entré il serra ajugge eins en son remitter. Et la cause est, pur ceo que si ascun home suist* Præcipe quod reddat *envers ascun tenaunt de franktenement, en quelle accion le demaundant ne recovera damages, et le tenaunt pledast† nontenure, mes autrement disclayma en le tenauncie, le demaundant ne poet averer son brief‡, que il est tenaunt come le brief suppose. Et pur celle cause le demaundant, apres ceo que juggement est done que le tenaunt alast sauns jour,*

---

* The common editions read this word *ousterment, utterly*, which is followed by *Sir E. Coke's* Transl. *Rastell's* Transl. accords with the text.

† In some copies of *Rastell's* Translation, this passage is rendered *pleadeth*, not *non-tenure*.

‡ *Rastell's* Translation renders this passage, *aver* in *the writ.*

enter into the tenements demanded, the which shall be as great advantage to him in law, as if he had judgment to recover against the tenant, and by such entry he is in in his remitter by force of the entail. But where the demandant recovereth damages against the tenant, there the demandant may aver that he is tenant as the writ supposeth, and this for the advantage of the demandant to recover his damages, or otherwise he shall not receive* the damages, which damages are or were† to him given by the law.

Action by disseisee against heir of disseisor, or disclaimer by heir, plaintiff remitted.

692 Also, if a man be disseised, and the disseisor die, his heir being in by descent, now the entry of the disseisee is taken away; and if the disseisee bring his writ of entry *sur disseisin* in the *per* against the heir, and the heir disclaim in the tenancy, &c., the demandant may aver *in* his writ that he is tenant as the writ supposeth, if he will, to recover

poet entrer en les tenementes demaundez, le quel serra auxi graund avantage a luy en la ley, sicome il avoet juggement de recoverer envers le tenaunt, et per tiel entré il est en son remitter per force del taille. Mes lou le demaundant recovera damages envers le tenaunt, là le demaundant poet averrer que il est tenaunt come le brief suppose, et ceo pur lavantage del demaundant pur recoverer ses damages, ou autrement il ne resceyvera ses damages, les queux damages sount ou fuerent† a luy dones per la ley.*

692 Item, *si home soit disseisi, et le disseisour devie, son heire esteaunt eins per discent, ore lentré de le disseisi est tolle ; et si le dissesi porta son brief dentre* sur disseisin *en le* per *envers leire, et leire disclayma en la tenauncie, &c., le demaundant poet averrer son brief que il est tenaunt come le brief suppose, sil voet, pur recoverer ses damages ; mes un-*

* This word in *Lettou & M.* and *Roh.* is printed as in the text ; but in *Machl., recovera.* In that copy of *Roh., penes Ed.*, the word *recovera* is substituted by a contemporary hand. *Rastell's* Transl. reads according to the text.

† The words *ou fuerent, or were,* are not given in *Lettou & M.*; but appear in *Machl.* and *Roh.* and all subsequent editions.

his damages; but yet, if he will relinquish the averment, &c., he may lawfully enter into the land because of the disclaimer, notwithstanding that his entry before was taken away; and this was adjudged before my Master Sir Robert Danby, late Chief-Justice of the Common Pleas, and his companions, [&c.*]

Sir Robert Danby was C. J. C. P., 2 E. 4, 1462.

693 Also, where the entry of a man is lawful, although he take estate to him when he is of full age, for term of life, or in the tail, or in fee, this is a remitter to him, if such taking of estate be not by deed indented, or by matter of record, which shall conclude or estop him (§ 58, 667, 693) (*e*):

Remitter by acceptance of estate.—Estoppel. *Claimant having right of entry taking estate is in his remitter.*

qore, sil voet relinquisher laverrement, &c., il poet loialement entrer en la terre per cause del disclaymer, nient obstaunt que son entré adevant fuist tolle; et ceo fuist ajugge devaunt mon Maister Sir Robert Danby, jadys Chief-Justice de le Comen Banc, et ses compaignons, [*&c.**]

693 Item, *lou lentré dun home est congeable, coment que il prent estate a luy quant il est de pleyn age, pur terme de vie, ou en le taille, ou en fee, ceo est un remitter a luy, si tiel prisel del estate ne soit per fait endente, ou per matere de recorde, que luy concludera ou estoppera: qar si home soit*

---

* This *&c.* is not given in *Rastell's* Transl., *Tottyl*, 1556, and subsequent editions; it appears, however, in the previous editions, and in *Marshe* 1556.

(*e*) With regard to an estoppel being worked by an indenture and not by a deed poll, see *ante*, § 58, p. 71 (*a*), where, in the case of lessor and lessee, the lessee is not estopped, though the lessor is by deed poll. What *Sir Edward Coke* states, in his comment on that section at 47, *b.*, is fully discussed in *Bacon's Abr. Leases* (*O*), and the authorities there cited.

It seems, however, that an estoppel can be worked by a deed-poll, if it be sealed by both parties, or there is contained therein any reciprocal covenants.—See *Plowd.* 421, 434; *Co. Lytt.* 143. *b.*, 352. *a.*, 363. *b.*; *Touchst.* 53, and authorities there cited.

Example. Disseisee to disseisor.

for if a man be disseised, and thereof take estate from the disseisor without deed, or by deed poll, this is a good remitter to the disseisee.

Second example. Alienee in fee of lessee for life to lessor.

694 Also, if a man let land for term of life to another, who alieneth to another in fee, and the alienee* make an estate to the lessor, this is a remitter to the lessor, because his entry was lawful.

Third example. Acceptance by disseisee of lease from disseisor, a remitter.

695 Also, if a man be disseised, and the disseisor let the land to the disseisee by deed poll, or without deed, for term of years, by which the disseisee entereth, this entry is a remitter to the disseisee: for in such case where the entry of a man is lawful, and a lease is made to him, albeit he claim by words in *pais*, that he hath estate by force of such lease, or saith openly, that he claimeth nothing in the land but by force of such lease; yet this is a remitter to him, for that such claim† in *pais* is nothing to the purpose. But if he claim†

Disclaimer in

disseisi, et ent prent estate de le disseisour sauns fait, ou per fait polle, ceo est bon remitter al disseisi.

694 Item, *si home lessa terre pur terme de vie a un autre, le quel aliena a un autre en fee, et lalienè* fait estate a le lessour, ceo est un remitter al lessour, pur ceo que son entré fuist congeable.*

695 Item, *si home soit disseisi, et le disseisour lessa la terre al disseisi per fait polle, ou sauns fait, pur terme des ans, per quel le disseisi entra, cest entré est un remitter a le disseisi: qar en tiel cas lou lentré dun home est congeable, et un lees est fait a luy, coment quil clayma per parolx en pais, que il ad estate per force de tiel lees, ou dit overtement, que il ne clayma riens en la terre si non per force de tiel lees; unqore ceo est remitter a luy, qar tiel clayme† en le* pais *nest riens a purpos. Mes sil clayme† en court de record, que il ad estate*

* In the three earliest copies this word is misprinted *alienour;* this error in that copy of *Roh. penes Ed.* is corrected by a contemporary hand.

† This is printed *disclaymer*, *disclaim*, in the later editions in both instances. *Rastell's* Transl. accords with the text.

in court of record, that he hath no estate but by force of such lease, and not otherwise, then is he concluded, &c.

court of record is an estoppel to a remitter.

696 Also, if two joint-tenants seised of certain tenements in fee, the one being of full age, the other within age, be disseised, and the disseisor die seised, and his issue enter, the one of the joint-tenants being then within age, and after that he cometh to full age, the heir of the disseisor letteth the tenements to the same joint-tenants for term of their lives, this is a remitter (as to the moiety) to him that was within age, because he is seised of the moiety which belongeth to him, in fee, for that his entry was lawful. But the other joint-tenant hath in the other moiety but estate for term of his life by force of the lease, because his entry had been taken away, &c.

Lease for life by heir of disseisor of joint-tenants, one of whom was under age, to both the joint-tenants: a remitter as to the moiety of the joint tenant disseised under age; but as to the other moiety the entry is tolled, and that joint-tenant only takes under the lease.

forsque per force de tiel lees, et nemye autrement, donques il est conclude, &c.

696 Item, *si deux jointenauntes seisis de certeyn tenementes en fee, lun esteaunt de pleyn age, lautre deins age, sount disseisis, et le disseisour morust seisi, et son issue entra, lun de les jointenauntes esteaunt donques deins age, et apres que il vient al pleyn age, leire le disseisour lessa les tenementes a mesmes les jointenauntes pur terme de lour vies, ceo est un remitter, quaunt al moyté, a cestuy qui fuist deins age, pur ceo que il est seisi de cest moyté que affiert a luy, en fee, pur ceo que son entré fuist congeable. Mes lautre jointenaunt nad en lautre moyté forsque estate pur terme de sa vie per force de le lees, pur ceo que son entré fuist tolle, &c.*

CHAPTER XIII.

WARRANTY.

The doctrine of warranty, a "curious and cunning learning," as *Sir Edward Coke* describes it, and which was one of the most copious and abstruse subjects in our law of real property, had its origin in tenure, and is derived from the obligation which was imposed on the lord, on his receiving homages, to defend his tenant in respect of the land holden of him, or, if he failed therein, to give him a recompense of equal value in other land.

This doctrine subsequently insinuated itself into contracts between parties who did not stand in the relation of lord and tenant; but as the livery of seisin, evidenced and accompanied by the deed of feoffment, was deemed equivalent to feudal investiture, the expedience of warranty naturally suggested itself to the parties, but became subject to this distinction: *viz.* that, insomuch as between lord and tenant, warranty was inherent and *implied* in the terms of investiture and from the effect of the feudal connexion, so, between the feoffor and feoffee, between whom no such relation subsisted, warranty became the subject of contract, and *expressed;* and upon this expressed warranty all the consequences of feudal or *implied* warranty have attached.

One of the most familiar operations of this doctrine was the derivative, or perhaps correlative, doctrine of *voucher,* which, with its accompaniment, *recompense in value,* formed the basis of *feigned recoveries,* a mode of assurance lately abolished, and for which more simple modes of conveyance have been substituted by the stat. 3 & 4 Gul. 4, c. 74.

Lyttleton illustrates this doctrine by examples and cases of the three kinds or instances of warranty known to our law, *viz.* warranty commencing by disseisin (§ 698—702), collateral warranty (§ 704, 709), and lineal warranty (§ 703, 706); and puts a case to shew that a lineal and collateral warranty might exist together at the same time (§ 710). The subject of this chapter is continued by illustration of the cases wherein the warranty of the tenant in tail barred his issue (§ 712—719). The learning of remainders is next touched upon in a discourse on *Rikhill's case*, in which an attempt to create future estates of freehold by way of springing uses, failed for want of compliance with the rules on which estates in remainder are founded, but more particularly on account of the invalidity of a limitation after alienation, such limitation being void as repugnant and inconsistent with the quality of the preceding estate (§ 720—723); although at this time a fee may be limited after a fee, and freehold estates be created to take effect *in futuro*, in contravention of those rules, by operation of the Statute of Uses; and the remaining portion of the chapter is occupied by an exposition of the effect of warranties, either as lineal or collateral, having regard to the persons by whom they are made, *viz.* by father (§ 729); by mother, wife of tenant in tail (§ 713); by wife, tenant in dower (whose warranty was restrained by 11 H. 7, c. 20) (§ 725); by husband, tenant by the curtesy, whose warranty was restrained at the time *Lyttleton* wrote by 6 E. 3, c. 1 (§ 724, 728); and by husband aliening his wife's estate (§ 731).

Warranty also might have been extinguished, 1st, by release (§ 748); 2ndly, by attainder (§ 745); 3rdly, by re-feoffment of the warrantor, by the warrantee; 4thly, *Sir Edward Coke* adds to these, defeazance.—*Co. Lytt.* 393, § 745.

Warranty always, as is the case with respect to remitter, descended upon the heir at common law, and not according to the course of any customary mode of descent (§ 735, 736).

A clause of warranty was usually annexed to all deeds of feoffment, and that clause bound the heirs of the feoffor (§ 711). In estates tail, where tenant in tail aliened, if to his feoffment was superadded a warranty, it barred the heir if assets descended, but not otherwise; and where no assets descended, a remainder-man or reversioner might be barred if he claimed as heir to the tenant in tail, whether assets descended or not. So that *lineal* warranty could only bar an estate tail if assets descended, to satisfy the heir for the lands warranted and aliened (§ 712). *Collateral* warranty barred in both cases, without assets (*Id.*); and a remainder-man or reversioner, claiming as heir under the entail, was barred: otherwise it was if such remainder-man or reversioner claimed from the donor, in which case the estate tail took effect.

The doctrine of collateral warranty had long been deemed a juridical sophistry; indeed it was founded on the mere assumption that the warrantor aliening would not deprive the heir *sans recompense* (*a*). This doctrine, however, was exceedingly restricted by stat. 4 & 5 Anne, c. 16, which made void all warranties by *tenant for life*, and all collateral warranties made by any ancestor *not having an estate of inheritance in possession.*

The doctrine of lineal warranty remained as at common law, that is to say, it bound the heir if assets descended; but by stat. 3 & 4 Gul. 4, c. 74, s. 14, *all* warranties of lands which shall be made after 31st December, 1833, by any tenant in tail thereof, shall be absolutely void against the issue in tail, and all persons whose estates are to take effect after the determination or in defeazance of the estate tail.

(*a*) *Sir E. Coke* says, that it had been attempted in Parliament that a statute should be made that no one should be barred by a collateral warranty, but where assets descend from the same ancestor, but it never took effect. *Rot. Parl.* 50 E. 3, num. 77.

The presumption that the warrantor (the uncle, § 709,) would not disinherit the heir unless with an adequate recompense or advancement, is derided by *March, viz.*—" A very strange presumption; how many *uncles* might a man find in this age, who, for a small sum of money, would not care to disinherit twenty heirs, if possibly so many could be, without the least scruple of conscience."—*Commonwealth's Friend.* 12mo. Lond. 1651.

Warranty commencing by disseisin was, where the ancestor that made the warranty is party to the wrong; and such warranty was not binding, because it cannot be presumed that one who is so unjust as to do wrong, will be so just as to leave a recompense to his heir: wherefore, such contracts were wholly rejected as collusive and founded on no consideration.—*Gilb. Ten.* 140, 141.

---

697 It is commonly said that there be three *kinds of* warranties, *scil.* warranty lineal, warranty collateral, and warranty that commences by disseisin. And it is to be understood, before the statute of Gloucester, all warranties which descended to them that are heirs to those who made the warranties, were bars to the same heirs to demand any lands or tenements against the warranties, except the warranties which commenced by disseisin ; for such warranty was never a bar to the heir, because the warranty commenced by wrong, *scil.* by disseisin (*b*).

Three kinds of warranties.

Before stat. of Gloucester (6 E. 1) all warranties, excepting those commencing by disseisin, barred the heirs upon whom they descended. § 725.

697 *Il est communement dit que trois garraunties y sount,* scil. *garrauntie lineall, garrauntie collaterall, et garrauntie que commence per disseisin. Et est assavoir, devaunt lestatuit de Gloucester, toutes garraunties queux descendont a eux queux sount heires a eux qui fesoient les garraunties, furent barres a mesmes les heires a demaunder ascuns terres ou tenementes encontre les garraunties, forspris les garraunties que commencerent per disseisin ; qar tiel garrauntie ne fuist unques barre al heire, pur ceo que la garrauntie commenca per tort,* scil. *per disseisin.*

(*b*) The stat. of Gloucester, 6 E. 1, provides that if assets descend, but to not the value of the land aliened, then the heir shall be barred for so much of the land aliened as that which is left amounts to, and no more. See *post*, § 724, where, by the same statute, the warranty of the tenant by curtesy did not bar the heir unless assets descended to him of the same value with the land aliened.

Examples of warranty commencing by disseisin, *(so called because the conveyance whereunto the warranty is annexed works a disseisin).*

698 Warranty that commences by disseisin is in such form, as where there is father and son, and the son purchaseth land, &c., and letteth the same land to his father for term of years, and the father by his deed thereof enfeoffeth another in fee, and bindeth himself and his heirs to warranty, and the father die, whereby the warranty descendeth on the son, this warranty shall not bar the son; for notwithstanding that warranty, the son can well enter into the land, or have an assise against the alienee, if he will, because the warranty commenced by disseisin: for when the father, that hath not estate but for term of years, made a feoffment in fee, this was a disseisin to the son of the freehold which then was in the son. In the same manner it is if the son letteth to the father the land to hold at will, and afterwards the father make a feoffment with warranty, &c. And as it is said of the father, so it may be said of every other ancestor, &c. In the same manner is it, if tenant by *elegit*, tenant by statute-merchant, or tenant by statute-staple, make a feoffment in

Which warranties do not bar the heir.

698 *Garrauntie que commence per disseisin est en tiel fourme, sicome lou il y est pere et fits, et le fits purchasa terre, &c., et lessa mesme la terre a son pere pur terme des ans, et le pere per son fait ent enfeoffa un autre en fee, et obligea luy et ses heires a garrauntie, et le pere devie, per que la garrauntie descendist al fitz, ceo garrauntie ne barrera mye le fitz ; qar nient obstant celle garrauntie, le fitz poet bien entrer en la terre, ou aver un assise envers lalienee, sil voet, pur ceo que la garrauntie commenca per disseisin : qar quant le pere, qui ne avoet estate forsque pur terme des ans, fist un feoffement en fee, ceo fuist un disseisin al fitz del franktenement que adonques fuist en le fitz. En mesme le manere est, si le fitz lessa a le pere la terre a tener a volunté, et puis le pere fait un feoffement ove garrauntie, &c. En sicome est dit de pere, issint poet estre dit de chescun autre auncestre, &c. En mesme la manere est, si tenaunt per* elegit, *tenaunt per statuit-merchant, ou tenaunt per statuit de lestaple, fait un*

fee with warranty, &c., this shall not bar the heir who ought to have the land, because such warranties began by disseisin.

699 Also, if guardian in chivalry, or guardian in socage, make a feoffment in fee, or in fee-tail, or for term of life with warranty, &c., such warranties are not bars to the heirs to whom the lands shall descend, because they commence by disseisin.

Case of guardian aliening with warranty.

700 Also, if the father and the son purchase certain lands or tenements, to have and to hold to them jointly, &c., and afterwards the father alien the whole to another, and bind himself and his heirs to warranty, &c., and afterwards the father die, that warranty shall not bar the son of the moiety which belongeth to him of the said lands or tenements, because as to that moiety which belongs to the son, the warranty commenced by disseisin, &c.

Warranty by disseisin as to one moiety, and lineal or collateral as to the other moiety. See § 708, where warranty may be, at the same time, either lineal or collateral.

701 Also, if A. of B. be seised of a mese, and F. of G., that no right hath to enter into the same mese, claiming the same mese to hold to him and to his heirs, entereth into the said

Another example of warranty by disseisin.

feoffement en fee ovesque garrauntie, &c., ceo ne barrera my leire qui doit aver la terre, pur ceo que tielx garraunties commencerent per disseisin.

699 Item, *si gardeyn en chivalerie, ou gardeyn en socage, fait un feoffement en fee, ou en fee-taille, ou pur terme de vie ovesque garrauntie, &c., tielx garraunties ne sount pas barres a les heires as queux les terres serront descendus, pur ceo que ils commencent per disseisin.*

700 Item, *si le pere et le fitz purchasent certeyn terres ou tenementes, a aver et tener a eux jointement, &c., et puis le pere aliena lentierté a un autre, et obligea luy et ses heires a garrauntie, &c., et puis le pere devie, celle garrauntie ne barrera mye le fitz de le moyté que a luy affiert de les dites terres ou tenementes, pur ceo que quaunt a cel moyté que affiert a le fitz, la garrauntie commenca per disseisin, &c.*

701 Item, *si A. de B. soit seisi dun mese, et F. de G., qui nul droit ad dentrer en mesme le mese, claymaunt mesme le mese u tener a luy et a ses heires, entra en mesme le mese,*

mese, but the said A. of B. is then continually dwelling in the same mese: in this case the possession of the freehold shall be always adjudged in A. of B., and not in F. of G., because in such case where two be in one house or other tenements, and the one claimeth by one title, and the other by another title, the law shall adjudge him in possession that hath right to have the possession of the same tenements. But if in the case aforesaid, the said F. of G. make a feoffment to certain barretors and extortioners in the country, to have maintenance from them, of the same house, by a deed of feoffment with warranty, by force whereof the said A. of B. dare not dwell in the house, but goeth out of the same house, this warranty commenceth by disseisin, because such feoffment was the cause that the said A. of B. left the possession of the same house, &c.

Where two occupy by different titles, the possession is in him who has the right of possession.

Terror and extortion a mode of disseisin.

702 Also, if a man that hath no right to enter into another's tenements, enter into the same tenements, and incontinently thereof make a feoffment to others by his deed with war-

Another example of warranty by disseisin.

mes le dit A. de B. adonques est continuelement demurraunt en mesme le mese: en ceo cas le possession de franktenement serra tout temps ajugge en A. de B., et nemy en F. de G., pur ceo que en tiel cas lou deux sount en un mese ou autres tenementes, et lun clayma per lun title, et lautre per lautre title, la ley ajuggera celuy en possession qui ad droit daver le possession de mesmes les tenementes. Mes si en le cas avauntdit, le dit F. de G. fait un feoffement as certeyn barretours et extorcionours en le pays, pur maintenaunce de eux aver, de mesme le mese, per un fait de feoffement ovesque garrauntie, per force de quele le dit A. de B. nosast par demurrer en le mese, mes se en alast hors de le mese, cest garrauntie commence per disseisin, pur ceo que tiel feoffement fuist cause que le dit A. de B. relinquast le possession de mesme le mese, &c.

702 Item, *si home qui nul droit ad dentrer en autri tenementes, entra en mesmes les tenementes, et incontinent ent fait un feoffement as autres per son fait ovesque garrauntie,*

ranty, and deliver to them seisin, that warranty commenceth by disseisin, because the disseisin and feoffment were made, as it were, at one time. And that this is law, ye may see in a plea, *Anno* 31 *E.* 3, in a writ of *Formedon* in the reverter.

Warranty lineal: *Example of.*

703 Warranty lineal is, where a man seised of land in fee, thereof maketh a feoffment by his deed to another, and binds himself and his heirs to warranty, and hath issue, and dieth, and the warranty descends on his issue, this is lineal warranty. And the reason why this is called lineal warranty, is not because the warranty descendeth from the father to his heir; but the reason is, because if no such deed with warranty had been made by the father, then the right of the tenements should descend to the heir, and the heir should convey the descent from the father, &c. 704 For if there be father and son, and the son purchase tenements in fee, and the father thereof disseiseth his son, and alieneth to another in fee by his deed, and by the same deed bindeth him and his heirs to warrant the same tenements, &c., and the father dieth; now

Rule or principle upon which lineal warranty is founded.—See also § 707, for the more strict rule.

Collateral warranty: *Example of. [See § 709, for example of like warranty on issue in tail.]*

et delivera a eux seisin, cel garrauntie commence per disseisin, pur ceo que le disseisin et le feoffement furent faitz, quasi uno tempore. *Et que ceo est ley, poies veir en un plee,* Anno xxxi. E. iii. *en un brief de* Formedon *en la revercion.*

703 *Garrauntie lyneall est, lou home seisi de terre en fee, ent fait feoffement per son fait a un autre, et obligea luy et ses heires a garrauntie, et ad issue, et morust, et la garrauntie descendist a son issue, ceo est lyneall garrauntie. Et la cause pur que ceo est dit lyneall garrauntie, nest pur ceo que la garrauntie descendist de le pere a son heire; mes la cause est, pur ceo que si nul tiel fait ovesque garrauntie fusoit fait per le pere, donques le droit de les tenementes descendroit al heire, et leire conveieroit le discent de le pere, &c.* 704 *Qar si soit pere et fitz, et le fits purchasa tenementes en fee, et le pere de ceo disseisist son fitz, et ceo aliena a un autre en fee per son fait, et per mesme le fait obligea luy et ses heires a garrauntir mesmes les tenementes, &c., et le pere morust; ore*

Rule on which collateral warranty is founded; and see also § 717.

is the son barred to have the said tenements; for he cannot by any suit, or other mean by the law, have the same lands, by reason of the said warranty: and this is a collateral warranty, and yet the warranty descendeth lineally from the father to the son; 705 but, because that if no such deed with warranty had been made, the son in no manner could convey the title which he hath to the tenements from his father unto him, insomuch that his father had not any estate or right in the tenements; therefore such warranty is called collateral warranty, insomuch as he that made the warranty is collateral to the title of the tenements: and this is as much as to say, that he upon whom the warranty descendeth could not to himself convey the title which he had in the tenements through him that made the warranty, in this case, if no such warranty had been made.

Example of lineal warranty. *Where the son must claim the land as heir to*

706 Also, if there be grandfather, father and son, and the grandfather be disseised, in whose possession the father releaseth by his deed with warranty, &c., and dieth, and after-

est le fitz barre daver les dits tenementes; qar il ne poet per ascun suyte, ou autre meane per la ley, aver mesmes les tenementes, per cause del dit garrauntie: et ceo est un collaterall garrauntie, et unqore la garrauntie descendist linealment de le pere a le fitz; 705 *mes, pur ceo que si nul tiel fait ovesque garrauntie ust este fait, le fitz en nul manere puissoit conveier le title que il ad de les tenementes de son pere a luy, entaunt que son pere navoit ascun estate ou droit en les tenementes; pur ceo tiel garrauntie est appelle collaterall garrauntie, entaunt que celuy qui fist la garrauntie est collaterall a le title de les tenementes: et cest ataunt adire, que celuy a qui la garrauntie descendist ne puisoit conveier a luy le title que il ad de les tenementes per mye celuy qui fist la garrauntie, en ceo cas, que nul tiel garrauntie fuist fait.*

706 Item, *si soit aiel, pere, et fitz, et laiel soit disseisi, en que possession le pere relessa per son fait ovesque garrauntie, &c., et morust, et puis laiel morust; ore le fitz est barre de*

wards the grandfather dieth; now is the son barred of the tenements by the warranty of the father. And this is called lineal warranty, because if no such warranty had been, the son could not convey the right of the tenements to him, nor shew how he is heir to the grandfather, but by means of the father*.

his grandfather, and yet because he can not make him self heir to his grandfather, but by his father, it is lineal.—Co. Lytt. 371. *a.*

707 Also, if a man have issue two† sons, and is disseised, and the eldest son release to the disseisor by his deed with warranty, &c., and die without issue, and afterwards the father dieth, this is a lineal warranty to the younger son, because although the elder son died in the life of the father, yet by possibility it might be, that he could convey to him the title of the land by (*i. e.* through) his elder brother, if no such warranty had been: for it might be, that after the death of the father the elder brother entered into the tenements, and

Example [*of* lineal warranty.] *Where the heir that is to be barred by the warranty is not to make his descent by him that made the warranty, as in the preceding case.*—Co. Lytt. 371. *b.*

*les tenementes per la garrauntie del pere. Et ceo est appelle lineall garrauntie, pur ceo que si nul tiel garrauntie fuist, le fitz ne puisoit conveier le droit de les tenementes a luy, ne monstrer coment il est heire al aiel, forsque per meane del pere**.

707 Item, *si home ad issue deux*† *fitz, et est disseisi, et leisne fitz relessa al disseisour per son fait ovesque garrauntie, &c., et morust sauns issue, et apres ceo le pere morust, ceo est un lineall garrauntie al puisne fitz, pur ceo que coment que leisne fits morust en la vie le pere, unqore* [*pur ceo que*‡] *per possibilité il puissoit estre, quil puissoit conveier a luy le title del terre per son eisne frere, si nul· tiel garrauntie fuisoit: qar il puissoit estre que apres la mort le pere leisne frere entroit en les tenementes, et morust sauns issue, et donques le*

* This passage will more readily convey the sense of *Lyttleton*, if the negative adverbs are rejected, when the text will be thus:—*The son could convey the right of the tenements to him, or shew how he is heir to the grandfather by means of the father.*

† *Three; Rastell's* Transl., *Tottyl* 1556, and subsequent editions.

‡ These words seem to be a redundancy.

died without issue, and then the younger son shall convey to him the title by the elder*. But in this case, if the younger son release with warranty to the disseisor, and die without issue, this is a collateral warranty to the elder, because that of such land as was to the father†, the elder by no possibility can convey to him the title by means of the younger son.

A warranty that is collateral *in respect of some persons, may afterwards become* lineal *in respect of others.*

708 Also, if tenant in the tail have issue three sons, and discontinue the tail in fee, and the middle son release by his deed to the discontinuee, and bind himself and his heirs to warranty, &c., and afterwards the tenant in the tail die, and the middle son die without issue, now is the eldest son barred to have any recovery by writ of *Formedon,* because the warranty of the middle brother is collateral to him, insomuch as he can by no means convey to himself by force of the tail any descent by the middle *brother,* and therefore it is a collateral warranty. But if in this case the elder son die without

puisne fitz conveiera a luy le title per le eisne. Mes en tiel cas, si le puisne fits relessa ove garrauntie a le disseisour, et morust sauns issue, ceo est un collateral garrauntie al eisne, pur ceo que de tiel terre que fuist al pere†, leisne per nul possibilité poet conveier a luy le title per le meane de le puisne.*

708 Item, *si tenaunt en le taille ad issue trois fitz, et discontinua le taille en fee, et le mulnes fitz relessa per son fait al discontinué, et obligea luy et ses heires al garrauntie, &c., et puis le tenaunt en le taille morust, et le mulnes fits morust sauns issue, ore est leisne fits barre daver ascun recoverie per brief de* Formedon, *pur ceo que la garrauntie del mulnes frere est collaterall a luy, entaunt que il ne poet per nul manere conveier a luy per force del taille ascun discent per le mulnes, et pur ceo cest une collaterall garrauntie. Mes si en ceo cas leisne fitz devie sauns issue, ore le puisne frere poet bien aver*

---

* *His elder brother; Rastell's* Transl.

† *Other; Rastell's* Transl., *Tottyl* 1556, and subsequent editions.

issue, now the younger brother can well have a writ of *Formedon* in the descender, and shall recover the same land, because the warranty of the middle *brother* is lineal to the younger son*, because it might be that by possibility the middle *brother* might be seised by force of the tail after the death of his elder brother, and then the younger brother might convey his title of descent through the middle *brother.*

709 Also, if tenant in the tail discontinue the tail, and have issue, and die, and the uncle of the issue release to the discontinuee with warranty, &c., and die without issue, this is collateral warranty to the issue in the tail, because the warranty descendeth upon the issue that cannot convey himself to the entail by means of his uncle.

Example of collateral warranty *on issue in tail.*

710 Also, if tenant in the tail have issue two daughters, and die, and the elder entereth into the whole, and thereof maketh a feoffment in fee with warranty, &c., and afterwards the elder daughter die without issue; in this case the younger

Warranty both lineal and collateral at one time. *Example of alienation by one parcener in tail.*

un brief de Formedon *en descendre, et recovera mesme la terre, pur ceo que la garrauntie le mulnes est lineall a le fitz* puisne, pur ceo que il puissoit estre que per possibilité le mulnes puissoit estre seisi per force del taille apres la mort son eisne frere, et donques le puisne frere puissoit conveier son title de descent per le mulnes.*

709 Item, *si tenaunt en le taille discontinua le taille, et ad issue, et deria, et luncle del issue relessa al discontinué ovesque garrauntie, &c., et morust sauns issue, ceo est collaterall garrauntie al issue en le taille, pur ceo que la garrauntie descendist sur lissue le quel ne poet soy conveier a le taille per meane de son uncle.*

710 Item, *si tenaunt en le taille ad issue deux files, et morust, et leisne entra en le entierté, et ent fait un feoffement en fee ovesque garrauntie, &c., et puis leisne file morust sauns issue; en ceo cas la puisne file est barre quaunt al un moyté, et*

* *Brother; Rastell's* Transl.

daughter is barred as to the one moiety, and as to the other moiety she is not barred: for as to the moiety which belongeth to the younger daughter she is barred, because that as to that moiety which belongeth to her, she cannot convey the descent by means of (*i. e.* through) her elder sister, and therefore, as to that moiety, this is a collateral warranty. But as to the other moiety, which belongeth to her elder sister, the warranty is not a bar to the younger sister, because she can convey her descent, as to that moiety which belongeth to her elder sister, by the same elder sister, and so as to that moiety which belongeth to the elder sister, the warranty as to that, is lineal to the younger sister.

The effect of lineal warranty *is to bar the heir of estate in* fee *without assets, and of estate in fee tail with assets.*

711 And note, that as to him that demandeth fee-simple by any of his ancestors, he shall be barred by warranty lineal, which descendeth upon him, unless it be restrained by some statute; 712 But he that demandeth fee-tail by writ of *Formedon* in *discender*, shall not be barred by lineal warranty, unless he have assets by descent in fee-simple by the same ancestor that made the warranty. But collateral warranty is

But collateral

quaunt al autre moyté ele nest pas barre: gar quaunt a la moyté que affiert a la puisne file ele est barre, pur ceo que quaunt a celle moyté que affiert a luy, ele ne poet conveier le discent per mye le meane de son eisne soer, et pur ceo, quaunt a celle moyté, ceo est un collaterall garrauntie. Mes quaunt al autre moyté, que affiert a son eisne soer, la garrauntie nest pas barre a la puisne soer, pur ceo quel poet conveier son discent, quaunt a celle moyté que affiert a son eisne soer, per mesme le eisne soer, et issint quaunt a celle moyté que affiert al eisne soer, la garrauntie quaunt a ceo, est lineall al puisne soer.

711 *Et nota, que quaunt a celuy qui demanda fee-simple per ascun de ses auncestres, il serra barre per garrauntie lineall, que descendist sur luy, si non que soit restreigne per ascun estatuit;* 712 *Mes il qui demanda fee-taille per brief de* Formedon *en descendre, ne serra my barre per lineall garrauntie, sinon queil ad assetes per descent en fee-simple per mesme launcestre qui fist la garrauntie. Mes collaterall gar-*

a bar to him that demandeth fee, and also to him that demandeth fee-tail without any other descent of fee-simple, except in cases which are restrained by the statutes, and in other cases for certain causes, as shall be said hereafter.

warranty bars the heir of both fee and of tail without issue.

713 Also, if land be given to a man and to the heirs of his body begotten, who taketh wife, and *they* have issue a son between them, and the husband discontinueth the tail in fee, and dieth, and afterwards the wife releaseth to the discontinuee in fee with warranty, &c., and dieth, and the warranty descends on the son, this is collateral warranty; 714 but if tenements be given to the husband and wife, and to the heirs of their two bodies begotten, who have issue a son, and the husband discontinue the tail, and die, and afterwards the wife release with warranty, &c., and die, this warranty is but a lineal warranty to the son: for the son shall not be barred in this case to sue his writ of *Formedon*, unless he have assets by descent in fee-simple by his mother, because their issue in writ of *Formedon* ought to convey to him the right as heir to his father and to his mother of their two bodies begotten, by

Warranty by mother, wife of tenant in tail, is collateral, and bars the son.

Husband and wife donees in special tail, husband's discontinuance and wife's subsequent release with warranty, is a lineal warranty on the son.

rauntie est barre a celuy qui demaunda fee, et auxi a celuy qui demaunda fee-taille sauns ascun autre descent de fee-simple, sinon en cases que sount restreignes per les statutes, et en autres cases pur certeyn causes, come serra dit en apres.

713 Item, *si terre soit done a un home et a les heires de son corps engendres, le quel prent feme, et ount issue fitz entre eux, et le baron discontinua le taille en fee, et devie, et puis la feme relessa al discontinué en fee ovesque garrauntie, &c., et morust, et la garrauntie descendist a le fits, ceo est collaterall garrauntie;* 714 *mes si tenementes soient dones a le baron et sa feme, et a les heires de lour deux corps engendres, queux ount issue fitz, et le baron discontinua le taille, et morust, et puis la feme relessa ovesque garrauntie, &c., et morust, cest garrauntie nest forsque une lineall garrauntie a le fitz: qar le fits ne serra barre en ceo cas de suer son brief de* Formedon, *sinon que il ad assetes per discent en fee-simple per sa mere, pur ceo que lour issue en brief de* Formedon *covient conveier a luy le droit come heire a son pere et a sa mere de lour deux*

form of the gift (*per formam doni*); and so in this case the warranty of the father and the warranty of the mother are nothing else but lineal warranty to the heir, &c.

Lineal and collateral warranty distinguished. See ante, § 707.

715 And note, that in every case where a man demandeth tenements in fee-tail by writ of *Formedon,* if any of the issue in the tail that hath possession, or that hath not any possession, make a warranty, &c., if he that sueth the writ of *Formedon* could by any possibility, by matter which could exist in fact, convey to him*self,* through him that made the warranty by the form of the gift, &c., (*per formam doni*), this is a lineal warranty, and not collateral.

Collateral warranty. *Gift by father to his eldest son in tail, remainder to the middle son in tail, remainder to the younger son in tail; the discontinuance of the elder son with warranty is collateral to the middle son.*

716 Also, if a man have issue three sons, and he giveth land to the elder son, to have and to hold to him and to the heirs of his body begotten, and for default of such issue, the remainder to the middle son, to him and to the heirs of his body begotten, and for default of such issue of the middle son, the remainder to the younger son, and to the heirs of his body begotten, in this case, if the elder son discontinue the tail in fee, and bind him*self* and his heirs to warranty,

corps engendres, per fourme del done; et issint en tiel cas la garrauntie de le pere et la garrauntie de la mere ne sount forsque lineall garrauntie al heire, &c.

715 *Et nota, que en chescun cas ou home demaunda tenementes en fee-taille per brief de* Formedon, *si ascun del issue en le taille que avoet possession, ou qui navoet ascun possession, fait une garrauntie, &c., si celuy qui suist le brief de* Formedon *puissoit per ascun possibilité, per matere que puissoit estre en fait, conveier a luy, per mye celuy qui fist la garrauntie per fourme del done, &c., ceo est un lineall garrauntie, et nemye collaterall.*

716 Item, *si home ad issue trois fites, et il dona terre al eisne fitz, a aver et tener a luy et a les heires de son corps engendres, et pur defaute de tiel issue, le remeyndre al mulnes fits, a luy et a les heires de son corps engendres, et pur defaute de tiel issue del mulnes, le remeyndre al puisne fits, et les heires de son corps engendres, en ceo cas, si leisne fitz discontinua le taille en fee, et obligea luy et ses heires a garrauntie, et mo-*

and die without issue, this is a collateral warranty to the middle son, and he shall be barred from demanding the same land by force of the remainder, because the remainder is his title, and his elder brother is collateral to that title which commenceth by force of the remainder. In the same manner it is, if the middle son hath the same land by force of the remainder, because his elder brother made not any discontinuance, but died without issue of his body, and afterwards the middle make a discontinuance with warranty, &c., and die without issue, this is a collateral warranty to the younger son. And also in this case, if any of the said sons be disseised, and the father that made the gift, &c., releaseth to the disseisor all the right, &c., with warranty, &c., this is collateral warranty to that son upon whom the warranty descendeth, *Causa qua supra.*

And so with respect to the discontinuance of the middle son between him and the younger son.

And father's release to a disseisor with warranty, is collateral to that son upon whom the warranty descends.

717 And so note, that where a man that is collateral to the title, &c., releaseth with warranty, &c., this is a collateral warranty, &c.

Collateral warranty. *The same rule as* § 705.

718 Also, if *the* father give land to his elder son, to have

Maxim. *Every warranty doth de-*

rust sauns issue, ceo est une collaterall garrauntie al mulnes fitz, et il serra barre a demaunder mesme la terre per force del remeyndre, pur ceo que le remeyndre est son title, et son eisne frere est collaterall a celle title qui commence per force del remeyndre. En mesme le manere est, si le mulnes fits avoit mesme la terre per force de le remeyndre, pur ceo que son eisne frere ne fist ascun discontinuaunce, mes morust sauns issue de son corps, et puis le mulnes fait un discontinuaunce ovesque garrauntie, &c., et morust sauns issue, ceo est une collaterall garrauntie a le puisne fitz. Et auxi en ceo cas, si ascun de les dites fitz soit disseisi, et le pere qui fist le done, &c., relessa a le disseisour tout le droit, &c., ovesque garrauntie, &c., ceo est collaterall garrauntie a celuy fitz sur qui la garrauntie descendist, Causa qua supra.

717 Et sic nota, *que lou home qui est collaterall a le title, &c., relessa ovesque garrauntie, &c., ceo est une collaterall garrauntie, &c.*

718 Item, *si pere dona terre a son eisne fitz, a aver et tener*

scend upon him that is heir to him that made the warranty, by the common law.—Co. Lytt. 376 *a.*

See § 602 *and* § 735—6, *that when the right of the land runs one way, and the warranty another, warranty is no bar.*

and to hold to him and to the heirs males of his body begotten, the remainder to the second son, &c., if the elder son alien in fee with warranty, &c., and hath issue female, and dieth without issue male, this is not collateral warranty to the second son, nor shall it hurt him *in respect* of his action of *Formedon* in the remainder, because the warranty descendeth upon the daughter of the elder son, and not to the second son; for every warranty which descendeth, descendeth upon him that is heir to him that made the warranty by the common law.

Gift in tail male, remainder to heirs female of donee, who makes feoffment with warranty, and hath issue a son and daughter, warranty is lineal *on them both, because she claims in remainder as tenant in female tail.*

719 Also, if land be given to a man and to the heirs males of his body begotten, and for default of such issue, the remainder thereof to his heirs females of his body begotten, and afterwards the donee in the tail maketh a feoffment in fee, with warranty accordingly, and hath issue a son and a daughter, and dieth, this warranty is but a lineal warranty to the son to demand by a writ of *Formedon* in the descender; and also it is but lineal to the daughter to demand the same

a luy et a les heires males de son corps engendres, le remeyndre a le second fitz, &c., si leisne fitz alienast en fee ovesque garrauntie, &c., et ad issue femelle, et morust sauns issue male, ceo nest pas collaterall garrauntie al second fitz, ne luy ledera de son accion de Formedon *en le remeyndre, pur ceo que la garrauntie descendist al file del eisne fitz, et nemy a le second fitz; qar chescun garrauntie que descendist, descendist a celuy qui est heire a luy qui fist la garrauntie per le comen ley.*

719 Item, *si terre soit done a un home et a les heires males de son corps engendres, et pur defaute de tiel issue, le remeyndre a ses heires femelx de son corps engendres, et puis le doné en le taille fait feoffement en fee, ovesque garrauntie accordant, et ad issue fitz et file, et morust, cest garrauntie nest forsque lineall garrauntie a le fitz a demaunder per brief de* Formedon en le descendre; *et auxint il nest forsque lineall a file a demaunder mesme la terre per brief de* Formedon en le

land by writ of *Formedon* in the remainder, if her* brother die without issue male, because she claimeth as heir female

See § 603, 735—6, *in confirmation of the maxim that warranty follows the cause of descent at law.*

remeyndre, *si son* frere deviast sauns issue male, pur ceo que ele clayme come heire femelle de le corps son pere engendre.*

---

* These words *si son*, *if her*, have been corrupted by a French edition by the *Stationers*, 1604, (from which it seems the text of the first nine editions of *Co. Lytt.* was taken,) into *sinon*, *unless*. This circumstance is noticed very fully in *Vaugh.* 369—376 (*e*).

(*e*) There is one case in *Lyttleton*, remarkable for many reasons, where the warranty of tenant in tail is lineal and not collateral to the person in remainder, and therefore binds not, if the case be law (as may be justly doubted), as *Lyttleton* is commonly understood. [Here is recited the present case, according to the corrupted reading, " unless the brother die without issue male.]

1. Here the warranty of the father, donee in tail, is but lineal to the daughter in remainder in tail; but she claims, saith the book, her remainder as heir female of the body of the donee in tail, which differs the case from other persons in remainder of an estate-tail.

2. And, by the way, in this case *Sir Edward Coke*, though he hath commented upon it, hath committed an oversight of some moment, by using a copy that wanted a critical emendation; for where it said, *That the warranty of the father is but lineal to the daughter, to demand the land by a* Formedon *in the remainder, unless the brother die without issue male, because she claims as heir female of the body of her father.* By which reading and context the sense must be, *That if the son die without issue male of his body, then the warranty of the father is not lineal to the daughter, cujus contrarium est verum:* for she can claim her remainder as heir female of the body of her father, and thereby make the father's warranty lineal to her, but only because her brother died without issue male.

That which deceived *Sir Edward Coke* to admit this case as he hath printed it, was a depraved French copy, thus, *Si non frere devyast sans issue male;* which, truly read, should be, *Si son frere devyast;* and the translation should be, not " Unless the brother die without issue male; " but, " If her brother die without issue-male."

Another reason is, that his French copy was depraved, because the French of it is, *Si non frere devyast sans issue male;* which is no

But if brother release to the discontinuee, his warranty thereupon is collateral to the sister.

of the body of her father begotten. But in this case, if her brother in his life release to the discontinuee, &c., with warranty, &c., and afterwards die without issue, this is a collateral warranty to the daughter, because she cannot convey to her*self* the right which she hath by force of the remainder by any means of descent by her brother, and therefore the brother is collateral to the title of his sister, and therefore his warranty is collateral, &c. (*f*).

Mes en ceo cas, si son frere en sa vie relessast al discontinué, &c., ovesque garrauntie, &c., et puis morust sauns issue, ceo est une collaterall garrauntie a la file, pur ceo que ele ne poet conveier a luy le droit que ele ad per force de le remeyndre per ascun meane de discent per son frere, et pur ceo le frere est collaterall a le title sa soer, et pur ceo son garrauntie est collaterall, &c.

---

language, for that rendered in English is, "Unless brother die." For it cannot be rendered as he hath done it, "Unless the brother die," without the French had been, "*Si non* le *frere devyast*," and not "*Si non frere devyast.*"

Sir Edward Coke's first edition of his *Lyttleton*, and all the following editions, are alike false in this section. I have an edition of *Lyttleton*, in 1604, so depraved, which was long before *Sir Edward Coke* published his; but I have a right edition, in 1581, which it seems *Sir Edward Coke* saw not, where the reading is right, *Si son frere devyast sans issue male*. Therefore you may mend all your *Lyttletons*, if you please; and in perusing the case, you will find the grossness of the false copies more clearly than you can by this my discourse of it.

And, after all, I much doubt whether this case, as *Lyttleton* is commonly understood, that is, *That this lineal warranty doth not bind the daughter without assets descending*, be law.—*Bole* v. *Horton*, *Vaugh.* 369.

(*f*) Here it appears, that whensoever the ancestor takes any estate of freehold, and in the same conveyance an estate is limited to any of his heirs, these latter words, "his heirs," are words of limitation, and not of purchase, although it be limited by way of remainder; and therefore here the remainder to the heir female vests in the tenant in tail himself: [so only, how-

720 Also, I have heard it said, that in the time of King Richard the Second, there was a Justice of the Common Pleas, dwelling in Kent, called Rykhill, who had issue divers sons, and his intent was, that his eldest son should have certain lands and tenements to him and to the heirs of his body begotten, and for default of issue, the remainder to the second son, &c., and so to the third son, &c., and because he would that none of his sons should alien or make warranty to bar or hurt the others that should be in the remainder, &c., he caused an indenture to be made to such effect, *scil.* that the

Rykhill's case. *Gift in tail upon condition that if the donees aliened, the estate should cease, void.*

[*Rykhill was C. J. C. P., 1389, an Irishman.*—Co. Lytt. 377. b.]

720 Item, *jeo ay oye dit, que en temps le Roy Richard le Second, il y fuist un Justice de le Comen Banc, demurrant en Kent, appelle Rykhill, qui avoit issue divers fitz, et son entent fuist, que son eisne fitz averoit certeyn terres et tenementes a luy et a les heires de son corps engendres, et pur defaute dissue, le remeyndre a le second fitz, &c., et issint a le tierce fitz, &c., et pur ceo quil voille que nul de ses fitz alieneroit ou ferroit garrauntie pur barrer ou leder les autres queux serront en le remeyndre, &c., il fist faire tiel endenture a tiel effecte,* scil. *que les terres et tenementes furent dones a*

---

ever, as to give *him* a remainder in tail female, and not by merger to destroy the remainder, and give him an estate tail general.—*Cov. readable Ed. Co. Lytt.*] And it is well to know this learning nevertheless it is dangerous to use such limitations in conveyances, as great inconveniences may arise thereupon; for if such a tenant in tail has issue divers sons, and they have issue divers daughters, or if tenant in tail has issue divers daughters, and each of them has issue sons, none of the daughters of the sons, nor the sons of the daughters, shall ever inherit to either of the said estates tail; and so it is of the issues of the issues, for (as hath been said) the issues inheritable must make their claim either only by males, or only by females, so that the females of the males, or males of the females, are wholly excluded in the heritage of either of the said estates tail: hence, therefore, it is proper, when the first limitation is to the heirs male, that the remainder should be to the heirs general, as then all the issues, be they females of males, or males of females, are inheritable.—*Co. Lytt.* 377. a. b.

Rule in Shelley's case.

lands and tenements were given to his eldest son upon such condition, that if the elder son should alien in fee, or in fee-tail, &c., or if any of his sons should alien, &c., that then their estate should cease and be void, and that then the same lands and tenements immediately should remain to the second son, and to the heirs of his body begotten, &c., upon the same condition, *scil.* that if the second son should alien, &c., that then his estate should cease, and that then the same lands and tenements immediately should remain to the third son and to the heirs of his body begotten, *et sic ultra*, the remainder to other of his sons, and livery of seisin was made accordingly.

One reason why remainders in this case are void, is because the remainder ought to pass out of the donor by the first livery, i. e. the remainder

721 But it seemeth by reason, that all such remainders in the form aforesaid made, are void and of no value, and this for three reasons. One reason is, because every remainder which beginneth by a deed, it behoveth that the remainder be in him to whom the remainder is entailed by force of the same deed, *at the time* when* the livery of seisin is made to

son eisne fitz sur tiel condicion, que si leisne fitz alienast en fee, ou en fee-taille, &c., ou si ascun de ses fitz alienast, &c., que adonques lour estate cessera et serroit voyde, et que adonques mesmes les terres et tenementes immediate remeyndront a le second fitz, et a les heires de son corps engendres, &c., sur mesme la condicion, scil. *que si le* ij. *fitz alienast, &c., que adonques son estate cessera, et que adonques mesmes les terres et tenementes immediat remeyndront al tierce fitz et a les heires de son corps engendres,* et sic ultra, *le remeyndre as autres de ses fitz, et lyverë de seisin fuist fait accordant.*

721 *Mes il semble per reason, que toutes tielx remeyndres en la fourme avauntdit faitez, sount voides et de nul value, et ceo pur trois causes. Une cause est, pur ceo que chescun remeyndre que commence per un fait, il covient que le remeyndre soit en luy a qui le remeyndre est taillé per force de mesme le fait, quant* le lyverë de seisin est fait a luy qui*

* This word has been printed *avant, before,* in almost every edition since the three earliest. *Rastell's* Transl. accords with the text.

him that shall have the freehold, [for in such case the growing and the being of the remainder is by the livery of seisin to him that shall have the freehold*], and such remainder was not to the second son at the time of livery of seisin in the case aforesaid, &c. 722 The second reason is, if the first son alien the tenements in fee, then is the freehold and the fee-simple in the alienee, and in none other; and if the donor had any reversion by such alienation, the reversion is discontinued; then how can it by any reason be, that such remainder shall commence its existence and its growth immediately after such alienation made to a stranger, that hath by the same alienation freehold and fee-simple? and also if such remainder should be good, then might he enter upon the alienee, where he had no manner of right before the alienation, which should be inconvenient. 723 The third reason is, when the condition is such, that if the elder

should vest at the same time with the particular estate.

The second reason is, a remainder depending upon a condition repugnant to or inconsistent with the estate previously granted, is void.

The third reason is, a remainder

avera le franktenement, qar en tiel cas le nessance et le estre de le remeyndre est per le lyverë de seisin a celuy qui avera le franktenement, et tiel remeyndre ne fuist al second fitz al temps de lyverë de seisin en le cas avauntdit, &c.* 722 *La seconde cause est, si le premier fitz alienast les tenementes en fee, donques est le franktenement et le fee-simple en lalienė, et en nul autre; et si le donour avoit ascun revercion per tiel alienacion, la revercion est discontinue; donques coment per ascun reason poet estre, que tiel remeyndre commencera son estre et sa nessance immediate apres tiel alienacion fait a un estraunge, qui ad per mesme lalienacion franktenement et fee-simple? et auxi si tiel remeyndre serroit bon, adonques purroit il entrer sur lalienė, lou il navoit ascun manere de droit avant lalienacion, que serroit inconvenient.* 723 *La tierce cause est, quant la condicion est*

---

* The passage within brackets is not given in those editions of *Rastell's* Transl., commencing *Tottyl* 1556, and continued by him and others to 1661; although it appears in *Marshe* 1556, and previous editions.

cannot depend upon a condition that the donee enter on breach of the condition.

son alien, &c., that his estate shall cease or shall be void, &c., then after such alienation, &c., may the donor enter by force of such condition, &c., as it seemeth, and so the donor and his heirs in such case ought sooner to have the land than the second son, that had not any right before such alienation, &c.; and so it seemeth that such remainders in the case aforesaid are void, &c.

Warranty by tenant in curtesy *is no bar to the issue, unless assets descend.*

724 Also, at the common law before the statute of Gloucester (6 E. 1), if tenant by the curtesy had aliened in fee with warranty accordingly, after his decease this was a bar to the heir, &c., as it appeareth by the words of the same statute; but it is remedied by the same statute, that the warranty of the tenant by the curtesy shall not be a bar to the heir, unless that he hath assets by descent by the tenant by the curtesy; for before the said statute this was a collateral warranty to the heir, because he could not convey any title of descent to the tenements by the tenant by the curtesy, but only by his mother, or other of his ancestors, &c.; and this is the cause why

tiel, que si leisne fits alienast, &c., que son estate cessera ou serroit voyde, &c., donques apres tiel alienacion, &c., poet le donour entrer per force de tiel condicion, &c., come il semble, et issint le donour et ses heires en tiel cas doient pluis tost aver la terre que le second fitz, qui navoit ascun droit devant tiel alienacion, &c.; et issint il semble que tielx remeyndres en le cas avauntdit sont voydes, &c.

724 Item, *a le comen ley devaunt lestatuit de Gloucester, si tenaunt per le curtosie ust aliene en fee ovesque garrauntie accordant, apres son decesse ceo fuist un barre al heire, &c., sicome appiert per les parolx de mesme lestatuit; mes il est remedie per mesme lestatuit, que la garrauntie le tenaunt per le curtosie ne serra mye barre al heire, sinon quil y ad assetes per discent per le tenaunt per le curtosie; qar devaunt le dit estatuit ceo fuist une collaterall garrauntie al heire, pur ceo que il ne puisoit conveier ascun title de discent a les tenementes per le tenaunt per le curtosie, mes tantsolement per sa mere ou autres de ses auncestres, &c.; et ceo est la*

it was collateral warranty. 725 But if a man inherited take a wife, who have issue a son between them, and the father die, and the son enter into the land, and endow his mother, and afterwards the mother alieneth that which she hath in her dower to another in fee with warranty accordingly, and afterwards die, and the warranty descendeth upon the son, now the son shall be barred to demand the same land by reason of the said warranty, because that such collateral warranty of tenant in dower is not remedied by any statute. The same law is, where tenant for life makes an alienation with warranty, &c., and dieth, and the warranty descendeth upon him that hath the reversion or the remainder, &c., they shall be barred by such warranty, &c.

Warranty of mother, tenant in dower, is collateral, where the land comes by the father, and bars the issue.

726 Also, in the said case, if it were so that when the tenant in dower aliened, &c., the heir was within age, and also at the time that the warranty descended upon him he was within age; in this case the heir may afterwards enter upon the alienee, notwithstanding the warranty descended, &c., because no laches shall be adjudged in the heir within age,

Warranty can be defeated or avoided by infant heir, by his entry, if descent cast, § 402.

cause pur que il fuist collaterall garrauntie. 725 *Mes si home enherite prent feme, les queux ount issue fitz entre eux, et le pere devia, et le fitz entra en la terre, et endowa sa mere, et puis la mere aliena ceo que ele ad en son dower a un autre en fee ovesque garrauntie accordant, et puis morust, et la garrauntie descendist a le fitz, ore le fitz serra barre a demaunder mesme la terre per cause de la dite garrauntie, pur ceo que tiel collaterall garrauntie de tenaunt en dower nest pas remedie per ascun estatuit. Mesme la ley est, lou tenaunt a terme de vie fait une alienacion ovesque garrauntie, &c., et morust, et la garrauntie descendist a celuy qui avoet la revercion ou le remeyndre, &c., ils serront barres per tiel garrauntie, &c.*

726 Item, *en le dit cas, il issint fuist que quant le tenaunt en dower alienast, &c., leire fuist deins age, et auxi al temps que la garrauntie descendist sur luy il fuist deins age; en ceo cas leire poet apres entrer sur laliené, nient contristeant la garrauntie descendus, &c., pur ceo que nul lachesse serra*

that he did not enter upon the alienee in the life of tenant in dower; but if the heir were within age at the time of the alienation, &c., and afterwards he cometh to full age in the life of tenant in dower, and so being of full age, he doth not enter upon the alienee in the life of tenant in dower, and afterwards the tenant in dower dieth, &c., there peradventure the heir shall be barred by such warranty, because it shall be accounted his folly, that he being of full age did not enter in the life of tenant in dower, &c.*

By equitable construction of stat. of Gloucester, c. 3, the heir of

728 Also, it is spoken in the end of the said statute of Gloucester, which speaketh of the alienation with warranty made by the tenant by the curtesy, in this form. Also, in

ajugge en leire deins age, que il nentra pas sur lalienè en la vie del tenaunt en dower; mes si leire fuist deins age al temps del alienacion, &c., et puis il devient a pleyn age en la vie de le tenaunt en dower, et issint esteant de pleyn age, il nentra pas sur lalienè en la vie del tenaunt en dower, et puis le tenaunt en dower morust, &c., là peraventure leire serra barre per tiel garrauntie, pur ceo que il serra rette sa folye, que il esteant de pleyn age nentra pas en la vie del tenaunt en dower, &c.

728 Item, *il est parle en le fyn del dit estatut de Gloucester, que parla del alienacion ovesque garrauntie fait per le tenaunt per le curtosie, en cest fourme. Ensement, en mesme le*

---

* Here follows in every French edition of *Lyttleton*, after *Tottyl* 1557, the following addition, which is noticed as such by *Sir E. Coke*, who thereupon refers to his commentary on § 697. This addition, which forms the 727th section of *West's* subdivision, 1581, appears in *Redm.* as part of the text; but in *Berth.*, *Middl.*, *Sm.*, *Powell*, and *Tottyl* 1554, it is given as a side-note, viz.—*But now by the statute made* 11 *Hen.* 7, c. 10, *it is ordained, if any woman discontinue, alien, release, or confirm with warranty any lands or tenements which she holdeth in dower for term of life, or in tail of the gift of her first husband, or of his ancestors, or of the gift of any other seised to the use of the first husband, or of his ancestors, that all such warranties, &c., shall be void, and that it shall be lawful for him which hath these lands or tenements after the death of the same woman to enter.*

the same manner, the heir of the wife after the death of the father and mother shall not be barred of action, if he demandeth the heritage or the marriage of his mother by writ of entry, that his father aliened in the time of his mother, whereof no fine is levied in the king's court. And so by force of the same statute, if the husband of the wife alien the heritage or marriage of his wife in fee with warranty, &c., by his deed *in pais*, this is clear law, that that warranty shall not bar the heir, unless he hath assets by descent, &c.

wife is not barred by the warranty of the husband unless with assets.

See post, § 732.

729 But the doubt is, if the husband alien the heritage of his wife by fine levied in the king's court with warranty, &c., whether this shall bar the heir without any descent in value, &c. And as to this, I will say here certain reasons which I have heard said in this matter. I heard my master Sir Richard Newton, late chief justice of the Common Place, once say in the same place, that such warranty as the husband maketh by fine levied in the king's court shall bar the heir, albeit he hath nothing by descent, because the statute saith, " whereof no fine is levied in the king's court, &c." and so

Point raised whether husband can by his alienation bar the heir of his wife by fine.

Opinion of Sir Richard Newton (who was C. J., C. P., in 18 Hen. 6), the affirmative.

manere, ne soit leire la feme apres la mort le pere et la mere barre daccion, sil demaunde le heritage ou le mariage sa mere per brief dentre, que son pere aliena en temps sa mere, dount nul fyn est levé en la court le roy. Et issint per force de mesme lestatut, si le baron del feme aliena leritage ou mariage sa feme en fee ovesque garrauntie, &c., per son fait en pays, ceo est clere ley, que celle garrauntie ne barrera mye leire, sinon que il ad assetes per discent, &c.

729 *Mes le doute est, si le baron alienast leritage sa feme per fyn levé en la court le roy ovesque garrauntie, &c., si ceo barrera leire sauns ascun discent en value, &c. Et quant a ceo, jeo voille icy dire certeyns reasons que jeo ay oye dite en cest matere. Jeo oya mon maistre Sr. Richard Newton, jadis chief justice de le Comen Banc, dire un foits en mesme le banc, que tiel garrauntie que le baron fait per fyn levé en la court le roy barrera leire, coment que il nad riens per discent, pur ceo que lestatut dit, " dount nul fyn est levé en la court le*

Whereas others argue contra, *viz. that such warranty does not bar the heir unless with assets: to which opinion* Lyttleton *inclines and argues* ab inconvenienti.

by his opinion this warranty by fine, &c., remaineth yet a collateral warranty, as it was at the common law, not remedied by the said statute, because the said statute excepteth alienations by fine with warranty. [730] And some others have said, and yet do say the contrary, and this is their proof; that as by the same chapter of the said statute it is ordained, that the warranty of the tenant by the curtesy shall be no bar to the heir, unless that he hath assets by descent, &c., although the tenant by the curtesy levy a fine of the same tenements with warranty, &c., as strongly as he can; yet this warranty shall not bar the heir unless that he hath assets by descent, &c. And I believe that this is law; and therefore they say, that it should be inconvenient to intend the statute in such form, that a man that hath nothing but in right of his wife can by fine levied by him of the same tenements which he hath but in right of his wife, with warranty, &c., bar the heir of the same tenements without any descent of fee-simple, &c., where the tenant by the curtesy cannot do it.

roy, &c.," et issint per son opinion celle garrauntie per fyn, &c., demourt unqore une collaterall garrauntie, sicome il fuist a le comen ley, nient remedie per le dit estatuit, pur ceo que le dit estatuit excepte alienacions per fyn ovesque garrauntie. [730] *Et ascuns autres ount dit, et unqore diont le contrarie, et ceo est lour prove; que come per mesme le chapitre de le dit estatut il est ordeigne, que la garrauntie le tenaunt per le curtosie ne serra mye barre al heire, sinon queil ad assetes per discent, &c., coment que le tenaunt per le curtosie leva un fyn de mesmes les tenementes ovesque garrauntie, &c., auxi fortement come il poet faire; unqore celle garrauntie ne barrera mye leire sinon queil ad assetes per discent, &c. Et jeo crey que ceo est ley; et pur ceo ils diont, que serroit inconvenient dentendre le estatut en tiel fourme, que un home qui nad riens forsque en droit sa feme purroit per fyn levé per luy de mesmes les tenementes queux il ad forsque en droit sa feme, ovesque garrauntie, &c., barrer leire de mesmes les tenementes sans ascun discent de fee-simple, &c.,*

731 But they have said that the statute shall be intended (*i. e.* understood) after this form, *scil.* where the statute speaketh, "whereof no fine is levied in the court of our lord the king," that is to say, whereof no lawful fine is rightfully levied in the same king's court; and that is, whereof no fine of the husband and his wife is levied in the king's court: for at the time of the making of the said statute, every estate of lands or tenements that any man or woman had, which should descend to his heir, was fee-simple without condition, or upon certain condition in deed or in law. And because such fine then lawfully might be levied by the husband and his wife, and that the husband and his wife and the heirs of the husband should warrant, &c., such warranty shall bar the heir, &c., and so they say that this is the meaning of the statute; for if the husband and his wife made a feoffment in fee by deed in pais, the heir after the decease of the husband and his wife shall have writ of entry *sur cui in vita, &c.*, notwithstanding the warranty of the husband; then if no such ex-

Intendment of the statute of Gloucester as to the barring the heir by fine, which fine, if made by the husband and by the wife, will bar the heir.

See ante, § 13.

Although feoffment by husband and wife would not bar the heir.

lou le tenaunt per le curtosie ceo ne poet faire. 731 *Mes ils ount dit que lestatuit serra entendus solonques celle fourme,* scil. *lou lestatuit parle, " dount nul fyn est levé en la court nostre seignour le roy," ceo est adire, dount null loyall fyn est droiturelement levé en mesme la court le roy ; et ceo est, dount nul fyn de le baron et sa feme soit levé en la court le roy : qar al temps de le fesaunce de le dit estatut, chescun estate de terres ou tenementes que ascun home ou feme avoit, que descenderoit a son heire, fuist fee-simple sauns condicion, ou sur certeyn condicion en fait ou en ley. Et pur ceo tiel fyn adonques loyalement poet estre levé per le baron et sa feme, et que le baron et sa feme et les heires le baron garraunteront, &c., tiel garrauntie barrera leire, &c., et issint ils diont que ceo est lentendement del estatut ; qar si le baron et sa feme firont un feoffement en fee per fait en pays, leire apres le decesse le baron et sa feme avera brief dentre* sur cui in vita, &c., *nient obstant la garrauntie de le baron ; donques si nul*

ception had been made in the statute, of the fine levied, &c., then the heir should have the writ of entry, &c., notwithstanding the fine levied by the husband and his wife, because the words of the statute before the exception of the fine levied, &c., are general, &c., that is to say, that the heir of the wife, after the death of the father and the mother*, be not barred of action, if he demand the heritage, or the marriage of his mother, by writ of entry, which *heritage or marriage* his father aliened in the time of his mother; [and so albeit the husband and his wife aliened by fine, yet this is true, that the husband aliened in the time of the mother†]; and so it should be in *the* case of the statute, except such words were, that is to say, "whereof no fine is levied in the court of our sovereign the king," and so they say that this is to be understood, "whereof no fine, by the husband and the wife, is levied in the court of our

tiel excepcion fuist fait en lestatuit, de le fyn levé, &c., donques leire averoit le brief dentre, &c., nient obstant le fyn levé per le baron et sa feme, pur ceo que les parolx de lestatuit davaunt lexcepcion de fyn levé, &c., sount generalx, &c., cestassavoir, que leire la feme, apres la mort le pere et la mere, ne soit barre daccion, sil demaunde leritage, ou le mariage sa mere, per brief dentre, que son pere aliena en temps sa mere; [et issint coment le baron et la feme alienont per fyn, unqore ceo est voire, que le baron aliena en temps la mere†]; et issint il serroit en cas destatut, sinon que tielx parolx fueront, cestassavoir, "dount nul fyn est levé en la court nostre soverain le roy," et issint ils diont que ceo est a entendre, "dount nul fyn, per le baron et la feme, est levé en la court nostre seignour le roy," le quel est loyalement levé*

---

* *Rastell's* Transl. renders these words, *husband and wife*, which according to the context is the same thing.

† The words within brackets are not given in *Rastell's* Transl., *Tottyl* 1556, and subsequent editions. *Marshe* 1556, and previous editions, retain them.

lord the king," the which is lawfully levied in such case; for if the justices have knowledge, that a man that hath nothing but in the right of his wife willeth to levy a fine in his name solely, they will not, nor ought not to take such fine to be levied by the husband alone without naming his wife, &c. *Ideo quære* of this matter, &c.

732 Also, it is to be understood, that in these words, "where the heir demandeth the heritage, or the marriage of his mother," this word "or," is a disjunctive, and is as much as to say, if the heir demand the heritage of his mother, *scil.* the tenements that his mother had in fee-simple by descent, or by purchase, or if the heir demand the marriage of his mother, *scil.* the tenements that were given to his mother in frankmarriage.

Intendment of words, "heritage" and "marriage," (which occur also at § 728).

733 Also, whereas it is put in divers deeds, these words in Latin, *Ego et heredes mei, &c., warrantizabimus et in perpetuum defendemus;* it is to be seen what effect hath that word, *defendemus*, in such deeds; and it seemeth that it hath not the effect of warranty, nor comprehendeth in it the cause of

The verb* "warrantizo" *only, has the effect of creating a warranty.

en tiel cas; qar si les justices ount conusaunce, que home qui nad riens forsque en droit sa feme voille lever un fyn en son noun solement, ils ne voillont, ne devoient prendre tiel fyn destre levé per le baron solement sauns nosmer sa feme, &c. Ideo quære *de cest matere, &c.*

732 Item, *est assavoir, que en ceux parolx, "lou leire demaunda leritage, ou le mariage sa mere," cest paroll "ou," est un disjunctif, et est a tant adire, si leire demaunda leritage sa mere,* scil. *les tenementes que sa mere avoit en fee-simple per discent, ou per purchase, ou si leire demaunda le mariage sa mere,* scil. *les tenementes que furent dones a sa mere en frankmariage.*

733 Item, *come est mote en divers faits, ceux parolx en Latin,* Ego et heredes mei, &c., warrantizabimus et in perpetuum defendemus; *il est a veier quel effecte ad celle parol,* defendemus, *en tielx faits; et il semble que il nad pas leffecte de garrauntie, ne emprent en luy cause de garrauntie; qar si issint*

warranty; for if it should be so, that it took the effect or cause of warranty, then it should be put into some fines levied in the king's court; and no one ever saw that that word, *defendemus,* was in any fine, but only this word, *warrantizabimus.* By which it seemeth, that this verb, *warrantizo, as, &c.,* creates the warranty, and the cause of warranty, and no other verb in our law.

Case illustrating maxim *that the heir shall never be bound by any express warranty, but where the ancestor was bound by the same warranty; for if the ancestor were not so bound, it cannot descend upon the heir.*

734 Also, if tenant in tail be seised of tenements devisable by testament according to the custom, &c., and the tenant in the tail alieneth the tenements to his brother in fee, and hath issue, and dieth, and afterwards his brother deviseth by his testament the same tenements to another in fee, and bindeth himself and his heirs to warranty, &c., and dieth without issue; it seemeth that this warranty shall not bar the issue in the tail, if he will sue his writ of *Formedon,* because this warranty descended not to the issue in the tail, insomuch as the uncle of the issue was not bound to warranty in his lifetime, neither could he warrant the tenements in his life, insomuch as the devise could not take any

serroit, quil prent effecte ou cause de garrauntie, donques il serroit mote en ascuns fyns levés en la court le roy ; et home ne veiet unques que celle parol, defendemus, *fuist en ascun fyn, mes tauntsolement cest parole* warrantizabimus. *Per que semble, que ceo verbe,* warrantizo, as, &c., *fait la garrauntie, et la cause de garrauntie, et nul autre verbe en nostre ley.*

734 Item, *si tenaunt en le taille soit seisi des tenementes devisables per testament solonques le custome, &c., et le tenaunt en le taille aliena les tenementes a son frere en fee, et ad issue, et devie, et puis son frere devisa per son testament mesmes les tenementes a un autre en fee, et obligea luy et ses heires a garrauntie, &c., et morust sauns issue ; il semble que cest garrauntie ne barrera mye lissue en le taille, sil voet suer son brief de* Formedon, *pur ceo que cest garrauntie ne descendist mye al issue en le taille, entaunt que luncle del issue ne fuist mye oblige a garrauntie en sa vie, ne puissoit garrauntir les tenementes en sa vie, entaunt que le devise ne*

execution or effect until after his decease. And insomuch as the uncle in his life was not held to warranty, such warranty cannot descend from him to the issue in the tail, &c., for nothing can descend from the ancestor upon his heir, unless the same had been in the ancestor. 735 Also, a warranty cannot go according* to the nature of the tenements by the custom, &c., but only according to the form of the common law; for if the tenant in tail were seised of tenements in Borough-English, where the custom is, that all the tenements within the same borough ought to descend to the younger son, and he discontinueth the tail with warranty, &c., and hath issue two sons, and dieth seised of other lands or tenements in the same borough in fee-simple, to the value or more of the lands entailed, &c., yet the younger son shall have a *Formedon* of the lands entailed, and shall not be barred by the warranty of his father, albeit assets descended to him in fee-simple from the same father according to the custom, &c.,

Borough-English. *The warranty of the ancestor does not bind unless it descend according to the course of the common law, therefore it cannot go according to the course of a customary descent; [nor shall the heir be charged upon a warranty by devise.—* [Plowd. Quæres, § 304.]

puissoit prendre ascun execucion ou effecte forsque apres son decesse. Et entaunt que luncle en sa vie ne fuist tenus de garrauntir, tiel garrauntie ne poet descendre de luy al issue en le taille, &c., qar nul chose poet descendre de launcestre a son heire, sinon que mesme ceo fuist en launcestre. 735 *Auxi, une garrauntie ne poet aler solonques* la nature des tenementes per le custome, &c., mes tantsolement solonques la fourme del comen ley; qar si tenaunt en le taille fuist seisi des tenementes en Boroghe-English, lou le custome est, que touts les tenementes deins mesme le boroghe devoient descendre a le fitz puisne, et il discontinua le taille ovesque garrauntie, &c., et ad issue deux fitz, et morust seisi des autres terres ou tenementes en mesme le boroghe en fee-simple, a le value ou pluis de les tenementes taillés, &c., unqore le puisne fitz avera un brief de* Formedon *de les terres taillés, et ne serra mye barre per la garrauntie son pere, coment que assetes a luy descendist en fee-simple de mesme le pere solonques le custome, &c.,*

* In *Lettou & M.*, *Machl.*, and *Roh.*, this word is misprinted *sans*.

because the warranty descendeth upon the elder brother, who is in full life, &c., and not upon the younger. And in the same manner it is of collateral warranty made of such tenements, where the warranty descended upon the elder son, &c., this shall not bar the younger son, &c. 736 In the same manner is it of tenements in the shire of Kent, which are called gavelkind, the which tenements are departible among the brethren, &c., according to the custom, &c.: if any such warranty be made by his ancestors, such warranty shall descend solely upon the heir that is heir by the common law, [that is to say, to the elder brother, according to the conusance of the common law*], and not to all the heirs which are heirs of such tenements according to the custom, &c.

And so in gavelkind. Warranty descends upon the heir at law; [for warranty runs with the land.]

737 Also, if tenant in the tail have issue two daughters by divers venters, and die, and the daughters enter, and a stranger disseise them of the same tenements, and one of the

Warranty does not descend upon or bar the half-blood.

pur ceo que la garrauntie descendist sur leisne frere, qui est en pleyn vie, &c., et nemy sur le puisne. En mesme le manere est de collaterall garrauntie fait de tielx tenementes, lou garrauntie descendist al eisne fitz, &c., ceo ne barrera mye le puisne fitz, &c. 736 *En mesme le manere est de tenementes en le conté de Kent, queux sont appelle gavelkynde, les queux tenementes sount departables entre les freres, &c., solonques le custome, &c.: si ascun tiel garrauntie soit fait per ses auncestres, tiel garrauntie discendera tantsolement al heire qui est heire per la comen ley, [cestassavoir, al eisne frere, solonques la conusauns del comen ley*], et nemy a toutz les heires quelx sount heires de tielx tenementes solonques le custome, &c.*

737 Item, *si tenaunt en le taille ad issue deux files per divers ventres, et morust, et les files entront, et un estraunge eux disseisist de mesmes les tenementes, et lun de les files re-*

* This passage between brackets does not appear in *Lettou & M.*, *Middl.*, *Roh.*, *Pyns.* 1516, *Redm.*, *Berth.*, *Middl.*, *Sm.*, *Powell*, and *Tottyl* 1554, or in *Rastell's* Translation.

daughters releaseth by her deed to the disseisor all her right, and bindeth her and her*self* heirs to warranty, and dieth without issue; in this case the sister that surviveth can well enter and oust the disseisor of all the tenements, because such warranty is no discontinuance nor collateral warranty to the sister that surviveth, because they are of half-blood, and the one cannot be heir to the other according to the course of the common law. But otherwise it is where there be daughters of tenant in the tail by one same venter.

738 Also, if tenant in the tail letteth the lands to a man for term of his life, the remainder to another in fee, and a collateral ancestor confirmeth the estate of the tenant for term of life, and bindeth him*self* and his heirs to warranty for term of the life of the tenant for life, and dieth, and the tenant in the tail hath issue, and dieth; now is the issue barred to demand the tenements by writ of *Formedon* during the life of tenant for term of life, because of the collateral warranty descended upon the issue in the tail. But after the decease of the tenant for term

A warranty may be raised by a confirmation which transferred neither estate nor right.
A warranty may be limited, and lands warranted as well for term of life, or in tail, as in fee.—Co. Lytt. 387. a.

§ 733, 706.

lessa per son fait a le disseisour tout son droit, et obligea luy et ses heires a garrauntie, et morust sauns issue; en ceo cas la soer que survesquist poet bien entrer et oustre le disseisour de toutes les tenementes, pur ceo que tiel garrauntie nest pas discontinuaunce ne collaterall garrauntie a la soer que survesquist, pur ceo que eles sount de demy sank, et lun ne poet estre heire a lautre, solonques le cours del comen ley. Mes autrement est lou y sount files del tenaunt en le taille per un mesme ventre.

738 Item, *si tenaunt en le taille lessa les tenementes a un home pur terme de sa vie, le remeyndre a un autre en fee, et un collaterall auncestre confirma lestate del tenaunt a terme de vie, et obligea luy et ses heires a garrauntie pur terme de vie del tenaunt a terme de vie, et morust, et le tenaunt en le taille ad issue, et devie; ore lissue est barre a demaunder les tenementes per brief de* Formedon *duraunt la vie le tenaunt a terme de vie, per cause del collaterall garrauntie descendue sur lissue en le taille. Mes apres le decesse de le tenaunt a*

Warranty annexed to an estate *pur autre vie.* *Heir of lessee shall have land let* pur autre vie, *on the decease of* cel qui vie.

of life, the issue shall have a *Formedon*, &c. 739 And upon this I have heard a reason, that this case will prove another case, *scil.* if a man let his land to another, to have and to hold to him and to his heirs for term of another's life, and the lessee* die living *celuy a qui vie* (*i. e.* he for whose life), &c., and a stranger entereth into the land, that the heir of the lessee can put him out, for this that in the case next aforesaid, insomuch as a man can bind him*self* and his heirs to warranty to the tenant for term of life solely during the life of the tenant for life, and that warranty descendeth on the heir of him that made the warranty, the which warranty is no warranty of inheritance, but only for term of another's life: by the same reason where tenements are let to a man, to have and to hold to him and to his heirs for term of another's life, if the lessee† die, living *celuy a qui vie*, his heir shall have the tene-

And so in case of an annuity, or any other thing lying in grant.

terme de vie, lissue avera un Formedon, &c. 739 *Et sur ceo jeo ay oye un reason, que celle cas provera un autre cas,* scil. *si un home lessa sa terre a un autre, a aver et tener a luy et a ses heires pur terme dautre vie, et le lessé* morust vivaunt celuy a qui vie, &c., et un estraunge entra en la terre, que leire le lessé luy poet ouster, pur ceo que en le cas proscheyn avauntdit, entant que home poet obliger luy et ses heires a garrauntie al tenaunt a terme de vie tantsoulement duraunt la vie le tenaunt a terme de vie, et celle garrauntie descendist al heire celuy qui fist la garrauntie, le quel garrauntie nest pas garrauntie denheritance, mes tantsoulement pur terme lautre vie : per mesme le reason lou tenementes sont lesses a un home, a aver et tener a luy et a ses heire pur terme dautre vie, si le lessé† morust, vivant celuy a qui vie, son heire avera les tenementes vivant celuy a qui vie, &c. Qar ils ont*

---

* Some of the copies of *Rastell's* Transl., by *Tottyl*, misprint this word *lessor*.

† *Pere, Father; Lettou & M., Machl., Roh., Redm., and Rastell's* Transl.

ments living *celuy a qui vie*, &c. For they have said, that if a man grant an annuity to another, to have and to take to him and his heirs for term of another's life, if the grantee die, &c., that afterwards his heir shall have the annuity during the life of *celuy a qui vie*, &c. *Quære de istâ materiâ.*
740 But where such lease or grant is made to a man and to his heirs for term of years; in this case the heir of the lessee or the grantee shall never have, after the death of the lessee or the grantee, that which is so let or granted, because this is a chattel real; and chattels real by the common law shall go to the executors of the grantee, or of the lessee, and not to the heir, &c.

A term of years being a chattel real, goes to executors or administrators, as well as a chattel personal, although limited to the heir.

741 Also, in some cases it may be, that albeit a collateral warranty be made in fee, &c., yet such warranty may be defeated and annulled: as if tenant in the tail discontinue the tail in fee, and the discontinuee is disseised, and the brother of the tenant in the tail releaseth by his deed to the disseisor all his right, &c., with warranty in fee, and dieth without issue, and the tenant in the tail hath issue and dieth; now

Maxim.
A warranty is defeated where the estate to which it is annexed is defeated.
§ 707.

dit, que si home graunta un annuité a un autre, a aver et percever a luy et a ses heires pur terme dautre vie, si le graunté morust, &c., que apres son heire avera lannuité duraunt la vie celuy a qui vie, &c. Quære de istâ materiâ.
740 *Mes lou tiel lees ou graunt est fait a un home et a sez heires pur terme des ans; en ceo cas leire le lessé ou le graunté navera unques, apres la mort le lessé ou le graunté, ceo que est issint lesse ou graunte, pur ceo que ceo est chatel real; et chatelx realx per le comen ley viendront al executours del graunté, ou de lessé, et nemy al heire, &c.*

741 Item, *en ascuns cases il poet estre, que coment un collaterall garrauntie soit fait en fee, &c., unqore tiel garrauntie poet estre defete et anientie: sicome tenaunt en le taille discontinua le taille en fee, et le discontinué est disseisi, et le frere del tenaunt en le taille relessa per son fait a le disseisour tout son droit, &c., ovesque garrauntie en fee, et morust sauns issue, et le tenaunt en le taille ad issue et devie;*

the issue is barred of his action by force of the collateral warranty descended upon him: but if after this the discontinuee enter on the disseisor, then can the heir in tail well have his action of *Formedon*, &c., because the warranty is annulled and defeated; for when the warranty is made to a man upon estate which he then hath, if the estate be defeated, the warranty is defeated. 742 In the same manner it is, if the discontinuee make feoffment in fee, reserving to him*self* a certain rent, and for default of payment a re-entry, &c., and a collateral ancestor releaseth* to the feoffee that hath estate upon condition, &c., and *the ancestor*† die without issue, although that warranty descended upon the issue in the tail, yet if afterwards the rent be behind, and the discontinuee enter into the land, &c., then shall the issue in the tail

Another case, illustrating the maxim, that where the estate to which warranty is annexed, is defeated, the warranty itself is defeated.

ore lissue est barre de son accion per force de collaterall garrauntie descendue sur luy: mes si apres ceo le discontinué entra sur le disseisour, donques poet leire en le taille aver bien son accion de Formedon, &c., *pur ceo que la garrauntie est anientie et defete; car quaunt la garrauntie est fait a un home sur estate que adonques il avoet, si lestate soit defete la garrauntie est defete.* 742 *En mesme le manere est, si le discontinué fait feoffement en fee, reservaunt a luy certeyn rente, et pur defaute de paiement un re-entre, &c., et un collateral auncestre relessa* a celuy feoffé qui ad estate sur condicion, &c., et morust sauns issue, coment que celle garrauntie descendist sur lissue en le taille, unqore si apres le rente soit aderere, et le discontinué entra en la terre, &c., donques avera lissue en le taille son recoverer per brief de* Formedon,

---

* In later copies, and in *Sir Edward Coke's* Transl., this passage is read thus, *viz., and a collateral warranty of the ancestor* is made *to the feoffee.*

† These words in *italics* are an emendation of the text by *Mr. Ritso*, who observes that it is not the discontinuee who is here spoken of, nor the feoffee who hath the estate upon condition, but the collateral ancestor of the tenant in tail, who made the warranty.—*Ritso's* Introd. 114.

have his recovery by writ of *Formedon,* because the collateral warranty is defeated. And so if any such collateral warranty be pleaded against the issue in the tail in his action of *Formedon,* he can shew the matter as is aforesaid, how the warranty is defeated, and so he can well maintain his action, &c.

Warranty defeated by extinction, where the warrantor take back as large an estate as he had created.

743 Also, if tenant in the tail make a feoffment to his uncle, and afterwards the uncle make a feoffment in fee with warranty, &c., to another, and afterwards the feoffee of the uncle doth infeoff again the uncle in fee, and afterwards the uncle infeoff a stranger in fee without warranty, and die without issue, and the tenant in the tail die*, if the issue in the tail will bring his writ of *Formedon* against the stranger that was the last feoffee†, and this by the uncle, the issue shall never be barred by the warranty that was made by the uncle to the said

pur ceo que la collaterall garrauntie est defete. Et issint si ascune tiel collaterall garrauntie soit plede envers lissue en le taille en son accion de Formedon, *il poet monstrer le matere come est avauntdit, coment la garrauntie est defete, et issint il poet bien meyntener son accion, &c.*

743 Item, *si tenaunt en le taille fait un feoffement a son uncle, et puis luncle fait un feoffement en fee ovesque garrauntie, &c., a un autre, et puis le feoffé del uncle enfeoffa areremaine luncle en fee, et puis luncle enfeoffa un estraunge en fee sauns garrauntie, et morust sauns issue, et le tenaunt en le taille morust*, si lissue en le taille voille porter son brief de* Formedon *envers lestraunge qui fuist le darrein feoffé†, et ceo per luncle, lissue ne serra unques barre per la garrauntie que fuist fait per luncle a le dit premier feoffé de son uncle, pur*

---

* The words, *and the tenant in the tail die,* are not given in *Rastell's* Transl., *Tottyl* 1556, and subsequent editions. These words appear in previous English copies, and in *Marshe* 1556.

† This passage is thus rendered in *Rastell's* Transl. :—*Against the stranger that cometh in by feoffment of the uncle, in this case the issue shall never be barred.*

first feoffee of his uncle, for this that the said warranty was defeated and annulled, because the uncle took back to him as great estate from his said first feoffee to whom the warranty was made, as the same feoffee had of (*i. e.* from) him. And the reason why the warranty is annulled in this case is this, *scil.* that if the warranty were in its force, then the uncle should warrant* to himself, which cannot be. 744 But if the feoffee had made an estate to the† uncle for the term of life, or in the tail, saving the reversion, &c., or if he make a gift in the tail to the uncle, or a lease for term of life, the remainder over, &c.: in this case the warranty is not altogether annulled, but is put in suspense during the estate that the uncle hath. For after this, that the uncle is dead without issue, then he in the reversion, or he in the remain-

Warranty suspended by warrantor's taking a lease for life, or a gift in tail.

ceo que la dite garrauntie fuist defete et anientie, pur ceo que luncle a luy prist cy graund estate de son dit premier feoffé a qui la garrauntie fuist fait, sicome mesme le feoffé avoit de luy. Et la cause pur que la garrauntie est anientie en ceo cas est ceo, scil. *que si la garrauntie esteroit en sa force, donques luncle garraunteroit* a luy mesme, que ne poet estre.* 744 *Mes si le feoffé fesoit estate al† uncle pur terme de vie, ou en le taille, savaunt la revercion, &c., ou quil fait done en le taille al uncle, ou un lees pur terme de vie, le remeyndre oustre, &c.: en ceo cas la garrauntie nest tout oustrement anientie, mes est mys en suspence duraunt lestate que le uncle ad. Qar apres ceo, que le uncle est mort sauns issue, donques celuy en la revercion, ou celuy en le remeyn-*

---

* *Should warrant* a fee-simple *to himself.* The editions of *Rastell's* Transl., by *Jane Yetsweirt* 1597, and *Stationers'* 1627, 1656.

† *Sir Edward Coke's* Transl. has rendered this word *al uncle,* to the *uncle,* his *uncle;* which error is noticed by *Mr. Ritso,* who remarks that *the* uncle refers to the uncle of the tenant in tail mentioned in the preceding section, and not *his,* the feoffee's uncle. And so again, in § 748, we should read, "if after (*i. e.* afterwards) the feoffee by his deed release to *the* uncle," and not "to *his* uncle."—*Ritso's* Introd. 114.

der, shall bar the issue in the tail in his writ of *Formedon*, by the collateral warranty in such case, &c. But otherwise it is where the uncle hath as great estate in the land of the feoffee, to whom the warranty had been made, as the feoffee hath of him. *Causa patet**.

745 Also, if the uncle after such feoffment made with warranty, or release made by him with warranty, be attainted of felony, or outlawed of felony, such collateral warranty shall not bar or affect the issue in the tail, for this, that by the attainder of felony, the blood is corrupted between them, &c. (*g*).

Warranty destroyed by corruption of blood, [for warranty of ancestor does not bind unless it descend].

746 Also, if tenant in the tail be disseised, and afterwards make deed of release to the disseisor with warranty in fee, and afterwards the tenant in tail is attainted or outlawed of felony,

The warranty of a tenant in tail disseisee will not bar his issue if his blood is cor-

dre, barreroit lissue en le taille en son brief de Formedon, *per la collaterall garrauntie en tiel cas, &c. Mes autrement est lou uncle avoet auxi graund estate en la terre del feoffé, a qui la garrauntie fuist fait, come le feoffé avoet de luy.* Causa patet*.

745 Item, *si luncle apres tiel feoffement fait ovesque garrauntie, ou reles fait per luy ovesque garrauntie, soit atteynt de felonye, ou utlage de felonye, tiel collaterall garrauntie ne barrera mye ne grevera lissue en le taille, pur ceo, que per le atteindre de felonye, le sank est corrupte entre eux, &c.*

746 Item, *si tenaunt en le taille soit disseisi, et puis fet fait de relesse a le disseisour ovesque garrauntie en fee, et puis le tenaunt en le taille est atteynt ou utlage de felonye, et ad*

* The edition of *Rastell's* Transl., by *Tottyl* 1556, and subsequent English copies, conclude this section with an *&c.*, without the *causa patet;* but *Marshe* 1556, and previous English copies, retain both the *&c.* and the *causa patet.*

(*g*) The statute 54 Geo. 3, c. 45, takes away *corruption of blood*, except in the cases of treason or murder.

rupted, for by the attaint warranty cannot descend but through the tenant attainted.

and hath issue and dieth; in this case the issue in tail can enter upon the disseisor: and the reason is, because nothing maketh discontinuance in this case but the warranty, and the warranty cannot descend upon the issue in the tail, for this that the blood is corrupted between him that made the warranty, and the issue in the tail. 747 For the warranty always abideth at (*i. e.* according to the course of descent of) the common law; and the common law is such, that when a man is attainted or outlawed of felony, which outlawry is an attainder in law, that the blood between him and his son, and all others which shall be said his heirs, is corrupted, so that nothing by descent can descend to any that may be said his heir by the common law: and the wife of such man that is so attainted of felony, shall never be endowed of the tenements of her husband so attainted. And the reason is, for that men should the more eschew to commit any felonies, &c. But the issue in the tail as to the tenements entailed is not in such case barred*, because he is inhe-

Warranty always follows the course of descent at law. § 711, 712. And by the doctrine of attainder the blood between the person attainted and those who claim through him is corrupted, and course of inheritance obstructed.

issue et morust; en ceo cas lissue en le taille poet entrer sur le disseisour: et la cause est, pur ceo que nul rien fait discontinuance en ceo cas forsque la garrauntie, et la garrauntie ne poet descendre al issue en le taille, pur ceo que le sank est corrupte perentre celuy qui fist la garrauntie, et lissue en le taille. 747 *Car la garrauntie toutz foitz demourt a la comen ley, et la comen ley est, que quaunt home est atteynt ou utlage de felonye, quell utlagarie est un atteyndre en ley, que le sank perentre luy et son fitz, et toutz autres queux serront ditz ses heires, est corrupte, issint que nul rien per discent poet descendre a ascun qui poet estre dit son heire per la comen ley: et la feme de tiel home que issint est atteynt de felonye, ne serra jammais endowe de les tenementes son baron issint atteynt. Et la cause est, pur ceo que homes pluis eschuerent de faire ascuns felonyes, &c. Mes lissue en le taille quant a les tenementes taillés nest pas en tiel cas barre*,*

---

* This word is omitted in the three earliest copies, evidently by an oversight: it appears in every other copy, French as well as English.

rited by force of the statute, and not by the course of the common law: and therefore such attainder of his father, or of his ancestor in the tail, &c., shall not put him out of his right [which he should have*] by force of the tail, &c.

748 Also, if tenant in the tail infeoff his uncle, who infeoffs another in fee with warranty &c., if afterwards the feoffee by his deed release to the† uncle all manner of warranties, or all manner of covenants real, or all manner of demands, by such release the warranty is extinct. And if the warranty in such case be pleaded against the heir in the tail that bringeth his writ of *Formedon* to bar the heir of his action, if the heir have and plead the said release, &c., he shall defeat the plea in bar, &c.; and many other cases and matters there be, whereby a man may defeat warranties, &c. *Warranty discharged by release.* *Many other means of defeating a warranty.*

749 And it is to be understood, that in the same manner as *A lineal war-*

pur ceo que il est enherite per force de lestatuit, et nemye per le cours de la comen ley: et pur ceo tiel atteyndre de son pere, ou de son auncestre en le taille, &c., ne luy oustera de son droit per force de le taille, &c.

748 Item, *si tenaunt en le taille enfeoffa son uncle, lequel enfeoffa un autre en fee ovesque garrauntie, &c., si apres le feoffé per son fait relessa al† uncle toutes maneres des garraunties, ou toutes maneres de covenantes realx, ou toutes maneres de demaundes, per tiel reles la garrauntie est extient. Et si la garrauntie en tiel cas soit plede envers leire en le taille qui porta son brief de* Formedon *pur barrer leire de son accion, si leire avoet et pledast le dit reles, &c., il defetera le plee en barre, &c.; et moltes autres cases et materes y sount, per que home poet defeter garraunties, &c.*

749 *Et est assavoir, que en mesme le manere come gar-*

---

* These words, *which he should have*, and which seem necessary to supply the full sense, are only given in *Rastell's* Transl.

† See *ante*, p. 685 (†).

ranty may be either defeated by matter in deed or matter in law, in the same manner as a collateral warranty; as in this case of issue in tail, who are barred by assets descended.

collateral warranties can be defeated by matter in deed, or in law, in the same manner can lineal warranties be defeated: for if the heir in the tail bring writ of *Formedon,* and a lineal warranty of his ancestor inheritable by force of the tail be pleaded against him, with this that assets descended to him of fee-simple, by the same ancestor that made the warranty; if the heir that is demandant can annul and defeat the warranty, this sufficeth him; for the descent of other tenements of fee-simple maketh nothing to bar the heir without the warranty, &c.

raunties collaterals poient estre defetes per matere en fait, ou en ley, en mesme le manere poient lyneall garraunties estre defetes : qar si leire en le taille porta brief de Formedon, *et un lyneall garrauntie de son auncestre enheritable per force de le taille soit plede envers luy, ovesque ceo que assetes luy descendist de fee-simple, per mesme launcestre qui fist la garrauntie; si le heire qui est demaundant poet adnuller et defeter la garrauntie, ceo suffist a luy; qar le discent des autres tenementes de fee-simple ne fait riens pur barrer leire sauns la garrauntie, &c.*

NOW HAVE I MADE to thee my son Three Books:

THE FIRST BOOK is of Estates which Men have in Lands and Tenements: that is to say, Of Tenant in Fee-Simple; Of Tenant in Fee-Tail; Of Tenant in the Tail after Possibility of Issue Extinct; Of Tenant by the Curtesy of

ORE JEO AY FAIT a toy mon fitz Trois Lyvers:

LE PREMIER LYVER est de Estates que Homes ount en Terres et Tenementes: cestassavoir, De Tenaunt en Fee-Simple; De Tenaunt en Fee-Taille; De Tenaunt en le Taille apres Possibilité dIssue Extient; De Tenaunt per le

England; Of Tenant in Dower; Of Tenant for Term of Life; Of Tenant for Term of Years; Of Tenant at Will by the Common Law; Of Tenant at Will by the Custom of the Manor*.

Curtosie dEngleterre; De Tenaunt en Dower; De Tenaunt a Terme de Vie; De Tenaunt pur Terme des Ans; De Tenaunt a Volunté per le Comen Ley; De Tenaunt a Volunté per Custome del Manor.*

THE SECOND BOOK is, Of Homage; Of Fealty; Of Escuage; Of Knight's-Service; Of Socage; Of Frankalmoign; Of Homage Ancestrel; Of Grand Serjeanty; Of Petty Serjeanty; Of Tenure in Burgage; Of Tenure in Villenage; Of Three Manners of Rents, *scil.* Rent-Service, Rent-Charge, and Rent-Seck: and these two small books I have made to thee, for the better understanding of certain Chapters of the Ancient Books† of Tenures (*g*).

LE SECOND LYVER est, De Homage; De Fealté; De Escuage; De Service de Chivaler; De Socage; De Frankalmoigne; De Homage Auncestrel; De Graund Serjeauntie; De Petit Serjeauntie; De Tenure en Burgage; De Tenure èn Villenage; De Trois Maners de Rentes, scil. *Rente-Service, Rent-Charge, et Rent-Sekke: et cest deux petitz lyvers jeo ay fait a toy, pur le meliour entendre certeyn Chapitres de les Auncieus Lyvers† dez Tenures.*

* *Tenant per le verge* does not form a separate chapter in the four earliest editions.—See p. 102 (*).

† This word, which *Sir Edward Coke* renders in his Translation, and also comments upon in the singular number, and as evidently referring to the book now known as *The Olde Tenures*, is printed, in every copy that the editor has seen, (except the French and English edition of 1671,) in the plural number; and *Rastell's* Transl. also renders, *books of tenures*.

(*g*) This book may well be accounted ancient, for it was composed in the reign of King Edward the Third, (as Justice *Fitzherbert*,

THE THIRD BOOK is, Of Parceners*; Of Jointenants; Of Tenants in Common; Of Estates of Lands and Tenements on Condition; Of Descents which toll Entries; Of Continual Claim; Of Releases; Of Confirmations; Of Attornments; Of Discontinuances; Of Remitters; Of Warranties, *scil.* Warranty Lineal, Warranty Collateral, and Warranty which commences by Disseisin.

LE TIERCE LYVER est, De Parceners; De Jointenauntes; De Tenauntes en Comen; De Estates de Terres et Tenementes sur Condicion; De Discents que tollont Entrees; De Continuel Claime; De Relesses; De Confirmacions; De Attournementes; De Discontinuaunces; De Remitters; De Garraunties,* scil. *Garrauntie Lyneall, Garrauntie Collaterall, et Garrauntie que commence per Disseisin.*

AND KNOW, my son, that I will not that you believe, that all which I have said in the said books be law, for this I will not to take upon me or presume; but of

ET SACHEZ, mon fitz, que jeo ne voille que tu cres, que tout ceo que jeo ay dit en les ditz lyvers soit ley, car jeo ne ceo voille enprendre ne presumer sur moy; mes de tielx choses

---

* Parceners by the custom do not appear as the subject of a separate chapter in the four earliest editions.—*Sup.* 297 (*).

---

in his Preface to his *N. B.*, saith), by a grave and discreet man.—*Co. Lytt.* 394. a.

There does not appear in the Preface to *F. N. B.* any notice of this ancient book; and *Sir Edward Coke*, in the Preface to the 8th and 10th *Reports*, assigns the date of H. 2 to this book, but this is doubtful, as that book refers to the Treatise upon Wards and Reliefs, since dignified by the name of the "Statute of Wards and Reliefs," unless the words referring thereto are an addition, which is not unlikely.—See p. 155. (a). (28 Ed. 1).

such things that are not law, inquire and learn of my wise masters learned in the law: nevertheless although certain things which are moved and specified in the said books are not law, yet such things shall make thee more apt and able to understand and apprehend the arguments and the reasons of the law, &c. For by the arguments and the reasons in the law, a man may sooner arrive at the certainty and the knowledge of the law.

Lex plùs laudatur quando ratione probatur.

que ne sount pas ley, enquerrez et apprendres de mes sages maisters aprisez en la ley: nientmeyns coment que certeyns choses queux sont motes et specifiez en les dits lyvres ne sount pas ley, unqore tielx choses serront toy plus apte et able de entendre et apprendre les argumentes et les reasons del ley, &c. Qar per les argumentes et les reasons en la ley, home pluis tost aviendra a le certeynte et a la conusaunce de la ley.

Lex plus laudatur quando ratione probatur.

EXPLICIUNT TENORES NOVELLI.

INDEX.

THE END.

Fructus Honos oneris: Fructus
Honoris onus.
I. L. 1639.

LONDON:
W. M'DOWALL, PRINTER, PEMBERTON-ROW, GOUGH SQUARE.